CADOGAN

London

Andrew Gumbel

P9-CKA-938

Cadogan Books plc
27–29 Berwick Street,
London W1V 3RF, UK
e-mail: guides@cadogan.demon.co.uk

**Distributed in the USA by
The Globe Pequot Press**
6 Business Park Road, PO Box 833, Old Saybrook,
Connecticut 06475–0833

Copyright © Andrew Gumbel 1995, 1998

Updated by Vanessa Letts and Bella Thomas

Book and cover design by Animage
Cover photograph by Sylvia Cordaiy/Humphrey Evans
Chapter title illustrations photographed by Tom Vaughan
and designed by Animage
Maps © Cadogan Guides, drawn by Map Creation Ltd

Series Editor: Rachel Fielding
Editing: Dominique Shead
Indexing: Ann Hudson
Production: Rupert Wheeler Book Production Services

ISBN 1–86011–019–3

A catalogue record for this book is available from the British Library

Printed and bound in the UK by Redwood Books.

To my mother and father

Acknowledgements

Much love and a big thank-you to Marion Frank, who provided an open house in Lancaster Gate, great food, lots of inspiration, a clutch of suggestions and a one-woman clipping service. Likewise my parents, who let me pester them for two weeks during the closing stages of the project, and Dana, Michael and the rest of the Prayssac crazies who cheered me up just when I needed it most. Thanks also to the London Tourist Board, the Greenwich, Southwark and Richmond tourist offices, the LDDC, the Palace of Westminster press service, Christine Brandt at Kew Gardens, the excellent London library service and all those museum curators who answered questions, handed out leaflets and provided excellent company. My editor and sometime Islington Person, Rachel Fielding, was a delight to work for, even when things got chaotic, as were the rest of the staff at Cadogan who walked my walks and taught me, rather late in life, the difference between right and left. Chris Schüler sorted my clerestories from my retrochoirs and recommended some good books. Finally, a special thank-you to Kathleen, who helped out in a million different ways, laughed at my bad jokes (well, some of them) and kept me smiling through to the end.

For the updating work on this edition, a big thank-you to Vanessa Letts, who not only provided a welter of new information, but also cast a quizzical, perceptive and gently challenging eye over the text. Thanks also to Bella Thomas for updating and expanding the practical sections, to Dominique Shead for coordinating the revised edit, to Tom Vaughan and Animage for respectively taking and designing the chapter title photographs, and to the whole Cadogan office, once again, for their insights and suggestions.

About the Author

Andrew Gumbel was born in a distant corner of that great anonymous expanse, the London suburbs. He first decided he loved London at the age of 10, and has been trying to make sense of it ever since. A journalist as well as a travel writer, he has returned to London periodically between lengthy periods abroad as a foreign correspondent for *The Guardian* and *The Independent*. He also wrote the Cadogan guide to Berlin.

Contents

Introduction

Oh thou, resort and mart of all the earth
Chequer'd with all complexions of mankind
And spotted with all crimes, in whom I see
Much that I love and more that I admire,
And all that I abhor...

William Cowper, *The Task, Book III* (1785)

London, you know, has a great Belly, but no palate, nor taste of right and wrong.

Thomas Hobbes, *Behemoth* (1680)

London, like all great cities, has a habit of going through drastic mood swings: grey, worthy and dull one minute, hip and ultra-modern the next. Down its long history it has been accused of everything from provincialism to irredeemable sinfulness; at times it has positively creaked under the weight of its own impossible size and complexity. At others, it has been hailed as everything a city could ever hope to be: a beacon of wealth, liberty, cosmopolitanism and artistic flair. And so, just when it was being written off as the crumbling capital of a dead empire, London has come roaring back to life. Freed from the shackles of empire and the bitter ideological divisions of the Thatcher years, it is enjoying a renaissance of extraordinary dimensions. The whole world is talking about its architects, its clothes designers, its film-makers, its musicians, its artists—even, in this most culinarily challenged of capitals, its chefs. No city in Europe is so desired, or so desirable.

London has recovered a belief in itself that would have seemed inconceivable even a decade ago, when gloom was perennially written on the hangdog faces of its citizens and the streets emptied as soon as the pubs closed. Now, in Soho or Notting Hill or Islington, you can barely move for people thronging to the latest designer shop, the newest art opening, or the hottest ethnic restaurant. The capital is being redefined by a new, highly creative generation of artists and designers iconoclastic enough to break down the fusty London of the past and rebuild it in their own image. Suddenly, everything seems possible and Londoners are embracing the changes with barely a whiff of scepticism or critical distance. The city invents and discards fads at an astonishing rate: rocket and shaved parmesan salad, the innovative food obsession of the mid-'90s, is already looking passé, along with Damien Hirst, Oasis and Vivienne West-wood. Old definitions no longer fit the new trends: sculpture and painting have given way to new mediums such as video art; the erst-while household design guru Terence Conran, meanwhile, has moved beyond the restaurant business into gastrodomes, veritable palaces of food consumption in custom-made settings like an old tyre factory, say, or a sports car showroom. This new London has even contrived to pretend that the weather is better: pavement cafés and al fresco dining are the new watchwords, along with Italian coffee and Mediterranean clothing styles.

Be warned, however. Amidst this creative frenzy, the old caveats about London still apply. It may be the most exciting city in Europe, but it is not the most beautiful, nor the easiest to get around. Indeed, there are times when it seems like one of those eccentric English aristocrats who deliberately dress in rags and forget to wash for weeks at a stretch. A city of its size is inevitably stricken with great swathes of dullness, not to mention air pollution, gridlocked traffic, creaky public transport, damp, ageing houses and all the other banal horrors of modern urban living. This is not a city that shouts its beauties from the rooftops, and many visitors who expect too much too quickly come away with a sense of bewildered disappointment.

There is an art to exploring London; you cannot simply do the rounds of its celebrated sights and museums and say you have seen it all. You have to engage on a personal level, ferreting out neighbourhoods you feel at home in, finding little backstreets you can admire without nec-essarily looking for them in a guidebook, discovering the museums and theatres and pubs that give you a sense of personal satisfaction. Two visitors meeting after a week in London might discover that one had hung around winebars in Kensington, taken a river trip to

Hampton Court and shopped at Harrods, while the other had sought out Freud's house, done some sketching in the Tate Gallery and sat in pub theatres at lunchtime. They would not have visited the same city at all, but they would both have been to London.

Once you have got over the sheer vastness and inconvenience, once you have traced out your route around the labyrinth, the sense of diversity and discovery can be immensely liberating. Nobody can know all of London—not poets, not politicians, not even guidebook writers. You have to make up your own version of it. Out of the chaos you produce a personalized sense of order, your own map of the city. Pop out of an Underground station at random and you may well find yourself in the sort of anonymous urban wasteland the city's millions of commuters pass through every morning and night; it is just possible, however, that you will discover a charming unknown corner of the metropolis you can call your very own.

My own idea of a perfect day in London, for what it is worth, might include a shopping trip along the upper stretch of Portobello Road, or a browse around Dillons bookshop on Gower Street; a cheap Indian meal in Drummond Street followed by a walk on Hampstead Heath; a wander through a section of the V&A, a play at the National or the Almeida, and perhaps a late-night bagel from Brick Lane. But don't take my word for it. The point is not to follow any of these recommendations; just be aware that the possibilities are endless.

A Guide to the Guide

The wit and raconteur Max Beerbohm once said that showing a visitor round London made him feel like Virgil accompanying Dante through the circles of hell. That may not sound like much of a compliment, but in one respect at least the observation is acute: the best way to orient yourself is to picture the city as a series of concentric circles. On the outside is limbo, that endless stretch of characterless suburbia that makes no sense to anyone except a mapmaker or a statistician; then comes the ring of inner suburbs, a zone of varied and often unexpected pleasures; finally, at the centre, is London's diabolical heart.

The centre is of course the part with most history, but that does not mean that it is necessarily the most interesting or most enjoyable to visit. What is central geographically may be only peripheral in terms of interest, and vice versa. As in Dante's *Inferno*, appearances can be deceptive. Certainly you should make sure you get to the National Gallery and St Paul's, but it would be a mistake to skip

The best of London

There's nothing more dreary than spending a week in London going round museum after museum. Variety should be the watchword, whether this is your first time in the city or your 50th. Don't worry if you miss out on some of the biggies—after all, plenty of Londoners have never been to the British Museum and are just waiting for the right occasion to get around to it. So treat the following not as a list of must-sees to check off one by one, but rather a rich menu from which to pick the items that suit you best on the day:

First-time visitors

National Gallery, Westminster Abbey and Tate Gallery (Walk II), Soho (Walk III), British Museum (Walk V), St Paul's (Walk VII), South Bank and the Museum of the Moving Image (Walk IX), Victoria and Albert Museum (Walk X), Portobello Market, Greenwich (including a boat ride down there).

Occasional visitors

Banqueting House and Houses of Parliament (Walk II), The Inns of Court and the John Soane Museum (Walk VI), St Stephen Walbrook and the Lloyd's Building (Walk VIII), The Clink and Old St Thomas's Operating Theatre (Walk IX), The Wallace Collection (Museums), Holland Park, Hampstead, Kew Gardens, Hampton Court.

Residents

Spencer House and the Queen's Chapel (Walk I), Westminster Hall and, if you can, the Foreign Office (Walk II), Jeremy Bentham's corpse (Walk V), St Etheldreda (Walk VII), Kensington Palace (Walk X), Leighton House, Carlyle's House, Highgate Cemetery, Christ Church Spitalfields, Rotherhithe. Note: some of these are pretty tough to get into, but the effort will be well rewarded.

If you are reasonably familiar with the tourist sights, here are a few more suggestions to bring the city to life:

Not been back lately

To catch a whiff of the extraordinary changes in London, all you really have to do is stand in the middle of **Soho** in mid-evening and marvel at the variety, exuberance and sheer numbers of the people around you. Eat at Terence Conran's futuristic gastrodome, **Mezzo**, or grab some conveyor-belt sushi served by robots on Poland Street. Further afield, there is the irrepressible trendiness of **Notting Hill** or the emerging bar and jazz club culture of **Hoxton Square**. For sight-seeing, the **South Bank** (Walk IX) is a must, particularly the newly refurbished **Oxo Tower**, the rebuilt **Globe Theatre** and the developments at **Butlers Wharf**—this is the spirit of the new London. Look out, too, for looming Millennium projects and quirky new places like the **Aquarium** at County Hall. If you remember **Bishopsgate** as a bombed-out wreck, go back now to see the magnificently refurbished church of **St Helen's**. Finally, you should try to take in some of the

new wave Britpack art. If there is nothing on at the **Saatchi Gallery** in **St John's Wood**, there may be a temporary show (check *Time Out*); failing that, the likes of Rachel Whiteread, Damien Hirst and Marcus Harvey can be found on display at the **Museum of London** and in restaurants like **Quo Vadis** and **The Pharmacy**.

Not been back in years

In addition to the above, you'll probably want to have a sniff round the **Docklands**, not just the monster tower at **Canary Wharf**, but also less obvious novelties like the riverfront at **Rotherhithe**. Go to the **Museum of the Moving Image** if that's new to you, and back to the action-packed **Science Museum** which has changed beyond recognition. If you remember the strict old licensing laws, you'll get a buzz just sitting in a pub mid-afternoon and ordering a drink. As for eating, just about anywhere should come as a startlingly pleasant surprise; try a modern riverside location (the **Blueprint Café**, Butlers Wharf, or **Canteen**, Chelsea Harbour).

Can't stand all this new-fangled stuff

If what you want is good, old-fashioned London, Walks II and IV (St James and Mayfair) are the places to start. No doubt you'll stay in a favourite quiet hotel in **South Kensington**, or even one of the posher establishments in **Mayfair**, but that shouldn't stop you dropping in on **Brown's** or the Ritz for tea—ideal stopping-off points during shopping sprees on Jermyn Street (bespoke clothes, as well as marmalade and Earl Grey at Fortnum's). Once you've exhausted sights like **Buckingham Palace** and the **Wallace Collection**, you might want to stroll around **Chelsea**, meet the eccentric pensioners at the **Royal Hospital**, or even venture out to the fine Adam houses at **Syon Park** and **Osterley**. Back in town, there are cocktails at the **Café Royal** and enticing dinner options around Covent Garden at **Simpson's**, **The Ivy** and **Rules**.

Multi-ethnic London

The world is all around you in London, but you can also seek it out, starting at places like the **Commonwealth Institute** on **Kensington High Street**, the **Africa Centre** in **Covent Garden** or the **Black Cultural Archives Museum** in **Brixton**. **Spitalfields Market** and **Brick Lane** in the East End are the centres of the Bengali community (look out for the Urdu street signs), while the Chinese are in **Chinatown** (Walk III). Food is the key to understanding between peoples, and might just spur you to travel out to **Southall** (London's most concentrated Indian community), **Golders Green** (for Jewishness and bagels from Carmeli's), **Clerkenwell** (for long-established Italian families and greasy-spoon lasagne joints), or **Green Lanes** (for Greek Cypriots who bake their bread fresh on Sunday afternoons). Admire the **mosque** in **Regent's Park**, or the Orthodox onion domes at the church of Agia Sophia on Moscow Road, **Bayswater**.

Romantic London

Okay, this isn't Paris or Venice, but London is more romantic than you might think. Anthony Minghella's film *Truly, Madly, Deeply* highlighted the heart-wrenching pleasures of **Kenwood** (those great views of the metropolis over the Heath) and the pavement cafés on the **South Bank** (don't forget the foyer jazz and cosy book-browsing possibilities inside the National Theatre, either). For dreamy walks, **Holland Park** or the riverside at **Richmond** and **Twickenham** are perfect. **Hampstead** is London's dinkiest neighbourhood—visit **Keats' house** to relive the poet's romance with Fanny Brawne, and find yourselves a quiet nook in the atmospheric **Holly Bush** pub. Otherwise try kite-flying on **Parliament Hill** (more good views as well as bracing air), or the canal walks and Georgian rows of **Canonbury** (plus the romantic association of penniless Lord Compton and the rich local merchant's daughter). **Hazlitt's** is a charming, centrally located hotel, while **Clarke's** (on Kensington Church St) or **Lemonia** (in Camden) make fine settings for a romantic dinner.

Hampstead, Greenwich or Kew just because they are not slap bang in the centre of town. In the same way, it would be foolish to spend too long in Mayfair or the City just because they happen to be where they are.

Central London is divided into 10 walks giving detailed instructions on how to get around. This takes up the greater part of the book simply because there are more stories to tell and more characters to sketch than in the outer reaches of the city. The first three walks start at Trafalgar Square, which is the closest thing that London has to a central pivot; the square itself is described as a preface to everything else.

London Area by Area covers the rest of the metropolis according to district and broad geographical direction. The section is not exhaustive, concentrating only on the areas that are really worth visiting. Some of these, like Spitalfields or Kensington, are very close to the centre; others, like Hampton Court, are barely in London at all. Some districts, for example Greenwich, are tailor-made for walking; others, like the Docklands, are too big to be covered on foot and require careful use of public transport. Where applicable at the end of each section, there are a few lines on districts further afield; these are mostly geographical pointers, not real recommendations.

The most important consideration when planning your excursions around London is the weather. Use the precious sunny days for all they are worth to visit the parks and street markets, to wander round the Inns of Court (Walk VI), to walk down Regent's Canal and stroll along the South Bank to Southwark (Walk IX). When it rains, there are any number of convenient shelters: the South Kensington museums (Walk X) should keep you busy all day without having to worry about an umbrella. Having said that, there will be few days when the rain is truly unbearable, and fewer days still when there is no rain at all, so it is worth getting used to the drizzle and learning not to complain too much. It is also worth thinking carefully about what you wear. You won't get into the Ritz (Walk I) or the House of Lords (Walk II) without a tie if you are a man, or a smartish outfit if you are a woman. Soho (Walk III), Brixton and Islington, on the other hand, require a more casual, hipper look. If you wore a tie in any of these places, you'd feel faintly ridiculous.

Travel

Getting to London

By Air

London is the spaghetti junction of the world's airways, with no fewer than five airports (at the last count) and planes from every conceivable airline zipping in from virtually every major city around the world. There should be no trouble finding a flight, even at the last moment, and you should be able to pick up a cheap deal without too much trouble—particularly if you are coming from North America or continental Europe. Shop around at several travel agents, and be prepared to consider Third World airlines as well as big names like British Airways, Qantas and the big North American carriers. North Americans wanting cheap flights to Europe can consult the worldwide web on: www.travelocity.com.

Travel times for direct flights are as follows: Paris or Dublin 1 hour, Rome or Madrid 2½ hours, New York or Montreal 6 hours, Los Angeles 9 hours, Australia or New Zealand 20–25 hours. Once your plane touches down, it is not necessarily all that easy to make your way into town. The choice of airports is as follows:

Heathrow, (✆ 0181–759 4321) the largest of London's airports with four passenger terminals, is about 15 miles west of the centre. Terminal 1 is mainly for short-haul British Airways flights; Terminal 2 for the European services of non-British airlines; Terminal 3 for non-British long-haul services; and Terminal 4 for British Airways intercontinental flights and Concorde. All terminals link up with the London Underground system, which runs from 5.30am to 11.30pm and is probably the least bad of a poor choice of ways of getting into London. The Piccadilly Line service gets you into the centre in about an hour for about £3.30. Watch out for long queues and unsympathetic staff at the ticket office. If you have a lot of luggage and your destination is not on the Piccadilly Line, it may be worth getting off at ✆ Earls Court or ✆ South Kensington and proceeding by taxi rather than trying to battle the crowds. There is also a bus service, which provides far more space for luggage but is also less frequent, slower (depending on traffic), quite a bit more expensive (about £6) and only runs until 8.45pm (✆ 0171–222 1234 for more information). The A1 goes to Victoria Coach Station, with stops on the way at Earl's Court, Harrods, Hyde Park Corner and Victoria railway station. The A2 goes to Russell Square in Bloomsbury with stops at the Kensington Hilton in Holland Park Avenue, Notting Hill Gate, Queensway, Paddington station and Marble Arch. If all this sounds like too much hassle, you can take a taxi, but it will set you back £30 or more and, if you arrive during the rush hour, could take as long as 90 minutes.

Gatwick (✆ 01293–535353), with two terminals, is about 20 miles south of London and handles a lot of charter flights and the less prestigious airlines. The only practical way into town is by the Gatwick Express train; this non-stop service to Victoria station (cost: £8.90) leaves every 15 minutes from 5am until 12am, and every hour for the rest of the night. Look out for the signs in your terminal. There is also a bus to Victoria Coach Station called Flightline 777 (✆ 0181–668 7261), which is cheaper but takes nearly three times as long. Don't even think about a taxi, which is no quicker than the bus and costs the same as a discount return flight to Paris.

Stansted (✆ 01279–680500) is the furthest from London, about 35 miles to the northeast, but in compensation is far and away the most pleasant. Only a few airlines, mostly arriving from continental Europe, use it for now, but it is likely to expand as pressure on Heathrow and Gatwick increases. Norman Foster's converted aircraft hangar design is pleasing to the eye and very efficient. Just pop down one floor by stairs, escalator or lift, and you are on the railway platform for London Liverpool St. The journey takes 40–45 minutes and trains leave every half hour. The fare is £10.

London City Airport (✆ 0171–474 5555), about nine miles east of the centre, serves mainly business passengers arriving from continental Europe. It too is modern and pleasant. Bus services (tickets £2–4) leave for Canary Wharf in Docklands and for Liverpool St every 20 minutes or so. A taxi ride into the City of London costs around £12. There is an executive helicopter service; if you need to ask the price, don't take it.

If you are lucky, you will never go anywhere near **Luton** airport as long as you live. It is inefficient, overcrowded and unfriendly. Mostly it provides charter flights for British tourists heading for the sun, but there is just a chance a foreign travel agent will be mean enough to book you through there. Almost as far away from London as Stansted, and in much the same direction, the airport has no direct rail link to the city. You have to take an airport bus to the station (paying for the privilege), and then take an invariably crowded commuter train in to King's Cross.

By Train

Unless you are coming from elsewhere in Britain, 'by train' really means 'by boat and train' or more likely, now the service is up and running and mostly rid of its early-day gremlins, by Channel Tunnel and train. The service from Paris or Brussels is a dream (three hours from door to door)—just as long as you aren't unfortunate enough to get stranded for hours as occasionally happens. In general, the service is wonderful until it hits the south coast of England, at which point the super-comfortable high-speed trains slow to a crawl along old-fashioned commuter lines (it is this sudden switch that has caused many of the breakdowns). With luck though, if you munch your designer sandwiches and keep reading your in-carriage *Financial Times* (depending what class you travel), the change of speed won't bother you unduly. The main ferry-train links bring you through Dover, Newhaven or

Portsmouth. If you are coming from Ireland, you can link up with the rather more efficient InterCity service to Paddington from your landing dock (Holyhead or Fish-guard). One word of warning: whatever your itinerary, be prepared to battle with a disastrously underfunded and badly managed network. Autumn leaves are often enough to bring the whole system to a halt, as is 'the wrong kind of snow'. A painful privatization a few years ago split the system up into separate companies according to activity—track, stations and signals under one management, rolling stock under another—a loopy idea that has wreaked organizational disaster and left the less profitable branch lines vulnerable to closure. Passengers are now referred to as 'customers', a sure sign that the railways are no longer considered a public ser-vice, but a business that functions only according to the ethics of the balance sheet.

London has eight main railway stations—Paddington, Euston, St Pancras, King's Cross, Liverpool St, Charing Cross, Waterloo and Victoria—all of which have their own corresponding Underground stations and, in some cases, inner London rail links. The Channel Tunnel terminus is temporarily at Waterloo station, in a con-course designed by Nicholas Grimshaw, but is due to switch to St Pancras and a terminus at Stratford once the British government gets its act together and lays down its own high-speed line. For information about the Tunnel call ✆ 01233–617575.

By Bus

National Express runs a network throughout Britain (✆ 0990–808 080) from Vic-toria Coach Station, while several companies including Eurolines (✆ 0171–730 8235 or 01582–404511) offer services to and from the continent. The coach sta-tion is about 10 minutes' walk along Buckingham Palace Road from Victoria proper, where you can find plenty of Underground links, buses and taxis.

By Car

The obvious thing to remember is that in Britain cars drive on the left-hand side of the road. This eccentricity goes back to the time when riders would walk alongside their horses by the road; since it was easier for most people to hold their animal's bridle in their right hand, it made sense for them to walk on the left-hand side of the road so they could be on the pavement. Logical, when you think about it.

Otherwise, driving is pretty straightforward, at least until you get into London itself (*see* below). You won't need an international licence if you are from any of the main English-speaking countries, although it is best to check with your local British consulate. Remember to get valid insurance before you leave and remember, too, that wearing seatbelts in Britain is compulsory, front and back. The quickest route across the Channel is Calais to Dover. Make sure you book in the summer months and be prepared for stiff high-season prices, although these are coming down because of a price war with the Channel Tunnel. The Tunnel, which starts at San-gatte near Calais and finishes at Folkestone, is well worth considering if the Channel is being tossed by a winter storm; otherwise it is not particularly advanta-geous since it takes just as long if not longer than the boat. You may want to consider arriving in Britain carless and then renting once you get there. Check out fly-drive deals before you leave home, since they are usually the cheapest. For rental companies in London, *see* below.

Border Formalities

Britain has opted not to join the eight-strong group of European countries practising an open-border policy (the so-called Schengen Group). So European Union citizens will still have to bring their passports or identity cards. That means a few delays and detours (particularly at the Channel Tunnel terminus at Waterloo), but basi-cally they can expect to breeze through customs; there is even a separate queue for them to avoid hold-ups. Anyone else can expect a fair grilling, particularly at air-ports and particularly if you are not white. There are very few customs restrictions if you are coming from another EU country. Otherwise, the usual limits on alcohol, cigarettes and perfume apply (roughly speaking, half a dozen bottles of wine or one bottle of spirits, plus 200 cigarettes). If you are a national of the United States, Canada, Australia, New Zealand, South Africa, Japan, Mexico or Switzerland, you won't need a visa to get in to the country if you are just on holiday or on a business trip. Other nationalities should check with their local British consulate.

Getting Around

For free information on planning bus and Tube journeys in London call the excel-lent London Transport 24-hour line on 0171–222 1234.

By Underground

London's Underground system (also known as the Tube) is 100 years old, and it shows. Creaky, unpunctual, smelly, unfriendly: it is everyone's favourite urban nightmare. The good news is that the authorities are aware of the problems and are working fairly efficiently to clean up stations, install new trains and work to elimi-nate the punctuality gremlins. The bad news, though, is that the cost of these improvements has made the Tube the most expensive city transport system in Europe, the most basic single adult ticket costing £1.30, compared with less than 40 pence in Paris. For better or worse, it is still the quickest way to cross London, especially during office hours, so you will just have to learn to love its shortcomings and consider yourself lucky you're not stuck in the fumes and gridlock above ground. Trains run from around 5.30am (7am on Sundays) until at least 11pm and as late as 1am on some lines (note that there is no service on Christmas Day).

Allow plenty of time for your journey; don't be surprised if you have to wait 20 minutes for a train to arrive, although in theory they should come every two or three. Do anything in your power to avoid the rush hour, when train carriages turn into solid packs of distressed human flesh and your face is ineluctably pressed into the sweaty armpit of a fat middle-aged accountant with bad breath. Don't, by the way, try to talk to anyone. There is a mysterious unwritten code of silence on the Underground, and any attempts at conversation will be countered with a row of steely stares. London commuters are a shy lot, at least below ground, and they like to suffer their Tube train misery alone.

The Underground fare system is organized in concentric zones, Zone 1 being the centre, and Zone 6 being the outermost ring including, among other things, Heathrow Airport. Pick up a map from any station and you will see that the lines are colour-coded to make them easier to follow. Among the worst lines are the Circle and District (particularly on their northernmost stretch from Paddington to Moorgate), the Metropolitan Line and the Northern Line. Among the best are the Victoria and Jubilee Lines, mainly because they were built most recently, and the refurbished Central Line. The East End and Docklands are served by the Docklands Light Railway, or DLR, an overground monorail which links up with the Tube at Bank and Tower Hill (you can call the DLR 24-hours travel hotline for advice on journeys on ✆ 0171–918 4000).

The most practical kind of ticket is a £3.50 One Day Travelcard, which you can buy to cover as many zones as you need and which is valid on buses and British Rail's Network SouthEast as well. Daily Travelcards are available after 9.30am; weekly and monthly passes are available any time, although you'll need a passport photo to get them; Zone 1 tickets are now sold in useful **carnets** which cost £10 for 10 tickets (saving you £3). If you arrive at Heathrow Airport but don't want a six-zone Travelcard, ask for a more restricted one, plus an extension for your journey into town.

By Bus

London's buses are slow, usually slightly cheaper than the Underground, and very often don't stop where they are supposed to because there are too many passengers on board already. On the plus side, at least you can see trees and sky, as well as the life of the city zipping by. And there *are* still bright red double-deckers (called Routemasters), with a conductor who issues tickets while the driver concentrates on driving. Since the late 1980s, when the bus system was deregulated, any number of vans, minibuses and coaches have been running services all over town. All are integrated into the London Transport network and charge similar (though often slightly lower) prices, based on the same zones as the Underground. Your best bet is to buy a Travelcard; individual fares might work out marginally cheaper but you can't change buses without paying all over again. If you plan to use the bus a lot, you should pick up a bus map, available from major Underground stations including Euston, King's Cross, Oxford Circus, Piccadilly Circus, Victoria and Heathrow. The number for London Transport enquiries (if you are patient enough to wait for them to answer) is ☎ 0171–222 1234.

There is a vast range of **tourist buses**. One useful one to know about is the Hop-on Hop-off, which takes you round all the main tourist sights of the centre and allows you to get on and off as many times as you like. Call ☎ 01708–631122 for details of the route so you know where to catch it.

By Train

British Rail's Network SouthEast is integrated into the London Transport system and can be useful for crossing large chunks of town, or else for accessing certain parts (for instance, the southeast) which the Underground neglects. Three useful services are the Thameslink, which starts at Luton Airport and snakes through West Hampstead, Kentish Town, King's Cross and Blackfriars through to the south London suburbs; the North London Line, which starts in Richmond and goes through Kew Gardens, Hampstead and Highbury on its way through to the East End; and the quick and efficient Waterloo and City line between Waterloo and Bank. There are also regular trains from Charing Cross or Cannon Street to Greenwich. The rail lines are all marked on the larger Underground maps (called Journey Planners), and you don't have to pay extra if you have a Travelcard.

By Taxi

Taxis are part of the mythology of London, perhaps because their drivers are the only people who can make sense of the great metropolitan labyrinth. Cabbies have to train for three years to take their qualifying exam, known as The Knowledge, in which they are expected to be able to locate every street, every major building and all the main tourist attractions as well as memorizing 468 basic routes. The test goes back to the very first days of motorized cabs, which first hit the streets in 1906. For years taxis conformed to a single sleek black design, but recently there have been some changes, notably the advent of advertising stickers and different body colours. You can still recognise them, however, by the distinctive For Hire signs on the roof which light up in orange when the cab is free.

During the day you can simply hail a taxi off the street. All licensed cabs are metered. They are more expensive than in most cities, but you can be confident of getting to your destination by the quickest route. If you do have a complaint, make a note of the driver's number displayed on his or her left lapel as well as the cab number and call the Public Carriage Office on ✆ 0171–230 1631. For lost property ✆ 0171–833 0996. If you want to order a taxi, contact **Dial-A-Black-Cab**, ✆ 0171–253 5000.

Black cabs are harder to find at night, and you may need to call a **minicab**. These tend to be cheaper, less reliable and occasionally a little hazardous. The best way to stay out of trouble is to call a reputable firm, like those listed below, and negotiate the price before you step into the car.

Atlas Cars, ✆ 0171–602 1234

Greater London Hire, ✆ 0181–340 2450

Town and Country Cabs, ✆ 0171–622 6222, ✇ 0171–622 6000, internet: www.taxi.co.uk. Good for South and Central London: male or female drivers, as requested, and with mini-televisions for passengers in every cab.

Lady Cabs, ✆ 0171–272 3019, a specialist service run by women for women passengers. Astonishingly, women did not drive cabs in London until the early 1970s.

By Car

Traffic in London moves at 11 miles an hour during the day—roughly the same speed as in the horse-drawn days of the 19th century. In other words, unless you are carrying your fridge around, you will be much better off forgetting about a car and using some other means of transport.

Speed is not the only consideration; parking is also a huge problem. Many of the spaces you will see are for residents only. Car parks and meters are very expensive and can prove ruinous if you outstay your welcome—around £30 for a parking ticket (or £60 if you leave it for longer than two weeks). If you're very unlucky you will have a nasty yellow clamp placed around one of your wheels. If this happens, look at the ticket to find out which Payment Centre you need to go to to liberate your vehicle (the main ones are at Marble Arch, Earl's Court and Camden). You will then have to fork out £38 to have the clamp removed plus a parking fine, and then return to your vehicle under your own steam. If you don't wait patiently for the declampers—and they can take up to four hours to arrive—you risk being clamped all over again. The only way to avoid hanging around for half a day is to call the Car Clamp Recovery Club (✆ 0171–235 9901) who will offer to recover your car for you for an additional £50 a year. There is one even worse horror that could befall you, and that is having your car towed away altogether. Call ✆ 0171–747 4747 to find out where your vehicle is and bring at least £135 in cash to the vehicle pound.

A car can nevertheless be a blessing in London, particularly in the evenings and for trips out of town. Familiarize yourself with the British Highway Code (available

from newsagents) and take particular note of the strict drink-drive laws. Technically you are allowed a glass of wine or two, but to be safe it's best either to stay
dry or to leave the car behind. The police will be businesslike but unforgiving if
they catch you over the limit. You don't need to carry your driving papers with
you, but if you are stopped you can be asked to show them at a police station
within five days.

If you are hiring a car, you need to be over 21 and have at least one year's driving
experience. Here are some addresses:

Hertz, lots of branches, central booking office ✆ 0990–996699.

Avis, lots of branches, central booking office ✆ 0990–900500, open 24 hours.

Supercars, 11a Greens End, SE18, ✆ 0181–317 1414. Much cheaper than the
multinationals.

On Two Wheels

In many ways, the bicycle is the perfect mode of transport in London. It is faster
than going by car, at least during the day, and 10 times more pleasant than the
Tube, especially if you make use of London's extensive parkland. There are draw-
backs, however: the city is too big and too hilly to make bikes practical for all
journeys (try going from Clapham to Highgate and you'll see the problem); it also
rains a distressingly large proportion of the time and can get very cold in winter.
Contrary to popular wisdom, however, the London streets are not particularly dangerous for cyclists as long as you assert yourself forcefully. Cars soon get out of the
way if you shout loud enough, and bus drivers are positively sympathetic as long as
you don't commit the cardinal sin of trying to overtake when they are signalling to
pull out of a bus stop. Here are a few bike hire addresses:

On Your Bike, 52–4 Tooley St (by London Bridge), ✆ 0171–378 6669. Wide
selection of bikes at reasonable prices.

Yellow Jersey Cycles, 44 Chalk Farm Road, Camden, ✆ 0171–485 8090.
More for the expert; ideal if you want to take a bike on the train and cycle in
the countryside.

Portobello Cycles, 69 Golbourne Rd, ✆ 0181–960 0444. Neighbourhood bike
shop off the Portobello Road.

You could also telephone **The London Cycling Campaign**, ✆ 0171–928 7220,
for advice and maps of safe routes around the city.

By River

An excellent Riverbus service that used to ply the Thames all day suffered a sad
demise in the summer of 1993; now you have to try your luck with a plethora of

commercial companies that run services from Westminster Pier or Charing Cross Pier, both just south of Trafalgar Square. Services upriver to Greenwich and the Thames Barrier—the most attractive destinations—run every half an hour between 10.40am and 3.20pm and take about 45–50 minutes (© 0171–930 4721 for up-to-the-minute information). In the other direction, services downriver to Kew, Richmond and Hampton Court are more erratic and may not run more than four times a day (© 0171–930 4097 for information). Hampton Court can be up to four hours' journey from the centre. The Pool of London Ferry operates a hop-on hop-off service between Tower Bridge and St Katharine's Dock (open 11–5, tickets £2 valid all day).

There are plenty of other stops and local services (for instance, from Richmond) all along the river, as well as along the canal from Little Venice to Camden and beyond: the London Tourist Board has a leaflet with full, up-to-date timetables, called Discover the Thames, available in tourist information centres. You can call for more information on © 0839–123432.

Practical A–Z

London has a packed programme of festivals and special events. Readers of P.G. Wodehouse will be pleased to know that the 'season', that mythical whirligig of balls, parties and sporting events for upper-crust Londoners and aspiring toffs from the country, really does exist, and you will be able to see them in action at the Royal Ascot races, the Wimbledon tennis championships and the Henley Royal Regatta. Dates for nearly all the events listed below change every year. Numbers for checking are given where possible:

January

1 January	*London Parade.* Display of 6000 real-American majorettes starting from Parliament Square at 12pm and finishing in Berkeley Square at 3pm.
Early January	Harrods' after-Christmas sale starts.
Mid-January to early February	*Chinese New Year* celebrations around Gerrard St in Soho. Lots of food and colourful floats.

February

Shrove Tuesday *Soho and Great Spitalfields Pancake Day Races.* Sprints down Carnaby Street and Spitalfields, with participants tossing pancakes in a pan; ✆ 0171–375 0441.

March

Second Week	*Ideal Home Exhibition* at Earl's Court Exhibition Centre, ✆ 01895–677677. Kitchens and bathrooms galore.
One Sunday	*Oranges and Lemons Service* at St Clement Danes in the Strand, at which local schoolchildren are given one orange and one lemon each in commemoration of a famous nursery rhyme (*see* p.262).

April

1 April	Check newspapers for April Fool's Day hoaxes.
Sat before Easter	*Oxford and Cambridge Boat Race.* Teams from the rival universities row their hearts out from Putney to Mortlake; ✆ 0171–730 3488.
Easter Sunday	*Easter Day Parade* in Battersea Park, complete with funfair and sideshows.
Mid-April	*London Marathon* from Blackheath to The Mall; ✆ 0171–620 4117 for details of route and how to enter.
Ascension Day	*Beating the Bounds.* Boys of St Dunstan's beat on the City's boundary markers with willow sticks in an ancient ritual. Starts at 3pm at All Hallows' by the Tower.

May

Early May
Museums Week—special events at 850 museums, internet: http://www.museumsweek.co.uk.

Late May
Chelsea Flower Show at the Royal Hospital Gardens. Funfairs on Hampstead Heath, Blackheath and Alexandra Park on Spring Bank Holiday Monday, ☎ 0171–828 1744.

June

First Saturday
Derby horse race at Epsom racecourse, Surrey.

Early June
Coin Street Festival, Gabriel's Wharf, London SE1: buskers and free street performances. *Greenwich Festival*: concerts, theatre and children's events, plus fireworks on the opening night; ☎ 0181–317 8687 for details. Also, *Hampton Court Festival*, opera music and dance; ☎ 0171–344 4444. Also, *Beating the Retreat*, floodlit evening display by Queen's Household Division outside Buckingham Palace.

Second Saturday
Trooping the Colour. The Queen's Guards in a birthday parade for Ma'am; ☎ 0171–414 2497.

June
Spitalfields Festival. Classical music in Christ Church, plus guided walks of the area; ☎ 0171–375 0441.

Mid-June
Royal Ascot. Society horse races at Ascot in Berkshire.

Late June–early July
Wimbledon tennis championships. Box office ☎ 0181–944 1066.

Late June–early July
Henley Royal Regatta. Rowers row on the Thames while very posh spectators get sozzled in their champagne tents.

June to August
Summer exhibition at the Royal Academy. More than 1000 works by living artists.

June to September
Kenwood Lakeside Concerts. Open-air concerts at the top of Hampstead Heath every Saturday. Magical if the weather's good; ☎ 0171–973 3427.

July

Gay Pride Day, first week of July on Clapham Common, ☎ 0171–737 6903. *City of London Festival:* classical concerts around the City; ☎ 0171–377 0540. Also, *Hampton Court Flower Show;* ☎ 0171–821 3042.

Late July
Royal Tournament. Fortnight of military pageants in Earl's Court; ☎ 0171–799 2323. Also, *Doggett's Coat and*

Badge Race, a rowing contest from London Bridge to Cadogan Pier. *See* p.332.

July to September   *The Proms* in the Albert Hall (*see* p.369); ✆ 0171–765 4475.

August

August to September   Buckingham Palace open to the public.

Last Sunday and   *Notting Hill Carnival.* Steel bands, dancing and general
Monday   Caribbean fun, occasionally broken up by police, around Portobello Rd and Ladbroke Grove (*see* pp.405–6).

September

Mid-September   *Chelsea Antiques Fair,* ✆ 01444 482514.

Third Week   *Open House Weekend,* ✆ 0181–341 1371: houses and buildings which are normally closed to the public open up for free, also walking tours.

Late September   *Clog and Apron Race.* A sprint through Kew by gardening students in strange attire; ✆ 0181–940 1171.

October

First Sunday   *Pearly Harvest Festival* at St Martin-in-the-Fields. Lots of folklore cockneys in their button-splashed coats playing ukeleles, ✆ 0171–930 0089.

November

5 November   *Bonfire Night.* Fireworks and bonfires, plus plenty of booze, in parks all over London (Highbury Fields and Battersea Park are good venues, but telephone the London Tourist Board ✆ 0839–123456 or check *Time Out* for details) to commemorate Guy Fawkes's attempt to blow up parliament in 1605 (*see* pp.63–5).

First week   *State Opening of Parliament.* The Queen sets out from Buckingham Palace for Westminster where she reads out the government's programme for the forthcoming year. Crowds follow her around.

First Sunday   *London to Brighton Veteran Car Run.* Starts in Hyde Park; ✆ 01753–681736 for details.

London Film Festival, based at the NFT on the South Bank but with showings all over town; ✆ 0171–815 1323.

Early November   *Lord Mayor's Show.* The new Lord Mayor goes on a grand procession through the City in his 18th-century gilded coach; ✆ 0171–332 1906.

| Sunday nearest 11 November | *Remembrance Day Service* to commemorate war dead at the Cenotaph in Whitehall. |
| November to December | Christmas lights go on in Oxford St, Regent St, Bond St and Trafalgar Square. |

December

| 31 December | New Year's celebrations beneath the Christmas tree in Trafalgar Square. |

Climate and When to Go

'When two Englishmen meet,' wrote Dr Johnson, 'their first talk is of the weather.' He might have added that their second, third, fourth and fifth talk are often the weather too. The English are weather-crazy, constantly hoping it will brighten up if it is raining—and it usually is—or else complaining about the heat on the rare occasions that the sun actually deigns to come out. In much the same way that Arabs are capable of asking after the health of every last family member for hours on end, so English people use the weather as a way of filling in embarrassing gaps in the conversation. Not for them the direct approach at parties ('So who are you then?'); rather they will begin with some meteorological platitude. 'Nice weather for the time of year, isn't it?' says the man sidling up to a woman with nice eyes. 'Yes,' she replies, impressed with his designer suit but shooting a worried glance at his sagging belly, 'but my garden could do with a bit more moisture before the summer sets in.' You quickly understand where Harold Pinter and Samuel Beckett found their inspiration.

The weather obsession is not just a matter of private speculation. It is all over the media. Turn on any radio station and you will hear a weather forecast almost as often as a Madonna song. Radio 4 fans enjoy the sheer excruciating boredom of listening to all 10 minutes of the shipping forecast, broadcast several times a day, in which some poor chump at the BBC has to give wind speeds, sea conditions and visibility reports for every sea area around the country. The weather announcers on television are national celebrities, true British eccentrics adored despite their nurdish manner and their often total inability to predict the next day's weather. One presenter, who shall remain nameless to spare his blushes, once assured a worried viewer on air that her fears of an impending hurricane were entirely groundless; 12 hours later half the trees in southern England had blown down. Incompetence only makes weathermen more endearing to the British public, though, and the presenter is still going strong, blinking nervously under the TV lights and stumbling over his words as he tries to explain the latest cold trough hovering over the west country. In his novel *London Fields*, Martin Amis predicts that before too long the weathermen will be fronting the evening news, with the newscasters put on for 30 seconds as an afterthought at the end of the bulletin. Most viewers, it is true, are far more interested in anti-cyclones and cloud banks than the trivia of international politics, famine and war.

The strange thing about the English weather is that there is nothing much to talk about. London's climate is so stable it could be on tranquillizers—rarely too hot, rarely too cold, rarely too sunny and rarely too wet, although you'll be lucky to get through a day without the odd spot of drizzle. The average temperature in July and August is 22° Celsius (75° Fahrenheit); in December and January it is 7° Celsius (44° Fahrenheit). So it rarely bakes and rarely freezes. Heat waves and snow are each so unusual that they tend to trigger a state of national panic. The rain is at its worst in November (2.5 inches or 64 mm on average), but keeps up a steady trickle all year. You rarely get drenched, but on the other hand you can't count on it staying dry for more than a few hours at a time, whatever the season.

Spring usually finds London at its best, with the trees in bloom and the air light and balmy. Autumn can also be magical, especially on Hampstead Heath and in the larger parks, while winter is ideal if you want to see lots of museums and plays. Summer is probably the worst time to visit: London can get surprisingly oppressive even in moderate heat, and the tourist buses quickly become a strain on the nerves. Don't think you'll escape the rain in the summer, either. July and August are two of the wettest months of the year.

Consulates in London

You can always find the number of your consulate or embassy by calling directory enquiries (℃ 192). Here are a few:

US Embassy, 24 Grosvenor Square, ℃ 0171–499 9000, open Mon–Fri 9–6. There is a 24-hour helpline for US citizens.

Australian High Commission, Australia House, The Strand, ℃ 0171–379 4334, open Mon–Fri 9–5.15.

Canadian High Commission, 38 Grosvenor St, ℃ 0171–258 6600, open Mon–Fri 8am–11am, with 24-hour telephone helpline.

Dutch Embassy, 38 Hyde Park Gate, ℃ 0171–590 3200, open Mon–Fri 9–5.30.

French Consulate, 21 Cromwell Rd, ℃ 0171–838 2000/2055, open Mon, Fri 9–12 noon; Tues–Thurs 9–4.

German Embassy, 23 Belgrave Square, ℃ 0171–824 1300, open Mon–Fri 9–3.30.

High Commission of India, India House, Aldwych, ℃ 0171–836 8484, open Mon–Fri 9.30–5.45.

Irish Embassy, 17 Grosvenor Place, ℃ 0171–235 2171, open Mon–Fri 9.30–5.

Japanese Embassy, 101–4 Piccadilly, ☎ 0171–465 6500, open Mon–Fri 9.30–1 and 2.30–4.30.

New Zealand High Commission, New Zealand House, 80 Haymarket, ☎ 0171–930 8422, open Mon–Fri 10–noon, 2–4.

South African Embassy, Trafalgar Square, ☎ 0171–930 4488. Check for opening hours.

Swedish Embassy, 11 Montagu Place (near Baker St), ☎ 0171–724 2101, open Mon–Fri 8.30–12.30 and 1.30–5.

Crime and Police

The British downmarket newspapers are full of lurid crime stories, usually involving children being attacked or abducted, or policemen being shot by crazed drug-dealers. Something of a siege mentality has set in, which is curious because serious crime in London has been stable for several decades. You won't be at greater risk in London than in any other biggish city in Europe; the greatest hazard is petty theft and pickpocketing, for which the usual precautions apply. Although usage is unmistakeably on the increase, drugs are yet to become the kind of overwhelming crime problem they are in the United States or parts of southern Europe; firearms are extremely uncommon and even police officers do not carry them (*see* pp.67–70). Don't hang around lonely neighbourhoods late at night—Hackney or Tottenham spring to mind—and don't leave valuables in your hotel room. Women have a far more hassle-free time in London than in Rome or Madrid, and it is accepted as normal for a woman to be out on her own. They should watch out on the Underground, however, particularly late at night.

You'll find the authorities very jumpy about the risk of terrorist attack, particularly since the huge Bishopsgate bomb planted in the City in 1992 by the IRA; wastebins have been removed from the Underground, automatic luggage lockers have been taken out of railway stations and many buildings bristle with security guards. Don't let reports of terrorist bombs put you off coming to London, though. You are more likely to die on the aircraft into London than in an attack once you get here; and you stand a far greater chance of being run over outside your house than ever dying on an aircraft. All of which might sound rather grim, but the basic message is cheerful: London is a safe place to go.

The police are usually friendly enough, although you might encounter suspicion or idle prejudice if you are Irish or black. If you need to go to the police to report a theft or other crime, simply visit your nearest station and you should receive a civil hearing—though you probably won't get your stolen goods back. In case of emergency, dial either ☎ 999 or ☎ 112. If you yourself get picked up by the police, you must insist, if you feel it necessary, on calling your embassy or consulate, or a lawyer if you know one. Keep your cool and remain polite at all times—the more cooperative you seem, the more leniently you are likely to be treated. Be particularly careful how you drive around Christmas time, as the drink-drive police is out in force.

Finally, to retrieve lost property, try the London Transport Lost Property Office at 200 Baker St, open weekday mornings only, © 0171–486 2496; or the Black Cab Lost Property Office, 15 Penton St, Islington, © 0171–833 0996, open Mon–Fri 9–4.

Disabled Travellers

London is reasonably wheelchair-conscious, certainly by comparison with the rest of Europe, and most of the major sights have proper access and help on hand if necessary. There are still problems, however, with the transport system and many theatres and cinemas. The London Tourist Board has a special leaflet which you can find in tourist offices called *Information for Wheelchair Users Visiting London* which covers hotels, tourists sights and transport. A fuller guide is *Access in London*, a booklet available at Books Etc on Charing Cross Road or by post from the Access Project at 39 Bradley Gardens, London W13 8HE (a donation of £7.50 for printing costs is requested). London Transport publishes *Access to the Underground* with information on lift-access to Tubes, available free from Tube stations or by post from the London Transport Unit for Disabled Passengers, 172 Buckingham Palace Road, London SW1W 9TN, © 0171–918 3312. Otherwise, bear the following addresses in mind:

Artsline, © 0171–388 2227. Free information on access to arts venues.

Holiday Care Service, © 01293–774535. Advice on hotels.

Shape, © 0171–700 8138. Offers cheap tickets for arts events.

Tripscope, © 0181–994 9294. Telephone helpline for people touring in London and the whole of Britain.

Finally The Greater London Association for Disabled People publishes a free *London Disability Guide*, available by post from 336 Brixton Road, London SW6.

Electricity

Britain uses three-prong square-pin plugs quite unlike anything else in Europe or North America. So far, the British government has resisted conforming to the rest of Europe on safety grounds—all British plugs have detachable fuses of three, five or 13 amps. So you will need an adaptor for any electrical device you bring in from abroad. The airport is as good a place as any to find one. Note also the electricity supply is 240 volts AC.

Gone are the days when gay celebrities had to flee London for the more tolerant climes of Paris. You won't catch any modern-day Oscar Wildes getting arrested in posh Knightsbridge hotels and slung into jail. More likely you'll find them out clubbing or demonstrating at Pride marches in Trafalgar Square. Male homosexuality was legalized in 1967, and although the age of consent was fixed for years at the anachronistically high age of 21 (heterosexuals are legal at 16), it is now down to 18 and likely to fall further. Female homosexuality, meanwhile, has never been criminalized because Queen Victoria did not believe it existed.

London has developed the most vibrant gay scene in Europe. For years Earl's Court was the focal point for gay clubs and bars, but recently the focus has shifted to Soho, Hampstead and Clapham. Old Compton Street in Soho has become something of a gay High Street, with specialist bars, shops, a travel agency, a hairdresser's and taxi company.

Some of London's best nightclubs, such as Heaven, The Fridge and Turnmills, either have a strong gay element or else are completely gay. There are also plenty of gay bars and cafés (see 'Entertainment and Nightlife' for clubs and bars, pp.539–40). The Angel, at 65 Graham St in Islington, is one of the most relaxed if only because there is a good even mix of men and women. You'll find zillions of other suggestions and write-ups in one of London's gay magazines, such as *QX, Thud* or *Pink Paper*. Here are a few addresses to get started with:

Lesbian and Gay Switchboard, ✆ 0171–837 7324. Advice and information 24 hours a day.

Gay's The Word, 66 Marchmont St, Bloomsbury. Leading gay bookshop in the capital.

Clone Zone, 64 Old Compton St. Multi-level shop with books, cards, clothes and leatherwear.

Covent Garden Health Spa, 29 Endell St. Strictly non-sleazy health club for men. Includes beauty therapy, jacuzzi and solarium.

The Backstreet, Wentworth Mews, Burdett Road, Mile End, open Thurs–Sun, ✆ 0181–980 8557. Out-of-the-way black leather and rubber nightclub for men, rather wilder than the clubs listed in 'Entertainment and Nightlife'.

Wilde About Oscar, 30 Philbeach Gardens, ✆ 0171–835 1858. Smart gay restaurant with garden.

For health issues, *see* below.

Health

Citizens of the European Union and some Commonwealth countries enjoy free medical care in Britain under the state National Health Service. The days when you could get free treatment on production of just a passport are probably over, so you'll need to fill out the appropriate paperwork before you leave home (in the EU the form is called an E111). Thus armed, the only things you will have to pay for are prescriptions and visits to the optician or dentist, although these should not cost more than a few pounds.

Anyone else, and that includes Americans, Africans, Indians and Canadians, should take out medical insurance.

If you need urgent medical treatment, you should head for one of the casualty departments (what in the United States are known as emergency rooms) of the major hospitals. These include St Thomas's on the South Bank, University College Hospital on Gower St in Bloomsbury, Guy's in Southwark, the Charing Cross Hospital on Fulham Palace Rd, Bart's in Smithfield and the Royal Free in Hampstead. You can call an ambulance by dialling © 999 or © 112.

There are several services dealing with HIV and AIDS including the Body Positive Helpline (© 0171–373 9124 or 0171–835 1045, from 7pm–10pm daily), the National AIDS Helpline (© 0800 567123, free of charge) and the Terrence Higgins Trust (© 0171–242 1010, open 3–10pm daily). Gay men with sex-related health problems should go to the special clinic at St Mary's Hospital in Paddington, Praed St, © 0171–725 1697, while lesbians can go to the Sandra Bernhard clinic for sexually transmitted diseases at the Charing Cross Hospital, Fulham Palace Rd, © 0181–846 1234.

Note also the following numbers:

Bliss Chemist, 5 Marble Arch. Stays open until midnight every day. Details of other late-opening chemists are available from police stations.

Great Chapel Street Medical Centre, 13 Great Chapel St, © 0171–437 9360, open Mon–Fri 2–4pm. An NHS general clinic that accepts EU, Commonwealth and Scandinavian visitors for free treatment.

Medical Advisory Service, © 0181–994 9874. Medical advice on all topics. Lines open 5pm–10pm daily.

Dental Emergency Care Service, © 0171–937 3951. An advisory service open 24 hours which will direct you to the nearest clinic for emergency dental care.

London Rape Crisis Centre, © 0171–837 1600. Open 24 hours.

Samaritans, ✆ 0171–734 2800. Helpline for any emotional problems, open 24 hours.

Acupuncture Council, ✆ 0181–964 0222. Phone for your nearest acupuncturist.

British Homoeopathic Association, ✆ 0171–935 2163. Gives information about a whole range of homoeopathic doctors and pharmacists.

Eye Care Information Bureau, ✆ 0171–928 9435. Will direct you to an eye specialist if necessary.

Healthline, ✆ 0345 678444. Free recorded information on 400 ailments.

Family Planning Association, ✆ 0171–636 7866. Will tell you where your nearest family planning clinic is and give you advice on morning-after pills, abortions and so on.

London for Free

You'll hear plenty of moans about the high cost of living in London, so here as an antidote is a list of things to do without spending a single penny:

Museums and Galleries: Many of London's best museums have traditionally been free, but it is turning into a losing battle because of wavering government commitment to the necessary subsidies. Museums still hanging on by their fingernails include the National Gallery, National Portrait Gallery, The RIBA Heinz Gallery, Tate Gallery (although it is considering charging for the new Museum of Modern Art at Bankside), British Museum, Sir John Soane Museum, Dulwich Picture Gallery, Bethnal Green Museum of Childhood, The Royal College of Art, The Percival David Foundation for Chinese Art, William Morris Gallery, the Petri Museum of Egyptian Archaeology, Keats' House and the National Army Museum. The Victoria and Albert Museum, Museum of London, Natural History Museum, Science Museum and Imperial War Museum all waive their charge from 4.30pm–5.50pm.

Other Sights: Churches, with the exception of Westminster Abbey and St Paul's Cathedral, are all free. So, too, are the Guildhall, the Changing of the Guard outside Buckingham Palace, court cases at The Old Bailey or The Royal Courts of Justice on the Strand, the Sunday afternoon haranguing sessions at Speakers' Corner and the more regular haranguing sessions at the Houses of Parliament. London's wonderful riverside walks and parks—St James's, Battersea Park, the 19th-century dinosaurs in Crystal Palace Park, Hampstead Heath, Hyde Park and Regent's Park—are always free. So also are the beautiful cemeteries in Kensal Rise, Highgate, Brompton and the Pet Cemetery in Hyde Park.

Window-shopping: Harvey Nichols, Fortnum & Mason, Selfridge's, Liberty, the Conran Shop, the design workshops in the Oxo Tower and even Harrods are well worth poking around even if you don't buy anything. Selfridge's often has special promotions and gives away free samples, particularly of cosmetics. Christies and Sothebys auction houses nearly always have pre-sale shows which are open to the public. Bookshops will let you browse to your heart's content, as will the computer and hi-fi shops on Tottenham Court Rd. Some of the fancier delicatessens in Soho and St James's (for example, the cheese sellers Paxton and Whitfield in Jermyn St) will give away free nibbles, although you are under some pressure to purchase something in return. Street markets can be colourful, especially Portobello Road (Sat), Petticoat Lane (Sun), Camden Lock (weekends only) and the Bayswater Road open-air art and painting display which takes place every Sunday. Food markets (try Berwick St for starters) sometimes knock down the price of fruit and vegetables at the end of the day so far they are as good as free.

Entertainment: There are free foyer concerts at the National Theatre and Barbican in the early evening. Covent Garden boasts plenty of street theatre and music, although you should offer something as the hat comes round. If you turn up to concert or theatre venues at the interval, you will often find people leaving and if you ask nicely they will give you their tickets. Shooting for the Royal Opera might be a bit optimistic but at the summer Proms at the Albert Hall, for example, you are virtually assured of getting in for the second half. Another option in the summer is to go up to Kenwood on Hampstead Heath on a Saturday evening. You can sit on the rolling hills and listen to the outdoor concerts there without actually paying to get in. The BBC Radio Ticket Unit, London W1A 4WW, hands out a lot of tickets for recordings of quiz shows like *The News Quiz* or *I'm Sorry I Haven't A Clue*, sometimes at quite short notice (© 0171 765 5243 or 765 5858). You can get tickets for TV shows on the BBC by sending a stamped addressed envelope to Audience Services, Room 301, Design Building, Television Centre, London W12 7RJ; or internet:http://www.bbc.co.uk/ tventertainment/tickets/html, email tv.ticket.unit@bbc.co.uk. Free tickets for comedy shows such as *Have I Got News For You* and *Clive Anderson Talks Back* are also distributed by the excellent Hat Trick Productions, but you must telephone in advance on © 0171–287 1598.

Maps

London is one city where wandering around clutching a map will not automatically mark you out as a visitor; few Londoners venture out of familiar territory without a copy of the *London A–Z Street Atlas*, an inch-thick book of maps with an index of street names to help you find your destination. Published by Geographers, this essential London survival tool comes in a variety of formats, from a simple black-and-white paperback to glossy colour editions with leatherette binding, and can be bought at almost any newsagent or petrol station.

Geographers A–Z also publish a series of nine sheet maps covering the whole of London area by area—Central, West, Northeast and so on. The central London map is particularly useful for sightseeing as it shows all the main sights on one sheet. The Clever Map Company's *London Backstreet Map* suggests routes from one part of Central London to another avoiding the major roads—a far more enjoyable and intriguing option than trudging along dusty dual carriageways.

Bus and Tube maps are available from most main Underground stations; the large Journeyplanner maps show both Tube and British Rail links. Motorists will need a road atlas with a good section on Greater London; the AA (Automobile Association) and the Ordnance Survey both publish excellent road atlases which are updated annually. Motorists who want to survive London's draconian traffic schemes and parking regulations should consult the *London Parking Map* and the *London Speed Trap Map*, both published by the Clever Map Company.

Cyclists will find the *Central London Cyclists' Map* a helpful guide to the quickest, safest and most pleasant routes through London's traffic mayhem. Published by the London Cycling Campaign, it can be bought from their office at 228 Gt Guildford Business Square, 30 Gt Guildford St, London SE1 0HS, ✆ 0171–928 7220 and from some bookshops and cycle shops.

The Ordnance Survey also publishes a sheet map of *Roman Londinium*, which marks all known features of the Roman city on the modern street plan, and details a Roman Wall Walk which takes in most of the remains still visible above ground—and, in one case, in an underground car park.

These and many other maps can be found at London's largest specialist map shop, **Stanford's**, 12–14 Long Acre, Covent Garden.

Media

Britain was once known for having both the best and the worst newspapers in the world. Its quality press was feared and respected for its opinions, its fine writing, its probing analyses and its depth of reporting both at home and abroad; the tabloid press, meanwhile, was feared and detested for its jingoism, its prurient muck-raking and its bewilderingly high circulation figures. In the world-weary 1990s, neither stereotype really holds true any more. The upper end of the market, made insecure by the power of television, the interference of big media barons and, in recent years, a damaging price war, has dropped its standards markedly in a bid to reach wider audiences. The tabloids, meanwhile, are as detestable as ever, but are getting some pretty stiff competition in the sleaze department from the supermarket fanzines and gossip rags.

Radio and television are going through a similarly difficult period, dropping some of their high standards and questioning long-held certainties as they face new challenges from cable, satellite and the Internet. With luck, this crisis of confidence will prove to be temporary. Britain, and London in particular, has a long history of pre-eminence in both print and broadcast journalism. Bland conformism has never held sway for long; whatever the shape of the new media landscape, it is hard to believe that Brits will not find a way to challenge, tub-tump and thunder as in the past. For the moment, though, the picture looks uncharacteristically grim.

Dailies: At the quality end of the range there is the *Daily Telegraph* (true-blue Tory, with some bright writing), *The Times* (maverick conservative, with a few good reporters), the *Independent* (once the pacemaker among the quality broadsheets, now struggling to keep up), the *Guardian* (bastion of the liberal left) and the *Financial Times* (a bellwether for the business world, printed on pink paper). All except the last of these are in significant financial trouble: the *Times* and *Telegraph* because of a vicious battle to grab each other's circulations, the *Guardian* because it chose to buy the loss-making Sunday *Observer*, and the *Independent* because of falling sales and the surrender of the bulk of its shares to proprietors at odds with its philosophy of intellectual and editorial freedom. The *Guardian*, which is keeping a healthy critical distance from the Labour government, is probably the best all-round read these days, while the *Financial Times* is certainly the most thorough in covering its chosen field, if a little dull.

Further down the greasy journalistic pole come the mainly right-wing middle-range papers: the *Daily Express* (very anti-Europe) and the *Daily Mail* (hot on society gossip and money advice). The *Mail*'s sister paper is the *Evening Standard*, which comes out in London in the afternoons and enjoys a captive commuter audience. It can be useful for information about the capital and has its entertaining moments, but watch out for some hair-raisingly reactionary comment pieces.

At the bottom of the pile come the real nasties, the downmarket 'tabloids' (so-called because of their format) with their lurid sex scandals and tone of moral righteousness. They have been a little tamer than usual of late, largely because of the anti-press furore in the wake of the car crash that killed Princess Diana. But tabloids never stay sober and remorseful for long. The *Sun*, notorious for its page-three topless pin-ups, is the biggest seller, followed by the very similar *Daily Star*. The *Sport* does not even attempt to cover news and devotes itself entirely to sex and phone sex instead. The *Daily Mirror* was once an excellent popular left-wing paper but has abandoned many of its principles for the sake of flashy celebrity scoops. What makes the tabloids so depressing is not so much their political line or news priorities as their cavalier attitude to the facts. Public figures (and sometimes ordinary people) are unjustly dragged through the dirt for the sake of spicing up a story, and political dogmas are hammered home with a blend of rabble-rousing and base prejudice. The truth, or at least a balanced truth, rarely figures at all.

The British press was once dominated by **Sunday newspapers**; now these tend to be owned by the daily titles and differ only slightly in tone from their sister publications. They are, however, two or three times as fat. The right-wing, establishment-bashing *Sunday Times* is the biggest-selling quality paper, but has some dubious journalistic ethics (inviting a neo-Nazi, for example, to edit Goebbels' diaries). The *Observer,* once the *Times*' stiffest competitor, is now a struggling offshoot of the *Guardian*, apparently waiting for the failure of one of its competitors to return to its glory days. The *Independent on Sunday* has an interesting review section. Most of the rest aren't worth the paper they are printed on.

Britain is relatively poor on **weeklies**. Anyone in London should buy *Time Out* (*see* Entertainment and Nightlife). Otherwise there is *The Economist* (conservative and informative, if a little patronizing), the *Spectator* (right-wing; occasionally witty but rather reactionary), the *New Statesman and Society* (centre-left; occasionally stimulating but rather dull), and *Punch* (owned by Alfie Head aka Mohammed Al Fayed and terminally dull). Every two weeks comes the satirical and often very funny *Private Eye*, which laughs at the establishment and occasionally digs up important scandals. For those with a more youthful sense of humour *Viz*, a cartoon magazine, is also very funny. Finally, you should take a look at *The Big Issue*, a magazine sold on the streets by the homeless, which offers a refreshingly different, if often depressing, view of the capital. Buying it will also help your seller build up a normal life again.

You can get hold of most foreign titles quite easily in London. Broadly speaking, the more cosmopolitan the area, the more varied its newspaper range. Two of the best shops are Moroni's, 68 Old Compton St, Soho, and Gray's Inn News, 50 Theobald's Rd, Bloomsbury. There are also two or three international shops at the top end of Queensway, north of ⊖ Bayswater.

Radio is still dominated by the public service BBC, which runs five national networks devoted respectively to pop (Radio 1, 98.8 FM), light entertainment (Radio 2, 89.2 FM), classical music (Radio 3, 91.3 FM), the spoken word in all forms (Radio 4, 198 kHz and 93.5 FM) and rolling news and sport (Radio 5 Live, 693 kHz or 909 kHz). Radio 4 is one of the great institutions of the airwaves, capable of great intelligence and wit in its news programmes, opinion forums, arts programmes, plays and quizzes. It even boasts its own soap opera, a tale of rural folk called *The Archers* which has been running for years. The BBC has had something of an identity crisis of late, fighting for an ever decreasing market share and trying to sort out its increasingly overloaded schedules. Some days you turn on the radio and all you hear is ball-by-ball cricket commentary. That's the time to turn the dial and look for something else, like Jazz FM (102.2 FM, devoted to jazz, blues and soul), Classic FM (100.9 FM), the news and phone-in channel London Newstalk (97.3 FM and 1152 kHz), or the commercial popular music station Capital FM on 95.8 FM, and its sister station which plays golden oldies, Capital Gold on 1548 kHz.

On **television**, network broadcasting is shared between the BBC and three independent channels, ITV (Carlton/LWT), Channel 4 and Channel 5. All five have their fair share of goggle-box trash, but—with the exception of the relatively new and so far underwhelming Channel 5—also produce excellent documentaries, news and arts programmes, comedies and drama serials, earning Britain an enviable reputation for some of the best television in the world. BBC1 and BBC2 carry no adverts (except wince-making self-promotions) and are supported by government subsidy and licence-payers. Channel 4 produces excellent films and caters to minority tastes of all kinds (Americans can catch the Superbowl here, as well as late-night country music bashes). The main news bulletins are at 6pm and 9pm on BBC1, 7pm on Channel 4 (lasting an hour) and 10pm on ITV. BBC2's more analytical *Newsnight*, perhaps the best digest of all, starts at 10.30pm.

That leaves just expensive **satellite TV**, dominated by Rupert Murdoch's five-channel Sky empire, which has stolen most of the world's important sporting events from terrestrial telly. The BBC recently started up a 24-hour rolling news channel, whose fortunes are yet to be determined. The better London hotels will also give you CNN, MTV and Eurosport. Happy landings.

Money and Banks

The currency in Britain is the pound sterling, divided into 100 pence. You'll come across notes worth £5, £10, £20 and £50, and coins worth 1, 2, 5, 10, 20, 50 pence and £1. London is also fully up to speed on credit card technology, and many shops, restaurants and hotels will accept Visa, Mastercard or American Express for all but the smallest purchases.

Minimum banking hours are Mon–Fri 9.30am–3.30pm, although many banks in Central London stay open later and, in some cases, on Saturday morning too. The biggest banks are Barclays, Midland, National Westminster and Lloyds. Most branches have automatic cash dispensers open 24 hours a day; check the stickers to see if your card and usual PIN number will be accepted, although if you don't have a British card you can expect your bank to charge a commission fee for any transaction.

You can change travellers' cheques at any bank or bureau de change, but remember to bring a passport or similar ID along with you. By and large, the big banks offer a better rate and lower commission fees, but shop around. If you need non-British currency, bureaux de change will be more likely to stock it. Try:

American Express, 6 Haymarket, ✆ 0171–930 4411.

Chequepoint, 548 Oxford St, and branches, ✆ 0171–723 1005.

Thomas Cook, Victoria Station, Marble Arch and many other branches, ✆ 0171–828 4442.

National Holidays

With the exception of Christmas and New Year's Day, Britain's national holidays, known as bank holidays, shift slightly every year to ensure they fall on a Monday. This avoids being 'cheated' out of holidays, as happens in continental Europe when they fall on the weekend, but it also leads to the absurdity of May Day being celebrated as late as 7 May. Banks and many businesses close down on bank holidays, but quite a few shops and most tourist attractions stay open. Public transport theoretically runs a Sunday service, but in practice tends to be very threadbare. The full list is: New Year's Day (plus the following Monday if it falls on a weekend), Good Friday, Easter Monday, May Day (first Monday in May), Spring Bank Holiday (last Monday in May), Summer Bank Holiday (last Monday in August), Christmas Day and the next day, known as Boxing Day (plus 27 December if one of them falls on a weekend).

Opening Hours

Traditionally, shops and offices stay open from around 9 to 5.30 or 6—significantly earlier than the rest of Europe. Pubs and bars still have fairly strict licensing rules (*see* p.505) and many of them will not serve alcohol after 11pm. Late opening for shops is becoming more and more common, however, particularly on Wednesdays and Thursdays, and even Sunday trading is becoming more flexible than in the past (Hampstead and Greenwich are particularly lively on the Day of Rest). In most areas of London you will find corner shops that stay open until at least 10pm; quite a few keep going all night.

Post Offices

Post offices are generally open Mon–Fri 9–5.30 and Sat 9–noon; avoid going at lunchtime as they can get very crowded. They are marked on most London maps (in the A–Z, for example, by a black star). You will be able to buy stamps and post letters and parcels at many newsagents', where you usually get a faster and friendlier reception. Two of the biggest post offices are at 24 King William IV St next to

Trafalgar Square (*open Mon–Sat 8–8*) and at King Edward St near St Paul's Cathedral. Both have stamp shops and a *poste restante* service, as well as a very useful mail collection on Sunday evenings.

If post offices are your thing, you might want to join one of the free guided tours of the Royal Mail Mount Pleasant Sorting Office on Mondays and Wednesdays at 2pm and 2.30pm; © 0171–239 2191 to book a place.

Postcodes: London postcodes are fairly confusing, and rely on an intimate knowledge of city geography to be intelligible. Postcodes begin with a direction (W for West, WC for West Central, N for North, NW for Northwest, and so on) and a number from 1 to 28. W1 covers Soho, Mayfair and Marylebone; WC1 is Bloomsbury; EC2, EC3 and EC4 cover the City; SE1 covers the South Bank and Southwark; W11 is Notting Hill; SW6 is Fulham; SW19 is Wimbledon. The full postcode then adds a letter immediately after the number, followed by a space, a number and two more letters. So a postcode might read EC1R 3ER—gobbledygook to anyone but a post office computer. This book uses postcodes sparingly, preferring to indicate the geographical district.

Pronunciation

Modern English spelling was standardized at the end of the 18th century by a small group of educationalists who evidently thought it would be hilarious to make pronunciation as difficult as possible for the uninitiated. Foreign tourists are forever inviting ridicule by asking for Glaw-sister Road or South-walk; it is hardly their fault if they are merely following the written word. Here is a survival guide to some of London's more common spelling anomalies:

Written	Spoken
Balham	Bal'm
Berkeley Square	Barkly Square
Berwick St	Berrick Street
Cadogan (Square or Books)	Caduggan
Charing Cross	Charring Cross
Cheyne Walk	Chainy Walk
Chiswick	Chizzick
Cholmondeley Walk	Chumly Walk
Clapham	Clap'm
Dulwich	Dull Itch
Gloucester Road	Gloster Road
Greenwich	Grin Itch
Grosvenor Place	Grove-ner Place

Holborn	Hoe Burn
Leicester Square	Lester Square
London	Lun Don
Southwark	Suth'k
Thames	Tems
Wapping	Wopping
Woolwich	Wool Itch

Religion

The state religion in Britain is Anglicanism, a peculiar hybrid of Protestant theology and Catholic ritual that developed after Henry VIII broke with the Roman Church to divorce his first wife, Catherine of Aragon. As discussed elsewhere, London's Anglican churches, particularly in the City, often show surprising accommodation with the business of money-making; to hear some businessmen speak about their faith and the ethics of wealth creation, you might think the money-changers had taken over the temple. Fortunately, the Anglican Church also has a strong liberal wing, which provides a powerful voice with which to denounce urban decay and establishment bigotry of all kinds. The admission of women priests to the Church of England in 1994 deeply upset traditionalists, many of whom have left and reverted to Catholicism. Unfortunately, this has failed to take the upper-class pomposity out of Anglicanism, but the advent of Tony Blair — a practising Christian and a missionary for modernisation — as prime minister might yet shake out some of the dead wood. Periodically the question of disestablishing the church comes up; if Prince Charles ever becomes king, he is in favour of modifying his role to become not Defender of *the* Faith, but Defender of Faith in general.

The biggest Anglican churches are St Paul's Cathedral, which has the finest organ in London, and Westminster Abbey. If you want to attend a service, a smaller church may be more to your liking. Leaf through some of the churches in the index for ideas. The biggest **Catholic churches** are Westminster Cathedral (off Victoria St) and the Brompton Oratory near the South Kensington museums. A more intimate place is St Etheldreda's in Ely Place off Holborn Circus.

London also has a sizeable **Jewish community**, concentrated in Hampstead, Golders Green and Stamford Hill, all in north London; one of the strangest sights in the whole city is watching 12-year-olds strolling down the Golders Green Road in their snazzy bar mitzvah suits on Saturday mornings. The main addresses are the Liberal Jewish Synagogue at 28 St John's Wood Road, ✆ 0171–286 5181, and the United Synagogue in Woburn House, Tavistock Square, ✆ 0181–343 8989, which offers information on orthodox services and activities.

The Pakistani immigrants of the 1950s, supplemented by Bengalis, Indians and Arabs from many countries, form the backbone of the **Islamic community**. The London Central Mosque at 146 Park Road near Regent's Park, ✆ 0171–724 3363, is a magnificent building which also contains a library and nursery school. Another popular place for Friday prayers is the East London Mosque at 84–98 Whitechapel Road, ✆ 0171–247 1357.

For other denominations, note the following addresses:

London Baptist Association, 1 Merchant St, Bow, ✆ 0181–980 6818.

The Buddhist Society, 58 Eccleston Square, Pimlico, ✆ 0171–834 5858.

Evangelical Alliance, Whitefield House, 186 Kennington Park Rd, ✆ 0171–582 0228.

Greek Orthodox Cathedral, Aghia Sophia, Moscow Rd, Bayswater, ✆ 0171–229 7260.

Hindu Centre, 7 Cedars Rd, Stratford, ✆ 0181–534 8879.

Central Church of World Methodism, Central Hall, Storeys Gate, Westminster, ✆ 0171–222 8010.

Assemblies of God Pentecostal Church, 141 Harrow Rd, ✆ 0171–286 9261.

Religious Society of Friends (Quakers), Friends House, 173–77 Euston Rd, ✆ 0171–387 3601.

Smoking

When smoking first became fashionable in Britain, James I called it 'a custom loathsome to the eye, hateful to the nose, harmful to the brain, dangerous to the lungs and, in the black stinking fume thereof, nearest resembling the horrible Stygian smoke of the pit that is bottomless.' The habit is not much better regarded now. Britain has caught on to the anti-smoking craze in a big way, and you will find total bans in theatres, cinemas, museums, buses and Underground stations. Most restaurants have non-smoking areas, and some bars and pubs are introducing a similar partition. If you are invited to someone's home, ask in advance if smoking will be tolerated. It is considered quite normal to send guests wanting a puff into the garden or street.

Students and Pensioners

Students and pensioners are entitled to discounts on transport passes, air and rail travel and entry to many museums and shows. You should have some appropriate ID; in the case of students, an ISIC card is the most practical and is recognized worldwide. Students with queries should address themselves to the University of London Union (ULU) in Malet St behind the British Museum, ✆ 0171–580 9551.

Telephones

In this era of privatisation and information superhighways, telecommunications is becoming a highly competitive field, with more servers offering their services all the time. The two biggest companies remain British Telecom, the former national monopoly privatized in 1984, and Mercury, its most prominent competitor. Watch out whose phone you use if you buy a phonecard (they are company-specific but widely available, for example from newsagents). Cash, of course, works fine anywhere. For prices and information on cheap times to call, check with your local post office (the rates are constantly changing). Obviously, though, evenings and weekends are cheaper, particularly for international calls.

London phone numbers come with one of two prefixes: 0171 for central areas and 0181 for outer ones. If you are in an 0171 area you only need to dial the prefix if you are trying to reach an 0181 number, and vice versa. Anyone calling from abroad must dial the prefix but without the first 0.

You can reach directory enquiries on © 192. If you get hold of a telephone directory, you'll notice that private numbers are collected in two volumes (A–L and M–Z) and businesses and services in a further volume. There are also yellow pages, ordering businesses by activity, which will only feature a name if the company has paid for an entry. The general operator's number is 100, the international operator is on 155 and international directory enquiries are on 153. The international dialling code is 00, followed by the country code in question (1 for the United States and Canada, 353 for Ireland, 33 for France, 39 for Italy, 49 for Germany, 61 for Australia, 64 for New Zealand). You'll find a vast range of services in the phone book, from a speaking clock to an alarm call service. These are rather expensive, and you'll probably spend less buying a basic clock of your own. The emergency number for police, ambulance, or fire brigade is either © 999 or © 112.

Finally, Britain has peculiar telephone jacks that are wider than the US variety. If you need to plug in a telephone or computer, make sure you buy an adaptor, available at decent-sized general stores.

Time

Britain is one hour behind the rest of western Europe, just to be difficult. During the winter (roughly the end of October to the third week of March) it follows Greenwich Mean Time; in the summer it follows British Summer Time which is one hour ahead of GMT. After years of poor synchronisation, Britain has at last agreed to change its clocks at the same time as the rest of Europe and North America. New York is 5 hours behind London time, San Francisco 8 hours behind, while Tokyo and Sydney are 10 hours ahead.

Tipping

Britain does not have the United States' established tipping code, but 10–15 per cent is considered polite in restaurants, taxis, hairdressers' and the posher hotels.

Toilets

The old-fashioned underground public toilets are disappearing fast—and with good reason, given their dubious hygiene record and reputation for attracting gay men on the prowl for casual sex. In their stead you will find free-standing automatic 'Super-Loos' which are coin-operated (20p) and smell of cheap detergent (there is one, for example, in Leicester Square). Generally speaking, you'll have a more salubrious experience in pubs, bars and restaurants. If you don't want to buy anything, just pop in to the toilets discreetly, and nobody should give you a hard time.

Tourist Information

London is one of the tourist brochure capitals of the world; show one faint sign of interest and you will be inundated in glossy paper. The main tourist offices, which can also help you find accommodation, can be found at the Underground station for Heathrow Terminals 1, 2 and 3; at Liverpool St Underground station; on the forecourt of Victoria Station; and in the basement of Selfridge's department store on Oxford St. Many districts also have local tourist information offices, which can be excellent and provide guides to show you round for the appropriate fee. The centres at Greenwich (© 0181–858 6376), Islington (© 0171–278 8787) and Richmond (© 0181–940 9125) also have accommodation services. The London Tourist Board has a recorded telephone service with up-to-date information (© 0839–123456); it is, however, rather expensive (up to 48p a minute, so look in the phone book or call 0171–971 0026 first to find out exactly which recording you want to access). The Tourist Board also has a website on www.London-Town.com with details on restaurants, shops, 3D maps and current attractions.

For more unusual tours of the city, contact the following: Supersky Trips, © 0345 023842: panoramic views from a 400ft-high balloon tethered in Vauxhall Spring Gardens (open 10–dusk, around £12 for 15 mins); Open Top Taxi Tours, © 01525-290800 (from £15 for 2 hours for up to five people): excellent tours of London in convertible taxis kitted out with sound systems, mini-fridges and instant cameras; Big City Scenic Flights, © 01275-810767: expensive aeroplane flights 1000ft over London with in-flight commentary.

There are any number of other guided tours, including guided walks. Hopefully, with this book in hand, you won't feel the need to resort to them, but if you do they are listed at tourist offices and in the pages of *Time Out*.

London in History

OLIVER
CROMWELL
1599
1658

> *When it's three o'clock in New York, it's still 1938 in London.*

Bette Midler

London is a city in love with the past. Not the unpleasant parts of it, mind you, not the grime, poverty and violence all too present in its long and turbulent history. No, the past that London cares about is glorious, colourful and just a little eccentric; strong on tradition, high on pomp and well larded with nostalgia. Its fondly preserved relics are in evidence everywhere: Beefeaters at the Tower, Horse Guards on parade, Savile Row suits, liveried assistants at Fortnum & Mason and red double-decker buses. History, at least according to folklore, has been very good to London: no foreign invasions since 1066, no major political upheavals since the Civil War, no grand-scale calamities since the Plague and Great Fire of 1665–6. Even when adversity has threatened, as it did during the summer of 1940, London has been strong enough to overcome it. Continuity has been the name of the game, or so London would like to believe.

Of course, London is kidding itself. Life in this most streetwise of capitals has been considerably more precarious than its folklore is prepared to admit. The pursuit of wealth, London's chief *raison d'être*, has always favoured the few at the expense of the many. Crime, disease, destitution and death have been constant blights, and popular revolt has all too often beckoned. The picture may be rosier in today's modern city, but insecurities about housing crises, transport failures and unemployment are never far from people's minds. It is not easy to face the present or look forward to the future with equanimity; hence the tendency—especially in times of recession—to take refuge in the 'good old days' of Empire and the Second World War, when Britain still counted as a global power and was not yet thrashing around for a role on the edge of Europe.

Much of London is dedicated to the deluded proposition that the old world is still with us. They're still changing the guard at Buckingham Palace, just as they did when Christopher Robin went down there with Alice circa 1910. The Queen is still on her throne, and the Queen Mother still wears flowery hats on important social occasions. Barristers and judges still wear wigs, and the Lord Mayor still arrives for his year in office in a gilded 18th-century coach. Of course these are just vestiges of the past, many of them absurdly if charmingly anachronistic, and in some cases actually bogus (*see* pp.76–80 on the fake traditions of the monarchy). The daily Ceremony of the Keys at the Tower, for example, has long since ceased to have a security purpose, if it ever had one. Likewise, the royal guards who stand to attention in their furry busbies and smart red uniforms are largely there for decoration. The more unpleasant aspects of the past have been either forgotten, or sanitized and co-opted into London's 'glorious tradition'. The great criminals of the past have been immortalized as ghoulish anti-heroes at Madame Tussaud's. Medieval torture is now considered a spectator sport for children. Even the punks on the King's Road, once considered an affront to common decency with their safety-pins and loud music, have become a harmless tourist attraction.

So London's history comes with a health warning: don't believe everything you are told. As V.S. Pritchett wrote in 1958: 'Dear, old-fashioned, leisurely, traditional, eccentric London is a legend we have successfully sold to foreigners—and to ourselves.' The gulf between this legend and the more complex, often more sordid reality helps explain many of London's insecurities about its place in the world. At times it is a city that yearns to modernize, to be hip and cutting-edge. At others, it likes to look back to a rose-tinted bygone age and sigh for the innocent youth it never had. London does not like to look squarely at its own past, but neither is it entirely able to escape it.

Origins: Rhinos, Romans and Revolt

London's habit of aggrandizing its own past began in the 12th century when Geoffrey of Monmouth, the man who elaborated the legends of King Arthur, spun tales about London being founded by a Trojan prince called Brutus and populated by heroic giants descended from the Celtic warrior King Lud. In fact, London in the pre-Christian era was an unpleasant swamp inhabited only by wild beasts. Excavations—at Heathrow Airport of all places—have unearthed evidence of elephants, mammoths, rhinoceroses and hippopotami. At the time of the first Roman invasion in 55 BC, there was no city on the Thames, and the main tribe in Britain, the Catuvellauni, had their capital further northeast at Colchester. It was the Emperor Claudius who built the first London Bridge to take his army over the Thames towards Colchester in AD 43, and Londinium grew up as a natural consequence on the north bank of the river. The settlement became an important transport hub as new roads radiated outwards towards Chester, Lincoln, Colchester, Dover, Lewes,

Brighton and Silchester. Colchester remained the capital for a while, but Londinium's position on the Thames made it an ideal trading centre. By AD 60, according to Tacitus, it was 'famed for commerce and crowded with merchants'.

Such prosperity was shortlived, however, for revolt was brewing among the Iceni of East Anglia, who had been double-crossed over the inheritance of their king, Prasutagus. Prasutagus had agreed to leave half his assets to the invaders in exchange for peace. But in AD 61 a group of Romans, taking advantage of the absence of their governor Suetonius Paulinus, decided to seize the other half as well. Prasutagus's Queen Boudicca (sometimes spelled Boadicea) was given a public flogging and her daughters raped. But Boudicca got her own back. She rallied an army and overran Colchester and St Albans before marching on Londinium, which she burned to the ground, hanging or crucifying any Romans she found in her way. It was the most serious revolt the Romans ever faced in Britain, and made Boudicca into a folk hero. Suetonius struggled long to win back the upper hand, but when he did he was merciless, slaughtering the Iceni indiscriminately and ravaging their territories. Boudicca herself took poison rather than face torture and execution at his hands.

Londinium was soon rebuilt, only to be beset by constant fires. The worst of them, in AD 130, did nearly as much damage as Boudicca's army. But the strategic position of the town served it well. The fact that it was on the edge of the Roman Empire kept it well out of the internecine rivalries rocking the rest of Europe, and allowed it to concentrate on selling cloth, hides, fur, gold, tin, lead and corn. In exchange it bought up pottery, glass, bronze, silverware, wine jugs and olive oil. The Romans fortified the town and built a cluster of public buildings, including a governor's palace, an amphitheatre, a Mithraic temple and a civic centre or *basilica* containing law courts, offices and administrative council rooms. The Roman walls, fragments of which survive at Tower Hill and at the Barbican, were completed by about 200.

The only threat to Londinium's prosperity came from the Pict and Saxon pirates of the North Sea. Towards the end of the 3rd century, an admiral named Carausius managed to beat back the invaders; soon, however, suspicion grew that he had helped himself to the pirates' booty rather than return it to its rightful owners. Rather than face punishment by the Roman authorities, Carausius declared himself emperor of Britain in 287. After six years of moderately successful rule, his fortunes began to wane and he was assassinated by his finance minister Allectus. Allectus was in turn overthrown by a new ruler sent from Rome, Constantius Chlorus. Londinium, now the fifth largest city north of the Alps, was clearly too important to Rome to be allowed to sink into civil strife.

The support from Rome did not last long. By the end of the 4th century, the empire was in terminal decline, and even Britain could not avoid feeling the effects. When a British-based career soldier called Magnus Maximus declared himself Roman emperor in 388, he took most of the colonial army off with him to Gaul and left Londinium at the mercy of the Picts, Saxons and Scots. He was just the first in a succession of pretenders to strip Britain of its garrison. In 410, as Romanized Britons appealed for help against the marauders, a hard-pressed Emperor Honorius could do nothing but tell them to organize their own defences. Nearly 400 years of Roman rule were over.

Saxons, Danes and Normans

At this point, London drops out of the history books for 200 years. Nobody knows for sure what became of the city in the 5th and 6th centuries. It seems, however, that it may well have been destroyed, because by the time records resumed London's street plan had changed and most of its citizens had moved out of the city walls to new settlements along the river. Christianity had arrived in a big way through the influence of St Gregory and St Augustine, and in 604 the ruler of the time, Ethelbert of Kent, undertook the building of the first St Paul's. The first Westminster Abbey followed later in the 7th century. This spiritual revival did nothing, however, to dampen London's trading instincts. By the 8th century, Bede noted London was 'a market place for many peoples, who come by land and by sea'. The wool trade, which was to form the basis of Britain's wealth for several centuries, began in earnest, and London grew fat as the chief entry point for consignments to and from the continent.

This peace and burgeoning prosperity was disturbed in the middle of the 9th century by new raiders, this time the Vikings, who swooped in from Denmark with horses in the holds of their ships and a terrifying array of battle-axes. Saxon Britain was quite unprepared to beat back their sophisticated army, and found itself overwhelmed. Only Alfred, King of Wessex, was able to stand up to them. He drove the Vikings out of his own territories in 871 and out of London 15 years later. On his orders, Londoners moved back inside the City walls as a defensive measure; the move paid off, since in 896 the townsfolk successfully repulsed a new Danish attack.

The situation remained tense but generally quiet for another century until King Ethelred (978–1016), nicknamed the Unready, decided he would prefer to pay the Vikings off than fight them. It was a disastrous decision. A band of marauding Danes kidnapped the Archbishop of Canterbury, Alfege, in 1011 and pelted him to death a year later. In 1013 the Danes took London after a brief siege and sent Ethelred fleeing for his life. Only after Ethelred's Norwegian ally Olaf pulled down London Bridge with ropes attached to his ships, so isolating the invaders, did the Danes call a truce and allow Ethelred back on the throne.

Ethelred was little more than a puppet, however, and his successor in 1016 turned out to be Canute, King of the Danes. Canute initially left London in the hands of Ethelred's son Edmund Ironside, basing himself at Winchester, but took over the city again after Edmund's death the following year. The Danish occupation brought new, unfamiliar customs to the city; one contemporary document records how Londoners resented having to wash as often as once a week, and complained about having to comb their hair to please Danish women—both activities considered unmanly in the extreme. This tyranny of gallant manners did not last long, however. Canute died in 1035 and his last son, Harthacnut, followed him to the grave seven years later. The new king was Ethelred's second son, Edward, who had spent the previous quarter-century in exile in Normandy.

Edward hoped that an alliance with the Normans would make Britain stable and keep the Danes out once and for all. He established his court and a new abbey at Westminster, earning himself the nickname The Confessor, and fostered strong ties with his former land of exile. Not everybody approved of his policies, and his chief rival Godwin seized control of the City in protest. When Edward died in January 1066, eight days after the consecration of his abbey, the scene was set for another showdown. Godwin's son Harold took the throne, and in retaliation Edward's Norman protegé William launched an invasion. As every schoolchild in the country knows, the two sides met at Hastings on the south coast, Harold was killed, and William (soon to be called the Conqueror) marched on victoriously to London.

Medieval London

William immediately showed he meant business by building a fortified tower at the eastern end of the City, so squashing any thoughts the citizens of London may have had about revolt. With the city merchants, William proved rather more malleable (they were, after all, the guarantors of the kingdom's wealth) and promised that their old trading rules would continue unhindered. Tensions between the City and the court at Westminster nevertheless persisted. One of the Tower's first constables, Geoffrey of Mandeville, tried to use his position to extort money from the merchants; he was so reviled that when he died he was left unburied for 20 years. The City made clear that it was not to be messed with, and slowly built itself into a powerful ideological counterweight to the king.

Over the next two centuries, the merchants organized themselves into a series of craft associations, or guilds, dotted around the City: saddlers in Fosters Lane, goldsmiths at the eastern end of Cheapside, plumbers in Clement's Lane, candlemakers in Cannon Street and shoemakers around St Mary-le-Bow. As their economic power grew, so too did their political confidence. They gave only limited support to

Richard the Lionheart in his efforts to raise money for the Crusades, preferring to support his brother John who was scheming to take over from him. At one point Richard commented in sheer frustration: 'If I could have found a buyer I would have sold London itself.' John became king on Richard's death in 1199, but immediately lost what credibility he had with the London merchants by demanding further taxes to fight a new war in Normandy. Eventually John's barons forced him to sign away a chunk of his powers in the Magna Carta declaration of 1215, obtaining amongst other things the right to elect a mayor for London annually without interference from the crown. Important though the document was for the development of the constitution, it would be a mistake to see the Magna Carta in itself as a great leap towards democracy. The barons were engaged in a power struggle and wanted primarily to look out for their own interests; the appointment of a London mayor gave them an important political platform. Then, as now, the mayor was appointed by the 24 aldermen of the City. His main job was to look after the interests of business; the people—ill-housed, ill-paid and without access to clean water or proper hygiene—did not come under any serious consideration.

Among the worst treated were the Jews, who had come over with William the Conqueror and settled north of Cheapside in the area still known as Old Jewry. From the start they had no legal rights. Barred from farming or any manufacturing trade, they were virtually forced into money-lending. They were also obliged to bury their dead outside the city walls, paying a spurious toll fee for the privilege. For a while they enjoyed a certain degree of protection from the king, but then the Crusades made anti-Semitism fashionable and they really began to suffer. When, at Richard the Lionheart's coronation, the crowd saw one Jew slipping into Westminster Abbey to offer gifts to the new sovereign, a mob formed and burned all the Jewish property it could find. The crown frequently fined Jews on the pretext that they had committed some heinous offence; if the king had no particular culprit in mind, he would simply fine the whole community. John's successor Henry III squeezed £160,000 out of the Jews this way, allowing him to pay for a good part of the rebuilding of Westminster Abbey. What the king couldn't steal from the Jews, he borrowed. There wasn't much difference; most Jews, after granting a loan to the monarch, never saw their money again.

The city merchants, meanwhile, went from strength to strength. As Henry III went deeper into debt, they bailed him out with loans and charged him extortionate interest rates. Henry railed and called them 'nauseatingly rich', but stopped short of imposing direct rule on London because he needed the merchants to plug his finances. The final showdown between Henry and the City came in 1263, when Simon de Montfort led a baronial rebellion to overthrow the king. Montfort won the support of Londoners of all classes with his promise of democratic reforms, but could not raise an army large or competent enough to topple the government. He perished at the battle of Evesham in 1265. Henry's revenge on London for its treachery was terrible. He fined the merchants £17,000 and wrote a new crime into the legal records: 'Offence, a Londoner'.

The City soon recovered, and when it did it refused all cooperation with the monarchy. Henry's successor Edward I was forced to turn to foreigners for money, inviting Lombard bankers to take up residence near Cornhill. Edward II meanwhile tried to curb the independence of London by force, with disastrous results. A furious mob chased the king through the streets, and when they failed to catch up with him they turned on his treasurer, the Bishop of Exeter, whom they tailed from Newgate to Cheapside shouting 'kill! kill!' before snatching him and hacking off his head with a breadknife. This incident contributed to Edward's deposition by parliament, and the disgraced king died a gruesome death, run through from behind with a red-hot poker at Berkeley Castle in Gloucestershire.

Riots and street fighting were a constant feature of medieval London and usually underpinned deep political tensions. In 1222 a wrestling match between Westminster and the City turned into a running battle. A century later, Italian traders fell victim to a mob accusing them of sleeping with English women and siding with the French in the Hundred Years' War. Sometimes the fighting would be the result of rivalry between two guilds, as in 1340 when the Skinners and Fishmongers pounced on each other. At other times anger was directed at the Crown, for example after Edward III licensed the export of wool exclusively to Westminster, rather than the City, in the 1340s. It was a dirty, precarious time to live, full of disease, dirt, crime and perverse punishment. Bad cooks were boiled alive, and crooked vintners were forced to drink their own foul wine in public. The Fleet river, running down from Smithfield Market to the Thames, was an open sewer overflowing with animal blood and offal. A baker called Richard drowned in human faeces when the floorboards he was standing on gave way and landed him in a cesspit.

Perhaps it was no surprise, given the teeming filth of the city, that the Black Death of 1348–9 hit London particularly hard. The population fell from 60,000 to less than 30,000 as the bubonic plague, carried by rats from Asia via continental Europe, ravaged house after house and street after street. Parliament moved temporarily out of Westminster because of an outbreak of plague there; the abbot and 27 of his monks died in a single month. Once the plague had done its worst, Edward III realized the importance of hygiene for public health and decreed that cattle should be slaughtered outside the city limits; largely as a result of his foresight, the population regained its former strength within 50 years.

Trouble soon beckoned again in the shape of the Peasants' Revolt. In 1381 a mob of peasants from around the country penetrated the capital demanding the repeal of the newly introduced poll tax, a universal levy so called because it penalized all citizens equally regardless of their ability to pay. The mob leader, Wat Tyler, demanded an audience with the 14-year-old King Richard II; while he waited, his men opened debtors' prisons, slaughtered lawyers, destroyed the residence of the unpopular and corrupt regent John of Gaunt, and burst into the Tower where they beheaded the Archbishop of Canterbury and his treasurer. The peasant leader eventually gained the royal ear, first at Mile End and then at Smithfield, where the king made vast concessions including the abolition of all feudal services. Many of Richard's courtiers could not believe their ears; William Walworth, the Mayor of London, drew his dagger and stabbed Tyler in fury at his presumption. The crowd erupted, and might yet have turned on Richard had the young king not stood up and offered himself as leader in Tyler's place. It was an extraordinary moment in English history: the mystical power of the monarch proving so great that the crowd took him at his word and dispersed peacefully. It was a bad call on their part. Richard immediately rescinded his promises (although, to deter further uprisings, he did abolish the poll tax) and hunted down and killed as many revolt leaders as his men could find. Tyler himself was dragged into Bart's hospital after his stabbing and then tortured and decapitated. Walworth, meanwhile, stayed in his post; his dagger was later incorporated into the arms of the City of London.

With so great a scare so early in life, Richard made sure henceforth that London and its citizens were well looked after. He established a Great Wardrobe to fit his court with lavish furniture and clothes, most of them ordered from City merchants like the celebrated mercer Dick Whittington. Whittington went on to be Lord Mayor four times, and under his guidance the City's power grew steadily, culminating in the construction of the magnificent Guildhall in the decade after Whittington's death.

The Wars of the Roses, a struggle for the crown between the Houses of Lancaster and York that dragged on throughout the mid-15th century, brought considerable disturbance to this calm. The City initially supported Edward IV and the House of York, but was happy to change its mind when political expediency demanded, not least because its champion was sleeping with the wives of a number of City merchants. Edward died in 1483 and his two young sons were subsequently murdered in the Tower of London. The hunchback Richard III, widely suspected of killing the young princes, took the throne for two years before going down in battle at the hands of the Earl of Richmond. Richmond, a Lancastrian, was crowned Henry VII and shrewdly ended the war by marrying a Yorkist.

Tudors and Stuarts: the Birth of Modern London

Political turmoil returned with a vengeance in the 1530s after Henry VIII's divorce from his first wife, Catherine of Aragon, in defiance of the Pope, and his consequent break with the Roman Catholic Church. Over the next 15 years a stream of churchmen, politicians and courtiers were executed, most of them at the Tower of London, as Henry closed the monasteries and cracked down on anyone who dared to challenge him. One of the first victims of this terrifying period was the humanist thinker Sir Thomas More, who refused to recognize the monarch as head of the church in England. Henry's second wife, Anne Boleyn, soon followed him to the scaffold on grounds of adultery, although her true crime (like Catherine of Aragon's) was giving birth to a daughter rather than a son and heir. Several ministers fell victim to Henry's growing megalomania, notably Cardinal Wolsey (who died on his way to execution) and Thomas Cromwell (who was beheaded at the Tower in 1540).

The political violence continued well after Henry's death in 1547 as the crown seesawed between Protestants and the Catholic Queen Mary. Not even children were spared if they happened to be politically inconvenient: Mary's 15-year-old cousin Lady Jane Grey and her equally callow husband Guildford Dudley were executed because of their families' Protestant allegiance. A modicum of order returned with the accession of Mary's Protestant sister Elizabeth in 1558, although she too had to resort to violence to fend off threats from her jealous relatives, particularly her Catholic cousin Mary Queen of Scots and her brother-in-law, Philip of Spain, who sent an unsuccessful invasion fleet, the Armada, to English shores in 1588.

Remarkably, the City kept its cool through this turbulence. For London, the Tudor period was one of unprecedented affluence. New industries, such as silk-weaving and glass manufacture, grew up and prospered. Commerce was so intense that the Thames turned into a multi-lane highway where boats were constantly obliged to raise their oars to allow traffic to pass. The richer merchants made a killing from the dissolution of the monasteries; they bought up the land on the cheap and then, thanks to the increasing speculative value of property in London, sold or rented it off again at enormous profit. Without doubt the key commercial event of the 16th century was the opening of the Royal Exchange in 1552; for the first time traders of all kinds could meet and fix bulk prices for their wares. It says much about the power of the merchants that in order to build the exchange, its founder Sir Thomas Gresham simply razed 80 houses along four different streets without so much as a thought for their inhabitants.

It was altogether a time of great social gulfs between the rich and the poor. As the population increased (from 75,000 in 1500 to 220,000 a century later), the greatest problem became access to clean and plentiful water. One Venetian ambassador to London in the early 16th century complained that he could detect the stink of the city cisterns even in his clean linen. A German called Pieter Morice alleviated the problem in 1572 by setting up a water wheel at London Bridge which pumped a supply up as far as Leadenhall market. A more permanent solution came 50 years later, when the City merchant Sir Hugh Myddleton had a trench dug all the way down from the underground springs of Hertfordshire. His New River provided a virtually unlimited water supply and heralded the enormous growth of London in the following centuries. Landed aristocrats moved into town, building palaces where monasteries had been, particularly on the land between Westminster and the City which we now know as the West End. This new district was not only near the royal court, it also enjoyed the benefit of the prevailing west wind which kept the stink of the City out of the aristocrats' nostrils.

England's peculiar Reformation, which after all had been motivated by Henry VIII's private interests rather than any theological rift with Rome, proved fragile at first. Soon, however, it was bolstered by the development of a radical anti-Catholic lobby inspired by Calvinist puritanism. The Puritans may have come in for a lot of bad press for their austere ways and their attacks on the Elizabethan theatre—John Manningham, a contemporary commentator, defined the Puritan as 'such a one that loves God with all his soul, but hates his neighbour with all his heart'. But politically they played a crucial role in questioning the powers of the monarch and the inequalities of English society. When the Stuart family—with its Catholic heritage and High Church sensibilities—came down from Scotland to take over the English crown in 1603, the Puritan agenda shot to the forefront of national debate.

The first Stuart king, James I, was so careful not to offend the Protestants that a group of disaffected Catholics decided to blow him up along with his parliament just two years after he came to power. The Gunpowder Plot was foiled at the last minute by a vigilant parliamentary watchman (*see* pp.63–5), thereby handing the Puritans a crucial propaganda victory and giving them virtually free reign to rant on about the evils of Roman Catholicism.

James's successor, Charles I, fatally underestimated the political importance of the Puritans. Because he was himself a Protestant, he failed to understand how his old-fashioned style of monarchy, based on privilege, favour and the divine right of kings, would anger them and push the country into civil war. The Puritans gained control of parliament and tried to force Charles towards reform. The king ignored their calls until 1641, when he was presented with a bill demanding the execution of his chief minister, the Earl of Strafford. He retaliated by dissolving parliament, only to find himself chased out of London a few months later. London had every reason to support the Puritan parliament; the merchants had always seen the crown as an obstacle to their aims, while many ordinary Londoners bitterly resented Charles's lavish spending and lack of interest in the common citizen. Once the fighting started, there was a purge of leading Royalists in the City including the Lord Mayor. Charles tried to lead his army against the capital in 1642, but could not overcome a tight ring of fortifications and turned back at Turnham Green near Hammersmith. Thereafter, the king did not set foot in London again until he was brought by force to be tried in Westminster Hall and executed outside his own beloved Banqueting House in 1649.

The architect of the Parliamentarians' military victory was Oliver Cromwell, a descendant of Henry VIII's ill-fated minister of the same name, who soon became de facto ruler of Britain. Cromwell turned out, however, to be despotic and unde-pendable. All talk of 'levelling' and democratic reform went out of the window when he closed down parliament in 1653 and accepted the title—and quasi-royal powers—of Lord Protector. By the time he died in 1658 he was almost universally reviled. John Evelyn described his funeral as 'the joyfullest that ever I saw, for there was none that cried but dogs'. Many influential London merchants had recon-verted to the royalist cause, and secret negotiations were soon under way to bring the future Charles II back from exile. Charles ascended the throne in 1660; Cromwell, on the other hand, was disinterred, hanged and decapitated, and his head displayed on the roof of Westminster Hall, the scene of Charles I's trial 11 years earlier. Despite this reversal of fortunes, the restored monarchy was a chas-tened institution: never again would a king assert his divine rights, nor would he dare to disdain the will of parliament.

Plague and Fire

The London of the 1660s was a prosperous city of a quarter of a million souls. The incipient trade in sea-coal was making it tremendously rich (and tremendously smog-ridden too). It was an unsentimental place, but at least it felt it could take any calamity in its stride. Fires would burn down a few buildings now and again, plagues would come along every few years and wipe out a few thousand people, but that was just the way life went. The overall mood, particularly among the gov-erning classes, was one of relentless optimism. Until, that is, the twin calamities of 1665 and 1666—an appalling plague followed by the worst fire in London's history.

The first bubonic plague victims in London were reported around Christmas 1664. The epidemic was initially checked by an exceptionally cold winter, but raged with a vengeance from the first warm days of April right through until November. The first sign of the disease was drowsiness, followed by headache, vomiting and delirious fever. Then the buboes would appear: at first no more than a rash, then full-blown black swellings under the arms and in the groin. The rash was called a 'token' which signalled almost certain death. These symptoms inspired the nursery rhyme:

> Ring-a-ring of roses
> A pocketful of posies
> A-tishoo! A-tishoo!
> We all fall down.

The 'roses' were the red skin rashes; the posies were medicinal herbs which the healthy carried around in the hope of warding off disease. The sneezing was a common sign of impending death.

What made the Great Plague particularly tragic was the complete abdication of responsibility by parliament, the City fathers and the king. Rich families moved out into the country from April onwards; Charles II prorogued parliament until September and followed them out, along with a swathe of politicians, municipal officials, doctors and clergymen. The economy started to collapse; shopkeepers went out of business for lack of customers and small companies were forced to close for lack of staff. Only quack doctors, selling amulets and concoctions of pepper and urine, managed to peddle anything resembling a living. Servants who had been abandoned by their masters either took work driving 'dead-carts' through the streets or else joined marauding gangs of looters and house-breakers. Gravediggers worked day and night. The corpses piled up in the streets and sometimes lay there for days at a time.

By midsummer, one Justice of the Peace decided to have the entire city population of cats and dogs exterminated, in the mistaken belief that it was they who carried the plague. Exterminators were paid two shillings for every animal corpse they could produce—the equivalent of two days' wages for a working man. Most of the cats and dogs were fed poisoned meat, or else clubbed to death. It was a crazy decision. The removal of all the cats gave free rein to the real villains, the plague-carrying rats, who now scurried around and multiplied with impunity. Fear and paranoia were rife. Londoners taking refuge in the country would not open a letter from the city without first washing it or heating it in front of a fire. Plague victims seeking a rural retreat were pelted with stones and manure to keep them away from healthy households. In London itself, any house with a victim was locked and guarded for 40 days, with all the inhabitants—sick or healthy—trapped inside.

As summer wore on, plague victims were seen foaming at the mouth and running naked through the streets. Some hurled themselves out of sheer despair into plague-pits reserved for the dead. The streets were filled with wailing and delirious moans. It was not until late autumn that the death toll began at last to wane; as late as Christmas there was still a stench of human putrefaction in the streets. Only when Charles II returned to the capital in February 1666 did London return to something like its normal state. The death toll from the plague was officially put at 69,000. It seems likely, however, that the figure was deliberately underplayed and that the real toll was nearer 100,000.

Catastrophe number two followed just a few months later. In the early hours of 2 September, a fire broke out at Farynor's bakery in Pudding Lane. Mr Farynor had almost certainly forgotten to damp down his oven, although he denied this in the subsequent investigation, and as a result sparks carried by a strong wind set fire first to the nearby Star Inn and then to the entire neighbourhood. The Farynor family scurried over the rooftops to safety, abandoning their maid who was left sleeping and burned to death. At first nobody thought much of the blaze. The Lord Mayor, Sir Thomas Bloodworth, was called out, but returned to bed declaring: 'Pish, a woman might piss it out!'

By morning, more than 300 houses and half of London Bridge were on fire. Soon the coal and tallow stores on Thames Street by the river were ablaze; then the London Bridge water wheel, which could have saved the day, was engulfed too. Attacking the inferno with water-filled leather buckets and primitive hoses, called squirts, did not do much good. The diarist Samuel Pepys was taken aback by the sheer heat: 'With one's face in the wind you were almost burned with a shower of fire drops,' he wrote. A scholar in Westminster, a mile away from the City, said he could read his Terence by the light of the flames. The glow was visible 50 miles away in Oxford. A worried Charles II ordered the mayor to pull down houses as a way of containing the fire, and dispatched a message through Pepys to that effect. But Bloodworth prevaricated once again, worrying about the cost of rebuilding what he personally destroyed, thus compounding the scale of the disaster. Believing the whole city to be lost, Pepys packed up his valuables and transported most of them by coach and boat to the countryside. His wine and Parmesan cheese he buried in his garden.

The fire raged for four days, destroying 13,200 houses, 44 livery halls and 87 churches including the medieval St Paul's Cathedral. 'London was, but is no more,' wrote the diarist John Evelyn. The damage might have been worse still but for King Charles who, realizing he could not count on Bloodworth, ordered the navy to break the fire by blowing up houses. By the time the flames came under control, the death toll was remarkably low—just eight victims. But the psychological damage was immense, as the fire gave rise to a sinister sort of instant fascism. Rumours spread that the fire had been started deliberately by foreign plotters or Catholics, and angry mobs began attacking French and Dutch families at random in the street. Some had to be locked up for their own protection. One Frenchman, Robert Hubert, was coerced into confessing responsibility for the fire at Farynor's bakery and hanged. King Charles, worried by the growing lynch-mob mentality, made a point of visiting homeless families camped around the city and disabused them of the foreign plot theory. But superstition persisted. Preachers noted that the blaze had started at Pudding Lane and ended at Pye Corner, near Newgate prison, and concluded that God was punishing the city for its gluttony.

In physical terms, London recovered with remarkable speed. The king rejected radical rebuilding schemes put forward by Evelyn, Christopher Wren and others, giving free rein instead to building speculators on condition that they used fireproof brick rather than wood. What this approach lacked in aesthetic finesse, it certainly made up for in practicality: by 1672 nearly everyone who had lost their home was rehoused. Public buildings were replaced with revenue from tax on seacoal; in this way the King's Surveyor of Works, Christopher Wren, refurbished scores of City churches and paid for his masterwork, the modern version of St Paul's Cathedral. Sadly, the atmosphere of intolerance and religious bigotry did not dissipate as easily as the physical scars of the fire. Catholics were scapegoated right, left and centre, notably by the followers of the notorious Protestant bigot Titus Oates (see p.64). As late as 1681, a plaque appeared in Pudding Lane blaming the fire on 'the malicious hearts of barbarous Papists'.

The death of Charles II in 1685 caused a constitutional crisis; despite siring several bastards, he had no legitimate son, leaving his brother James—an ardent Catholic—to inherit the throne. James II suppressed an uprising by Charles's illegitimate but popular son, the Duke of Monmouth, but could not consolidate his military victory with political backing. After three years, James was forced to flee, and parliament invited his son-in-law, the Dutch prince William of Orange, to come to England and take over. 1688 is known as the year of the Glorious Revolution, so called because parliament once and for all fixed its legislative role and decreed that no Catholic would be allowed to take the English crown again. The somewhat inglorious corollary of this revolution, however, was the institutionalized persecution of Catholics, particularly in Ireland where William took an army to defeat James at the Battle of the Boyne. The merchants of London did not let this bother them unduly, and they returned to the important business of making money. They established trading links with the Orient through the East India Company and, as the industrial age beckoned, laid the foundations of the modern capitalist system.

Gin, Corruption and Glory: London's Golden Age

The 18th century was London's golden age. Every great city has one, a defining moment in its history when all its best characteristics (and usually all its defects) are most saliently in evidence. One thinks of Paris in the 19th century, or New York in the first half of the 20th. Hanoverian London was simply and effortlessly ahead of the rest of the world. For one thing, it was much larger than any other city: its population of 650,000 at the beginning of the century grew to nearly a million by the end, making it twice as big as its nearest rival, Paris. One in 10 of the population of England and Wales lived in London, compared with one in 40 Frenchmen in their capital. The empty spaces between Westminster and the City filled with Palladian mansions, new residential squares, shops, offices and churches. Further building stretched south of the river, west towards Kensington and north around Hampstead and Highgate. This urban sprawl, which bewildered every commentator of the age, was the direct result of London's economic wealth, boosted by advances in science and commerce and reinforced by the creation of the British Empire.

Along with this physical and economic growth came a flowering of the arts: a newfound appreciation of architecture on the Palladian model; the emergence of British painting through Hogarth, Reynolds and Gainsborough; the rise of the theatre under the influence of the actor-manager David Garrick; and above all a thriving literary scene populated by satirists (Swift and Pope), novelists (Smollett and Fielding) and the towering personality of the journalist, lexicographer, literary critic and general man-about-town, Dr Samuel Johnson.

It would be a grave mistake, however, to take this general prosperity and cultural richness as a sign of contentment and well-being. The truth was quite the opposite. If the 18th century saw London at its most typical, that was because it also saw it at its dirtiest, most crime-ridden and most divided by class, wealth and ambition. The Hanoverian monarchs were corrupt and lazy, and parliament acted as their stooges. There was little pretence at democracy; the country was run by a cartel of rich aristocrats feeding off the misery of the majority. Most ordinary citizens spent their time in a gin-befuddled haze to forget their troubles. London, in the words of the historian J.H. Plumb, was 'filled with violence and aggression, with coarse language and gross manners, with dirt, disease and lust'.

The 18th century was, then, a golden age predicated not just on glory but also on corruption and grime. London was the prototype big city, and it presented urban life at its rawest and most compelling. 'Human life is everywhere a state in which much is to be endured and little to be enjoyed,' said Dr Johnson. But he also remarked that by seeing London, 'I have seen as much of life as the world can show.' London contained every form of existence, from the fopperies of powdered aristocrats stuffing themselves with rich food and gambling away their fortunes at the card table, to the desperation of ordinary people dying of hunger on the streets. It was an age of unreasonable appetites and colossal deprivations. The streets were for the most part unlit, unpaved and unnumbered; filth and refuse was stacked shoulder-high on street corners; the sky was often thick with fog. For the first half of the century the Fleet river (modern Farringdon Street) was an open sewer, and the Thames stank of rotting carcasses and industrial effluent.

Many of the century's most extraordinary figures were rogues or crooks. Conditions were so terrible that anyone who stood up to authority, even by breaking the law, was hailed a folk hero. Gossip on the street was not about politicians or aristocrats, but about such figures as Jonathan Wild, thief-taker extraordinary, or Jack Sheppard, the master jail-breaker. Their stories are detailed elsewhere in this book. Londoners lived at the mercy of a cruel and arbitrary legal system that proposed absurd punishments for trivial offences. Imitating a Chelsea pensioner was a crime punishable by death, as was planting a tree anywhere near the prime minister's office in Downing Street. One wonders what perverse pleasure was derived from such an eccentric system of crime and punishment; the Justices of the Peace, who were largely responsible for controlling crime in the capital, were described by Edmund Burke towards the end of the century as 'the scum of the earth'. The government used the law as a way of waging war on the lower classes, deterring them from revolt through fear. While the authorities might hang a child for stealing a single spoon, they were quite happy to let marauding bands of rich young men roam the streets and terrorize the city population. The most notorious of these gangs were the Mohocks, who took pleasure in torturing nightwatchmen, throwing housemaids out of windows or forcing prostitutes to stand on their heads in barrels. Few were ever brought to book.

London desperately needed a radical figure to counter this atmosphere of fear and corruption, and it found one in the unlikely form of John Wilkes. The cross-eyed son of a wealthy Clerkenwell distiller, Wilkes was a notorious libertine, drunk and member of the Hell-Fire Club which organized bizarre Satanic banquets. He burst on to the political scene in 1762 with the publication of the pamphlet *North Briton*, in which he hurled insults at all the leading figures of the age. At first Wilkes was treated as a bit of a joke and was appreciated mainly for his quick wit. On one occasion, the Earl of Sandwich told him in parliament: 'Egad, Sir, I do not know whether you will die on the gallows or of the pox.' Wilkes replied: 'That will depend, my Lord, on whether I embrace your principles or your mistress.'

Wilkes pushed his luck a bit too far in 1763, when issue number 45 of *North Briton* attacked the king's speech at the state opening of parliament. Wilkes was arrested and imprisoned in the Tower of London before being packed off into exile. To his astonishment, however, he attracted a large following of ordinary people who demanded his freedom with the slogan 'Wilkes and Liberty'. When the City hangman tried to burn copies of *North Briton* outside the Royal Exchange, a crowd gathered to pelt him with dirt and recover pamphlets from the flames. In 1768 Wilkes returned to London and tried to get re-elected to parliament as member for

Middlesex. Three times he stood and won, but each time the authorities cancelled the poll. Once Wilkes was thrown back into jail, another time a group of his supporters were gunned down by government troops. Eventually, however, the establishment realized what damage it was doing to itself and allowed Wilkes to enter the political arena via the City of London. This might seem an odd place for a radical to thrive, but the City merchants had shown in the past that they were not averse to firebrands as long as they could use them as weapons against the power of parliament and the crown. Wilkes became Lord Mayor in 1774, and although his agenda for universal suffrage, freedom of the press and reform of the legal system did not come about overnight, he put them irrevocably on the political agenda.

By this stage, popular anger was so great that it could have boiled over at any time. The explosion came, as it turned out, from a revolt led by one of the most trenchant anti-Catholics in parliament. Lord George Gordon was bitterly opposed to a Relief Bill allowing Catholics to inherit land and establish schools, and set up a Protestant Association to give vent to his opinions. In June 1780 the Association brought a vast crowd to St George's Fields in Lambeth for a demonstration; soon London had a full-scale riot on its hands. By no means all the protesters were anti-Catholic fanatics; rather they used Lord Gordon's demagogy to launch a general popular protest against the establishment. The mob burned down five prisons, including Newgate, and released the inmates into the streets; they attacked the prime minister's office at Downing Street and tried unsuccessfully to burst into the Bank of England. They also meant to roast the Archbishop of Canterbury alive along with other luminaries, but had to content themselves with plundering the Lord Chief Justice's house and tossing his extensive book collection on to a bonfire. The fighting, looting and burning lasted for five days and only abated when government troops opened fire, killing at least 285 people.

The violence of the Gordon Riots scuppered any chances of achieving any concrete political aims. Official reports made much of the fact that a brewery in Holborn had been looted, and dismissed the rioters as drunken hooligans. Politically, the *ancien régime* barely paid any attention to the uprising. Lord Gordon, as an aristocrat, was acquitted of treason and spared his life, while 21 members of the riot mob were picked out more or less at random and hanged. Once again, the Hanoverians showed there was one law for the rich, another for the poor.

The tide was slowly turning, however. Resentment of the Hanoverian order was growing, not only among working people but also within the establishment itself. The ageing, doddery and finally insane George III came to look as much of an anachronism as his less fortunate contemporary Louis XVI in France. Luckily for him, it was Louis who fell first, losing his head as well as his crown in the fervour of the French Revolution; the shock of events across the channel proved something of a respite for George since the establishment rallied together to prevent similarly radical ideas taking root at home. From 1792 to 1815 Britain was at war with France, rather than with itself, and the Hanoverians clung on a while longer.

What finally brought their order to an end was not a plot or a popular uprising—although the Cato Street conspiracy of 1820 (*see* p.68) came close—but rather the disrepute the monarchy brought upon itself. No episode better exemplifies this than the strange tale of George IV and his wife, Caroline. George first met Princess Caroline of Brunswick in 1795 when he was Prince of Wales. A few weeks earlier, with their marriage already in prospect, she had sent him one of her teeth which she had had drawn specially as a token of affection. It was not a good portent. When the two came face to face, George's first words were: 'I am not well. Get me a glass of brandy.' He then swore at his emissary, Lord Malmesbury, and ran out of the room. A stunned Caroline remarked: 'Does he always behave that way? What a fat man! How ugly he is.' This was not destined to be a marriage made in heaven, and the two parted ways almost as soon as they were officially pronounced man and wife.

That might have been the end of it, had Caroline not suddenly reappeared shortly after George's accession to the throne in 1820 and demanded her full rights as queen. Caroline had been living abroad for years, and most people had forgotten all about her, so George dismissed her claim as ridiculous. But the king's enemies, who detested George's decadent lifestyle and extravagant use of the public purse, saw a marvellous opportunity to get back at him and promptly supported Caroline's claim. In parliament, the Whig party depicted Caroline as a wronged woman who had suffered in silence while George conducted his innumerable affairs. The Tory party, meanwhile, took George's side and argued that Caroline herself was an adulterer who deserved to be dumped and divorced. The case went to the House of Lords, which astonished the nation by upholding Caroline's case and deeming a divorce inadmissible. A full-scale constitutional crisis threatened, but the Whigs decided they had embarrassed the king enough and decided not to take the issue any further. They had had no particular sympathy for Caroline and, having used her for their own purposes, simply abandoned her. At George's coronation in 1821, the queen was not only left out of the ceremony, but suffered the indignity of being turned away from Westminster Abbey. The doorman told her that since she did not have a ticket, she could not come in. Broken by the experience, she died just a few months later.

George's extraordinarily lavish coronation proved to be the last hurrah of the Hanoverian order. Having tarnished him in the Caroline affair, parliament proceeded to veto most of his plans to transform the centre of London into a new stately capital. After the appointment of the Duke of Wellington, hero of the

Napoleonic Wars, as prime minister in 1828, George barely got a look in. On his death in 1830, *The Times* wrote: 'There never was an individual less regretted by his fellow creatures than this deceased king.'

Victorian London

The Victorians liked to think of themselves as the champions of progress in London. To a large extent they were right. Thanks to them, the capital acquired street lighting, sewers, railways, buses, an Underground system, a regular police force, fine hotels, clubs, new theatres and, ultimately, a democratic government of its own: in short, all the trappings of a modern civilized city. The trouble was that in the process they savaged London's soul.

Their reaction to the Hanoverian era was a vicious backlash: having established that they did not like it, the more zealous among them set about destroying its every last vestige. They did not just turn away from neoclassical architecture, they destroyed whole chunks of it. They did not merely disapprove of the moral laxities of the Georgian era, they established a code of behaviour so repressive it was just as reprehensible as the one it replaced. It was a time of desperate hypocrisy, not least because many leading Victorians were by temperament as ill-disposed towards democracy and social justice as their forebears. Their doctrine was one of 'non-interference', which meant maintaining the status quo under a veil of liberal rhetoric. In their concern for industrial progress and economic prosperity, they very nearly lost control of London altogether. The city population jumped from one million to four million between 1800 and 1880, creating slums and desperate poverty on a scale never seen before. Because of London's instinctive abhorrence of central planning, the city lost all shape and purpose. As early as the 1820s, William Cobbett described it as 'the great Wen', and the epithet stuck. London came to be seen as a place to be feared, not enjoyed. The overriding preoccupation of the country's leaders was to avoid the kind of political violence rocking other European capitals. Reform—for example, the 1832 Act extending voting rights, which followed closely on the heels of the 1830 uprising in Paris—was almost always a reaction to the threat of revolt rather than a stroke of political enlightenment.

London in the 19th century above all lacked imagination. While the heroes of the Georgian era were criminals and radical politicians, now they were worthy bureaucrats like Edwin Chadwick and Joseph Bazalgette who, for all their qualities (and, on occasion, considerable defects), were never exactly going to set the world on fire. The most exciting event of the century, the Great Exhibition of 1851, certainly injected an air of cosmopolitanism into the city but it was never properly followed up. Paris may have been a far more traumatic place politically, but its palaces, boulevards and shopping arcades of iron and glass far outshone the bulky neo-

Gothic palaces of Victorian London. Its bright lights and lively nightlife made the British capital look unwieldy and dull.

The lack of imagination showed itself all too clearly in 1848, when most European capitals were being set alight by revolutionaries demanding a new democratic order. The Chartist movement, which campaigned for universal suffrage, organized a demonstration in Trafalgar Square on 6 March, which turned violent after the police panicked and started attacking participants. Instead of following this up, however, the Chartists withdrew into internal debate for a whole month. By the time they actually marched on parliament from St George's Fields on 10 April, the 79-year-old Duke of Wellington was waiting for them with 170,000 special constables as well as the full array of the Metropolitan Police force. Then it started raining, and the Chartists dispersed before they had even crossed the river. 'My poor friends,' said Hector Berlioz, the French composer, who was in London at the time, 'you know as much about starting a riot as the Italians about writing a symphony.'

In fact, the government had carefully laid the ground to ensure the failure of the Chartist uprising. In 1829, the Home Secretary Robert Peel had instituted the first uniformed police force in London, choosing not to arm them in a bid for popular support. Then in 1846 the government repealed the highly unpopular Corn Laws, which had discriminated against consumers by keeping prices high. In so doing, it isolated the Chartist movement from the urban middle class and ensured its eventual demise. When new movements like the trade unions and the socialists sprang up later in the century, the government was again happy to accommodate part of their demands if it meant averting a showdown. Further electoral reform came in 1867, and the right of workers to form trade unions was recognized soon after. Only once did a demonstration turn nasty. On 13 November 1887, subsequently known as Bloody Sunday, grenadiers with fixed bayonets fired into a crowd of socialists in Hyde Park, killing two people and injuring scores more. Compared to the carnage of the Paris Commune 17 years earlier, the losses were tiny. But they did much to mobilize the working class into a political force and so create the modern Labour Party.

The Victorians followed the same principle with social problems as they did with political discontent: containment. The government did little to alleviate the plight of the poor until the effects of poverty, such as crime and disease, started affecting the rest of society. 'Let those who are anxious to improve the health of the poor... prove to people of property that the making of these reforms will pay,' wrote the influential political thinker Herbert Spencer. Starting in the early 1830s, London was hit by a series of cholera epidemics. Edwin Chadwick, in his landmark *Inquiry into the Sanitary Condition of the Labouring Population of Great Britain* (1842), made a clear link between disease and poverty and deplored the sanitary conditions in London, particularly the water supply which was at the root of the epidemics. At first Chadwick's report was ignored, but when cholera started hitting the middle classes in the late 1840s and 1850s, the authorities began to sit up and take notice. Disraeli, the Tory leader and future prime minister, described the Thames to the House of Commons as 'a Stygian pool, reeking with ineffable and intolerable horrors'. A Metropolitan Board of Works was established in 1855, and under its chief engineer Sir Joseph Bazalgette built an embankment for the Thames and established the city's first network of underground sewers. The Great Stink subsided and the quality of water, which the reformer Sydney Smith had once described as containing 'a million insects in every drop', improved dramatically.

The problems of poverty, however, were not so much overcome as displaced. Slums in central London were pulled down and replaced with broad avenues. The inhabitants were forced to move out to equally miserable lodgings further afield. The East End, grimy home to thousands of workers in the London docks and scene of the Jack the Ripper murders in the 1880s, became the most notorious slum of all, which the Board of Works did little or nothing to improve.

Our Finest Hour

The late Victorian and Edwardian eras saw the growth of the suburbs and the gradual waning of the inner-city population; the City itself turned into a glorified office development, described by one member of parliament as 'a strange animal pickled in the spirits of time', and the Lord Mayor was no more than a figurehead for its business interests. By the time the London County Council, the capital's first overall governing authority, came into being in 1889, there was little it could do to influence the urban sprawl. The LCC's proudest achievement, the Clean Air Act which finally rid London of its thick fogs, did not make the statute books until 1956.

London in the late 19th and early 20th century lost much of its glamour. The empire had spread around the globe, and many of the country's brightest hopes set off for India or Egypt rather than face the prospect of a drab career in grey old London. The city was turning into little more than an entry and exit point for goods coming through its docks, a metropolis of contented tradesmen and petty bureaucrats. Joseph Chamberlain described it in 1904 as 'the clearing-house of the world'; but who wants to live in a clearing-house?

It took two World Wars and the collapse of the Empire to shake London out of its torpor. The first scare came with a series of German zeppelin raids in 1915. The LCC silenced Big Ben and drained the pond in St James's Park so that its reflection would not guide the German pilots to Whitehall and Buckingham Palace. The raids proved shortlived, however, and provided only a taste of what was to come in the appalling winter of 1940–1.

The sustained German air raids on London known as the Blitz began on 7 September 1940 and lasted for 76 consecutive nights bar one, 2 November, when the weather was too stormy for the Germans to fly. Around 20,000 people died, thousands more were injured and more than 1½ million properties were damaged or destroyed. Buckingham Palace was hit on 13 September but suffered relatively minor damage. St Paul's Cathedral survived the bombing virtually unscathed despite being at the centre of some of the heaviest raids of all. But whole blocks in the City and surrounding areas such as Holborn, Shoreditch and Southwark were wiped off the map. Londoners spent night after night either in specially designed corrugated steel shelters in their gardens, or else in the relative safety of the Underground stations.

Despite the suffering, Londoners look back on the Blitz with a strange fondness. It is remembered as 'our finest hour', when the threat of German invasion was thwarted through a blend of skill and stiff-upper-lip bravery on the part of an outnumbered and woefully unprepared Royal Air Force. Londoners remember the tremendous community spirit that accompanied the air raids and see the Blitz as a time of great social levelling when everyone, regardless of background, simply mucked in.

All of these memories have a certain degree of truth in them, of course, and certainly the community worked together with far greater cohesion than it had during earlier disasters in London like the Great Plague and Great Fire. But in truth the Blitz, like so many memories of the Second World War, was not quite as glamorous as the folklore version of it would have us believe. The people were chivvied along by the popular press and, in particular, some amazingly stirring speeches by the prime minister, Winston Churchill, who vowed to fight the Germans with 'blood, toil, tears and sweat'. The first great 'triumph' of the Battle of Britain was the evacuation of the British Expeditionary Force across the Channel from Dunkirk, where it had been pushed back by the advancing German army. As Ed Murrow, London correspondent for CBS news, remarked laconically at the time: 'There is a tendency... to call the withdrawal a victory and there will be some disagreement on that point.'

As for the air war itself, it was not true that the British were outnumbered. Both sides had about 1000 aircraft at the start of the conflict, and as the battle wore on the British managed to replenish their stock with downed German planes, an advantage their enemy did not share. It was not true, either, that the British were unprepared. They managed to detect the enemy with radio-direction-finding stations (later known as radar) which had been installed *four years* earlier in 1936. Indeed, there were so many ground defences that some historians believe shrapnel from anti-aircraft artillery killed more people than the German bombs.

In London itself, social levelling was more limited than was readily admitted. Grand hotels like the Dorchester or the Savoy converted their basements into comfortable dormitories for their guests (the Savoy even had a special section for heavy snorers), and most expensive West End restaurants offered all-night shelter as part of their service. By contrast poor Londoners, especially those made homeless by the bombing, had little option but to shelter in the Underground stations, which had no sanitary facilities and stank of urine, sweat and carbolic. Rats and lice thrived, and at one stage the government feared an outbreak of typhoid. The Underground was not completely secure either: 100 people were killed at Bank station after a bomb ripped through the water mains, and similar incidents occurred at Marble Arch, Bethnal Green and Balham. Some people became so addicted to sleeping in the Underground that they stayed long after the bombing was over. Others preferred to stay in their own homes despite the risks. One woman in Poplar had a lucky escape when a bomb struck during a bath. The blast turned the bathtub over and protected her from the brick rubble tumbling down around her. Rescuers found her naked, embarrassed, but quite unharmed.

From Multiculturalism to Sado-Monetarism and Beyond

High on the Dunkirk spirit, London recovered quickly after the Second World War. The Labour government of 1945–51, together with the LCC, established the modern social security system, provided free health care for all, began constructing social housing and organized the 1951 Festival of Britain to kick-start the arts. While the collapse of the British Empire might have been bad for the country's standing internationally, it did wonders for London. Not only did the city reassert itself as a centre of British culture, it absorbed much of the culture of the former colonies. Mass immigration began in the early 1950s and continued more or less unabated for 15 years. The main waves were from the Caribbean, India, Pakistan and Hong Kong. Drab pre-war neighbourhoods began to echo to the sound of steel bands, markets filled with exotic vegetables and spices and unusual new languages took root in the inner city. As a new youth culture grew up in the late 1950s and 1960s, the immigrant wave was a strong influence. Students ate cheap Indian or Chinese food, and danced at clubs playing salsa and conga. London latched on to the jazz craze in the 1950s and, after the advent of rock'n'roll, discovered an extraordinary musical talent of its own. The Rolling Stones, the Yardbirds, the Who and Eric Clapton all came from the London area and attracted vast followings. There had been nothing this exciting since Henry Purcell. Young people grew their hair and wore eccentric clothes that shocked the sober older generation. London, so the saying went, was swinging.

Well, up to a point. The young of London were pretty conservative compared to their Parisian counterparts, and they didn't put up much of a show in 1968 when students in the rest of Europe and the United States were out in the street demanding social revolution and an end to the Vietnam War. Some youth movements like the Teddy Boys were overtly racist and vented their hostility at the new immigrant population. Much of London society was as inward-looking and xenophobic as it had been when the Jews and Lombards arrived in the Middle Ages. In 1968, the Conservative politician Enoch Powell gave legitimacy to the new anti-immigrant mood with a speech in which he forecast doom if any more foreigners were to be allowed into the country. 'Like the Roman,' he said, 'I seem to see the Tiber flowing with much blood.' This so-called 'Rivers of Blood' speech inspired the growth of the neo-fascist National Front in the 1970s and found legislative expression in a raft of tough laws introduced by the Conservatives after Margaret Thatcher brought them to power in 1979. The black community in particular became stigmatized and slumped to the bottom of the social pile, leading to an explosion of anger in 1981 when riots broke out in Brixton, a major centre of London's Caribbean community, and again in Tottenham in 1985 when a police constable was hacked to death with machetes on the Broadwater Farm estate.

Under Thatcher, the fabric of London changed almost beyond recognition. Her aggressive free-market policies (which she liked to term a return to 'Victorian values' but which one adversary wittily described as 'sado-monetarist') deprived many public services, particularly the transport system, of badly needed funds. She waged war against the left-wing councils running many of London's boroughs by imposing a ceiling on the rates they were allowed to charge their local residents. Finally she abolished rates altogether in favour of the flat-rate poll tax—a short-lived experiment, as it turned out, which led to riots in Trafalgar Square in April 1990 and eventually to her downfall as prime minister.

Most seriously of all, Thatcher lost patience with the Greater London Council, the LCC's successor which had been created in 1965. Despite the fact that the GLC was a democratically elected—and popular—assembly, Thatcher decided she could not longer tolerate its radical Labour leader, Ken Livingstone, and simply abolished it in 1986. London was left with no single political body to oversee its affairs; the work was divided between five government departments, 33 borough councils and around 60 committees and quangos, all of them quite unaccountable to the electorate. The consequences of this erosion of city democracy were grave. Public housing became desperately short, the Underground grew ever creakier, and new developments like the Docklands were left with utterly inadequate amenities or links with the rest of the city.

To many Londoners, the Thatcher years were a nightmare from which they are only now beginning to wake up. In her messianic determination to challenge the old certainties of British life and replace them with her narrow vision of self-reliance and wealth creation, she created deep ideological divisions that served only to bring out the worst in London's social structure. The streetwise boys from suburban Essex who were allowed to make their fortunes in an increasingly unfettered City may have adored her, but to many others she was an object of undiluted hatred.

This drastic sense of polarisation lingered on under Thatcher's successor, John Major, but vanished almost overnight as Tony Blair's Labour Party swept to a land-slide election victory on May Day 1997. London suddenly felt rejuvenated and optimistic again; even people who had not voted for Blair (and there were some) sensed the excitement of change. The Conservative legacy was no longer a cause for grudges, but an opportunity to be seized in both hands. Instead of moaning about the erosion of public funding for the arts, the new government triggered a slew of public works projects for the Millennium using the proceeds from a Tory-era innovation, the National Lottery. Instead of exacting revenge in kind for the Conservative onslaught on Labour borough councils, plans were made for a refer-endum to reintroduce a London-wide government with a directly elected mayor.

Quite how long the initial optimism of the Blair era will last remains to be seen. London clothing fashions, London chefs, London music and London avant-garde art are all the rage at the moment. But the city's biggest problem remains its struggle for durable modernity: how to square its obsession with new fads and fash-ions with an old and drafty housing stock, a down-at-heel public transport network and a bureaucratic structure that is stuck somewhere in the latter days of empire. The point is not for London to turn its back on the past, or worse still to pickle it in briny nostalgia, but to take a cool unflinching look at its history, sort out the good from the bad, and use it as a springboard into the future.

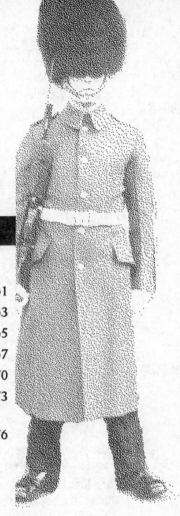

London Myths

> *The city does not speak its past, it contains it like lines on a hand; it is written in the corners of its streets, in the grills of its windows, in the banisters of its staircases, in the antennae of its lightning conductors, in its flagpoles, every segment notched in its own way with scratches, saw marks, incisions, knocks.*
>
> Italo Calvino, *Invisible Cities*

Every city needs its myths; they are the bedrock on which a sense of identity is founded. At their most harmless, myths provide people with a common culture and stories to tell their children. At their most sinister, they encourage nationalist fervour, jingoism, racial hatred and wars. The purpose of myths is to revise and reshape the past to make it seem more palatable. Reality is either glamorized or sanitized; thus crooks and scoundrels become folk heroes, despots become enlightened, and suffering either becomes picturesque or disappears altogether. What makes London peculiar is the extraordinary quantity of its myths, some of them so deep-rooted that they operate at an altogether unconscious level. Most cities conjure up just one or two images: lights and pavement cafés in Paris, skyscrapers and the promise of limitless wealth in New York, gondolas and romance in Venice. But London has many mythical identities. In different guises, it is a glamorous capital of royalty and aristocracy, a haven of middle-class decency and tolerance, or a Gothic labyrinth of fog and foul crime. Each of these images serves a distinct and often complex purpose: to play down the rigidity of the class system, perhaps, or to give a respectable mask to intolerance, or to justify inaction against poverty.

For a long time, London has treated its past not as history to be studied and argued over, but as a heritage to mould and dispose of as it sees fit. Nobody knows the real Dick Whittington any more; in the popular imagination he has *become* the poor boy who rose to the office of Lord Mayor with the help of his cat. Likewise, the pomp and ceremony surrounding the royal family is accepted without question as ancient and traditional; few people realize how recent and phoney much of it is. Seeing history as heritage has always appealed to London's ruling classes, serving to legitimize them as inheritors of a glorious tradition. In recent years, as Britain has declined as a world power and waves of recession have gripped the economy, this manipulation of the past has become a veritable industry. Museums, attractions and heritage centres have sprouted with extraordinary speed. As the manufacture of tangible goods has declined, the manufacture of nostalgic dreams has taken over to fill the void. Even advertising exploits images of the 'good old days' to sell anything from soap to sliced white bread.

London myths are not fixed, but are subject to startling mutations. One of the characteristics of the Thatcher years was to question the validity of institutions underpinning British life; one of the consequences of this was to plunge the institutions into deep crisis. The monarchy, in particular, has undergone a sea-change in public attitudes, with the myth of the marvellous Windsors now replaced with the new myth of Diana, saint and martyr. Tracing the trajectory of such public perceptions and their fallacies is not intended to ruin anyone's fun, but rather to alert you to the often amusing absurdities of myth-making and some of its dangers.

Come Again, Whittington

At the bottom of Highgate Hill, a few miles to the north of central London, is a stone inscribed with the words:

> *Sir Richard Whittington*
> *Thrice Lord Mayor of London*
> *1397 Richard II*
> *1406 Henry IV*
> *1420 Henry V*

This is the spot where, as little more than a boy, the future Lord Mayor Dick Whittington is supposed to have heard the bells of St Mary-le-Bow calling him back to the City of London, just as he was about to give up hope of ever making his fortune there. Dick Whittington is in many ways the emblematic Londoner, and his story is known to every London schoolchild through storybooks and Christmas pantomimes. It is a touching tale of a poor boy made good, a salutary lesson teaching us never to give up hope and that even the most modest of us can rise to the top of the social ladder. Unfortunately the story bears no relation to the way medieval London worked, and certainly has nothing in common with the life of the real Richard Whittington.

The fable—with apologies to those who know it—runs something like this. Young Dick makes his way to London with no other possession in the world except his cat, persuaded that he will find the streets paved with gold. His dreams are quickly dashed, and he finds employment only as a kitchen-boy in the house of a well-to-do merchant. The merchant is about to embark on a trading voyage to Barbary, and generously invites each of his servants to contribute something to the cargo so they can benefit from the profits of the trip. Poor Dick has nothing to give but his cat, who is duly dispatched upon the high seas. Subject to abuse in the kitchen and left with no friends in the world, Dick grows increasingly desperate and resolves to leave London. As he reaches Highgate, however, he hears the loud peal of the Bow Bells ringing out to him with the words:

> Turn again, Whittington
> Thrice Lord Mayor of London

Dick heeds the bells' advice, and on his return to the merchant's house discovers that he is rich beyond his wildest imaginings. Evidently the king of Barbary had a severe problem with rat infestation, and was delighted to buy Dick's cat for a fantastic sum. Dick marries his master's daughter, Alice, and eventually fulfils the prophecy of the bells.

The real Richard Whittington was not poor at all, but the third son of a well-to-do merchant from Pauntley in Gloucestershire. Thanks to his father's connections he became apprenticed to a mercer's company in the City of London and worked his way up to become one of the richest men of his times. He was Master of the Company of Mercers three times before attaining the office of Lord Mayor, which he held four times, not three as the Whittington Stone claims. He was never knighted, so the 'sir' is also erroneous. His wife, who was indeed called Alice, was the daughter of the City merchant Sir Ivo Fitzwaryn. As for the 'cat', that was a medieval word for a trading boat; Whittington had a fleet of them, which made his fortune by carrying wares to and from the continent. If he captured the imagination of his contemporaries at all, it was as a generous philanthropist. He refurbished Newgate Prison, provided a ward for unmarried mothers at St Thomas's Hospital and founded the College of Priests next to St Michael Paternoster Royal, the City church where he was buried in 1423. He made his real mark, however, by increasing the economic and political power of the City through the expansion of the wool trade and the wider use of bills of exchange. He was the first London mayor to be called Lord, and his riches went a long way to paying for the City's magnificent 15th-century palace, the Guildhall.

Interestingly, the fairy-tale version of the Whittington story only evolved in the early 17th century, a moment of great social flux when a fable about social mobility was a convenient foil for the burgeoning mercantile order. It was not the first myth to justify the increasingly unequal distribution of wealth in London. Fifty years earlier, the extremely well-born founder of the Royal Exchange, Sir Thomas Gresham, had invented a similar rags-to-riches tale about himself, saying he had been abandoned in a field as a child and that only the chirping of grasshoppers had stopped him from slumping into unconsciousness and dying. Gresham decorated his Royal Exchange and much of the City of London with grasshopper images to spread the tale—hoping the populace would forget that his wealthy father, Sir Richard Gresham, had used the grasshopper emblem before him.

On closer inspection, both the Gresham and Whittington stories undermine their bogus promises of social mobility. They suggest that their subjects were called to high office by a supernatural force (speaking through grasshoppers for Gresham and bells for Whittington), the inference being that the rich deserve their riches because they have been chosen from on high. One can draw a perverse parallel between the Whittington tale and the story of St Peter, who was scurrying away from Rome when Christ appeared to him in a vision and called him back with the words *Quo vadis?*. Both stories are about men losing their nerve and then, after a supernatural revelation, finding new inner strength. The difference, of course, is that Peter was fleeing persecution, not poverty, and returned to a martyr's death, not untold riches. The parallel, which would have been clear to 17th-century audiences, certainly has disturbing implications. In the City of London's curious system of thought, it seems making money is a virtue, even a form of redemption, on a par with the crucifixion of one of Christ's apostles.

No Catholics, Please, We're British

> *'Remember, remember the Fifth of November,*
> *Gunpowder, treason and plot.'*
>
> English Nursery Rhyme

Every year on the evening of 5 November, English families venture out into the cold for a peculiar kind of street party. People stand around, usually in a field or large garden, and watch a stuffed dummy being burned on a bonfire while fireworks whizz through the air above them. The dummy represents one of the great villains of English history, Guy Fawkes, who on 5 November 1605 was caught trying to blow up James I and all his ministers inside the Houses of Parliament.

Bonfire Night, as it is known, is usually a good-humoured affair, with children setting off Catherine Wheels and rockets while the adults roast sausages on a barbecue and down whiskies to keep warm. Most people assume it is a sort of displaced Halloween, or perhaps an adapted version of an ancient harvest festival. They even think of Guy Fawkes as a bit of a lad for daring to blow the establishment into the stratosphere. In fact the original purpose of the festival was not to commemorate Fawkes but to revile him, because he embodies every prejudice in the book against Roman Catholics.

Catholics have come in for a tough time in Britain ever since Henry VIII decided to break with Rome to divorce his first wife, Catherine of Aragon, in 1530. The ensuing attempts to keep Catholics off the throne, plus the never-ending English spates of ethnic cleansing *avant la lettre* in Catholic Ireland, have translated down the centuries into extraordinary outbursts of bigotry and hatred that jar completely with the tolerant self-image the English like to project. Guy Fawkes was one of a group of conspirators bitterly disappointed by James I's failure to ease the repression of Catholics introduced by his predecessor, Elizabeth I. The Gunpowder Plotters were hanged, drawn and quartered for their presumption, their severed heads displayed on pikes around London. Later in the 17th century, the Great Fire of London was widely blamed on Papists, and Catholics were chased through the streets by lynch-mobs. In the 1670s, an extraordinary Protestant zealot called Titus Oates had three dozen Catholics executed on trumped up charges of subversion and treason.

On one occasion, 100,000 of Oates's followers gathered at Smithfield to burn an effigy of the Pope; the dummy was stuffed with live cats which squealed as the flames licked up around them. In 1689, after the flight of Britain's last Catholic king, James II, anti-Catholic hooligans trashed properties and burned Catholic chapels; they appeared in the streets waving oranges on sticks, prefiguring the ritual beloved of the Protestant Orange Order in Northern Ireland. The same year, Catholics were formally banned from ever taking the crown again; laws followed in 1699 that stopped them inheriting land or establishing their own schools. A Relief Bill intended to relax these measures in the late 18th century fuelled the Gordon Riots, led by virulent anti-Catholics. Catholics were not allowed to worship in their own churches until 1792, and did not establish a functioning hierarchy in Britain until well into the 19th century. Even then ordinary people equated Catholicism with Irish nationalism, particularly after a series of Fenian terrorist attacks in London in the 1880s.

Nowadays Catholicism is coming back into fashion, boosted by the desertion of traditionalists from the Church of England over the issue of women priests. Even a member of the royal family, the Duchess of Kent, has decided to convert to the Roman Church. The decline of religious practice in general, and the growing irrelevance of the religious habits of the country's rulers have made most people forget the virulence with which discrimination against the Roman church operated. But the Catholic problem is still with us in the form of the Irish question; in Northern Ireland until very recently Protestants and Catholics were still shooting at each other, and the Catholics, by and large, were getting all the blame.

Ostensibly, Guy Fawkes seems to have little to do with this long history of rancour and ill-will. After all, he was hardly the first person to conspire against the crown. He was not even the ringleader of the Gunpowder Plot, merely the man who squealed on his comrades. He was not even a prominent advocate of Catholic rights. But Fawkes was the man unlucky enough to be caught with 36 barrels of gunpowder and a match in his hand in the cellars of the Palace of Westminster, and so became a vivid public symbol of treason and dastardly Catholic plotting. James I's advisers were all too aware of his propaganda value, and they inaugurated the commemoration of 5 November by a special Act of Parliament. The Church of England's Book of Common Prayer was amended to include a line about 'malignant and devilish papists' conspiring against the state and against God (the Protestant variety, that is); this sentence was not removed until 1859. After the overthrow of James II, with anti-Catholic feeling at its height, a ritual search of the parliamentary cellars was inaugurated on the eve of the State Opening of Parliament, a ritual which continues to this day. Bonfire Night is still imbued with a latent viciousness quite out of step with other British festivals. Every few years the dummy of Guy Fawkes is replaced by a current hate figure like Adolf Hitler, Saddam Hussein or Margaret Thatcher. And yet by now it is all laughed off as harmless fun. Children spend the days leading up to 5 November on charity runs asking for a 'penny for the Guy', quite unaware that they are reciting the first line of a vindictive anti-Catholic ditty. The full text goes:

> *Penny for the Guy*
> *Hit him in the eye*
> *Stick him up a lamp post*
> *And there let him die.*

Pea Soup in the Sky

Everyone knows about the London fog, right? The damp and stifling gloom that shrouds the streets in mystery and allows people to pop up and disappear at will; the swirling chaos where criminals can operate without fear and where lone women hazard out at their own peril; the sickly yellow industrial smog known as a 'pea-souper' that burns your eyes and tingles your throat. To some people, the fog is what makes London romantic—back in 1841, Benjamin Haydon called it 'the sublime canopy that shrouds the City of the World'. To others, it is what makes the city repellent; generations of snotty Frenchmen have refused to set foot in the place because they are afraid they won't see anything through the smoke and rain. So strong are the images inherited from poets, novelists and artists that many people, not just snotty Frenchmen, remain under the delusion that fog still inhabits the city today. In fact, the atmosphere was cleared by act of parliament shortly after the Second World War, and there has not been a pea-souper in London since 1962.

The fog, on the whole, was invaluable in creating some sense of mystique in workaday, mercantile London and has provided rich inspiration for the city's artists. Without the fog we would not have the tremendous opening to Dickens's *Bleak House*:

> *Fog everywhere. Fog up the river where it flows among green aits and meadows: fog down the river where it rolls defiled among the tiers of shipping, and the waterside pollutions of a great (and dirty) city...*

Nor would we have the dramatic cityscape paintings of Turner, Whistler and Monet. Indeed, so impressed was Oscar Wilde with the artistic possibilities of the fog that he could scarcely believe the phenomenon really existed:

> *At present people see fogs, not because there are fogs, but because poets and painters have taught them the mysterious loveliness of such effects. There may have been fogs for centuries in London. I dare say there were. But no one saw them, and so we do not know anything about them. They did not exist until Art invented them.*

Wilde was, of course, exaggerating for his own artistic purposes. Fogs most certainly did exist, and not just as a side-effect of the notoriously gloomy English weather. They were the result of burning sea-coal, the commodity that made London's export traders rich from the 17th century onwards. As early as 1661, the diarist John Evelyn complained about 'that hellish and dismal cloud of sea-coal' and vainly recommended planting flowers around the city to disperse it. By the early 19th century, the fog was so thick that it could last for days at a time. On 27 December 1813, the Prince Regent tried to leave London for Hatfield House in Hertfordshire but had to turn back because his coachman could not make out the road ahead of him; on the return journey, one of the prince's outriders fell into a ditch.

The fog almost certainly contributed to an increase in crime, and did few favours for Londoners' lungs. Hundreds of people died each month from the effects of atmospheric pollution. If you ever visited the cities of eastern Europe, with their brown-coal stoves and asbestos factories, before the opening of the Berlin Wall in

1989, you will know what the London fog must have been like: pungent enough to make your eyes water and your chest burn. Londoners would habitually walk around with a handkerchief over their mouth and nose to fend off what Robert Southey described in 1808 as 'a compound of fen-fog, chimney-smoke, smuts and pulverized horse-dung'.

The longest pea-souper of all lasted from November 1879 until March 1880; fogs persisting for several weeks remained common right up to the 1950s. Finally the government passed a Clean Air Act in 1956, gradually banning all industrial chimneys from the metropolitan area. In a macabre last hurrah, the fog caused a serious rail accident at Lewisham in 1957, killing 87 people. The worst of its effects were over, however, and five years later the skies were clear.

The Boys in Blue

In the early 1960s, the newspapers drew attention to the extraordinary Stakhanovite feats of a London police detective. 'Sergeant Challenor worked 102 hours in one week,' announced *The Times* in one headline. He was credited with 'new crime-fighting methods' and commended 17 times by his superiors for tireless dedication to the job. Once, according to his wife, he walked home 17 miles in the pouring rain just 'to keep fit'.

Detective-Sergeant Harold Challenor seemed the very model of a dedicated British bobby. And yet the real story was downright sinister. The new crime-fighting methods he advocated consisted essentially of planting evidence on his suspects. In 1963 he picked out a demonstrator during a visit by the Greek royal family and arrested him with the priceless line: 'You're fucking nicked, my old beauty.' Back at the police station, Challenor pulled a brick out of a drawer and tut-tutted: 'We have got to stop them throwing bricks at royalty.' The suspect said he was beaten up seven times on the way to the police station alone. On another occasion, Challenor tried to coerce a prisoner into leaving his fingerprints on an iron bar. When the prisoner refused, Challenor punched him in the face.

Perhaps the most astonishing thing about Challenor is that he was the first British policeman ever to be investigated for malpractice (he was eventually struck off the force in 1965). Even today, he is not considered anything more than an unfortunate blot on the glorious history of the London Metropolitan Police and its criminal investigation department at Scotland Yard. While in most countries the police force arouses at least a touch of suspicion or fear, in Britain officers are looked upon more like teddy-bear uncles than figures of authority.

The London bobby, with his trademark blue uniform and silver-starred helmet, is by reputation friendly, helpful, sanguine and efficient, kind to children and always gentlemanly, even with the most hardened of criminals. If he has a defect, it is perhaps to be a little too trusting, even dim-witted at times. But whatever his faults, there is no doubt that he is on the side of good in the struggle against evil.

This image is, of course, nine parts fantasy to one part truth. The one truly remarkable feature of the British police is that they have never regularly carried firearms. This has no doubt spared bloodshed on innumerable occasions and inspired a high degree of public trust. But that does not necessarily make London policemen more efficient or friendly than their continental European counterparts. They owe their enviable reputation not so much to their exploits as to a steady stream of sympathetic depictions in novels, on stage and on television. Dickens's decent detective Inspector Bucket in *Bleak House* is perhaps the prototype; a generation later Gilbert and Sullivan had a whole chorus of good-humoured policemen lampooning themselves and complaining that their lot was not a happy one in *The Pirates of Penzance*.

When the detective novel got going in the late 19th and early 20th century, the prowess of the police was usually pushed into the shade by the razor-sharp brains of Sherlock Holmes, Father Brown and Hercule Poirot, but even then their main fault was only to be a bit slow and bumbling. By the time of the film *The Blue Lamp* (1950), starring Dirk Bogarde, the boys in blue were very much back in charge as heroes against the dastardly forces of evil. *The Blue Lamp* spawned a long-running and highly popular television series called *Dixon of Dock Green* whose hero had in fact been killed off at the end of the film. The genial PC Dixon, played by Jack Warner, took on great moral authority, partly as a result of his resurrection, and ended each episode with a little lecture straight to the camera on why crime does not pay.

If bobbies have been spared the accusations of sleaze and corruption that stock to most other police forces, perhaps it is because they are a recent phenomenon. Before 1829 there was no uniformed force in London at all, merely an outfit of private detectives known as the Bow Street Runners (*see* p.209). The Runners' proudest exploit was to foil the Cato Street Conspiracy of 1820, when a group of anarchists planned to murder the prime minister, Lord Castlereagh, and his entire cabinet. The group was betrayed by one of its own members, who tipped off the Runners about a meeting in Cato Street off the Edgware Road. The ringleader, Arthur Thistlewood, stabbed one of the Runners to death before being overcome; he and his co-conspirators were later hanged.

The Cato Street affair made government ministers nervous about the informal organization of the Bow Street Runners and the possibility of infiltration by anarchist spies. Nine years later, Home Secretary Robert Peel—originator of the nickname 'bobby' and the less frequent 'peeler'—legislated to create a full uniformed force. His main aim was to reassure the public, not scare them ('Liberty does not consist of having your house robbed by organized gangs of thieves,' he told the House of Commons), so he decided firearms would be inappropriate.

The 19th century saw a sharp increase in crime in London, largely as a result of deepening poverty, and the new police soon had their work cut out. In 1841 they made their first big blunder when they allowed Daniel Good, a Roehampton man who had murdered and chopped up his wife, to slip through their fingers. Although they eventually caught him on his way to the coast, they decided they needed a special criminal investigation department. The result was Scotland Yard, which began operating in 1842 from offices in Whitehall (later moved to Northumberland Avenue).

The Yard's record is far from unblotted. Its most famous case, the hunt for Jack the Ripper (*see* below), has never been solved. Moreover, it has a disturbing record of botching sensitive investigations, especially when they have involved foreigners. In 1894 a 26-year-old French tourist called Martial Bourdin was caught in a bomb explosion outside the Royal Observatory in Greenwich and died of his injuries; it later emerged he was the victim of a plot by undercover police agents trying to discredit foreign anarchists. In 1911 policemen tracked down a gang of jewel thieves to a house in Sidney Street in the East End. The police believed the thieves included a notorious Russian anarchist called Peter the Painter, and brought in a troop of marksmen to start shooting. The gangsters fired back, but after a five-hour siege (during which the unflappable local postman continued his deliveries undaunted), the house caught fire and everyone in it perished. The police persisted in their theory that a foreign anarchist plot had been in the works, but no evidence ever emerged to back up their assertions or their heavy-handed tactics. Recent research suggests that Peter the Painter, who became a bogeyman to generations of children, was not in the building at all.

In recent times the blunders have mainly involved black immigrants and Irish terrorist suspects. In the 1970s police extracted confessions under duress from Irish suspects accused of setting off bombs in Guildford and Birmingham; as a result 10 innocent men and women spent more than 15 years in jail before being vindicated. In London, the police's reputation took a nosedive after the 1981 Brixton riots, when a public inquiry charged them with open hostility towards the black community. Four years later they were accused of fabricating evidence after the murder of a policeman on a mainly black housing estate in Tottenham; the three men sent to prison for the murder were eventually exonerated.

For a while in the 1980s, the Dixon of Dock Green image looked in serious danger of falling apart. Newspapers gleefully carried stories about police prejudice and brutality, such as the following from the *Daily Telegraph*:

> *PC Alcock denied using any violence. He said he could explain the fact that polish found on the zip of Mr Torrance's trousers was identical to that on his shoes.*

Or this from the *Guardian*:

> *A police inspector told an inquest yesterday that he was not immediately concerned at the sight of a prisoner tied up with a rope, a belt and two pairs of handcuffs, who was being held around the head by a colleague on the floor of a police station.*

The 1990s have seen a certain amount of sympathy return to the police, if only because a number of them have been killed while hunting down crack-dealing gangs in the capital. In response, one category of special police was given permission to carry handguns in 1994 without first seeking clearance from their superiors. The police may still be heroes, but nobody is pretending any more that they are *nice*. Short of another resurrection, PC Dixon wouldn't survive very long in today's world with his simple truncheon, his home-spun philosophy and ready smile.

I Made My Excuses and Left

In the late 1980s, the *Sunday Times* reporter Liz Hodgkinson made a big splash by announcing in her weekly column that she and her husband had given up having sex. Celibacy, she argued, was a much healthier way of living and took nearly all the tension out of her marital relationship. God knows what the bar-room gossip at the newspaper was like, especially since her husband Neville also worked for the *Sunday Times*, but in the country at large she was treated with a mixture of bewilderment and strange admiration. The English have a reputation for being rather uninterested in sex; indeed they sometimes wear their indifference like a badge of pride. The confessions of Mrs Hodgkinson only seemed to confirm the old adage pronounced by the Hungarian-born humorist George Mikes in the 1950s: 'Continental people have a sex life; the English have hot-water bottles.'

Of course, this supposed indifference to the pleasures of the flesh is pure tosh. The English are as interested as anyone in getting their leg over (as their charming phrase has it). Back in the 18th century, to go back only that far, aristocratic young men used to have sex with prostitutes in the bushes of St James's Park without hint of shame, while around the corner at the Temple of Health and Hymen on Pall Mall, couples with fertility problems were encouraged to come and make love beneath a mirrored dome on horse-hair mattresses. The literature of the time was peppered with explicit amorous encounters; even pornographic novels like John Cleland's *Fanny Hill* were considered respectable in polite company.

The prudishness which set in during the 19th century was not specific to Britain, but perhaps under the matronly eye of Queen Victoria it found its most eccentric and extreme expression. London middle-class society (where the puritan ethic was strongest) was organized around two exclusively male environments, the work-place and the club. Women were hidden away at home and only brought out on special occasions. Sex was strictly for procreation, at least in theory; female orgasms weren't supposed to exist, and male ones, unless produced in a God-fearing cause, were supposed to make you blind. In fact, sex was rampant—particularly among those middle-class men who set all the moralistic rules in the first place—and certainly not all pious in intent. Roughly one in every 60 houses in London was a brothel (a commentary on the poverty as well as the sexual hypocrisy of the age); men who did not believe their wives could have orgasms would regularly let themselves be taken in by prostitutes faking theirs.

Beneath this essentially misogynistic state of affairs lay a strong latent streak of homosexuality. Middle-class boys were thrust together in one hothouse environ-ment after another, from boarding school to sports field to office to dining society. The Empire fostered unmistakably homo-erotic images of muscular, sun-tanned young men making deep bonds of comradeship as they sought glory together in the Near East and India. Single-sex intimacy was the defining code of male Victorian behaviour, even if homosexuality itself was officially considered a criminal offence.

It took decades for the hypocrisies of the Victorian era to begin to wear off. A turning point was the trial in 1960 which succeeded in unbanning D.H. Lawrence's *Lady Chatterley's Lover*, hitherto deemed obscene. Just a few years later, rock stars were the new role models, getting through girlfriends faster than clean shirts and calling their behaviour a sexual revolution. Free love was in, and sex became an instrument of rebellion against the fusty older generation. Sexual intercourse—according to that most furtive and sardonic of English poets, Philip Larkin—began in 1963, 'between the end of the *Chatterley* ban/And the Beatles' first LP'.

Well, the inhibitions didn't quite all disappear in a Reichian puff of smoke. The Conservative Party, to its cost, persisted in preaching high moral values and then counted the cost when one of its cabinet ministers, John Profumo, was caught out in an embarrassingly sordid sex scandal. In the auspicious year of 1963, Profumo was found to have slept with a high-class call-girl, who in turn had been sleeping with the defence attaché at the Soviet Embassy. The affair had the effect of a bomb-shell, exploding every myth of buttoned-up sobriety ever connected with the British establishment. 'In the late spring of 1963,' wrote the newspaper columnist Bernard Levin, 'men and women all over Britain were telling, and others believing and embellishing and repeating, such stories as that nine High Court judges had been engaging in sexual orgies, that a member of the Cabinet had served dinner at a private party while naked except for a mask, a small lace apron and a card round his neck reading "if my service don't please you, whip me", that another member of the Cabinet had been discovered by police beneath a bush in Richmond Park where he and a prostitute had been engaging in oral genital sex...' Profumo was, of course, forced to resign—although for misleading parliament rather than any breach of morals or security—and the following year a humiliated Conservative government tumbled to its first election defeat in 13 years.

Despite the Profumo affair, prudishness has never quite gone out of fashion in Britain. The sexual revolution had its backlash, particularly in attitudes to censorship in the media. In the 1970s, the most robust campaigner—the closest thing in Britain to a Moral Majority—turned out to be a prim sexuagenarian called Mary Whitehouse, who seemed to spend her whole time reading and watching filth, and then writing incensed letters about how disgusting she found it all. Through her efforts, a poem describing a Roman centurion's erotic fantasies about the crucified Christ, which first appeared in the homosexual journal *Gay News* (what was a nice old lady doing reading *that*?), was banned on grounds of blasphemy in 1975. Likewise, she managed to influence the British Board of Film Classification to cut or ban a number of films with what she perceived as an overdose of sex or violence. A lot of trash went unmissed, but serious films like Derek Jarman's *Sebastiane* (incidentally the first feature film ever shot in Latin) had the greatest difficulty in reaching the audience they deserved. Film censors have shown frequent sympathy for Mrs Whitehouse's views; one, back in the 1960s, remarked: 'Anything that turns me on, I cut.'

This persistent prudery has returned to haunt the Conservative Party in recent years. In 1983, Margaret Thatcher's anointed successor Cecil Parkinson was forced to resign because making his secretary pregnant was not deemed consistent with the 'Victorian values' that Thatcher was touting at the time (although of course such behaviour was perfectly normal by Victorian standards; his only mistake was to be found out). A decade later, as Thatcher's successor John Major was pushing the slogan 'Back to Basics' and blaming many of society's ills on the break-up of the traditional family, one minister was forced to resign for siring an illegitimate family without telling his wife, another was humiliated for making love to his mistress in football socks and a Conservative MP was found asphyxiated in his London flat, apparently as a result of a sexual misadventure involving women's underwear, a plastic bag and an orange spiked with amyl nitrate.

The hypocrisy inherent in all these scandals has been compounded by the attitude of the downmarket press, whose own attitude to sex epitomizes all that is most hateful and prurient about Victorian morality. The *Sun* and the *Star* claim to be 'family' newspapers, yet between their covers are countless tales—told in a tone of phoney outrage betrayed by an evident voyeuristic glee—of three-in-a-bed romps, lecherous priests and shameless temptresses luring happily married men into trouble. When it comes to political sex scandals, you can sense the tabloid editors salivating with delight even as they pontificate on the disgustingness of it all. Their skewed attitude is evident from their vocabulary, peppered with words like 'peek-a-boo', 'curvy' and 'buxom' that come straight out of a 1950s timewarp of giggly schoolboy smut. More than 30 years on from the sexual revolution, reporters still pretend to be selfless martyrs to the cause of investigative journalism as they wander from brothel to peep-show to strip-joint in search of scandal.

There are signs that the public is no longer willing to be shocked by such puerile nonsense. The new intake of MPs in the 1997 election for the first time included a number of declared homosexuals, one of whom, Ben Bradshaw, overturned a large Conservative majority in Exeter partly because of his adversary's patently obnoxious attempt to make political capital out of his sexuality. A few months later, the new Foreign Secretary, Robin Cook, managed to weather a media storm and survive after leaving his wife and moving in with his secretary. More recently still, London has tittered and gasped (but not keeled over in holier-than-thou horror) at tales of couples having sex behind the American Memorial in St Paul's Cathedral, or in a private box at the Victoria Palace Theatre during a packed performance. It seems that what the public hates is not the sexual transgression so much as the revolting double standards that so often go with it. Conservatives are still getting caught in honey traps and living in fear of being 'outed' for some misdemeanour or another. But even they must be getting the message that a little honesty can save a thousand blushes. After all, the Victorian era ended a long, long time ago.

Everybody's Favourite Serial Killer

In France he is Jacques L'Eventreur, in Italy Jack Lo Squartatore, in Spain Jack El Destripador. He is the most famous criminal in the universe, and yet nobody has ever found out who he was. Jack the Ripper really needs no introduction—the man who terrorized prostitutes in the East End of the 1880s, the world's first sex murderer to be labelled as such, the Hannibal Lecter of old London Town. Certainly, his is a grim legacy. But what is it about him that captures the imagination so? To read some accounts of his handiwork, you would have thought that crime never existed in London until he invented it.

In fact, old Jack was remarkable neither for the heinousness of his crimes, nor even for his targeting of prostitutes. Of the 900,000 inhabitants of the East End of the time, 11,000 lived in a state of absolute misery and more than 100,000 lived below what we would now consider to be the poverty line. More than half the children born there died before they reached the age of five, and 10 per cent of those who reached elementary school were mentally defective as a result of cold, hunger and exhaustion. Not only was prostitution rife in this environment, many unfortunate women also came to appalling ends at the hands of pimps or customers. Five months before the Ripper killings began, for example, a street-walker called Emma Elizabeth Smith was found in Limehouse with her ear severed and a spike up her vagina. She eventually died in agony of peritonitis. Violence was a daily reality.

What made Jack special was not so much his psychotic behaviour as his appeal to newspaper editors. In 1888, the year of the Ripper murders, the popular press was just beginning to hit the big time; circulation of the leading paper, the *Lloyd's Weekly News*, was edging towards the one million mark. Every newspaper loves a good story, and Jack the Ripper had it all—sex, violence, mystery, squalor and the possibility of endless speculation about suspects. By the time the popular Sunday papers were through, the list of possible Rippers included Walter Sickert the painter, Sir William Gill (Queen Victoria's personal physician), and even the Duke of Clarence, the syphilis-ridden son of the Prince of Wales.

There were deeper reasons, too, why Jack the Ripper appealed to late Victorian audiences. The senseless violence he perpetrated was a startling expression of the urban alienation of the age. The city was monstrously large, choked in smog, and racked by appalling gulfs between rich and poor. The narrow alleys and squalid tenements of the East End were a part of London which few people knew or cared to explore; most of the time the area was pushed, like a guilty secret, to the back of their minds. The Jack the Ripper saga presented an opportunity for them to exorcise, at a safe distance, their anxieties and feelings of responsibility for the chaos of the city. The sex angle was also cathartic in its way, sending a frisson of guilt-ridden excitement down the spine of every buttoned-up Victorian prude; remember this was the age in which table legs were covered to spare ladies' blushes and prostitutes described, if at all, as 'daughters of joy'.

The facts of the case, it's true, are pretty gruesome. The Ripper first struck on 31 August, slitting the throat and abdomen of Mary Ann Nichols in Buck's Row in Whitechapel. The next victim was Annie Chapman, mutilated and decapitated on 8 September at the back of a lodging house in Hanbury Street (now the site of a brewery). Murders three and four took place on 30 September—Elizabeth Stride in Berner Street and Catherine Eddowes in Mitre Square in the City, the latter found with her intestines pulled out.

The newspapers omitted some of the more lurid details from their reports, but nevertheless succeeded in creating a sensation, not least in the East End itself. Women would joke that they were 'the next for Jack'. A lynch-mob mentality grew up, and bands of men would pounce on strangers at random, particularly foreigners and Jews. Shortly after Eddowes' murder, a message appeared on the wall behind her body: 'The Jewes [sic] are the ones that will not be blamed for nothing.'

More than a month went by, and then the killer struck for a final time, killing Mary Jane Kelly in Miller's Court off Dorset Street. By now every bar room in the country was discussing who the killer might be, speculating what his motives were and suggesting how to catch him. One particularly unpleasant theory was that Jack the Ripper had syphilis and, following an ancient Chinese superstition, used women's genitals to suck the virus off his ulcers. Among the intriguing ideas for tracking down the culprit was a plan to place springed dummies of women in dark alley-ways that would sound an alarm as soon as they were touched. Just as all this gossip reached fever pitch, however, the killings suddenly stopped. Nobody knows why. Two prostitute murders the following year were initially attributed to Jack the Ripper, but the connection was subsequently dropped on forensic grounds.

So who was Jack the Ripper? At first the most popular theory was that he was a doctor, since the mutilations betrayed a knowledge of anatomy and seemed to have been carried out with medical instruments. But soon the wildest conspiracy theories grew up, linking the murders to anyone and everyone from Oscar Wilde to the queen herself. The most likely (and therefore, to Ripperologists, the least interesting) suspect was a certain Dr Montague John Druitt, a doctor not of medicine but of law who disappeared soon after Mary Kelly's murder and whose corpse was subsequently found floating in the Thames with stones in his coat pockets. Sir William Gill was also an attractive suspect, not least because he was often seen wandering around Whitechapel. As for the Duke of Clarence, his main link was a physical resemblance to Druitt, and a rumour that he had gone soft in the head because of venereal disease.

The fascination of the Ripper case has only increased with the years, and every literary, criminological and scientific school has come up with its own theory. Books on the subject are so numerous that nobody has yet managed to compile a complete bibliography. The attraction, aside from the obvious draw of an unsolved mystery, is perhaps the extraordinary number of London myths that the case evokes—crime, bobbies, fog, class, hang-ups about sex, and, peripherally, the royal family. One hypothesis dear to certain psychologists is that the Ripper was James Kenneth Stephen, the Duke of Clarence's old tutor from Cambridge, the theory being that Stephen was in love with Clarence and killed the prostitutes to avenge his unrequited homosexual passion.

Conspiracy theorists have become convinced there was an official cover-up, particularly since Scotland Yard mysteriously closed the files on the case in 1992. Feminists (or anti-feminists, depending on which way you look at it) have speculated about a Jill the Ripper, suggesting that she was a crazed backstreet abortionist. Even murderers have looked to Jack for inspiration; a killer operating among the sex shops and peep shows of Soho in the 1960s quickly earned the nickname Jack the Stripper.

By now the Ripper is not just a historical figure, but an icon of popular culture. Stories and novels have variously imagined the Ripper emigrating to America to carry on his evil deeds, or repenting and taking holy orders, or undergoing a sex change and calling himself Jane the Ripper. He has starred in the parodic musical *Eine kleine Rippermusik*, inspired a play (Frank Wedekind's *Lulu*), an opera (Alban Berg's version of Wedekind's story) and numerous films. Alfred Hitchcock's silent classic *The Lodger* is essentially the Ripper story; in Stanley Kubrick's *Dr Strangelove*, the mad Brigadier-General who unleashes nuclear armageddon is called Jack D. Ripper. Jack has popped up on *Star Trek*, lodged as an evil force inside the computer on the Starship Enterprise. He even dominates the menu of a café in Charlottesville, Virginia, where you can order Elizabeth Stride sandwiches (featuring a mixture of cold meats), Annie Chapman tuna fish rolls, Poor Old Jack's roast beef and Mary Kelly cheesecake.

Perhaps the most perverse twist to the Ripper story is in Michael Dibdin's novel *The Last Sherlock Holmes Story* (1979). The idea of pitting the great detective of Baker Street against Victorian London's most notorious criminal is not unique: Ellery Queen wrote a mystery story on this premise and James Hill turned it into a successful film starring Peter Cushing called *A Study in Terror*. But in Dibdin's book, it turns out that Sherlock Holmes *is* Jack the Ripper. Watson catches his friend *in flagrante* as he skins the mutilated body of Mary Kelly and hangs strips of her flesh from a picture rail, all the while jauntily humming *La donna è mobile* from Verdi's *Rigoletto*. The ultimate battle between good and evil then takes place at the Reichenbach Falls, not between Holmes and Moriarty, but between Watson and Holmes. Conan Doyle, a man with a wicked sense of humour of his own, would no doubt have enjoyed the joke.

Keeping the Anachronism Alive: The Royal Family

Mention the House of Windsor and most people will think of divorce, dysfunction, breathless late-night phone calls, toe-sucking in the South of France and, of course, that ghastly car crash under the Pont de l'Alma in Paris. Crisis and scandal seem to be the only things keeping the British royals in the newspaper headlines any more; to predict the imminent demise of the monarchy has become the journalistic commonplace of the decade.

And yet one forgets quite how recently those same newspapers were revelling in the timeless mysteries of kingship, in the glories of Britain's royal heritage and the magnificent example that the Windsors set for family life up and down the realm. Back in the mid-1980s, the Queen was marvellous and kind and decent, Prince Philip a bit tactless but charming enough; Charles and Diana were living in fairy-tale bliss; Andrew had forgotten his ex-porn star girlfriend and married the bubbly Fergie; Princess Anne was showing extraordinary dedication in her work for Save the Children, and even the wimpy Prince Edward was doing all right as an apprentice to the maestro of the modern British musical, Andrew Lloyd Webber. Every few years a royal wedding or jubilee would bring the crowds out into the streets waving their Union Jacks and brandishing their Chaz'n'Di coffee mugs. 'Modern societies still need myth and ritual,' the Conservative politician Ian Gilmour observed back in the 1970s. 'A monarch and his family supply it.'

One might think Gilmour's words had been proved hopelessly wrong, that the romance of the royals had been forever tarnished by the realisation that they cannot begin to maintain the high standards expected of them. That is what the newspaper columnists love to write. The British people, the argument goes, now know they were conned into potty true-blue adulation and aren't going to fall for it any more. But the issue is considerably more complicated than that. Look at what happened in the week after the death of Princess Diana. While the newspapers were lambasting the Windsors for their apparent heartlessness and failure to register appropriate public grief, millions of people packed the streets of London for her funeral and treated the very same Windsors with utmost respect as the funeral cortege made its way from Kensington Palace to Westminster Abbey. The nation put on a funeral service as magnificent as any imaginable, and half the world sat glued to its television screens to watch. If this was the end of the road for the monarchy, it was a pretty strange way to go.

The truth is, the British monarchy is doing what it has done ever since the country's unhappy experiment with republicanism in the 17th century: searching for ways to adapt and survive even though its discernible usefulness has long since been exhausted. The last few years have seen a profound crisis, no question, but such episodes are by no means unprecedented. One only has to think of Queen Victoria sulking away in Balmoral after the death of her husband Prince Albert; she all but abandoned her institutional duties and, horror of horrors, the country began to realise that it didn't make much difference.

What saved the monarchy on that occasion was a complete image overhaul. When Victoria put herself dangerously out of commission in the 1860s, one of her most astute subjects, the political philosopher Walter Bagehot, wrote a kind of users' manual for royalty called *The English Constitution*. It was to prove the primer for all Victoria's successors. Bagehot decided the royal family's chief role should be not government, but entertainment. The English, he said, 'defer to what we may call the theatrical show of society... the climax of the play is the Queen'. Bagehot defined with astonishing precision the modern love-hate relationship between the royal family and the media; the monarchy, he said, should 'commonly be hidden like a mystery, and sometimes paraded like a pageant'. In other words, too much publicity would ruin its magic, while too little would whittle it away.

The royal family didn't have much pageantry to speak of in 1867, the year Bagehot's book was published, so a great slew of it had to be invented. In 1877 Victoria was named Empress of India in a lavish but thoroughly meaningless ceremony; in 1887 her Golden Jubilee was marked with street parties and parades, and in 1897 her Diamond Jubilee was celebrated in similar vein. For Edward VII's coronation in 1901, a new set of Crown Jewels was manufactured along with a few lavish state coaches. Westminster Abbey, the coronation venue since time immemorial, acquired a new organ, electric lights and red cassocks for its choristers. London's architects, under the direction of Aston Webb, built Admiralty Arch, the Victoria Memorial and the present East Front of Buckingham Palace. Reams of patriotic music was written, including Edward Elgar's Pomp and Circumstance suite and coronation anthems by Arthur Sullivan. Meanwhile, the souvenir merchants started showering the shops with royal mugs, commemorative pottery and all the other tourist trappings we have learned to love to hate.

It all worked like a dream. The man behind the facelift was Reginald Brett, Viscount Esher, who understood the true value of 'tradition', no matter how bogus, in lending legitimacy to the crown. He managed to invent a whole new royal ceremony, the Investiture of the Prince of Wales, and pass it off as a throwback to ancient ritual even though it was nothing of the kind. Brett also knew how to handle the media, and soon they were eating out of his hand. The royal family was no longer the bunch of in-bred halfwits, tyrants, fornicators and drunks that it had been for centuries; now it was a model of decent middle-class living in tasteful aristocratic surroundings—what the historian David Cannadine has called the 'Balmorality play'.

The illusion held during the Second World War, when George VI and his wife, the current Queen Mother, boosted national morale during the Blitz with their appearances at bomb sites (though imagine how different things might have been if George's elder brother Edward VIII, a known Nazi sympathizer, had not abdicated in 1936 to marry an American divorcee). The illusion persisted, too, for the first 40-odd years of Queen Elizabeth's reign. Her televised coronation in 1953 was the most lavish—and most phoney—ever, featuring amongst other things a group of seven 'state' coaches rented from a film production company. She went one better than Lord Esher by having Charles invested as Prince of Wales in 1969 at the telegenic Welsh castle of Caernavon (again, for no good historical reason). She had her cousins, the Mountbattens, market royal dinner plates, royal cookery books and coffee-table adornments like *The English Dog at Home*, a portrait album devoted to royal pooches. She pulled off the public relations coup of the century by persuading the world that Charles loved the fragile, virginal Lady Diana Spencer. And she spun a careful web of mystique around her many state visits around the world. She never travels without her own tea set, or her own toilet seat (specially fitted by aides wherever she goes); for a four-day trip to France a few years ago she dragged dozens of courtiers and 147 pieces of luggage.

The first bubble to burst was the myth of the Happy Family, and the woman who punctured it was undoubtedly Princess Diana. Recruited into the Windsor fold to provide fresh blood after all those generations of in-breeding, Diana succeeded triumphantly in renewing the image of the royals, but for reasons that nobody—not even she—could have imagined on her wedding day. In exchange for the privilege of marrying into the House of Windsor, she was expected to wear hideous dresses that didn't suit her, stand dutifully by her husband's side when he was in the country and stay quietly out of sight in draughty state apartments when he wasn't. As time went by and her public opinion ratings went up, she found the barbarities of the modern monarchy ever more unbearable and the reasons to tolerate them less and less compelling. At last she decided to go into print, with the help of the tabloid journalist Andrew Morton, and revealed all those notorious tales of her bulimia and of Charles's long-standing love affair with the woman she called The Rottweiler, Camilla Parker Bowles.

Time will tell whether Diana really demolished the House of Windsor, as her detractors claim, or whether in fact she showed it the way to move forward. One thing is certain: she built up a myth around herself that cast the fusty image of her in-laws deep into the shadows. The more she revealed of her personal misery, the more the public loved her. The less she wore those awful frilly outfits, preferring private fittings by Gianni Versace, the more the photographers chased after her. The more she shunned the military establishment and campaigned to abolish anti-personnel landmines, the more she increased her profile worldwide. She preferred battered women and AIDS victims to the debutante circuit, but she also danced with John Travolta at the White House and hobnobbed with Elton John. Instinctively, she understood exactly what Bagehot and Ian Gilmour had been writing about and worked out how to adapt it to the 1990s. If the royals wanted to capture the spirit of the age, they had to behave like movie stars.

If Diana had lived, perhaps she would have eclipsed the Windsors altogether—sweet revenge for being thrown out after her divorce from Charles. As it is, her death has brought about its own hefty dose of myth-making; after all, she is now in the same stratospheric category as James Dean and Marilyn Monroe (and she even managed, posthumously, to snatch Elton John's song about Marilyn for herself). The Windsors may not have her star quality or her extraordinary appeal, but they have got public sympathy back on their side. If they drop all that pompous non-sense about happy families and the glories of ancient ritual, they might end up surprising everyone and lasting several troubled generations longer.

Architecture: the Growth of the City

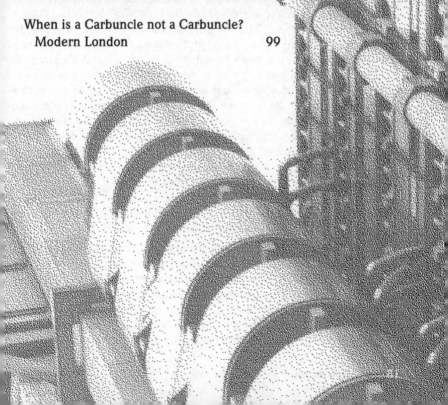

> *It is the disaster of London, as to the beauty of its figure,*
> *that it is thus stretched out in buildings, just at the pleasure*
> *of every builder, or undertaker of buildings, and as the*
> *convenience of the people directs, whether for trade or*
> *otherwise; and this has spread the face of it in a most*
> *straggling confus'd manner, out of all shape, incompact*
> *and unequal... whither will this monstrous city then extend?*
> *and where must a circumvallation or communication line of*
> *it be placed?*
>
> Daniel Defoe, *A Tour Through the Whole*
> *Island of Great Britain (1724–7)*

A mess, a maze, a muddle, a monster: writers and critics describing London since the early 18th century have without fail been overawed by its sheer size and unmanageability. In the generation after Defoe, Tobias Smollett had visions of the entire county of Middlesex being covered in brick (and he was not wrong). A century later William Cobbett christened the city 'the Great Wen'; for William Booth it was the 'Slough of Despond'; H.G. Wells had fantasies of it bubbling over into the Home Counties like some grotesque vat of viscid fluid. One can understand why Defoe, writing in the 1720s, was so bewildered by the rate of London's growth. In his lifetime it was the biggest city in the world; urban sprawl did not exist as a concept until London invented it. But one wonders how it was that this monstrous growth continued into the 19th and 20th centuries, unabated, unchecked and seemingly beyond control. There seems to be something endemic to the place; London is like an obese child that keeps on growing to the despair of its parents. The urban equivalent of crash diets, such as the Great Fire or the Blitz, have had only a temporary effect in countering the spread of great rolls of suburban adipose tissue. Even when the overall population of London has fallen, as it has since the Second World War, the buildings and office blocks and housing estates have still continued to sprout. Where will the city bulge out to next? What can we do to stop it? The questions posed by Defoe have never really gone away.

And yet the reasons behind the phenomenon are not as mysterious or as unfathomable as some of the more florid writers in the London literary canon like to make out. Public policy towards the architecture and development of the capital has been remarkably consistent down the centuries. London has always been essentially a merchant city, and the ethos of the marketplace has infused nearly all its monumental buildings and housing projects. London, alone among the great European capitals, is a private enterprise city. The landlord, not the prince, has been its inspiration and its master builder. Nobody has ever succeeded in imposing a single, overarching vision, and for that reason London is a city of disparate parts, not a unified whole. There have been few attempts to realize civic projects on a truly grand scale in London; these have always been short-lived and usually ended in failure.

There are those who see a positive advantage in this lack of a grand plan—hurrah for the libertarian tradition that shuns the tyranny of the state; three cheers for the triumph of English pragmatism over continental dogmatism; long live the right of the people to organize their city as they see fit. 'London is remarkable for the freedom with which it developed,' wrote the architectural critic John Summerson. 'It is the city raised by private, not public, wealth; the least authoritarian city in Europe.'

While diversity is one of London's great strengths, the mess-maze-muddle of the modern city suggests a certain flaw in this argument. The flaw is that the freedom to build has been almost exclusively the reserve of aristocratic landowners, whose estates were developed by building speculators. The freedom of the people never entered into it. London may not be a planned city in the same way as Paris or Chicago, but the development of its land in individual, privately owned parcels was certainly just as prescriptive and undemocratic. Instead of suffering the monopoly of the state, London has suffered the caprices of the private sector. It is merely planning under a different and less efficient guise.

One result of this laissez-faire attitude to urban development has been a cavalier disregard for London's historical landmarks and monuments. Too many have been wantonly destroyed, almost always for reasons of commerce and short-term gain. Those that have survived are often tucked into back-alleys or obscured from view by monolithic office blocks. Fine buildings have tended to survive only as long as there is still a utilitarian need for them: take John Soane's Bank of England, savaged in the 1920s because it was no longer big enough; or the Georgian arch at Euston Station, knocked down in the early 1960s because it interfered with British Rail's modernization plans. The taste for demolition has waned appreciably in recent years, but that has not necessarily been a sign of a new aesthetic sense. It is merely a switch of priorities. Nowadays the authorities do not knock down old buildings; they pickle them in nostalgia, dress them up as tourist attractions and market them as part of a London heritage package. Why destroy history when you can sell it off instead?

The prevailing tendency in London towards speculation and jerry-building has, generally speaking, left little room for manoeuvre for imaginative architects. Embellishing London with fine buildings has for centuries been something of a hit and miss operation. It was easier in the Middle Ages, when the crown, the religious orders and the city merchants all wielded sufficient power to commission such landmark buildings as Westminster Abbey, Bermondsey Abbey or the first Royal Exchange. After the Great Fire and the beginning of the housing boom, monumental architecture came to depend on parliamentary whim and the vagaries of fortune, such as the frequent fires that afflicted the city. There might be a chance to build a few churches here, a government building there, but no steady stream of work for any but the most favoured of artists such as Wren or Nash. The talents of less fortunate but equally gifted architects such as Hawksmoor or Soane were largely squandered.

And yet it would be wrong to think of London as a place of little stylistic imagination. Style wars between architects, city planners and landowners have been going on since the early 17th century. London's architectural history has been one long struggle between traditionalists and progressives, from the slow acceptance of Palladian ideals in the 17th and 18th centuries, to the Victorian clash between classical and Gothic styles, right up to the present-day disputes over modernism and its successor movements. The trouble is, the traditionalists have nearly always won, successfully spreading fear of the new and stunting the city's development. The banality of the modern cityscape belies the incredible fertility of architectural imagination at work in London. Sadly, much of that creative energy has gone to waste.

London in the Age Before Style

The Danish architect and critic Steen Eiler Rasmussen famously described London as a 'scattered city', in contrast to the more familiar 'concentrated' cities of the continent. The reason for London's straggly nature, he argued, was that the original citadel built by the Romans was simply too small. A second centre at Westminster grew up as a result, and London never recovered its equilibrium. When the Saxons began settling in the late 4th century, they preferred to set up river communities along the Thames rather than move into the City, which had fallen into decline in the dying days of the Roman empire. An abbey was established on Thorney Island (what we now know as Westminster) in the 7th century, and the royal family set up its residence in Aldwych.

It was not until 886 that the Saxons, under Alfred the Great, moved back inside the city walls—largely, it seems, as a defensive measure against the invading Danes. Westminster retained its growing importance, however, and was confirmed as London's second centre when Edward the Confessor decided to take up residence in a revamped Westminster Abbey. London's lingering sense of structural unity was gone forever, and the City never got another chance to expand. Indeed, the modern Square Mile is scarcely any bigger than at the time of the Norman invasion in 1066.

Roman and Saxon London have almost entirely disappeared from view. You can see sections of the 3rd-century Roman wall near the Tower and the Barbican, and there are various relics scattered around the City churches and in the Museum of London. But the earliest complete building to survive into the modern era is the Norman keep of the **Tower of London**, better known as the White Tower. The chapel of St John inside the tower features one of the few examples extant in London of round Norman arches (you can also see them in the church of St Bartholomew the Great and in the crypt of St Mary le Bow).

In the 12th century, builders began experimenting with pointed Gothic arches alongside the traditional rounded ones in a style known as Transitional. You get a good idea of the techniques used in the **Temple Church**, where points are formed by the intersection of rounded arches, and in some of the older sections of St Mary Overie, now incorporated into **Southwark Cathedral**. These are only relatively minor works, however: the greatest buildings of the age, including the vast medieval version of St Paul's, have been lost.

England developed its own Gothic tradition—see, for example, the retro-choir of Southwark Cathedral, the Lady Chapel of St Bartholomew the Great, or the crypt of St John's in Clerkenwell—but it was not until Henry III decided to rebuild **Westminster Abbey** that London enjoyed its first major monument in the same decorated, or 'flamboyant', style as the great cathedrals of northern France. Henry knocked down Edward the Confessor's Abbey with the somewhat spurious excuse that it was dilapidated and started work on the version we know today, erecting much of the east end and the magnificent **Chapter House**. Financial problems and the distraction of the Hundred Years' War delayed work on the nave for 100 years, and it was only under Richard II that construction went into full swing. From 1375 the man in charge of the work was Henry Yevele, the first named architect in London's history, who scrupulously respected the ground plan as originally conceived while adding some decorative touches in the Perpendicular style, a late Gothic idiom peculiar to England. The **Henry VII Chapel**, completed in 1517, is at once the high point of the Abbey and, with its astonishing fan-vaulted ceilings, the apotheosis of English Gothic.

Finding remnants of medieval London is no easy task, since so much of it was destroyed during the dissolution of the monasteries in the late 1530s or else burned down in the Great Fire. Brick was not used to build houses until the Tudor era and did not become popular until the reign of James I in the early 17th century. As a result there are precious few frontings from the era, although **Staple Inn** on High Holborn and **Prince Henry's Room** in Fleet Street are notable exceptions. Among the few examples of medieval architecture left in the City are the churches of **St Etheldreda** and **St Helen's Bishopsgate**, and the crypt of the

Guildhall. There are splendid hammerbeam roofs in the **Middle Temple Dining Hall**, **Westminster Hall** and **Eltham Palace**. For the most striking building of the Tudor age, though, you have to head all the way out to Henry VIII's palace at **Hampton Court**, the pinnacle of what is now known as English Renaissance. The term is something of a misnomer, since England largely ignored the artistic revolution going on in Italy and other parts of the continent in the 15th and 16th centuries. For its real Renaissance, London had to wait another 100 years and the advent of Inigo Jones.

Jones versus Wren: the Style Wars Begin

Inigo Jones (1573–1652) was London's first modern architect and a man with an uncompromising mission: he sought single-handedly to impose the tenets of Palladian Renaissance architecture back home in England. The son of a Smithfield clothworker, Jones spent much of the early part of his career as a stage designer and worked closely with Ben Jonson in the production of theatrical masques. Then in 1613 he was invited by Lord Arundel to spend 18 months in Italy. The experience was tantamount to a religious conversion. Jones became an assiduous student of Andrea Palladio's *I Quattro Libri dell'Architettura* and, like his Italian mentor, became fascinated with the theories of Vitruvius and other architects of classical antiquity.

Like many converts, Jones ended up more zealous than the man who inspired him, more Palladian than Palladio himself. He became a mathematical purist, one might say a fundamentalist, who believed in an architecture that was 'solid, proportionable according to the rules, masculine and unaffected'. Even Michelangelo, with his flights of Mannerist fancy, failed to pass muster in Jones's book.

Such ideas were little short of revolutionary in an England still stuck in a 200-year-old Gothic time warp, and the shock was soon felt when Jones was appointed Surveyor-General to James I on his return from Italy in 1615. His first, and arguably most impressive, completed building was the **Banqueting House** (1622) at Whitehall, which he intended to be the centrepiece of a massive new royal palace—until a row over his style caught up with him.

Jones's fate as an architect became inextricably linked with the political fortunes of his most influential patron, James's son Charles I, who got him to complete the **Queen's House** at Greenwich and encouraged Francis Russell, the fourth Earl of Bedford, to execute Jones's plans for an arcaded piazza at **Covent Garden**. When it was first built in the 1630s, Covent Garden offered a vision of urban planning that could have set a precedent for the whole of London: a genuinely public space where the populace could meet and go about their commerce surrounded by fine aristocratic buildings. At first the scheme appeared to be a success, and Jones began work on a similar development in Lincoln's Inn Fields. But then the Civil War broke out, and his notions of urban planning, deemed anti-Puritan, were ditched along with the monarchy itself. Covent Garden began its slow decline and Jones, an ardent monarchist, had to flee London for his life. He was bundled out of Basing House in the City in a blanket in 1647 after the place was set on fire.

Hostility to Jones's aesthetics did not wane following the return of the monarchy in 1660. Jones's plans to restore the medieval cathedral of St Paul's were ditched and a new architect, the young **Christopher Wren** (1632–1723), was appointed to take over the task. In fact Wren so wholly eclipsed Jones that a generation later he felt confident enough to ask King William if he could tack a Corinthian colonnade on to the façade of the Banqueting House to create a new royal residence. William only turned him down because he felt living so close to the river at Whitehall might be bad for his asthma.

A comparison between Jones and Wren helps explain much about London's aesthetic sensibilities. Both were visionary, multi-talented men (Jones worked in the theatre; Wren was a professor of astronomy at Oxford as well as a first-rate mathematician), with boundless energy and technical expertise. And yet the former was reviled while the latter became the most revered architect Britain has ever known. What did Jones do wrong? As we have seen, the political climate in the years leading up to the Civil War was against him. He did not live long enough to seize the rebuilding opportunities that fell into Wren's lap after the Great Fire of 1666. Most of all, though, he was simply ahead of his time in a country unbending in its cultural conservatism. Palladio may have died 35 years before Jones even discovered him, but London simply was not ready to receive such pure classicism at the beginning of the 17th century.

Wren, on the other hand, was a pragmatist who somehow managed to hit the right note with his patrons. He successfully blended the lessons of Renaissance classicism with those of Baroque to produce a style that was majestic but at the same time not over-assertive. It was just this lack of ostentation that the London authorities were looking for—new, but not too new—and soon the commissions were pouring in. Not only did Wren design the new **St Paul's**, he oversaw the rebuilding of more than 50 City churches and worked extensively in Greenwich and elsewhere. Not that he didn't have his failures. He had to tone down his plan for St Paul's and only managed to sneak the dome—deemed too Baroque and hence too Roman Catholic—past the authorities by a sly piece of political subterfuge. He also failed to realize his ambition to rebuild the City on a rational grid plan after the Great Fire. Wren wanted to dispense with the old medieval layout and create a series of radiating roads spreading out from two focal points, St Paul's and the Royal

Exchange, but the authorities deemed the notion too disruptive and revolutionary. Both Jones and Wren tried to act as ambassadors for the new styles being developed on the continent, and the English critics acted as a peculiar breed of customs officer, approving the more acceptable tenets of classicism and Baroque while turning down the more rigorous, flashy, or Papist notions contained within them. In doing so, they probably sentenced London for ever to a watered-down, generally unadventurous architectural heritage. In Wren (and arguably in Wren alone), at least London had a genius who could make the most of the limiting conditions. Wren used the tall steeples of his churches to create a graceful skyline for London even though many of his façades were forcibly hidden behind other buildings. He also made revolutionary changes to church interiors, opening them up to make them airier and focusing attention on the pulpit and lectern as well as the altar. In Wren, the Church of England found its perfect architectural voice: his churches removed much of the mystery of Catholic ritual and for the first time made the priest visible, and audible, to the whole congregation.

Too Square for Squares: the Rise of the Landlords

The rejection of Jones's aesthetics was more than a question of style: it affected for ever the way Londoners were destined to live. At the time of the Great Fire, there were only two residential squares in the rapidly growing chunk of London between Westminster and the City: Covent Garden and the brand new development of aristocratic houses at **St James's Square**. They represented two very different models of urban living. While the former was a space open to people of all classes (and, from the middle of the 17th century, the site of the West End's main fruit and vegetable market), the latter was conceived as the exclusive reserve of the aristocratic tenants who had set up home there. Covent Garden was a public space in the manner of an Italian piazza or the Place des Vosges in Paris; St James's a hallowed and very private domain. Jones's defeat in the style wars meant it was St James's that proved the model for virtually all subsequent development in London. Future squares were not necessarily so exclusive, but they were all obsessively private. Indeed, most squares built in the 18th and 19th centuries were little more than an extension of the upper-middle class drawing room; often the entrance would be guarded by a caretaker, while the garden in the middle would be fenced off with railings and locked. 'We have been capable of building pretty squares,' wrote V.S. Pritchett, 'but we are constitutionally incapable of the *grande place*.'

If the squares of London's West End are not all as up-market as St James's, it is largely because the Great Fire transformed the housing market in the capital, creating an urgent need to provide the largest possible number of houses in the shortest possible time. One man soon hit upon the winning formula: he was Thomas Wriothesley, the fourth Earl of Southampton. After the Great Fire, the Earl devised a system of development which has persisted to this day: the leasehold. At **Bloomsbury Square**, which he had begun developing in the early 1660s, he divided the land into plots and leased them out individually at a low rent for 42 years, on condition that the properties all be built to a prescribed style. It was a system that worked with great efficiency. Building speculators leapt at the chance to develop land cheaply, erecting their houses as tall and as thin as they could to extract maximum profit from the ground space. The tenants were given a strong incentive to leap in near the beginning of the lease; all the while, the landowner retained overall control over the property.

So successful was the Earl of Southampton that over the next 150 years or so, other aristocrats followed his example and developed their agricultural estates, usually at enormous profit: the Dukes of Bedford in Covent Garden and Bloomsbury; the Dukes of Westminster in Mayfair, Belgravia and Pimlico; and the Duke of Portland in Marylebone. Only the royal parks, the crown's former hunting grounds, escaped the encroachment of bricks and mortar. The names of the speculators who moved in on these estates are commemorated in the street names of the West End: Panton, Clarges, Storey, Bond and Frith. The squares around which the buildings were arranged were intended primarily to increase the value of the property; they offered space and light and a place where coaches could comfortably draw up. There was no question of letting the public in. One speculator, Thomas Neale, tried to dispense with the square to squeeze more money out of his land at Seven Dials north of Covent Garden. The result of his star-shaped development was catastrophe: nobody wanted to live on dark, narrow streets and the area quickly deteriorated into slumland.

The consequences of the leasehold were manifold. On the plus side, it provided decent and plentiful housing to make up for the losses of the Great Fire and to accommodate the fast-growing population. In some quarters, the uniform series of estates inspired admiration: John Evelyn described Bloomsbury Square as the 'epitome of town planning'. As time went on, however, abuses in the system led to poor building standards and the entire subordination of aesthetics to the profit motive. In the late 18th century, Sir John Soane commented that the leasehold system was necessarily 'opposed to sound construction, whereby not a year passes without lives being lost through this wretched practice.' The Lighting and Paving Acts of 1761 and the Building Act of 1774 curbed the worst excesses of the jerry-builders but only accentuated the conformity of design through their various prescriptions. The estate-building went on largely unabated well into the 19th century and beyond.

The most lasting effect of the leasehold system was one of lifestyle: it made the house, rather than the flat, the norm for residential living. Speculators could cut down on their ground rent by building narrow, tall houses destined for one family each, rather than gambling on grander developments subdivided into apartments. London thus became the only European capital to opt for 'vertical' rather than 'horizontal' living. The architecture of the houses reflects this. In 1709 the sash window began to replace the more mundane casement to provide more light for the family living room; in the absence of public squares, sunken gardens at the front or rear became popular. While the fronts of houses looked out on to the squares, the backs gave on to narrow alleys known as mews where horses were tethered. The French traveller Louis Simond described the Georgian London home thus in 1817: 'These narrow houses, three or four storeys high—one for eating, one for sleeping, a third for company, a fourth underground for the kitchen, a fifth perhaps at the top for the servants—and the agility, the ease, the quickness with which the individuals of the family run up and down, and perch on the different storeys, give the idea of a cage with its sticks and birds.'

Palladio Returns

Ceremonial building did not stop in the Georgian era, but Sir Christopher Wren was a hard act to follow and it took some time for London's architects to regain their confidence and find their niche. In his long lifetime, Wren eclipsed even the most talented of his students, such as Nicholas Hawksmoor and John Vanbrugh, who only came fully into their own towards the end of their master's life. Their chance came in 1711, when the newly elected Tory parliament passed an act for the building of 50 new churches. The act was over-pompous in its ambitions, and only a dozen or so of the churches were ever completed, but these included Hawksmoor's **Christchurch Spitalfields** and **St Anne Limehouse** and James Gibbs's **St Martin-in-the-Fields** and **St Mary-le-Strand**. The dour grandeur of Hawksmoor's work expressed the full if somewhat belated flowering of English Baroque, while Gibbs, in his experiments with models from antiquity, signalled a surprising comeback for classicism in general and Palladianism in particular.

Two books favoured Palladio's return to good odour in England, both of them published in 1715 thanks to the enthusiasm of a new Italophile, the youthful aristocrat-cum-architect Lord Burlington. The first publication was an edition of Vitrivius's designs, while the second was Palladio's own *Quattro Libri*, the manual much annotated and consulted by Inigo Jones but never before made available to the public in England. Clearly, those critical customs officers who had previously rejected Palladio decided that he could now safely be taken out of quarantine. Why this change of heart? As Sir Reginald Blomfield has pointed out, maybe he was just too useful to be ignored. 'With the touch of pedantry that suited the times and invested his writings with a fallacious air of scholarship,' Blomfield wrote in his

Studies in Architecture, 'he [Palladio] was the very man to summarize and classify, and to save future generations of architects the labour of thinking for themselves.' Certainly, London's first outing in neo-Palladianism, the **Mansion House**, did not exactly herald the flowering of an exciting new movement. It took half a century to complete, and ended up as rather less than the sum of its parts. But, in two architectural forms at least, Palladian classicism came fully into its own in Georgian England: the smart town house and the stately country home.

In London, Lord Burlington set the ball rolling with **Burlington House** (1720), now home to the Royal Academy in Piccadilly. This was followed by such masterpieces as Burlington's **Chiswick House** (1729), **Marble Hill House** in Twickenham (1729) and **Spencer House** in St James's Place (1766). The two greatest exponents of the Palladian tradition in London were probably the much underrated William Kent, who worked largely on interiors such as the exquisite staircase inside **44, Berkeley Square**, and Robert Adam. Adam, along with his brothers William, John and James, perfected the art of creating lively but regular exteriors and matching them with graceful, finely detailed interiors. There are examples dotted all over London: **Chandos House** in Cavendish Square, or **Home House** in Portman Square. Sadly, much of the Adams' work was wrecked by the Victorians who found it offensive to their High Church sensibilities. The gravest of these losses was surely the **Adelphi** (1773), a riverside housing development near the Strand which was vandalized to make room for the Thames Embankment in 1867 and then pulled down and replaced with a crude Art Deco monolith in 1937.

The Adelphi was one of only very few 18th-century projects to be sponsored by the crown. Although it too was initially developed as a leasehold (for the Earl of St Albans), George III recognized its aesthetic qualities and successfully appealed to parliament to put up the money for its completion according to the Adam brothers' wishes. Perhaps the king, along with many London residents, was influenced by John Gwynn's landmark book *London and Westminster Improved* (1766), which brought home just how straggly and ill-formed London had become. Gwynn described the new London and its leasehold estates as 'inconvenient, inelegant, and without the least pretension to magnificence or grandeur'. He encouraged a number of changes, including the introduction of stucco to liven up the drab façades of the brick buildings, and welcomed the invention of Coade stone, a cheap but very hardy imitation of ornamental terracotta. With these materials, London's houses could at least be livened up, like a middle-aged face dusted with rouge and powder. Under Gwynn's influence, architects were encouraged to exercise their imaginations once more, and slowly they started dreaming of grand projects to give London some of the monumental glory that it lacked. England's victory in the

Napoleonic Wars, and the rise to power of the Prince Regent (later to become George IV) provided the political and financial opportunities for such dreams to be realized. Everyone started drawing up plans to change the face of London.

Nash versus Soane: the Clash of Ideals

The two most prominent architects of the moment were John Nash and John Soane. Of the two, there is little doubt that **Sir John Soane** (1753–1837) was the more talented. He had studied classical models more profoundly, his structures were more interesting and innovative and his buildings, those that made it into bricks and mortar, were more solidly built than Nash's. And yet Soane missed out on nearly every major commission going under the benevolent regency of the Prince of Wales. If you visit the John Soane Museum in Lincoln's Inn Fields, you will gain some insight why: Soane's grandiose schemes for royal palaces and neo-classical parliament buildings, on display on the first floor, were hopelessly idealistic and paid scant attention to the strictures of space or budget. He may have been a creative genius, but he was also a grand eccentric. Instead of trying to tame Soane, the authorities decided instead to ignore him and as a result only a few major London projects of his made it to completion. Sadly, none of these have survived in their original form; all that is left of Soane's Bank of England is a mutilated version of his exterior curtain wall and a few bowdlerized rooms inside.

John Nash (1752–1835) was an idealist too, and a spendthrift to boot, but for reasons that have never been entirely explained he won the Prince Regent's near-exclusive favour and ended up doing more than any architect since Christopher Wren to change the face of London. His early career was hardly auspicious: he was declared bankrupt after dabbling in a doomed property scheme in Bloomsbury Square and retreated to Wales where he concentrated on designing fanciful country houses. The turning point came in 1798 when, at the age of 46, he married the 25-year-old Mary Ann Bradley. The story goes that Bradley was a mistress of the Prince Regent's, and that Nash nobly pitched in with an offer of marriage to save George's embarrassment at the first of five pregnancies. True or not, there has yet to be a more convincing explanation for Nash's meteoric rise from provincial obscurity to national stardom.

Nash thought big and managed to persuade the Prince Regent, a fellow spendthrift, to sponsor his projects for **Regent Street** and **Regent's Park**. This involved developing the newly available Marylebone estates into a series of terraces overlooking a landscaped park, and a grand avenue leading down between Mayfair and Soho all the way to George's palace at Carlton House Terrace. The mixed fortunes of the scheme are detailed in Walk IV. Nash also laid the foundations of **Trafalgar Square** and started work on **Buckingham Palace**. At his best, Nash was capable of buildings of great charm and elegance (for example, the admirable sweep of Park Crescent at the entrance to Regent's Park). But at other times he could be sloppy, with a tendency to kitsch (his indiscriminate use of stucco at Chester Terrace was once described as 'spray-on architecture'), and his contemporaries found his primacy in the architectural community ever harder to take. Foreign observers tended to be more indulgent about his weaknesses, simply because nobody before had so ambitiously taken central London by the scruff of the neck and tried to shake it into shape. The German landscape architect Prince Pückler-Muskau wrote: 'It cannot be denied that his buildings are a jumble of every sort of style, the result of which is rather "Baroque" than original—yet the country is, in my opinion, much indebted to him for conceiving and executing such gigantic designs for the improvement of the metropolis... Now for the first time, it [London] has the appearance of a seat of government, and not an immeasurable metropolis of shopkeepers.'

Nash's fortunes, like those of Inigo Jones, depended in the end on the popularity of the monarch of the day: when George IV died in 1830, Nash's career was over. He was immediately dismissed from work on both Buckingham Palace and Trafalgar Square and allowed to sink back into the obscurity from which George IV had plucked him. At the time nobody gave the matter a second thought; Nash was just one of many architects around at the time, and not generally considered more than minor in importance. With hindsight we can appreciate his tremendous impact, and also begin to understand why his sensibilities were deemed so out of place in the London of the 1830s. The social make-up of the city had altered radically as the population shot up from just under one million in 1801 to nearly two million in 1837. A banking crisis in 1825 had severely squeezed state funds. Industrialization was developing apace and poverty was spreading rapidly. This was not the right atmosphere for the refinements of classical architecture; London was seemingly sinking into anarchy and parliament desperately sought some sort of moral as well as practical guidance. It found its answer in a peculiar mixture of architecture and fundamentalist religion.

Victoriana: the Bigots Have it

The demise of Nash did not entirely banish classical style from London. The tail-end of the classical movement, known as the **Greek Revival**, lasted through to the 1840s and classical architecture made periodic comebacks throughout the Victorian era. The chief architects of the Revival were Robert Smirke, designer of the **British Museum**, William Wilkins (**University College** as well as the non-Revivalist National Gallery) and Decimus Burton (the **Athenaeum Club** and the **Ionic Screen** at Hyde Park Corner). What *did* die with Nash, however, was his idealistic dream of a new rational city. Ideas kept pouring in, particularly plans for a new royal palace or a grand sewerage system. There were 120 proposals for

Trafalgar Square alone, including a Coliseum, a statue of Nelson at the base of a giant mast and several pyramids. But parliament rejected every one of these schemes. Austerity and practicality were in; grand dreams and lavish spending were deemed mere frivolity.

One of the most eccentric architectural entrepreneurs of the age (and arguably the least successful architect of all time) was an Irish colonel and member of parliament who rejoiced in the delightfully pugnacious name of **Frederick William Trench**. Trench tirelessly stood up in the House of Commons with ingenious new schemes, quite undeterred by his total lack of success over a 40-year period. In 1823 he wanted to build a triumphal avenue leading directly from St Paul's to a new royal palace in Hyde Park; the fact that this would annihilate the Temple Church and Covent Garden, among other historic sites, did not seem to deter him unduly. For Trafalgar Square he came up with a pyramid; later on in his career, he suggested turning Buckingham Palace into a laundry for half-pay officers. Trench's despairing colleagues in parliament tried to shut him up by offering him regular promotion: first a knighthood in 1832, then an elevation to the rank of general in 1854. But still the wacky ideas kept coming (he did not die until 1864). Trench's nearest miss was a scheme for a Thameside embankment in the late 1820s. But, in a cruel twist of fate, his two main sponsors both died as plans were reaching a crucial stage and Trench was sent scurrying back to the drawing board. An anonymous satirist immortalized the hapless Irishman in verse at the time of his embankment scheme:

> *Yet I like thee pleasant Tre—*
> *Though the sages of the bench*
> *Would not give a single stiver*
> *For your bridge along the river...*

Any smiles were wiped off the face of the architectural community in 1836, when **Augustus Welby Pugin** (1812–52) published his pamphlet 'Contrasts'. In one fell swoop Pugin, a fanatic and a genius, dealt the deathblow to English classicism and heralded a return to Gothic forms. As far as Pugin was concerned, there had been no decent urban planning worthy of the term since about 1440. The classical movement was for him an irreligious aberration: 'This mania for paganism is developed in all classes of buildings erected since the 15th century—in palaces, in mansions, in private houses, in public erections... What madness, while neglecting our own religious and national types of architecture and art, to worship at the revived shrines of ancient corruption, and profane the temple of a crucified Redeemer by the architecture and emblems of heathen Gods.' Pugin rejected Protestantism as the root of all moral decay and called for a 'revival of Catholic art and dignity'. He soon got his chance: the Palace of Westminster burned down in 1834, and he was nominated to work with Charles Barry to rebuild it. The detail of

Pugin's work on the new parliament, notably in the interiors, testified to his prodigious talent, but that did not alter the fact that his mind was a touch possessed. Cardinal Newman said of him: 'He is intolerant and, if I may use a stronger word, a bigot.' Pugin was as severe a critic of himself as he was of others, and died in the madhouse at Bedlam at the age of 40.

Pugin's was, in essence, a crude nationalist manifesto that invoked religion and notions of 'good taste' to stir the hearts of men bewildered by the sheer pace of the industrial revolution. But it worked. Others quickly rallied to his point of view, most notably John Ruskin, who described classicism as 'base, unnatural, unfruitful, unenjoyable and impious'. To a new generation of architects, Pugin was a rousing inspiration. **George Gilbert Scott**, one of the chief exponents of the Gothic Revival, wrote: 'I was awakened from my slumber by the thunder of Pugin's writings.' Gothic Revival meant a profusion of brick turrets and highly embellished terracotta, a rejection of the bland white of classicism for a profusion of reds and greys and purples. Scott flexed his Revivalist muscles most notably with the frontage of **St Pancras Station** (1874). Other striking examples of the genre are G.E. Street's **Royal Courts of Justice** (1881) and William Butterfield's highly ornate interior of **All Saints Margaret Street** (1849).

Pugin's watchwords were 'the Beautiful and the True'; nowadays we tend to think of such overblown Victoriana as the Albert Memorial in Hyde Park (by Scott) more in terms of the Ugly and the Bloated. But whatever our instinctive revulsion to these monuments, they remain fascinating as indications of the deep contradictions in Victorian thought. On the one hand, this was supposed to be the age of Progress; on the other, here were the age's leading artists peering far back into the medieval past for inspiration. The 19th century saw the rise of capitalism in all its shining ghastliness; and yet the Victorians liked to think of themselves primarily as devotees of God, not Mammon.

The Victorians' greatest contribution to the age was, of course, material not spiritual: the development of the docks, which had begun in 1800; the building of countless bridges, river tunnels and railway stations; and, eventually, the development of the world's first underground railway. It was also the Victorians who finally installed a proper sewerage system and built the Thames Embankment (although only after the health of the middle classes came under serious threat from cholera). 'Railway termini and hotels are to the 19th century what monasteries and cathedrals were to the 13th century,' wrote *Building News* in 1875. 'They are the only truly representative kind of buildings we possess.' But London could not in the 19th century keep up with a city like Paris with its new boulevards, department stores, and monumental architecture. The public displays of grandeur and style that made Paris what it was were considered distasteful in conservative London, and the typical materials of 19th-century Paris, iron and glass, were scarcely exploited in the British capital at all. One exception was Joseph Paxton's wondrous **Crystal Palace**, built for the 1851 Great Exhibition, which went thoroughly unappreciated by the architectural critics of the day who considered it at best a feat of engineering, not an aesthetic achievement. Ruskin dismissively called it 'a cucumber frame between two chimneys', and the Palace was soon put out to grass at Sydenham in southeast London, where it eventually burned down in 1936. The very idea of a Great Exhibition had been rather continental in the first place, encouraged by the cosmopolitan Prince Albert who wanted to landscape part of South Kensington along Parisian lines into a municipal park dotted with great museums and centres of learning. The scheme was only partly realized at the time of Albert's death in 1861 and severely truncated thereafter.

If the Victorians were shy about construction, they showed no such compunction about tearing down parts of the city and rearranging them to meet their own requirements. Armies of church restorers went about 'improving' Wren's interiors, tinkering with the geometry and the furnishings and wrecking his lighting effects by putting stained glass in the windows. The anti-classical backlash also produced a veritable orgy of destruction of Georgian masterpieces that continued well into the 20th century. Among the victims were William Kent's royal stables (pulled down to make room for the National Gallery), the first Westminster Bridge, an Adam house in Grosvenor Square, the old criminal law courts designed by Sir John Soane and large chunks of Georgian Whitehall. The Victorians could not very well destroy the Georgian town house because it had spread so far over the city, but they did turn it upside down. Servants were now put below stairs, not at the top of the house. The Victorian household was like a microcosm of the Empire: rulers on top, underlings and natives below. New housing spread through the London hinterland with the rage of a forest fire: first in Belgravia and Pimlico, thanks to the entrepreneurial zeal of the speculator Thomas Cubitt, then throughout Kensington, Chelsea, Bayswater and Notting Hill, and finally out towards such established villages as Wimbledon, Richmond, Ealing, Hampstead and Highgate.

With the population mushrooming, Victorian London also saw a growing anonymity in the city. The binds that tied small communities loosened under the sheer weight of people; street life disappeared and even the clothes became greyer and less distinctive. Commuting, that most alienating of urban rituals, started in earnest in the 1860s. Privacy and, by extension, home-owning became something of a cult. The house became, in Jonathan Raban's felicitous phrase, a machine for believing in. Property was the means by which parvenus could prove that they had made it in the big city: it was the Victorian age that popularized the expression 'an Englishman's home is his castle'. Living in a house rather than a flat was still a point of great pride for middle-class Londoners, despite the growing shortage of space in the city. The apartment was considered a foreign vulgarity allowing little privacy because the neighbours could register every entrance and exit. It was also thought profoundly immoral because of the proximity of the living rooms to the bedrooms. Worst of all, flat courts encouraged the mingling of different classes on the stairs. 'As for the ladies,' commented *The Architect*, 'it is difficult to assign a limit to the distress and shame that would be occasioned by an habitual encounter on mutual steps between one caste and another.' Blocks of flats did, nevertheless, make their first hesitant appearance in the 1850s, usually provided with plenty of entrance ways to keep those unpleasant cross-cultural encounters down to a minimum, and often described not as 'flats' but as 'mansions' to give them a more refined social cachet.

Here Come the Suburbs

In 1856 the *Saturday Review* described London as 'the least beautiful city in the world'. A generation later, the disapproval had taken on strong moral tones. William Morris wrote idyllic poems about a utopian London 'small and white and clean', and described the monstrous urban sprawl as a 'spreading sore ... swallowing up in its loathsomeness field and wood and heath without mercy and without hope, mocking our feeble efforts to deal even with its minor evils of smoke-laden sky and befouled river'. Clearly, it was time for the middle classes to get out, and they deserted in their thousands to the suburbs.

The immediate effect of this suburbanization was simply to spread the metropolitan jumble out into the Home Counties. 'The deadening uniformity that we noted in the terrace-houses of the City reaches its peak in the suburbs,' wrote the architectural critic Hermann Muthesius. 'There are no bends, no variety, no squares, no grouping to relieve the unease that anyone who strays into these parts must feel.' The lower middle-classes had effectively been conned. True, they had escaped the inner-city slums, but at the price of overwhelming dullness. Families settled in one anonymous corner of the city only to have to spend a good part of their day commuting to another, often equally anonymous, one. Even interior décor became heavy and oppressive, relieved only by the flights of fancy in wallpaper and furniture pioneered by William Morris's Arts and Crafts movement.

What about wealthy families? Clearly, they were not going to stand by and watch this distressing trend grow if they could help it. Some stayed in town, picking exclusive riverside locations like Cheyne Walk to build new houses, or else indulging in a new fad for exotica. **Leighton House** in Holland Park, for example, was kitted up for the painter Lord Leighton as an oriental palace with fountains, mosaics and patterned tiles from Cairo and Damascus. Escapism duly became the architectural watchword well into the Edwardian era. Like cooks trying to liven up a bland dish with hot spices, designers called forth every style they could think of to breathe a little new life into the city. There was a Tudor Revival (James Pennethorne's **Public Record Office**, for example) and even a Baroque revival of sorts, dubbed the Wrenaissance—good examples are **Kodak House** in Kingsway and the **Port of London Authority building** on Tower Hill.

Meanwhile, there was a concerted effort at urban improvement. The authorities cleared the slums around St Giles to create Shaftesbury Avenue and Tottenham Court Road. Theatres, dance halls and smart hotels took the place of miserable working-class dwellings. Slum clearance also attracted the attention of such philanthropists as the American businessman George Peabody, who left half a million pounds on his death in 1869 for the construction of decent low-rent dwellings. The forbidding, prison-like **Peabody Estates** designed by H.A. Darbishire are still with us today (for example, in Old Pye St in Westminster or Greenman St in Islington). Pevsner described them as 'familiar but nonetheless detestable'. They did nothing to make London more beautiful, and had only a limited impact on the city's housing problems.

Towards the end of the Victorian era, a new generation of architects grew up with the belief that the only enduring solution to London's problems was to abandon the metropolis and start again in the surrounding countryside. The chief theorist of this movement was **Ebenezer Howard** (1850–1928), who pioneered the concept of the garden city. His idea was to create a balanced environment for a community outside the city centre where there was plenty of space and greenery for children to play and respectable adults to go about their daily business. New towns duly sprouted in Hertfordshire, Berkshire and Surrey, and many comfortably-off families moved there. Closer to London, architects designed islands of upper middle-class respectability such as Hampstead Garden Suburb. The problem with Howard's vision was that its liberal veneer concealed a profound hostility to the lower classes. One of his ideal drawings of London shows the inner city divided carefully into secure areas to contain waifs, drunks and the insane, while respectable folk are placed safely out in suburban communities with pious names like Concord, Morrisville and Gladstone. Despite his earnest good intentions, Howard only succeeded in creating ghettos of pleasantness for a relatively narrow band of society. 'Ebenezer Howard's garden city was a place for Christopher Robin to go hoppety-hop,' wrote Jane Jacobs in her *Death and Life of Great American Cities*.

The move to the suburbs and the commuter belt beyond had deleterious effects on the inner city. Architecturally, the first 40 years of the 20th century were a disaster in London. The kind of monumental architecture popular on the continent found only a muted echo in Edwardian London; schemes like County Hall, Admiralty Arch and the Victoria Memorial were hardly on the same scale as the Grand Palais and the Gare d'Orsay in Paris. The newly formed London County Council commissioned eccentric projects like an upright Tower of Pisa and an imitation Tower of Babel, both from Albert Brunel, but failed to generate enough interest to make them worth building. There was even a project to build an imitation Eiffel Tower. Sadly, the site picked for the monument was way out in Wembley, where the miserable and rather distant view over London hardly warranted a journey to the remote northwestern suburbs. Work began on the Wembley Park Tower, as it was officially known, in 1891 but stopped again three years later when visitors to its first completed viewing platform failed to materialize. The Tower never grew any further, earned the nickname the 'London Stump' and in 1907 was finally blown up with dynamite.

The interwar years were even more barren for London architecture. Of the few buildings to be commissioned in that time, perhaps only the Art Nouveau **Michelin Building** on the Fulham Road, Sir Giles Gilbert Scott's **Battersea Power Station** and the occasional purpose-built cinema showed any sign of innovation or liveliness. The rest were an amorphous and unpleasant mass of grey, none more so than the breathtakingly ugly **Senate House** of London University, which George Orwell used as the model for his Ministry of Truth in *Nineteen Eighty-Four.* 'Those 1930s buildings were all shut in and negative,' says a character in Colin MacInnes's *Absolute Beginners,* 'with landlord and broker's man written all over them.' Meanwhile, the destruction of the city's Georgian heritage, begun in the Victorian era, continued apace. Regent Street was pulled down and rebuilt in drab stone, as was Soane's Bank of England. It was not until the postwar generation that anybody seemed to notice or care about what was going on. 'It was of course in no meek abandon but in positive orgies of philistinism that throughout the 1920s and 1930s the British people once and for all jettisoned their sorely tried architectural tradition,' the traditionalist critic James Lees-Milne wrote in his 1947 book *The Age of Adam.* 'In concerts of jubilation bishops, aldermen and captains of commerce urged the tearing down of churches by Wren, bridges by Rennie, terraces and town palaces by Adam...' Even Hitler's bombs could not eclipse that kind of unthinking architectural barbarism.

When is a Carbuncle not a Carbuncle? Modern London

The bombsites left all over London after the Blitz presented a wonderful opportunity for architectural improvement throughout the city, an opportunity that was for the most part entirely squandered. The one beneficial side-effect of the Nazi bombing campaigns was to slow down the growth of the suburbs and encourage the creation of a Green Belt around the outside of the city where building could be strictly controlled. Inside London, the postwar building boom became an architectural disaster as vacant lots fell prey to the worst kind of functionalism. The modern movement hit London like a slab of concrete landing on a bird's nest, creating soul-less inner-city housing estates and residential tower blocks. The new generation of publicly subsidized housing projects, while laudable in intent, was built on the cheap by speculators interested only in short-term profit. This is what Jane Jacobs, in her attacks on the modern movement, described as 'the Great Blight of Dull-ness', or what the American writer Bill Bryson more flippantly called the Fuck You school of architecture. New generations of Caribbean and South Asian immigrants were turned into slum dwellers at the mercy of bigoted landlords and bootboys. The best buildings of the 1950s and 1960s, such as the South Bank Centre, at least made up in practicality what they lacked in aesthetic appeal. But most of the pro-jects of the period were eyesores that should not have passed the planning officer's desk, such as Knightsbridge Barracks, the Centre Point building or the Shell Centre.

It was not all bad. Whatever the new buildings might have been like, it was the old buildings that underwent the greatest transformation. London was becoming a place of great social and racial diversity, and all those stuck-up Victorian town houses were quickly gutted and filleted and converted into series of two- and three-room flats. Mews properties, considered fit only for horses in the 18th century, became hotly sought after for their seclusion and bijou elegance. Failed middle-class areas like Notting Hill and Brixton were repopulated and reinvigorated by young Jamaicans and Nigerians alongside bohemian white students. For a moment, London forgot its mercantile instincts and let its hair down. While the modern movement was pointing misguidedly to a monolithic brave new world, the old Victorian certainties of bricks and mortar were melting visibly.

Reaction to the modern movement came in several waves. First, in the 1970s, came the remorse, signalled by a decision to call a halt to the building of insipid skyscrapers. Then came nostalgia, and a veritable hankering for the lost elegance of the past. The fashion was to prettify and restore old houses rather than destroy them, as previous generations had done. The redevelopment of Covent Garden after the fruit and vegetable market moved out in the early 1970s was a turning point: the GLC initially wanted to turn the area into office blocks and roads but was persuaded to transform it into the recreation and tourism centre you see today.

It was only in the 1980s that new building emerged with any confidence. The two key events were the deregulation of the City in the mid-1980s and Margaret Thatcher's free-for-all invitation to private speculators to develop the derelict docks. The profit motive has proved a rather unreliable promoter of civic order, however, and the results have been distinctly uneven. Among the notable failures is the NatWest Tower in Bishopsgate, which has little to recommend it except its height. Among the successes are Richard Rogers' hi-tech Lloyd's of London in the heart of the City, Norman Foster's ITN headquarters on the Gray's Inn Road, Terry Farrell's reworking of Charing Cross railway station as a glasshouse complex called Embankment Place and Ray Moxley's aluminium tower at Chelsea Harbour. The redevelopments in the Docklands have come in for vehement criticism because of the social upheavals they have caused and the lack of basic services such as transport and shopping (*see* pp.436–7). Some of the new buildings there are nevertheless rather successful, at least as pieces of architecture—the new marina at Surrey Quays, for example, or the refurbished warehouses of Hay's Galleria or Tobacco Dock. Even Cesar Pelli's monstrous 800ft tower at the heart of Canary Wharf is impressive in its way, if only for its sheer audaciousness in an architecturally timid city like London. But you don't have to look far for the horrors, a prime example being the Cascades housing estate on the Isle of Dogs, which has become a seedbed of new far-right nationalism.

Plenty of people began asking themselves whether all this unrestricted construction was really wise, among them Prince Charles who took the architectural community completely by surprise in 1984 by slagging off a slew of new building projects in a speech to the Royal Institute of British Architects (RIBA). The heir to the throne lambasted the postwar world for its 'deep aesthetic idleness' and accused modernist architects of ignoring the needs and tastes of ordinary people. He described a Mies van der Rohe design commissioned for the City as a 'glass stump', and ridiculed a proposed extension to the National Gallery as 'a carbuncle on the face of a much-loved and elegant friend'. What Charles wanted to see was a return to solid, tasteful architecture that people could enjoy as part of an integrated urban environment.

Reaction to the prince's speech was fast and furious. Many architects accused him of turning his back on progress and yearning for a nostalgic and non-existent past. Berthold Lubetkin, a veteran modernist on the RIBA board, compared him to Stalin for his over-eagerness to pour scorn on the professionals. Could one really put all the blame on architects without considering the priorities of the planners and speculators? Was the National Gallery extension really as bad as the tower blocks of Hackney and Camberwell? By scorning all modern and postmodern architecture, regardless of merit, Charles revealed his true agenda: a nostalgic return to 'traditional' building forms, that is to say imitations of Georgian classical design. His main objection to the National Gallery extension was that it did not look like William Wilkins's (less than successful) original. In other words, the Prince of Wales was just saying his bit for the heritage industry: old is good and new is bad.

The effect of his speech was astonishing. The Mies van der Rohe project was dropped and the National Gallery extension recommissioned from a more conservative firm of American architects. Traditionalist buildings started popping up everywhere, including a neo-Georgian riverside development by Quinlan Terry in

Richmond. Terry's work prompted even Charles Jencks, an architectural adviser to the Prince, to ask: 'Is this architecture or pastiche?' The more adventurous among the architectural community were appalled. Richard Rogers said: 'Modern architecture is in danger of being obliterated by an indiscriminate wave of nostalgia.'

The future shape of London is near-impossible to predict. Since the abolition of the GLC in 1986 there has been no city-wide government to mastermind planning, and little state cash to encourage buildings with a truly civic purpose. Hopefully these things will return if London is given a new city government as planned. Hopefully, too, the city will make the most of the ambitious public works projects underway to mark the millennium. Among the dozen or so schemes being mooted are new footbridges across the Thames, a rethink of the South Bank complex including a transparent canopy by Richard Rogers, a reorganization of the British Museum including a new concourse around the old Reading Room of the British Library, a giant ferris wheel by the river in Lambeth affording vertiginous views over the whole city and, most spectacular and controversial of all, a huge Dome rising out of the derelict docks of north Greenwich. If the millennium project succeeds, it will be an event to rank in London's architectural history alongside the Great Exhibition and the 1951 Festival of Britain. Certainly, optimism is riding high as it has not done for decades.

All will depend on London finding a sense of vision. The Docklands redevelopment was also supposed to be a vast project to reinvigorate London. But Margaret Thatcher's big mistake was to give carte blanche to private capital investment, allowing speculators to build to their hearts' content in the old docks without planning restrictions. Their buildings, ranging from the innovative to the god-awful, were not supported by adequate urban infrastructure and turned into a financial and social nightmare, a virtual wasteland of unoccupied and unwanted office and housing developments. Throughout its history, London has refused to learn the lesson that private enterprise alone cannot build a successful city. That is why so much of London is a mess, and will continue to be unless the government takes some bold and energetic planning decisions. Maybe, on the brink of the third millennium, the message is finally sinking in.

London in the Arts

103

The city as a form is uniquely prone to erode that boundary between the province of imagination and the province of fact.

Jonathan Raban, *Soft City*

In a celebrated passage from Smollett's epistolary novel *Humphrey Clinker*, the bilious hero Matthew Bramble launches into a lengthy rant about the shortcomings of London. It is an 'overgrown monster', he says, a place of 'luxury and corruption', full of noise, confusion, glare and glitter but without elegance or propriety. His lodgings are frowzy and small, the air is vile, the water filthy, the wine undrinkable and the food adulterated and expensive. Over and over this passage has been seized upon as evidence either of Smollett's own ill-tempered view of life or of the appalling social conditions in London in the mid-18th century. But it seems some critics skip over the letter in the middle of all this written by Bramble's travelling companion Lydia Melford. She says: 'All that you read of wealth and grandeur, in the Arabian Nights Entertainment and the Persian Tales, concerning Bagdad, Diarbekir, Damascus, Ispahan and Samarkand, is here realized.' Clearly, Smollett cannot be accused of merely venting his own spleen. In fact, in these passages he encapsulates the same conflicting feelings about London (while taking them to satiric extremes) that surface throughout its rich literary canon.

Writers have often found London vile *and* fascinating, irresistible *and* frightful. Images of Bagdad or Babylon, with all their connotations of splendour as well as decadence, are among the most used in English literature. Smollett's critics, particularly his contemporaries, found it convenient to misread him for their own purposes; it is a fate that many writers on London have shared. London-bashers like to pick out quotations stressing the dirty, dangerous, crowded, fog-ridden aspect of the big city; only too often they have quoted Shelley's *Letter to Maria Gisborne*:

*London, that great sea, whose ebb and flow
At once is deaf and loud, and on the shore
Vomits its wrecks, and still howls on for more*

but have conveniently forgotten the next line, which reads:

Yet in its depth what treasures!

In similar but opposite fashion, the high priests of the London tourist trade have rummaged through the quotation books in search of suitably upbeat one-liners, often completely misrepresenting the original authors in the process. The same old chestnuts appear again and again in the brochures and leaflets: William Dunbar's 'London thou art the flower of cities all', Samuel Johnson's 'When a man is tired of London, he is tired of life' or Wordsworth's 'Earth has not anything to show more fair'. In fact, the poem attributed to Dunbar was little more than a piece of flattery concocted for a royal banquet given by Henry VII in 1501, and says little about London except how great it is ('thou are of towns A *per se*', it begins). As for Johnson and Wordsworth, their lines have been so overused that the original sense has been almost entirely lost. I return to them below.

For the tourist trade, the literature of London is also a commodity to be packaged and sold. Blue plaques pinpoint the dwelling-places of bygone literary giants, however briefly they occupied them, while Poet's Corner in Westminster Abbey provides them with tombstones, whether or not they are actually buried there. You can go on literary walking tours, or buy literary companions which explain in painstaking detail which author wrote which work in which house in which year. The house where Dr Johnson wrote much of his dictionary has been opened to the public. So, too, has one of Dickens's houses. In both cases the premises have been specially kitted out with period furniture and memorabilia culled from elsewhere to make them more 'authentic'. These reconstructed shrines often confuse the line between fiction and reality. The fact that Sherlock Holmes was a figment of Arthur Conan Doyle's imagination is no obstacle to visiting his famous offices at 221b Baker Street. Manette Street in Soho is named not after a real person but after Dr Manette from Dickens's *Tale of Two Cities*; even the goldbeater's workshop described in the novel has been 'reconstructed' in the doctor's honour. Sometimes fiction can form the basis of a whole tourist enterprise. There is no evidence, for example, that the Old Curiosity Shop off Lincoln's Inn Fields was the building that inspired Dickens to create Little Nell; like Juliet's alleged balcony in Verona, it is just a pretty and plausibly old-looking site exploited for commercial gain.

What these tourist shenanigans show is, amongst other things, the extraordinary power of fiction to reshape a city in our imagination. As Jonathan Raban suggests in *Soft City*, each of us has a personalized city in our heads which conforms not to the contours of a map but to our own individual experience. The larger the city (and London is as large as they come), the harder it is to get a grip on the place as a whole, and the greater the need to reinvent it; we have to create images for what we do not, and perhaps cannot, know for ourselves. Novels and other art-forms help create just the kind of coherent vision that a city-dweller might need. No wonder, then, if some books and authors manage to enter the collective consciousness. Dickens in particular succeeded in reshaping London for generations of readers. We still refer today to 'Dickensian' conditions to denote certain kinds of destitution, and might call someone we meet a 'Dickensian' character. Of course Dickens did not invent urban poverty, or the larger-than-life heroes and villains that stalk the metropolis, just as Conan Doyle did not invent the modern detective. But through fiction authors have helped frame the terms of our imaginative vision. To read the literature of London is not merely to acquire culture in an abstract sense. It is to get to know a parallel London, which in a perverse way is just as real as the city of bricks and mortar and motor cars, and certainly just as influential: the London of the imagination.

Pepys and Evelyn: Diarists for Posterity

Nowadays we know Samuel Pepys as the greatest diarist in English literature, a painstaking recorder of London in the 1660s. And yet he nearly missed the most dramatic event of his lifetime, the Great Fire. Pepys actually woke up on the night that the fire started, but decided it did not look like much and went back to bed. Unlike the incompetent Lord Mayor Thomas Bloodworth, who made the same mistake, though, Pepys quickly made up for lost time and proceeded to describe the fire in minute detail, first from the vantage point of his home in the City and then, as the blaze spread, from Bethnal Green and Woolwich. It is to him and his fellow diarist, John Evelyn, that we owe nearly all our knowledge of the traumatic events of September 1666. In many ways, Pepys and Evelyn also gave London its modern taste for literature and literary gossip.

London had featured in the English literary canon throughout the Middle Ages, notably in Chaucer who used it as a backdrop for a number of his Canterbury Tales. But nobody before the Tudor era set about describing the city itself in any detail. The literary scene changed profoundly with the invention of the printing press; both William Caxton and his pupil Wynkyn de Worde set up presses in London, Caxton in Westminster and Worde in Fleet Street. William Fitzstephen gave an account of medieval life in the capital in the *Cronycle of England* in 1497; a century later John Stow provided the first rigorous topographical and historical picture in his *Survey of London*. The author who did most before Pepys and Evelyn to give us something of the city's atmosphere and flavour was Ben Jonson, in such colourful plays as *Bartholomew Fair*, set in Smithfield market. It is the diarists, however, who have better stood the test of time as chroniclers of the burgeoning metropolis.

Pepys (1633–1703) was a top-flight civil servant who sealed the success of his career when he helped bring Charles II back from exile in 1660. Appointed Clerk of the Acts to the Navy Board, he began writing his diary as a chronicle of political events at the outset of the Restoration. It was never meant for public consumption, and indeed was written in a personal shorthand telescoping words and phrases and peppered with a handful of foreign languages. As the diary goes on, Pepys's personal life intrudes more and more: what he has eaten, what he has seen at the theatre, his troubles with servants, his relationship with his wife Elizabeth, his worries about his eyesight and, ultimately, his affair with his wife's companion Deborah Willett which caused him to break off his diary in 1669. Because the journal is essentially private (it was not published until 1825), it is not given to great literary flourishes; it is unspectacularly written, but dense and highly detailed nonetheless. Pepys enjoyed access to Charles II, and provides much royal gossip; it is through him that the legend of Charles hiding in an oak tree at the Battle of Worcester in 1651 has been handed down.

Evelyn's journal, by contrast, was always intended for public consumption and is a much better read, even if its subjects are described without Pepys's obsessive attention to detail. Evelyn (1620–1706) was a man of independent means who never had to work for a living; his diary reads rather like a modern gossip column. He tackled a huge variety of subjects: engravings, vineyards, navigation, tree planting and different types of salad. It was Evelyn who discovered the sculptor Grinling Gibbons, finding him at work at a cottage near his house in Deptford. The one subject on which Evelyn kept almost entirely silent is himself. The only personal anecdote concerns a visit by the Russian Tsar, Peter the Great, to the Deptford dockyards. The royal party requisitioned Evelyn's house, Sayes Court, and filled it 'full of people right nasty'. By the time the royal party left, 300 window panes had been smashed, and Evelyn's prize holly hedges had been ruined because the tsar had insisted on being hurtled through them in a wheelbarrow.

Grub Street Blues

In the late 17th century, literature in London became an industry and Grub Street was its sweatshop. The street, suitably enough a former refuse ditch near the church of St Giles Cripplegate, filled with hack writers and literary hopefuls who wanted to be near the printing presses and bookshops of Fleet Street and Ludgate Hill. It was the literary equivalent of Tin Pan Alley, a street of sweet dreams and dashed hopes, of burning ambitions and broken bank balances. Thanks to the poet Andrew Marvell, the magnificently evocative name entered the language, becoming a byword for cheap literature, mass-produced journalism and the subculture that went with them. Dr Johnson's dictionary says of Grub Street: 'Much inhabited by writers of small histories, dictionaries, and temporary poems; whence any mean production is called *grubstreet.*' Johnson's reference to writers of dictionaries suggests he considered himself as much a part of the Grub Street phenomenon as anyone; the whole literary scene was implicated, from the giants at the top to the ink-stained drudges in the gutter.

The big names associated with the street's subculture are Alexander Pope (1688–1744) and Jonathan Swift (1667–1745), who exposed the rotten core of life in the capital in their poems and essays. Indeed one of the images of Grub Street is of hacks spending their time worming away at the myths of London with their satires of excess and horror. Pope's *Dunciad,* first published in 1728, is an extended fantasy on the chaos of the city and its literary scene. He wrote:

> *Not with less glory mighty Dulness crowned*
> *Shall take through Grub Street her triumphant round;*
> *And her Parnassus glancing o'er at once,*
> *Behold an hundred sons, and each a dunce.*

Swift's poems also emphasize the grotesque, stinking side of London; his is a place of dead cats, dung and blood. Indeed he and Pope can be said to have produced the literary equivalent of Hogarth's satirical paintings and engravings. 'The subject matter of Pope, Swift and Hogarth is replete with obnoxious details,' writes the critic Pat Rogers. 'Their recurrent motifs are squalor, pestilence, ordure, poverty: their mode is one of physicality, their tone often that of outrage or disgust.' But the Grub Street crew was not above compassion, especially when it came to their fellow-writers struggling to make a living. The playwright Oliver Goldsmith wrote a touching epitaph on one hack called Edward Purdon:

> *Here lies poor Ned Purdon, from misery freed,*
> *Who long was a bookseller's hack:*
> *He led such a damnable life in this world,*
> *I don't think he'll wish to come back.*

The imagery of Grub Street remains potent to this day, with echoes in Karl Marx's remark that a writer is a worker in as far as he enriches his publisher, or again in Raban's assertion that 'the freelance writer, like the professional diner-out, lives off the slack in the metropolitan economy'. Grub Street itself, however, bears few physical traces. In 1830 its name was changed to Milton Street, after the man who owned the land on which it stood, and in the 1950s it became part of the stark concrete landscape of the Barbican.

When a Man is Tired of Quoting Dr Johnson

For as long as tourists have been visiting London, they have been beaten over the head with Dr Johnson's assertion that 'When a man is tired of London, he is tired of life'. Taken out of context, it sounds more like a threat than an exhortation: you had better like London, or else you might as well admit you are an unimaginative squirt and quietly curl up in a corner and die. That is not at all what the good doctor meant. The phrase comes not directly from Johnson, but from his biographer James Boswell. Under an entry for 29 September 1777, towards the end of Johnson's life, Boswell has him say: 'Why, Sir, you find no man, at all intellectual, who is willing to leave London. No Sir, when a man is tired of London, he is tired of life; for there is in London all that life can afford.' In other words it is not that London is necessarily *likeable*, but that it offers an array of life in all its forms that is fascinating to anyone with a curious mind.

Those who cling on to the notion that Johnson loved everything about his city need look no further than his poem entitled *London*, written at the beginning of his career in 1738. In it he describes London as 'the needy villain's gen'ral home' and remarks:

> *Here malice, rapine, accident conspire*
> *And now a rabble rages, now a fire;*
> *Their ambush here relentless ruffians lay*
> *And here the fell attorney prowls for prey:*
> *Here falling houses thunder on your head*
> *And here a female atheist talks you dead...*

Johnson is expressing the same conflicting feelings about London as his contemporary Smollett: it is violent and unpleasant, but it is also fascinating. Significantly, 'When a man is tired of London' asserts that the city can be seen as a microcosm of life itself; it is an encyclopedia into which any intelligent person can dip and draw inspiration. To see the city in this way is to give it shape and meaning, in some sense to limit it and make it intelligible. The phrase reflects the times in which Johnson lived: he witnessed the first great growth of London, and like other writers of his time he tried to make sense of it through literary metaphor. In other words, London was no longer graspable through ordinary perception alone; it required the power of the imagination.

Elsewhere in his *Life of Johnson*, Boswell takes up the same theme as his mentor. London, he says, is a different place for different people, but the intellectual 'is struck with it, as comprehending the whole of human life in all its variety, the contemplation of which is inexhaustible.' This image of the city as a microcosm of life itself recurs again and again in the literature of London. A century after Boswell and Johnson, Henry James reacted to the much expanded and far greyer capital in strikingly similar vein. He wrote in his *Notebooks* in 1881:

'It is difficult to speak adequately or justly of London. It is not a pleasant place; it is not agreeable, or cheerful, or easy, or exempt from reproach. It is only magnificent... You may call it dreary, heavy, stupid, dull, inhuman, vulgar at heart and tiresome in form... But for one who takes it as I take it, London is on the whole the most possible form of life.'

A Confused William Wordsworth

In 1802, William Wordsworth (1770–1850) came down to London from the Lake District and wrote his famous *Sonnet Composed Upon Westminster Bridge*, which begins:

> *Earth has not anything to show more fair:*
> *Dull would he be of soul who could pass by*
> *A sight so touching in its majesty...*

Another good piece of advertising copy for the London Tourist Board? It certainly seems that way. This is London without its bustle, its dirt, its immensity. 'Ne'er saw I, never felt, a calm so deep,' Wordsworth says. Even the river, which in 1802 was notorious for its stink of industrial effluent and raw sewage, 'glideth at his own sweet will'. Gone, too, is the fog: the skyline is 'bright and glittering in the smokeless air'.

What kind of a London is this? Wordsworth's poem seems more of a romantic idyll of the countryside than a description of the metropolis. How did he ever find London so quiet and attractive? The answer is that he got up at five o'clock in the morning, long before anybody else, and chose a particularly clear and crisp day to enjoy the sunrise over the distant spires and towers. Wordsworth did not set out to describe London in a complete or typical way; he was actively seeking out a moment, however transient, at which the over-developed city could still be said to be in touch with nature. In 1802 the docks were under construction and the industrial revolution was about to change the old rural world forever. The success of the poem demonstrates that Wordsworth found his magic moment. But the sonnet is not a celebration of the glories of London; rather it is an elegy for all the glories it was in the process of losing.

In Book VII of *The Prelude*, written a few years later, Wordsworth returns to London and this time describes it in the daytime. There is quite a difference. No longer a sight 'touching in its majesty', it is 'a monstrous ant-hill on the plain of a too-busy world'. Urban reality is something the poet can barely comprehend, and he mixes the muddle in his head with the chaos he sees all around him:

> *Oh, blank confusion! true epitome*
> *Of what the mighty city is herself,*
> *To thousands upon thousands of her sons,*
> *Living amid the same perpetual whirl*
> *Of trivial objects, melted and reduced*
> *To one identity, by differences*
> *That have no law, no meaning, and no end—*

Earth may indeed have nothing to show more fair than London, but only at the crack of dawn on a clear day with a strong prevailing west wind. Otherwise it is just as grimy and shapeless as ever.

Dickens Reshapes a City

'Dickens,' wrote his contemporary Walter Bagehot, 'describes London like a special correspondent for posterity.' It is the peculiar achievement of Charles Dickens (1812–70) to have succeeded in his vast body of fiction in outstripping the achievements of a whole century's worth of historians, journalists and social researchers. His imaginative vision has managed to convey more of the flavour and density of life in Victorian London to more people than any profusion of facts or faithfully recorded observations. In the popular consciousness, his work far surpasses even the brilliant achievements of Henry Mayhew, whose four volumes of social reportage, *London Life and the London Poor*, also provide a compendious portrait of the times. In Weinreb and Hibbert's *London Encyclopedia*, which is after all a historical companion, not a literary one, Mayhew merits just six entries while Dickens enjoys an astonishing 81.

Dickens was the first, and arguably the only English novelist to embrace the whole metropolis in his fictional world without flinching or growing incoherent. His labyrinthine plots and vast social backdrops create an illusion of the complexity of the city itself. To read Dickens is to take on the metropolis and come away feeling as though you have conquered it. And yet the London of his novels is very much an artificial one: his characters have names, like Veneering or Pecksniff or Gamp, that are far too absurd to be plausible; likewise their personalities exaggerate identifiable reality to the point where they become grotesque. With Dickens you are always wavering between realism and caricature, between the city you know and the free flight of your imagination.

The defining experience of the metropolis in Dickens is surface. His London is so big that it is hard to penetrate anyone beyond the outward signposts to their character: clothes, physical features, manner of speech and so on. Surface, not substance, is paramount in determining social status. A book like *Our Mutual Friend* is all about the fragility of identity in the big city and the ease with which one social mask can be exchanged for another, particularly through the power of money. Appearances are everything, for the middle-class snob Mr Podsnap, for the parvenu Veneerings, even for the modest Mr and Mrs Boffin. When the Boffins come into an unexpected fortune, they understand that their characters must change along with their status. 'Our old selves wouldn't do,' Mr Boffin tells his wife. Characters grow rich, grow poor, get lost and are found again with terrifying arbitrariness in this profusion of surfaces that is Dickensian London. The fog is a recurring metaphor; characters pop out of the gloom at crucial moments and then sink back again into anonymity and isolation. The modern city is a lonely place. Dickens wrote in one of his journalistic pieces: 'It is strange with how little notice, good, bad, or indifferent, a man may live or die in London.' It is a sentiment that infuses much of his fiction.

One of the most appealing facets of Dickens is his compassion, a quality which not only brings his characters to life but also makes him seem at times like something of a social crusader. His moving descriptions of the poorhouse, or the slums of St Giles (called Tom-all-Alone's in *Bleak House*), or the stink of Smithfield market, or the barbarity of Newgate jail and its gallows, have all been interpreted as appeals for greater social equality; at the same time, his satirical indictments of bureaucracy, whether in the legal system or in parliament, suggest grave disillusionment with the way Britain was governed.

And yet Dickens turns out to be more slippery about politics than he appears on first sight. In 1869 he made a remarkably equivocal statement when addressing the Birmingham and Midland Institute. He said: 'My faith in the people governing is, on the whole, infinitesimal; my faith in the People governed is, on the whole, illimitable.' Quite a few people in his audience who did not have the advantage of seeing the capital P in print thought he was advocating authoritarianism, although Dickens later insisted on the opposite. The ambiguity is significant and crops up elsewhere in his work.

Dickens decries drunkenness as the consequence of poverty one minute, then speaks out against the degeneracy of drinkers the next. His description of Tom-All-

Alone's may be humane and touching, but he also talks about its 'corrupted blood' which 'propagates infection and contagion' as though poverty itself were a sort of disease.

What this indicates is that Dickens was infused with the contradictions of his age, and in particular the contradictions of the big city. Fortunately, he was a good enough writer not to allow preachiness to take precedence over his powers of observation; maybe he was too unsure of his own prejudices to know how to let them intrude. As a result, he could be read and appreciated by just about anyone. The 'bran-new' Veneerings are depicted with such verve and humour that even social climbers of the same ilk could read about them without taking offence. George Orwell wrote that Dickens 'seems to have succeeded in attacking everybody and antagonizing nobody'. Dickens encapsulated a vision of the city so coherent and apparently complete that to take exception to his novels would have been to admit a deficient appreciation of life itself.

The Art of Detection

London in the late 19th century took on a more sinister and bewildering aspect than ever before. Never had the city been so large or so anonymous. The suburbs were sprouting, the population was mushrooming, and all the old codes of city life—the surfaces that Dickens revelled in—were flattening out and disappearing. The slums of the East End were filled with more human misery than anyone dared contemplate; meanwhile the new railway stations were packed with thousands of identical commuters in uniform-like grey suits. Pickpockets and petty thieves could operate with virtual impunity because they had become as faceless as the rest of the urban population. The city seemed incomprehensible and dangerous. Who could make sense of such a place?

Enter Sherlock Holmes, detective extraordinaire, who from his first appearance in *A Study in Scarlet* in 1887 stunned and delighted thousands of avid fans with his powers of observation and deduction. Sir Arthur Conan Doyle's creation, with his trademark deerstalker hat and meerschaum pipe, was a detective whose time had come. A generation after Dickens, the city had become too confusing, too diffuse, too anonymous for a single imagination to grasp. Holmes, exceptionally, knew how to decode the bewildering surfaces and restore a sense of order. What's more, the dramatic context of the stories—mystery tinged with melodrama—gave back to the city its lost sense of variety and excitement. Crime became a thrill, not a threat.

'It has long been an axiom of mine that the little things are infinitely the most important,' says Holmes in the story *A Case of Identity*, as he proceeds to reel off an astonishingly detailed list of facts about a woman he has never met before.

Attention to small signs and clues has by now become an axiom of city life, the key to becoming fashion-conscious and streetwise. But it was a mildly disturbing idea in late Victorian London, where a sense of propriety and moral uprightness was maintained precisely by *not* observing too much or asking too many questions. In many of his adventures, Holmes acts or talks in a way that outrages those around him, not least the police, who are always powerless until he comes to their aid. He puts his narrator Dr Watson through humiliation after humiliation because of his inferior detecting skills, but nevertheless expects unswerving loyalty.

Holmes is a disconcerting figure who can see into the hearts not only of criminals but of all men. His pronouncements come with a peculiar note of moral authority and he uses them to draw out the innermost secrets and thoughts of both his suspects and his associates; Holmes acts as a kind of secular Father Confessor for the sins of the modern city.

Despite his knack for unearthing hidden desires, Holmes is also a supremely rational detective. One of his greatest attractions to the late Victorians was that he proved, or appeared to prove, that deductive logic could provide the answer to any problem, no matter how great. At a time when London's growth seemed to have veered out of control, here was a man who could make sense of it all. It must have been every civil servant's fantasy to see through the muddle of London with Holmes-like clarity and bring the whole heaving monster under control. Elementary? If only.

Yearning for the Age of Innocence

The Sherlock Holmes stories illustrate the sense of moral degeneration that accompanied the rapid expansion of London. But Holmes's level-headed reaction to his environment was unusual in the literature of the time. More often, the city inspired diabolical fantasies such as Robert Louis Stevenson's *Dr Jekyll and Mr Hyde*, or grimly atmospheric depictions of urban paranoia like Joseph Conrad's *The Secret Agent*. Everywhere was a sense of disgust. For William Morris the city was a 'spreading sore', for H.G. Wells it was 'vast and incomprehensible', for George Gissing it was 'the devourer of rural limits', for Jack London it was simply 'the abyss'. It is surely significant that in Wells's *War of the Worlds*, the Martians land in the commuter town of Woking, which at the time was on the fault line between suburbia and the unbroken countryside beyond.

Escapism was a common theme. Wells opted for suburban romance in such books as *Love and Mr Lewisham* (1900) and *Kipps* (1905) before turning to science fiction, the most escapist genre of all. In *The Napoleon of Notting Hill* (1904), G.K. Chesterton depicted a London neighbourhood declaring its independence from the rest of the city in an attempt to recover its community spirit. His fantasy harked back to the medieval concept of a citadel defending itself against invaders, and was to find many echoes in the post-war Ealing film comedy *Passport to Pimlico*, which starts from a similar premise.

Escapism acted like nostalgia: it expressed a yearning for the innocence of a bygone age, for a time when the city was attractive and shiny, and the countryside unadulterated by its rapacious appetites. Much of the urban literature of the late 19th and early 20th centuries has been forgotten precisely because of the false premise of that nostalgia; such an age of innocence never existed. Even a novelist as talented as E.M. Forster turned his back on the most troubling aspects of the city and focused instead on such subjects as property (the ultimate middle-class concern) and the lure of Italy (the ultimate middle-class escapist fantasy). In *Howards End* (1910), Forster states explicitly that the working classes do not interest him; they are 'for the statistician or the poet'. The most troubling figures are the novel's only lower-middle class characters, the downtrodden clerk Leonard Bast and his wife. Perhaps it says something about Forster's own prejudices that Mrs Bast makes a plot-stirringly drunken scene and then conveniently drops out of the action, while Leonard is killed off at the end to ensure that he troubles the middle-class order no further. Nevertheless it is Bast who best illustrates the understated viciousness of Edwardian society, and who best expresses the age's yearning for innocence. At the height of his frustration over his inability to get ahead, he simply gets up and walks all night until he is out of London; as he comes to a wood strewn with bluebells he understands, or thinks he understands, that a better, purer world is still within his reach.

Such illusions feature little in the avant-garde of the modernist movement, which made a link between urban alienation and the fragmentary nature of human personality to draw radically new portraits of the city in central Europe (Kafka), Dublin (Joyce) or London (Virginia Woolf). In Woolf's work, and particularly her novel *Mrs Dalloway*, the city figures only incidentally in the interior monologue of the narrator. The metropolis is no longer something solid and graspable, but a patchwork of fragments that can link individuals in spontaneous ways, or just as easily isolate them from one another. The characters in *Mrs Dalloway* find common points of reference in the ringing of church bells or the appearance of a royal coach in the centre of London; but the links are constructs of their imagination, not something the city has imposed upon them. In Woolf's writing, the city has lost its unitary character altogether.

The rise of the labour movement in the 1920s and 1930s led to a greater realism about working life, and a more trenchant analysis of the class system. The left-wing critic Cyril Connolly said that London was 'for rich young men to shop in, dine in, ride in, get married in, go to theatres in, and die in as respected householders...not for the poor.' George Orwell gave an unflinching view of life at the bottom of the pile in *Down and Out in Paris and London*. Interestingly, he also turned the escapist fantasy genre on its head in *Nineteen Eighty-Four*, in which the London of his imagination is not clean, neat and commodious, but a frightening dictatorship in which control of the city has been bought at the price of its citizens' freedom to think. The old Victorian moral certainties are turned on their heads: War is Peace, Freedom is Slavery, Ignorance is Strength. All progress is open to political manipulation, even the development of broadcasting.

In 1949 the BBC was seen as the flagship of free speech; Orwell turned radio and television into the prime instruments of political repression in his dystopian world. In Orwell's London the degeneration of the city is no longer moral and physical, it is political and spiritual. Yearning for innocence has become impossible.

Multicultural Melting Pot

The newcomer has always been a compelling figure in the literature of the city, and the immigrant wave of the 1950s and 1960s provided ample material for new writers. Together with the profusion of foreign cultures came a melting of the old class strictures and a celebration of youth: what more could a novelist want? Newly arrived Caribbean writers such as George Lamming and Samuel Selvon began describing their experiences in novels like *The Emigrants* and *The Lonely Londoners*. Meanwhile, the homegrown writer Colin MacInnes captured the jazzy excitement and novelty of the time in his London trilogy (*City of Spades*, *Absolute Beginners* and *Mr Love and Justice*) which appeared in the late 1950s. His characters embark on labyrinthine and inter-connecting journeys around the city, finding new life in stuffy old neighbourhoods and allowing their old ideas to be exploded by the environment evolving around them. The narrator of *Absolute Beginners* finds his north Kensington neighbourhood so teeming and exotic that he calls it Napoli. The continuity of the Victorian family has been broken; for the immigrants because they have left theirs behind, for the native Londoners because the trauma of the war has sparked the desire to create a new, more communal society.

MacInnes's is a relentlessly optimistic view of postwar London, one that is not entirely endorsed by the immigrants he writes about. Some of the best postwar novelists have come from the former colonies: V.S. Naipaul from India via Trinidad, Salman Rushdie, also from India, and Ben Okri from Nigeria. They too describe the new exotic streak in the city, the smell of spices and the rhythm of African and Caribbean music. In *The Satanic Verses*, which aside from all the controversy is an outstanding novel about the immigrant experience, Rushdie fantasizes about London acquiring the climate of Bombay, its buttoned-up citizens suddenly exposed to tropical heat and passion. But he also focuses on the immigrant's paradox of belonging and not belonging—a theme he shares with many of his fellow immigrant writers. Rushdie is much more bitter about the insidious effects of racism than a writer like MacInnes, particularly when he describes the Thatcher era with its return to 'Victorian values'. One of Rushdie's characters notes bitterly: 'No pitched battles these days... The emphasis is on small-scale enterprises and the cult of the individual, right? In other words, five or six white bastards murdering us, one individual at a time.'

In the 1980s, the decade that cultivated greed as a virtue, novelists began to satirize the city as a place where anything can be had, anything can be consumed, by a person ruthless and hungry enough to want it. Material excess and the concomitant erosion of the human spirit are the central themes of Martin Amis's *Money* (1984), a black comedy whose narrator, John Self, is addicted to his own power of consumption. Mostly he consumes pornography and junk food, the trash of the city, and his morality is the morality of a man who cannot believe what he is getting away with, but is happy to get away with it anyway:

'We all seem to make lots of money. Man, do we seem to be coining it here. Even the chicks live like kings. The car is free. The car is on the house. The house is on the mortgage. The mortgage is on the firm—without interest. The interesting thing is: how long can this last?'

The answer is it cannot last, but in the meantime the fabric of society is collapsing entirely. Both *Money* and Amis's later *London Fields* are shot through with a sense of impending doom. *Money*, we are warned from the start, is a suicide note, while in *London Fields* the imminent disaster is no less than the end of the world. In both books, London is crawling with shysters unaware of and quite indifferent to the chaos they are wreaking. People care about nobody but themselves. The old novelistic themes of love and marriage make no sense. Love, like everything else, is a commodity; love, in the words of a character in Julian Barnes's novel *Talking it Over* (1991), is just a system to get someone to call you darling after sex. There are no human feelings any more. All that the city can offer in the late 20th century is consumption, then death.

The Visual Arts

London is not a visually compelling city. It has never paid a great deal of attention to its own physical appearance; it is a worldly, not an aesthetic capital, a place of much chatter and gossip but little visual flair. Until the 18th century, few artists bothered to draw or paint London at all, and those that did were for the most part gifted foreigners—there was no home-grown talent to speak of. What

finally began to inspire painters and draughtsmen was not a straightforward view of London, but an oblique, skewed vision that evoked
its murky and grotesque passions rather than just the mundane rows
of bricks and mortar. Two kinds of artists have thrived in London:
the social satirist, for whom the cityscape was an expression of the
overweening ambition and furtive appetites of its citizens, and the
Romantic, for whom the London fog above all provided limitless
opportunities for experimentation with light, colour and fantasy.
Victorian strictures about morality put the satirists out of fashion,
while the Romantics were cruelly robbed of their greatest inspiration
after the passing of the Clean Air Act in 1956. London barely features in the major works of late 20th-century painting, photography
or even film, and when it does its depiction often reflects artistic
visions of the past rather than a new aesthetic approach. London is
still a city in search of visual inspiration.

In Search of Style: London Before Hogarth

Perhaps the earliest representation of London is a gold medallion showing the triumphant arrival of the 3rd-century Roman emperor Constantius Chlorus. It gives
precious little away about the shape of the London of the time, showing Constantius riding through a generic city gate to a warm welcome from the townsfolk.
Eight centuries later, the pictorial image was scarcely more sophisticated: the depiction of Edward the Confessor's funeral procession in the Bayeux Tapestry (11th
century) is no more than a sketch marking the Abbey of St Peter at Westminster. A
more detailed picture emerges in a woodcut featured in Wynkyn de Worde's edition of the *Cronycle of England* (1497), in which London appears as a dense
cluster of turrets and spires. But there is no sense yet of distance or perspective; it
was only when artists began to use the river as a reference point that they managed
to provide a focus for the urban clutter.

The river features prominently in a remarkable manuscript painting of Charles
d'Orléans in the Tower of London (*c.*1500) by an unknown Flemish artist. The picture, which is sporadically on display in the British Library, clearly shows Traitor's
Gate, the White Tower (which really was white in those days) and some of the
riverside houses. The importance of river transport is highlighted by a cluster of
boats in front of London Bridge; one can even see the perilous currents beneath the
bridge's thick stone arches.

The rise of London as a mercantile capital in the 16th and 17th centuries was not
accompanied by a flourishing of the visual arts, to the embarrassment of the royal
court; the Tudors and Stuarts were forced to draft in painters and craftsmen from

abroad. The German Hans Holbein the Younger (1497–1543) was the undisputed master of the Tudor portrait, as evidenced by his work in the National Portrait Gallery; Henry VIII even sent him off round Europe to capture the likenesses of potential wives. A century later, Charles I called on Peter Paul Rubens (1577–1640) and Anthony Van Dyck (1599–1641) from Flanders to lend pictorial weight to his assertion of the divine right of kings. Rubens's crowning achievement in London was the frescoed ceiling of the Banqueting House in Whitehall.

Van Dyck was a portraitist who painted Charles every which way: on horseback, in his most pompous robes and, memorably, in triplicate. Both artists feature prominently in the National Gallery and in the stately homes of the period. Their work bears the unmistakable mark of their patron, reflecting Charles's supreme, fatally misjudged self-confidence; perhaps fortunately, both artists died before the Civil War and so escaped the Puritans' revenge for their royal flattery.

The Great Fire of 1666 made Londoners realize they had almost no pictorial record of their city, and a new mania arose for cityscapes and maps. John Ogilby's 5x8ft post-Fire map, published in 1676, was the first detailed and accurate chart the city had ever known. There is a copy of it in the Guildhall Library. The Flemish engraver Wenceslaus Hollar, meanwhile, was the period's most assiduous visual recorder. He drew small-scale maps showing the devastation of the fire, and etched numerous cityscapes that give a full, if unimaginative, idea of what London looked like at the time. The greatest aesthetic achievement of the late Stuart period was probably Abraham Hondius's striking series of pictures of Frost Fairs on the frozen Thames, which are in the Museum of London.

Hogarth and His Followers

It was not until the advent of William Hogarth (1697–1764) that London acquired a painter who could hold his own against the best in Europe. Hogarth had his nose rubbed in the dirt of the city from the day he was born. Brought up just a stone's throw away from the live cattle market in Smithfield, he was lucky to survive his infancy, never mind climb up the social ladder far enough to be able to live off his art. That he did so was a testament not only to his skill, but also to his extraordinary popularity. Prints of his paintings and engravings hung on the walls of thousands of households all over London.

Hogarth's genius was to adapt classical modes of satire to the peculiarly rich, if putrid, atmosphere of 18th-century London. His pictures capture the greed and bloated ambition of the aristocratic classes, while retaining an extraordinarily human touch. He makes fun of his subjects, he disapproves of them, but he rarely reduces them to pure caricature. His pictures burst with life in all its forms, from the elegant to the revolting. You see the rich in their palaces and the poor begging on the street; tavern brawls and mayhem at the madhouse at Bedlam; extraordinary scenes of riotous drunkenness, overeating and lustful groping. Among the most accessible works are *The Rake's Progress,* a series of eight paintings charting the rise and fall of a young aristocrat from the gambling house to the lunatic asylum, and *The Election,* a brilliant dissection of corrupt Hanoverian politics (both of these in the John Soane Museum in Lincoln's Inn Fields); *Marriage à la Mode,* a more restrained series satirizing aristocratic mores (in the National Gallery); and *Gin Lane,* an engraving showing the terrifying effects of drink on the population of London (in the British Museum but not always on display).

Hogarth's followers were many; among the more distinguished were Thomas Rowlandson (1756–1827), who took special delight in sending up the outrageous fashions and ageing flesh on display in the city's pleasure gardens; and James Gillray (1757–1815) who specialized in political caricature. George Cruikshank (1792–1878) bewailed the sprawling growth of the city and the rape of the countryside in such prints as *London Going Out of Town* or *The March of Bricks and Mortar* (the latter to be found in the Guildhall Library). Hogarth's influence continued to be felt in the 19th century, if only in the cartoons which flourished in the growing popular press. One can also see the effect he had on a novelist like Dickens, whose characters share Hogarth's cartoon-like, larger-than-life quality. But the engravers of the 19th century failed on the whole to match the licentiousness and cutting satirical edge of their predecessors, and tended to be more heavy-handed in their treatment of social issues. Most notable among them was the French illustrator Gustave Doré, who produced his series *A Pilgrimage* in London in the late 1860s and early 1870s. His much reproduced engravings give a bleak view of the City which is almost Dickensian in its sympathy for the destitute and the down-trodden of the backstreets.

The Romance of Fog

Painters struggled with a more realistic approach to London throughout the 18th century, largely without success. Canaletto was in the city from 1745 to 1754, but his clear-cut, topographical style which worked so well in Venice was peculiarly ill-suited to a city best known for its grey skies and thick fogs. It was not until the advent of J.M.W. Turner (1775–1851) that artists realized what a great asset the fog was. In the early 1830s, Turner painted the *Thames above Waterloo Bridge* with a veil of industrial smoke to heighten the effects of colour and light. Then in 1834 he witnessed the burning of the old Houses of Parliament and produced an extraordinary painting mingling black soot with the burnished gold of the flames and their reflection in the river. The picture (now in Philadelphia) astounded his contemporaries and earned some ridicule from *John Bull* magazine, which found the picture so heavy on yellows that it likened it to a dish overlaced with curry powder. The work could not have been more different from the city scenes of his contemporary and rival, John Constable, who painted a small, rustic London from the vantage point of his house in Hampstead. Turner was vindicated by most critics, including John Ruskin who wrote a vigorous defence of him in his *Modern Painters* of 1843. In his later years, Turner went on to produce even more daring and innovative canvases such as *Rain, Steam and Speed* (in the National Gallery), which almost abandons recognizable forms altogether to depict the impact of the railways on the countryside just outside London.

The middle of the century saw a flowering of moderately interesting English art, including John Ritchie's *Hampstead Heath* and Augustus Egg's triptych of a fallen wife wandering destitute beneath the arches of the Adelphi, *Past and Present*. But it took another foreigner, the American James Whistler (1834–1903), to take up where Turner had left off. Whistler, who settled in London in 1860, caused a furore with his *Nocturne in Black and Gold* (1874), a brilliant and moody piece (now in Detroit) evoking a firework display in the soot-filled sky above the Thames. It was the perfect illustration of what Hippolyte Taine, the indefatigable French traveller, had noted a few years earlier: 'In this livid smoke, objects are no more than phantoms and nature looks like a bad drawing in charcoal which someone has smudged with his sleeve.' Ruskin blamed the bad drawing on Whistler, not on London, and said the picture was like 'flinging a pot of paint in the public's face'. Whistler won a farthing in libel damages for the remark but bankrupted himself with the legal fees he incurred.

The French Impressionists also made much of the London fog, particularly Claude Monet who first came to London in 1870 and returned at regular intervals. 'It is the fog that gives [London] its magnificent amplitude,' he wrote towards the end of his life. 'Its regular and massive blocks become grandiose in that mysterious mantle... How could the English painters of the nineteenth century have painted the houses brick by brick? Those people painted bricks they did not see, that they could not see!' Monet's *Thames from Westminster* (1870), showing the brand new Victoria Embankment, is in the National Gallery; for his mean and moody *Houses of Parliament* of 1903, however, you'll have to hotfoot it to the Met in New York.

As Monet suggested, native English painters were way behind their foreign rivals when it came to depicting London. Even the vicissitudes of the English upper classes were recorded more memorably by a Frenchman, James Tissot, than by any homegrown talent. The home team caught up somewhat with the founding of the Impressionist-inspired Camden Town group by Walter Sickert in the early years of the 20th century. Sickert was a specialist at portraits and interiors, particularly the London music halls; the other members of the group included Harold Gilman, Spencer Gore and Charles Ginner. Theirs were worthy efforts, but scarcely revolutionary; indeed, right up to the Second World War, Whistler was still the overriding influence on cityscape painting in London. The Tate Gallery has two impressive examples from the 1940s of this rather derivative strain of English painting: Victor Pasmore's *Thames at Chiswick* (1943–4) and Graham Sutherland's *Devastation: An East End Street* (1941).

A Detour into Cinema

As it turns out, the gloomy, near-monochrome feel of Sutherland's picture, relieved only by twinkles of white and yellow, is remarkably close to the visual design of Mike Leigh's 1993 feature film *Naked*. Even in the closing years of the century the wells of aesthetic inspiration are still very much the same as those of the past. Perhaps the smokeless capital just isn't exciting enough for visual artists any more. The best-known modern painters to have worked in London, such as David Hockney, Francis Bacon and the 1990s Britpack (*see* below), have barely addressed the city as a subject at all. Photographers have likewise sought subject-matter elsewhere—although Bill Brandt, with his moody encapsulations of the darker side of London life, is a notable exception.

In the case of film, the paucity of London features is due in large part to the bureaucratic nightmare of location shooting. Classics like Fritz Lang's *Ministry of Fear*, Alfred Hitchcock's *Number 17* or Michael Powell's *Peeping Tom* describe a London largely recreated in the film studio; even a film as visually compelling as Michelangelo Antonioni's *Blow Up* cannot do more than hint at London through occasional glimpses away from the main hurly-burly of city life. At least until the 1970s, London was arguably best filmed in low-key 'kitchen-sink' productions like *Up the Junction* and the television play *Waterloo Sunset*, whose heroine is a bag lady.

In the last decade, two very different kinds of London film have emerged. The first tends to be grittily realistic, relieved only by forays into satire and the grotesque. *Naked*, the story of a homeless man caught up in the anonymity and random violence of the big city, falls firmly into this category, as do the films of Stephen Frears (*My Beautiful Laundrette* and *Sammy and Rosie Get Laid*—both scripted by Hanif Kureishi) and Ken Loach (*Riff Raff*). The second kind tends to be a nostalgic foray into the faded glories of the past. There is little violence, little sex and no bad language, just beautiful costumes and lots of quiveringly understated emotions. Examples include John Boorman's *Hope and Glory*, about the Blitz, and Merchant-Ivory productions like *Howards End*, based on the Forster novel of Edwardian love and property.

So different are the two schools of film-making that harsh words have inevitably flown from one to the other. The British director Alan Parker (who long ago decamped to Hollywood) once dismissed Merchant-Ivory as 'the Laura Ashley school of film-making'; conversely, the right-wing historian Norman Stone has described the work of Frears *et al* as flat, two-dimensional and representing 'a nasty part of their producers' brains'. Broadly speaking, the realists have been rather more successful than the traditionalists in producing arresting and innovative work.

Certainly outside of England they have attracted far greater and more favourable critical attention. Back home, however, they have all too often been overlooked or deemed distasteful by the likes of Professor Stone. The problem is that film-makers like Frears or Loach depict a London most people would rather not think about. It is a city of racism, poverty, crime and dirt, a place where bigots bruise ahead and idealism is crushed. Given Britain's track record for cultural conservatism, perhaps we should not be surprised that the last place these films are appreciated is the country that they describe to such devastatingly powerful effect.

101 Ways to Chop Up a Dead Cow: the '90s Britpack

After years of aimless plodding, the London art scene suddenly exploded in the early 1990s thanks to the exploits of a tight-knit group of graduates from Goldsmiths art college who transformed themselves from apprentice craftsmen into superstars virtually overnight. First out of the starting blocks was Damien Hirst, whose *Physical Impossibility of Death in the Mind of Someone Living* (1992) turned out to be a 14-foot tiger shark suspended in a formaldehyde tank. As if that wasn't arresting enough, Hirst was soon pickling whole sheep and slicing cows into curious anatomical sections and putting them on display at the Saatchi Gallery in St John's Wood.

His fellow graduates, meanwhile, started experimenting with elephant dung and clitorises cut out of porn magazines (Chris Ofili), using the hand prints of children to produce a collage of the notorious child-murderer Myra Hindley (Marcus Harvey), making a head bust out of eight pints of the artist's own frozen blood (Marc Quinn), or depicting acts of appalling brutality and sexual violence with the help of mutilated shop mannequins (the Chapman brothers). The Britpack, also known as the YBAs (young British artists), had arrived with a vengeance.

Their works may not have been a visual reflection on London itself, but they nevertheless took London, and the whole country, by storm, particularly in the wake of the stunning *Sensation* exhibition at the Royal Academy in 1997 that brought them the first whiff of establishment approval. The tabloid newspapers were appalled and mounted a series of campaigns against what they saw as an offence to common decency. The Myra Hindley piece was savaged twice by irate members of the public, forcing the curators to install some high-octane security. Many of the Royal Academy's grandees were themselves outraged and nonplussed; three of them resigned over the decision to bring such vile objects into their hallowed space in Burlington House. This was a shallow grab for attention, they felt, not a show-case for serious artistry. 'Any opportunity to see pickled fish and tumescent penises is great fun,' the traditionalist painter Anthony Green conceded, 'but it has little to do with art that will survive beyond the millennium.'

It's probably several decades too soon to judge whether the arresting nature of the Britpack's work is mere hype, or the sign of something genuinely new and thought-provoking. Some of it probably is flashy for the sake of being flashy, a suspicion that is only deepened by the media-hugging antics of the likes of Damien Hirst (who is now moving into that other must-do activity of '90s London, restaurant-owning). But then again we live in an age of glittering superficiality and passing fads, some-thing that works of art are entirely within their rights to reflect. The first lesson of the Britpack, perhaps, is that artistic work in this image-saturated era *has* to grab people's attention or else risk going unnoticed altogether.

Music in London

Music? Did you say English music? Well I've never heard of any.

Frederick Delius, English composer

Musical composition, historically speaking, has not been London's strong point. 'The English do not love music, they respect it,' sneered Antonin Dvorak, who passed through London in the late 19th century. A generation later, the irascible conductor Sir Thomas Beecham commented: 'English music is a state of perpetual promise. Indeed it might be said to be one long promissory note.'

It is certainly true that whole centuries have gone by without the emergence of a single significant home-grown composer. The royal court, in particular, has suffered from this dearth of talent and, as with painters, has frequently had to draft in foreigners to satisfy the call of the Muse. But it would be wrong to think of England as an entirely unmusical nation, or London an unmusical city. Music has been a feature of both street life and high society living since Roman times; if first-rate composers and musicians have not always come to the fore, it has been due at least in part to political circumstance and class prejudice. During the Commonwealth, Oliver Cromwell's Roundheads banned concerts and smashed up organs in London's churches; two centuries later, the Victorians treated street musicians as vagrants and drew the odious, still persistent distinction between 'classical' music, which was for respectable ladies and gentlemen, and 'popular' music, which was for the riff-raff and didn't really count.

The electronic age and the advent of jazz, rock and blues has banished for ever the notion that the English have no musical talent. London in the 1960s was the springboard for the two most influential groups of all time, the Rolling Stones (who were London-bred) and the Beatles (who came, of course, from Liverpool but settled in the capital as soon as they became famous). London remains one of the biggest centres in the world for music of any kind, with umpteen orchestras, a prestigious operatic tradition, lots of great jazz and offbeat rock venues and quite a few creative artists of world repute. If something is still missing, it is perhaps a sense of local inspiration, of connection between musicians and the city in which they live. We can all think of passionate musical paeans written about Paris, or Vienna, or Naples, or New York—but what about London? Nobody has sung about how much they love Piccadilly in the springtime, or how they want to wake up in a Battersea that never sleeps... The best London has managed to come up with is the distinctly lukewarm *'Maybe it's because I'm a Londoner, that I love London so'*. Not a song that Piaf or Sinatra ever thought of covering.

From Plainsong to Byrd Song

The first music that we know about in London came from Rome. Brass bands and percussion accompanied the Roman soldiers who occupied Britain for the first 400 years of London's existence; then when St Augustine came to convert King Ethelbert in 597, he sang Roman liturgical songs with his crowd of followers. At first, music was used as an accompaniment, not as an entertainment in itself. It cropped up most commonly in church, at performances at court, and in street shows given by troubadours, minstrels, jugglers and dancers—the precursors of folk or popular musicians.

In early medieval times, music consisted essentially of plainsong, a simple single line of melody repeated with variations known as tropes—embellishments often made on one sung word like 'alleluia'. One of the earliest enduring English melodies is the song *Sumer is icumen in*, written around 1140 in canon form for four voices. The first known English composer was **John Dunstable** (*c.*1390–1453), from whom around 60 musical scores survive. His most famous song, *O Rosa Bella*, was a smash hit all over Europe.

It was not until Tudor times that London's musical star really began to rise. Henry VIII was himself an accomplished musician and composer, and he in turn attracted the talents of **Thomas Tallis** (1505–85), who injected a new sensuality into English music with such works as *The Lamentations of Jeremiah* and the striking 40-voice motet *Spem in Alium*. The madrigal, an unaccompanied song usually written for four voices, became popular thanks to Elizabethan and early Stuart composers like **Thomas Morley** (1557–1630), **William Byrd** (1543–1623) and **Orlando Gibbons** (1583–1625).

Gibbons took notes on the hawkers about town to write his *Cries of London*, while he and Byrd, in a reflection of the evolution of new instruments, published the world's first collection of keyboard music. The most prolific and popular composer of the period was **John Dowland** (1563–1626), an Irish lute-player who built up a formidable reputation for deeply melancholic songs first at the Danish court and then in London.

Music was increasingly in demand, and musicians were courted in the homes of aristocrats as well as princes. The Elizabethan theatre provided further opportunities; indeed Shakespeare wrote songs specially for inclusion in his plays. This was also the age in which the organ began to transform church music; Morley, in particular, wrote liturgical works by the ream and established the first musical traditions of the newly established Anglican Church.

Such efforts were stifled, however, by the Puritans, who believed that religion was far too serious a subject for the frivolities of music. After the Civil War, organs were smashed in churches all over London and street musicians were prevented from performing, at first just on Sundays and then completely. Music was either suppressed or pushed underground. 'Ten years of gloomy silence seem to have elapsed before a string was suffered to vibrate, or a pipe allowed to breathe, in the kingdom,' wrote the musical historian Charles Burney.

Purcell, Handel, er, that's it

The philistinism of the Commonwealth dealt a severe blow to London's musical fortunes, and the golden age came to an abrupt end. Charles II tried to introduce the French music he had heard in exile on the other side of the Channel, but without much luck. The craze for opera, which was sweeping continental Europe, barely made any impression in England. Until, that is, the advent of **Henry Purcell** (1659–95). Purcell was born into a musical family in London, and already at the age of 17 took over as organist at Westminster Abbey. He, along with all the recognized composers of his day, trained in the ecclesiastical setting of the Chapel Royal at St James's Palace, but was soon to make his name with secular entertainments. One of his earliest major works, *Dido and Aeneas* (1689), was a straight imitation of the Italian opera of the time, in which the music continued without interruption from beginning to end. Thereafter, Purcell modified his operatic style somewhat, introducing breaks for conversation to vary the dramatic pace in such works as *King Arthur* (1691) and *The Fairy Queen* (1692). So exhilarating, so effortlessly impressive, and at times so intensely tragic was Purcell's work that he earned the nickname 'Orpheus Britannicus'. Thanks to him, the royal court—and London at large—acquired an appetite for music that it was never to lose again.

A second musical giant emerged a generation later in the shape of **George Frideric Handel** (1685–1759), a German by birth who ended up in London more by accident than design, but who arguably contributed more to English music than anyone else before or since. Handel was born in Halle, south of Berlin, and established himself as a composer first in Italy, then Hamburg, and then at the court of the elector of Hanover (later George I of England), where he was Kappellmeister. He came to London in 1711 to put on one of his Italianate operas, *Rinaldo*. So great was his success, however, that he was persuaded to stay and produced an extraordinarily prolific body of work over the next half-century: his output of music, both sacred and profane, both courtly and popular, was greater than that of Bach and Beethoven put together.

Today Handel is known chiefly for his oratorios, particularly *The Messiah*; in his own time, however, he was above all a popular composer of Italian operas (*Atalanta, Scipione, Giulio Cesare in Egitto*, etc), which were performed not only before well-to-do audiences but also in public, notably in the fashionable London pleasure gardens of the time. 'The love of music,' wrote one 18th-century social historian, 'is now descended from the Opera house in the Haymarket to the little public houses about this metropolis, and common servants may now be met with, who pretend as much judgement of an opera tune as my Lady Duchess.' Handel may have been a master of musical structure and harmony, but he also knew how to please an audience, how to 'hit them straight on the drum of the ear' as he put it. And he was not the only one.

This was also the era of John Gay's *The Beggar's Opera* (1728), which drew on traditional melodies as well as the music of another expatriate German, John Pepusch. Music's ability to break down class barriers made some people uncomfortable, however, and every intellectual argument was used to denigrate opera. 'A curse on this damned Italian pathic mode,' wrote one detractor, Henry Carey. The critic Charles Dibdin described Handel's music as 'floods of German nonsense'. Dr

Johnson was more laconic in his observation that opera was 'an exotic and irrational entertainment which has always been combatted, and has always prevailed'.

No section of the establishment was more suspicious of music than the Anglican church, which so discouraged devotional compositions that it lost large chunks of its flock to the new nonconformist Methodist movement. The father of Methodism, **John Wesley**, was an unambiguous admirer of Handel and the other great composers of the age; far from believing that music denigrated religion, he once remarked of a rendering of *The Messiah*, 'I doubt if that congregation was ever so serious at a sermon, as they were during this performance'. Wesley and his brother Charles were prolific hymn-writers; ironically, their compositions proved so popular that even the Anglican authorities fell for them and they are now the mainstay of Sunday morning services across the country.

The mid-18th century saw the onset of a long crisis in English music. Perhaps in part as a result of the prevailing conservative attitudes, no composer emerged who could even begin to match the stature of Purcell and Handel. Interest in music itself did not wane; indeed, the revolutions in composition being set in motion by Haydn, Mozart and Beethoven only increased the appetite for symphonic and operatic performances in London. Unable to raise any local talent, London drafted in as many famous foreigners as it could. Johann Christian Bach was persuaded to come to England in 1762 and stayed until his death 20 years later; an eight-year-old Mozart passed through in 1764; Haydn also made a number of visits and wrote no fewer than 12 London symphonies. Over the next century or so, eminent musical residents of London were to include Weber, Mendelssohn, Berlioz, Brahms, Bruckner and Fauré.

The local talent did not disappear entirely. Street music became a prominent feature of London life in the 18th century, and stayed that way for a century. Henry Mayhew, in his *London Life and the London Poor* of 1851, found more than 250 ballad singers in the capital, as well as hurdy-gurdy players, organ grinders, bagpipers, violinists and clarinettists. The din generated by all these competing musicians was satirized as early as 1740 by Hogarth and others. In Victorian times, however, parliament moved to outlaw the buskers. At first householders were given the power to tell street musicians to move on 'on grounds of illness or any other reasonable cause'; then in 1864, under the Metropolitan Police Act, buskers were banned altogether.

Music thus became a class issue in 19th-century London. Whereas a century earlier opera had been a near-universal art form, under the Victorians it became a lavish spectacle for the middle and upper classes only. Admittedly London was far from the only city where this transformation took place; but in London music appreciation was endowed with arguably more snobbery than any other capital. At the beginning of the 19th century, the ordinary folk of London had rioted when Covent Garden tried to put up its prices; by mid-century, when Edward Barry's new opera house was constructed, most ordinary folk had given up hope of gaining admittance at all.

Popular music entertainment moved out of the opera house and into the music-hall, where performers like Marie Lloyd and Albert Chevalier were soon attracting larger crowds than the regular theatres with their mixture of popular song and cabaret performance. 'Classical' music became the preserve of the elite, and its appreciation something of an excuse for pretentiousness and condescension towards the lower orders. It is surely significant that in E.M. Forster's novel *Howards End*, written in 1910, the lowly clerk Leonard Bast begins his ill-fated attempt at social climbing at a performance of Beethoven's Fifth Symphony.

The only time the concert-going public let its hair down was at the tongue-in-cheek, camp operettas of Offenbach or London's very own **Gilbert and Sullivan**. Works like *Trial By Jury*, *H.M.S. Pinafore*, *The Mikado* and *The Pirates of Penzance* were all the rage in the London of the 1880s and 1890s. These were certainly fun (although by now somewhat dated fun), but they were hardly pinnacles of musical achievement.

Roll Over Vaughan Williams

Out of this rather sterile atmosphere came a surprising revival in English music. The talents of **Edward Elgar**, **Ralph Vaughan Williams**, **Frederick Delius** and **Gustav Holst** may not have triggered any musical revolutions, but at least they represented the resumption of some kind of English tradition where virtually none had existed for the previous 150 years. Elgar (1857–1934) was almost certainly the most talented of them, although his career got off to an inauspicious start with the premiere of his oratorio *The Dream of Gerontius* at the inauguration of the Roman Catholic Westminster Cathedral in 1900. The musicians could not keep up with Elgar's rewrites, the choir master died in mid-rehearsal and as a result the première was greeted with an outpouring of critical invective. It took years for the oratorio to build up its reputation as one of the finest choral works of the 20th century. Elgar was not bothered, however, and proceeded to produce further remarkable works characterised by his subtle harmonies and understated passions, including the *Enigma Variations*, a violin concerto and a celebrated cello concerto.

In the same period, Holst (1874–1934), an English-born composer of Scandinavian origin, produced his famous suite *The Planets*, and Vaughan Williams (1872–1958) began exploring the roots of English music, both sacred and profane, in his sizeable output of symphonies, operas and choral music. Not all composers of the period have stood the test of time equally. Frederick Delius (1862–1934) was once described by the newspaper columnist Bernard Levin as producing 'the musical equivalent of blancmange'.

The new-found strength of the English classical tradition continued well into mid-century, thanks to the likes of **William Walton** (1902–83), famous for his film music and the oratorio *Belshazzar's Feast*, **Benjamin Britten** (1913–76), who wrote several operas and a remarkable *War Requiem*, and **Michael Tippett** (born 1905), who has continued to produce challenging and politically committed operas well into old age. It must be said there is nothing particularly London-ish about these composers, nor necessarily even English; the advent of the technology of mass reproduction of sound—through radio, film and records—has blurred the cultural specificity of all music and made the national or other origin of composers of only incidental interest. Britten may have chosen English subjects for his operas, but Tippett has proved more eclectic and is as well known in the United States or Australia as he is at home. With the waning of royal patronage, traditional composers have taken an ever greater interest in folk, jazz and popular song, not to mention electric sound and computer-generated noise.

The technological revolution, and the resulting emergence of certain kinds of popular music as the dominant cultural trend across the world, has not pleased everyone; the conservative core of the classical music world is distinctly uninterested in modern music—whether classical or popular—and regards it as vulgar and noisy. It has closed its eyes and ears almost entirely to the explosion of musical talent that has hit London since the advent of rock and roll. Happily, through force of circumstance, this is now beginning to change.

Rocking All Over the World

The most important influences of the mid to late 20th century—jazz, blues, rock and the stage musical—all came, of course, from the United States. But London learned to take advantage of them all and produced its own distinguished exponents of each genre. Ronnie Scott's jazz bar in Soho was crucial in bringing black American musicians to London and waking the postwar generation up to the possibilities of be-bop and blues. Among the new addicts to these forms of music were Brian Jones, later one of the **Rolling Stones**, and **Eric Clapton**, who spent most of his unhappy childhood in the south London suburbs figuring out ways to emulate the likes of Buddy Guy, Robert Johnson and Muddy Waters.

Muddy Waters later said of Mick Jagger, lead singer of the Stones: 'He took my music, but he gave me my name.' The English groups of the 1960s were popularizers, but they also opened the public's eyes up for the first time to musical traditions of all kinds. Clapton and Jack Bruce were in the vanguard of the English blues movement, while folk-rock bands of the late 1960s and early 1970s like

Fairport Convention blended new musical forms with the folk traditions of England and Ireland. Groups like the **Kinks** (and, a decade later, Squeeze) provided a further sub-genre with their affectionate winks to the English music hall tradition.

What made the Beatles and the Stones so exceptional and so popular, apart from their immediate musical talent, was their ability to create an image—for themselves, for rock music as a whole and for an entire generation. Flower Power, the Summer of Love and the rest were as crucial to their mystique as their songs were; these things gave an identity to young people around the world as they protested against the Vietnam War, hailed the shortlived Prague Spring, or manned the barricades at the student riots in Paris. The delirious rhythms of rock music and the effect they had on young audiences were an ideal vehicle for revolt; to traditionalists and reactionaries, rock was 'the music of the devil' and its practitioners immoralists who appeared to be dismantling the pillars of civilized society.

It seems laughable now that the censors of the 1960s should have got so worked up about the insidiousness of songs like the Stones' *Let's Spend the Night Together* or the Beatles' *Lucy in the Sky with Diamonds*. A decade later, real anarchy was on the loose in the shape of the shortlived punk movement, with its ripped tee-shirts, dyed hair and safety pins in every imaginable bodily orifice. 'We're not into music, we're into chaos,' said Johnny Rotten, who helped form the **Sex Pistols** in the mid-1970s. The Pistols had no musical talent to speak of, nor did they write lyrics that bear repeating in any context except the wild janglings of their songs. But they voiced a certain anger and disgust which in hindsight seem surprisingly healthy given the smug shenanigans of the money-conscious 1980s that were to follow. 'Punk let people in on the secret of the future,' wrote the style author Peter York, 'namely that there wasn't one.'

After punk, rock music—at least in Britain—lost much of its cutting edge and for the most part turned into a depressingly crass exercise in commercialism. Despite some signs of life, music in Britain has become little more than a satellite of the (by now) well-established American industry. Songs that were once deemed innovative and interesting, like The Clash's *Should I Stay or Should I Go* or Cream's *I Feel Free*, have now been co-opted as backing tracks to television commercials. The subversive music of the past is being gradually absorbed into the mainstream. Arguably the most exciting musical events after 1979 were the all-star Live Aid concert of 1985, and the similar 1988 bash in London in honour of Nelson Mandela. At least they showed some kind of vitality and political awareness. Otherwise, the music world has fallen into a swoon of nostalgia for its corrupted youth, and seems to have little to say about the present or future. The darlings of the 1990s Britpop movement, **Blur** and **Oasis**, are a self-conscious throwback to the glory days of the Beatles. Even rap, the new musical craze of the States and parts of continental Europe, has had only a limited impact in London despite its sledge-hammer attempts at being controversial. Interesting things are happening, particularly in more marginal new genres such as trip hop and drum'n'bass, but they are getting hard to locate without expert guidance.

The Marxist philosopher Theodor Adorno once said that popular culture was necessarily trash because it was a product of high capitalism. The 1960s and 1970s proved him wrong once; to prove him wrong again, the London scene needs to ditch the consumerism and let the inspiration flow once more.

Central London: The Walks

Walking in central London is not as hard to enjoy as it looks. Behind all those intimidating traffic-clogged trunk roads are some delightful alleys, narrow backstreets and riverside paths. As you follow these routes you will get to know a city most Londoners rarely see: a London of grace and charm and, generally speaking, without the hassle and the heated tempers.

The inner London walks, plus the preface on Trafalgar Square, cover the oldest and most interesting historical areas of the city. Don't think, however, that you will see only museums and monuments. Many of the areas—such as Soho or Bloomsbury—have a distinctive atmosphere worth soaking up for its own sake. Others are rich in parkland, where the achievements of the metropolis mingle with the pleasures of nature.

Each walk is intended to capture a different facet of the big city, often focusing on a particular institution: parliament in Walk II, for example, or the Law Courts in Walk VI. Along the way you will find most of the tourist biggies—Buckingham Palace (Walk I), Westminster Abbey (Walk II), the British Museum (Walk V), St Paul's (Walk VII), the Tower of London (Walk VIII) and the South Kensington museums (Walk X).

If there is anything you can't find, just check the index. If it is not in this section, the chances are it will be in Outer London or, at the outside, in the Museum chapter.

Trafalgar Square

Stiff on a pillar with a phallic air,
Nelson stylites in Trafalgar Square.

Lawrence Durrell

Back in the 1810s and 1820s, when Britannia really did rule the waves and London was the capital of a burgeoning empire, a hitherto taboo concept suddenly came into fashion: urban planning. Previously it had been considered perfectly proper for London to develop organically according to the whims of private landowners. But then industrialization arrived, threatening to stifle the capital in factory smoke if the laissez-faire planning policy persisted. At the same time, Britain's victory in the Napoleonic Wars unleashed a broad desire for some decent monumental architecture. The Prince Regent, an ardent patron of grand building schemes, was only too happy to sponsor major projects, and soon architects were putting forward proposals for the wildest and most outlandish schemes, transforming the London of their imaginations into a grid of broad avenues and grand palaces.

It was in such an atmosphere that Trafalgar Square was first conceived. The Prince Regent (later crowned George IV) and his chosen architect, John Nash, wanted to create a vast open space glorifying the country's naval power which would also provide a focal point from which other urban projects could spread. It was a fine idea, but one that was destined to be cruelly truncated by the vagaries of history. George developed a reputation as a spendthrift and a philanderer, and as economic crisis gripped the nation in the mid-1820s all his dreams were brought to a halt by a hostile parliament. Nash was dismissed as soon as George died in 1830, and from then on Trafalgar Square was left at the mercy of successive parliamentary committees who argued for the best part of a generation over its final form.

The end result has all the allure of a pizza pie concocted by a bevy of squabbling chefs. Its centrepiece, Nelson's Column, has certainly captured the imagination of both tourists and anti-government demonstrators as a symbol of imperial Britain, but it is a monument entirely at odds with its immediate surroundings. What should, and could, have been the centrepiece of a grand modern city is today a noisy, dusty traffic hub of little grace or architectural distinction. If it is the fate of London to be a shapeless jumble with no place to call its heart, then the story of Trafalgar Square goes a long way towards explaining why.

The site first entered the history books in 1293 when Edward I built **Charing Cross** as a memorial to his late queen, Eleanor of Castile. Eleanor had died three years earlier in Nottinghamshire, and Edward erected 12 crosses, one at each of the points where her funeral cortège had stopped on its way to Westminster Abbey. Charing Cross was the last stop. Time and historical whimsy have conjured up the impression that the name Charing is a corruption of the French *chère reine* (dear queen). In fact, the name predates Eleanor and is probably derived from the Anglo-Saxon word *cerr* meaning a bend in the river. You can see a 19th-century replica of the original Caen stone cross in the forecourt of Charing Cross station, just off the Strand. The badly decayed original, which used to stand at the top of what is now Northumberland Avenue, was pulled down in 1647 and put to practical use, both to fashion knife-handles and to renovate paving stones in Whitehall.

A bronze equestrian **statue of Charles I** was commissioned from the French sculptor Hubert Le Sueur to take the place of the cross, but could not immediately be erected because of the outbreak of the Civil War. A brazier by the name of John Rivett was ordered to destroy it, but Rivett was a secret royalist and buried it instead in his garden. He made his fortune selling relics he claimed were fashioned from the statue's melted-down metal, then astounded everyone by producing the figure intact after the restoration of the monarchy. The statue was finally erected, atop a pedestral carved by Grinling Gibbons, in 1675.

In the 18th century, Charing Cross developed into a popular meeting spot for both the rich in their sedan chairs and the poor who frequented the raucous nearby taverns; Dr Johnson famously remarked that 'the full tide of human existence' appeared to gather there. The main attractions were the public pillories—branding, nose splitting and ear lopping—that took place beneath Charles's haughty figure. In their enthusiasm, the public regularly hacked off chunks of the statue, which became so dilapidated that in 1810 the sword buckles and straps fell off.

Modern Trafalgar Square evolved partly out of a desire to raise the tone of the Charing Cross area. Nash pulled down the old King's Mews (incidentally, a fine Georgian building by William Kent) to make room for his planned ensemble of grand classical buildings. But he never got to build them before his fall from grace. The whole Trafalgar Square project might have been abandoned had it not been for a lingering determination to bestow grand honours on Horatio Nelson, the country's legendary naval commander who had died at sea during the Battle of Trafalgar in 1805. The victory that the English scored against the French there brought Nelson the kind of adulation one might expect for a martyred saint. In 1808, the essayist William Wood wrote a rousing eulogy of England 'proudly stemming the torrent of revolutionary frenzy', and proposed erecting a giant pyramid to his hero. Over the years 120 official proposals were submitted, including a myriad of columns, pyramids and even a Coliseum.

In the absence of a coordinating architect, however, the scheme made painfully slow progress. Where Nash had been extravagant, the special select committee of the House of Commons proved downright stingy. The new planners were not interested in producing monumental architecture unless it could be done on the cheap. The only halfway decent building in Trafalgar Square to make it into bricks and mortar, the National Gallery, was severely compromised by a long list of parliamentary stipulations about its design (*see* below).

As for **Nelson's Column**, it did not see the light of day until 1843. Originally, the committee was actually against building a column, arguing (correctly) that it would dwarf the new National Gallery and surrounding neighbourhood. But, as so often in London's chequered planning history, nobody had the guts to propose anything more daring, and when a competition was launched in 1838, William Railton's 145ft high hunk of granite won the day.

The Corinthian column, topped by an unremarkable and scarcely visible likeness of Nelson in his admiral's three-cornered hat, by E.H. Baily, was erected on a sloping concrete basin prepared by the neoclassical architect Charles Barry. Railton based his design on a triumphalist precedent from ancient Rome, the Temple of Mars in the Forum of Augustus. The bronze bas-reliefs at the base of the column represent Nelson's four greatest victories, at Cape St Vincent, the Nile, Copenhagen and Trafalgar, while the surrounding statuary is of Nelson's generals. They all face *away* from the National Gallery, accentuating the lack of cohesion in the square's overall design. The two granite fountains at the base arrived in 1845, while the bronze lions, the most appealing feature of the ensemble, appeared a quarter of a century later. These were the work of the landscape gardener Edwin Landseer, a novice at sculpture called in after a previous commission turned out to be too embarrassing to put on display.

Once finished, Trafalgar Square proved a success in one respect only, as a symbol of the nation and its imperial past. Adolf Hitler was so impressed with Nelson's Column that he ordered his bombers to leave it alone, harbouring ambitions instead to haul it off to Berlin once he had invaded and conquered Britain. The square's symbolism has not been lost, either, on generations of political demonstrators who have met here to demand everything from universal suffrage (under the Chartists in 1848) to the abolition of Margaret Thatcher's hated poll tax. Aesthetically, though, the square is a disaster, its overall effect sterile, monolithic and impersonal. The only time it ever comes to life is on New Year's Eve when thousands of people gather in a somewhat drunken crush beneath a vast Christmas Tree donated each year by the Norwegian government. The rest of the year it is grey, noisy and unremarkable.

> *Trafalgar Square is the point from which all measurements in London are drawn; there is a plaque indicating this on the corner of Charing Cross Road. On the eastern side of the square is South Africa House, where anti-apartheid protesters maintained a constant vigil through the latter part of Nelson Mandela's 26-year imprisonment. Next door is James Gibbs's church of St Martin-in-the-Fields (see Walk III). In the southeastern corner stands a lamp-post known as the smallest police station in the world, which contains a telephone linked up to police headquarters at Scotland Yard. On the western side, in a building designed by Robert Smirke, builder of the British Museum, is Canada House, home to the Canadian High Commission.*

> *The grand entrance to the Mall to the southwest, Admiralty Arch, is dealt with in Walk I. Of the statues in the square, that of George IV in the north-eastern corner was originally commissioned to stand atop the Marble Arch at the entrance to Buckingham Palace. When the arch was moved to Hyde Park, the statue was dumped here, purportedly until a more suitable spot could be found. The main outstanding attraction, however, is on the northern side, the **National Gallery** (open Mon–Sat 10–6, Sun 2–6; free).*

The National Gallery: Creation and Controversy

The National Gallery is an astonishing collection of West European painting from the 13th to the early 20th centuries, including masterpieces from virtually every major school. Its great names include Leonardo da Vinci, Piero della Francesca, Van Eyck, Raphael, Titian, Veronese, Rubens, Poussin, Rembrandt, Velazquez, Caravaggio, Turner, Constable, Delacroix, Monet, Van Gogh, Cézanne and Picasso.

The National Gallery is very much a 19th-century phenomenon: a catalogue of paintings from the Grand Tradition reflecting the pride and power of the collector nation. It was founded in 1824 when George IV persuaded the government to buy an initial 38 pictures, including a handful of Raphaels, Rembrandts and Van Dycks, from the estate of the recently deceased marine insurance broker and philanthropist John Julius Angerstein. Many of the gallery's masterpieces were bought in the Victorian era, particularly under its first director Charles Eastlake, who went on a series of annual spending sprees in Italy in the 1850s and 1860s. The picture-buying has continued ever since; and although money has grown tighter in recent years the annual budget remains well over £2 million.

The building was commissioned from William Wilkins soon after the acquisition of Angerstein's collection, but the project, like the rest of Trafalgar Square, fell victim to parliamentary penny-pinching. By the time it was finished in 1838 it was widely derided and nicknamed the 'national cruet stand' because the cupola reminded critics of a mustard pot and the bell-towers looked like pepper casters. More serious reservations focused on its lack of grace, its awkward symmetries and the apparently needless decision to build a broad 12ft-high staircase up to the main entrance. 'This unhappy structure may be said to have everything it ought not to have, and nothing which it ought to have,' wrote the review *All Year Round* in 1862. 'It possesses windows without glass, a cupola without size, a portico without height, pepper-boxes without pepper, and the finest site in Europe without anything to show upon it.' But Wilkins was given a near impossible task since most of the features which earned him derision, including the cupola and the bell-towers, were stipulated in the original commission. Awkwardly, he was asked to incorporate part of the frontage of the demolished royal palace at Carlton House in his façade—all this, and a measly budget of just £100,000. Wilkins kept his cool and did what he was told, even coming in £45 under budget. If the building ended up less than the sum of its parts, it was not entirely his fault.

Architectural controversy was to dog the National Gallery again a century and a half later. In the early 1980s the supermarket chain Sainsbury's sponsored a new extension at the western end of the gallery, and a competition was duly held. The winning entry, by the British firm Ahrends Burton and Koralek, was an audacious modernist design in glass and steel that set out to be a bit different and lend a provocative new tone to staid old Trafalgar Square. For the first time in years, it looked as though London might be serious about following Paris's example in commissioning ground-breaking new buildings. But then Prince Charles, heir to the throne, stunned everybody in a speech to the Royal Institute of British Architects in 1984 in which he called the proposed extension a 'monstrous carbuncle' and called for a return to traditional architectural values.

The National Gallery competition was hastily scrapped and a new, more sober extension commissioned from the American architects Robert Venturi and Denise Scott Brown, which was completed in 1991. There is nothing much wrong with their version of the Sainsbury Wing, which unlike ABK's goes out of its way to blend in with its surroundings. But its bland conformism is a constant reminder of the design opportunities missed. Charles's remarks proved a severe blow to the morale of young architects promoting bold and innovative design. ABK did not work again for 18 months after the 'carbuncle' speech. Competitions are now few and far between, as are genuinely exciting new buildings. Meanwhile the real carbuncles—the speculator-driven monstrosities in Docklands and elsewhere—continue to sprout with impunity.

The first work of art, which most visitors miss, is a mosaic of Greta Garbo's head by Boris Anrep (1933) on the floor of the main entrance hall. Pick up a floor plan from the information desk and you'll see that the gallery's four wings each concentrate on a different historical period, starting with early medieval Italian painting in the Sainsbury Wing and moving gradually eastwards towards the 20th century.

Rooms devoted to individual painters are clearly marked. At the entrance to each wing, you are given the names of the major paintings to look out for. The gallery is magnificently lit, with intelligent explanations displayed alongside each picture. There is a computer database in the Micro Gallery in the Sainsbury Wing, where you can look up and print out detailed information on pictures or artists.

There are also organized lectures on individual pictures, as well as a constantly changing special exhibition in the Sunley Room to the left of the central hall, where paintings from the collection are grouped to illustrate a specific theme. And if that is not enough for you, there are hundreds of minor paintings stored on lower floors available for public view.

The Sainsbury Wing (1260–1510)

The National Gallery's early Renaissance collection concentrates almost exclusively on Italian and Dutch painters. In an annexe off the first room here, Room 51, is Leonardo's magnificently expressive *Cartoon*, a full-size chalk sketch for a painting of the Virgin and Child with Saint Anne and John the Baptist, which was commissioned in 1508 for the altar of the church of SS. Annunziata in Florence. The figure of Saint Anne, pointing up to heaven, is the main talking point since she looks no older than her daughter Mary. Some critics believe she is in fact Saint Elizabeth, the mother of John the Baptist whom she is holding. The *Cartoon* has for years been kept behind thick glass in reduced lighting because of its fragility. In the early 1980s it was nearly lost forever when an over-emotional visitor fired a couple of shotgun blasts at close range. As it happened, the attack turned out to be a perverse sort of blessing. The picture underwent the restoration work it had desperately needed for years and now looks good as new; the gallery earned plenty of sympathetic publicity, and various curators and restorers won awards for their brave efforts.

We now jump back pre-1400 to the mostly religious paintings of Duccio and the Italian school. A striking oddity is the *Wilton Diptych* (Room 52), a piece of propaganda for Richard II which depicts the young English king protected by John the Baptist, St Edmund and Edward the Confessor as he kneels before the Virgin and a host of angels. Painted by French artists in the late 14th century, it is a striking statement on the divine power of kingship. One begins to appreciate how Richard could end the Peasants' Revolt with little more than a hand gesture.

Room 55 contains some of Uccello's set-piece experiments with movement and perspective, notably the *Battle of San Romano* (1450) with its sea of colour and broken lances.

Then in Room 56 is one of the most beautiful and influential paintings of the early Renaissance, Jan Van Eyck's *Arnolfini Marriage* (1434). The precision and detail in this portrait of an Italian merchant and his new wife in their house in Bruges is astounding. Notice the lapdog, the broom and the pair of clogs—each object swelling the mood of fastidious bourgeois contentment. The wife looks about 16 months pregnant; in fact she is merely bunching her thick green dress against her stomach to symbolize the couple's hopes for a fecund future. Technically most fascinating is the concave mirror on the back wall, which reflects the whole scene including the painter and his easel like a wide-angled photograph. Generations of later artists have borrowed such gimmicky use of reflection, notably Velazquez (see his *Rokeby Venus* in Room 29).

Bellini is well-represented (see his portrait of *Doge Leonardo Loredan* in Room 61), as are Antonello and Mantegna. Then in Room 66 is Piero della Francesca's *Baptism of Christ*, a peculiarly central Italian interpretation of the baptism story. The limpid colours and burnished summer light are unmistakeably those of Piero's hometown of Borgo Sansepolcro. Christ is baptized not in a broad river, as northern European painters have usually imagined it, but in a trickle of a stream beneath an olive tree.

West Wing (1510–1600)

The smallest of the display areas (just eight rooms), the West Wing is also the weakest although it features some fine set pieces such as El Greco's *Christ Driving the Traders from the Temple* (Room 7) and Veronese's *Family of Darius before Alexander* (Room 9). More unusual is Holbein's *Christina of Denmark* in Room 2, one of a series of portraits of eligible European women that he undertook for Henry VIII after the king's third wife Jane Seymour died in 1538. Perhaps influenced by Holbein's rather glum depiction, Henry did not ask for Christina's hand but turned to Anne of Cleves instead, whom he quickly divorced. Tintoretto's *St George and the Dragon* (Room 7) is curious because it makes the damsel in distress the main subject of the painting. The work is bathed in an ethereal light beaming down from the heavens. The valiant George barely gets a look in.

North Wing (1600–1700)

Room 15 neatly compares two idealized harbour scenes, Claude Lorrain's *Embarkation of the Queen of Sheba* and Turner's much later Lorrain-influenced *Dido Building Carthage*. There is more Lorrain (whom the National refers to as Claude) in Room 19, including his dreamy *Enchanted Castle*. On the way there are two rare Vermeers in Room 16, *Woman Standing at a Virginal* and *Woman Sitting at a Virginal*. Room 20 contains Poussin's *Adoration of the Golden Calf*, a magnificently decadent study of the power of Mammon. Curiously and rather suitably, the Golden Calf looks like Nigel Lawson, Britain's corpulent Chancellor of the Exchequer during the most venal of the Thatcher boom years in the 1980s (a newly downsized Lawson has since been making a career out of boasting how thin he has become, but that is another story).

Some of the very best of Rubens is in Room 22, including two versions of the *Judgement of Paris*. The later one (1630) is simpler, more pastoral and more satisfying to the modern eye than the earlier one, all rosy-cheeked buttocks and over-voluptuous thighs. In *The Rape of the Sabine Women*, the sensuality of the painting takes on a sinister and frightening quality. *Samson and Delilah* depicts the moment of the Biblical strong man's arrest as he lies draped over Delilah's suggestively exposed midriff. You have to be a sucker to believe it was just a haircut that made him so exhausted.

Room 27 is devoted to Rembrandt, notably two of his highly expressive self-portraits. The first, done when he was 34, is self-assured and vigorous while the second, painted in the last year of his life, is darker and more reflective. Rembrandt beautifully captures the intimacy of the moment in his near-monochrome *Women Bathing in a Stream*, while in *Belshazzar's Feast* he shows his talent for depicting sheer drama. The look of astonishment on Belshazzar's face is at once shocking and almost funny. The words written on the wall in Hebrew read *mene mene tekel upharsin* (you have been weighed in the balance and found wanting). One of Rembrandt's contemporaries, Gerrit van Honthorst, painted an equally dramatic (and gruesome) picture of the martyrdom of Saint Sebastian by arrows, which is in room 14 (next to Room 28).

Velazquez's *Rokeby Venus* in Room 29 was Spain's first nude, although it bows to contemporary sensibilities by portraying the subject with her back to the viewer. The mirror reflecting her face is a joke on the part of the artist: according to the angle at which it is held, what we should be seeing is the full splendour of Venus's voluminous bust. In Room 30, we come to a series of state portraits, many of them commissioned by Charles I. It is a display that highlights much of the Stuarts' pomp and self-satisfaction.

The best painting is probably Van Dyck's *Equestrian Portrait of Charles I*, the classic encapsulation of a vainglorious monarch convinced that nothing can touch him. The picture loses some of its power when you remember that in life Charles measured less than 60 inches in his stockinged feet. It was, of course, only a few years before the Civil War and Charles's death on the scaffold. Room 32 is most notable for two Caravaggios, the *Supper at Emmaus* depicting Christ breaking the bread to reveal who he is, and *Salome Receiving the Head of John the Baptist,* a moody piece contrasting the deep suffering etched on the severed head of John and the near total indifference of a frowning Salome.

East Wing (1700–1920)

Venice dominates Room 34, notably in the vast panoramas of Canaletto's two set pieces *The Basin of San Marco on Ascension Day* and *Regatta on the Grand Canal.* Both depict major city festivals, the former the marriage of Venice and the Sea at which the Doge ritually tosses a golden ring into the Adriatic. The room also contains a handful of Guardis, whose softer-edged versions of the floating city contrast with Canaletto's geometric precision.

Room 35 is devoted to Turner, the ultimate English Romantic painter whose dramatic watercolours of shipwrecks and sunsets experiment boldly with light and colour. The guides all push you towards *The Fighting Téméraire*, a sumptuous tribute to a battleship being dragged out to its watery grave by a modern steamer. But the most innovative work here is arguably *Rain, Steam and Speed*, a delicate contrast of the industrial and natural worlds. The Great Western Railway express hurtles straight towards the viewer, the steam from its engine mingling with the colours of the morning mist and the murky River Thames at Maidenhead. Critics who first saw the picture in the 1840s thought it was preposterous; in fact it was a good three or four decades ahead of its time, anticipating the light and colour experiments of the Impressionists.

English painting dominates the following rooms, from Gainsborough, Reynolds and Hogarth (don't miss his brilliant satirical series on upper-class life, *Marriage à la Mode*) to the idyllic country scenes of John Constable including *Salisbury Cathedral from the Meadows* and *The Hay Wain* (Room 40). There is some interesting non-English Romantic painting here too, notably Paul Delaroche's *Execution of Lady Jane Grey* (Room 41) and Caspar David Friedrich's magnificently lit picture of a cripple praying in the snow, *Winter Landscape* (Room 42).

Rooms 43–5 are devoted to the Impressionists and their followers. Many of the pictures are so famous they need no introduction—Van Gogh's *Chair*, Seurat's *Bathers at Asnières*, Cézanne's *Les Grandes Baigneuses* and views of Mont Sainte Victoire, Monet's *Water Lilies* series, Henri Rousseau's *Tropical Storm with Tiger.*

More unusual are Monet's *Gare St Lazare*, a study of Paris at its industrial zenith, and his *Thames from Westminster*, painted in 1871 when the Victoria Embankment with its (then) wooden piers had just opened. No English-born painter has ever captured the moody, foggy atmosphere of industrial London better than Monet. Also don't miss Degas's *Miss La La* for its dramatically angled glimpse of a trapeze artist at the Cirque Fernando clenching the rope between her teeth.

The very last room, 46, is devoted to Picasso and in particular his work from the 1930s. The only major piece here is *Minotauromachia*, a monochrome etching featuring mythical hybrids of bull and man. In imagery and technique it prefigures *Guernica*, his nightmare vision of the Spanish Civil War.

I: St James's and Royal London

Start: ⊖ *Trafalgar Square.*
Walking time: *about 2 hours.*

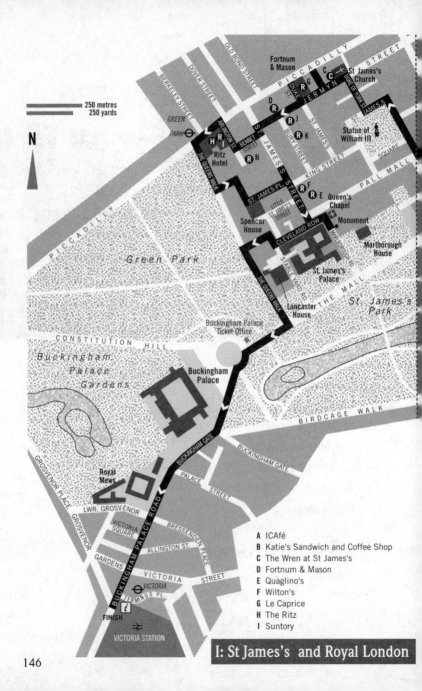

250 metres
250 yards

N

OLD BOND STREET
BERKELEY STREET
DOVER STREET
PICCADILLY
Fortnum
& Mason
DUKE ST.
JERMYN
STREET
St James's
Church
DUKE OF YORK ST.
G
R
C
C
D
R
R
J
R
K
Statue of
William III
ST. JAMES'S
SQUARE
GREEN
PARK
ARLINGTON ST.
BENNET
STREET
BURY STREET
ST. JAMES'S STREET
H
I
R
H
THE QUEEN'S WALK
Ritz
Hotel
ST. JAMES'S PL.
LITTLE
ST. JAMES'S
STREET
R
F
F
E
Queen's
Chapel
KING STREET
PALL MALL
Spencer
House
CLEVELAND ROW
Monument
MARLBOROUGH RD.
Marlborough
House
St. James's
Palace
Lancaster
House
THE QUEEN'S WALK
STABLE YARD RD.
THE MALL
St. James's
Park
PICCADILLY
Green Park
CONSTITUTION HILL
Buckingham Palace
Ticket Office
BIRDCAGE WALK
Buckingham
Palace
Gardens
Buckingham
Palace
GROSVENOR PLACE
Royal
Mews
BUCKINGHAM GATE
BUCKINGHAM GATE
PALACE STREET
LWR. GROSVENOR
GROSVENOR GARDENS
VICTORIA
SQUARE
BRESSENDEN PLACE
ALLINGTON ST.
BUCKINGHAM PALACE ROAD
VICTORIA STREET
TERMINUS PL.
VICTORIA
FINISH
i
VICTORIA STATION

A ICAfé
B Katie's Sandwich and Coffee Shop
C The Wren at St James's
D Fortnum & Mason
E Quaglino's
F Wilton's
G Le Caprice
H The Ritz
I Suntory

I: St James's and Royal London

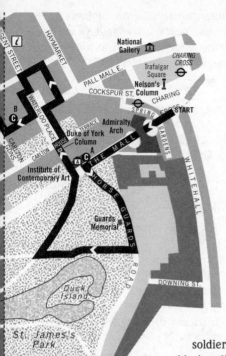

St James's is the fairyland of London, a peculiarly British kind of looking-glass world where everyone (well, nearly everyone) eats thickly-cut marmalade sandwiches and drinks tea from Fortnum & Mason, where the inhabitants are for the most part kindly middle-aged gentlemen with bespoke tailored suits and ruddy complexions, where shopkeepers are called purveyors and underlings wear livery coats. What's more, this fairyland comes with its very own queen, who lives in a palace surrounded by broad lush parks and guarded by toy soldiers in busby hats and red, blue and black uniforms. Everything is clean and beautiful in fairyland, even the roads, some of which have been coloured pink to add to the general feeling of well-being.

St James's is the preserve of the establishment, not the vulgar money-making classes of the City but an older, rarefied pedigree which whiles away the hours in the drawing-rooms of fine houses and private clubs. It is a world that has been endlessly depicted and lampooned on film and on television; incredibly, it still exists. Think of it as a zoo for that endangered species, the upper-class Englishman. It is eccentric, and not without its dark side, but it is not to be missed.

Perhaps inevitably, many of the buildings on this walk keep their doors firmly shut to the great unwashed. If you want to see Buckingham Palace you'll have to come between August and the beginning of October (and preferably before 2000, when it might just close again). The Changing of the Guard is at 11.30am daily during the summer and on alternate days the rest of the year. The Royal Mews are usually open on Tuesdays, Wednesdays and Thursdays only (less frequently in the winter), while visits to Spencer House are restricted to Sundays. Take your pick.

---

lunch/pubs

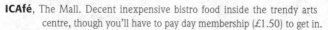

The most atmospheric (if not necessarily most appetizing) option in this part of town is one of the old gentlemen's clubs. The snag is, you either have to be a member or know one who will invite you. Otherwise pickings are on the expensive side.

ICAfé, The Mall. Decent inexpensive bistro food inside the trendy arts centre, though you'll have to pay day membership (£1.50) to get in.

Katie's Sandwich and Coffee Shop, 15a Pall Mall. Home-made sandwiches to eat in or out. The most unpretentious spot in St James's.

The Wren at St James's, St James's Church, Jermyn St or Piccadilly. Cheap, wholesome vegetarian fare: chili beans casseroles, soups, salads and home-made cakes. £4–7.

Piccolo Prince, Prince's Arcade. Excellent value Italian sandwiches (parma ham, mozzarella, artichokes and fresh basil) in an otherwise expensive area.

Wiltons, 55 Jermyn St, best to reserve in advance on ☎ 0171–629 9955. English food, strong on fish and game, in a setting resembling that of a gentleman's club. £30.

Il Vicolo, 3–4 Crown Passage. Excellent, traditional Italian trattoria, good pasta etc. from £15–20.

The Avenue, 7/9 St James's St. Attempt at a Manhattanesque sophisticates' restaurant and elegant 'modern' food (coq au vin, tarte tatin, risotto, fish cakes, crab spring rolls, etc.). The set lunch is specially good value: from £17.50 for two course (☎ 0171–321 2111 for reservations).

Fortnum & Mason, Jermyn St and 181 Piccadilly. The luxury food shop has three traditional English restaurants, the posh Patio (£20 for a basic lunch menu), the even posher Fountain on the ground floor, and the St James's on the fourth (serving afternoon tea for £12.50). Something of a tourist trap and overpriced, but good nonetheless.

Le Caprice, Arlington House, Arlington St. Top-notch English grill-room with French frills. Dress smart. Around £30 for lunch, reservations advisable on ☎ 0171–629 2239.

The Ritz, Piccadilly (entrance on Arlington St). De rigueur for society teas (currently £21 per head) in the ornate Edwardian Palm Court. Dress smart.

Quaglino's, 16 Bury St. Ferociously trendy Italian food in an ornate ballroom setting. £25 or so for lunch, reservations on ☎ 0171–930 6767.

Matsuri, 15 Bury St. Laidback Japanese food in basement specialising in grill-cooked food and delicious noodle soups, from £10–15.

Leave Trafalgar Square at the southwestern end, opposite the National Gallery, taking the next turning round to the right from Whitehall.

A sense of place, and occasion, is immediately invoked by the grand concave triple entrance of **Admiralty Arch**, the gateway to St James's and start of the long straight drive along The Mall up to Buckingham Palace. The stone arch, designed by Aston Webb in 1910 as part of an architectural ensemble in memory of Queen Victoria (see the Latin inscription to this effect across the top), is one of the few monumental buildings from the Edwardian era in London. Traffic passes through the two side-gates and the larger central gate is opened only for royal processions; the interior of the arch was used for naval offices and living quarters for the First Sea Lord until 1997, when it was given to a housing charity called Centrepoint and turned into a refuge for the homeless.

*Passing through the arch, you'll appreciate the full splendour of St James's Park ahead to your left; notice, too, the white stone frontings to your right. These are part of **Carlton House Terrace**, the remnants of one of London's more lavish—and ultimately futile—building projects.*

In the early 18th century this site was home to Henry Boyle, Baron Carlton, whose much-admired gardens extended most of the way up towards Buckingham Palace. The Prince of Wales (later George IV) decided he rather liked the place and hired the architect Henry Holland to spruce up the house to the standards of a royal palace. For 30 years Holland and his associates toiled away, adding Corinthian porticoes here, brown Siena marble columns there, and decking out each room with sumptuous decorations. One contemporary critic said the end result stood comparison with Versailles; that did not stop the extravagant George from declaring himself bored with the new palace shortly after he acceded to the throne in 1820 and having most of it demolished.

The portico columns were incorporated into the National Gallery in Trafalgar Square, while many of the furnishings were removed to the new royal residence being built down the road, Buckingham Palace. It was left to George's favourite architect, John Nash, to salvage what he could from the wreckage of Carlton House and construct these elegant terraces in their place. They have housed many a club and eminent society in their time; now the most interesting address is No.12, the **Institute of Contemporary Arts**. Perhaps surprisingly given the setting, the ICA is a mecca for the 'Britpack' school of art, the pre-post-avant-garde and the obscure in all areas of the arts. Come here for lectures on the finer points of post-structuralism seen through the eyes of a reconstructed Lacanian, or the latest in performance art dancing, or for films with titles like *Life is Cheap but Toilet Paper is Expensive*. Art shows have been known to draw on blackcurrent drink adverts and pop videos to illustrate their point. The Royal Opera House this is not, even if it looks from the outside like it might be. There is a modest day membership fee to get into the main shows and the excellent café; otherwise you are restricted to the foyer and bookshop, with their right-on political postcards and learned tomes highlighting undercurrents of lesbian eroticism in 19th-century French literature.

> *Cross the Mall and turn down Horse Guards Road, which skirts the eastern end of the park. You pass what looks like a bomb shelter, a heavily reinforced bunker covered in ivy called the Citadel which was built to house the wartime headquarters of the Royal Navy in 1940. Just beyond, on the left, is the broad open space known as* **Horse Guards Parade***.*

The Horse Guards in question are the queen's very own knights in shining armour, properly known as the Household Division. Altogether, seven regiments are allocated the task of dressing up in chocolate-soldier costumes and parading in front of Buckingham Palace (although they occasionally engage in more serious business, too, like peacekeeping in Bosnia). Housed both here and at Wellington Barracks on the south side of the park are the Household Cavalry (look out for the horses), the Life Guards, the Blues and Royals, the Grenadiers, the Coldstream Guards and the Scots, Irish and Welsh guards. The best time to see them is on the first weekend in June, when they all take part in a grand parade in front of the Queen known as Trooping the Colour. Otherwise you can make do with the Changing of the Guard (outside the Horse Guards at 11am daily or outside Buckingham Palace at 11.30am daily from May–Aug, and every other day the rest of the year), when the detachment on duty outside Buckingham Palace (three officers and 40 men) is relieved in a colourful series of manoeuvres.

This has been parading territory since Henry VIII's day, when Horse Guards Parade was built as an extension to Whitehall Palace. The present-day barracks are Georgian, the work of William Kent; notice the arch leading to Whitehall, which is so low that Hogarth once painted a coach coming through it with a headless driver.

> *Turning your back to Horse Guards Parade, you see in front of you the* **Guards Memorial***, commemorating the fallen of the First World War. Beyond is the dreamy expanse of* **St James's Park***.*

The park explains much about the spirit of the neighbourhood. Certainly it seems perfectly spruce nowadays, even rather romantic in a restrained sort of way, with its tree-lined pond and proliferation of city wildlife; but its elegance is a cunning artifice created to overcome centuries of turbulence and squalor. Back in the early 12th century, Queen Matilda founded a women's leper colony on the site of what is now St James's Palace.

The park was a marshy field where the lepers would feed their hogs. By the mid-15th century leprosy had subsided and the hospital was turned into a special kind of nunnery; special because its young occupants were better known for administering to the flesh rather than to the spirit of the eminent men who called on them. These so-called *bordels du roi* lasted barely more than 50 years and were closed by Henry VIII, who built St James's Palace in their place and drained the marsh to create a nursery for his deer. The first formal gardens were laid out under James I, who installed, among other things, an aviary (hence the name of the street on the south side, Birdcage Walk) and a menagerie of wild beasts including two crocodiles. The setting was romantic enough for Charles II to use it as a rendezvous with his mistress, Nell Gwynne; unfortunately it also attracted upper-class hooligans in search of both trouble and rumpy-pumpy with the local whores.

In 1672 Lord Rochester described the park as a place of 'buggeries, rapes and incest', a state of affairs not improved even after a decree issued by Queen Anne banning dogs, hogs, menials, beggars and 'rude boys' from the premises. James Boswell lost his virginity to a whore in St James's Park on 20 March 1763, an experience which brought him 'but a dull satisfaction' (the same might, incidentally, be said about reading his books). Boswell's lack of enthusiasm did not stop him coming back for more, and with great regularity, as readers of his *London Journal* will know. Not everyone found St James's Park a big turn-on: the great Venetian philanderer Casanova gave up all thoughts of fornication after seeing 'six or seven people shitting in the bushes with their hinder parts turned towards the public'. Casanova's English hosts could not understand his disgust; for them, the sight of aristocrats pooping in the park was nothing out of the ordinary.

It was only under George IV that the park developed its present dignity. George landscaped the lake as we see it today and added gas lighting to deter the ladies of the night. The sex-crazed aristocrat gave way to an altogether gentler breed, the birdwatcher, as St James's filled with more than 30 ornithological species. Look out for the pelicans, ducks, geese and gulls which have made the lake their home.

> *Make a small loop round the park, return to the Mall outside the ICA and climb the staircase away from the park to reach* **Waterloo Place.**

The stone steps, part of Nash's Carlton House Terrace development, lead you to the **Duke of York Column**, a towering 124ft monument to the glory of Frederick, second son of George III and commander-in-chief of the British armed forces during the Napoleonic Wars. Yes, he was *that* Duke of York, the one who, at least in nursery rhyme, marched his men to the top of the hill and then marched them down again. So high is the statue that contemporary wags said the duke was trying to escape from his creditors—he left around two million pounds in debts on his death. The £25,000 that went towards this memorial was met by collecting one day's pay from every soldier in the army (and, because they had a soft spot for the old duke, they didn't seem to mind). Originally the design was to have been a replica of Trajan's Column in Rome, but unfortunately the pay of British soldiers at the time did not leave enough money to clad the memorial in relief sculptures.

Just behind the Duke of York, on the south side of Pall Mall, is an equestrian bronze statue of Edward VII, complete with shrapnel marks from the Second World War. The two buildings on the corners of Waterloo Place and Pall Mall are the Institute of Directors and the Athenaeum (a gentlemen's club); we shall return to them presently. Just north of Pall Mall is another Guards' memorial, this time honouring the 2162 soldiers of the Household Division who died in the Crimean War.

> *This walk now takes a detour to the right down Pall Mall and then up to the left through **Royal Opera Arcade**, London's earliest covered shopping street (1818) featuring Regency shop fronts designed by John Nash.*

The shops here still sell a full range of traditional hunting, shooting and fishing gear. The arcade derives its name from the pre-Covent Garden Royal Opera building, which burned down in the 1860s and was replaced with the modern Her Majesty's Theatre on the corner of Haymarket and King Charles II Street.

> *From the top of the arcade, glance to your right at the elegant Corinthian portico of the Theatre Royal, Haymarket, built by Nash in 1831, which stares at you from Charles II St. To return to Waterloo Place, turn left, then left again down Lower Regent St to Pall Mall.*

If you enjoyed birdwatching in St James's Park, maybe you should pull your binoculars back out for some ornithological study of a different kind here in Pall Mall, the high street of London's **clubland**. The rare bird you are after is male, 50-ish and invariably well-dressed; he tends to stagger somewhat, especially after lunch, and looks rather like one of those old salt-of-the-earth types that Jack Hawkins or Trevor Howard used to play. Note the stiff upper lip sporting a trimmed moustache, the tailored suit and, in some of the finer specimens, the bowler hat. *Homo clubiensis* does not tend to have many bodily markings apart from some ruddy splotches on the cheeks and nose and perhaps a port stain on his sleeve or a gravy spatter on his tie. Be sure to address members of the species as 'Sir' at the very least, and 'Colonel' if you really want to get chummy.

The author and former club *maître d'* Anthony O'Connor has defined the London club as a place 'where a well-born buck can get away from worries, women and anything that even faintly smacks of business in a genteel atmosphere of good cigars, mulled claret and obsequious servants.' The club phenomenon speaks volumes about English class relations; it shows that in London the middle-class gentleman, at least at the height of the British empire from about 1850 until the Second World War, sought his entertainment privately and in the company of his peers, while the lower orders remained safely in the street and his family stayed for-lornly at home. Nowadays the phenomenon is more restricted—largely to former public school boys, Conservative Party members, and the upper echelons of the armed forces—but still reflects the English predilection for keeping in with one's own and casting disparagement on everyone else.

Despite their exclusivity, clubs became popular because they were relatively cheap. One club aficionado wrote in 1853 that 'a man of moderate habits can dine more comfortably for three or four shillings (including half a pint of wine) than he could have dined for four to five times that amount at the coffee houses and hotels.' To the comfortable but not excessively rich businessman, the club atmosphere gave the feeling of acting and being treated like a lord in his mansion, with a library, smoking room, card room and any number of conference rooms at his disposal.

As London mushroomed in size in the mid-19th century and increasing numbers of the well-to-do moved out to the suburbs, the club also became a convenient home-from-home where a member could drop off his things and stay over for a modest rate. Of course a big attraction was the prospect of spending raucous nights with the boys without fear of intrusion by wife or children. 'I'll be at my club' became the catch-all excuse for every conceivable piece of marital negligence or indiscre-tion, and one that no wife could ever hope to disprove.

Clubs did not exactly do much for Victorian family values; the contemporary French commentator Jacques-Ignace Hittorf, more used to the open café society of his native Paris, reflected that they encouraged 'the cult of egoism, the abandon-ment of family virtues, the exclusive taste for material pleasures, and a deplorable laxity of morals'.

Not that the traditional clubs were particularly comfortable places. The food was usually indifferent at best, more like school dinner than a restaurant meal. The rooms were usually poorly heated and the beds awkward and narrow. Only the ser-vice was impeccable. There were clubs in the 1920s where the lackeys really did iron the newspapers and scrupulously washed any loose change they found in gen-tlemen's pockets. Maybe we should not wonder if such a peculiar environment spawned its special breed of fuddy-duddies who buried themselves away in arm-chairs with *The Times* newspaper and told their war adventures to nobody in particular while drinking themselves into a pleasant stupor.

Anthony O'Connor tells how at the Oriental one Colonel who habitually fell asleep over his cigar and port managed to set his chair on fire a record 14 times. The cele-brated chemist Michael Faraday died in his armchair at the Athenaeum in 1867, and rumour had it he had lain hidden under his newspaper for three days before anybody noticed there was something amiss.

The end of the empire and the emancipation of domestic servants brought about a sharp decline in clubland. With staff no longer prepared to work for a pittance and endure all manner of abuse from members, the establishments could no longer make ends meet. Before the Second World War there were 120 clubs in London; now there are less than 40. Apart from the food and beds, standards have risen and so have prices. Many have taken the previously unthinkable step of admitting women; even the arch-conservative Carlton Club broke its strict men-only code to welcome in Margaret Thatcher. The atmosphere at the clubs remains rarefied, although some of the carefree indolence of the past has disappeared.

As the gloriously named Captain Flickerton-Heyhew-Smythe remarked sometime in the 1960s: 'It seems incredible now that the vast resources of a huge Empire were reserved for a chosen few, the few who spent their lives gazing out of bow windows while they waited for another session of backgammon.' That does not mean that decadence is entirely out: in the 1990s a new club surfaced called School Dinners, at whose functions gaggles of stuffy young men are served boarding-school culinary horrors like bubble-and-squeak and spotted dick (don't ask what these are, if you don't know you don't want to know) by waitresses in short skirts and fishnet tights. The idea is to get very drunk, feel up the waitresses and then throw the food liberally around the room. Fun fun fun.

Facing you on Waterloo Place are the splendid buildings housing the **Institute of Directors** *to the left and the* **Athenaeum** *to the right.*

The Institute of Directors building is the older of the two, originally designed by Nash in 1827-8 to house the United Service Club and incorporating a number of features from Carlton House, notably the main staircase. The exterior was given a facelift in the late 1850s to look more like the Athenaeum opposite; both now have neoclassical friezes just below the roof awnings. The Athenaeum, designed by Decimus Burton, is one of the best Greek Revival buildings in London, its frieze inspired by the relief sculptures from the Parthenon housed in the British Museum. The club was known in the 19th century as the haunt of the intellectual elite, which explains the gilt statue of Athena, goddess of wisdom, above the entrance and the Greek letters of Athena's name in the mosaic above the porch.

As you walk past the Athenaeum down Pall Mall, look out for the brass plates announcing a host of other clubs, including the Travellers', the Reform, the Royal Automobile, the United Oxford and Cambridge and the Army and Navy Club.

Schomberg House at Nos.80–82 is an elegant mansion built in the Dutch style in the 1680s. In the late 18th century it housed the eccentric Temple of Health and Hymen, where couples with fertility problems would come to make love beneath a mirrored dome on mattresses stuffed with the tail hair of English stallions. The originator of this enterprise, the Scottish doctor James Graham, ended up, perhaps unsurprisingly, in a lunatic asylum. The Reform Club, at Nos.104–5, is where Jules Verne's fictional hero Phineas Fogg made his wager and set out to travel around the world in 80 days. It was also traditionally the bastion of the Whig party and, if you have sufficient effrontery, is worth infiltrating for a glimpse of its extremely elegant interior and mirrored double staircase (by Charles Barry) in which members are reflected in a tunnel of ever more gloomy infinity.

As in all St James's clubs, long rolls of ticker tape are posted on lecterns at the entrance, detailing the latest news headlines. Further into the interior are several libraries, a snooker room, bedrooms and a dining room with an unusual portrait of Gladstone at the tender age of 24.

*Before moving on, a word on **Pall Mall** itself.*

The street's curious name derives from an ancient Italian ball game called *palla a maglio*, literally ball and mallet, a form of croquet which entailed hitting a ball through metal hoops. The sport, which was known in England first by its French name, *paille maille*, then as *pell mell*, proved wildly popular on its introduction in the mid-16th century. Charles II liked it so much that he built this pall mall alley close by St James's Palace (he even installed his mistress, Nell Gwynne, in a house overlooking it). In the early 18th century the ball game disappeared, but the street remained fashionable as a row of upper-crust shops and cafés. The Star and Garter, the pub where Byron was arrested after killing his cousin Mr Chaworth in a duel, stood at No.100. Café society gave way to the club craze in the 19th century; now Pall Mall is increasingly the preserve of blue-chip companies such as Rothmans and P&O, which have their headquarters in its grand buildings.

*The first or the second turning to the right leads you into the leafy expanse of **St James's Square**.*

This square was where St James's turned from a mere adjunct to the royal palaces into a fashionable residential district in its own right. Just before the Great Fire of 1666, Charles II had granted a lease to Henry Jermyn, Earl of St Albans, charging him to build 'palaces fit for the dwelling of noblemen and persons of quality'. The result was to set the tone for nearly all of London's squares, creating a haven of privacy and seclusion with little resemblance to the more public urban spaces familiar in the rest of Europe (*see* pp.86–90).

St James's Square was for three centuries the *sine qua non* of fashionable London living, not because the architecture was remarkable but, as an 18th-century commentator pointed out, because of its 'prevailing regularity throughout, joined to the neatness of the pavement'. It also boasted a fine central garden, marred occasionally in the early days by the dumping of offal and dead animals from a nearby market. The equestrian statue in the middle is of William III; his horse has one hoof atop the molehill which caused the king's fatal riding accident in 1702.

Nowadays there are no more private residences in the square's spacious, mainly Georgian houses; they have been replaced by a succession of clubs, eminent institutions and company offices. Notice, for example, the East India, Devonshire, Sports and Public Schools Club at No.16 (with large bay windows you can peer through for a glimpse of the toffs in the dining room); and in the northwest corner the London Library, a superb open-shelved literary and historical book collection founded by Thomas Carlyle in 1841. No.4, on the eastern side, was the headquarters of De Gaulle's Free French during the Second World War, while General Eisenhower directed the First Allied Army and planned the North African and Normandy campaigns from Norfolk House at No.31.

No.5 was until recently home to the Bureau of the People's Jumhurya, a.k.a. the Libyan Embassy. In 1984 one of the embassy staff took a potshot and killed a woman police constable, Yvonne Fletcher, during an anti-Libyan demonstration in the square. The police began a tense siege, culminating in the severing of all diplomatic ties between London and Tripoli. Fletcher is commemorated by a plaque on the spot where she died.

> Leave the square on the north side by Duke of York St, which leads straight up to the church of **St James Piccadilly** (open daily, with lunchtime recitals and evening concerts; call ahead on ℂ 437 5053 for details).

St James's parish church (1684) seems curiously at odds with the rest of the neighbourhood, being totally unmarked by either pretention or exclusivity. Nowhere here do you see the trappings of wealth or snobbery; instead there is a flea market in the churchyard (Wednesday–Saturday, with an antiques market on Tuesday), a vegetarian restaurant ('The Wren') in the annexe, a Centre for Healing, and a message of warm welcome on the noticeboard in the porch. This is the visitors' church, a place where everyone in London can find an open door (or rather two open doors, one to the north and the other to the south).

Nevertheless, from an architectural point of view, St James's is an object lesson in effortless grace and charm. It is the only church that Christopher Wren built from scratch in London (the others were all renovations or rebuildings on medieval sites), and as such most clearly expresses his vision of the church as a place where the relationship between the priest and his congregation should be demystified.

St James's is airy and spacious, with the altar and pulpit in full view and accessible to all. An elegant gilded wooden gallery with rounded corners runs around the

western end, supported by Corinthian pillars in plaster adorned with intricate decorations. There are some beautiful carvings by Grinling Gibbons, notably on the
limewood reredos behind the altar (fruit and nature motifs) and on the stone font
(depictions of Christ and his apostles). The exterior is a simple affair in brick and
Portland stone. The uncomplicated but effective spire is a comparatively recent
addition (1968) although it was designed by Wren; for two centuries St James's
was topped by a nondescript bellcote put together at a cut-price rate by one of
Wren's carpenters.

> *Leave the church the way you came in, by the south door. The street
> stretching to left and right is **Jermyn Street**, which boasts some of the
> fanciest shopping in town. For the purposes of this walk, you need to turn
> right, but by all means wander a little in the other direction first.*

Royal and aristocratic patronage has showered down over the years on the old-
fashioned emporia lining Jermyn Street. Already the names of the establishments
hark back to another era: Turnbull and Asser the shirtmakers, George Trumper,
barber and perfumer, or Bates the hatter (the full spectrum, from flat caps to
bowlers). The shop assistants more closely resemble manservants from the great
aristocratic houses of the past than paid employees of ongoing business concerns.
Deference and attention to detail are the watchwords, sometimes pushed to rather
absurd extremes.

At Trumpers clients are still asked, at the end of a haircut, if Sir would like 'anything for the weekend' (a wonderfully euphemistic way of avoiding any mention
of the dread word 'condom'). Anyone buying a shirt is in for a treat of careful measuring, discreet compliments and nonchalant chitchat about the fluctuating
quality of modern cloth (try Harvie and Hudson at No.97, with its attractive mid-
Victorian fronting). Another fine establishment is Paxton and Whitfield the
cheeseseller at No.93, where the freshest cuts of the day are advertised on a black-
board behind the counter and samples of unusual cheese types are offered for
tasting with water biscuits.

> *On your right along Jermyn St you pass two arcades lined with more pur-
> veyors of quality goods: first Princes Arcade, with its brown and white
> décor and then, after Duke St, the lower-ceilinged, green and white Pic-
> cadilly Arcade. Halfway between them is the back entrance to **Fortnum &
> Mason,** the ultimate old-fashioned English food shop (open till 8pm with
> a good value afternoon tea for £12.50 from 3–5.15pm).*

However awful the reputation of English food down the centuries, one establishment, at least, has managed to escape the opprobrium with remarkable ease.
Fortnum & Mason is the kind of luxury food shop that would cause the mouth of

even the most suspicious of French gourmets to water: wonderful potted meats, home-made breads, smoked fish and caviar, all beautifully packaged and served with fervent attention (although at a price you might want to think twice about). Charles Fortnum was one of George III's footmen, and he and his friend John Mason opened their first shop in St James's in the 1770s. The rest, as they say, is history.

The briskest trade has traditionally been in tea, marmalade and potted Stilton cheese; gift packs of all of these are stored at the front of the shop (on the Piccadilly side) and attract hordes of American and Japanese tourists every day (so many that in 1997 the shop doubled in size and expanded into the next door building). Aside from popular items like the Fortnum and Mason hamper, there are less obvious pleasures, too, particularly at the cheese counter where Hawes Wensleydale, Ticklemore goat cheese and organic Pencarag more than hold their own against the fine French and Italian varieties sitting next to them.

The building itself is less alluring. Completed in 1925, its centrepiece is a turquoise mermaid fountain in rather dubious taste. One more recent addition is quite fun—the clock above the entrance (1964). As the hour strikes, articulated figures of Mr Fortnum and Mr Mason emerge from their boxes and bow to each other.

*Return to Jermyn Street and continue to the junction with St James's St. Nearby is the entrance to **White's**, the oldest club in London (1693). Cross St James's St and walk down Bennet Street into Arlington St, which boasts some fine Georgian houses, notably the mansions designed by William Kent at Nos.21 and 22. At the top end of Arlington St, on the corner of Piccadilly, is the entrance to the **Ritz Hotel**.*

Tea at the Ritz (a steep £21 a head) is a London institution, a challengingly priced but worthwhile indulgence that permits you to spend an hour or two immersed in an Edwardian paradise of gilded statues, ornate filigree roof decorations, interior waterfalls and exotic plants in the Palm Court. The food isn't bad either: platefuls of cucumber or salmon sandwiches, plus scones with clotted cream and strawberry jam (a cheaper and less filling alternative to tea would be to have a quiet cocktail at the bar).

This is the sister hotel to the original Paris Ritz, and opened in 1906, eight years after its illustrious relative. The London Ritz has always been quite independent however; César Ritz may have lent it his name, but he had already retired from public life at the time of its opening and was later to die in a Swiss clinic from a debilitating venereal disease. If you are lucky you will meet the unflappable *maître d'* Michael Kopf. Bend his ear and he will regale you with stories of the hotel's most famous guests, some of whom are celebrated in a mural in the foyer.

Walk onto Piccadilly, turn left and continue until you reach the edge of
Green Park.

This pleasantly undulating expanse of greenery has much the same history as St James's Park. It was originally a burial ground for Queen Matilda's lepers (and, in deference to the dead beneath it, has never been planted with flowers). Henry VIII made it a royal park, and Charles II laid out its walkways. Green Park, like its neighbour, was a haunt of trouble-makers and duellists in the 18th century. On one occasion, Count Alfieri returned to the Haymarket Theatre for the last act of a play after sustaining a duelling wound to his arm from Lord Ligonier, his mistress's husband. Later he joked: 'My view is that Ligonier did not kill me because he did not want to, and I did not kill him because I did not know how.'

Turn left down Queen's Walk, which affords some of the best views of the park. A little way down to the left is a narrow alley leading through to St James's Place, a particularly attractive L-shaped street filled with Georgian houses. The finest of these, at No.27, is **Spencer House** *(open Sun 10.30–5.30, last adm 4.45, except Jan and Aug; adm expensive. Visit by guided tour only; tours begin at regular intervals and last an hour).*

This gracious Palladian mansion was born in sorrow: its original backer, Henry Bromley, ran out of money and shot himself moments after reading his will over with his lawyer. The site was then taken over by the Spencer family (ancestors of Princess Diana) who hired a bevy of architects including John Vardy and Robert Adam to produce one of the finest private houses in London. Completed in 1766, Spencer House boasts magnificent parquet floors, ornate plaster ceilings and a welter of gilded statues and furniture. The highlight is Vardy's Palm Room, in which the pillars are decorated as gilt palm trees with fronds stretching over the tops of the arched window bays.

James Stuart's Painted Room features classical murals, graceful chandeliers and a fine, highly polished wooden floor. The whole house was renovated by its current owners, RIT Capital Partners, in 1990 and looks magnificent. Unfortunately only eight rooms are open to the public; the rest are kept for the pleasure of the financial executives who occupy it during the week.

St James's Place leads back to **St James's Street.** *One block to your left are its two most interesting buildings,* **Brooks Club** *on the corner of Park Place to the left, and the 1960s* **Economist Building** *in its own small piazza to the right.*

Along with Pall Mall, this street is clubland *par excellence*, although in the past it has enjoyed a less than irreproachable reputation because of its gambling dens. White's, the oldest London club (which we passed a little earlier), may well have instituted the national mania for bets and betting in the mid-18th century when it ran books on everything from births and marriages to politics and death. 'There is nothing, however trivial or ridiculous, which is not capable of producing a bet,' wrote *Connoisseur* magazine in 1754.

White's was soon eclipsed, however, by Brooks down the road. One particularly obsessional gambler, Charles James Fox, ran up debts of £140,000 and was seen cadging money off the waiters at Brooks before his father, Lord Holland, stepped in to bail him out in 1781. Horace Walpole, who saw bailiffs removing Fox's furniture from his digs a little way down the street, defined Brooks as a place where 'a thousand meadows and cornfields are staked at every throw, and as many villages are lost as in the earthquakes that overwhelmed Herculaneum and Pompeii.'

St James's Street has changed quite a bit in the 20th century. The bottom end, at the junction with Pall Mall, is dominated by two turn-of-the-century office buildings by Norman Shaw. More striking still is the Economist Building at Nos.25–7, a series of three concrete hexagonal towers designed by Peter and Alison Smithson for the weekly news magazine *The Economist* and completed in 1964. Much praised at the time, the building is certainly one of the more successful of London's experiments in 1960s modernism; now, a bit like *The Economist* itself, it looks impressive but stylistically seems a little dated.

> *Pause for a moment at No.24 next door, the address where the satirical cartoonist James Gillray threw himself out of a window to his untimely death in 1815. Then head back down St James's St; at the end stands the fine Tudor gatehouse of **St James's Palace** (closed to the public).*

For more than 300 years this was the official residence of England's kings and queens; indeed, foreign ambassadors are still formally accredited to the Court of St James even though they are received, like every other official on royal business, at Buckingham Palace. As noted above, Henry VIII built St James's to replace the whorehouse posing as a nunnery that had been established on the site two generations earlier.

Although endowed with fine buildings (of which only the octagonal towers of the gatehouse survive), St James's Palace became known as a raucous place of ill manners and debauchery, particularly under Queen Anne and the early Hanoverians who used it to hold drunken banquets. Anne was well known for her unseemly appetite for food and drink, particularly brandy, and for the bodily noises she frequently emitted at table (inspiring Thomas D'Urfey to write his satirical poem *The Fart*, in which the queen's courtiers reluctantly accept responsibility for the stink caused by Her Majesty). Dinner guests had the distressing habit of urinating in front of their peers, usually but not always into bowls provided for the purpose.

Not suprisingly, the place soon came to be described as 'crazy, smoky and dirty'. The Prince Regent celebrated his disastrous marriage with Caroline of Brunswick here in 1795, spending his wedding night fully dressed in a drunken slumber in the fireplace of the bridal chamber. Soon afterwards he moved into Carlton House, and the palace's somewhat tarnished glory days were over. A fire destroyed most of the original buildings in 1809; the rebuilt courtyards now house offices for members of the royal household.

Just to the left of the gatehouse is the entrance to Marlborough Road and **Marlborough House.**

Queen Anne leased this part of the grounds of St James's Palace to her closest friend Sarah, Duchess of Marlborough. The two called each other by common names as a joke (the Queen was Mrs Morley, the Duchess Mrs Freeman), but fell out after the Duchess complained she had once been kept waiting 'like a Scotch lady with a petition'. They never spoke again. In the meantime, the Duchess asked the ageing Christopher Wren and his son to build Marlborough House, instructing them to use the red bricks that her husband had used as ballast in his warships returning from Holland. The house was retouched periodically over the next 200 years, at one point housing the Museum of Manufactures, forerunner of the Victoria and Albert Museum.

Its heyday came under Victoria's heir Prince Edward and his wife Alexandra, who made it the epicentre of London society. Edward employed an army of liveried servants, including a page boy in full Highland dress on the door, and entertained his friends nightly. Alexandra lived here after her husband died in 1910, and buried her three dogs Muff, Tiny and Joss in the garden. Now Marlborough House is the headquarters of the Commonwealth Secretariat and not generally open to the public.

Marlborough Road contains two curiosities: near the bottom an Art Nouveau bronze memorial plaque to Queen Alexandra by Alfred Gilbert in Marlborough Gate and, a little further up, the **Queen's Chapel.**

The chapel, the first neoclassical church in England, was built by Inigo Jones in 1623 to celebrate the prospective marriage of the future Charles I and the Infanta of Spain, although as it turned out Charles married a French princess, Henrietta Maria, instead. It is extraordinarily simple, little more than a box livened up with the odd flourish of stucco; but it is graced with attractive furnishings, including a reredos carved by Grinling Gibbons and a painting of the Deposition by Annibale Carracci. Above all, it is uplifted by the light that pours in through the large windows above the altar. This is where the Princess of Wales' lead coffin was laid in the week before her funeral. Unfortunately the chapel is almost never open and does not welcome casual visitors. The only way to get in is to attend a Sunday service in spring or summer (come by to check times).

> *Return to the top of Marlborough Road. Turn left and keep going, passing Stable Yard Road on your left, which contains one of the palace's courtyards, Ambassadors Court. Straight on but slightly to the right, re-enter Green Park through a small alleyway, and turn left. On your left is **Lancaster House**.*

This was destined to be the residence of Frederick, the bankrupt Grand Old Duke of York encountered earlier. An architectural wrangle delayed the project too long, however, for the duke to live to see it. Robert Smirke, architect of the British Museum, was first hired for the job, then fired in favour of Benjamin Wyatt. The final result is an elegant three-storey rectangle in Bath stone with a tall neoclassical portico and elegant Louis XV fittings in its state rooms. After the Duke of York's death it was never used by the royal family, but passed instead through a succession of aristocratic owners. It is now used for high-level conferences and was the scene of the agreement that secured independence for Rhodesia, subsequently known as Zimbabwe, in 1979.

> *Queen's Walk brings you back to The Mall. Turn right and before you is the gilded figure of Victory which hovers over the white marble Victoria Memorial (a mush of allegory and sentiment by Aston Webb); right behind are the much-photographed railings and façade of Buckingham Palace.*

Buckingham Palace

> *I must say, notwithstanding the expense which has been incurred in building the palace, no sovereign in Europe, I may even add, perhaps no private gentleman, is so ill-lodged as the king of this country.*

The Duke of Wellington (1828)

On 7 August 1993, miracle of miracles, Buckingham Palace opened its doors to the public for the first time. For generations, royalists had invoked the need to preserve the mystery of the monarchy and refused, in the words of Walter Bagehot, to 'let daylight in upon its magic'. But by the early 1990s the British monarchy was in a crisis of quite astonishing proportions. Two royal marriages had broken up in quick succession, Princess Diana's struggles with bulimia and depression had been made glaringly public, Prince Charles had allegedly been taped telling his mistress on the telephone how he fantasized about being her tampon and, to top it all, half of Windsor Castle had burned down.

Little knowing the revelations and tragedies that were still to come, the Queen herself dubbed 1992, the year of most of these misfortunes, her 'annus horribilis'. To rally public opinion back behind the monarchy she made two unprecedented concessions. The first was to agree to pay income tax for the first time (although, as nobody knows quite how much the Queen earns, it is not clear just how much she is prepared to plough back into the Exchequer). The second was to unveil some of the mysteries of Buckingham Palace for two months of the year, for an initial period of five years (now it will stay open until at least 2000).

As a public relations coup, opening the doors of the queen's official residence proved less than spectacular. Quite a few newspaper critics, their knives already well sharpened by the preceding flurry of royal scandals, complained that the tour was impersonal, poorly put together and even boring. The public seemed more forgiving, fawning happily over every precious object listed in the official catalogue, but did not turn up in quite the numbers anticipated.

The disappointment was nothing new for Buckingham Palace, a residence with a past more chequered than a dozen chessboards. The site was part of the swamp inhabited by lepers in the 12th century; James I then planted mulberry trees in an attempt to drain the soil and attract silkworms. Unfortunately he grew the wrong kind of trees and the silkworms stayed away. Then in 1702 John Sheffield, Duke of Buckingham, built himself a modest little mansion called Buckingham House. The royal family liked it so much that they bought it off Buckingham's illegitimate son in 1762 and called it the King's House.

So the place might have remained, had it not been for the extravagant ambitions of George IV, who decided that Carlton House was not grand enough and asked John Nash to build a new palace on this site. It was a crazy scheme, impractical in financial terms and quite unnecessary given the number of plush residences George had already built for himself in his time as Prince Regent. Nash nevertheless forged ahead with a vast three-sided building with more than 600 rooms, and a triumphal arch (the Marble Arch which now sits at the top of Park Lane) at its entrance. George meanwhile pulled the wool over parliament's eyes by making out that his pet architect was merely undertaking some 'improvements' to Buckingham House.

In 1828 the Duke of Wellington, no friend of George's, became prime minister and, faced with the mounting costs of the king's folly, did his best to pull the plug on the whole project. 'If you expect me to put my hand to any additional cost, I'll be damned if I will,' he told his royal master.

Wellington cut the weekly budget from £10,000 to £2500, but even he had to acknowledge that the project was too far advanced to be ditched. It was truncated instead. George died in 1830, Nash was fired for his 'inexcusable irregularity and great negligence', and the solid but unimaginative Edward Blore took over as master builder. 'Blore the bore' reined in Nash's plans, built an unimaginative east wing (later adorned with a triple-porticoed façade by Aston Webb) and completed the interior fittings at the lowest possible cost. The result was a total mess. The drains did not work, the lavatories stank, bells would not ring, doors would not close and several of the palace's 1000 windows would not open.

George's successor, William IV, stayed clear of the place altogether, believing it would best be converted into a barracks, while Queen Victoria described it as a 'disgrace to the country'.

Victoria nevertheless stuck it out, even growing quite fond of the place. But then in 1861 her husband Albert died and she decamped, seemingly indefinitely, to her Scottish retreat at Balmoral. The early 1860s were a low point both for the monarchy and for Buckingham Palace, with Victoria showing little enthusiasm for her calling; indeed in 1864 a notice appeared on the railings outside the palace declaring: 'These commanding premises to be let or sold, in consequence of the late occupant's declining business.' Under growing pressure from her advisers, Victoria managed to pull herself together.

She gradually re-established her own mystique, and by the end of her reign in 1901 had made Buckingham Palace the nerve-centre of the modern monarchy. Its reputation went from strength to strength in the course of the 20th century. Most British people instinctively adored it, although they probably could not say quite why, beyond the firm belief that the home of the royal family must inevitably be tinged with magic. The public's starry-eyed view was not always shared by the royals inside; Edward VIII, who abdicated in 1936 to marry Wallis Simpson, the American divorcee he loved, wrote in his memoirs that it seemed 'pervaded by a curious, musty smell that still assails me when I enter its portals'.

The palace's modern misfortunes have included some amusing lapses in security. Three German tourists once camped in the gardens for the night, believing themselves to be in Hyde Park. More recently, an enterprising amateur pilot flew on to the roof in a light aircraft. The most alarming incident was in 1982, when an intruder called Michael Fagan walked in unchallenged through the master of the household's office, tried out the thrones in the throne room, then slipped through a hidden door into the Queen's private apartments and found his way into her bedroom. The queen, confronted by a barefoot stranger clutching a broken ashtray in a blood-stained hand, pressed her panic button but had to sweet-talk her visitor for six minutes before help arrived.

It was a security fiasco, but in the end nobody was hurt. Fagan was treated as a harmless basket-case, acquitted of the one charge brought against him (stealing half a bottle of wine) and allowed to return home after a few months in a psychiatric hospital. Nobody has ever quite worked out his motives, although it seems he spent most of his time with the Queen talking about his personal problems.

Interviewed at his home in Islington shortly before the public opening of Buckingham Palace, Fagan said he would like nothing more than to be hired as a tour guide. 'After all,' he said, 'I know my way around.'

So what exactly is all the fuss about? What do you get to see? Certainly not a glimpse of the 'working palace' constantly alluded to by the Queen's public relations flaks. The tour takes in just 18 of Buckingham Palace's 661 rooms, and even these feel as though they have been stripped down to the bare minimum to ensure they are not sullied by the savage hordes. The original carpets are rolled away each summer and replaced with industrial-strength red Axminster rugs that clash awkwardly with the fake marble columns, greens, pinks and blues of the flock wallpapers and gold and cream ornamental ceilings.

The place feels hollow and spookily empty; in fact it is hard to imagine that anybody lives or works in such soulless surroundings. Perhaps it's just as well that there is no café or refreshment stall for the public, as the toilets are right at the end of the tour, in some tents in the Palace gardens. As for the personal touch, there is not so much as a photograph of the royal family on the whole tour, let alone a flesh-and-blood prince or princess to welcome the guests. As one American tourist commented, 'At least Mickey Mouse is always present in *his* Disneyland.'

> *The tour route leads you to the inner courtyard and thence to the back part of the palace overlooking the gardens. The Grand Staircase, with its elegant wrought-iron banister, leads up to the first of the state rooms, the Green Drawing Room. The guide that follows only mentions the highlights, and not necessarily in the order in which you will encounter them; the attractions are on the whole fairly obvious, and although there is no free groundplan to help you get your bearings the wardens are exceptionally helpful and friendly. (Open Aug and Sept, at least until 2000, 9.30–5.30 daily, last entry 4.15, ticket office closes at 4; adm expensive; ℗ 0171–321 2233 to book tickets in advance and avoid the queues. The ticket office, an elegant tent structure designed by architect Michael Hopkins, is at the western end of St James's Park just off the Mall, and the entrance is at Ambassadors' Court on the south side of the building. These days the Palace has its own web site on http://www.royal.gov.uk.)*

The effect sought by Nash was above all a theatrical one. All these rooms are filled with ostentatious chandeliers, somewhat chintzy furniture and ornate gilt and painted plaster ceilings. Whether you are in the Green, Blue or White Drawing Room you can't help feeling as though you are trapped in a Dairy Milk chocolate box. Much of the decoration has been imported from the fire-damaged rooms of

Windsor Castle; there are, however, some impressive pieces giving a hint of the flamboyant tastes of George IV, who acquired most of the treasures in Buckingham Palace.

In the **Green Drawing Room**, for example, there is a delicate, beautifully painted Chelsea pot-pourri vase depicting courtly figures in a rustic setting; notice also the Regency-era chandelier featuring three weeping women standing back to back. The **Blue Drawing Room** was originally red and has a handsome marble astronomical clock from the 18th century, while the **White Drawing Room** contains a vast mirror which swings open to reveal a hidden cabinet. According to the guards, Elton John played the grand piano in the **Music Room**, and Princess Diana practised tap-dancing on the rather slippery looking floor.

The **Throne Room** (the second room on the tour) is an almost laughable exercise in kitsch, with his'n'hers thrones in pink and yellow adorned with the initials EIIR for Elizabeth and P for Philip. On the walls is a plaster frieze, adorned with scenes from the Wars of the Roses, that only adds to the artificial atmosphere. This could be the set of a Gene Kelly musical; in fact it is the room where the queen receives heads of state and ambassadors. (The adjacent State Ballroom, where the Queen ennobles knights of the realm while a string quartet plays a bizarre medley of tunes from Mozart to Mary Poppins, is off-limits to the public, partly because it's used in the summer as a storage space for the Palace carpets.)

The incidental decoration does not really improve as the tour goes on, although there are some nice French clocks in the State Dining Room and some fine if disconcerting Gobelins tapestries depicting famous rapes (Proserpine and Europa) on the Ministers' Staircase. The real highlight is the 155ft-long **Picture Gallery** (the third room on the tour) which is crammed from floor to ceiling with the cream of the royal collection of some 10,000 paintings.

The walls are a bit crowded for comfort, but the gems stand out easily enough: Van Dyck's idealized portraits of Charles I, Rembrandt's *Lady with a Fan, Agatha Bas* and *The Shipbuilder and His Wife*, landscapes by Ruisdael, Poussin and Claude Lorrain, portraits by Frans Hals, Rubens' underwhelming *St George and the Dragon*, Albert Cuyp's *Landscape with a Negro Page*, and much more besides. Apart from Charles I, the only royal to receive anything like pictorial justice in Buckingham Palace is Victoria, whose family is cosily captured in Franz Winterhalter's 1846 portrait in the East Gallery (the room after the Picture Gallery).

The lower floor of the tour holds few new surprises, although you can have some fun in the 200ft Marble Hall with its yards of sculpture—look out for Canova's sensuous *Mars and Venus*, which George IV commissioned from Napoleon's pet artist after the British victory at Waterloo. A saunter through the Bow Room brings you out into the garden where Palace 'air hostesses' will deliver any bags and coats checked in at the beginning of the tour.

Here in the garden you may linger and enjoy some fine views, before moving on to the highlight of the tour which is the souvenir shop. In many ways this is the most telling part of the trip, with mugs and videos and other royal memorabilia displayed to the public in Argos-style glass cabinets. At the top end of the scale, you can pick up a perfectly frightful crystal bowl or enamel box for roughly the same price as a dinner in a three-star restaurant.

Better value (and more appetizing) are the Buckingham Palace Belgian Chocolates moulded into the shape of the crown, or the attractive-looking Buckingham Palace gold tooth-mug, only a moderate rip-off at £12.50 and an ideal Christmas present for regally-inclined mothers-in-law.

---

*A little further along Buckingham Gate is the entrance to the **Queen's Gallery**, a further, rather small selection of paintings from the royal collection (closed between exhibitions, but otherwise open daily 9.30–4.30, last adm 4; adm). The works exhibited rotate fairly regularly, so if you are lucky you can see some rare Leonardo or Vermeer; if you are unlucky you might get lumbered with a lot of boring furniture.*

*For a final dose of royalty, keep going along Buckingham Gate until it turns into Buckingham Palace Road, where a prominent gateway to the right leads to the **Royal Mews** (open Wed 12noon–4 all year round; March–Aug Tues and Thurs too (same hours); Aug–Oct Mon–Thurs, 10.30–4.30.)*

This is the royal equivalent of the Batcave, where the blue-blooded celebs undergo a mysterious transformation before bursting out into the public arena through the grand entrance arch in their ceremonial clothes and outrageous vehicles. The Batmobiles here wouldn't do much to impress Bruce Wayne, though: not so much as an engine in sight. Instead there are rows of gaudily painted wagons, a fine 18th-century Riding House by William Chambers, and stables for the thoroughbreds. Here you can take a close look at the Gold State Coach commissioned by George III for coronation ceremonies; Queen Victoria's Irish Coach used for the State Opening of Parliament; the Glass State Coach built in 1910 for royal weddings; and many more besides.

Back in the 18th century, royal coaches were little different from the carriages owned by a hundred wealthy men around London (as anyone who has seen the ludicrously lavish Lord Mayor's Coach in the Museum of London will appreciate).

It was not until the age of the automobile that they really made the royal family stand out from the crowd; now they are an essential part of the royal mythology, another pleasing anachronism with which to charm the public.

> *From here, the nearest Underground station is at Victoria, a five-minute walk down Buckingham Palace Road. That's also where you will find buses to take you pretty much in any direction around the city.*

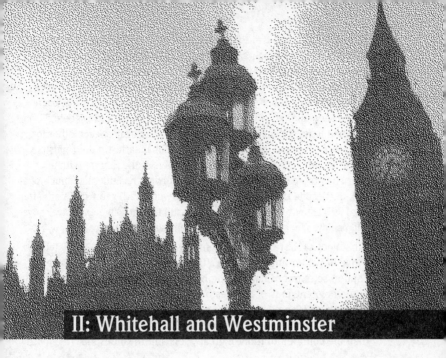

II: Whitehall and Westminster

Start: *Trafalgar Square.*

Walking time: *2 hours, not including time spent in Westminster Abbey and the Tate Gallery.*

Westminster means two things: the Mother of All Parliaments, that august institution which has set the benchmark for democratic assemblies all over the world; and the mother of all London churches, Westminster Abbey. Actually, there is nothing very motherly, or even feminine, about either place. This part of town has for centuries been the preserve of men of power. It conjures up images of kings being crowned in full splendour, of noblemen plotting against each other for control of the grand institutions of state, of mandarins in their plush offices sealing the fate of the furthest corners of the Empire with a flourish of the pen. Women have not, until very recently, had much of a look-in. Despite the election of 102 new women MPs to parliament after the 1997 Labour victory, Westminster still has the same exclusive, boys-will-be-boys feel as the clubland of St James's across the park.

What goes on here may be essentially serious, but it is alleviated by a love of banter and ceremony. There is arguably no experience in London so extraordinary as the high verbal gymnastics and low schoolboy tantrums of debates in the House of Commons. The atmosphere is somewhat more sober, but no less pompous, next door in the Abbey, with its grand Gothic architecture and larger-than-life commemoration of great poets and royal despots.

This is a nourishing but not over-long walk, beginning with the splendours of the Banqueting House and ending with one of London's most stunning art galleries, the Tate (which will be reorganizing itself as the Tate Gallery of British Art by 2001). Most of the sights are open every day, although you'll have to do quite a bit of work to get into the Houses of Parliament (*see* below).

---

lunch/pubs

It's a good idea to squeeze as much of the walk as possible in between meals, since the eating possibilites are distinctly limited.

The Footstool, St John's Smith Square. Decent café in the crypt with reasonably priced pub food and occasional art shows. £5–10.

Pret à Manger, 75b Victoria Street. Tasty and sophosticated sandwiches and sushi, on the pricey side, but always excellent. £5.

Tate Gallery. A downstairs café (decent but pricey and usually with queues) plus a proper slightly stuffy restaurant serving reliable English food and redeemed by the famous epicurean mural by Rex Whistler. Restaurant £25–35, café from £5, all non-smoking.

II: Whitehall & Westminster

A The Footstool
B Prêt à Manger
C Tate Gallery
D Shepherd's
E Pimlico Tandoori
F Pomegranates

Map labels:

250 metres
250 yards

N

National Gallery
Statue of Charles I
Trafalgar Square
CHARING CROSS
CHARING CROSS STATION
COCKSPUR ST.
CHARING CROSS
START
EMBANKMENT
Admiralty Arch
NORTHUMBERLAND AVE.
THE MALL
WHITEHALL
GREAT SCOT. YARD
Old Admiralty
WHITEHALL PL.
Old War Office
St James's Park
HORSE GUARDS ROAD
Horse Guards Parade
HORSE GUARDS
Banqueting House
Ministry of Defence
VICTORIA EMBANKMENT
Foreign Office
DOWNING ST.
RICHMOND TER.
Cenotaph
Cabinet War Rooms
KING CHARLES ST.
PARLIAMENT STREET
WESTMINSTER
BIRDCAGE WALK
GREAT GEORGE ST.
BRIDGE ST.
WESTMINSTER BRIDGE
STOREY'S GATE
Methodist Central Hall
St Margaret's Westminster
Parliament Square
Big Ben
to ST JAMES'S and B
BROAD SANCTUARY
Westminster Abbey
Old Palace Yard
Houses of Parliament
Dean's Yard
Abbey Gdns.
Jewel Tower
Westminster School
GT. COLLEGE ST.
MILLBANK
Victoria Tower Gardens
GT. PETER ST.
MARSHAM STREET
TUFTON STREET
SMITH SQUARE
St John's
River Thames
HORSEFERRY ROAD
THORNEY ST.
LAMBETH BRIDGE
PAGE ST.
THORNEY ST.
JOHN ISLIP STREET
Tate Gallery
FINISH
to PIMLICO and E and F
ATTERBURY ST.
MILLBANK

171

Shepherd's, Marsham Ct, Marsham St. a smart British restaurant with imaginative but expertly presented food: game in season, beef on trolley etc. £21.50–25 for a two- or three-course lunches, best to book ahead on ℂ 0171–834 9552.

Pimlico Tandoori, 38 Moreton St (near ⊖ Pimlico). One of the better Indian restaurants around this part of town. £10–15.

Pomegranates, 94 Grosvenor Road (near ⊖ Pimlico). Excellent and imaginative eclectic menu in small basement restaurant, closed for lunch on Sat and Sun; lunch from £10.

You can't really get lost on the first part of this walk as it is a straight line from Trafalgar Square down Whitehall to the Houses of Parliament. As you leave the square, pause for a moment by Hubert Le Sueur's equestrian statue of Charles I (see p.136 for details), the king who lost his head just down the road outside the Banqueting House. Charles's diehard fans gather here every year on the anniversary of his death, 30 January, and lay a wreath in his honour.

In Charles's time, the view down **Whitehall** was rather different. Instead of today's busy traffic funnel lined with self-important neoclassical offices, the street was a grand thoroughfare flanked on either side by the Renaissance buildings of Whitehall Palace. At the top of the street was the three-storey stone and flint Holbein Gate, a magnificent entrance to the royal area that was thoughtlessly pulled down in 1759 to facilitate the flow of coach traffic. The palace itself was built and established as the main royal residence by Henry VIII in the early 1530s. It continued to be embellished until 1689, when William and Mary decided to move to Kensington Palace and the court decamped to St James's; then in 1698 the whole complex, with the exception of the Banqueting House, burned to the ground after a Dutch laundry woman left a stove on overnight. Whitehall has since become a synonym for the British Civil Service, which moved in during the 18th and 19th centuries to take advantage of the close proximity to parliament. Among the bronze plates you'll see on your way down are the Ministry of Defence, the Ministry of Housing and, on the corner of Parliament Square, the Treasury. None of the government buildings is open to the public.

On your right as you walk down Whitehall is the Whitehall Theatre, which built up a reputation for staging light farces in the 1950s and 1960s (farce apparently being the preferred fare of all those grey-faced bureaucrats after a long day's juggling with the paperclips). The theatre is nowadays home to the tedious Jack Docherty Chat Show, screened every weeknight on British TV, but it is worth seeing for a glimpse of the theatre's fine Art Nouveau interior alone (free tickets available from 5.30pm for the show which starts at 6pm, ℂ 0171–287 4718 for more *details). A little beyond the theatre is the back entrance to the Horse Guards (see p.150), followed immediately by the elegant 18th-century façade of Dover House, once an aristocratic mansion and now used as the Scottish Office. The highlight of Whitehall is directly across the road, just south of the junction with Horseguards Avenue: the **Banqueting House** (open Mon–Sat, 10–5; adm; may close at short notice for government functions, © 0171–930 4179 if in doubt).*

The Banqueting House was the first building that Inigo Jones, the Palladio-crazy King's Surveyor of Works, constructed on returning from his expedition to Italy in 1615. The royal family had somehow managed without a permanent dining hall for more than 80 years; the wood and canvas structure on this site in which the Tudors entertained foreign guests was described by James I as an 'old, rotten, slight-builded shed' and pulled down. Jones's replacement, completed in 1622, was the first Italianate building in London, a sober design of elegant proportions which enthused foreign visitors but left the home-grown critics stone cold. Jones was not really ahead of his time; the rest of London was just living about 150 years in the past, and it took more than a century before the Banqueting House attracted the architectural admiration it deserved.But the building was much more than a place where royalty ate dinner; it became an essential symbol of Stuart kingship, especially after Charles I commissioned the breathtakingly beautiful but supremely arrogant **ceiling frescoes** by Rubens in the main dining hall on the first floor. The theme of these frescoes is the divine right of kings, no less. Of the three main panels, the first is an allegorical celebration of the union of England and Scotland under James I; the second a celebration of James's virtues; and the third, directly above the throne, a depiction of the peace enjoyed under James's reign. For James I you could just as easily read Charles I—this was very much a glorification of the present monarch, rather than a fond tribute to his father. In fact, Charles had less in common with James I than with Richard II, whose own claim to the divine right of kings 250 years earlier is so brilliantly captured in the Wilton Diptych (in the National Gallery). Charles should have remembered how Richard II was deposed and murdered for his presumption; a few years later, he wound up on an executioner's block right outside this dining hall.

The Banqueting House inevitably became something of a Royalist shrine after the restoration of the monarchy in 1660, and was chosen as the venue for Charles II's coronation celebrations. James II tried to turn it into a Catholic shrine, and stuck a weather vane on the roof to warn him of any 'Protestant wind' that might blow him off his royal perch. The Protestant wind did indeed come, in the shape of William of Orange, who deposed James and promptly used the Banqueting House for a joint feast with Queen Mary in 1689 to celebrate their accession. Jones's building survived the Whitehall Palace fire of 1698, but its ceremonial role faded fast. For 200 years it was stuffed full of religious paraphernalia and used as a royal chapel. It was only restored to its original form for its public opening in 1963. It is still occasionally used for a royal ceremony on Maundy Thursday, the day before Good Friday, when the queen distributes specially minted coins, known as Maundy money, to charitable institutions and the poor.

> *Keep walking down Whitehall, cross the road and you come to the turning for* **Downing Street**, *home to British Prime Ministers on and off since 1735. Unfortunately, you won't be able to sidle up to the famous Georgian front door at No.10 without a security pass; the best you can hope for is a glimpse through the heavy iron gates installed in 1990 under prime minister Thatcher. Next door at No.11 is the Chancellor of the Exchequer, the British equivalent of treasury secretary or finance minister, and next door to him, at No.12, is the government whips' office, where the party in power keeps tabs on its members in parliament.*

It is rather pleasing to think that this street, the scene of many a heated cabinet meeting and ministerial bollocking, was once an open venue for cock-fighting. A theatre dedicated to the proposition that encouraging animals to tear each other apart with spurs is just as entertaining as watching politicians doing the same thing in the Palace of Westminster stayed in business on this site alongside the Axe brew-house until about 1675. It was only then that a rather modest building development, later to become the powerhouse of the British establishment, was undertaken by one George Downing, a slippery fellow who managed to spy for both Oliver Cromwell and Charles II during the Civil War and come out of it not only alive but stinking rich into the bargain. It was more accident than design that led to Downing Street's lasting fame. When the prime minister, Robert Walpole, succeeded a certain Mr Chicken as tenant in 1735 he never meant to establish No.10 as an official residence, and indeed many of his successors preferred to con-duct the business of government from their more lavish homes elsewhere in London. Only in the early 19th century was 10 Downing Street kitted out with proper facilities, such as John Soane's sumptuous dining room (eating always seems to be the last priority of the British governing classes); only in 1902 did it become the prime minister's home as well as office. The shortcomings of the place have never gone away, though; when Tony Blair became prime minister in 1997, he installed his family in the more spacious No.11 next door, swapping places with his unmarried Chancellor, Gordon Brown.

It certainly appeals to the British establishment's keen sense of understatement that 10 Downing Street should be such an ordinary-looking seat of power. Many of the prime ministers who have lived here, however, have been less than enthralled and must have yearned for the majesty and space of an Elysée Palace or a White House.

Certainly, the comparative modesty of the place has been no guarantee of immunity from attack. The kitchen was destroyed by a German bomb in 1940 (on which occasion the housekeeper Mrs Landemare rather comically ran up and down the staircases fretting over her ruined soufflé). Then in 1992 the IRA drove a lorry up the back of Whitehall and lobbed a howitzer into the Downing Street garden in the general direction of the cabinet room where prime minister John Major and his colleagues were meeting. The mortar broke a few windows but injured nobody; Major, so the story goes, rose without a flicker of alarm and suggested simply that the cabinet adjourn to another room.

A little further down from Downing St, in the middle of the road, is the **Cenotaph**, *the nation's chief memorial to the dead of the two world wars (designed by Edwin Lutyens in 1920) and the site of an official ceremony attended by the Queen and senior politicians of all parties every Armistice Day, 11 November.*

One such ceremony, in 1981, caused a political storm because the then leader of the opposition, Michael Foot, turned up in a coat described by the popular press as a 'donkey jacket'. The good citizens of Britain were outraged, and did not let him forget his supposedly cavalier attitude to the war dead when the Falklands War broke out six months later. Shortly thereafter, Foot and his Labour Party went down to the biggest election defeat for 52 years; Labour leaders, never previously known as the snappiest of dressers, took great care over sartorial codes for years afterwards. Only recently have the likes of Gordon Brown dared to turn up to an official dinner at the Mansion House in a lounge suit rather than a dinner jacket, ruffling those establishment feathers all over again.

Whitehall at this point becomes Parliament St; take the first turning to the right, King Charles St, which forges between two imposing sets of government offices.

To the right is the **Foreign and Commonwealth Office**, once the control tower of a vast empire and a building that caused one of the biggest architectural rows in London's history when it was commissioned in the 1860s. The architect commissioned for the job, Sir George Gilbert Scott, was a dedicated Gothic Revivalist who initially came up with a hallucinatory complex of turrets and courtyards that looked like an over-ornate version of the Loire chateau at Blois. The ageing prime minister, Lord Palmerston, had more classical tastes, however, and consigned this plan to the dustbin with a withering attack in parliament. 'We all know that our northern climate does not overpower us with an excess of sunshine,' Palmerston blustered. 'Then, for Heaven's sake, let us have buildings whose interior admits, and whose exterior reflects, what light there is.' Sent scurrying back to the drawing board, Scott came up with an updated sort of Venetian palace which blended Italian and

Byzantine styles and featured a profusion of rounded arches. Again Palmerston voiced his displeasure, calling the new proposal 'neither one thing nor t'other, a regular mongrel affair', and again Scott was told to start from scratch.

This time, the architect was savvy enough to realize that his Gothic fantasies would never satisfy his political masters. 'I bought some costly books on Italian architecture and set vigorously to work,' he explained. The end result was certainly lavish, but unlike his earlier proposals eminently forgettable. The best things about the Foreign Office are its ornate interior courtyards. Unfortunately, unless you know someone who works there and can let you in, you are unlikely ever to see them.

> *At the end of King Charles St, as you come out into St James's Park, you'll see a pile of wartime sandbags to your left. These mark the entrance to the* **Cabinet War Rooms***, the underground world where British leaders met in secret during the Second World War and the essential work of government was carried out (open daily, 9.30–5.15, and from 10 in the winter; adm)*

Winston Churchill had the basement of a number of government buildings converted in preparation for war in 1938, and he, his cabinet and 500 civil servants worked down here throughout the conflict, protected from the bombing by several layers of thick concrete. The floor below the present exhibition contained a canteen, hospital, shooting range and sleeping quarters. The upper floor, on public display, was where the cabinet met and communications were maintained with the outside world. Churchill, whose office was quite literally a converted broom cupboard, kept a direct line open to President Roosevelt in Washington; all other telephone connections were operated from an unwieldy old-fashioned switchboard and scrambled, for perverse reasons of security, via Selfridge's department store on Oxford Street.

The War Rooms, with their Spartan period furniture and maps marking the British Empire in red, are a magnificent evocation of the wartime atmosphere. A pity, then, that the curators do not allow the place simply to speak for itself. They have piled on the nostalgia with broadcasts of Churchill's wartime speeches, wailing air-raid sirens in the corridors and any number of absurd nostalgia-trip souvenirs in the gift shop: 'careless talk costs lives' mugs and even a ration-ticket recipe book.

> *Turn left on to Horse Guards Rd, and then left again on to Great George St which leads into* **Parliament Square***. The square is full of monumental statues to British statesmen including Palmerston, Disraeli and Winston Churchill (the stooping Churchill, as fashioned by Ivor Roberts-Jones in 1974, is heated from within to stop the pigeon droppings sticking). Straight ahead is the distinctive tower of Big Ben, and to the right loom the flying buttresses of Westminster Abbey.*

Westminster started out as a piece of swampy, brambly ground called Thorney Island, a backwater more than a mile upstream from Roman Londinium. Little is known for certain about its development before Edward the Confessor established it as his centre of government in the 11th century. Folk tales nevertheless abound about its origins. One story has it that St Peter himself pointed out the site of the future abbey to a humble 7th-century fisherman called Edric, who then managed to sell his miraculous story to King Sebert of the East Saxons. An abbey of some sort was almost certainly built at the time, but it did not take on political importance until the reign of Edward the Confessor.

After Edward, there was a significant shift in London's balance of power, the City remaining the preserve of the merchants while Westminster became the centre of the royal court. The two poles competed for centuries; a wrestling match between Westminster and the City in 1222 degenerated into a running battle lasting for days. The printer William Caxton set up his press in Westminster in the late 15th century, while his pupil Wynkyn de Worde operated from St Bride's in the City. The division between the two centres is still felt to this day, even if the geographical gap between them has been reduced by urban development and modern transport. Regrettably, both have lost something of their human touch. Most residents moved out of the two areas long ago, and they are almost exclusively given over to their prime pursuits: commerce in the City, politics here in Westminster.

The Palace of Westminster

*To visit the **Houses of Parliament**, you should head for St Stephen's entrance, which is roughly half way along the complex of buildings. Visiting arrangements for parliament are phenomenally complicated, and vary according to your nationality; you might well find that telephoning in advance (© 0171–219 3000 , or © 219 4272 for information on what is being debated) will avoid wasting time. The usual timetable (always open to interruption according to the day's agenda) is as follows. For debates in the House of Commons (open to all): Mon–Thurs, 2.30–10 and Fri, 9.30–3. For Question Time, the daily duel between ministers and their detractors: Mon–Thurs, 2.30–3.30; to be sure of getting in you need to apply in advance to your MP if you are British, and to your embassy if you are not. If you turn up on spec, you must queue outside St Stephen's entrance; don't expect to sit down before 5pm. Debates in the House of Lords: Wed from 2.30pm (until debates finish), Thurs from 3pm, Fri from 11am, and occasionally Mon. Note that both houses have long recesses, particularly in the summer, and that debates of particular public interest are likely to be very crowded. To see the rest of the Palace of Westminster* *(notably Westminster Hall) you need to apply for a permit about two months in advance from your MP or embassy. It's a good idea whatever your arrangements to bring your passport and leave behind any large bags or cameras. You should also dress reasonably formally. The one bit of good news amid all this mayhem is that the Houses of Parliament, once you get in, come free of charge.*

The best way to approach the Palace of Westminster is to imagine it as a multi-layered onion. Most of today's building is the dizzy virtuoso work of Charles Barry and Augustus Pugin, two Victorian architects working at the height of their powers to replace the old parliament destroyed by fire in 1834. Their building's neo-Gothic luxuriance is both an expression of Victorian self-confidence and a throwback to the medieval origins of the English parliamentary system. As you wander through its corridors and peer into its grand chambers, you have a sense of several moments in history converging at one point: matters of pressing actuality are debated inside a Victorian secular cathedral, which in turn is modelled on buildings and institutions dating back to the 11th century.

The story of the palace begins with **Westminster Hall**, which has survived the centuries more or less intact. The hall was originally a banqueting chamber built by King William Rufus, the son of William the Conqueror, in 1097. Its true glory dates from the end of the 14th century, when Richard II's architect Henry Yevele raised the walls, and Hugh Herland built the magnificent oak hammerbeam roof. The Hall was the meeting-place of the Grand Council, a committee of barons which discussed policy with the monarch in an early incarnation of parliament. Westminster Hall also became the nation's main law court, where such luminaries as Anne Boleyn, Sir Thomas More and Charles I were tried and condemned. After the restoration of the monarchy, royalists avenged themselves for Charles's execution by digging up the body of his parliamentary foe Oliver Cromwell and sticking his head on the roof of Westminster Hall; there it remained until a strong wind blew it away in 1675. The old Hall was a rowdy place, with shops and entertainments to distract the lawyers. Henry VIII built a court for real tennis (an early indoor version of the modern game) next door, and as late as the 1940s restorers found balls jammed in the roof. Monarchs were naturally attracted to the Hall's splendour and until 1821 used it for their coronation banquets. These were not always an unqualified success. When George III and Queen Charlotte celebrated their investiture in 1761, their dinner was lit by 3000 candles. The wax dripped on to many a fine dress, and scores of honoured guests had to be carried out after fainting from the heat. From about 1550, the lower house of parliament, known as the House of Commons, began meeting in St Stephen's Chapel in the main body of the palace. It may seem odd to convene parliament in a religious setting, but the juxtaposition is curiously appropriate: ever since the Reformation, parliament has been a symbol of the primacy of Protestantism in English politics. Pugin and Barry recognized this, and incorporated the chapel into their design. It was only when St Stephen's was destroyed in the Blitz that the House of Commons became an entirely secular chamber, but even today's reconstructed version has an unmistakably religious aura. The benches on which members sit look like choir stalls; the Speaker's chair is like an altar before which members bow on their way in and out; the division lobby, where votes are counted, resembles a vestry or ante-chapel. If the atmosphere of the medieval parliaments has persisted, the same cannot exactly be said for procedure. Parliament's power in the early days was precarious to say the least and depended in large measure on the indulgence of the reigning monarch. The change began with a provocation that even parliament could not tolerate. In 1621 King James I tore out pages in the *Commons Journal* asserting the right of members to deal 'with all matters of grievance and policy'; parliament felt so antagonized that it took steps to bar royalty from its proceedings altogether. In 1642 Charles I became the last monarch ever to set foot in the House of Commons, and seven years later parliament abolished the monarchy outright—albeit temporarily—at the end of the Civil War.

The role of the modern parliament was largely defined by the Glorious Revolution of 1688, which overthrew the despotic James II and forever banned Catholics from occupying the crown. Henceforth legislation was decided by parliament alone; the monarch had the right only to advise and, in exceptional circumstances, block new laws by refusing the Royal Assent. There was no provision, however, for the very key to a democratic society, universal suffrage. For much of the 18th century, parliament was in the hands of a few special interest groups that took little or no interest in the well-being of the vast proportion of the population. It was not until 1832 that the first Reform Act broadened the base of voters beyond a clique of influential aristocrats and their cronies, and not until 1928 that all adult voters, male and female, had the right to cast their ballot. The swing towards democratic representation was largely the result of fear; fear that the popular revolutions sweeping France in the early 19th century might take hold in Britain if concessions were not made to the will of the people. It is worth remembering that Barry and Pugin set to work in the middle of this transition period; the changing times are to a large extent reflected in their building.

Pugin Rubs his Hands and Wins the Commission of a Lifetime

The inadequacies of the old Palace of Westminster were recognized as early as the 1820s. A new building might have been proposed there and then, but ministers baulked at the cost of such a scheme so soon after the Napoleonic Wars. It took a calamity to spring them into action. On 16 October, 1834, the Clerk of Works, a

Mr Richard Wibley, was asked to destroy several bundles of old talley-sticks in a cellar furnace. The fire raged out of control, and the whole palace was soon engulfed in flames. *The Times* newspaper wrote jocularly the following day that the 'motion for a new House is carried without a division'.

Augustus Pugin had been an eyewitness to the 1834 fire and revelled in every minute of it. He hated classical architecture and neoclassical architects and was only too happy to see their various improvements to the old parliament go up in smoke. 'There is nothing much to regret and much to rejoice in a vast quantity of Soane's mixtures and Wyatt's heresies effectually consigned to oblivion,' he wrote. 'Oh what a glorious sight to see his composition mullions and cement pinnacles and battlements flying and cracking...' Fearing that a neoclassical architect would be asked to design the new parliament, Pugin put his name forward and, although he was only 24 at the time, was named assistant to the older, more experienced Charles Barry. Theirs was a near perfect partnership. Barry sketched out the broad lines of the design, while Pugin attended to the details of ornamentation. Some of Pugin's work was lost in the bombing of the Second World War; you can nevertheless admire the sheer fervour of his imagination in the sculpted wood and stone, the stained glass, tiled floors, wallpaper and painted ceilings that abound along every corridor and in every room. Despite Pugin's rantings against the classicists, he was happy to go along with Barry's essentially classical design and Gothicize it to his heart's content. The Palace of Westminster's blend of architectural restraint (Barry) and decorative frenzy (Pugin) is one of its most appealing aspects.

Pugin went mad and died in 1852, and so never lived to work on the most famous feature of the new building, the clock tower at the eastern end known universally by the name of its giant bell, **Big Ben** (*visits to the clock must be arranged through an MP or serving member of the House of Lords, or for horologists with a specific interest in the clock, directly through Chris Hillier on © 0171–219 4874*). Nowadays the clock is renowned for its accuracy and its resounding tolling of the hour, but the story of its construction is one of incredible incompetence and bungling. The 320ft-high clock tower was finished in 1854, but because of a bitter disagreement between the two clockmakers, Frederick Dent and Edmund Beckett Denison, there was nothing to put inside it for another three years. Finally a great bell made up according to Denison's instructions was dragged across Westminster Bridge by a cart and 16 horses. But, as it was being laid out ready for hoisting into position, a 4ft crack suddenly appeared, and the bell had to be abandoned. Similar embarrassments ensued over the next two years, until a functioning, but still cracked bell was at last erected at the top of the tower. It remains defective to this day.

Why the name Big Ben? The most common explanation is that the bell was named after Sir Benjamin Hall, the unpopular Chief Commissioner of Works who had to explain all the cock-ups in his project to an unimpressed House of Commons. Another theory has it that Big Ben was in fact Benjamin Caunt, a corpulent boxer who owned a pub a couple of hundred yards away in St Martin's Lane. The chimes, which are well-known around the world because they are broadcast by the BBC World Service, are a bastardized version of the aria 'I Know That My Redeemer Liveth' from Handel's *Messiah*. Denison filched the idea from the similar chant emitted by the bells of St Mary's church in Cambridge, where he had been an undergraduate. The words accompanying the bong-bong-bong-BONG are:

> *All through this hour Lord be my Guide*
> *And by Thy Power no foot shall slide.*

After such an inauspicious beginning, the clock has had a remarkably uneventful history, only seriously going wrong during the Second World War, when the belfry stage of the tower was damaged and the clock-face shattered by bombing. Once, in 1949, the hands stopped turning under the weight of a flock of starlings. Since then, apart from a dry bearing which stopped the clock twice in 1997, Big Ben has proved unfailingly accurate. The tower itself has a shadier, less well-known side, though, as an occasional prison. Emmeline Pankhurst, the suffragette pioneer, spent several days in confinement there in 1902.

Order, Order and Chaos in the House

From the moment that Barry and Pugin's building opened in 1852, it set an entirely new tone to proceedings in parliament. It was no longer just a legislative assembly, it was a *club*, the best club in London, as Winston Churchill liked to say. Like so many British institutions, parliament is a place of deeply embedded rituals, established by a ruling order intent on protecting itself and its idiosyncratic ways; even if the institution has changed, the rituals have survived out of a quirky fondness for the past. Whatever its modern way of functioning, parliament still *feels* like the exclusive terrain of upper-class men who drink and smoke cigars together and decide the fate of the nation in an atmosphere of elegant sparring.

Debates at Westminster are famous for their witty repartee and banter, which all too often takes precedence over the substance of the topic itself. 'Stop a minute, what did we decide?' the early Victorian prime minister Lord Melbourne once asked the Lords in confusion. 'Is it to lower the price of bread, or isn't it? It does not matter what we say but, mind, we must say it all the same.' The daily gruelling of ministers known as Question Time, which once a week features the prime minister, is an opportunity for the opposition to prove its debating abilities as much as its prowess in unnerving or embarrassing the government.

The floor of the House of Commons has produced some wonderful rhetorical moments, not least when one member has sought to insult another. The Victorian statesman Benjamin Disraeli had a particular talent in this department, once saying of his self-satisfied Whig rival William Gladstone: 'He has not a single redeeming defect'; or again of a bumptious young member called John Bright: 'He is a self-made man, and worships his creator.' Churchill described Clement Attlee as a 'sheep in sheep's clothing' and 'a modest little man with much to be modest about'. More recently, Labour's Denis Healey said that being attacked by the ineffectual Conservative minister Geoffrey Howe was 'like being savaged by a dead sheep'.

But members of parliament are also capable of extraordinarily puerile behaviour, even in the quasi-religious atmosphere of the House of Commons. Some of the masculine stuffiness has been tempered by the arrival of over a hundred new women MPs in the 1997 intake, but even they have been forced to submit a formal complaint about sexist taunts ('Get back in the kitchen!', 'She's got PMT!', etc.) thrown across the chamber. No image of the place is more memorable than that of the Speaker yelling 'Order! Order!' to get unruly members to shut up and listen. To see debates in which backbenchers chant, shout out jibes and cheap jokes and generally ensure that they drown out whoever is speaking at the time is to realize that we have not come that far from the atmosphere of 1782, when the German Lutheran pastor Carl Philip Moritz noted with horror: 'It is not all that uncommon to see a member lying stretched out on one of the benches while others are debating... Some crack nuts while others eat oranges...' But in parliament there is bad behaviour and bad behaviour. Like any self-respecting club, Westminster has its rules. And while it might be fine to scream your head off as a member of an opposing party is trying to put his or her point across, certain other lapses are not. Members must not address each other by name, but rather by the constituency they represent, or at the very least 'my honourable friend' if it is a party colleague or 'the honourable member' if it is an opponent. The Speaker can call a member to order for instances of what is deemed to be 'unparliamentary language'. Accusing an MP of lying or being drunk is unacceptable; rather they must be demonstrated to have been 'witholding certain facts', or uttering 'terminological inexactitudes', or 'appearing to be tired and emotional'. Terms to which Speakers have taken objection in the past include: blackguard, coward, git, guttersnipe, hooligan, rat, swine, stoolpigeon and traitor. A member must withdraw such a word if called upon to do so; otherwise he or she faces disciplinary proceedings that can include expulsion from the chamber for a certain number of days.

The Good, the Bad and the Doddery: the House of Lords

If the House of Commons sometimes seems a touch out of date, it is a paragon of modernity compared to the fuddy-duddy anachronisms of the **House of Lords**. The 650 members of the Commons are at least democratically elected; the 1000-odd peers in the Lords (nobody seems to know quite how many there are) earn their place either by appointment or, *mirabile dictu*, by heredity. More than half of these superior parliamentarians, whose job it is to check and in some cases delay Commons legislation, owe their position entirely to an accident of birth (and, to be sure, it is only male heirs who enjoy the privilege). Luckily, most of the hereditary peers stay well away from the Lords. The place is nevertheless peopled with a fair smattering of octogenarian upper-class degenerates, not to mention a well-known massage-parlour frequenter and a convicted thief. The political parties use the Lords as a place to kick their senior no-goodniks upstairs, or as a place to park their elder statesmen once they have outlived their usefulness in the Commons. The place is not without its remarkable figures working assiduously to exploit the parliamentary system to the full (and, in some cases, working to obstruct the more objectionable pieces of Commons law-making), but this hard core is hardly helped by the anachronistic absurdity of the immediate surroundings.

Back in 1909, Lloyd George described the peers as 'broken bottles stuck on a park wall to keep off radical poachers from lordly preserves'; if the institution was out of date then, it is even more out of date now. If you attend a Lords session (incidentally, in the finest of Pugin's rooms, all glistening with red and gold) you'll notice how, in stark contrast to the fun and games of Question Time in the Commons, the debates drone on interminably. This is because, unlike in the Commons, there are never any time limits. If an inbred country squire with a grievance about hunting dogs wants to stutter on until four o'clock in the morning, nobody can stop him as long as his remarks pertain in some way to the debate at hand. If you think the Commons habit of calling another member of parliament 'honourable member' is strange, come to the Lords where modes of address include 'my noble kinsman' or even (for the 26 Anglican bishops) 'the right reverend prelate'. And all this for a crowd whom Lloyd George castigated for having no credentials ('They only require a certificate of birth—to prove that they are the first of the litter. You would not choose a spaniel on these principles'). Everybody recognizes that the House of Lords is undemocratic, and yet reform has been a long time a-coming. For years the Conservative Party assumed it could count on the Lords' support in times of crisis (if necessary by shaking a few bushes on country estates to round up the hereditary crew), and Labour—while in opposition—found the place too useful as a forum for authoritative swipes against the government. Tony Blair has now promised some sort of overhaul, but no details have been given at the time of this writing. So for the moment the British political scene will continue to be punctuated by the likes of Viscount Montgomery of Alamein (imagine *him* as president of the European Commission), Lord Archer of Weston-super-Mare (better known as the airport novelist Jeffrey Archer) and the magnificently named Thomas Galloway Dunlop de Roy de Blicquy Galbraith, the noble Lord Strathclyde. It sounds like the *dramatis personae* of a play by Oscar Wilde, but it's no way to run a country.

*If you are interested in the origins of the parliamentary buildings, you should make a detour at this point to the **Jewel Tower**, which is on Abingdon St opposite the far tower of the Palace of Westminster (open daily 10–1, 2–6 exc Oct–Mar when it closes at 4; adm).*

Along with Westminster Hall, this is the only surviving relic of the 1834 fire and is now a museum containing a collection of pre-fire remains. Unfortunately there are no more jewels left; instead you can enjoy an excellent exhibition detailing the history of the Houses of Parliament ('Parliament Past and Present'). There is also a small but mind-crushingly dull display on weights and measures, the legacy of the Jewel Tower's 70 years as a public office for this peculiarly uninspiring topic.

*With or without the detour, you should now return to Parliament Square and walk round to the left where the first church building you come across is **St Margaret's Westminster**.*

This white stone church is best known for its society weddings: its marriage register includes such names as Samuel Pepys, John Milton and Winston Churchill. The building itself, which does not usually get much attention what with Big Brother the abbey standing next door, is a patchwork of relics and architectural styles dating back to the late 15th century. Edward VI's evil protector Lord Somerset tried to demolish it to provide stones for Somerset House but was rebuffed by angry parishioners who chased his men away with clubs and bows. St Margaret's suffered more serious damage in the Second World War and has been extensively rebuilt since. Its most prized possession, the east window, is a stained-glass depiction of the betrothal of Catherine of Aragon to Prince Arthur, the eldest son of Henry VII. The window, commissioned from Spanish craftsmen, celebrates a fatefully shortlived union, since Arthur died and Catherine married his brother, the future Henry VIII, before it could be installed. The glass was tactfully removed to Waltham Abbey in Essex and only brought back in 1758.

*Leaving St Margaret's, hug close to the abbey to the left and walk round to the western entrance. Before you turn the corner you'll notice an elegant Beaux Arts-style building on the other side of the street. This is the **Methodist Central Hall**, a popular venue for organ recitals and public meetings. To your right you'll see a 1960s monstrosity, the Queen Elizabeth II Conference Centre, on which the less said the better. Turn instead to the wonders of **Westminster Abbey**.*

Westminster Abbey

Admission to the Abbey is free for services or prayers. For visitors the nave is open Mon–Fri 9.20–4.45, last adm 3.45, and Sat 9.20–2.45 and 3.45–6; adm charged from March 1998 onwards. The Cloisters are open daily 8–6;

free. The Royal Chapels, Statesman's Aisle and Poets' Corner are open Mon–Fri, 9–4.45 and Sat, 9–2.45; adm. The Chapter House, Pyx Chamber and Undercroft Museum are open daily 10.30–4; adm. Guided tours conducted by the vergers are also available © 0171–222 7110 to book.

It is impossible to overestimate the symbolic importance of Westminster Abbey in English culture. This is where monarchs are crowned and buried, where the Anglican Church derives its deepest inspiration, and where the nation as a whole lionizes its artistic and political heroes. To construct an equivalent in Paris you would have to roll Notre Dame, the Panthéon and the Père Lachaise cemetery all into one, and probably add a bit of the Invalides and Versailles as well. No other country invests so much importance in a single building. There is, quite literally, nowhere like it.

The comparison with France is an apt one, since architecturally the abbey derives its inspiration from the great cathedrals at Reims and Amiens and the Sainte-Chapelle in Paris. 'A great French thought expressed in excellent English,' one epithet has it. The abbey's origins go back to the mists of the Dark Ages; it found a mystical patron in Edward the Confessor, saint and monarch; it was rebuilt from scratch in the finest Gothic traditions from the 13th until the 16th century; and it was completed in 1745 when one of England's finest architects, Nicholas Hawksmoor, added the towers at the western end. Thus the abbey spans virtually the whole of modern English history. To be buried there, or at least to have a plaque erected, is still the highest state honour for an English citizen. The tombs of the medieval kings and other relics bestow much of the legitimacy to which the modern monarchy can still lay claim. If St Paul's (*see* Walk VIII) is a monument to the secular wealth of London, Westminster Abbey enshrines the mystical power of the crown.

The story of Edric the fisherman, told above, is only one of the founding myths of the abbey church of St Peter at Westminster. Bishop Mellitus, the builder of the first St Paul's, is said to have consecrated an early version in the 7th century; St Dunstan is also believed to have worked on building an abbey here 300 years later. The only thing for certain is that a religious institution was on the site when Edward the Confessor became Saxon king in 1042. Edward's abbey was consecrated just eight days before he died in 1066, and features in a panel of the Bayeux tapestry depicting his funeral ceremony. The importance of Westminster as a royal counterweight to the City was reinforced when Edward's protegé William the Conqueror had himself crowned in the new abbey on Christmas Day 1066. The link between Christ the King and William the King could not have been made more explicit; to reinforce the point William's men attacked and killed several members of the crowd outside whose cries of enthusiasm they mistook for the start of a riot.

Edward the Confessor was canonized in 1161, and a monk called Osbert de Clere began singing about his great merits, not least his chastity (for which there is scant evidence). The Edward cult served the crown well, not least in its political struggle with the City merchants, and it is perhaps no surprise that a king with more than his fair share of trouble with the City, Henry III, should decide to rebuild a bigger, finer abbey in his ancestor's honour. Henry's excuse for knocking down the old church, that it was 'consumed with excessive age', was a spurious excuse for a bit of self-glorification. The effort almost bankrupted him, and he had to pawn his own jewels to pay successive master-builders—Henry de Reyns, John of Gloucester and Robert of Beverley—and complete work on the east end. The nave remained untouched for another two centuries, and was not finished until 1532. The long delay was all to the abbey's benefit, however, for it allowed architectural techniques to catch up with construction; the final result includes such pinnacles of English Gothic as the Chapter House (based closely on the Sainte-Chapelle) and the fan-vaulted Henry VII Chapel in the late Gothic extension to the east end.

It was Westminster's association with the crown that saved the abbey during the dissolution of the monasteries in the late 1530s, when it escaped with just a few smashed windows and broken ornaments. Its revenues were severely depleted, however, and transferred to the coffers of St Paul's (hence, at least according to folklore etymology, the expression 'robbing Peter to pay Paul'). To this day the abbey remains a 'royal peculiar', which means it is run directly by the crown rather than the Church of England. The royal connection made it a target during the Civil War, when Cromwell's army used it as a dormitory and smashed the altar rails. Cromwell succumbed to its lure once he was Lord Protector, however, and had himself buried in the abbey after his death in 1658. His body, as noted above, was dug up at the Restoration and eventually reburied at the foot of the gallows at Tyburn. After the Civil War, the abbey was once again given over to burials and coronations. Aside from royals, the place is stuffed with memorials to politicians (in the Statesman's Aisle), poets (in Poets' Corner), actors, scientists and engineers.

The coronation ceremony has become familiar around the world thanks to television re-runs of the investiture of Elizabeth II in 1953, the first coronation to be televised. But ceremonies have not always gone as smoothly as the establishment might have liked. Richard I had a bat swooping around his head during his ceremony, a sign perhaps of bad luck to come. Richard II lost a shoe in the Abbey, while James II's crown wobbled and nearly fell off during his parade down Whitehall. George IV was so weighed down by his outrageously extravagant coronation garb that he nearly fainted and had to be revived with smelling salts.

Perhaps he was distressed by the thought that Queen Caroline had been locked out of the Abbey and was banging on the doors throughout the five-hour ceremony. In the words of one commentator, George looked 'more like an elephant than a man', but he still found time to flirt with one of the ladies in the congregation before the Archbishop of Canterbury's sermon. In reaction to such licentiousness, George's successor William IV had a coronation so austere it was dubbed the 'Half-Crownation'. The new king, who thought the ceremony 'a pointless piece of flummery', chattered all the way through and left early. Talking out of turn was a problem, too, at Victoria's coronation in 1837 when two incompetent trainbearers disrupted proceedings with a quarrel about how to walk down the aisle. Furthermore, the officiating clergy got their seats muddled, one lord of the realm tripped and fell down the stairs from the throne and the Bishop of Bath nearly ended the ceremony prematurely by turning two pages of the order of service at the same time. Most embarrassingly of all, the Archbishop of Canterbury forced a ruby ring intended for Victoria's little finger on to her ring finger, causing the young queen to wince with pain. 'Some malignant spell broods over all our most solemn ceremonials and inserts into them some feature which makes them all ridiculous,' lamented Robert Cecil, the future Lord Salisbury, in 1860.

The mishaps continued into the 20th century. Edward VII's archbishop stumbled while carrying the crown of state and nearly put it the wrong way round on Edward's head. At a rehearsal for George VI's coronation, the Orb went missing until the six-year-old Princess Margaret was found playing with it on the floor. It was only with the arrival of television that the royal retinue pulled out all the stops to put on a faultless show (reaching a pinnacle of perfection at the funeral of Princess Diana—when Elton John played *Candle in the Wind* to the largest worldwide live television audience ever known).

> Pick up a floor plan at the entrance of the abbey; what follows is a list of the main sights starting at the west end and proceeding clockwise around the abbey complex. Everything west of the choir screen is free; beyond is the old east end, now St Edward's Chapel; and beyond that the late Gothic extension including the Henry VII Chapel. The cloisters and Chapter House are off the end of the south transept.

The Nave

Measuring 103ft from floor to ceiling, the nave of Westminster Abbey is by far the tallest in England, an indication of the influence of French architects for whom height was an important means of expressing their awe before the Almighty. But height was not something that the abbey's architects, notably Henry Yevele in the late 14th century, wanted to emphasize too strongly, and its effects are diluted in a number of ways. The nave is very long as well as high, giving an impression of general grandeur but not necessarily of loftiness. The columns, made of Purbeck marble, grow darker towards the ceiling, thus further deadening the effect of height. And the ceiling decorations push the eye not upwards, but along towards the altar. Overall, ornamentation is just as important as effects of perspective. As you come in, there is a 14th-century gilded painting of Richard II. The north aisle of the nave has become crowded with memorials and stones to politicians, earning the nickname **Statesman's Aisle**. From the relief memorial to William Pitt the Younger above the west door, to the monument to the Earl of Stanhope against the choir screen, you can spot the names of those who did most influence British political life in the 18th and 19th centuries. Among the characters who crop up elsewhere in this book you can find Sir Robert Peel (founder of the Metropolitan Police), prime ministers Palmerston, Gladstone and Disraeli, Chamberlains Joseph and Neville, Lloyd George and Clement Attlee. Plenty of other walks of life are celebrated in this part of the abbey, notably scientists and engineers including Michael Faraday (a memorial tablet) and Sir Isaac Newton (a splendid monument against the choir screen by William Kent).

The Choir and St Edward's Chapel

The first attraction beyond the ticket counters, the choir screen, is a 19th-century reworking by Edward Blore of the gilded 13th-century original. Note the elegant black and white marble floor, and the heraldic shields commemorating the families who gave money to construct the abbey in the 13th century. Behind the High Altar is St Edward's Chapel, the epicentre of the abbey with its memorials to medieval kings around the Coronation Chair. Until November 1996, when it was finally removed to Edinburgh Castle, the simple gilded wooden chair contained the Stone of Scone, the most sacred symbol of the kings of Scotland, which was stolen by Edward I in 1279 and arrogantly kept for five and a bit centuries here in England. Of the tombs, the finest certainly used to be the golden memorial encrusted with jewels which Henry III built for Edward the Confessor. All that remains now is the base. Henry himself lies nearby, in a simple chest built so that the body could be removed at any time and the bones extracted in case the English army wanted to brandish them on their next campaign in Scotland. Richard II and his wife Anne of Bohemia lie together on a single tomb. Their effigies used to hold hands but their arms have snapped off. Richard's jawbone was removed by an enterprising pupil from Westminster School who pulled it out through a hole in the tomb in 1776; the missing bone was only returned to poor old Richard in 1916. Henry V, the man who beat the French at Agincourt, has his own mini-chapel towards the back featuring sculpted scenes of his exploits. Until the 18th century it was possible to see the corpse of Henry's widow, Catherine of Valois, lying embalmed in an open tomb. The diarist Samuel Pepys came to Westminster Abbey on his 36th birthday and gave himself a treat by kissing the leathery ex-queen full on the lips. Perhaps to discourage such behaviour, the abbey authorities bundled her into a tomb in St Nicholas's chapel in 1776.

Henry VII Chapel

The penny-pinching Henry VII managed one great feat of artistic patronage during his reign, this extraordinary fan-vaulted chapel which is nominally dedicated to the Virgin Mary but is in fact a glorification of the Tudor line of monarchs. It is a supreme example of Perpendicular style—an English offshoot of late Gothic that flowered at a time when most of Europe was already well stuck into the Renaissance. Henrys VII and VIII, Edward VI, Mary and Elizabeth I are all buried here in style, along with a healthy sprinkling of their contemporaries and successors. Elizabeth shares her huge tomb with her embittered half-sister Mary in a curious after-death gesture of reconciliation. The bodies believed to be the two princes murdered in the Tower of London in 1483 also have a resting place here, as do two of James I's children, Sophia and Mary, who died in infancy. The highlight of the chapel, though, is the decoration. The wondrous ceiling looks like an intricate mesh of finely spun cobwebs, while the wooden choirstalls are carved with exotic creatures and adorned with brilliantly colourful heraldic flags.

Poets' Corner

The south transept and the adjoining St Faith's Chapel are part of the original 13th-century abbey structure, and boast a series of wall paintings and some superbly sculpted figures of angels. Geoffrey Chaucer was buried in the south transept in 1400, and ever since other poets and writers have vied to have a place next to him after their deaths. When Edmund Spenser, author of *The Faerie Queen*, was buried in 1599, several writers tossed their unpublished manuscripts into the grave with him. His contemporary, the playwright Ben Jonson, asked modestly for a grave 'two feet by two feet' and consequently was buried upright. Few of the writers commemorated in Poets' Corner are actually interred here; among the 'genuine' ones are Dryden, Samuel Johnson, Sheridan, Browning and Tennyson. Having a memorial in Poets' Corner is deemed the ultimate accolade for a writer. Shakespeare nevertheless had to wait 130 years for his, William Blake 150, Anthony Trollope 111; a campaign to have Virginia Woolf honoured is still under way. To free up more space in the increasingly crowded corner, the abbey authorities have recently installed a stained glass window with new memorials to parvenus such as Pope, Herrick and Wilde.

Chapter House, Pyx Chamber, Abbey Museum

A pretty cloister (note the flamboyant tracery of the windows) leads to these three annexes to the abbey. The octagonal Chapter House, completed in 1255 and used sporadically as the meeting-place for medieval parliaments, reproduces in miniature the techniques of weight distribution used at the Sainte-Chapelle in Paris. A single central shaft supports a vaulted roof and eight bays containing tall stained-glass windows. The intricate floor tiles, bearing heraldic symbols, are generally reckoned to be the finest examples of their kind in England. The Pyx Chamber, which dates back to Edward the Confessor's abbey, is named after the box, or pyx, containing standard pieces of medieval gold and silver. These coins are still checked and counted in a ritualistic annual ceremony at Goldsmiths' Hall in the City. Finally, the Abbey Museum (*extra adm*) contains many treasures once displayed inside the church proper, including the military gear Henry V used at Agincourt. The museum also acts as a kind of medieval Madame Tussaud's, with its collection of wax effigies of royalty and other VIPs that were once used in funeral processions.

---

*Emerging from the cloisters, you come into Dean's Yard, a pretty square flanked by abbey buildings which is unfortunately crowded out by parked cars. Through a narrow passage to the left is Little Dean's Yard and the complex of buildings of **Westminster School**. These are not usually open to the public, so walk around discreetly.*

Westminster is one of England's most famous 'public' schools. Public confusingly means precisely the opposite of what it says, and Westminster, along with Eton, Harrow and Winchester, is one of most exclusive private schools in the country. Originally part of the abbey next door, its buildings date back to the 11th century. There have been many additions since, including Lord Burlington's College building (1722–30), inspired by a Palladian theatre in Vicenza. The school boasts a fine pedigree of old boys including Ben Jonson, Christopher Wren, Edward Gibbon, John Gielgud and Andrew Lloyd Webber. Pupils are easy to spot because they wear their smart clothes with a fashionable degree of shabbiness and talk like BBC announcers. Westminster is one of the more progressive of the public schools—it has admitted girls aged 16–18 since 1972—but nevertheless holds on to some eccentric old traditions. Every Shrove Tuesday the school cook throws a pancake into a jostling scrum of pupils; the one who grabs the largest piece of batter wins a guinea (just over £1) from the dean of the abbey.

Return to Dean's Yard and continue down to the left where the square runs into Tufton St. The third turning on the left, Dean Trench St, leads *to the church of **St John's Smith Square** (entrance on both north and south sides).*

This attractive open-plan Georgian church, designed by Thomas Archer and completed in 1728, was grossly under-appreciated in its first 200 years; Queen Anne compared it to an upturned footstool (and indeed the crypt café is called The Footstool). Now the church has been converted into a concert hall staging excellent concerts. There are rehearsals most afternoons which are well worth gate-crashing. The atmosphere is light and airy and the acoustics excellent.

*Leave St John's Smith Square by Dean Stanley St, opposite the way you came in. Turn right onto Millbank and keep walking for about 10 minutes, passing Lambeth Bridge along the way, until you come to the Tate Gallery. Before you go on, cast your glance across the Thames to **Vauxhall Cross**, a large, upsettingly futuristic building that houses MI5, Her Majesty's Secret Service (see p.420).*

The Tate Gallery

Founded at the end of the 19th century by the sugar baron Sir Henry Tate of Tate & Lyle fame, this is the second great London art collection after the National Gallery (*open Mon–Sat, 10–5.50, Sun 2–5.50; free, with free guided tours Mon–Fri at 11am, 12 noon, 2pm and 3pm*). In spring 2000 the collection will divide into two: 20th-century international art will move across the river to the massive new **Tate Gallery of Modern Art at Bankside** (*see* p.333); the gallery here will be renamed the **Tate Gallery of British Art** and the entire building will be devoted to a chronological survey of home-grown works from the Renaissance until now. This will vastly increase the proportion of art on display: for now, only 15 per cent of the Tate's total collection of over 5000 paintings and 50,000 drawings and sketches is viewable at one time.

If you're visiting the gallery before spring 2000, you will see a collection which breaks down clearly into three distinct parts: British art, 20th-century modern art, and James Stirling's attractive Clore Gallery extension, which opened in 1987 and contains an outstanding collection of paintings by the great 19th-century artist J.M.W. Turner.

Just inside the main entrance you will notice one of the main attractions of the gallery—a fascinating transparent collection box for donations. Although this grabs the attention of nearly every visitor to the gallery, it was created by a design company (Casson Wheeler) rather than an artist. From here you can pick up a free floor plan of the gallery and its exhibits. You will probably wish to choose your own itinerary, depending on your tastes: what follows is a description of some of the highlights. By spring 2001, all visitors will have direct on-line access to information about the British art collection; the collection will be arranged chronologically and there will be five new galleries, nine renovated galleries, and a new lower level space for temporary exhibitions.

British Art

British Art may not sound like a promising subject, but the Tate makes it beguilingly attractive. To be sure, there are lots of stuffy, uninteresting portraits and endless country scenes. But the Tate also owns a large number of outstanding examples of Hogarth, Gainsborough, Stubbs, William Blake, Constable, Turner, Whistler, Spencer, Nicholson and Henry Moore. Contemporary painters in the collection include Anthony Caro, Richard Hamilton, David Hockney, Eduardo Paolozzi, Lucian Freud, Howard Hodgkin (winner of the 1985 Turner prize), Richard Long and Frank Auerbach. Highlights include Room 2, which is almost entirely devoted to **Hogarth**'s finest satire, *O the Roast Beef of England*, a depiction of the greed and corruption of France seen through the soldiers, priests and beggars of Calais. Hogarth himself appears, sketchbook in hand, drawing the famous gates of the city while a detachment of soldiers prepares to arrest him. Aside from this picture, however, the Tate catches Hogarth in uncharacteristically sober mood as portrait painter to the great and good, including Thomas Herring, Archbishop of Canterbury. The next few rooms trace the careers of Gainsborough and Zoffany, soft-focus portrait painters in the Watteau mould, Stubbs the horse specialist (who used to paint the horses and then fill in the background later) and the founding president of the Royal Academy, **Sir Joshua Reynolds**. Reynolds adopted the ideal style and classical themes pioneered in Renaissance Italy, adding to it something of the fragrance of the English countryside. His *Three Ladies Adoring a Term of Hymen*, for example, turns four upper-class English sisters into gossiping Greek nymphs with delicate complexions and dainty clothes.

Room 7 is devoted to the terrifying Manichean world of **William Blake** (1757–1827), a man who turned his vivid Biblical and literary nightmares into extraordinarily enigmatic poetry, pen and ink watercolours and prints. We see Adam and Eve in horror as they discover the murdered body of Abel, Nebuchadnezzar crawling in rags like vermin, and Job in all stages of his trials. Blake was a radical anti-materialist, who saw human progress as essentially displeasing to the Almighty. Look at his portrait of Isaac Newton, showing the father of modern physics as a misguided, ape-like classical figure making drawings in the dirt; or his *Ghost of a Flea* in which the painter is told that fleas are inhabited by the souls of bloodthirsty men. Among the most lyrical works here are Blake's illustrations to the *Divine Comedy*, which capture all of Dante's comic perversity as well as the horror of the whirlwinds, the contorted bodies and various tortures including the grue-some well of fire reserved for Pope Nicholas III.

The section on **Victorian painting** starts with the Romantic John Constable and his lyrical depictions of Malvern Hall in Warwickshire and Salisbury Cathedral; it then moves on to John Martin's hallucinogenic visions of heaven with bands of angels suspended from dramatic day-glo clouds. Martin serves as a useful counter-foil to the **Pre-Raphaelites**, the group of mid-Victorian painters who strove to reject the ideal style symbolized by Raphael and his followers, in favour of a natu-ralistic approach more in tune with the real world. The works of Rossetti, Millais, Waterhouse and Burne-Jones cannot really be said to be realistic, however; their strong colours and heart-rending emotions are redolent of a heightened reality, like the application of belladonna to a beautiful pair of eyes. Among the works to look out for are Waterhouse's *Lady of Shalott*, Burne-Jones's *King Cophetua and the Beggar Maid* and Millais' *Ophelia*, shown floating lifelessly in a marshy brook. There are some other Victorian curiosities, notably the work of Richard Dadd, a lunatic asylum inmate who murdered his father, and Augustus Egg's triptych of a fallen woman called *Past and Present*. The final section of the British collection is on Impressionists and Cubists—not the famous French variety, but the little-known sideshoot from across the Channel. The likes of Walter Sickert, Philip Wilson Steer, Augustus John and Stanley Spencer make only a limited impact (although Spencer's vision of bodies emerging from tombs in the country village of Cookham has a cer-tain Hammer-horror compulsiveness). The best pieces here are by foreigners working in England, like the American James Whistler whose *Nocturne in Blue-Green* is a compelling cityscape of the Thames at Chelsea (echoed in later British pictures of London such as Victor Pasmore's *Thames at Chiswick*).

Turner Collection—The Clore Gallery

Joseph Mallord William Turner (1775–1851), the predominant British painter of the 19th century, made arrangements for the bulk of his work to be kept as a national treasure. Although many of his most famous paintings can be found in the National Gallery, this is where students and art lovers can best assess his work—there are more than 300 oil paintings and 37,000 works on paper. Turner was a true pro, rarely seen in public without his sketchpad or his easel. A diehard Romantic, he specialized in seascapes and idealized classical scenes à la Claude Lor-rain. As his work progressed he grew more audacious in his use of light and colour, prefiguring in many ways the experiments of the French Impressionists and often bewildering the artistic establishment in London. Much of his work is a wistful look at the passing of the old rural world and the advent of the industrial revolu-tion; his classically inspired paintings are often penetrating allegories of the aspirations and cruelties of the British Empire. It is hard to pick out individual pictures, especially since the displays tend to change, but try to see some of the following: *Rome from the Vatican* (1820), an idealized portrait of the Eternal City reflecting many of Turner's artistic preoccupations; *Snow Storm: Steam-boat off a Harbour's Mouth*, a virtuoso whirl of chaos on the waves; *A City on a River at Sunset*, a gorgeous, warm study of sky and water, probably in Rouen; and *Peace— Burial at Sea*, a tribute to Turner's fellow painter David Wilkie in which light, mist and smoke mingle in Turner's typical sea setting.

Modern Art

The modern collection is the most popular section of the Tate and it includes well over 5000 works of art (including Carl André's infamous *Equivalent Viii*, a stack of 120 firebricks which caused such a furore when the Tate bought it for a six-figure sum in 1986 that it now qualifies as the gallery's most famous acquisition ever). Works on display at any one time are regularly rotated, and it is hard to predict what will be on display when you visit. One of the best rooms is the excellent **Art Now Space** (see floor plan for directions). This is devoted to contemporary art, and frequently shows some excellent installations, such as Tacita Dean's sound and video exhibit on foley artists, or *Border*, Michal Rovner's video of flocking birds.

Highlights in the main modern galleries include Magritte's disturbing dreamscapes and the desolate cities of Giorgio de Chirico (*Uncertainty of the Poet*). Excellent examples of **German Expressionism** include the nightmare visions of Kirchner, Kokoschka, Nolde and Grosz; Grosz's typically grim *Suicide* is a red-stained view of a man shooting himself while a prostitute looks on apathetically. **Matisse** dominates Room 24, particularly his early *Inattentive Reader* (1919) and his experiment with paper cut-outs, *The Snail* (which one of the guards insists is called the Snail because a tiny nick at the very top of the picture looks exactly like a snail making its way slowly across the picture). Thereafter, the collection veers off in a hundred directions. **Francis Bacon**'s contorted, all-too human forms, especially the series of pictures of his friend George Dyer, are fascinating to some people, as are **Giacometti**'s gravely pessimistic series of stick-like figures. Abstract painting is well represented by Jackson Pollock and Mark Rothko; Pop Art by Roy Lichtenstein's comic-book *Whaam!* and Andy Warhol's *Marilyn Diptych* which parodies the movie superstar's transformation into a vulgar commodity.

> *From the Tate Gallery catch the 3, 77a or 159 bus back to the West End; otherwise it is a 10-minute, rather meandering walk to ⊖ Pimlico. From the main entrance, turn right and right again into Atterbury St, then left into John Islip St, right on the Vauxhall Bridge Road, left into Drummond Gate and finally round to the right on Bessborough St which leads to the Underground station.*

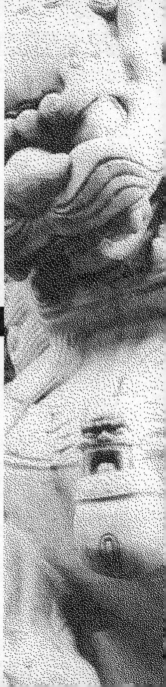

III: Covent Garden and Soho

Start: *Trafalgar Square.*

Walking time: *2½ hours, not counting time lingering in bars or museums.*

III: Covent Garden and Soho

200 metres
200 yards

N

OXFORD STREET

TOTTENHAM
COURT ROAD

French
Protestant
Church

St Patrick's
Church

SOHO

CHARING CROSS ROAD

DENMARK ST.

SQUARE

BATEMAN'S BLDGS.

MANETTE ST.

GREEK STREET

FRITH STREET

FLITCROFT ST.

PHOENIX ST.

WEDGEWOOD

K

MENS

O

R

Foyle's
Bookshop

DEAN STREET

BATEMAN ST.

G

L

R

B

WARDOUR STREET

MEARS ST.

BOURCHIER ST.

OLD COMPTON ST.

N

C

Cambridge
Circus

BROADWICK STREET

DUCK LA.

BERWICK STREET

Berwick St
Market

M

C

F

Palace
Theatre

LEXINGTON STREET

G

PETER ST.

WALKER'S COURT

BREWER ST.

RUPERT STREET

SHAFTESBURY

AVENUE

NEWPORT ST.

CHINA-
TOWN

DANSEY
PL.

MACCLD ST.

GERRARD STREET

R

P

LEICESTER COURT

Left-handed
Shop

GT. WINDMILL ST.

To **E** **R**

WARDOUR ST.

LISLE STREET

LEICESTER ST.

BEAR ST.

FINISH

LEICESTER

COVENTRY STREET

SQUARE

National (

A

A Belgo
B Mezzo
C Café in the Crypt
D Spaghetti House
E Country Life
F The French House
G Wagamama
H Calabash
I Orso
J Neal's Yard Dining Rooms
K Mildred's
L Maison Bertaux
M Patisserie Valerie
N Bar Italia
O Quo Vadis
P The New Diamond

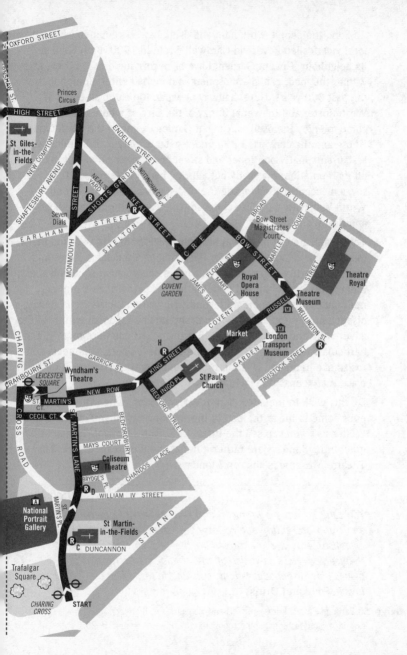

N. OXFORD STREET

HIGH STREET

Princes Circus

ENDELL STREET

St Giles-
in-the-Fields

NEW COMPTON

SHAFTESBURY AVENUE

MONMOUTH STREET

SHORTS GARDENS

NEAL'S YARD

DRURY LANE

BROAD

J R

A R

NEAL STREET

NOTTINGHAM CT.

Seven
Dials

SHELTON STREET

EARLHAM

LONG

ACRE

BOW STREET

Bow Street
Magistrates
Court

MARTLETT COURT

Theatre
Royal

COVENT
GARDEN

JAMES ST.

MART ST.

FLORAL ST.

Royal
Opera
House

Theatre
Museum

RUSSELL STREET

WELLINGTON ST.

COVENT

Market

London
Transport
Museum

R I

H R

KING STREET

GARDEN

R

GARRICK ST.

CRANBOURN ST.

Wyndham's
Theatre

LEICESTER SQUARE

NEW ROW

INIGO PL.

BEDFORD STREET

St Paul's
Church

TAVISTOCK STREET

ST. MARTIN'S CT.

CECIL CT.

ST. MARTIN'S LANE

MAYS COURT

BEDFORDBURY

CHANDOS PLACE

Coliseum
Theatre

BRYDGE'S PL.

R D

WILLIAM IV STREET

National
Portrait
Gallery

A

ST. MARTIN'S PL.

St Martin-
in-the-Fields

STRAND

R C

DUNCANNON

Trafalgar
Square

CHARING
CROSS

START

CHARING CROSS ROAD

'In Soho the people work hard and drink hard—tremendously hard,' a local vicar called Reverend Cardwell wrote in 1900. Both Soho and its neighbour, Covent Garden, have been thriving on the booze, as well as the food, genial atmosphere and myriad entertainments, for the past 300 years. Here, halfway between the clubbish pomp of Westminster and the venal frenzy of the City, is where Londoners come to enjoy themselves. Covent Garden, home to the Royal Opera House and the converted fruit and vegetable market, is teeming with restaurants, natty boutiques and street performers. Soho still thrives off its reputation as a seedy but alluring hang-out for exotic freaks and sozzled eccentrics who made the place famous after the Second World War with their jazz clubs, low-life bars, alternative bookshops and fleapit cinemas.

The establishment has always been suspicious of this area: too many foreigners and loose morals for the liking of respectable ladies and gents. The artistic community has never shown such squeamishness; indeed this is the heart of London theatreland with its haunted nooks and much elaborated legends. Nowadays the sleaze is slowly disappearing, supplanted by the flashy cars and modish whims of the advertising and media darlings. But the naked power of money, and particularly the pressure of the property developers, still meets stiff resistance here; and it is the robust, unpretentious old spirit of the place that keeps Soho swinging.

Do this walk in the afternoon or early evening, when the bars and pubs come to life at the end of the working day. If you come on a Wednesday you can see the inside of St Paul's Covent Garden at lunchtime. Sundays are rather quiet as the theatres are dark. The Theatre Museum is shut on Mondays.

lunch/pubs

You can't go very far wrong around here—Covent Garden and Soho are eating-out country par excellence. *Some establishments are mentioned in the text as sights in themselves. Here is a list of the cheaper, less formal places. For further suggestions, consult the restaurant listings in* **Food and Drink**.

Belgo, 50 Earlham Street. Frites, mussels and Belgian beer, high-tech interior décor, and fashionable metropolitan crowd; lunch from £10–20.

Mezzonine, 100 Wardour Street. Ultra sophisticated brasserie food in massive restaurant owned and operated by interior designer Terance Conran; with a 2-course £7 before 7pm special.

Café in the Crypt, church of St Martin-in-the-Fields. Self service, hot and cold food in this atmospheric vaulted brick crypt. Main dishes around £5–6.

Spaghetti House, 30 St Martin's Lane. Functional but efficient Italian chain restaurant with tasty food. Set menu £7.95.

Country Life, 3–4 Warwick St. Very cheap and tasty vegetarian salads and main dishes sold, New York style, by weight from £5 for a full lunch.

The French House, 49 Dean St. All very Sohoesque, with a pub below and a small but attractive dining room above, best for meat and game: pig's trotters, sweetbread, liver and tongue. £20–30; reservations on ☎ 0171–437 2477.

Wagamama, 10A Lexington St. Busy and popular Japanese noodle restaurant, where you sit at long communal tables.Be prepared to queue. £5–10.

Calabash, 38 King St. Come here for unusual and excellent dishes from all over Africa (grilled plantain, cous-cous, groundnut stew, etc.). Downstairs in the Africa Centre. Main dish £6.50–7.50.

Orso, 27 Wellington St. One of the most authentic Italian restaurants in town: fashionable but not too dear, with pasta made on the premises, and excellent veal, hare and liver. Lunch from £20–25, or less for pasta as a main course; open from 12 noon to midnight, 7 days a week.

Neal's Yard Dining Rooms, 14 Neal's Yard. Cheap, tasty and filling home-made vegetarian 'worldfood', from Mexican to Indian and African street food. £5–10 for a full meal.

Mildred's, 58 Greek St. Classy vegetarian fare, including felafel, stir-fries and home-made ice-cream. Very popular. Less than £10.

Maison Bertaux, 28 Greek St. Mouthwatering French pastries. Lovely stopping-off point for excellent-value tea, gateaux and pastries.

Patisserie Valerie, 44 Old Compton St. More delicious croissants, cakes and savoury vol-au-vents. Very crowded and a bit self-consciously arty.

Bar Italia, 22 Frith St. Open 23 out of 24 hours, a Soho institution for everyone from after-hours clubbers to tourists: arguably the best espresso and cappuccino in town. Some snacks.

Quo Vadis, 28 Dean Street, ☎ 0171–437 9585. Swanky French/English cuisine by superchef Marco Pierre White in restaurant decorated with works by Damien Hirst and Marcus Harvey, with a two-course set lunch from £15.

The New Diamond, 23 Lisle St. One of the best establishments in Chinatown (though there's not much to pick between them), with an enormous menu and seating on two floors. £7–15.

Covent Garden

The church of **St Martin-in-the-Fields** is the oldest building on Trafalgar Square, and the only one truly to benefit from the exposure the square affords; its curious combination of Greek temple façade and Baroque steeple quickly catches the eye, even if the mix is a little awkward. James Gibbs's design, built over four years from 1722 to 1726 to replace a decaying 16th-century original, became popular with the royal family which had several babies christened here. Its churchyard, now a day-time junk market (*open daily 10–5.30*), contains the graves of Charles II's mistress Nell Gwynne and the 18th-century painters Reynolds and Hogarth. In recent times the church has become popular for its concerts and resident orchestra, the Academy of St Martin-in-the-Fields.

The portico's cold stone Corinthian columns lead to a rather bland interior enlivened only by some kitschy plaster cherubs on the ceiling. Look out for the alabaster font, a relic of the original medieval church, and the ornate 19th-century oak pulpit with its delicately twisted banister rail. The greatest curiosity is the vaulted brick crypt, used after the First World War to shelter homeless soldiers returning from the front and again during the Blitz as an air-raid shelter. St Martin's celebrated vicar Dick Sheppard held the first broadcast service here in 1924. Now the crypt contains a restaurant, gallery and brass rubbing centre.

> *Turn right outside the church and you come to St Martin's Place. In front of some elegant Georgian façades, now private offices, is a* **statue of Edith Cavell**, *the feisty Red Cross nurse who became a symbol of national outrage when the Germans shot her in Belgium in 1915 for helping prisoners of war to escape.*

George Frampton's singularly unattractive marble and granite monument (1920) completely misread the wounded spirit of the nation after the Great War. His effigy, with its exhortation to devotion and sacrifice in the service of king and country, is imbued with exactly the same high patriotic sentiment that created so much tragedy in the first place. As Cavell's last words, inscribed here, say: 'Patriotism is not enough.' Margot Asquith, the prime minister's wife, remarked at the unveiling that the statue was as likely to make the British blush as the Germans. Regrettably, red faces have yet to solicit the services of the demolition men.

> *Across the road you'll see the entrance to the* **National Portrait Gallery** *(open Mon–Sat 10–6, Sun 2–6; free).*

This gallery is unique, and a true oddity. Unique, because no other Western country has ever assembled a similar collection of portraits of the glorious names populating its history. Odd, because the kings, generals, ministers, pioneers, inventers and artists on display here have not been chosen according to the quality of the painting—in fact some of it is downright lousy. They are here because the Victorian aristocrats who originally founded the gallery believed that it would serve as a stern kind of history lesson. As prime minister Palmerston told parliament soon after the collection was inaugurated in 1856: 'There cannot ... be a greater incentive to mental exertion, to noble actions, to good conduct on the part of the living than for them to see before them the features of those who have done things which are worthy of our admiration.'

The gallery is a forceful argument for Thomas Carlyle's view that the history of the world is 'but the biography of great men' (and, very occasionally, great women), and that the proper duty of the lower orders is to shut up and be grateful. Of course, this was a highly convenient notion at a time when the aristocratic ruling order was under threat from both the industrial middle classes and the disgruntled urban poor, and spoke volumes about the insecurity of the establishment. (Only a few years earlier Lord Liverpool had warned: 'One insurrection in London and all is lost.') Don't be too surprised, then, to find that in here you will see no revolutionaries, few union leaders, few true dissidents; nobody, in fact, who might be deemed out of place at a society dinner party. Well, almost nobody. In the 20th Century Galleries there is a portrait of Arthur Scargill, Marxist miners' leader, erstwhile Thatcher-baiter and, to judge by his blow-dried blond quiff, aspiring dictator of some eccentric Balkan mini-state.

The gallery has far more pictures than space: over 9000 portraits with only five narrow floors to exhibit them (a café on the roof is planned for 2002). You only get to see a small, rotating fraction—check the computer database provided. Chronologically, the collection starts at the top with the Tudor age and works its way down towards the present day, with a magnificent new 20th-century wing designed by Piers Gough. The best paintings, technically speaking, are probably Holbein's vividly life-like versions of Henrys VII and VIII and Sir Thomas More. There are also magnificent renditions of the 19th-century prime ministers Disraeli and Gladstone by Millais, self-portraits by Hogarth and Reynolds, a distinctly ambivalent Churchill by Walter Sickert (all yellows and greens) and a Cubist T.S. Eliot by Jacob Epstein. Some of the portraits are so reverent as to be absurd. Lawrence of Arabia appears in stone effigy like some medieval king imbued with divine powers. Jacques-Emile Blanche's James Joyce looks ludicrously respectable in a smart suit in front of an orderly writing desk. You suspect he's dying to light that cigarette dangling between his fingers.

The most entertaining pictures, though, are the modern royals on the first floor, largely because they are all so bad. Alison Watt's Queen Mother looks like a bag lady who has stumbled into the wrong person's living room. The Queen, draped in the red robes of the Order of the British Empire, is given an air of grandeur and benign severity she simply does not possess in real life. The artist, Pietro Annigoni, said he did not want to paint her as a film star, but a film star is exactly what she looks like: she could be auditioning for Joan Crawford's role in *Johnny Guitar*. Or maybe she is just trying to look tough for Margaret Thatcher, a prime minister she never made much secret of disliking, whose portrait lurks on the staircase around the corner. In Rodrigo Moynihan's hands, Thatcher is no longer the bossy, strident nanny of the nation. He casts her in flattering soft-focus; she looks like she couldn't hurt a fly.

> *Cross the road again and head up St Martin's Lane, past a huge modern post office. Soon after on the right, is what must be one of the city's narrowest allies, Brydges Place. You can barely squeeze your shoulders through its crack of an entrance, although there's not much reason to as it is rather dank and smelly. Instead look up to the distinctive globe of the* **Coliseum** *theatre, home, at least for now, to the English National Opera.*

Built in 1904, this was the first theatre in England with a revolving stage. The globe used to revolve too, until it was deemed a hazard by Westminster City Council. Now the whole place is under threat, with the government planning to move the ENO into Covent Garden along with the Royal Opera and Ballet. So catch it while you can.

Already you have stepped into London's theatreland, as the black strip at the bottom of the street signs says. The theatres along St Martin's Lane—the Albery and Duke of York's as well as the Coliseum—all date from the turn of the century and so were among the last great playhouses to be built in London. But as early as the 18th century the street was attracting such artistic residents as Joshua Reynolds, first president of the Royal Academy, and Thomas Chippendale, the furniture maker. Back then it was still a rough neighbourhood: there was a whipping post and a small prison opposite St Martin-in-the-Fields, where the constables regularly got drunk and mistreated their charges. Nowadays it's strictly the preserve of the chattering classes. Even the sandwiches around here look urbane and smart, all wholemeal, pastrami and oozing mozzarella.

> *Take a detour to the left down* **Cecil Court**, *a charming pedestrian alley stuffed full of prints, antiques and second-hand books. Mozart first stayed here when he came to London as a child prodigy of eight in 1764. If you want, you can extend the detour by walking to the end, turning right on Charing Cross Road past Wyndham's Theatre and then doubling back on St Martin's Court, another pedestrian alley full of popular pre-theatre pubs. That way you come back out on St Martin's Lane opposite New Row, another pleasant pedestrianized street lined with cafés and*

antique shops. Walk down it, turn right at the end down Bedford Street and then take the first left into Inigo Place and the churchyard of St Paul's (church open Mon 9.30–2.30, Tues–Fri 9.30–4.30, and for services on Sun 11am).

Don't be surprised if you feel you are sneaking up to this church from behind. That is exactly what you are doing. Properly speaking, St Paul's is part of the original Covent Garden piazza (*see* below) which Inigo Jones built in mock-Italian style in the 1630s. Jones made one crucial oversight, however. He and his low-church patron, the Earl of Bedford, thought they could get away with putting the altar of their church at the western end, so breaking with convention which insists it should be in the east. The Bishop of London, William Laud, was in no mood to be so indulgent. This was the first new church to be built in the capital since the Reformation, and the arch-conservative Laud was keen not to stir up controversy. He ordered Jones to put the altar where it traditionally belongs, in this case flush against the planned main entrance. Until the 19th century you could still enter by one of the two side doors on the piazza, but in 1871 they were blocked up by the restorer William Butterfield, presumably to ensure that godfearing churchgoers would not have to mingle with the drunken riffraff in the market. Now the only way in is here, by the pretty and secluded churchyard rose garden. St Paul's has ended up back to front. The interior is of disarming simplicity: a double square, 100ft by 50ft. Horace Walpole relates how the Earl of Bedford, Francis Russell, was anxious not to spend too much money on the church (he was more or less talked into building it, along with the rest of Covent Garden, by King Charles I). 'In short, I would not have it much better than a barn,' Russell told Inigo Jones. Jones is said to have replied: 'Well then, you shall have the handsomest barn in England.'

St Paul's is one of the few pre-Great Fire buildings still left in London, and the only significant part of Inigo Jones's piazza still standing. An overzealous restorer called Thomas Hardwick began reworking the whole interior in the late 1780s, but changed his mind after a devastating fire in 1795 which he took as a providential sign. He ended up rebuilding the whole church as it had been before. A fine new organ was added in 1861, incorporating part of the casing of the original.

St Paul's quickly won the affections of the theatre folk of Covent Garden, who preached here as well as attending services. They nicknamed it the Actors' Church. Several luminaries of the stage are buried here, including Ellen Terry, the *grande dame* of the late-Victorian theatre, whose ashes are marked by a plaque in the south wall. There is also a curious floor stone in memory of Claude Duval, a highwayman hanged in 1670 who gained his notoriety as much by womanizing as by robbing the rich. He was once seen dancing under the moonlight with an eminent lady he had just held up on a road on Hounslow Heath. The floor stone reads:

> *Here lies Du Vall: Reader, if male thou art*
> *Look to thy purse; if female to thy heart...*
> *Old Tyburn's glory, England's illustrious thief*
> *Du Vall, the ladies' joy, Du Vall the ladies' grief.*

It's an elegant little verse, but in fact it is doubtful whether Duval was ever buried here since there are no records of him in the parish register. This could just be the Actors' Church doing a bit of acting of its own.

> *You can go back the way you came, but normally the iron gate leading into King St is open. King St is where you want to head anyway: turn right when you get back to the corner of New Row and Bedford St. The Georgian mansion at 26 King St houses the famous tailors Moss Bros, where you can rent out a morning coat or tails from assistants who seem to have stepped straight out of the 19th century. No.38 is the Africa Centre, a great place to linger whether for its arts and crafts shop, its bookstore, readings, concerts, art exhibitions or its food (in the Calabash restaurant). A few paces further and you reach* **Covent Garden** *itself.*

There are those who find modern Covent Garden too ritzy and spoiled with its boutiques, upmarket jewellery stalls and prettified pubs; too much of an easy crowd-pleaser with its mime artists and handclapping bands belting out yet another rendition of *I'm a Believer* or *The Boxer*; too much—heaven forbid—of a *tourist attraction*. Looking into the past, however, one should perhaps be relieved it is even half as pleasant as it is. When the wholesale fruit and vegetable market moved out to the south London suburbs in the 1970s, the London authorities initially wanted to build office blocks and a major roadway through here. Wouldn't that have been fun? It was the local traders and residents who saved Covent Garden with protests and petitions; it is also the locals who, by and large, have the run of the place today. Dig a little, and behind the obvious tourist draws are plenty of quieter, more discreet spots. If Covent Garden seems a little derivative, it is because it deliberately and self-consciously echoes its own past—a dash of Inigo Jones's original piazza with its street life and sideshows, several measures of Charles Fowler's covered market, plus plenty of the eating, drinking and general revelry that have always characterized this neighbourhood.

Covent Garden originally had an extra 'n'—it was pastureland belonging to the Convent of St Peter at Westminster, the original Westminster Abbey. After the dissolution of the monasteries, the crown gave the land to the Earl of Bedford and his family. Francis Russell, the fourth earl, fancied himself as a building speculator and, with the encouragement of the King, hired Inigo Jones, the King's Surveyor of Works, to construct houses 'fit for the habitations of gentlemen'. Jones, who had become famous for designing the Banqueting House in Whitehall (*see* p.173), duly obliged with an arcaded piazza heavily influenced by his studies of Palladian buildings in Italy. Smart terraced houses on three sides looked on to a large public square where coaches could linger and strollers enjoy the grace of their surroundings. Modern architects have compared it to the Piazza d'Arme in Livorno or the Place des Vosges in Paris. It was a light, elegant piece of work, but failed to make much impression on Jones' contemporaries, who were unused to the concept of the public square and found it simply too un-English. One bilious critic said his work was 'like Bugbears or Gorgon heads'. For a while the piazza enjoyed a certain novelty value—there had never been anything like it in London—and attracted fashionable tenants. But within 30 years the rich nobs had largely moved back west to St James's. To them, the idea of a square encouraging street life and the mingling of the classes seemed horrifying. When market stalls started appearing in the 1670s, the piazza lost any remaining kudos and fell into rapid decline. Nobody seemed to care much about Jones' fine buildings, which were allowed to disintegrate and disappear. Bedford House, the first and finest house on the piazza, was demolished in 1706 to make room for a row of shops. That tells you something about London's planning priorities.

In the 18th century Covent Garden attracted a totally different species of humanity. 'One would imagine that all the prostitutes in the kingdom had picked upon the rendez-vous,' spluttered Sir John Fielding, blind half-brother of the novelist Henry who was magistrate for the district in the 1750s. Covent Garden became a byword for vice, a den of iniquity and immorality where criminal gangs ran extortion rackets, gambling houses and brothels. Vice has a funny way of attracting respectable folk, however, and Covent Garden became a favourite drinking haunt of literary types including Henry Fielding, Pope, Sheridan and Goldsmith. Boswell writes unabashedly in his *London Journal* about picking up two prostitutes and taking them to the (long defunct) Shakespeare Tavern: 'I ... solaced my existence with them, one after the other, according to their seniority.'

Meanwhile, the market grew in importance, especially after the closure of Stocks Market in the City in 1737. But importance was not always a guarantee of quality, and rotting or adulterated food became increasingly common. Smollett's character Matthew Bramble remarks sourly in *Humphrey Clinker*: 'It must be owned that Covent Garden affords some good fruit; which, however, is always engrossed by a few individuals of over-grown fortune at an exorbitant price.' Most of the produce, he complains, is vile and filthy, and the strawberries a 'pallid, contaminated mash'.

Bric-à-brac traders gradually joined the fruit and veg sellers, causing such congestion and chaos that by the early 19th century parliament was forced to reorganize the market's licensing system and authorize the building of a proper market hall. The result was Charles Fowler's grand structure of Tuscan columns and pretty arcades, completed in 1830, which largely survives as the centrepiece of the piazza today. Over the next 80 years, further market halls followed—Floral Hall (1860), the Flower Market (1871) and the Jubilee Market (1904). Covent Garden became a bustling, popular focal point for central London where people of all classes could mingle. It is no accident that in *Pygmalion*, Bernard Shaw's play unravelling the savage eccentricities of the British class system, his characters Henry Higgins and Eliza Doolittle first meet outside the classical portico of St Paul's. In time, however, the market grew too big for the space available and, after decades of overcrowding, the fruit and veg stalls moved out in 1974 to roomier, more modern premises at Nine Elms south of the river.

With the loss of the market, Covent Garden has undoubtedly lost its rough edges. The main hall, once littered with crates and stray vegetables, is now spick and span, while the Flower Market houses museums devoted to transport and the theatre. Unlike the disastrous redevelopment of Les Halles in Paris, however, the place has not lost its soul. Both the burger barons and the filofax-and-caviar brigade have been kept at bay. You can still buy roast chestnuts or a greasy baked potato from a street vendor as Dickens did, or watch clowns and jugglers performing in front of St Paul's where Punch and Judy shows first caught the public imagination in the 17th century.

> *Linger outside St Paul's (or take a cheapish ride in the 'Spaceball', a transparent ball used to prepare astronauts for zero-gravity) and then wander through the main hall, following signs directing you to the wonderful* **Cabaret Mechanical Theatre** *on the lower level of the market (open weekdays, 10–6.30, Sat 10–6.30 and Sun 11–6.30; adm cheap, children under five free, web site http://ourworld.compuserve.com/home-pages/barecat).*

This small and eccentric compendium of automata is guaranteed to amuse practically anyone from anywhere, instantly. On one side there's a quirky but jolly amusement arcade, with handmade machines costing 10–20p a go; on the other a fascinating exhibition of over 64 push-button automata (defined by the owners as 'inanimate objects that imitate the actions of living things'). Tickets to the exhibition are stamped by a wooden mechanical man; once you're inside everything—from Keith Newstead's Heath Robinson *Rabbit Eradicator* to Paul Spooner's erotically heaving Manet's *Olympia*—is push-button operated and free. All the nutty and satirical automata on display (except for the pianola) are one-offs, hand-made in the last 15 years out of scraps of tin, wood and ingenious clockwork mechanisms. The collection grew haphazardly after the owner Sue Jackson began displaying automata in her crafts and toy shop in Falmouth in the 1970s; in the small shop here at the Cabaret Theatre there's a range of make-your-own-automata for sale.

*Walk through the market to the other side. A little way up on the right is the **London Transport Museum** (open Sun–Thurs and Sat 10–6, Fri 11–6; adm, full disabled access).*

Londoners like to grumble about London Transport, but in their heart of hearts they are really rather fascinated by it. This cheerful museum celebrates everything that is excellent about the system, from the red London Routemaster bus to the London Underground map, designed in 1931 by Harry Beck, and never surpassed. In the main gallery, a glass walkway takes you past a series of historic buses, trams and steam locomotives, including the oldest surviving double-decker horse tram (dating from 1882, when 1000 tonnes of horse dung were deposited on the streets of London every day). In adjoining galleries you can see an original watercolour of Beck's Underground map, and a superb collection of Art Deco period posters. For children (and adults too) there's a simulated Tube train driving seat, actors dressed in period costume, educational 'Action Zones' and a museum shop. The museum also organizes a programme of talks and events (including a regular tour and lecture on London's disused Tube stations, ✆ 0171–379 6344 for details.)

*Around the corner on Russell St is the **Theatre Museum** (open Tues–Sun 11–7; adm). In June 1998 the top floor will include a new exhibit on Cameron Mackintosh musicals (Miss Saigon, Cats and Les Misérables).*

This museum is a bit grotty at first glance and confusingly laid out; by far the best way to see it, unless you're an expert on theatre, is to join one of the very informative guided tours led by actors three times a day and free with the price of admission (*tours leave daily at 11.30am, 2pm and 3pm*). A vast number of exhibits covers the history of the English stage from the Elizabethan public playhouses to the rise of the National Theatre, illustrated by period costumes and plenty of model theatres. Unfortunately all this wonderful stuff—from Edmund Kean's death mask to the psychedelic hand-printed costumes used by the Diaghilev Ballets Russes to premiere 'The Rite of Spring' in Paris in 1913—is displayed behind the smudged glass of dully lit fish tanks. Rather more engaging fun is to be had by submitting yourself to the free make-up displays; you may have noticed some eccentric-looking people with werewolf faces or Mr Hyde expressions on your way in.

*Two of the most famous London theatres are a mere stone's throw away: the **Theatre Royal Drury Lane**, which is not in Drury Lane but on the corner of Russell St and Catherine St (you can see it as you come out of the Theatre Museum to your right); and the **Royal Opera House**, better known simply as Covent Garden, which is off to the left down Bow St.*

The Theatre Royal was one of the first establishments to open after the Restoration, holding a performance of *The Humourous Lieutenant* by Beaumont and Fletcher at its premiere in 1663. Nell Gwynne made her debut here, as did David Garrick and Edmund Kean in subsequent centuries. Once famous for its classical repertoire, it turned to spectacular dramas in the latter part of the 19th century when its manager Augustus Harris, a theatrical Cecil B. De Mille, staged horse races, snowstorms, earthquakes and avalanches.

The theatre's constant curse, however, has been fire. In 1809, the playwright and politician Richard Sheridan, who was then manager, was alerted to the flames spewing out of his theatre while embroiled in an important debate in parliament. Stoically, he refused to go to the site until his business at Westminster was done. He was later seen nursing a stiff drink at the scene of the fire and commenting with characteristic wry humour: 'Surely a man may take a glass of wine by his own fireside.' Benjamin Wyatt was responsible for the rebuilding, completed in 1812. In 1840 the theatre acquired a different kind of curse, when a man was found in one of the walls with a knife poking through his ribs; a ghost has appeared in the circle from time to time ever since, particularly at matinées.

Fire has also been a scourge at the Theatre Royal's illustrious neighbour. The Covent Garden theatre was advertised as the most luxurious in London when it opened in 1732, but quickly became known for its calamities as much as its performances. An angry mob ripped up the boxes and orchestra pit in 1763 after management broke with the custom of granting free entry for the third act. There was further violence in 1792 when the theatre tried to raise gallery prices to pay for costly restoration work. Then in 1808 a fire razed the theatre to the ground. A new building designed by Robert Smirke was opened in record time just over a year later, but again when the management had the temerity to raise prices the result was fighting in the streets. The Old Price Riots lasted more than two months until the theatre finally relented to the demands of its rowdy audience.

The second Covent Garden fire broke out during a ball in 1856, just a few years after the theatre had become established as an opera house. The orchestra desperately played *God Save the Queen* to persuade everyone to leave the building. In the end nobody was seriously hurt, but nothing remained of the theatre apart from the portico frieze *Tragedy and Comedy*. The new architect, Edward Barry, incorporated it into his new design, which is the building you see today.

Nowadays the drama focuses around the scaffolding, flying sparks, lunging cranes, exposed steel, concrete frames and girders and pungent circus smells as intensive construction works begin on a massive £230 million redevelopment of the opera house and an imaginative extension of the site surrounding it. These works are long overdue: the 1858 building has had no real maintenance since the 1960s, and the cramped and stifling back-stage facilities used by two separate companies (The Royal Ballet as well as The Royal Opera) and a leaking roof were in dire need of repair and technical updating. The redevelopment—by architects Jeremy Dixon and Edward Jones—will integrate the Opera House with Covent Garden market for the first time, replacing the Georgian houses on the north side of Russell Street with shopping arcades (also containing cafés, restaurants and a box office) and a loggia walkway above, all based on Inigo Jones's original Piazza.

The extension will also include a Studio Theatre, a new, cheaper and more informal auditorium seating up to 400 people; new accommodation and rehearsal studios for The Royal Ballet; and a restoration of The Floral Hall, a Crystal Palace-style glass canopied market hall facing Bow Street which was damaged by fire in the 1950s and used since as a scenery store. Inside the opera house itself backstage facilities will be modernised, front of stage sight lines will be improved and 100 new low-price seats will be added.

There is just one snag to these grand plans, and that is that the whole place is going bust. To avert the nightmare of a beautifully restored opera house with no opera company left to perform in it, the government has proposed merging the Royal Opera and Ballet with the English National Opera (*see above* under the Coliseum). This announcement has shocked and dismayed almost everyone concerned, and it looks like we are in for a good old-fashioned wrangle about the future of a precious corner of London.

*Opposite the entrance to the Opera House is the old **Bow Street Magistrates' Court** where the Fieldings, Henry and John, held court in the 18th century.*

Henry, who was a trained barrister as well as the author of *Tom Jones*, used his tenure here to set up the Bow Street Runners, an informal plainclothes police force that worked to crack down on underworld gangs and challenge the infamous official marshals, or 'thief-takers', who were usually in cahoots with the thieves themselves. Most infamous of all the thief-takers, and the subject of one of Fielding's own books, was Jonathan Wild, who built up an entire criminal empire by repossessing property he had more often than not stolen and sold on in the first place. His success depended on playing an elaborate game of deception and counter-deception with his own men; during his career he turned in several dozen of his accomplices to keep his nose clean.

As long as Wild did not hold on to any of the goods he stole, it was hard for the magistrates to pin anything on him. In desperation, parliament passed a special Act in 1718 designed to make it easier to catch Wild; it stated that any profit from a crime was as serious a matter as the crime itself. Wild lasted another seven years before finally being captured, tried and sentenced to death in 1725. He was so scared of the public humiliation he knew he could expect on the way to the gallows that he tried to take his own life with laudanum. He drank so much of it, however, that he was violently sick and survived to be jeered and pelted all the way to Tyburn.

The idea behind the Runners was to end such corruption in the judicial system; investigators, according to Fielding, should be beyond reproach and resist the temptation to make deals with the criminal community. The Runners proved remarkably effective and soon became famous throughout the land, particularly for their role in thwarting the Cato Street conspiracy in 1820 (see p.68). Until Robert Peel's uniformed bobbies appeared in the 1830s, they were the closest thing to a police force that London had.

When ill health forced Henry to retire in 1754, his half-brother took over and introduced foot patrols to keep an eye on known felons. Legend has it that the 'Blind Beak' could recognize 3000 thieves by their voices alone. The present building dates from 1881; sadly a police museum that once stood here has closed down.

> *Walk to the end of Bow St and turn left onto Long Acre, once a centre for coachmakers and cabinet makers (Chippendale lived here) and now a bustling if somewhat touristy shopping street. Stanford's, reputed to be the biggest map seller in the world, is down the far end at No.12. This walk turns off rather sooner, however, to the right down* **Neal St**.

This pedestrian alley is a pleasant throwback to the hippy era, all beads, home-made earrings and wholefood. While Carnaby Street, the in-place in the 1960s, has faltered and died, Neal Street, a development from the late 1970s, has survived largely thanks to its jolly shops and cheap vegetarian cafés. Turn left down Shorts Gardens and you come to distinctly New Age **Neal's Yard**, a tranquil triangular oasis planted with trees and climbing plants, and an excellent place to sit down, away from the traffic fumes and confusion. There are plentiful cheap vegetarian eats here, a world food café, a bagel café, a walk-in backrub parlour, an excellent bakery, a natural cosmetics shop, and the famous Neals Yard Therapy Rooms, offering the gamut of 'alternative' therapies, from acupuncture to lymphatic drainage, from past-life counselling to 'rolfing'—something to do with realigning the body in relation to gravity.

As a last resort, there's a New Age shop stuffed with crystals and books on mystical healing. On your way in, don't miss the Heath Robinson clock above the Neal's Yard Wholefood Warehouse. A tube marking off the minutes slowly fills with water. Then, on the hour, the water races into watering cans which tip into a gutter filled with flowers mounted on floats. The flowers rise into view as though they had just grown, then subside as the water drains away.

On the other side of Shorts Gardens is **Thomas Neal's Arcade**, filled with designer boutiques and shops. With its wrought iron lamps and glass roof, this is another derivative piece of modern London architecture, this time a throwback to the arcaded emporia of the 19th century, but one that seems to be setting the pace for the changing atmosphere of the area with its emphasis on conspicuous consumption and designer chic.

Continue along Shorts Gardens to a curious confluence of roads called **Seven Dials**.

Neal refers to Thomas Neale, Master of the Royal Mint in the late 17th century, who dabbled unwisely in property speculation. Neale's number one priority was to squeeze every last penny out of his investment, and felt that building a square would be a waste of precious leasable land. So instead he constructed a star-shaped development with seven streets leading off from an ornamental Doric pillar in the centre. The pillar had a sundial on each of six sides, as well as acting as a sundial itself—hence the name Seven Dials. Neale's stinginess caught up with him: the narrow maze of streets he constructed may have saved space, but it was also an ideal meeting place for criminals. The area degenerated into an appalling slum frequented only by street vendors scraping for a living. In the late 18th century rumours circulated that the monument concealed a vast treasure in its base. The authorities, worried that a riot might break out, took the pillar down in 1773 and only dared to re-erect it a century later, well away from London on the green at Weybridge in Surrey. It returned here in the late 1980s.

Seven Dials is part of the neighbourhood of St Giles (appropriately enough, named after the patron saint of outcasts and lepers), which was effectively destroyed in the mid-19th century in a slum clearance scheme that gave rise to the broad avenues you see today. The Victorians were so determined to drive out the locals that at one point in the mid-1840s they pulled the roofs off a row of houses earmarked for demolition. Many of the residents stayed put all the same, successfully holding up the rebuilding scheme for another 30 years. By the 1870s, however, with the advent of Shaftesbury Avenue and Charing Cross Road, the poor had fled north to Islington and Stoke Newington, and St Giles breathed its last.

Turn right up Monmouth St and you come to St Giles Circus, a soulless traffic junction that highlights how much life the Victorians sapped from the area. To the left down St Giles High St stands the elegant, if slightly dilapidated church of **St Giles-in-the-Fields**.

Queen Matilda established a leper colony here in 1101 (hence the dedication to St Giles) and handed out a cup of charity to condemned prisoners who passed on their way to the gallows at Tyburn. The present church, heavily influenced by St Martin-in-the-Fields with its classical Portland stone portico and tall spire, was built in 1753 by Henry Flitcroft, the son of William of Orange's gardener.

Unfortunately the church is rarely open. If you do get in, look for the stone commemorating the Restoration poet Andrew Marvell, who died in 1678.

> *Turn left down Denmark St, a street renowned for its sheet music and instrument shops which was nicknamed Tin Pan Alley in the 1950s and 1960s. Andy's Guitar Workshop, a favoured haunt of guitarists since the early days of rock'n'roll, is still going strong, and hosts blues bands most nights of the week in the Twelve Bar Club, which is held in a converted forge behind the shop. At the end of Denmark St you come out on* **Charing Cross Road**.

Opposite you at Nos.119–125 is Foyle's, the most famous bookshop on a street of bookshops. Don't be deluded by its reputation, however, which dates from the inter-war years: inside it is a chaotic, antiquated mess. Foyle's fame largely rests on the boast that you can find any book at all on its well-thumbed shelves. Sure you can, as long as you have about 36 hours to spare and the patience of a saint. There is no rational categorization to speak of, the shelves are in a hopeless state of disorder and the books are often grubby from all that thumbing.

The modern chains just up the road, Books Etc and Waterstone's, are far more efficient general stores. Charing Cross Road's charm, however, lies in higgledy-piggledy secondhand bookshops such as Quinto (think *84 Charing Cross Road*) or its specialist shops. Collet's, the celebrated left-wing bookshop at No.66 where radicals lectured on revolution in the 1930s, sadly went bankrupt in 1993. However, the expensive art bookshop Zwemmer's, at Nos.76–80, is still going and so are places like the Silver Moon Women's Bookshop up the road.

> *It's worth taking a little detour down Charing Cross Rd to Cambridge Circus to admire the swirling terracotta façade of the* **Palace Theatre** *(1891), built as an opera house and now semi-permanent home to the permantenty booked out hit musical Les Misérables which opened here originally in 1985. In the southeastern corner of Cambridge Circus is a curious clock held up by a sculpted naked woman. Returning back up Charing Cross Road, turn left into* **Manette Street**, *the narrow road next to Foyle's.*

About three-quarters of the way down on the left, notice the small figure in the wall of a goldbeater's arm. This, along with the street's name, is a folly taken straight from Dickens's *Tale of Two Cities*. One of the characters in that novel, Dr Manette, is described as living 'in a quiet street-corner not far from Soho Square' near a goldbeater's workshop. The street, originally Rose Street, was duly renamed in 1895 and this curious ornament erected.

> *The archway at the end of Manette St, next to the Pillars of Hercules pub, brings you out into Greek St and the heart of* **Soho**.

Soho

'Better a seedy Soho than a tarted-up tourist attraction like Covent Garden,' opines Daniel Farson in his entertaining book *Soho in the Fifties*. Seediness has always proved strangely alluring in this wild and cosmopolitan district, so distinct from the sober calm of the rest of central London. Soho started off as a refuge for French Huguenots, and now counts whole communities of Italians, Cypriots, Greeks, Poles, Chinese, Thais and Bengalis who along with the new wave trendies run the area's zillions of restaurants and bars. Here are the clashing smells of oregano and lemongrass, the competing sounds of jazz and Hong Kong pop, the unlikely mix of bohemian intellectuals, hip zoot-suiters and peepshow pimps.

The curious name is a medieval hunting call, as in the quaint 15th-century exclamation quoted by the Oxford English Dictionary: *'Sohoe, the hare ys founde!'*. The district was indeed hunting territory up to the 17th century, although it seems Soho took its name not from the cry itself but—not unsuitably given the character of the district—from the name of an inn. Its first patron was Charles II's illegitimate son James Scott, Duke of Monmouth, who was granted the lease of Soho Fields (now Soho Square). He proved an appropriate figurehead for the district. Dashing, hotheaded and staunchly anti-establishment, Monmouth took up arms against Charles's successor James II at the Battle of Sedgemoor in 1685 where he made 'Soho!' his battle cry. He was eventually captured and executed at the Tower, where it took five swings of a particularly blunt axe to sever his head. The executioner had to finish him off by hacking at his neck with a knife. Monmouth's family and followers brought the body home and stitched it back together.

Low life and aristocrats have always dwelled side by side in Soho. In the 18th century it was fashionable with salon hostesses as well as artists and whores. In Victorian times it was full of cowsheds and slaughterhouses, with animal droppings littering the street. For polite society, the area became a byword for depravity and lack of hygiene. 'Untidy, full of Greeks, Ishmaelites, cats, Italians, tomatoes, restaurants, organs, coloured stuffs, queer names, people looking out of upper windows, it dwells remote from the British Body Politic,' John Galsworthy wrote in his middle-class epic *The Forsyte Saga*.

Galsworthy's characters would have been even more horrified by what was to come: erotic revues, peep-shows and the rise of pornography. In 1931 the Lord Chamberlain authorized nudity on stage for the first time for a revue at the Windmill Theatre, although he stipulated that the lighting had to stay low and the showgirls were not allowed to move while they showed off their bodies. The rules remained unchanged during the Second World War, when showgirls often found themselves standing stock still as everyone around them dashed for shelter from German V-bombs.

It was after the war that Soho really came into its own. In the 1950s it became the centre of the avant-garde in jazz, new writing, experimental theatre and cinema. In many ways Soho prefigured the social upheavals of the 1960s, creating a youth subculture based on rebellion, permissiveness, *joie de vivre*, booze and drugs. This was the world of Colin MacInnes's *Absolute Beginners*, of John Osborne and the other Angry Young Men, of Kenneth Tynan and his risqué revue *Oh Calcutta!*. Above all, Soho developed its own community of intellectuals and eccentrics, people of all classes mingling, chatting, borrowing money off each other and getting pleasantly tippled in pubs or illicit 'near-beer' bars that stayed open outside the stringent licensing hours.

Walk into the right place and you would meet Nina Hamnett, known as the Queen of the Bohemians, who boasted that Modigliani had credited her with 'the best tits in Europe'; or Ironfoot Jack, an impresario with one leg six inches shorter than the other who went around in colourful silk scarves; or Jeffrey Bernard, a journalist who sat in the Coach and Horses pub in an alcohol-induced stupor writing a column called Low Life for the *Spectator* magazine.

Like all golden ages, 1950s Soho and its low life came to a somewhat sorry end. Nina Hamnett was eventually reduced to an incontinent wreck hobbling round Soho with a permanently damaged thigh bone she broke in a drunken fall, the celebrated local bookseller David Archer died of a drugs overdose and most of the famous writers moved out to Camden or Notting Hill. The liberalizations of the 1960s and 1970s brought peepshows and strip joints galore that nearly caused the destruction of the neighbourhood. The planning authorities, outraged by prostitutes openly soliciting on every street, threatened to bulldoze the whole district to make way for office blocks. Only Jeffrey Bernard valiantly hung on in there, turning out his column as regularly as his liver would permit (he finally died in 1997, but not before Peter O'Toole had turned him into a legend on the West End stage with the one-man show *Jeffrey Bernard Is Unwell*).

It wasn't until the mid-1980s that new laws regulated the pornography business and Soho regained some of its spirit. The number of peepshows is strictly controlled, and most of the prostitutes now solicit via cards left in telephone booths rather than on the streets. The developers have largely been kept out by the Soho Society, set up in 1972, which succeeded in having the district declared a conservation area. So attractive has Soho become that the trendies have inevitably moved in to join the fun. The quirky hipness of the 1960s has evolved into a social free-for-all, drawing in movers and shakers in the music, film and advertising worlds, comediennes and television personalities, journalists, artists, dealers and agents, hangers-on and drop-outs, sleazeballs and whackos. Not a week goes by without a new bar, a new restaurant, a new fad. Today it might be sushi served by robots, or caramelised onions; next week these will be passé and the new obsession will be pine-scrubbed noodle bars, or cafés that look like middle-class living rooms. Is the fashion wind blowing towards East Soho, or West Soho? Against the odds, the area has become glamorous and limitlessly desirable, the very image of a vibrant new London. James Scott would have loved it.

> *Before you head off, notice the snail emblem across the road at 48 Greek St advertising the French restaurant L'Escargot. For this walk, you need to turn right on Greek St into* **Soho Square**.

This was where Scott built his mansion, Monmouth House (long ago destroyed and now occupied by Bateman Buildings on the south side of the square). A contemporary statue of Charles II by Caius Gabriel Cibber still stands in the square gardens, looking somewhat worse for wear behind a mock-Tudor toolshed which covers an underground air vent. On the north side of the square is the French Protestant Church, originally built for the Huguenots and then reworked by the Victorians in flamboyant neo-Gothic style. To the east is the red-brick tower of St Patrick's Roman Catholic Church, which holds weekly services for the local Spanish and Cantonese communities in their own languages.

On the corner of Greek Street is a stern Victorian establishment, the **House of St Barnabas**, which by its own definition 'offers a temporary home for women who have the necessary recommendations'. Founded in 1846 (although the building dates back a century earlier), the House set out to improve the lot of the poor through Christian teaching. This was where William Gladstone, that pillar of Victorian politics, would take prostitutes during his extraordinary night-time walks through the area in the early 1850s. His declared aim was to talk them out of their sinful ways and offer them temporary relief from poverty, but inevitably cynical tongues soon began wagging. 'He manages to combine his missionary meddling with a keen appreciation of a pretty face,' remarked one member of parliament, Henry Labouchere. As often as not, Gladstone would offer to take the prostitutes home. 'What will your wife say?' his permanent secretary asked him in horror while accompanying him on one such trip. 'Why,' Gladstone replied, all innocence and sweet reason, 'it is to my wife that I am bringing her.'

> *Head down Frith St, past the Frith Street Gallery (a small gallery at no.60 specialising in works on paper) Ronnie Scott's jazz club (Scott, a jazz saxophonist, died in 1996, but his dingy basement club still gets high profile bookings) and a plethora of restaurants including Jimmy's, a basement Greek café serving cheap moussaka and chips that has changed little since the Rolling Stones ate there in the 1960s. Turn right on Bateman St and you come to* **Dean Street**.

Many phantoms haunt this particular street. No.49 is the **French House**, which became the official headquarters of the Free French forces under Charles de Gaulle during the Second World War. Now it's a lively pub-cum-wine bar with a dining room above and its walls covered with photographs of famous Frenchmen. Two clubs further down the street illustrate the changes in Soho since the 1950s. The Colony, at No.41, was once described as 'a place where the villains look like artists and the artists look like villains ... burglars and millionaires, tramps and poets, students and countesses are all given an identical welcome.' Drunken artists, from Francis Bacon to Geroge Melly, have gathered here since time began. The Groucho—so called because of Groucho Marx's one-liner that he never wanted to join a club that would have him as a member—opened at No.44 in 1985 and has been a hit with the world of television, music, comedy, publishing and film ever since.

Quo Vadis, the restaurant at No.28, became instantly trendworthy in 1996 after it was bought from its original Italian owners by Marco Pierre White (famous London superchef) and Damien Hirst (Britpack conceptual artist-cum-restaurateur) and completed refurbished. Downstairs are works by Hirst and Marcus Harvey. Upstairs is where Karl Marx lived with his family from 1851–6 in a two-room attic flat in conditions of near abject penury (now a building site as it undergoes extensive refurbishments).

Not only did Marx have next to no money, he did little to set about earning any. While he spent his days in the British Library reading room, his wife Jenny struggled to bring up their growing family in a garret without ready access to toilets or running water. Three of their children died of pneumonia. For a while the Marxes shared their digs with an Italian chef, and readily invited all-comers to their dwelling to share what little they had. Then Karl started an affair with the family maid Lenchen, managing to get both her and his wife pregnant at the same time. In the end, the arrival of inheritances from Jenny Marx's mother and uncle saved the family from the poorhouse and they left for the healthier climes of Primrose Hill.

> *From Dean St, turn right into **Old Compton St**, which in many ways is the archetypal Soho street. Here you'll find cafés like the Patisserie Valerie at No.44, restaurants, delicatessens, gay clubs and bars, and modest-looking newsagents stocking every conceivable title on the planet. Turn right on **Wardour St**, once known for its furniture and antique stores but now occupied by film companies who advertise their forthcoming productions in the high glass windows on the left-hand side of the street. Turn left into Broadwick St, and then turn left again into **Berwick Street**, home to the best fruit and vegetable market in London (Mon–Sat 9–4).*

You'll hear the barrow-boys hawking their collies and taters as you come round the corner. Berwick Market always has beautifully fresh produce at incredibly low prices for central London. Ever since Jack Smith introduced the pineapple to London here in 1890, the market has also had a reputation for stocking unusual and exotic fruit and veg such as salsify or starfruit. The houses behind the stalls date, like the market itself, back to the 18th century, although there is plenty to distract you from even noticing them. There's a couple of old pubs (The Blue Posts is the most salubrious), a scattering of noisy independent record stores and several excellent old-fashioned fabrics shops specializing in unusual silks, satins, velvets, Chinese printed silks and printed cottons, sold by the metre and the place to go if you're looking for something exotic for yourself or your sofa.

> *At the southern end of Berwick St is a pokey passage called Walker's Court, dominated by peepshows and the London equivalent of the Moulin Rouge, Raymond's Revue Bar. At the end of the passage, turn right on to **Brewer Street**.*

This street is the ultimate Soho mixture of sex-joints and eclectic shops. As you wander down it you will notice discreetly signposted peep-shows, an excellent fishmonger's, a well-stocked poster shop and, at No.67, the shop **Anything Left-Handed**. If, like Michelangelo and John McEnroe, you are what the specialists call sinistro-manual, you might be delighted to find an entire shop full of left-handed scissors, can-openers, cutlery, pens and gardening tools. There are even left-handed mugs. Left-handed mugs? Of course, so all us southpaws can see the illustration on the mug while we are holding it.

> *Return to the corner of Walker's Court and turn right down Rupert St, where the market stalls continue but are rather quieter and less attractive than in Berwick St. At the end of Rupert St, turn left on Shaftesbury Avenue, then right down the lower end of Wardour St and then left again into Gerrard St, centre of London's **Chinatown**.*

London's Chinese population came mostly from Hong Kong in the 1950s and 1960s, victims not so much of the political upheavals in the region as the cruel fluctuations of the Asian rice market. Back then Gerrard Street, like the rest of Soho, was cheap and run down and relatively welcoming to foreigners. It took more than a generation for the new community to be fully accepted, however, and it was not until the 1970s that this street was pedestrianized and kitted out with decorative lamps and telephone boxes styled like pagodas—a spectacular backdrop to the Chinese New Year celebrations which take place here at the end of January or early February. Many of the older generation have only a rudimentary grip of English, and remain suspicious of their adoptive environment. The younger generation has integrated rather better; those born here are mockingly nicknamed BBCs (British-born children). London's Chinatown is still very small—just this street and Lisle Street really—and the trade is overwhelmingly in food and restaurants. There are a few craft shops, and there's always been a discreet illegal business in gambling—underground dens for mah-jong, pai-kau and fan tan. Triad gangs keep a relatively low profile in London, although there have been occasional outbursts of mob violence since the early 1980s. In 1982 a Soho gambling den was firebombed, while in 1989 four people were burned alive in an amusement arcade.

> *The eastern end of Gerrard St and Newport Place are crowded with Chinese supermarkets and craft shops, which are well worth poking around for a bargain. From Newport Place, walk straight down Leicester Court and turn right into **Leicester Square**, the finishing point of this walk.*

Towards the end of the 19th century, Leicester Square was *the* place to be seen of an evening, especially for middle-class men looking to let their hair down and flirt with 'unrespectable' women. Attractions included the gaudily decorated Alhambra Music Hall (now replaced by the Odeon cinema), Turkish baths, oyster rooms and dance halls. Nowadays the square is a pale shadow of its former self, a characterless jumble of first-run cinemas and hamburger joints. All the fine buildings of the past, including the 17th-century Leicester House which gave its name to the square, are long gone. The Blitz was largely responsible for destroying the buildings and spirit of the place. On 8 March 1941, several high-explosive bombs crashed into the Rialto cinema and caused the roof of the Café de Paris nightclub to cave in. Thirty-four people were killed, including the trumpeter Ken 'Snake-eyes' Johnson whose band was playing at the time. To make matters more distasteful, several people, including members of the fire brigade, were caught stealing rings and jewellery from the dead and dying.

Leicester Square has nowadays recovered some of its happy-go-lucky spirit; the square has been pedestrianized and the central garden tidied up. Come here at more or less any time of the day or night and you will find a rough and ready crowd of cinema-goers, student tourists, buskers, street performers, portrait painters and pickpockets. For the dedicated sightseer, however, the only historical curiosity is a bronze statue of Charlie Chaplin with his bowler hat and walking stick, but it is marred by the trite dedication: 'The comic genius who gave pleasure to so many.'

IV: Mayfair and Regent Street

Start: ⊖ *Piccadilly Circus.*
Walking time: *2 hours.*

That most society-conscious of 19th-century Whig reformers, the Reverend Sydney Smith, once said of Mayfair: 'The parallelogram between Oxford Street, Piccadilly, Regent Street and Hyde Park encloses more intelligence and human ability, to say nothing of wealth and beauty, than the world has ever collected in such a space before.' The area certainly does not want for high-class pedigree; if you have ever played the London version of Monopoly, you will know that Oxford Street, Bond Street, Regent Street, Park Lane and Mayfair itself are the most expensive and desirable properties on the board. But Mayfair has not lived up to the promise Sydney Smith saw in it. It is cosmopolitan and expensive, but not really fashionable; elegant and well-maintained, but not sophisticated; central and self-important, but at the same time strangely quiet. In short, the place does not buzz.

So why visit at all? The main reason is a certain quirky charm which most visitors to the big shops of Oxford Street and Regent Street fail entirely to find. The eccentrically built jewellery shops on Old Bond Street, the anachronisms of Burlington Arcade, the bustle of Shepherd Market and, a little further away, the outrageous neo-Gothic splendour of All Saints, St Margaret Street: these are all little-known curiosities within a stone's throw of the hordes that mill through London's main thoroughfares every day. Here in the heart of London you can enjoy a gentle stroll among Georgian mansions and fine shops, while having the streets virtually to yourself. Pretty much any day is good for visiting, but the Faraday Museum is closed on weekends.

lunch/pubs

Plenty to avoid in this part of town: the fast-food joints around Piccadilly Circus and the overpriced pizzas and steakhouses of Oxford St. But plenty to savour too, particularly in Shepherd Market where you can pay a king's ransom to hobnob in style with Mayfair's finest or bolt down a plate of bangers and beans for next to nothing.

The Criterion, 224 Piccadilly (at Piccadilly Circus). Quality cuisine in a wondrous high decibel neo-Byzantine grotto, decorated with gold mosaics; worth visiting for the interior alone. £14.95 for a two-course meal is one of London's better restaurant bargains, though service is a bit of a rush job.

Da Corradi, 47 Curzon St. All-day breakfast in this high-quality Italian greasy spoon. £10.

Boudin Blanc, 5 Trebeck St. Cheap French bistro food. Popular, atmospheric and wonderful value with a two-course set lunch from £5.95.

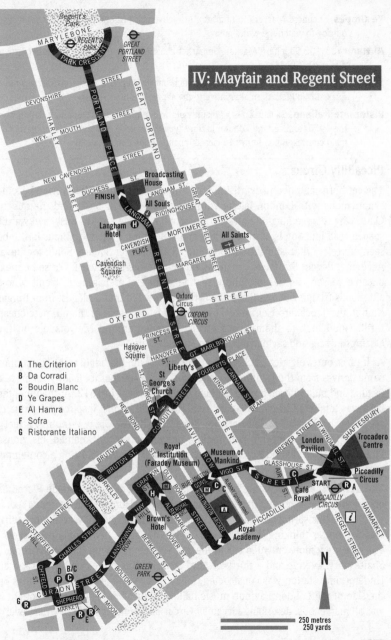

IV: Mayfair and Regent Street

A The Criterion
B Da Corradi
C Boudin Blanc
D Ye Grapes
E Al Hamra
F Sofra
G Ristorante Italiano

250 metres
250 yards

N

221

Ye Grapes, Shepherd Market (no number). Attractive pub just opposite L'Artiste with seats outside to watch the world go by.

Al Hamra, 31–33 Shepherd Market. Upmarket Lebanese fare. Delicious but rather expensive. £20–30.

Sofra, 18 Shepherd Market with another branch on 18 Shepherd Street. Attractive, more relaxed Middle Eastern alternative to the above, this time Turkish. £16–21.

Ristorante Italiano, 54 Curzon St. Quaintly old-world, much-loved restaurant dating from the 1950s and serving London literary types with good traditional Italian pasta and main courses; lunch from £15 closed lunchtimes on Sat and all Sun.

Piccadilly Circus

The car horns and neon advertising hoardings of **Piccadilly Circus** have become synonymous with London, along with red double-decker buses and the queen. Quite why is something of a mystery; the dominant smell of this busy, awkwardly shaped road junction is of traffic fumes and stale chips. Piccadilly Circus has to be seen more for what is in the surrounding area (Leicester Square, Soho, the Royal Academy, Regent Street etc.) than for anything in the place itself. For some inexplicable reason, hordes of European teenagers are prepared to spend whole afternoons trudging across Piccadilly Circus's crowded traffic islands, from Burger King to the Trocadero Centre to Tower Records, in search of the ultimate cheap thrill. Good luck to them. It's a bit like hanging around McDonald's on the Champs-Elysées and saying you've seen Paris.

As it turns out, vulgarity has long been a feature of the Piccadilly area. The strange name derives from the fortunes of Robert Baker, a 17th-century tailor who made a fortune and built himself a mansion here on the proceeds in 1612. At the time, the land was totally undeveloped apart from a windmill (which inspired the name of the street leading off to the north of Piccadilly Circus, Great Windmill Street). Baker's peers thought his ostentation ridiculous and nicknamed his house Pickadilly Hall to remind him of his humble origins, a *pickadil* being a contemporary term for a shirt cuff or hem.

The development of St James's and Mayfair in the 18th century made Piccadilly one of the busiest thoroughfares in London. In 1791 Horace Walpole remarked: 'I have twice this spring been going to stop my coach in Piccadilly, to inquire what was the matter thinking there was a mob, but not at all; it was only passengers.' The area grew more crowded still in the late 19th century with the construction of Shaftesbury Avenue and a flurry of new theatres. Bus routes multiplied and an Underground station was constructed, followed by vast advertising hoardings on the side of the London Pavilion music hall. Virginia Woolf and others thought it was all marvellous, describing Piccadilly Circus as 'the heart of life ... where everything desirable meets'. After the Second World War the ads went international—Coca Cola rather than Bovril—and electric, giving a touch of modernity to the 'swinging' city of Europe. Even in this Age of Aquarius, it takes a certain perversity to think of Piccadilly Circus as swinging any more; in the 1970s it was in the news mostly for its sprawling Underground station where drug addicts and men in dirty raincoats used to lurk in the toilets.

Two curiosities are nevertheless worth a moment's attention. The first is the **Criterion Restaurant** on the south side of the Circus, which has a long dining room sumptuously adorned in neo-Byzantine style, with a gilt ceiling, marble pillars and ornamental tiles. An enthusiastic team of restorers reopened the restaurant in 1992, since when it has proved so popular that it has been snapped up by Marco Pierre White and turned into a fast-moving showcase for his cuisine. The second attraction of Piccadilly Circus is the **Eros statue** at its centre, a winged aluminium figure fashioned by Sir Alfred Gilbert in memory of the Victorian philanthropist Lord Shaftesbury and unveiled in 1893. Londoners have developed a strange fondness for this statue, an audacious and rather un-British experiment in homo-erotic art; strange because it was designed without a shred of enthusiasm, detested by the critics who first saw it and plagued ever since by corrosion and overzealous tourists who like to clamber all over it. The figure is not in fact supposed to be Eros, the cherubic god of love, at all; Gilbert intended it to be an Angel of Christian Charity, in memory of Lord Shaftesbury's work with destitute children. The identity problem (not exactly surprising, given the statue's state of undress and the bow in its right hand) was only one of several sources of anguish for Sir Alfred Gilbert. He was reluctant to embark on the project in the first place, describing Piccadilly Circus as 'an impossible site on which to place any outcome of the human brain except possibly an underground lavatory'. Then, having accepted the commission, he tried in vain to have the statue mounted atop a wide basin lapped by gushing fountains. He was overruled by his masters, the Shaftesbury Memorial Committee, which shuddered at the thought of the public getting splashed. So angry was Gilbert at this and other setbacks that he refused to attend the official unveiling by the Duke of Westminster. The statue has been plagued by misfortune ever since. George Bernard Shaw called it 'hideous, indecent and ludicrous'; it spent the two world wars and most of the time between away from Piccadilly Circus; more recently, it was found to be suffering from cracks and corrosion, and spent most of the 1980s being mended.

> *The best thing about Piccadilly Circus is the view down Lower Regent St towards St James's Park and the Houses of Parliament. On the corner of Piccadilly and Regent St is a gargantuan branch of Tower Records which might be a nice place to shop were it not for the incessant crowds of*

walkman-zombies who bump into you every five seconds. We will return to Regent St, but first a quick tour round the real horrors of this part of town. Head out of Piccadilly Circus on Coventry St (another name familiar from Monopoly!). On the corner of Haymarket, you'll notice a flamboyant and truly hideous sculpture called The Horses of Helios *by Rudy Weller (1992), and just down from it, at No.34 Haymarket, a stranded mid-Georgian shopfront now occupied by Paperchase. Back on the north side of Coventry St, is the* **London Pavilion**.

This was once a music hall but has now been tarted up and revamped as the **Rock Circus** (*open 11–9, except Tues noon–9 and Fri and Sat 11–10; adm expensive*). This can be quite fun in a tacky sort of way—a sanitized history of rock'n'roll told with the help of wax figures from Madame Tussaud's and a vast array of lighting tricks, and a revolving theatre featuring an automaton of The Beatles. The soundtrack is pumped straight into your ears via a personal headphone set you receive at the entrance, so there's no need to pay attention to the hordes of spotty young males making fools of themselves with imaginary guitars all around you.

Right opposite the London Pavilion, with entrances on Great Windmill St, Coventry St and, round the back, on Shaftesbury Avenue, is the **Trocadero Centre**.

It would be no great loss to visit London and miss out on this, arguably the city's brashest, least salubrious attraction. Take a quick look and gasp at the mesmerising atrociousness of it all—the overpriced theme-u-rants (Planet Hollywood and the Thunderdome Café), the screaming kids and intimidating teenagers. Amidst the horrors, there are some thrilling and expensive virtual reality simulators, a dodgem ride (also thrilling and expensive) and a 3-D IMAX cinema. If these are your idea of fun, go ahead. If not, you should be able to see the whole place and be out again in about 20 seconds.

Return to Piccadilly Circus, via Shaftesbury Avenue if you can, just to vary the route and to take in the clump of theatres (Lyric, Apollo and Shaftesbury) on the north side of the street. Cross over Glasshouse St and you begin the slow curve around the quadrant of **Regent Street**.

Regent Street was once the finest street in London, although you might not think so to look at it now. In fact, all it boasts are a few fine shops (particularly men's clothes stores), the new *Cheers* theme-u-rant (at 72 Regent Street, overpriced and depressingly anonymous) and some rather stuffy, impersonal buildings livened up just once a year by the overhead display of electric Christmas decorations. The street could scarcely be further from the original plan, drawn up in 1813 by John

Nash for the Prince Regent, which intended to bring revolutionary changes to the way London was organized. Nash's idea was to make Regent Street the main north-south artery linking the prince's residence at Carlton House on The Mall to the newly landscaped expanse of Regent's Park; as such it would have been the centrepiece of a carefully planned ensemble of squares, palaces and public thoroughfares. The prince was effusive about the scheme and predicted it would 'quite eclipse Napoleon'. Parliament, however, was not so sure and fretted about how much the whole thing would cost. The main problem was the lack of precedent for urban planning in London; one by one suspicious noblemen whose land lay on the proposed route for Regent Street raised objections to selling out to the crown. By the time Nash had haggled his scheme to completion, Regent Street was no longer the straight line of his plans, but a series of curious wiggles that had to be bent and twisted into something resembling an elegant shape.

One such wiggle was here at Piccadilly Circus. Nash converted it into a graceful quarter-turn and christened it The Quadrant, endowing it with arcades and balustrades that provided the perfect walkway for strollers in central London. 'Those who have daily intercourse with the public establishments in Westminster may go two-thirds of the way on foot under cover,' wrote Nash, 'and those who have nothing to do but walk about and amuse themselves may do so every day in the week, instead of being frequently confined many days together to their houses by rain.' The idea caught on, and Regent Street became the centre of fashionable London society, with shops that attracted customers from around the world. Nash himself took lodgings in a spacious flat at No.16—quite a novelty in a city where everyone, at that time, lived in houses.

The splendour of The Quadrant was not to last. The Victorians had no time for Nash, and little more for Georgian architecture in general. Shopkeepers complained that the arcaded pavements were too dark and attracted too many louche characters, particularly in the evenings. As a result, the authorities decided in 1848 to pull down the colonnade, thus wrecking the harmony of Nash's design. At the beginning of the 20th century, the buildings themselves came under attack, again because of the complaints of shopkeepers who said their floorspace was too restricted. Demolition began in 1916 and the present desperately unimaginative buildings were in place by the mid-1920s. The reconstruction represented a triumph of commerce and petty-mindedness over imagination, a problem that has beset London more than once in its long history.

Nobody has mourned Regent Street more eloquently than E.M. Forster in his elegiac essay *London is a Muddle*, written in the 1930s: 'It was not great architecture, but it knew what it was doing, and where it was going... Here are monuments that do not adorn, features that feature nothing, flatness, meanness, uniformity without harmony, bigness without size. Even when the shops are built at the same moment and by architects of equal fatuity, they manage to contradict one another. Here is the heart of the Empire, and the best it can do. Regent Street exhibits, in its most depressing aspect, the Spirit of London.'

> *One address that has not changed too much is the **Café Royal** at No.68 on the right-hand side of The Quadrant. Even its present owner, Granada, has vowed to leave it alone. If you're feeling tired, this is a good stopping off point for a cocktail or afternoon tea from 3pm–5pm (from £5 for afternoon tea, to £15 for a 'champagne high tea').*

A liveried doorman stands guard over one of the most fashionable addresses of the decadent years leading up to the First World War. Its extravagant mirrors, velvet seats, marble table-tops and caryatid sculptures have remained more or less as they were when Oscar Wilde, Aubrey Beardsley and Edward, Prince of Wales, held court here in the naughty 1890s.

Legend has it that the café's founder, a Parisian wine merchant called Daniel Nicolas Thévenon, had just £5 to his name when he set up shop in 1865. Nowadays you'd be lucky to get a coffee for that amount. Despite and perhaps because of a certain snootiness, the café has proved enduringly popular with Top People. During the Second World War, Winston Churchill regularly rang up to order dinner at Downing Street; his favourite order, dispatched with two waiters in a taxi, was six smoked salmon, six tournedos Rossini and plenty of Stilton. Just as well nobody knew about that particular indulgence when Churchill was giving his rousing speeches about common sacrifice and fighting them on the beaches.

> *Low arches lead off to left and right into Air St; the Piccadilly Arcades, a series of covered shops, are off to the right just beneath the Sun Alliance Insurance building. A little further on, turn left down Vigo St and walk down to the first four-way junction. To your right is the quintessential address for men's bespoke tailoring, **Savile Row**. The street has hit hard times recently, although you'll still find some atmospherically traditional establishments, such as Gieves and Hawkes at No.1. The roof of No.3 was where the Beatles held their famous impromptu concert in 1969, their first live performance in public for three years, which formed the basis of their farewell film and album* Let It Be. *Opposite Savile Row, on the other side of Vigo St, is the driveway to the **Albany**.*

This elegant Georgian building is one of the most beautiful in London and was once a prestigious address for eminent bachelors including Lord Palmerston, Robert Smirke, William Gladstone, Graham Greene and Terence Stamp.

Straight ahead is Burlington Gardens, a short street dominated on the left-hand side by a building adorned with outsize statues of the great philosophers, from Locke to Leibniz to Linnaeus (and that's just the ones beginning with L). Until it moved to the British Museum in December 1997, this was the Museum of Mankind (see p.241). The building itself was constructed in the 1850s to house the administrative offices of the University of London. Its new role is yet to be determined.

*The last building on the left at the end of Burlington Gardens is a **folly** built in 1926 for Atkinsons the outfitters, since supplanted by the fashion house Ferragamo. The building looks more like a church than a shop, with its spire and carillion of 23 bells. The brickwork is further adorned with gilded crests and a grasshopper, symbol of the Elizabethan Lord Mayor of London, Sir Thomas Gresham. Returning towards the Museum of Mankind, the first turning on the right is **Burlington Arcade**.*

London never really went in for shopping arcades the way that Paris did at the beginning of the 19th century; nowhere in this city will you find the graceful iron and glasswork of the Parisian *passages*, the precursors of the modern department store. Arcades nevertheless enjoyed a brief popularity in the final decade of George IV's life. The Royal Opera Arcade (*see* p.152) was the first, and there are others dotted around Piccadilly and St James's which are mentioned either in this walk or in Walk I. The most famous, however, is Burlington Arcade (1819), no doubt because of its top-hatted beadles who enforce the arcade's quaint rules: no whistling, no singing and no running. The arcade was not, it must be said, commissioned predominantly for aesthetic reasons; Lord Cavendish, the owner of Burlington House next door, was fed up with passers-by throwing oyster shells and other rubbish into his garden and thought the arcade would be a suitable barrier. Originally it had a magnificent triple-arched entrance, but in 1931 the shopkeepers of the arcade demanded more girth to take deliveries, and the arches were destroyed (another depressing example of Forster's Spirit of London). Nowadays it is elegant enough, its high-ceilinged halls decorated in green and white, but you probably won't be tempted by its overpriced upmarket clothes shops.

*The south end of the arcade comes out on Piccadilly. Turn left and left again to enter Burlington House, home to the **Royal Academy of Arts** (open 10–6 daily; adm).*

In 1714, the third Earl of Burlington took a trip to Italy and, rather like Inigo Jones exactly one century earlier, came back an ardent convert to Palladian architecture. But where Jones failed to start a general trend, Lord Burlington succeeded triumphantly; Palladian buildings were soon sprouting all over London. One of the first was the earl's private residence here in Piccadilly, completed in 1720 to the designs of James Gibbs, Colen Campbell and the earl himself. The gate leads into a grand courtyard graced with a beautiful graced colonnade. The house was based on Palladio's Palazzo Porta in Vicenza, a classic exercise in harmony and simple lines. The poet John Gay was much impressed, writing: 'Beauty within, without proportion reigns.' But Palladian mansions soon gained a reputation for being more comfortable to look at than to live in. Viewing such a house, another contemporary poet, Alexander Pope, remarked sardonically:

> *Thanks Sir, cried I, 'tis very fine*
> *But where d'ye sleep and where d'ye dine?*

Burlington House was nevertheless lived in for more than a century, until the government bought it in 1854 to house the Royal Academy of Arts. It has been one of London's most important exhibition venues ever since, staging major retrospectives ('Monet' in 1991) as well as the famed Summer Exhibition, a traditional but fairly underwhelming showcase for over a thousand amateur British artists in which most of the works offered for sale seem to feature pictures of cats, sunny Italian landscapes or vases of anemones. The RA does put on more cutting-edge exhibitions, most of these under the wing of its outspoken secretary, Norman Rosenthal, who looks like a boy scout but is actually one of the most influential movers in the British art world. Rosenthal was responsible for 'A New Spirit in Painting' in 1981 which featured controversial neo-expressionist works by Julian Schnabel and Anselm Kieffer, and for the highly controversial 'Sensation' exhibition in 1997, Charles Saatchi's collection of Young British Artists (*see* pp.123–4).

The RA also has a permanent collection with works from each of its prestigious members (Reynolds, Gainsborough, Constable and Turner for starters), as well as a marble relief sculpture by Michelangelo of the *Madonna and Child with the Infant St John*. You won't get much sense of the original Palladian mansion, however, because the building was radically altered by the Victorian architect Sydney Smirke in 1872. Smirke added a second storey, thus upsetting the harmony of the original, rearranged the interiors and stuck statues of famous artists on to the outside walls above the windows—look out for Leonardo, Michelangelo, Titian and Christopher Wren. The bronze statue in the centre of the courtyard is of Sir Joshua Reynolds, the founder of the Royal Academy, shown with palette and paintbrush. It dates from 1931.

> *Leaving Burlington House, walk back past Burlington Arcade and turn right up* **Old Bond Street**.

Two kinds of shopkeeper dominate Bond Street: jewellers and art dealers, whose gaudy if not always particularly attractive shop fronts make for a diverting stroll. Old Bond Street, the lower part of the thoroughfare, concentrates mainly on jewellery and includes all the well-known international names including Tiffany's at

No.25 (note the fine gold-trimmed clock hanging above the entrance) and Chatila at No.22, with its curious gargoyles above the window displays. Evidently these establishments have kept going through the recession thanks to the patronage of the Russian mafia, which has made London its main foreign outpost. Old Bond Street brought a rare piece of good luck to the inveterate 18th-century rake and gambler, Charles James Fox, who once made a bet with the Prince of Wales on the number of cats appearing on each side of the street. No fewer than 13 cats appeared on Fox's side, and none on the Prince of Wales's. Maybe, though, Fox should have taken his inauspicious number of cats as an omen and steered clear of the gambling dens of St James's, since he later went bankrupt and had to be bailed out by his father.

*The turning on the left just after Stafford St is the **Royal Arcade**. Built in 1879, it is one of the kitschier examples of the genre with caryatids painted orange and white above the entrance. Walk through the arcade to emerge on Albermarle St. Across the road on the right is one of the entrances to **Brown's Hotel**.*

This old-fashioned hotel remains one of the quintessential addresses of aristocratic London. Founded by a former manservant in 1837, it retains the kind of service one imagines to have been quite commonplace in the houses of gentlemen of quality. Franklin and Eleanor Roosevelt spent their honeymoon here, while in room 36 the Dutch government declared war on Japan during the Second World War. Nowadays, the time to come is for tea when, for a slightly cheaper rate than the Ritz (*see* p.158), you can fill up on scones and cucumber sandwiches and enjoy the attentions of demure waiters in tails. Dress smart or they won't let you in.

*Across the road from Brown's, at 21 Albermarle St, is the **Royal Institution** (open Mon–Fri, 10–6; adm).*

This building, with its pompous façade based on the Temple of Antoninus in Rome, is to science what the Royal Academy is to the arts: the most prestigious association of professionals in the land. Founded in 1799, the Institution built up a formidable reputation thanks to early members such as Humphrey Davy (inventor of the Davy Lamp for detecting methane down mines) and his pupil, Michael Faraday. The small museum (the only part of the building regularly open to the public) is in fact Faraday's old laboratory where he carried out his pioneering experiments with electricity in the 1830s; his work is explained with the help of his original instruments and lab notes. The Royal Institution also organizes excellent lectures, including series specially designed for children.

*Just beyond the Royal Institution, at the top of Albermarle St, is the ultimate shop for country gents, **Asprey's**, whose windows are packed with rifles, shooting-sticks and waders. If you walk through the shop to the*

Bond St side you can also enjoy its extraordinary collection of military jew-ellery, including tanks and fighter jets made of gold and silver. Eventually you need to turn left onto Grafton St (named after the same family as the famous street in Dublin, though with no reason to be as famous), then round the bend first into Dover St and then right into Hay Hill. At the junction with Berkeley St, look right for a moment into Berkeley Square (to which we shall return) and notice the mock-Tudor grey house on the corner. Almost directly across from Hay Hill is Landsdowne Row, which leads into Curzon St and the heart of **Mayfair**.

The May Fair was once exactly that: an annual festival of eating, drinking, enter-tainments and (usually) debauchery that took place in the first two weeks of May. The custom began in 1686 when the area was in its infancy; by the middle of the 18th century, the neighbourhood had gone so far upmarket that the residents described the fair as 'that most pestilent nursery of impiety and vice' and made sure it was shut down for good. Mayfair has been pretty staid ever since, the preserve of London's *beau monde* who want nothing more than to be left alone. You will nev-ertheless notice, particularly around Curzon St, some fine 18th-century houses and a few oddities. Notice, for example, the dramatic Edwardian façade of the Christian Science Church at No.7. 'Cleanse the Leper, Raise the Dead, Heal the Sick,' reads the inscription. It is only on closer inspection that you realize that the façade is all that remains, the rest having been bombed away in the war; inside is a modern office complex which the Christian Scientists share with an assortment of commer-cial enterprises.

Shortly after the church, turn down one of the passages off Curzon St to the left and you come to **Shepherd Market**.

There may not be any more May Fairs in Mayfair, but this enchanting warren of cafés, restaurants and small shops nevertheless comes as a nice surprise after all the stuffiness of its surroundings. Back in the 17th century, this was where the fire-eaters, jugglers, dwarves and boxers would entertain the crowds in early spring. The entrepreneur Edward Shepherd then turned the area into a market in 1735 (notice the attractive low Georgian buildings), and it has been a focus for rather more low-key entertainment ever since. Recently there has been another battle against 'impiety and vice' in the form of high-class prostitutes who come here in the evenings to pick up rich businessmen.

Returning to Curzon St at the far end of the market, turn left and then immediately right onto **Chesterfield Street**, *the best preserved Georgian street in the district with characteristic stuccoed brick façades. At the top, turn right into Charles St, and keep going until you emerge at the south-western corner of* **Berkeley Square**.

This is a key address for debutantes and aristocratic young bucks, who come for the annual Berkeley Square Charity Ball and vie to join the square's exclusive clubs and gaming houses. The chief interest to the visitor is the elegant row of Georgian houses on the west side. The highlight is No.44, described by Nikolaus Pevsner as 'the finest terraced house in London', which was built in 1742–4 for one of the royal household's maids of honour. Unfortunately the house is now a private casino called the Clermont Club, and its stunning interior, including a magnificent double staircase designed by William Kent, is out of bounds to the general public. They say the house is haunted by the ghost of its first major-domo, who can be heard coming down the stairs with his slight limp; one can only hope that one day he will spook the gamblers off the premises and allow everyone else a closer look.

Leave Berkeley Square on the eastern side by Bruton St, which leads into Conduit St at the junction with **New Bond Street***, worth a brief detour to look into the showrooms of art dealers like Bernard Jacobson and Le Fevre (or, round the corner on Cork Street, Waddington and Victoria Miro). Sotheby's, the famous auctioneers, are at Nos. 34–35 New Bond Street; above the front door is the oldest outdoor sculpture in London, an ancient Egyptian figure made of igneous rock dating back to 1600 BC. After the detour, continue down Conduit St, then turn left on St George St to* **St George's Hanover Square***.*

A neoclassical church with a striking Corinthian portico, St George's was built in 1721–4 as part of the Fifty New Churches Act. It is the parish church of Mayfair and has proved enduringly popular as a venue for society weddings, including the match between Shelley and Mary Godwin. The interior, restored at the end of the Victorian era, has some fine 16th-century Flemish glass in the east window and a painting of the Last Supper above the altar attributed to William Kent. Notice also the cast-iron dogs in the porch; these once belonged to a shop in Conduit St and were brought here in 1940 after their original premises were bombed.

Walk round the back of the church and return to Conduit St via Mill St. After one block to the left you come back to Regent St. Across the road is the department store **Liberty's***, famous for its silks and fabrics which in the 19th century carried designs by William Morris. It still stocks some attractive furniture from the Arts and Crafts period on the top floor and excellent kitchenware, women's clothes and jewellery on other floors. Duck under the arch directly opposite Conduit St and you come into Foubert's Place, a busy pedestrian alley. In Kingly St to the left you can see the bridge leading from the main Liberty's building to its fake-Tudor timbered extension. Continuing on Foubert's Place, you come to that byword of 1960s London culture,* **Carnaby Street***.*

Don't be deluded by the name—the caftans, beads and marijuana that once characterized this street have given way to cheap tee-shirts, Union Jack underpants, plastic
bobby helmets and crass souvenir models of Buckingham Palace and the Tower of
London. Carnaby St simply became too famous for its own good and deteriorated
into tourist trash. More seriously, in the late 1980s it became a hangout for neo-
Nazis who openly paraded racist literature on the stalls. The most attractive building
is the Shakespeare's Head pub on the corner of Foubert's Place. Look up above the
doorway and you'll see a painted bust of the playwright smiling down on the crowd.
For some reason lost in the mists of time, the figure has one hand missing.

> *Return to Regent St via Foubert's Place or Great Marlborough St, then
> continue on up to Oxford Circus, where Regent St meets **Oxford Street**.*

Oxford Street is forever packed with shoppers and tourists, for whom its wide pavements and large department stores symbolize the very essence of the big city. This
rather puzzling mystique is not at all borne out by the reality, which is impersonal,
uniform and unremittingly grey. In 1825 John Wilson Croker called Oxford Street
'thou lengthy street of ceaseless din', and the description still applies; even if cars
have been banned during the daytime, there is still plenty of noise from the zillions
of buses and taxis. Oxford Street has only its shops, and they are nothing to write
home about. The most prestigious address, a few blocks off to the right beyond
Duke Street, is Selfridge's, which for sheer size and range of goods is the closest
rival in London to Harrods. The other department stores, such as Debenhams and
John Lewis, are not nearly as much fun (or as cheap) as the specialist shops dotted
around more intimate parts of London. For the most part, Oxford Street can only
offer outsize outlets of high street regulars like Marks & Spencer, River Island and
The Gap—evidence that Oxford Street is really just Nowheresville plopped into the
centre of London.

> *This is where Mayfair ends, but as a coda to this walk you can continue a
> little further up Regent St. The second turning to the right is Margaret St
> which leads, beyond the junction with Portland St, down to the aston-
> ishing **All Saints Church**.*

Ruskin once said of All Saints, Margaret Street, that it was 'the first piece of architecture I have seen built in modern days which is free from all signs of timidity and
incapacity'. That was probably an understatement. William Butterfield's church,
completed in 1859, is the apogee of the Victorian Gothic Revival; a riot of colour,
decoration and rather sinister charm. Its arches, pillars and vaulted ceiling are
almost aglow with coloured granite, marble, alabaster and painted tiles. Its tall spire
(227ft) is spooky enough to warrant an appearance in a horror film. All Saints is not
a church that leaves you indifferent; either you will find it breathtakingly audacious
or else it will revolt you as a sanctimonious piece of Victorian excess.

*This is a particularly forlorn corner of the West End, so hurry back to Regent St either by the way you came, or one block higher along Mortimer St, home to the Middlesex Hospital and some attractive cafés. Either way, you come out on a bend called **Langham Place**.*

Langham Place was one of the wiggles that John Nash had to contend with when building Regent St. The problem was Sir James Langham, who agreed with some reluctance to have his house demolished but refused to sell his back garden. Nash was forced to steer his thoroughfare to the left, but graced the turn with the round church of **All Souls**, whose façade and curious spire guides the eye easily around the corner. Nash's church was much ridiculed at the time of its construction (1822–4), often likened to an exclamation mark, but now is loved for its warm yellow stone and temple-like appearance.

Its most loyal visitors are from **Broadcasting House** next door. This rather grim 1930s building is the nerve centre of the British Broadcasting Corporation, better known by its initials, BBC. The Beeb (or Auntie as it is sometimes referred to) still runs its main radio operations here; television, however, has moved out west to Shepherd's Bush, and the World Service, heard by millions around the world, is based at Bush House in Aldwych.

There never used to be much for the visitor to see around here, but now the broadcasting grandees have thought fit to provide something called 'The BBC Experience'. This includes a guided tour of the building, a look at a collection of Marconi's earliest radio equipment, a shop and café, and various inevitable interactive displays in which visitors have the opportunity to direct a soap opera, read the weather forecast or 'be' a sports commentator (*open 9.30–5.30 daily, © 0870 6030304 for bookings; adm on the pricey side*).

Broadcasting House has spawned a thousand stories, especially from the war years when its journalists abandoned their customary objectivity to lend their weight to the allied war effort (in a less polite country this would be called propaganda; it certainly played its part in boosting morale). On 15 October 1940, a bomb exploded in the building and killed seven people in the middle of the Nine O'Clock News; the news reader, Bruce Belfrage, proved quite unflappable and continued his broadcast to the end. A more humorous occasion was a visit by the exiled King of Norway, Haakon VII. The king approached the front desk, gave his name to the receptionist and waited to be called to a studio. The receptionist picked up her phone, hesitated a moment, and then asked: '*Where* did you say you were king of, dear?'

The third building of interest is the **Langham Hotel** across the road. Built in 1865, this was the prototype luxury hotel in London, which became *the* place for eminent visitors to stay. Napoleon III, Toscanini and Mark Twain all passed through. The composer Antonin Dvorak once scandalized the management by asking for a double room for himself and his grown-up daughter to save money. But in the end it was not doubtful morals that proved the Langham's downfall so much as its inability to keep up with the latest technological advances. Its rooms were all serviced by a single giant tank containing 38,000 gallons of water. When a German landmine landed in 1940, the tank burst and the hotel was ruined. It only reopened, as part of the Hilton chain, in 1991.

From here, bus and walking possibilities are many. To find the nearest Underground station, either return to Oxford Circus or else continue north on the section of Regent St called Portland Place, which was first laid out by the Adam brothers in the 1770s and contains a handful of original Georgian buildings as well as the elegant Art Deco headquarters of the Royal Institute of British Architects at No.66 (open Mon–Fri 8–7 and Sat 9–5; free). The RIBA has an excellent year-round exhibition programme showing work by the likes of Bernard Tschumi, Rem Koolhaas and Zaha Hadid, and focusing on contemporary architectural projects both here and abroad. Every Tuesday at 6.30pm there are talks by some of Britain's leading architects (© 0171–631 0460 for the programme or check Time Out *for details). Portland Place leads to Nash's glorious Park Crescent (see pp.382–3) and* ⊖ *Regent's Park.*

Start: ⊖ *Holborn.*

Walking time: *2 hours, plus several more for a good look round the British Museum.*

V: Bloomsbury & the British Museum

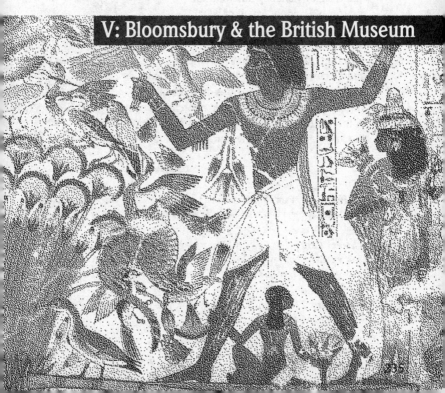

Bloomsbury, according to William the Conqueror's survey *The Domesday Book*, started life as a breeding ground for pigs, but it has acquired a rather more refined pedigree since. Home to London University, the British Museum, the new British Library and countless bookshops and cafés, it is the intellectual heart of the capital. George Bernard Shaw, Mazzini, Marx and Lenin all found inspiration among the tomes of the Reading Room in the British Library. Bertrand Russell and Virginia Woolf helped form an intellectual movement here, the Bloomsbury Group, whose members invited each other for tea and gossip in the area's Georgian town houses.

More recently, Bloomsbury has become a favoured location for the publishing trade and the new wave of independent television production companies. It is a quiet, slightly shabby but youthful quarter of London. Much of your energy will inevitably be devoted to the vast collections of the British Museum, with their echoes of empire and distant civilizations. But there's a good sprinkling of other curiosities on the walk as well, including some eccentric churches, a couple of interesting museums, the new British Library, and the jolly corpse of Jeremy Bentham sitting in a corner of University College.

lunch/pubs

Garden Café, 32 Museum St. Sophisticated sandwiches and salads, French gateaux and chocolate, and freshly squeezed juices. Eat in or take away.

Museum Street Café, 47 Museum St. Slightly overhyped but nevertheless excellent bistro-style café with exquisitely presented home-made food, with a good value two-course set lunch from £12.50.

The Coffee Gallery, 23 Museum St. Potato and artichoke frittata, roasted winter vegetables with pesto, and scrumptious Sicilian salads.

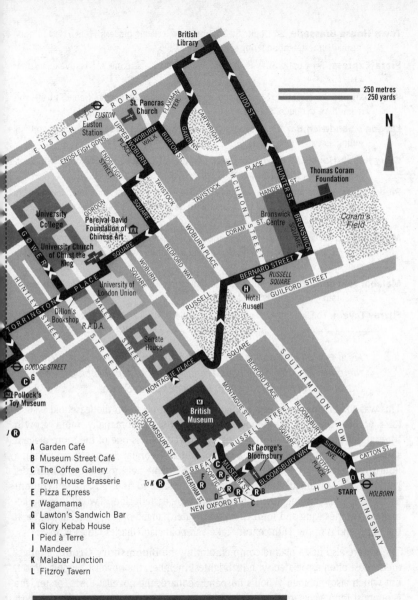

250 metres
250 yards

N

British Library

St. Pancras Church

Euston
Euston Station

EUSTON ROAD

ENDSLEIGH GDNS.
ENDSLEIGH STREET

UPPER WOBURN PLACE
WOBURN WALK

FLAXMAN TERR.

CARTWRIGHT GARDENS

BURTON ST.

JUDD ST.

HUNTER ST.

HANDEL ST.

MARCHMONT STREET

Thomas Coram Foundation

Coram's Field

University College

GORDON SQUARE

Perceval David Foundation of Chinese Art

TAVISTOCK SQUARE

TAVISTOCK SQUARE

WOBURN PLACE

CORAM ST.

Brunswick Centre

BRUNSWICK SQUARE

University Church of Christ the King

HUNTLEY STREET

GOWER STREET

TORRINGTON PLACE

MALET STREET

WOBURN SQUARE

BEDFORD WAY

University of London Union

RUSSELL

BERNARD STREET

RUSSELL SQUARE

H Hotel Russell

GUILFORD STREET

Dillon's Bookshop

R.A.D.A.

Senate House

SOUTHAMPTON ROW

GOODGE STREET

C G

Pollock's Toy Museum

/ R

MONTAGUE PLACE

BLOOMSBURY STREET

GREAT RUSSELL STREET

MONTAGUE ST.

BEDFORD PLACE

BLOOMSBURY SQUARE

M British Museum

St George's Bloomsbury

RUSSELL STREET

BLOOMSBURY WAY

SICILIAN AVE.

CATTON ST.

To K R

STREATHAM ST.

COPTIC ST.

MUSEUM ST.

A
F C R
R E R
D R B
C

NEW OXFORD ST.

BLOOMSBURY SQUARE

SOTON PLACE

HOLBORN

HOLBORN

KINGSWAY

START

A Garden Café
B Museum Street Café
C The Coffee Gallery
D Town House Brasserie
E Pizza Express
F Wagamama
G Lawton's Sandwich Bar
H Glory Kebab House
I Pied à Terre
J Mandeer
K Malabar Junction
L Fitzroy Tavern

V: Bloomsbury and the British Museum

237

Town House Brasserie, 24 Coptic St. Sophisticated, eclectic modern French 'fusion' food in smartish restaurant offering set lunch for £9.95.

Pizza Express, 30 Coptic St. Very acceptable pizza in a striking Art Nouveau setting. £10–15.

Wagamama, 4 Streatham St. Cheap, popular, delicious Japanese noodle ('ramen') bar—you might have to queue. £5–10.

Lawton's Sandwich Bar, 7 Goodge St. Wide variety of sandwiches in busy, unpretentious setting. Eat in or take away.

Glory Kebab House, 57 Goodge St. Greek Cypriot restaurant of long standing, with enormous portions, reasonable prices and ultra friendly waiters. £7–10.

Pied à Terre, 34 Charlotte St. One of the best in Fitzrovia, modern French food. Its speciality dish—get this—is braised pig's head with deep fried brains and ears. Lunch a good bargain from £19 upwards.

Mandeer, 21 Hanway Place. Elegant but cheap vegetarian Indian restaurant a stone's throw from Tottenham Court Rd Tube, serving a fantastic value canteen-style lunch for under £5. Wonderful value.

Malabar Junction, 107 Great Russell St. Set lunch from £7.95 in sleek but laidback Indian restaurant close to the British Museum.

Fitzroy Tavern, 16 Charlotte St. Drinking hole of the 1940s literati. *See* below.

From ⊖ Holborn, walk north up Southampton Row, then take a left down the pretty arcades of Sicilian Avenue (look out for Skoobs, an excellent cheap second-hand book shop) into Bloomsbury Square.

This was the original London housing development based on the leasehold system (*see* pp.88–90), and the model for the city's phenomenally rapid growth throughout the 18th and 19th centuries. Nowadays it is one of the more elegant squares in central London, with a ring of stately Georgian homes surrounding a flourishing garden. The Gordon rioters of 1780 came here to tear the Lord Chief Justice, Lord Mansfield, limb from limb but, unable to find him, had to content themselves with burning down his house (on the eastern side). Two of the troublemakers, Charles King and John Gray, were later hanged on the site. The statue at the north end is of the 18th-century rake and politician Charles James Fox.

The square also has a plaque commemorating the **Bloomsbury Group**, a movement most often associated with its brightest member, the novelist Virginia Woolf, but which also included Woolf's husband Leonard, the novelist E.M. Forster, the economist John Maynard Keynes, the philosopher Bertrand Russell and the essayist Lytton Strachey. The group had no manifesto or specific aim; rather it was a loose association of like-minded intellectuals (most of them politically on the soft left) who met to exchange ideas. Following the teachings of the philosopher G.E. Moore, they believed that the appreciation of beautiful objects and the art of fine conversation were the keys to social progress—an admirable if somewhat elitist outlook on life. Many of the names have disappeared into the historical ether: who now, at least outside Britain, has heard of Clive and Vanessa Bell, Roger Fry, David Garnett or Duncan Grant? You still see plaques outside their houses around Bloomsbury; otherwise they have largely disappeared from sight.

> *Turn left on to Bloomsbury Way, and a little way along on the right is the church of **St George Bloomsbury**.*

This eccentric Baroque church is the work of Nicholas Hawksmoor, 18th-century specialist in the spooky and the bizarre. The portico presents a sober classical façade, its plain pediment supported by two rows of Corinthian columns; but behind is an extraordinary stepped steeple that looks a bit like an elongated pyramid topped by a wobbly statue of George I in a toga. The steeple, which is in fact based on Pliny's description of the mausoleum at Halicarnassus in Crete, prompted ridicule as soon as it was unveiled in 1731. Horace Walpole captured the mood of disdain for both the church and the exclusively German-speaking king in the following lines:

> *When Henry VIII left the Pope in the lurch*
> *The Protestants made him head of the church*
> *But George's good subjects, the Bloomsbury people,*
> *Instead of the Church, made him head of the steeple.*

The interior of St George's is again a model of sobriety, typical of the plain open style pioneered by Wren. For a taste of Hawksmoor's more lugubrious side, you should walk round the outside to the left where a meandering alley ducks under arches and weaves around the church's blackened contours.

> *The alley brings you out on Little Russell St. The name Russell, incidentally, alludes to the same family of Earls of Bedford who built up Covent Garden; Bloomsbury is full of streets called Russell, Bedford and Southampton (the Earl of Southampton being the builder of Bloomsbury Square). Turn left on Little Russell St, and then right on to Museum St with its elegant rows of cafés and rare bookshops that lead straight up to the main entrance of the British Museum.*

The British Museum

Back in the 1770s, the grumpy novelist Tobias Smollett complained that the fledgling British Museum was too empty and lacked a decent book collection. The museum has certainly made up for both deficiencies since. Stuffed with treasures gathered from the farthest reaches of the British Empire, and boasting one of the finest and fullest libraries in the world, it has become an irresistible magnet for visitors and scholars of every temperament and interest. It is by far the most popular tourist attraction in London, catering to nearly seven million visitors a year: triumphant proof that real quality beats the tackiness of the Tower of London or Madame Tussaud's any day.

The museum started as a depository for the art collections of the 18th-century physician Sir Hans Sloane, who bequeathed his possessions to the state on his death in 1753. Parliament decided to put Sloane's *objets d'art* together with the Earl of Oxford's extensive collection of manuscripts under the same roof in Montagu House, the predecessor to the present building. Early visitors had to undergo an extraordinary bureaucratic procedure to be admitted, applying ahead of time in writing to seek the approval of the chief librarian, who allowed no more than 10 people in at a time. It was not until 1879 that access became free and unrestricted.

The collections grew at an astonishing pace. In 1757 George II donated the entire royal library, containing some 10,500 books dating back to Tudor times; over the next half century, books, manuscripts, state papers, antique vases, ethnographic objects, Egyptian relics and Oriental pottery came flooding in. In 1801 the British armed forces brought back some of Napoleon's priceless booty after defeating him at Alexandria. Fifteen years later Lord Elgin brought the celebrated marble friezes of the Parthenon back from Athens.

The British Museum was turning into a storehouse of the spoils of empire, and it was also bursting at the seams. The man chosen to build a new, larger museum was Robert Smirke, an adventurer who had disguised himself as an American to see the art treasures of Paris during the Napoleonic Wars and who later toured Greece with a mob of hired gangsters for protection. His design, which took more than 20 years to complete, pioneered what was later to be called the Greek Revival. His ultra-regular, many-pillared building looks like a temple from antiquity spruced up with Victorian touches. The pediment, for example, contains a very classical-looking relief depicting that most 19th-century of concerns, the progress of civilization. Originally, Smirke's building had a large and airy courtyard. In 1852 Charles Barry put forward a scheme to cover the courtyard with a glass roof using methods of construction recently used in the Crystal Palace. But the proposal was rejected in favour of a scheme to build a new reading room, and in 1854 Smirke's brother Sydney built the British Library's Round Reading Room on the site, covering it with a vast copper dome.

Still the British Museum was not large enough, and over the years some of its departments were farmed out elsewhere. The emergence of the South Kensington museums in the late 19th century provided a new home for its natural history, science and decorative arts collections. In 1970 the Museum of Mankind in Piccadilly took charge of its ethnography department. By the 1990s, the vastness of the museum became so overwhelming that a radical new plan was developed. Its realization is still underway.

A 21st-Century British Museum

Between 1997 and 2000, the Museum is organizing its most exciting and complicated reshuffle ever, as the British Library moves to new premises in St Pancras (*see* p.249 below). The move (especially the removal of the Library's ugly postwar bookstacks) is liberating a massive 40 per cent of the Bloomsbury site for redevelopment under a scheme devised by Norman Foster.

First, Smirke's elegant Greek Revival inner courtyard (which contained the British Library's bookstacks and has been hidden to the public since 1857) will be liberated and opened up into the Great Court. This spectacular and vast space will be covered with a vaulted glass canopy and filled with light. Around it will be galleries, restaurants and bookshops, including the anthropological collections stored until recently at the Museum of Mankind at Piccadilly.

The centre of the Great Court will be dominated by the walls and dome of the Round Reading Room, revealed to the public gaze for the first time in 150 years. A new double staircase and a raised walkway will wrap around the exterior of the Reading Room, giving visitors access to the upper floors of the main museum. Inside the Reading Room the original azure, cream and gold decor will be restored, and part of the room will become a new reference library with an ultra-sophisticated computer database for the collections.

Finally, beneath the Great Court two large staircases will lead down to a new Centre for Education, with two large new auditoriums and five seminar rooms for lectures, seminars and films.

> *The British Museum is open Mon–Sat 10–5, Sun 2.30–6; free; internet information on http://www.british-museum.ac.uk; guided tours (adm) are available. There is more in the museum than can possibly be described below; what follows is a guide to its most famous and appealing artefacts. Your best strategy is to pick up a floor plan and make up your own mind what to see. Roughly speaking, the highlights are as follows. Ground floor: the Reading Room, Western Asia (Assyrian sculptures including the royal lion hunt reliefs from Nineveh), Egypt (the Rosetta stone) and Greece (the Elgin marbles). Upper floor: Egypt (mummies and sarcophagi), Rome (the Portland vase), Romano-British collection (Lindow Man, Mildenhall Treasure) and Medieval (Lewis chessmen).*

Ground Floor

The Round Reading Room

(Between 1997 and 1999 the Round Reading Room and the area around it will be completely redeveloped and still out of bounds to the general public—see above.)

This is one of the best loved rooms in the world, with a beautiful cavernous dome bigger in diameter than St Paul's or St Peter's in Rome. Although designed by Sydney Smirke, it was the brainchild of Sir Antonio Panizzi, an Italian exile who invented the systems for labelling and cataloguing that are used in libraries to this day. A steady stream of the world's political thinkers and revolutionaries came to this wonderfully spacious domed circular room, among them Marx (who wrote *Das Kapital* in Row G), Mazzini and Lenin. Other writers who have found inspiration, consolation and even, occasionally, love among its eighteen million tomes include Macaulay, Thackeray, Hardy, Dickens and Yeats.

It was with considerable reluctance that scholars and researchers gave up their seats of learning here in 1997, bemoaning not only the wonderful architecture they left behind, but also the acoustics; reading here was like reading in a fishtank—no sudden crashes, and all conversation reduced to a sweet-sounding blur. Gissing described the pallor of readers wandering here 'in the shadow of the valley of books'. In the 1940s, the writer and wit Sydney Carter was even moved to write a poem about it:

> When I was a young I used to read books
> In a place called the British Museum
> There were plenty of women who gave me strange looks
> But somehow I just didn't see 'em.
>
> Now I am ninety and weary of books.
> Of knowledge (I think) I have plenty.
> Now I'm beginning to notice the girls—
> They are most of them round about twenty.
>
> If I polish my glasses I see them quite well,
> And some are exceedingly pretty.
> It occurs to me that I have wasted my life
> And there goes the bell, what a pity!

Western Asia

Western Asian treasures are spread throughout the British Museum, but the most accessible, the Assyrian relics of Nineveh, Balawat and Nimrud, are here on the ground floor. The Assyrians, occupying an exposed area in what is now northern Iraq, built up a civilization essentially built on war with their neighbours, especially the Babylonians, between the 9th and 7th centuries BC. Their palaces are decorated with figures of wild animals, mythical creatures and magic symbols as well as depictions of conical-helmeted soldiers at arms with their chariots, battering rams and pontoons. Nimrud was the stronghold of Ashurnasirpal II (883–859 BC). His palace doorway was flanked by two huge stone lions with human heads and wings, which have survived almost entirely intact. There is a statue of the king himself, and stone reliefs illustrating his campaigns. From Balawat comes a reconstruction of the similarly adorned gates built by Shalmaneser II; the cedar wood, bolstered by strips of bronze, is original. The apotheosis of Assyrian civilization, though, was at Nineveh under King Ashurbanipal (668–627 BC). The reliefs from his palace show him routing the Arabs and defeating the Elamites at the Battle of the River Ulai (note the detail of the palm trees and musical instruments in the royal victory parade). The most extraordinary artwork depicts a **royal lion hunt**; the dying animals, shot through with arrows, are sculpted with great emotional force.

Egypt

There are more lions here in the Egyptian sculpture gallery, this time red and black ones carved in granite and limestone for the tombs of Pharaohs; Ruskin described them as 'the noblest and truest carved lions I have ever seen'. Among the huge Pharaohs' heads and ornate sarcophagi, look for the likeness of Amenophis III, an 18th Dynasty ruler, and the gilded coffin containing Henutmehit, the Chantress of Amen-Re, from around 1290 BC. Many of the riddles of the ancient Egyptian world were solved through the **Rosetta Stone**, a slab of black basalt discovered by Napoleon's army in the Nile Delta in 1799, which by extraordinary good fortune reproduces the same text in three languages: Greek, demotic and Egyptian.

The subject of the stone is not exactly inspiring; it is a decree issued at a general council of priests meeting in Memphis in 196 BC. But it offered the first opportunity for modern scholars to crack the code of Egyptian hieroglyphics. The man who takes the greatest credit is the French Egyptologist Jean François Champollion. But, as the patriotically-minded museum display points out, he was greatly helped by the British scholar Thomas Young, who was the first to realize that hieroglyphics could have phonetic as well as symbolic value.

Greece

Two monuments overshadow the Greek collections: the Nereid Monument and the Elgin Marbles. The **Nereid Monument** is a reconstruction of a vast tomb found at the Greek colony of Xanthos in Asia Minor. Built like a temple with a pediment supported by Ionic columns, it is a stunning tribute to the Lycian chieftains who are buried there; it also features remarkable frieze sculptures of men in battle, noblemen at court, an animal sacrifice and a hunting expedition.

Dating from around 400 BC, the Monument was destroyed at some stage by an earthquake and only rediscovered during an expedition by the archaeologist Charles Fellows in 1838. Painstakingly put back together, it reached its present state only in 1951.

As for the **Elgin Marbles**, they have aroused so much controversy for being in Britain rather than Greece that their artistic merit is sometimes entirely overlooked. To set the record straight: Lord Elgin, the British Ambassador to the Ottoman Empire, discovered the stones lying forlornly on the ground when he visited Athens in 1800. The Parthenon, from which the marbles came, had been half wrecked in a skirmish between the Turks and a Venetian fleet besieging them in 1687, when a supply of gunpowder kept in the building exploded and brought many of the colonnades crashing to the ground. Elgin obtained a licence from the Turkish Sultan in 1802 and proceeded to transport the treasures back home.

The British are probably right to assert that the marbles would not have survived if they had stayed in Greece; the Turks never lifted a finger to restore the Acropolis and at one stage ground down some of the stones that Elgin left behind to make cement. The Greek government claims that its own national sentiments should be taken into consideration; fair enough, but it is worth remembering that the Parthenon Museum in Athens already has many of the best relief sculptures (the remainder being in Paris and Copenhagen). The British Museum has shown no sign of giving in to the Greek demands, and is not likely to in the foreseeable future.

The Elgin Marbles are the frieze reliefs from the Parthenon, the temple to Athena on top of the Acropolis, and are considered some of the finest sculptures of antiquity. Depicting a Panathenaic festival to commemorate Athena's birthday, they reveal a remarkable mastery of detail and human feeling. The British Museum has them displayed in a vast room giving an idea of the scale of the Parthenon itself.

The best way to view the sculptures is as a kind of cartoon strip. The grand procession includes riders in their chariots, city elders, musicians, pitcher bearers, attendants, sacrificial victims, beautiful girls carrying libation bowls, tribal heroes and, in the east frieze, the gods Hermes and Dionysus. On the south side is a depiction of a brawl between the Lapiths of Thessaly and their guests the mythical Centaurs, who have got drunk and attempted to drag off the Lapith women. The exhibition also includes fragments of the east pediment, depicting the birth of Athena, and the west front, showing the battle between Athena and Poseidon for control of Attica, the region around Athens.

Oriental Collections (halfway between Ground and Upper Floors)

These rooms cover a huge amount of ground, from Chinese Tang dynasty glazed tomb figures to Turkish and Syrian ceramic work, by way of Thai banner painting and religious monuments from India and Nepal. Perhaps the most impressive section for the non-specialist is the room devoted to South and Southeast Asia. There is some magnificent filigree work in a 19th-century altar screen from Nepal; some beautiful doors to a Balinese palace made of jackfruit wood, with gilded leaf motifs on red lacquer; some beautiful stone figures of Vishnu, Shiva and other gods from 11th-century central India; and, at the end of room 33, large chunks of the 3rd-century Great Stupa at Amaravati in Andhra Pradesh. This is a grand domed Buddhist temple, with narrative scenes of the life of Buddha decorated with lotus motifs.

Upper Floor

Egypt (continued)

The display of **Egyptian mummies and sarcophagi** is the most popular section of the British Museum, no doubt for its addictive gruesomeness. Here is the Egyptian way of death in all its bizarre splendour: rows and rows of spongy bodies wrapped in bandages and surrounded by the prized belongings and favourite food of the deceased. It took 70 days to prepare a body for interment in ancient Egypt. The body was either dried out or soaked in a solution of natron and water. The viscera were then cut out or dissolved with chemicals; the brain was drained out through the nostrils with the help of an iron hook. Only the heart, which the ancient Egyptians believed to be the centre of understanding, remained in the corpse at burial. After disembowelling, the bodies were washed with palm wine and sewn up, bandaged and strewn with valuables. The effect of all this is ghoulish in the extreme. The headrests used to prop up the mummies look distinctly like gallows blocks; the food, including bread, cake and pomegranate dating back to 1250 BC, looks almost as putrid as the barely-preserved human flesh. Most unsettling of all is the body of a man from 3400 BC in a reconstructed grave pit.

Western Asia (continued)

The collection is more eclectic here than downstairs: Bronze Age tools from Syria, a mosaic column from Tell-al-Ubaid, reliefs from Kapara's palace in Tell Halaf (now in northeastern Syria) as well as further relics from Nimrud (ivory carvings) and Nineveh (tablets from the royal library). The two highlights are a collection of magnificently preserved funerary busts from Palmyra dating from the 1st and 2nd centuries AD, and the extraordinary sculpture *The Ram in the Thicket* from Ur, the birthplace of Abraham. Made of gold and lapis lazuli, this delicate figure dates back to 2600 BC, when Ur was part of Chaldea in southern Babylonia. It was found in a pit at the entrance to Ur's royal cemetery, along with other treasures including a golden royal cup, a silver lyre and a splendid lapis and carnelian headdress.

The Italy of the Greeks, Etruscans and Romans

As a prelude to this section, have a look down the western staircase, which is adorned with a Roman mosaic. On the walls are more mosaic fragments, this time from Greek palaces in Halicarnassus, Ephesus and Carthage. The collections themselves are a bit of a mixed bag: Greek red-figure vases found in Lucania and Apulia in southern Italy (1400–1200 BC), a carved stone Etruscan sarcophagus found at Bomarzo north of Rome (3rd century BC) and plenty of bronze heads of Roman emperors. Anyone who knows Rome will appreciate the terracotta reliefs that once decorated the Pantheon, with their orgiastic depictions of Cupid, Bacchus and a number of satyrs; there are also fragments of wall paintings from Nero's Golden House in the Forum. The highlight of the Roman collection, though, is the **Portland Vase**, so called because the Barberini family sold it to the Dukes of Portland. The vase, made around the time of the birth of Christ, is of cobalt-blue glass and coated in an opaque white glaze depicting the reclining figures of Peleus and Thetis, with Cupid and his love arrows hovering overhead. The vase has had a traumatic time of it since arriving in England; first a rival of the Portland family did his best to smash it, and then in 1845 a drunken visitor succeeded in breaking it into 200 pieces. He was later charged, not with criminal damage to a priceless treasure, but with the comparatively harmless offence of glass breakage. The vase has been lovingly put back together and you would scarcely notice the difference.

Romano-British Section

The oldest and most gruesome exhibit here is **Lindow Man**, the shrivelled remains of an ancient Briton preserved down the centuries in a peat bog. The body, which has been dated between 300 BC and AD 100, shows evidence of extreme violence. Evidently he was the victim of ritual slaughter, perhaps by druids, who stripped him, garotted and bled him, put his body in a bag and then threw him into unconsecrated ground in the middle of a bog at Lindow, near the town of Moss in Cheshire. There he lay until 1984 when a digging machine rooting around in the peat became entangled in the lower half of his body. All you see here is his torso and crushed head, freeze-dried like instant coffee, with a hologram giving you a better idea of what he originally looked like.

Excavations in Britain have provided more pleasant surprises, notably the **Mildenhall Treasure**, 34 remarkably well-preserved pieces of 4th-century silver tableware dug up from a field in Suffolk in 1942. There are some beautiful mosaics, the largest of them a 4th-century floor from Hinton St Mary in Dorset which appears to be Christian in inspiration. The fish symbol much used by the early

Christians features prominently, and the figures representing the four winds at the edges of the mosaic could also stand for the four gospels. A mosaic from Thruxton in Hampshire, from the same period, is more carefree in spirit, depicting Bacchus (whose head is unfortunately missing) in a pastoral setting.

Medieval Antiquities

Here you will find more extraordinary finds from digs around the British Isles. An excavation at Sutton Hoo on the Suffolk coast brought to light an extraordinary haul from a burial ship loaded up in homage to an early 7th-century British king, possibly Raedwald who died in 624. In the manner of the ancient Egyptians, the king's courtiers piled up everything he could possibly want for the afterlife: gilded ivory drinking horns, lyres, maplewood bottles, silver platters, gold jewellery, coins and more besides. You should not miss the **Lewis chessmen**, a collection of 78 pieces in walrus ivory discovered in the remote Outer Hebrides in 1831.

The farmer who first came across them fled thinking they were elves and fairies, and it was only the fortitude of his wife that persuaded him to go back for another look. The figures do not make up complete chess sets and are thought to have been left by a travelling salesman, possibly from Scandinavia, sometime in the 12th century.

Prints and Drawings

It is hard to predict what you will see here as the museum's vast collection is displayed in rotation. On a good day, though, you can find Michelangelo's sketches for the roof of the Sistine chapel, etchings and sketches by Rembrandt and a large selection of anatomical studies by Albrecht Dürer. Look out, too, for William Hogarth's satirical engravings, notably *Gin Lane* which castigates the corrupting influence of drink on 18th-century London, and his extraordinary series on cruelty.

Leave the museum by the Montague Place exit, then turn left. At the end of the street you come into **Bedford Square***, one of the best preserved Georgian squares in London (1775–80). Note the elegant symmetry of the brick terraces and the Coade stone decoration around their doorways. The square was once a mecca for publishing firms, but the advent of computers has persuaded most of them to relocate to more high-tech surroundings. Walk back down Montague Place to* **Russell Square***, the large and rather characterless centre of Bloomsbury. On the western side looms* **Senate House***, one of the spookiest buildings in London, which stands at the heart of the schools and colleges of the* **University of London***.*

For the first 1800 years of its history, London had no university at all, and only acquired one after non-Anglicans found they were barred from admission to

Oxford, Cambridge and the other British universities. From the time that University College (*see* below) opened in 1828, London has been a relatively progressive and unusually secular centre of learning. In 1878 London became the first British university to let women sit for degrees, and in 1912 was the first to appoint a woman professor.

The London School of Economics (off Aldwych) has a particularly strong track record of political radicalism and was the focus of the rather half-hearted British student response to the Paris revolt of May 1968. For many years the university, which like Oxford and Cambridge is made up of several federated colleges, was administered from Burlington House in Piccadilly, now the Royal Academy. Then in 1936 the architect Charles Holden built the Senate House, a terrifyingly inhuman white hulk of a building. It looks better suited to bureaucrats than academics, and during the Second World War was taken over by the Ministry of Information. George Orwell turned it into the Ministry of Truth in his totalitarian nightmare *Nineteen Eighty-Four*. Now it contains the university library, as well as several smaller departments including the School of Slavonic and East European Studies. Those former Kremlinologists must feel right at home.

> *The School of Oriental and African Studies (SOAS) sits in the northwest corner of Russell Square. To the northeast, on the corner with Bernard St, is the **Hotel Russell**, a late Victorian extravaganza in terracotta with brightly decorated marble halls inside. Bernard St takes you past the Brunswick Centre, a 1960s concrete shopping mall without redeeming features except the excellent Renoir art cinema. Turning left, however, to circle Brunswick Square, you come across a pleasant expanse of greenery. In the northeast corner of the square is a bronze statue of Thomas Coram and the entrance to his **Foundation for Children** at No.40 (open by appointment only until 1998 when the foundation will be opening a new museum of British 18th-century art and social history. Call ahead on ℅ 0171–278 2424 for details).*

Coram, a sea captain, founded his hospital for waifs and strays in 1739. It has a high artistic pedigree—Hogarth encouraged his artist friends to contribute their work. The collection includes his sober portrait of Coram, also works by Gainsborough, Reynolds and Benjamin West (whose *Suffer Little Children* takes up the theme of the hospital) and the original manuscript of Handel's *Messiah*, bequeathed by the composer. The hospital was demolished in 1926, leaving a large open field that has since been partially reclaimed by a local primary school. Of the original building, only a reconstruction of the governor's Court Room and an oak staircase survive.

*From here you can enjoy a walk around some of Bloomsbury's prettier streets and squares. Retrace your steps along the north side of Brunswick Square and turn right into Hunter St which, along with its extension Judd St, has some attractive cafés and small shops. Continue walking up Judd Street as far as the Euston Road, and facing you on the other side of the road on Midland Street is the new **British Library** (open from April 1998, with guided tours, bookshops and a restaurant).*

The history of this new building has been such a shambles that it came as a shock to most people when it finally opened, a decade late, in November 1997. Construction work on Colin St John Wilson's building began back in 1978 and took longer than the building of St Paul's cathedral. By the time it was completed, Wilson had overspent by £350 million, his practice had dissolved, and the building itself had been exposed to that peculiarly violent brand of venom that the British reserve for new architectural projects. A parliamentary committee report in 1994 described it as 'one of the ugliest buildings in the world', resembling 'a Babylonian ziggurat seen through a funfair distorting mirror'. Prince Charles called it a 'collection of brick sheds groping for significance'; others have compared it to a provincial shopping mall.

Now that it has finally opened, Londoners will probably get used to the building, and then become fond of it (following a long-established pattern). Ironically, the building's most vicious critics have been stunned and delighted by the spectacular interior, with its vast scale, open tracts of white Travertine marble, and complex and fascinating spaces flooded with light. The building opens to the public in April 1998. If the red brick exterior fills you with initial fear and loathing, remind yourself that the building is worth seeing for its three exhibition galleries and art treasures alone.

The big attraction is the library's vast number of manuscripts, from the sacred to the profane, from the delicate beauty of illuminated Bibles to the frenzied scrawl of Joyce's first draft of *Finnegan's Wake*; from musical scores to political documents, notebooks and private letters. Among the greatest treasures are the **Lindisfarne Gospels**, the work of a monk named Eadfrith who wrote and illuminated them on the island of Lindisfarne (also called Holy Island) off the northeastern coast of England in honour of St Cuthbert. The decorative pages look like Oriental carpets for their bright colours and attention to detail. In the text itself, look out for the English words scrawled in between the lines of Latin during the 10th century by Aldred, Bishop of Durham. It is the oldest known English translation of the Bible, and anticipates by 400 years the work of John Wycliffe, the first Englishman to render both Testaments, not just the Gospels, into the vernacular.

The other star exhibit is the **Magna Carta**. The British Library has two of the four surviving copies of this document, one of the founding texts of the modern democratic system signed by King John at Runnymede under pressure from his barons in 1215. Its 63 clauses are written in a fine if somewhat illegible hand. An excellent display case provides the full text in modern print and discusses its historical importance. Among the other manuscripts are examples of royal correspondence, written out by hand long after the advent of printing; the Duke of Wellington's despatch from the battlefield at Waterloo; and William Gladstone's notes on cabinet meetings. Look out, too, for Lenin's reapplication for a reader's ticket which he made under the pseudonym Jacob Richter. There is an extensive collection of literary manuscripts, including an illuminated version of Chaucer's *Canterbury Tales*; original texts by Ben Jonson, Dryden, Marvell, Dickens, George Eliot, Trollope and Virginia Woolf; part of the correspondence between George Bernard Shaw and Ellen Terry; and—arguably the highlight—Lewis Carroll's beautifully neat handwriting and illustrations in the notebook version of *Alice in Wonderland* (then called *Alice's Adventures Under Ground*), which he gave to his niece Alice Liddell for Christmas in 1864.

Stamp lovers should head for the **Philatelic Collections** which include first issues of nearly every stamp in the world from 1840 to 1890, and an extraordinary range of those issued since. If you think stamps are a bore, look instead at the beautiful Japanese, Indian and Arabic manuscripts here, including a Buddhist cosmology from Burma and Sultan Baybar of Cairo's gold leaf-embroidered Koran of 1304.

As the library gets up and running, look out for other alternatives including striking sculpture by Edward Paolozzi (a 3-D version of William Blake's grim depiction of Isaac Newton) and others. Also opening here from May 1998 will be the **British Library National Sound Archive** (*open daily 10–8; free*). This wonderful collection includes early gramophones and record sleeves, and a series of priceless historical, literary and musical recordings: Florence Nightingale and Gladstone, Paul Robeson in a live performance of Othello, James Joyce reading from *Ulysses*, The Beatles interviewed by Jenny Everett, Charlie Parker's club performances (recorded on wire), and Stravinsky in rehearsal.

> *Leave the library, cross the road and walk a short way east along the Euston Road. At the junction with Mabledon Place, turn left. This leads into* **Cartwright Gardens**, *an attractive late Georgian crescent (1807) which has often been associated with political reformers, including Major John Cartwright himself, who lobbied for universal suffrage and the abolition of slavery; the anti-cholera campaigner Edwin Chadwick; and the liberal preacher Sydney Smith. Burton Place, off the western side of the crescent, leads to Burton St; turn right and then left into* **Woburn Walk**,

*a short pedestrian street of beautifully preserved bow-fronted buildings dating from 1822. Look out for the plaque marking W. B. Yeats's house. At the end, turn right up Upper Woburn Place; on your right is the Greek façade of **St Pancras New Church**.*

The coming of the railways in the mid-19th century was responsible for this rather splendid church. Old St Pancras, which dates back to the 7th century, found itself inconveniently wedged between the two termini at King's Cross and St Pancras and fell into a state of oblivion (you can still see it on Pancras Rd, although it has suffered from overzealous restoration). Far more impressive is the Greek Revivalist building, completed at great expense in 1822 by the father and son team of William and Henry William Inwood. Inspired in part by the Erechtheion in Athens, the church boasts a broad pediment propped up by an Ionic porch and a fine two-tiered octagonal tower. The interior is long, dark and brooding. If you walk round the back, there are pavilions at either side of the church supported by classical caryatids.

Returning down Upper Woburn Place, you come into Tavistock Square. The first building on your left is the headquarters of the British Medical Association; the second has a plaque marking the house where Dickens wrote Bleak House *in 1856–7. The square has an attractive garden with a kneeling figure of Mahatma Gandhi, a reminder of the pacifist links of the Bloomsbury Group, surrounded by flowers. Walk round to the southwest corner of the square, where it links with Gordon Square. On the first corner of Gordon Square proper is the **Percival David Foundation of Chinese Art**.*

This fine collection of imperial porcelain (*open Mon–Fri 10.30–5; free*) is named after the philanthropic collector who acquired its treasures. With its extensive library and superb ceramics, this is a vital stopping-off point for China scholars. The vases, which are beautifully documented and dated, range from the Sung dynasty of the 10th century up to the Qing dynasty of the 18th.

*Cross Gordon Square. At the opposite corner you come to Byng Place and the entrance to the **Church of Christ the King**, an attractive and undervisited neo-Gothic building originally built for a Victorian Catholic sect but now used by the university. The road running north of here is **Gordon Street**, a popular address for the Bloomsbury Group as the many blue plaques testify. This was also where the British Fascist leader Oswald Mosley printed his propaganda rag Action in the 1930s. The Bloomsbury Theatre, on the left, hosts both student and professional productions; the Bartlett, a singularly unlovely building on the corner of*

*Endsleigh Gardens, houses the university architecture school. Return to Gordon Square and walk along Byng Place, which twiddles round a corner and turns into Torrington Place. We are back in the heart of university territory. On the corner of Malet St is the students' union (ULU). If you happen to be a student yourself, you can use its good cheap bar. Halfway down Malet St is **Birkbeck College**, which in 1823 became the first college in England to run evening courses for the working classes. It joined London University in 1920. Continuing down Torrington Place, you come to **Gower Street**.*

The blackened brick terraces of Gower Street sum up everything the Victorians hated about Georgian building. Ruskin called it 'the nec plus ultra of ugliness in street architecture'. You can see what he meant: the sameness of the houses, relieved only by the occasional splash of paint on the lower storey, and the arrow-like straightness of the street. The one Victorian building on the street is **Dillons** bookshop on the corner of Torrington Place.

*Turn right up Gower St and continue until you reach the entrance to **University College** on the right.*

The college is a fine, if rather heavy, example of the Greek Revival style by William Wilkins, the architect of the National Gallery. Many Victorians hated the place, combining their dislike of classical architecture with their disapproval for what they called 'the godless College in Gower Street'; soon after it opened, a group of committed Anglicans set up in competition at King's College on the Strand. Visitors should head straight for the South Cloister in the far right-hand corner. Not far from the doorway is the glass cabinet containing the stuffed body of Jeremy Bentham, the utilitarian philosopher and political reformer who died in 1832.

Bentham had helped set up University College, and himself asked for his body to be preserved in this way. It is a surprisingly jolly monument. The skeleton, dressed in flamboyant clothing, is original apart from the skull, which has been removed to the College safe and replaced with a smiling wax model topped with an eccentric straw hat. Once a week Bentham is carted off in his wheeled cabinet to attend meetings of the board of governors, where he is registered as 'present but not voting'. He is also invited to university parties where as often as not some old buffer clutching his fifth glass of port can be seen engaging him in deep conversation.

Opposite the College is University College Hospital, founded at the same time and still a major London teaching hospital. This is, however, a rather unpleasant corner of Bloomsbury, wedged between the thundering traffic of the Euston Road and several streets' worth of severe Victorian student lodgings to the west. Retrace your steps back to Dillons, then turn right away from the university down the continuation of Torrington Place. This brings you out on to the **Tottenham Court Road**.

As late as the 1870s, cows grazed along this road which is now all too crowded with traffic. Its main attractions are its discount computer and hi-fi shops, and its furniture stores—Heals (very classy and upmarket), Habitat (cheaper but duller) and shop after anonymous shop specializing in sofa-beds and futons.

Directly opposite Torrington Place is the American Church, an innocuous enough looking building but which was once **Whitefields Tabernacle**, the biggest non-conformist church in the world, with room for a congregation of 8000. The church was badly damaged in the Second World War and rebuilt as a memorial chapel.

Turn left down Tottenham Court Rd and right into Tottenham St. This is an area of cafés, cheap Greek restaurants and the occasional fancy shop. Turning left on Whitfield St, you come to the unmissable **Pollock's Toy Museum** *on the corner of Scala St.*

Benjamin Pollock was the leading Victorian manufacturer of toy theatres, and this small but very attractive museum (*open Mon–Sat 10–5; very cheap adm*) is based on the collection that he left. It's an atmospheric place, the four narrow floors connected by creaky staircases. The theatres are on the top floor, and exhibits also include board games, tin toys, puppets, wax dolls, teddy bears and dolls' houses. Not least amongst the museum's attractions is an excellent shop which sells beautiful reproduction toy theatres which children assemble themselves out of wood and card and then use to stage their own plays. The shop also sells a vast number of cheap and cheerful stocking-fillers.

Scala St comes out on Charlotte St, the centre of **Fitzrovia**.

This was one of the key addresses of 1940s and 1950s London, a villagey extension of Soho with plenty of cheap food and drink and a colourful cast of literary eccentrics. Dylan Thomas, Theodora Fitzgibbon, Julian MacClaren Ross, George Orwell and Augustus John drank at the Fitzroy Tavern, which gave its name to the area, and their pictures are displayed in the Writers and Artists bar in the basement. 'What will you have to drink?' the landlord used to ask the permanently sozzled Dylan Thomas. 'Anything that goes down my throat,' came the reply.

Unfortunately, the television crowd moved into Charlotte St during the 1980s, pushing the area several notches upmarket. Locals still mourn the loss of Schmidt's, a magnificent German deli which closed in the 1970s, and Bertorelli's, which was one of the first Italian food shops in London, and something of a revelation to a whole generation of Londoners brought up on ration food.

As you walk northwards up Charlotte Street you are gradually overshad-
owed by the **Telecom Tower,** *a sparkplug skyscraper built in 1965 to*
redirect London's telephone, radio and TV signals. You used to be able to
climb its 580ft tower and eat in a revolving restaurant at the top; now,
unfortunately, it is closed to the public. As you approach it, Charlotte St
turns into Fitzroy St and eventually comes out into **Fitzroy Square.**

Both George Bernard Shaw and Virginia Woolf lived at No.29 (though not, of
course, at the same time), and another Bloomsbury Group acolyte, the artist Roger
Fry, set up his Omega Workshops here. Unfortunately the elegant Georgian houses
on the south and east sides, designed by the Adam brothers, were destroyed by
wartime bombing and replaced with an unpromising 1960s concrete development.

Transport is not a problem from here. Either walk back via Grafton Way to
Tottenham Court Rd, where there are loads of buses, or keep walking
north to Euston Rd. ● *Warren St is a few paces to the right;* ● *Great Port-*
land St and ● *Regent's Park just a few minutes' walk to the left.*

VI: The Inns of Court and Fleet Street

Start: ⊖ *Embankment.*
Walking time: *about 3½ hours.*

'Sir,' said Dr Johnson in typically expansive mood to one of his visitors, 'if you wish to have a just notion of the magnitude of this great City you must not be satisfied with seeing its great streets and squares but must survey the innumerable little lanes and courts.' Johnson was speaking from the heart: he lived around Fleet Street and the Inns of Court for most of his adult life and was addicted to the furtive clubbishness of the labyrinthine narrow backstreets. Everyone knows Fleet Street as the original home of British journalism, and the Inns of Court as the cradle of the English legal system. But if you walk down the main thoroughfare from the Strand to Ludgate Circus, you see only the faintest signs—maybe a bookshop or an appropriately named pub—of these two professions. The real activity, or what's left of it, goes on in the warren of buildings and quadrangles on either side, which resemble not so much the heart of a big city as a medieval university town.

The topography of the area gives a hint of its peculiar, rarefied atmosphere. The Inns of Court in particular have always shrouded themselves in secrecy and ancient ritual as a way of asserting their special place in the social order. Even today, maintaining the traditions of wearing wigs and gowns and eating formal dinners is considered every bit as important as knowledge of the law itself. There is no less a sense of mythology surrounding the great printing presses and journalists' back-street pubs that once characterized the eastern end of Fleet Street. They, however, have almost all gone, victims of new technology which has pushed the newspapers out to computerized premises in the City and

A Ye Olde Cock Tavern
B Temple Bar Tandoori
C Ye Olde Cheshire Cheese
D Café Sofra
E Cittie of York
F Prêt à Manger

THEOBALD'S ROAD

GRAY'S INN ROAD

Gray's Inn Gardens

Gray's Inn

RED LION STREET

BROWNLOW ST.

FULWOOD PL.

E F
P C

CHANCERY LANE **FINISH**

HOLBORN

Holborn Circus

250 metres
250 yards

N

HOLBORN

FINISH

HOLBORN GATE

KINGSWAY STREET

Sir John Soane's Museum

LINCOLN'S INN

Gothic Chapel

New Hall & Library

Royal College of Surgeons

Lincoln's Inn Field

FIELDS

Stone Buildings

Lincoln's Inn

Old Hall

Gatehouse

Public Record Office

Staple Inn

CHANCERY LANE

FETTER LANE

SHOE LANE

Dr Johnson's House

GOUGH ST.

WINE OFFICE COURT

C P

Ludgate Circus

D
R

Old Curiosity Shop

PORTUGAL ST.

CAREY STREET

SERLE ST.

NEW SQUARE

BELL YARD

Royal Courts of Justice

St Dunstan's in the West

FLEET STREET

P R
A B

Temple Church

WHITEFRIARS ST.

St Bride's Church

BOUVERIE ST.

ALDWYCH

St Clement Danes

St Mary-le-Strand

STRAND

ARUNDEL ST.

Temple Bar

MILFORD LA.

ESSEX ST.

Middle Temple

MIDDLE TEMPLE

Inner Temple

KING'S BENCH WALK

Inner Temple Garden

INGTON ST.

ALDWYCH

King's College

TEMPLE

VICTORIA EMBANKMENT

LANCASTER PL.

SAVOY ST.

Savoy Chapel

Somerset House

WATERLOO BRIDGE

River Thames

oria nkment dens

Cleopatra's Needle

Docklands. To the horror of the scribblers who used to work here, most of their old office buildings have been demolished or taken over by accountancy firms.

This is very much a working area, so come during the week.

---

lunch/pubs

When the journalists left Fleet Street, they took with them the unique atmosphere that characterized its pubs and restaurants. This is a pretty sterile place to eat now and you might do better to detour to Covent Garden. The following aren't bad though:

Ye Olde Cock Tavern, 22 Fleet St. Roomy and historic pub (see description below) with good food and friendly service. £5–8.

Temple Bar Tandoori, 23–28 Fleet St. Excellent, smartish Indian with great chicken tikka and tandoori specials. £15–20.

Ye Olde Cheshire Cheese, Wine Office Court. Another famous and atmospheric inn, excellent for lunchtime drinking. Best to avoid the overpriced, insipid food.

Café Sofra, 101 Fleet Street. Excellent Turkish chain, selling full and very tasty Turkish lunch from £9.

Cittie of York, 22–3 High Holborn. Admire the long bar and enjoy reasonable pub food in one of the wood-panelled recesses. £5–10.

Prêt à Manger, in two locations, 28 Fleet Street and 122 High Holborn. Reliable chain for superior sandwiches and freshly squeezed juices.

---

*This walk begins with a 30-minute prelude, which you can cut if you are in a hurry by heading straight for the Royal Courts of Justice (✆ Aldwych or Temple). Starting from ✆ Embankment, take the Villiers St exit and turn right through the gate into **Victoria Embankment Gardens**, part of the land reclaimed when Sir Joseph Bazalgette's Metropolitan Board of Works built the Embankment in the 1860s as a buffer against flooding and disease. It's a pleasant enough park, full of worthy statuary, but its main attraction is its view over one of London's more unusual landmarks, **Cleopatra's Needle**, which you can see off to the right about halfway through the park.*

A 60ft granite obelisk probably wasn't the most practical present the Turkish Viceroy of Egypt, Mohammad Ali, could have offered as a mark of his esteem for the British back in 1819. Still, he must have laughed himself silly when he saw what a hash the great empire made of transporting it back home. It took the British a staggering 59 years, and even then the best place they could think to put it was here between the river and a four-lane highway. The French, given a similar monument by Ali in the 1830s, gave theirs pride of place in the Place de la Concorde.

Cleopatra's Needle has always been a bit of a joke, and it's scarcely surprising. It's almost impossible to get close enough to admire the carvings and symbols dating back to 1450 BC which honour not just Cleopatra but Pharaohs Tethmosis III and Ramses II too. When the British were first presented with the obelisk in Alexandria, it was lying helplessly in the sand, having toppled over several hundred years earlier. For decades nobody could work out how to move it. Then in 1877 the engineer John Dixon built an iron cylindrical pontoon and towed it out to sea, where it was nearly lost in a gale. The original site planned for the Needle, in front of the Houses of Parliament, turned out to be no good because of ground subsidence. When it finally went up on the present site in 1878, it was realized in horror that the contractor had planted the sphinxes at its base the wrong way around. A contemporary piece of graffiti read:

> *This monument one supposes*
> *Was looked upon by Moses*
> *It passed in time from Greeks to Turks*
> *And was stuck up here by the Board of Works.*

The Board of Works nevertheless took the monument very seriously and buried mementoes beneath it for posterity. Somewhere under the 186 tons of granite are a selection of Victorian newspapers, some coins, a razor, a box of pins, four Bibles in different languages, Bradshaw's *Railway Guide* and photographs of the 12 best-looking Englishwomen of the day.

*Leave the gardens on the north side by the **York Water Gate**.*

Built in the 1620s, this chunky Baroque portico is the only surviving relic of York House, a mansion which was destroyed in the 1670s. The Water Gate, as its name implies, used to be right on the riverfront. The nearby streets spell out the full name of one of York House's last residents, George Villiers, Duke of Buckingham: George Court, Villiers St, Duke St and so on. There even used to be an Of Alley, but it was renamed York Place.

The Water Gate leads into Buckingham St; turn right at the top into John Adam St, and walk to the end.

Bazalgette's Embankment may have created some new gardens, but it also destroyed one of the most handsome housing developments in London, the **Adelphi**, which was built here in the 1770s by the Adam brothers. The much-admired wrought-iron balconies of their 24 terraced houses overlooked the river from an imposing height. With the arrival of the Embankment a century later, however, the Adelphi was half-demolished, lost its riverside position and with it much of its charm. The shady arches where the Thames once lapped became a hide-out for criminals and vagrants. It wouldn't have been hard to remedy the situation, but in 1936 the whole development was simply knocked down. It was one of the more shameless pieces of destruction in London's history, which the uninspiring new building by Colcutt and Hemp did little to mitigate. A few of the original Adam houses survive, notably the stuccoed centrepiece right in front of you, and, to your left, 10 Adam St, with its curved black brick façade and elegant bay window.

> *Walk up Adam St to the **Strand**, a noisy and largely soulless thoroughfare which, as the name implies, once formed the riverfront. Head east, and a couple of streets to your right is the narrow entrance to the **Savoy Hotel**.*

You'll notice that the taxis making their way into the hotel drive on the right rather than the left; this is the only street in Britain where traffic conforms to the rest of Europe, for reasons explained only by the eccentricity of the hotel's founder Richard d'Oyly Carte. When the Savoy opened in 1889, it was the most modern luxury hotel in the world with electric lifts and lights and an unusually large number of bathrooms per floor (*en suite* washing facilities being a strictly 20th-century phenomenon, and something which appalled the in some ways conventional Oscar Wilde who exclaimed that he would rather have water brought to his room than share his quarters with hot and cold running taps). César Ritz was the first general manager and Auguste Escoffier first head chef; the pair of them absconded nine years later to found the Ritz Hotel in Paris. With them they took the Savoy's enviable guest list, as well as such recipes as Peach Melba which they concocted for the delectation of the Australian opera singer Nellie Melba.

In the Middle Ages the hotel, and much of the ground to the east of it, was the site of the **Savoy Palace**, an imposing fortified waterside residence occupied at various times by the Black Prince and John of Gaunt, regent for the infant Richard II. John tried to introduce the much-detested poll tax and as a result became one of the main hate figures of the Peasants' Revolt of 1381. The mob ripped out his furnishings and hangings, tossed his gold and silver on to a giant bonfire and slaughtered his physician and serjeant-at-arms. Remarkably they were careful only to vandalize, not steal, all the better to vent their moral indignation. One man caught pillaging ended up being thrown on the bonfire himself. Although John survived the onslaught, the palace did not. The cellar collapsed, trapping 32 men who had gone down there to sample its choicer wines. Then the Great Hall came crashing down after a box containing gunpowder was accidentally fed to the flames.

The building never recovered. It was a hospital under Henry VII, then fell into a slow decline until, by the 19th century, there was next to nothing left. The only vestige is the **Savoy Chapel** on Savoy St, which has been so altered that it bears little resemblance to the original. Once popular for society weddings, partly because it tolerated the remarriage of divorcees, it is now the Chapel of the Royal Victorian Order.

*Continue along the Strand, and past a row of shops after the turn-off to Waterloo Bridge on the right is the entrance to **Somerset House**.*

Somerset House was the first Renaissance palace in England, built for one of the biggest thugs in the country's history. In 1547 the Duke of Somerset was named Lord Protector for the new king, nine-year-old Edward VI, and set about building a home grand enough to match his overweening ambitions. He knocked down two bishops' palaces, an inn of chancery and a church to make room for his super-palace, and pillaged two more churches to provide the stone. He even tried to quarry St Margaret's Westminster, but the parishioners there chased his lackeys away. Such a man could not last long, and Somerset was executed in 1552. But his palace lived on, at least for a while, as a residence for royalty and a venue for peace conferences. It fell out of fashion in the 17th and 18th centuries and, despite boasting a chapel by Inigo Jones and the first example of parquet flooring in Europe, was demolished in the 1770s. The replacement, used to house a succession of Royal Societies, various public records and the Inland Revenue service, is a fine Georgian building by William Chambers. The imposing courtyard used to lead down to the river bank and still has a good view over the water.

Somerset House's chief attraction is the **Courtauld Institute**, with its exquisite collection of paintings, particularly of Impressionists and post-impressionists (*closed until Oct 1998 for architectural refurbishment, from Oct 1998 onwards open Mon–Sat 10–6, Sun 2–6; adm; full disabled access, café, entrance is to the right on the way in to Somerset House, © 0171–873 2526*). Most of the paintings were a bequest by the philanthropist Samuel Courtauld, who also set up a school of fine art affiliated to London University. An elegant staircase leads to 11 smallish rooms spread over two floors. There is a magnificent *Adam and Eve* by Lucas Cranach the Elder, some fine Rubens including his early masterpiece *The Descent from the Cross*, and a roomful of unusual 18th-century Italian art including a series of Tiepolos. The Impressionists include a copy by the artist of Manet's *Le Déjeuner sur l'Herbe* (the original being in the Musée d'Orsay in Paris), some wonderful Degas studies of dancers and moody Cézanne landscapes. Highlights from the 20th century include Kokoschka, Modigliani and some excellent contemporary British works donated in the early 1980s.

*Next door to Somerset House is **King's College London**.*

Behind the unlovely modern concrete entrance is a fine, late neoclassical quadrangle designed by Robert Smirke. The college, founded by the Duke of Wellington, was originally intended to be a place of high Christian principles in contrast to the 'godless institution', University College, which had opened a few years earlier. It specialized in theological studies throughout the 19th century. King's is now part of London University teaching a wide range of subjects, and has a highly regarded medical school in South London.

*Returning to the Strand, straight ahead of you, in an island in the middle of the road, is **St Mary-le-Strand** church.*

Built in 1724, St Mary-le-Strand was James Gibbs's first full church commission and borrows heavily from classical models. The round porch, for example, is a straight steal from Santa Maria della Pace in Rome where Gibbs had studied, and the steeple is pure Wren. Still, it won Gibbs a handsome reputation as the English vogue for classicism took off. Originally, the church stood on the north side of the street, but turned into an island in 1910 as the advent of the motor car prompted the Strand to be broadened. The interior of the church was refitted in the 19th century and is unremarkable except for the thick unornamented interior walls, made that way to keep out traffic noise.

St Mary is now dedicated to the women of the Royal Navy, a military connection it shares with Christopher Wren's **St Clement Danes** (1682), a couple of blocks further on. St Clement belongs to the Royal Air Force, which footed the bill for renovating its elegant steeple after the Second World War. The place contains several war memorials and lists of honour for the men who died fighting Nazi Germany. Outside the church entrance are statues to Air Chief Marshal Lord Dowding, hero of the Battle of Britain, and Arthur 'Bomber' Harris, who masterminded the destruction of Dresden and other German cities towards the end of the Second World War.

Nowadays Harris is viewed as rather less than a war hero for his relentless and deliberate savaging of civilian targets in Germany. His strategy did little or nothing to bring forward the end of the war; it merely killed hundreds of thousands of people and wantonly destroyed some of Germany's great cities. At the unveiling of the statue in 1992, a crowd of protesters gathered to voice their disapproval at the description of Harris as 'a great commander' and tried to daub the figure in spray-paint. The army boys did their best to drown them out with several verses of 'For he's a jolly good fellow'.

Every March, the pupils of St Clement Danes Primary School come here to receive an orange and a lemon in a ceremony echoing the words of a famous London nursery rhyme about the chimes of the city's church bells: *Oranges and lemons/Say the bells of St Clement's.* In fact the ceremony is somewhat phoney, since the church in the rhyme is almost certainly St Clement's Eastcheap, near the wharves where citrus fruit used to arrive from the Mediterranean. The tune is played out on the church carillon.

*Cross on to the north side of the road and in front of you to the left is the gargantuan Gothic extravaganza known as the **Royal Courts of Justice**, London's civil law courts (open Mon–Fri, 10–4.30; free; no court cases in the August recess, © 0171–936 6000 for any other information). Leave your bags and cameras at the entrance and gape in wonder.*

The architect, George Edmund Street, had always wanted to build a cathedral, and it shows. This building is an astonishingly complex work of high vaulted ceilings, ornately carved halls, burrow-like corridors and crazy spires and towers. There are more than 1000 rooms including 58 chambers for court hearings and 3½ miles of corridors. The 230ft-long Great Hall, which you see as you come in, looks like the nave of a great church with its high vaulted arches and ornamented windows. This is one of the grandest examples of English Victorian Gothic. The effort of building it stretched parliament's budget to breaking point, harried and alienated several groups of workers, and so exhausted poor old George Street that he died of a stroke shortly before his masterpiece was completed in 1882.

Fourteen years earlier, Street had been chosen from a ferociously competitive group of architects including George Gilbert Scott, E.M. Barry and Alfred Waterhouse, to build a permanent site where civil cases could be heard in the High Court. (Criminal cases are tried at the Old Bailey—*see* pp.289–91.) At the time, the legal profession was busy reforming itself into something close to its modern shape. Only a few years earlier, Dickens had published *Bleak House*, a rousing indictment of the bureaucratic, self-serving, expensive muddle surrounding legal suits, and the injustice meted out to innocent parties as a result. In 1875 the Supreme Court of Judicature replaced the old superior courts and established the Court of Appeal and the High Court as they are known today. The High Court is divided into three sections—the Family Division, which deals with divorce and private property disputes; Chancery Division, which covers company law; and Queen's Bench Division, which handles major libel and other prominent suits.

Street's ambition was, like the judiciary's, very much one of moral improvement. The grand figures gazing down from the roof as you walk in are Solomon (left), Alfred the Great (right) and Jesus Christ (centre, on the highest point of the upper arch). At the back, above the northern entrance to the Courts, is a fourth figure, that of Moses, the ultimate lawgiver. Inside, at the far end of the Great Hall and half way up the staircase, Street deliberately left out one column as a sign to the Almighty that he acknowledged his own imperfections. Clearly, the architect hoped to impart some of his Christian idealism to the legal profession.

Despite Street's lofty ideals, little of the bureaucratic fog denounced by Dickens cleared as a result of the reorganization of the judiciary. Indeed Street's grandly elaborate building, for all its architectural merits, could not have better expressed the Byzantine complications of the legal process. It is imposing, but ultimately expresses only the supreme self-confidence of all those Lord Chancellors and Lord Chief Justices whose statues line the Grand Hall. 'I often used to wonder,' wrote H.V. Morton, 'why one should have to be divorced or sued for libel in a building which, more than any other recent addition to the metropolis, suggests an inconvenient medieval stronghold.'

It is all too easy to be sucked into Street's vision of the law as a gift from God and forget that litigation is chiefly a pursuit of the rich, if not the greedy. While powerful tycoons like the late Robert Maxwell rush to the courts to stop papers printing unpleasant truths about themselves, ordinary citizens only rarely secure the financial support they need to fight their legal battles. Civil justice may at its best be efficient, but it is rarely magnanimous. To find the most appropriate symbol in this building, you should look not to those grand figures on the roof, but to the emblem above the judges' entrance on the northern side of the law courts. It shows a cat and dog tussling with all the base animal instincts of litigants.

It all boils down, in the end, to class. The lawyers are usually well-educated and middle-class and so are their clients. One of the most memorable recent cases heard at the Royal Courts was a libel suit brought by the best-selling author Jeffrey Archer against the *Daily Star* newspaper in 1986. Archer, who was also deputy chairman of the Conservative Party at the time, had been seen at Victoria Station handing over £2000 in cash to a prostitute, and the *Star* had had the temerity to suggest that something improper might have gone on between them. Archer claimed he had been set up and that the prostitute had been trying to blackmail him. In the end it was no contest. Archer had impeccable breeding, the best connections and packets of money; the prostitute had nothing except a tenuous alliance with a newspaper generally sneered at in polite company. The affair hinged on the prostitute's assertion that she had seen spots on Archer's bare back; Archer's dutiful wife Mary, described approvingly by the judge as 'fragrant', testified his back was in fact smooth. Archer duly won the case and collected record damages of £500,000. Maybe he deserved to win, maybe he didn't; the point was he, as a gentleman, was taken at his word and the prostitute was not.

There is nevertheless something very seductive about the ritualistic drama of the law, a drama heightened in England by the adversarial confrontation of lawyers, even in civil cases, and the continuing tradition of wearing gowns and wigs in court. You can see an exhibition of legal costumes, from the workaday to the ceremonial, to the right as you walk into the Great Hall. Back in the 18th century wigs were common among many of the professions because they recalled the military perukes worn at the Battle of Blenheim in 1704. Only three groups kept wearing them for any length of time—lawyers, clergymen and coachmen. Today it is only the lawyers (plus the coachmen of the royal household) who persist in the tradition, although there are occasional campaigns to scrap them. Perhaps wigs lend an air of gravitas that the law desperately needs. Or maybe it is a sense of fun. 'The law is a tedious profession,' writes V.S. Pritchett, 'and it relieves the boredom by its own little comedies.'

Sit in on one of the hearings (they are all open to the public, just ask at the information desk for advice on which to attend) and you get the feeling that advocates and judges are merely glorified actors playing out their roles on a privileged stage. Whatever the gravity of the words spoken, you feel that it is not the content but the performance that counts. Pritchett, in his excellent book *London Perceived*, cites one example of courtroom banter where a pun made by a prosecuting lawyer falls flat. 'Not one of your best,' murmurs the judge. Counsel replies red-faced: 'An inadvertence, m'lud.' It is as though the outcome of the case depended more on the quality of the wit than the arguments. No surprise, perhaps, that the catering company which supplies the canteen at the Royal Courts is called *Go Bananas*.

> *Turn left towards Fleet St; in front of you, in another traffic island, a monument called the **Temple Bar** marks the entrance to the City of London .*

In the Middle Ages the Bar was quite literally a barrier to control comings and goings into the City. So independent and powerful were the City fathers that any unwelcome visitors were simply slung into the jail that stood on the site. The unlucky ones had their heads and pickled body parts displayed on spikes. Even the sovereign had to ask permission to pass this way, a tradition that has lasted in ritualistic form into the modern era. If the queen wants to enter the City on official business, she stops here to request entry from the Lord Mayor. The Lord Mayor then agrees and offers his sword as a demonstration of loyalty. The sword is immediately returned to show that the sovereign is in the City under the mayor's protection and she continues on her way. It is not a common ceremony; the last time it took place was during the Queen's Silver Jubilee celebrations in 1977.

For 200 years an arched gateway designed by Wren marked this spot, but in 1878 it was removed because of traffic congestion and replaced with the present, rather modest monument by Horace Jones. The bronze panels depict Queen Victoria and Edward, Prince of Wales, entering the City of London. The bronze griffin on top is one of the City's emblems, introduced by the Victorians who remembered that the griffins of mythology guarded over a hidden treasure of gold. They presumably forgot, however, that griffins also tore approaching humans to pieces as a punishment for their greed.

> *Cross to the south side of Fleet St where you will see the entrance at 229–30 Strand of the private lawyers' retreat, the Wig and Pen club. Thereafter the first turning on your right, beneath a 16th-century wooden*

*gateway, is Middle Temple Lane which leads into the first of the **Inns of Court** on this walk.*

The Inns of Court

'What, all lawyers?' spluttered George III when introduced to a group of them at a parade in Hyde Park in 1803. 'Call them the Devil's own!' Sometimes it is hard to tell whether the four Inns of Court—Middle Temple, Inner Temple, Lincoln's Inn and Gray's Inn—are lawyer's associations or the meeting grounds of some quietly cabalistic sect. Their practices seem strange, if not incomprehensible, to anyone not fully initiated into them, and their history is steeped in semi-secret ritual. The Inns do little to elucidate their own mysteries; indeed they seem to thrive on their very inscrutability.

First of all, the Inns are not open to all lawyers, only the part of the profession known as barristers. English law divides lawyers into two groups: the majority who deal with clients directly and advise them on points of law, as well as representing them in the lower courts, known as solicitors; and the barristers, who alone are entitled to go to the High Court to plead a case. Historically the difference between the two kinds of lawyer was one of class. For centuries only the independently wealthy could afford to study at an Inn, or *read for the bar* as the jargon has it. Becoming a solicitor was a vocation for the more lowly orders only. The Inns were, and to some degree still are, rarefied clubs where the upper classes could mingle with their own. Barristers were the aristocrats of the profession who concentrated on giving an eloquent performance in court, while the solicitors, acting as their underlings, did all the preparatory work and instructed the barristers on the facts of each case.

Things have changed in as far as solicitors, especially in the City, have attained far higher status over the years; they still consult barristers on the finer points of law but command equally high salaries. The Inns have also broadened the social range of their intake. Where once it was forbidden to take employment while reading for the bar, nowadays it is perfectly normal. Scholarships are available, especially for overseas students. But the old hierarchical division between barristers and solicitors is still felt, if only because the traditions of the Inns continue very much as before. Students still have to eat formal dinner three times a term in the dining hall of their Inn to ensure that their social skills are developed alongside their legal ones; indeed you could be forgiven, from the way that some Inn members talk, for thinking that the dinners were the only qualification that counted. As an article in *The Times* unkindly remarked back in 1846, a barrister 'need not have the capacity to earn a dinner, provided he has the necessary appetite for eating one'. Perhaps things haven't moved on all that much since the 15th century when Sir John Fortescue, the head of Lincoln's Inn, stipulated that students be taught not the rudiments of the law, but 'all commendable qualities requisite for gentlemen'.

Much of the mystery of the Inns of Court is bound up in history. The first people to occupy the site were the Knights Templar, the most fervent of all the Crusaders, who moved here half way through the 12th century and set up a lucrative trading business along the River Thames. These fighting monks took their name, and the name of this area, from Jerusalem's holiest of holies, Temple Mount, where shrines to Judaism, Christianity and Islam co-exist on the same site. One of those shrines, the Dome of the Rock, was the inspiration for the knights' trademark round churches (*see* Temple Church below). The Knights Templar had peculiar customs and secret initiation rites which gave them an air of mystery similar to the one surrounding the lawyers today. Some of the folklore was passed on directly. Lawyer's briefs, for example, are still signed with a kind of loop that evolved from the Templars' special sign of the cross.

The wealth and power of the Templars incited the envy of secular authorities, who violently suppressed the order in 1307 and handed over the Temple buildings to their rivals, the Knights Hospitaller. The place soon fell into decline, and lawyers began renting the empty space. The legal profession organized itself very much as the knights had done, with a division between the Middle and Inner Temples (the Outer Temple, to the west, was never occupied). The two Inns developed distinct and to some degree competing identities. You can tell immediately which building belongs to which Inn because each is stamped with the appropriate emblem: a pascal lamb and flag of innocence to denote Middle Temple, a winged horse or Pegasus for Inner.

The knights were thrown out after the dissolution of the monasteries in 1539, but the lawyers were not able to gain full control of the property until 1609, when James I offered it to them on condition that they guarantee the upkeep of its historical buildings. This the lawyers did, though to judge by the wild revelries that went on it is scarcely believable that the church and master's house stayed in one piece. The students were forever putting on music and dance shows (in fact these were part of the curriculum). They gambled, fought duels and drank until they dropped. By the 16th century the Temple elders felt constrained to appoint Lords of Misrule to impose some semblance of order. Spanish cloaks and rapiers were banned by royal decree.

The lawyers were not much more diligent in subsequent centuries. Often they would go fishing in the Thames all afternoon and had to be called in by a horn blast. Fleet Street's Apollo Club (now long gone) used to have a sign above its kitchen clock which barristers heeded with deep reverence: 'If the wine of last night hurts you, drink more today and it will cure you.'

If life is more civilized nowadays, it is probably because of the pressing need to earn a living and meet the Inns' astronomically high rents. Many barristers have moved out altogether, while some of the rooms on the upper floors have been taken over by rich individuals or small private companies unconnected with the law. You still see plenty of lawyers around, though, their black gowns flapping in the breeze as they scurry round the courtyards and up the poky staircases.

Walk down Middle Temple Lane and you'll pass several buildings and squares where the barristers have their offices, or chambers as they are known.

Each entrance-way is numbered and has a painted wooden board indicating the names of the occupants inside. The ground floor is usually occupied by a clerk who does administrative work for all the barristers on his staircase. One of the great peculiarities of the barristers' professional code is that they are not allowed to form associations or companies; each one must be self-employed and, nominally, independent (the idea being that they are less corruptible this way). What makes this notion so curious is that the Inns are so manifestly a kind of association. Formal dinners and staircase camaraderie ensure constant contact between members of the profession. It is usually through friends or mentors that young barristers get their first jobs; often they will act as second fiddle to a senior barrister on a big case. It is not a particularly honest state of affairs, since independence clearly means one thing in principle and another in practice. Pulling strings for friends and associates is all right; formalizing the arrangement is not, presumably because it might draw too much attention to the essentially exclusive and clubbish nature of the Inns and their working practices. If barristers formed companies, then—well—any old person might be able to join the profession. And that wouldn't do at all, would it?

*Brick Court (first on the right) was once occupied by the playwright and occasional lawyer Oliver Goldsmith; now the court has been partly converted into a car park. Pump Court (first left) is one of the oldest parts of the Inn whose deep wells were used to provide water during the bombing of the Second World War; the pump itself was destroyed and never replaced. Fountain Court (second right) still has the single water jet that gives it its name. On the corner of Fountain Court and Middle Temple Lane is the beautiful **Middle Temple Hall** (often closed, ask at the gatehouse for permission to see it).*

This magnificent Tudor dining hall, completed in 1573, perfectly expresses the fulsome self-confidence of the legal profession. Admiring the grandeur of the double hammerbeam roof and the beautiful screen, both fashioned from solid English oak, it is easy to understand how Ben Jonson could describe the Inns of Court as 'the noblest nurseries of humanity and liberty in the kingdom'. The long table on the raised platform, where the senior members of the Inn traditionally sit, was made from a single oak tree donated by Queen Elizabeth I. The smaller table in front of it, known as the Cupboard, was cut from the wood of the *Golden Hind*, the ship which Sir Francis Drake led against the Spanish Armada in 1588. Above the high table are the portraits of monarchs from Charles I through to William III. The other walls are emblazoned with the coats-of-arms of the Middle Temple's Readers, or senior lecturers. Everything is heavy with the weight of tradition, and yet is effortlessly elegant and light at the same time.

In Tudor and Stuart times the Hall was used for lavish entertainments, particularly plays; Shakespeare's *Twelfth Night* had its première here in 1601. This was also where students would gather for their gambling sessions. When workmen replaced the floor in 1730, they discovered hundreds of dice beneath the old wooden planks. A century earlier James I had sanctioned dice-playing to allow students a break from the tedium of studying their dusty casebooks.

> *Turn right down Middle Temple Lane and you pass the **library**, where you can see a copy of the US Declaration of Independence.*

The Middle Temple enthusiastically supported the end of British rule in America and several of its members, notably Edmund Burke, were involved in drawing up both the declaration of independence and the US constitution. A special relationship with the United States continues to this day. The **garden**, which stretches out behind the library towards the river, is traditionally the place where the Wars of the Roses started in 1455. The start of hostilities, at least as recounted in Shakespeare's *Henry VI*, came as the warring houses of Lancaster and York plucked their respective emblems, a red and white rose, from the Temple flower beds.

> *Walk back up Middle Temple Lane and turn right onto Crown Office Row, which takes you into the **Inner Temple**. Notice the Pegasus symbol on the entrance gate. Immediately you come to the magnificent lawns of the Inner Temple's own garden. This is an ideal picnic spot in good weather, tranquil and surrounded by fine buildings. On the eastern side is **King's Bench Walk**, a fine brick terrace designed by Christopher Wren.*

In the 1730s this was where William Murray, later Lord Chancellor, had his chambers. Murray evidently spent rather more time sitting in the neighbourhood drinking establishments than he did working, since his clients all complained they could never find him in. The Duchess of Marlborough was so incensed by his absences that she turned up one night incognito and waited until midnight. Still Murray did not show. When bystanders asked the clerk about the visitor, he replied: 'I could not make out who she was, for she would not tell me her name; but she swore so dreadfully that I am sure she must have been a woman of quality.'

Turn left up King's Bench Walk and then turn left again after the library.
Many of the Inner Temple's buildings, including its dining hall, were
destroyed by wartime bombs. Straight ahead, however, more or less
intact, is the **Temple Church** *(open 10–4 Mon–Sat, Sun services at 8.30*
and 11.15).

London's only surviving round church dates back to 1185 when the Knights Templar moved to this area from their original London home in Holborn. It is often said to be modelled on the Church of the Holy Sepulchre in Jerusalem, the supposed site of the crucifixion, but in fact the attribution makes no sense. The Holy Sepulchre is neither round nor on Temple Mount, and the inspiration is much more likely to have been the Dome of the Rock. Either way, this church is a fine example of English Transitional style. The circular western end is Romanesque, while the nave (completed in around 1240) is Gothic. One of its charms is the way in which the semicircular arches of the earlier style intersect to form the peaked arches of the later. It is a simple design that has been much tinkered with over the years, notably by Wren who added the buttresses and the carved reredos, and by the 19th-century architects Sydney Smirke and Decimus Burton, who ensured, in the words of Walter Godfrey, that 'every surface was repaired away or renewed'. The gravest damage was wrought in the Second World War when incendiary bombs brought in the roof, cracked the Purbeck marble columns and crashed into the nine effigies of Crusader knights at the western end of the church. The damage is now largely repaired, and there is a memorial to the bombing in a choir window which depicts the flames licking around St Paul's Cathedral.

When James I handed over the church to the lawyers in 1609, he made Middle Temple responsible for the northern half, Inner Temple for the southern. They still sit that way today. They have not, however, had recourse recently to the Templars' penitential cell, on the northern side towards the back. Prisoners in the 12th and 13th centuries would be left in the tiny room for weeks, fed only with bread and water left in a recess at the bottom. They could follow services through the slit at the front. Many succumbed to the hardship and were carried out of the cell feet first.

At the western end of the church, turn right up Inner Temple Lane which
takes you back into Fleet St. The gateway is a magnificent piece of 17th-
century half-timber work, one of the few surviving examples of pre-Fire
construction in wood in London. On the first floor (entrance at No.17
Fleet St) is **Prince Henry's Room** *(open Mon–Sat, 11–2; adm).*

Henry was the son of James I, and this room was built on the occasion of his being named Prince of Wales in 1610. The site was scarcely grand, however, merely the upstairs room of an inn. The chief attraction is the beautifully preserved oak panelling and the ornamentation on the moulded plaster ceiling bearing the letters P.H. The room also houses a collection of memorabilia of the celebrated 17th-century diarist Samuel Pepys, who used to do a fair amount of his drinking around here. It includes extracts from his diary (written in a peculiar shorthand only properly deciphered in the 19th century) as well as various household objects and spectacles (Pepys was forever convinced he was about to go blind).

One of Pepys's drinking haunts was the **Ye Olde Cock Tavern** down the road at No.22, which still has fine wood panelling, although it was rebuilt in the late 19th century. In Pepys's day it was a much-frequented chop house. His diary entry for 23 April 1668 describes in a macaronic mixture of languages how he turned up for an assignation with an actress called Mrs Knipp. He got well tanked up, 'did tocar her corps all over and besar sans fin'. Pepys, it must be said, was not the most beautiful of human specimens, and it's hard to imagine him ravishing anyone, let alone an actress. Nevertheless, Pepys recounts that when he got home that night, his irate wife extracted a confession and came at him with a red-hot pair of tongs.

*The stretch of **Fleet Street** from here down to Ludgate Circus was, until the mid-1980s, the epicentre of the British press.*

Fleet Street

It was an exciting place to visit. The stench of newsprint emanated from the very bowels of the buildings where the presses ran all night. At the crack of dawn the first pubs and cheap cafés opened to feed the typesetters, printers and early-shift reporters. The drinking and chatter would then go on all day and evening within the tight constraints of the licensing laws; a few private clubs would stay open uninterrupted. The atmosphere was irreverent and rowdy, giving the journalists a refreshingly sleazy reputation in respectable circles. One celebrated *Punch* verse of the 19th century satirized it thus:

> *You cannot hope to bribe or twist,*
> *Alas, the British journalist*
> *But seeing what he'll do*
> *Unbribed, there's no occasion to.*

British journalists are probably no more corruptible than their counterparts elsewhere. But nowadays they are certainly less of an exuberant and high-spirited pack. Fleet Street has all but died; the newspaper offices have been taken over by accountants and solicitors or, in the case of the downmarket *Sun* and *News of the World*, turned into a multi-storey car park. Meanwhile most of the pubs and restaurants have either closed down or become sterile and expensive. The major titles which once all huddled around this small area are now scattered to the four winds—

Docklands, the City, Kensington. Only the Press Association, the national news agency, soldiers on alone at No.85.

So what happened? The death of Fleet Street happened in two stages: first slowly, and then virtually overnight. From the 1970s onwards, it became clear that computerization was going to transform the newspaper industry. There was considerable resistance to modernization, particularly from the powerful print unions who correctly foresaw disaster for thousands of their members. For a while, newspapers struggled on with antiquated machinery and whole armies of surplus staff.

Then in 1986 the Australian media baron Rupert Murdoch, who had carefully bought up a number of struggling titles over the previous few years, simply fired all his unionized workers and moved the offices of *The Times*, *Sunday Times*, *Sun* and *News of the World* to a new site with state-of-the-art technology in Wapping. The unions were furious, but there was little they could do except vent their anger on the street. It was the end of an era, and everybody knew it. Within three years the *Daily Telegraph* moved to Docklands, the *Daily Express* to the other side of the Thames and the *Evening Standard* and *Daily Mail* to Kensington.

The move to new technology may have been necessary, but Murdoch's typically abrasive gesture did far more than simply replace printing presses with computer terminals. It handed a handsome victory to the prime minister, Margaret Thatcher, in her battle to dismantle organized labour in the name of free enterprise. The handful of proprietors who, like Murdoch, could afford to treat their workers with impunity gained enormous power. By and large, they refashioned the content and structure of their publications to suit their own business-driven values, encouraged unpleasant and dishonest pryings into private lives by the downmarket tabloids, and left little room for dissenting or investigative voices. Such is their power, however, that they are courted by political leaders of all colours. Murdoch, notably, was wooed by Tony Blair as part of his successful election strategy in 1997. The industry has become a more insecure place to work, and the few independent titles have almost no protection from the big sharks of the media market place.

All this has left precious little for the visitor to peruse in Fleet Street. Ironically, one of the street's more objectionable establishments is still going strong. Historiallly El Vino's wine bar at No.47 must be one of the most reactionary drinking holes in London. Women were only served—reluctantly—after an appeal court ruling upheld their customer rights in 1982. On the other side of the street, a little further on, is the old Telegraph building (now occupied by Goldman Sachs) with its fine clock and, beyond Shoe Lane, the grotesque but impressive Art Deco black glass front of the old Express building, nicknamed the Black Lubianka for its resemblance to the more triumphalist architectural products of Stalinist Russia. Directly opposite, back on the south side of the street, is the Press Association building (shared, until recently, with the international news agency Reuters).

*Turn off into the passage beyond the Press Association building and you come to the journalists' church, **St Bride's**.*

This spot was where Fleet Street's association with newsprint began. William Caxton's apprentice Wynkyn de Worde moved his printing press to a site next to St Bride's church in 1500. Thanks to all the lawyers and priests in the area, he had the perfect market for his books on his doorstep. Thereafter Fleet Street became a literary haunt, attracting such figures as Dryden and Milton and encouraging Christopher Wren to rebuild St Bride's after the Great Fire. In 1701 he finished off his renovation with the impressive spire, made up of four arched octagons of diminishing size, which inspired a local pastry cook called Mr Rich to make the world's first tiered wedding cake.

The body of the church was destroyed by a German bomb in December 1940, and it has since been fully if unspectacularly repaired. You should not miss the crypt, where archaeologists have unearthed stones dating back to Roman times, including the remains of no fewer than seven previous churches built on the site. For centuries the land here was used as a burial ground and charnel house. The display also gives an excellent history of Fleet Street, from its origins as the main artery of Saxon Loudenwic up to the trauma of the 1980s print union strike. One of the objects on display is an iron coffin with a sprung lid dating from 1818. The lid was a defence against 'resurrectionists', medical students who snatched the bodies to further their illicit studies of anatomy.

*Return to Fleet St, cross the road and turn left back towards the law courts. A few steps away on your right you will see a dark low passage called **Wine Office Court**.*

This side of Fleet Street is as full of winding alleys and dark back streets as the Temple. Wine Office Court, as the name suggests, was one of the great drinking haunts of the 18th century. One contemporary records that 'nothing but a hurricane' would have induced Dr Johnson to drink anywhere else. The pub that still stands here, the **Ye Olde Cheshire Cheese**, retains much of the atmosphere of that era with its oak decor and hearty menu. Unfortunately the Cheese has become a little too touristy for its own good, but the beer, if not the food, is still to be recommended. At the turn of the 20th century its star attraction was a parrot named Polly who did impressions. On Armistice Night in 1918 Polly imitated the sound of a champagne cork popping 400 times before fainting from exhaustion. When she died in 1926, obituary notices appeared in more than 200 newspapers.

At the top of Wine Office Court is a vile modern development (1989)
called Gunpowder Square with a cannon in the middle. Turn left here and
*you come into Gough Square where, at No.17, is **Dr Johnson's House***
(open Mon–Sat, 11–5.30, and 11–5 Oct–April; cheap adm).

This is the elegant 17th-century house where the good Doctor lived from 1748 to 1759. For many of those years he was busy compiling his famous dictionary, the first of its kind in the English language. He worked in the attic, sitting in a rickety three-legged chair that somehow supported his vast bulk and ordering about his six clerks, who must have had a tough time keeping up with his boundless energies and inexhaustible wit. Boswell said the attic looked like a counting house.

The chief legacy of the dictionary to modern lexicographers is its scrupulous references to literary texts. But it is also full of jokey definitions that poke fun at anyone and everyone, including Johnson himself; a lexicographer is defined as 'a writer of dictionaries, a harmless drudge'. The dictionary, published in 1755, made Johnson's reputation as both a serious academic and a great wit. His wife Tetty, however, did not live to see his moment of glory. Described by Joshua Reynolds as 'always drunk and reading romances in her bed', she died here in 1752.

The house is of interest more for its atmosphere than its contents. The furniture is from the right period, but little of it ever belonged to Johnson. There is, of course, a first edition of the dictionary, along with portraits of Johnson and his friends, a chair which the Doctor sat on when he drank at the Cock Tavern and—most bizarrely—a lump of rock said to be part of the Great Wall of China.

Return to Fleet St through the maze of small alleys and turn right. Just
*after Fetter Lane is the curious church of **St Dunstan-in-the-West**.*

You can't help noticing the clock, which looks like something out of *The Flintstones* with its two muscular figures in gold loincloths who beat a gong every 15 minutes with their hefty clubs. Believe it or not, this dates from the 17th century when it was erected by the parishioners of St Dunstan as a token of thanks for surviving the Great Fire along with their church. Nobody knows who the two figures are meant to represent, the best guess being Gog and Magog, the legendary giants of the City. The church dates back to the 13th century, but was completely rebuilt in the 19th and is now shut most of the time.

William Tyndale preached here briefly in 1523 before the publication of his English-language Bible forced him to flee the wrath of the church authorities. Notice the memorial bust on the outside to Lord Northcliffe, pioneer of the trashy downmarket newspaper and spiritual father of today's powerful press barons. Northcliffe never believed what he read in the papers and never particularly cared to. He used to tell his journalists: 'Never lose your sense of the superficial.'

*Take the next turning on the right, Chancery Lane. Up ahead of you on the right are the turrets and pinnacles of the massive mock-Tudor mansion housing what used to be the **Public Records Office**, now moved out to Kew. Take the first left, Carey St, which takes you past the back entrance to the Royal Courts of Justice. The grey building up ahead on the right is the bankruptcy court. This walk turns off before that, into the passage that leads past the second-hand law bookseller Wildy and Son and into New Square, part of **Lincoln's Inn**.*

In many ways this is the most beautiful of the Inns of Court, with its broad meadows and grand buildings. The heart of this Inn is at the top of New Square to the right. You'll have to ask permission to see the **Old Hall**, built in 1492, which has a fine arch-braced roof, panelled walls and carved screen. It also boasts a large Hogarth painting, *Paul Preaching before Felix*, commissioned by the Inn in 1750. Next door is the Gothic **Chapel**, which looks medieval but in fact dates back only to the early 17th century—an indication of how backward English architecture was before Inigo Jones came to shake it up. To reach the interior, which has been largely refurbished, you have to climb a stone staircase. Beneath is a fine undercroft where, beneath the arches, students at the Inn used to meet and hold classes.

Further up on the same side is a fine Palladian ensemble known as the **Stone Buildings**, built by Robert Taylor in 1774 (note the scars left on the stonework by a German zeppelin raid in 1917). On the other side of the lawn are the **New Hall** and **Library**, built in red brick in neo-Tudor style by Philip Hardwick in 1843–5.

*Look at the magnificent Tudor **Gatehouse** (1518) leading from the east side of the Inn into Chancery Lane; above the heavy oak doors are the arms of two distinguished members of Lincoln's Inn, Thomas More and Thomas Lovell, as well as those of the Inn's founder, the 14th-century Earl of Lincoln. For the purposes of this walk, however, you should head out on the other side, past the New Hall and into **Lincoln's Inn Fields**.*

This square was Inigo Jones's second attempt, after Covent Garden, at piazza architecture in London. Like its predecessor, though, it fell out of fashion almost as soon as it had been built in the early 1640s. Only one of the original mansions, Lindsey House at Nos.59–60, has survived, albeit with a stuccoed façade added in the 18th century. The grassland in the centre of the square was never properly developed and soon turned into a brawling ground and general rubbish dump. Nowadays it is little more than a nondescript field, the allure of its greenery marred by ugly wire fencing to prevent the homeless from sleeping there.

Try to see the **Royal College of Surgeons** at Nos.35–53, a classical building revamped by Charles Barry in the 1830s, which has an extraordinary collection of anatomical specimens. It is not officially open to the public, but ask nicely and they may let you in. The collection, started by the 18th-century physician John Hunter, includes the skeleton of Jonathan Wild, the notorious thief-taker, plus a giant of 7ft 8in and a dwarf measuring just 20 inches.

> *On the north side of Lincoln's Inn Fields, at No.13, is the highlight of the square,* **Sir John Soane's Museum** *(open Tues–Sat, 10–5, with a £3 guided tour—which is free to students—on Saturdays at 2.30 and with visits by candlelight on the first Tuesday of each month from 6–9; free, but any donations are gratefully accepted).*

John Soane (1753–1837) was a great English eccentric and also one of the great architects of his age. He was a fanatical student of antiquity, and one of the towering figures of the neoclassical movement in Britain. His greatest single achievement was the Bank of England, which sadly fell victim to the philistinism of the City fathers in the 1920s. For the most part, Soane's other works were too idiosyncratic or too fantastic to win public competitions. One contemporary described him as 'personal to the point of perversity'.

Soane did not seem unduly bothered by the relative paucity of high-profile commissions; he stayed busy throughout his professional life and won a formidable reputation as a lecturer on the architecture of his contemporaries. In later life he bought up and converted three adjacent houses here in Lincoln's Inn Fields, adapting each room to his quirky style and filling them with objects from his remarkable art collection. In 1833 (four years before his death in 1837), Soane saw through a private Act of Parliament in which he bequeathed the whole collection to the public, leaving money for upkeep and payment of staff, with the stipulation that the museum should be maintained forever as it was on the day of Soane's death. It is a unique monument to one man's fertile imagination.

One of the highlights is the Picture Room on the ground floor, containing two great satirical series of paintings by Hogarth: *The Rake's Progress*, which follows the rise and fall of a degenerate young man from the moment he comes into his inheritance to his untimely end in the madhouse, and *The Election*, four scenes satirizing the greed and corruption surrounding political ambition.

Nowhere will you see better examples of Hogarth's unfailing eye for the grotesque and the debauched; these pictures are great black comedies but also express serious outrage at the excesses of the age. The Picture Room also includes studies by Piranesi and architectural drawings by Soane himself. Soane ingeniously accommodated this sizeable collection of paintings, drawings and prints into a minuscule room by hanging the whole lot on a series of false walls which he called 'picture planes'. These open out one after the other, until eventually they reveal a window looking down to the basement and a small alcove containing a plastercast from Castle Howard of a nymph, gently undraping herself.

Soane's other prized exhibit is the sarcophagus of the Egyptian Pharaoh Seti I (1303–1290 BC) in the Sepulchral Chamber in the basement. This is the finest example of a sarcophagus you can see outside Egypt, beautifully preserved and covered in hieroglyphics honouring Osiris and Ra and adorned with a painted figure of the goddess Nut, to whom Seti had pledged allegiance, on the inside. The sarcophagus came originally from the Valley of the Kings from which it was plundered by an interesting character called Giuseppe Belzona, a former circus strongman and tomb robber who eventually died in the jungle trying to find the source of the Niger. Initially, Belzona offered the sarcophagos to the British Museum, but the curators dithered and tried to haggle over its expensive price tag. In 1824 Belzona took it to Soane, who snapped it up for the full asking price, a princely £2000.

It would be a mistake, however, to visit this museum merely for its artistic highlights. Every room yields surprises, whether it is the enormous collection of plaster casts Soane made from classical models, or the classical colonnade running along the upstairs corridor, or simply the amazing ambiguities of light, which Soane manipulated so intriguingly in every area of the house with the aid of concave and then convex mirrors. Above the picture room on the first floor is a beautiful glass dome; in the basement you suddenly come across catacombs, or an atmospheric Monk's Parlour that looks like the setting for a Gothic horror novel.

In the Drawing Rooms upstairs you see the plans Soane made to transform London into a rational city, including one proposal for a giant royal palace in Hyde Park and another for a new neoclassical parliament building. Try to imagine Westminster with this understated, elegant architecture instead of the actual neo-Gothic extravagance by Barry and Pugin. London would be quite a different city altogether.

> *This is the end of the walk, more or less. From here, head for the northwestern corner of Lincoln's Inn Fields and go right up Gate Street towards* ⊖ *Holborn. If, however, you still have some energy left, there is still one Inn of Court and a couple of other curiosities to discover. Head towards the northeastern corner of Lincoln's Inn Fields, turn left on to Newman's Row and you come out on High Holborn. Cross the road, turn right and continue until you reach the Citie of York pub, which boasts the longest bar in England. The passage off to the left leads to* **Gray's Inn**.

This, the last of the four Inns of Court, suffered most from wartime bomb damage and has largely been rebuilt in unimaginative imitation of the graceful brick original. The first open space you come to, South Square, has one elegant older building left at No.1. This was where Dickens began his working life, as a 15-year-old legal clerk. The **chapel** contains some original 17th-century stained glass, and the **Hall** has managed to preserve its 16th-century wooden screen. The greatest pleasure is the long **garden** at the back, first planted by Francis Bacon in 1606 and popular ever since for lunchtime strolls and picnics.

> *Returning to High Holborn, turn left and cross over Gray's Inn Road, past*
> ✱ *Chancery Lane, and you come across another Victorian Gothic extrava-*
> *ganza, this time in red brick and terracotta.*

This used to be **Furnival's Inn**, one of nine so-called Inns of Chancery which acted as a sort of overflow for the main Inns of Court. Lawyers had their offices here and some students would pursue their studies while waiting for admission to the Temple, Lincoln's Inn or Gray's Inn. All the Inns of Chancery have now disappeared. The present building, designed by Alfred Waterhouse and completed in 1879, was constructed for the Prudential insurance company, which still has its offices here. It is a surprisingly graceful, if somewhat overstated, Victorian palace, leading you through a series of fine courtyards and elaborately arcaded passages.

> *As you re-emerge on to High Holborn, you see across the road one of the*
> *few pre-Fire shop frontings left in London.*

The 16th-century timber houses lead into another former Inn of Chancery, **Staple Inn**, whose quiet squares and graceful brick houses are now occupied by the Institute of Actuaries. This is a postwar reconstruction of the original 14th-century buildings, but retains the atmosphere of uncanny calm that struck Dickens a century ago. Writing in *The Mystery of Edwin Drood*, Dickens pinpointed the atmosphere of cosseted seclusion common to all the Inns on this walk: 'It is one of those nooks, the turning into which out of the clashing street imparts to the relieved pedestrian the sensation of having put cotton in his ears, and velvet soles on his boots.' Enjoy it as surreptitiously as you can: Staple Inn is not officially open to the public, but nobody will stop you wandering quietly in.

Start: ⊖ *St Paul's.*

Walking time: *about 2½ hours, but allow a good half day to see St Paul's and the Museum of London properly.*

VII: The City—St Paul's to the Barbican

This is a walk round a distinctly unfashionable side of the City, one that delves beyond the stereotypical shiny office fronts and pin-striped businessmen explored in Walk VIII, to rediscover something of the sounds and smells that once characterized the heart of London. Here, a few steps away from the financial high-jinks and the executive lunch spots, is an area of markets, street traders, law courts and hospital buildings—a reminder that until the 17th century the City *was* London, a place not only of wealth creation but also of poverty, blood, shit and disease. Here are the vestiges of a time when the City was a maze of winding medieval streets, where stockjobbers mixed with bakers, priests with thieves, and genteel ladies with penniless whores.

Wren's churches, and St Paul's Cathedral in particular, grace the skyline, but the area is also characterized by the bloody carcasses of Smithfield meat market and the grim legacy of Newgate prison, now converted into the Central Criminal Court. The contrast between the old, grimy City and its slick modern incarnation is a constant theme of this walk. This is the London whose contrast of affluence and wretchedness was described by Thomas Paine two centuries ago as being 'like dead and living bodies chained together'. Today it may be the affluent who lay claim to the area, but the traces of a more turbulent and violent past are still visible.

This is a walk to do during the week, preferably in the morning to capture the full atmosphere of Smithfield Market. Note that the Museum of London is shut on Mondays.

---

lunch/pubs

Smithfield market is the hub of the area's (increasingly upmarket) pubs and restaurants. This is a part of town where you can find breakfast at 5.30 in the morning and still be drinking at 11 at night. At lunchtime the choice is enormous.

The Place Below, St Mary-le-Bow, Cheapside. Award-winning, very popular, nutritious and vegetarian salads and soups in the basement undercroft of this historic City church. £10–15.

St Etheldreda's Pantry. Dirt cheap lunches (£2–3) inside the walls of the pre-Fire Roman Catholic church.

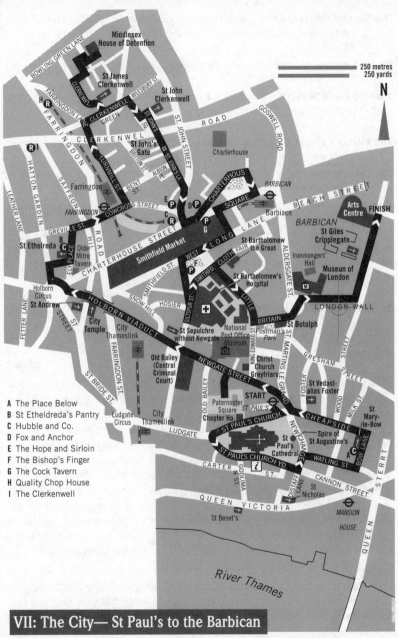

250 metres
250 yards

N

Middlesex
House of Detention

BOWLING GREEN LANE

St James
Clerkenwell

St John
Clerkenwell

AYLESBURY ST.

CLERKENWELL GREEN

GOSWELL ROAD

FARRINGDON LANE

CLERKENWELL

ST JOHN'S SQ.

ST. JOHN STREET

ROAD

Charterhouse

CHARTERHOUSE

BARBICAN

BEACH STREET

Arts
Centre

FINISH

FARRINGDON

St John's
Gate

TURNMILL ST.

BRITISH ST.

ALBION PL.

ST JOHN'S LA.

BENT ST.

Farringdon

HATTON GARDEN

SAFFRON HILL

FARRINGDON ROAD

COWCROSS STREET

CHARTERHOUSE SQUARE

Barbican

BARBICAN

St Giles
Cripplegate

FARRINGDON

CHARTERHOUSE STREET

Smithfield Market

LONG LANE

St Bartholomew
the Great

WEST SMITHFD. CLOTH FAIR

Ironmongers'
Hall

ALDERSGATE ST.

Museum of
London

LEATHER LANE

GREVILLE ST.

St Etheldreda

ELY PLACE

HILL

Olde
Mitre
Tavern

SMITHFIELD ST.

St Bartholomew's
Hospital

LONDON WALL

Holborn
Circus

St Andrew

FETTER LANE

HOLBORN VIADUCT

SNOW HILL

HOSIER

GILTSPUR ST.

LITTLE BRITAIN

St Botolph

GRESHAM STREET

WOOD ST.

City
Temple

City
Thameslink

ST. ANDREW ST.

FARRINGDON STREET

St Sepulchre
without Newgate

National
Post Office
Museum

KING EDWARD ST.

ST. MARTINS LE GRAND

Postman's
Park

St Vedast-
alias Foster

FOSTER LANE

MILK ST.

St Mary-
le-Bow

ST BRIDE ST.

Old Bailey
(Central
Criminal
Court)

NEWGATE STREET

Christ
Church
Greyfriars

CHEAPSIDE

Ludgate
Circus

City
Thameslink

LUDGATE

Paternoster
Square

Chapter Ho.

OLD BAILEY

ST PAUL'S

START

ST PAUL'S CHURCH

St
Paul's
Cathedral

NEW CHANGE

Spire of
St Augustine's

WATLING ST.

BOW LANE

C

ST PAULS CHURCH YD.

CARTER ST.

GODLIMA ST.

DISTAFF LANE

CANNON STREET

St Nicholas

QUEEN VICTORIA

St Benet's

MANSION
HOUSE

QUEEN STREET

River Thames

A The Place Below
B St Etheldreda's Pantry
C Hubble and Co.
D Fox and Anchor
E The Hope and Sirloin
F The Bishop's Finger
G The Cock Tavern
H Quality Chop House
I The Clerkenwell

VII: The City— St Paul's to the Barbican

281

Hubble and Co, 55 Charterhouse St. Stylish wooden-floored French wine bar with good, solid bar food and light, modern French and Italian dishes in the main restaurant. £15–25.

Fox and Anchor, 115 Charterhouse St. Famous Smithfield pub serving full breakfast (£6.50) and steak for lunch from £10–20.

The Hope and Sirloin, 94 Cowcross St. Pub with upstairs restaurant famous for its champagne breakfasts (£17) as well as more standard morning nosh-ups (£7.50 for a full cooked breakfast of bacon, eggs and eight other items).

The Bishop's Finger, 9–10 West Smithfield. Unspoiled, traditional meat market pub with rowdy atmosphere and decent pub food. Open early.

The Cock Tavern, East Poultry Market, Smithfield. Pub open for breakfast or lunch. Cheap, slightly shabby but very lively.

Quality Chop House, 94 Farringdon Rd. High-class gloss on working-class English food in mid-Victorian surroundings. Popular, so worth booking on ✆ 0171–837 5093; lunch from £20.

The Clerkenwell, 73 Clerkenwell Road. Sophisticated Mediterranean lunches, good for delicately cooked pasta and fish; telephone ahead for lunch bookings on ✆ 0171–831 7595.

St Paul's Cathedral

> *A huge, dun Cupola, like a foolscap crown*
> *On a fool's head—and there is London Town!*

Lord Byron, *Don Juan*

St Paul's is more than just a cathedral or famous landmark. It is an icon for a whole city. Get to know St Paul's and you understand many of the ambitions and failings of London itself. For nearly 1400 years, succeeding buildings on this site have sought to express the material confidence of a powerful capital while at the same time delineating its spiritual aspirations. Back in the 7th century, St Paul's was England's first major Christian temple; in its medieval incarnation it was the largest single building in the land. In the hands of Christopher Wren, who rebuilt it from scratch after the Great Fire, it was hailed as an architectural masterpiece. Since then St Paul's has dutifully propped up all the myths of the nation: as the burial place for heroes during the glory days of empire, as a symbol of British endurance during the Second World War when it miraculously survived the Blitz, or as the fairy-tale setting for Prince Charles's marriage to Lady Diana Spencer in 1981.

And yet St Paul's has often shared more with the commercial world outside its doors than with the spiritual world celebrated within. Back in the Middle Ages the cathedral was itself a kind of market, with horses parading down the nave and stallholders selling beer and vegetables to all-comers. Even today, the first thing confronting the swarms of tourists who come here is a cash register, a sign of St Paul's peculiar ease in reconciling religious faith with the handling of money. It is a cool, cerebral place. While we admire Wren's pure lines and lofty vision, we feel little warmth or sense of a living church community. 'Throughout London's history,' writes the historian Robert Gray, 'the affairs of this life have generally claimed precedence over those of the next, and when Londoners have spared time from their businesses to take account of their souls, they have tended to bring the ethos of the market place to their spiritual transactions.' St Paul's is a monument to wealth first, and God second.

No wonder, then, if it has a little of the atmosphere of the counting-house. Its history goes back to the earliest days of Christianity in England. Ethelbert of Kent, the first Anglo-Saxon king to convert, began building it in 604 at the behest of Pope Gregory's personal envoy Mellitus, later the first Bishop of London. Its name was probably chosen because both St Paul and Ethelbert were late converts to Christianity. But Paul turned out to be an appropriate patron in other ways. He, above all other early Christians, addressed himself to the question of material gain in ways that have won the admiration of conservative rulers and politicians down the ages. Margaret Thatcher, in an address to the Church of Scotland in 1988, defended her own free-market ideology by quoting a line from Paul's second epistle to the Thessalonians: 'If a man will not work he shall not eat.' From this she concluded that Paul was advocating a kind of Thatcherite philosophy predicated on individual rather than collective responsibility. Her argument may not have impressed too many theologians, but it reflected a long tradition of regarding Paul as an appropriate figurehead for the City and its material preoccupations.

Ethelbert's cathedral burned down within a few decades, and its immediate successor was demolished by the Vikings in 962. The third St Paul's was the one that made everyone sit up and take notice. It was a monster, 585ft long with a 450ft spire, making it the largest building in England and bigger by far than Wren's cathedral. It was not so much a church as a mini-city all of its own, incorporating ecclesiastical buildings, schools and colleges. It was the focus of all processions and ceremonies in the city, and, thanks to St Paul's Cross, a popular meeting place for citizens of all classes. By 1385 the cathedral had become so rowdy that the bishop issued a formal ban on ball games and beer-selling and introduced fines for window breakages. A century later an order went out banning wrestling on the premises.

The Reformation brought further decadence. The nave became known as Paul's Walk, a convenient thoroughfare for market stallholders bringing their food, beer and animals through from Carter Lane (to the south) to Paternoster Row (to the north). In 1554 a vain order was issued to ban horses and shooting inside. Bishop Pilkington described the nave thus in 1560: 'The south side for popery and usury, the north for simony; and the horse-fair in the midst for all kinds of bargains, meetings, brawlings, murders, conspiracies; and the font for ordinary payments of money, as well known to all men as the beggar knowns his bush.' Services were little more than a diversion, and restricted to the choir.

Not surprisingly, the building started falling to pieces. When the spire was struck by lightning and collapsed in 1561, it was not replaced, even after a public lottery held inside St Paul's a few years later. The proceeds went to the nation's naval harbours instead, which says something about the priorities of the diocese. One character in the anonymous late-Elizabethan play *Arden of Feversham* remarks that he only goes into St Paul's to spit. By the time of the Great Fire, old St Paul's was so dilapidated that several architects wanted to pull it down and rebuild it from scratch. In 1634 Inigo Jones had started revamping the building in classical style, but never got beyond a new portico at the western end. During the Civil War the roof fell in, the windows were smashed and most of the statuary vandalized beyond repair. Christopher Wren, commissioned to consider the cathedral's future in 1663, called it 'defective both in beauty and firmness ... a heap of deformities that no judicious architect will think corrigible by any expense that can be laid out upon it.'

He did not have to lobby long for the merits of demolition. On 4 September 1666, the first flames of the Great Fire reached St Paul's and proceeded to engulf it entirely. John Evelyn, the diarist, recorded: 'The stones of St Paul's flew like grenados, the melting lead running down the streets in a stream, and the very pavements glowing with fiery rednesses, so as no man nor horse was able to tread on them.' Only a statue of the 17th-century poet John Donne, a former dean of St Paul's, survived the inferno. Macabrely, the heat also catapulted the corpse of Robert Braybrooke, Bishop of London 250 years earlier, out of his tomb and into the churchyard. Crowds gathered to look upon the flesh still covering his skeleton, which Samuel Pepys described as 'tough like a spongy dry leather'.

Nothing was easy about the rebuilding. Wren initially used gunpowder to clear the wreck of old St Paul's but had to resort to battering rams instead after terrified locals complained of rogue pieces of stonework flying through their living-room windows. As for the design, Wren set his heart on building a dome in the manner of the great Italian Baroque churches. That idea, too, met stiff resistance—it was considered excessively Popish in those religiously sensitive times. Twice Wren (who was by now the King's surveyor-general) tried to convince the project's commissioners of the merits of his plans, and twice his plans were rejected, to his understandable consternation. You can see his magnificent 20ft oak replica of the Great Model (plan number two, and a longer, sleeker version of the present building) on display in the crypt. Eventually the dome problem was solved through a mixture of guile and compromise. Wren submitted a third plan dispensing with a dome in favour of a steeple, and had it approved in 1675; in return the royal warrant giving him the go-ahead granted him the liberty 'to make some variations rather ornamental than essential, as from time to time he should see proper'. By the time the cathedral opened 35 years later, the dome was back, as were many of the architect's other rejected ideas.

Already wary, Wren shrouded the building work in secrecy. He constructed a wall around the site and ensured that work proceeded evenly across the whole ground plan to deny his patrons the possibility of pointing to an isolated section and proposing modifications. By the time the main body of the church became visible, it was too late for his critics to change anything. Wren did not have it all his own way, however. In 1697 the parliamentary committee supervising him became so angered by his secretive tactics and slow progress that it docked half his annual salary; he did not receive his arrears until a change of government 14 years later.

*From ➋ St Paul's, follow the signs to the cathedral (these should be to your left). As you turn off Cheapside into **St Paul's Churchyard**, the contours of the massive dome emerge from behind the plane trees.*

The churchyard is no more than an alleyway and, besides housing the cathedral Chapter House (a redbrick building designed by Wren in 1712) and deanery, has never been particularly religious in purpose. Before the Great Fire it was the centre of the London book trade. It was also the site of St Paul's Cross, a kind of popular gathering place which Thomas Carlyle described as '*The Times* newspaper of the Middle Ages'.

The cross was a bizarre combination of speaking platform, pulpit and gallows. Ordinary people assembling there might hear news of forthcoming royal marriages, or witness theological arguments, or see condemned books thrown into a bonfire. In 1605, it was the site chosen to hang, draw and quarter some of the Gunpowder Plotters (the rest, including Guy Fawkes, met their grisly end in Westminster). The cross was finally dismantled and destroyed in 1673; an unremarkable memorial statue of St Paul on a tall column was erected in its place in 1910.

*The churchyard takes you round to the entrance of **St Paul's Cathedral** (℗ 0171–236 4128, open Mon–Sat 8.30–4; adm) at the western end.*

The sheer imposing scale of St Paul's is apparent as soon as you approach the entrance at the west front. The broad staircase leads up to a two-tiered portico upheld by vast stone columns and flanked by two clocktowers. Dominating the high pediment in the centre is a statue of St Paul, with St Peter to his left and St James to his right. It is surely no coincidence that these three figures look down on the sovereign of the day, Queen Anne, whose statue stands on the ground outside the entrance. The ensemble, the work of a single artist, Francis Bird, forges a clear mystical link between the City, the crown and the church. The symbolism was not lost on the lampoonists of the time, who seized on the fact that Anne is facing *away* from the cathedral towards the drinking taverns of Ludgate Hill and Fleet Street. She was known as a bit of a tippler herself, and one popular rhyme went:

> *Brandy Nan, Brandy Nan, you're left in the lurch,*
> *Your face to the gin shop, your back to the church.*

The nave is vast but remarkably simple in its symmetries; concentrate on the harmony of the architecture and try to blank out the largely hideous statuary and incidental decoration added well after Wren's time. As you walk beneath the dome look down at the marble floor and you'll see the famous epitaph to Wren, added by his son after his death in 1723, '*Lector, si monumentam requiris, circumspice*' (Reader, if you seek a memorial, look around you).

Look, in particular, up towards the magnificent dome. This is something of an optical illusion, nowhere near as big on the inside as it is on the outside. In fact, Wren built a smaller second dome inside the first to keep the interior on a manageable scale. The story goes that the first stone used to construct the dome was a relic from the old St Paul's which by coincidence bore the Latin word *resurgam* (rise up). Wren took it as a good portent and had the word inscribed in the pediment above the south door, adorning it with an image of a phoenix rising from the ashes.

> *You can climb up into the dome, or domes, from a staircase on the south*
> *side of the cathedral, in exchange for another cash contribution.*

The first stopping-off point is the **Whispering Gallery** 100ft up, so called because you can murmur with your face turned towards the wall and be heard with crystal clarity on the other side of the dome, 107ft away. You can also admire James Thornhill's series of frescoes on the life of St Paul which stretch all the way around the gallery. Vertigo permitting, you can continue on up to the Stone Gallery, the Inner Golden Gallery and the Outer Golden Gallery, offering panoramic views over London from just below the ball and cross at a height of 365ft. In the latter stages of building, the septuagenarian Wren used to be hoisted up here in a basket every Saturday to inspect the work. In deference to his age, however, he left it to his son to lay the final and highest stone.

The solidity of the dome more than proved its worth during the Blitz. An incendiary bomb made a direct hit on 29 December 1941, but by good fortune it fell out on to the Stone Gallery where further damage was prevented by the swift action of the volunteer fire-fighting group, the St Paul's Watch. Throughout the war, St Paul's offered a symbol of resistance to the nation as time and again it evaded the German bombing. Twice, bombs landed but failed to go off; on several other occasions the cathedral remained unscathed while the buildings all around collapsed and burst into flames. One of the most famous photographs of the war shows St Paul's standing proud in a sea of fire and smoke. In the end it suffered only relatively light damage to the altar and north transept.

Back on *terra firma*, you can explore all the junk added to St Paul's in the generations following Wren. Until 1795 there were no monuments inside the church, its greatest ornaments being the magnificent organ, built by Wren himself, and the attractively carved choir stalls by Grinling Gibbons. Henry Moore's statue *Mother and Child,* on the north side behind the choir, is also worth admiring. Oh, but what a disaster the rest is, particularly the execrable Victorian mosaics of the Creation in the choir and the grotesque monuments to General Gordon of Khartoum and the Duke of Wellington. The *baldacchino* in front of the altar is a shameless steal from St Peter's in Rome, built as a war memorial in 1958. Holman Hunt's fine pre-Raphaelite painting *The Light of the World*, a lush depiction of Christ opening the door to a man's soul, hangs on the south side of the nave—but only reluctantly is it admitted that this is not the original, which is in Keble College, Oxford.

And so down to the **crypt** (entrance near the south door), whose highlight is undoubtedly Wren's Great Model (*see* above) and the fine exhibition that accompanies it. Most of the space, though, is taken up with tombs commemorating Britain's military leaders. Among the rows and rows of nonentities you can find the Duke of Wellington (again) in his pompous porphyry casket and, directly beneath the dome, the black marble sarcophagus honouring Horatio Nelson. The Florentine sarcophagus, by Pietro Torrigiano, was originally commissioned by Cardinal Wolsey back in the 16th century, but was deemed too good for him and spent three centuries unused and neglected in Windsor Castle until Nelson's mourners unearthed it for his funeral in 1805.

> *Returning to the nave, leave by the west door, the way you came in, and walk round the outside of the cathedral to the left.*

The streets on the hill leading down to the river to the south, such as Carter Lane and Peter's Hill, give a flavour of the labyrinthine medieval City—half-timbered houses, inns and churches. The medieval inns survive in modern form, offering lunchtime pints to businessmen. After the Great Fire, Wren oversaw the reconstruction of 52 of the 87 churches damaged or destroyed by fire, and his work is still very much in evidence throughout the City.

Looking down Godliman St, for example, you can see the dome and short spire of **St Benet**, an attractive building in dark red brick and Portland stone. At the bottom of Distaff Lane is the conical steeple of **St Nicholas Cole Abbey**, the very first church Wren worked on which was completed in 1677. Walking round the back of St Paul's on to New Change, you see the surviving tower of **St Augustine's** inside the modern buildings of the cathedral choir school. The rest of the church was destroyed in the Blitz; note, however, the fibreglass spire, based on Wren's original.

---

*From New Change, turn right into Watling St, named after the original Roman road that ran from Dover to St Albans but not actually on its route. Take the second turning on the left, Bow Lane, which leads you to Cheapside and one of the most impressive of Wren's churches, **St Mary-le-Bow**.*

Wren almost certainly left the bulk of his church renovations to subordinates; it is hard to imagine that he had time to redesign all 52 himself. This church, however, bears all the signs of his own imprint. It is famous for two reasons. First for its massive, distinctive steeple, which soars 217ft into the sky, and secondly for its Bow Bells which have formed part of the mythology of London for centuries. It was their resounding peal that persuaded the fairytale Dick Whittington to turn again and return to London in search of fame and fortune. Ever since, the tradition has been that anyone born within earshot of the bells can call himself a true Londoner. The bells no doubt owe their reputation to the fact that for a long time they were the loudest in the City. In the 14th century they were rung to signal a curfew. During the Second World War, the BBC used them to introduce its radio news broadcasts. Now, unfortunately, they are rarely used and survive largely as a folk memory. There is a third, less well known, reason why you should visit St Mary-le-Bow: its magnificently preserved Norman crypt. Along with the Guildhall's, it is one of the few left in London. This was where William Fitzosbert, nicknamed Longbeard, took refuge and was finally smoked out after the failure of his rebellion against Richard the Lionheart's war taxes in 1196. The round arches of the crypt probably gave the church its name; the space is now used as a restaurant with tasty home-cooked food.

*Turn left onto Cheapside and head back towards ☉ St Paul's where the walk started. As you pass Foster Lane on the right, note the Italianate spire of another Wren church, St Vedast-alias-Foster. When you reach the Underground station, walk straight ahead past the roundabout on to Newgate St. To your right is the ruin of what was once one of Wren's finest reconstructions, **Christ Church Greyfriars**.*

In the Middle Ages this was the second largest church in the City after St Paul's. It became popular for funerals after Henry III buried the heart of his wife Eleanor of Provence here in 1291; the dead were often interred in monk's habits to speed their passage to heaven. Gutted in the Great Fire and then destroyed again in the Blitz, Christ Church can now only boast its steeple, decorated with urns, and the ruined shell of the nave.

> *From here you can take a quick detour up King Edward St for a look at the* **National Postal Museum** *(open Mon–Fri, 9.30–4.30; free), in the post office in King Edward Building on the left-hand side of the road. This is a stamp collector's wet dream: three floors of postal memorabilia, from rare stamps to uniforms, Bantams (the motorbikes used for delivering telegrams) and red and green post boxes dating back to the 1850s.*

> *Returning to Christ Church, cross the road and look for the pedestrianized entrance to* **Paternoster Square***.*

Once the site of Newgate meat market, where hundreds of sheep were slaughtered each day, Paternoster Square has become a battleground for London's architectural factions. The present development, all 1960s concrete, is justifiably regarded as vile by all parties. Prince Charles memorably referred to it as 'the continuation of war by other means'. But nobody has yet come up with a viable replacement. Lively, innovative plans by Richard Rogers and Arup Associates fell victim to London's structural inability to make planning decisions, as the Corporation of London (the City's local government body), the dean of St Paul's and lobby groups such as English Heritage squabbled endlessly about their merits. Prince Charles effectively gave the kiss of death to any plan that might be at all daring by complaining of architects who 'wrecked the London skyline and desecrated the dome of St Paul's with a jostling scrum of office buildings'. In 1991 a sober neoclassical design by John Simpson, Terry Farrell and Thomas Beeby was presented to a distinctly mixed reception. Building work of any kind has yet to begin.

> *Return to Newgate and turn left. Near the top of Warwick Lane, the next turning on the left, is the elegant Victorian terracotta front of* **Cutler's Hall***, headquarters to one of the City livery companies. Two streets further on is the* **Old Bailey***, once the site of Newgate Prison and now home to the Central Criminal Court.*

The Old Bailey

> Leonard Vole: *But this is England, where I thought you never arrest, let alone convict, people for crimes they have not committed.*
>
> Sir Wilfrid: *We try not to make a habit of it.*
>
> from Billy Wilder's film *Witness for the Prosecution* (1957)

The soaring gilt statue of Justice rising from the roof of the Old Bailey *(accessible via several flights of stairs only, open Mon–Fri, 10.30–1 and 2–4.30, no cameras, large bags, drink, food, pagers, radios, gas canister etc., no children under 14, no cloakroom for bags; free)* has become such a potent symbol of temperance in the English legal system that it has eradicated virtually all memory of the barbarity once associated with this site. Until 1902 this place was Newgate Prison, one of the most gruesome of all jails, which Henry Fielding once described as a prototype for hell. Generations of prisoners were left here, quite literally, to rot; to this day judges wear posies of sweet-smelling flowers on special occasions as a grim reminder of the stench that used to emanate from the cold, filthy cells.

Newgate became the City jail as early as the 12th century, although its notoriety grew only after the Great Fire when it was entirely rebuilt. On arrival prisoners were regularly bullied and robbed by the governor and his warders. They were then slung into dark underground dungeons without ventilation or running water. The only way to avoid starvation was by bribery. Jail fever, a virulent strain of typhoid, was rife and the whole place stank of disease and human flesh. Many of the prisoners had little to look forward to except one last walk on the way to the gallows at Tyburn (now called Marble Arch). The unluckiest were pressed to death in their cells for failing to confess their crimes.

Few ever hoped to escape from such a place. And yet in the 18th century one man, the burglar and highwayman Jack Sheppard, managed to do so twice. The first time Sheppard picked the lock of his condemned cell with a nail file. The second time he made his getaway, quite incredibly, from a third floor cell in a bell-tower where he had been handcuffed, manacled and chained to the floor. As a result he became an overnight celebrity, an unfortunate side-effect for a man on the run and one that precipitated his recapture. Back in prison he was visited by an eminent former inmate of Newgate, Daniel Defoe, who wrote one of several contemporary accounts of his life, and by James Thornhill, the king's portraitist, who painted him. When he was finally carted off to Tyburn in 1724, a large crowd came out to cheer him. Just before the hangman pulled the rope over his neck, a penknife was found concealed in his clothing. Even *in extremis*, Sheppard had been planning another escape.

Gradually a campaign started to reform Newgate, and in the 1770s the prison was entirely rebuilt to a design by George Dance the Younger. It did not stand for long, since it was one of the targets of the Gordon Riots of 1780. The mob demanded the release of all prisoners, and when their demand was not met they smashed open the prison gates with crowbars, set the place alight and chased the keeper and his family over the rooftops. About 300 prisoners, many in chains, rushed out into the streets to join the riot, while scores of others, trapped inside their cells, screamed in terror as fire devastated the premises. When the prison was rebuilt, for the second time in 10 years, one of its first new inmates was the riot leader himself, the anti-Catholic fanatic Lord George Gordon, who died there of jail fever in 1793. Conditions scarcely improved, and indeed the prison only gained in notoriety as the gallows were moved from Tyburn to a site just outside the front door in Newgate Street.

When the social reformer Elizabeth Fry visited women prisoners at Newgate in 1813, she found many of them lying starving and drunk on the cold stone floor. Dickens professed a 'horrible fascination' for the place and included it in a clutch of his novels. But eventually Newgate's reputation proved its undoing. The public hangings came to an end in 1868 and the prison itself was demolished in 1902 to make way for the criminal courts you see today.

The mood now could not be more different. The nickname Old Bailey, referring to the alley running off Newgate Street, conveniently avoids all reference to the old prison. Ask about the place's history and you will be given a list, not of the horrors of incarceration, but of the famous names whose trials have taken place here: Oscar Wilde; the Edwardian wife-murderer Dr Crippen; and William Joyce, known as Lord Haw-Haw, who broadcast enemy propaganda from Nazi Germany during the Second World War.

You are welcome to attend a court hearing in one of the public galleries, although the tightly arranged wooden benches are not exactly designed for comfort. The rituals are similar to those of the civil courts (*see* pp.263–5), although the mood is inevitably more sombre. Over the years, the system's confidence has been shaken by a spate of miscarriages of justice, particularly in cases involving IRA bombings and police murders. In the early 1990s the appeal court quashed a whole series of convictions because the evidence, often based on uncorroborated confessions, did not stand up to close scrutiny. Some of the prisoners, originally sentenced in the 1970s, were framed by the police and spent half their lives in jail before being vindicated. The fate of the Guildford Four, the Birmingham Six and the rest has sparked an anxious debate on the justice system's ability to handle delicate issues. Fortunately for the released prisoners, the death sentence was abolished in Britain in 1965.

The legend above the entrance to the Old Bailey reads: 'Defend the children of the poor and punish the wrongdoer'. On both these counts, the place has been less successful than it thinks.

*Return to Newgate St and across the road to your left, just beyond Gilt-spur St, is the church of **St Sepulchre without Newgate**.*

When the condemned prisoners of Newgate heard the great Bell of Bailey inside the tall tower of this church ring out at dawn, they knew that their final hour had come and that they were soon to begin the long final journey to Tyburn. Back in 1605 a parishioner by the name of Robert Dowe thought he would give the prisoners a little more notice of their fate and paid for a handbell to be rung at midnight along a tunnel which connected St Sepulchre to the prison. He also wrote a few lines for the bellman to recite:

> *All you that in the condemned hole do lie*
> *Prepare you for tomorrow you shall die*
> *Watch all and pray; the hour is drawing near*
> *That you before the Almighty must appear.*
> *Examine well yourselves, in time repent,*
> *That you may not to eternal flames be sent.*
> *And when St Sepulchre's Bell in the morning tolls*
> *The Lord have mercy on your souls.*

The bellman would approach the condemned cell and shout the last lines through the keyhole, just to make sure the message got through. It's a wonder nobody told him to shut up and keep his bad poetry to himself. The bell itself is now locked in a glass case on the south side of the church.

St Sepulchre is an interesting mixture of styles. Its 15th-century fan-vaulted porch and part of the tower survived the Great Fire; the rest, largely rebuilt in the 1670s, has been tinkered with and restored right up to the present day. St Sepulchre is now known as the musicians' church and prides itself on its lunchtime concerts. The Musician's Chapel on the north side includes a stained-glass window dating from the early 1960s which depicts Dame Nellie Melba as Mimi in *La Bohème*.

At this point Newgate St becomes Holborn Viaduct, once a crossing over the River Fleet (which gave Fleet St its name) and now a mundane and noisy road that arches over Farringdon Rd below.

Welcome to **Holborn**, district of unexciting offices and only occasionally exciting shops sandwiched in between the City and the more obvious delights of Bloomsbury. The only consolation of this nondescript corner of London is that it was a lot worse in the 17th and early 18th centuries, when the Fleet was a notorious open sewer, filled with dead cats and rotten meat from Smithfield market as well as all the stinking ordure of the City.

The Fleet was eventually filled in in 1747; the Victorians then tried to jolly up the district, none too successfully, by building this brightly decorated bridge over

Farringdon Rd and adorning it with allegorical statues of Commerce, Agriculture, Science and Fine Arts.

*Rest assured, this walk merely skims round the edge of Holborn, mainly for a quick look at three of its churches. The first two, the **City Temple** and **St Andrew's Holborn**, are on your left just after the bridge.*

From the outside City Temple has an extremely elegant three-tiered tower dating from 1874. The non-conformist church acquired a reputation in the 1920s as a forum for debate on taboo subjects like birth control. It was bombed in the Blitz and the large interior is seriously 1950s, with a wedding cake pulpit, fifty foot high cross, Wedgewood plaques, even the occasional 'Jesus Lives' banner. You'll want to run back out as fast as you can. Just beyond is the white tower of St Andrew's.

This church was famous during the Civil War for its courageous rector John Hackett, who carried on reading from the Book of Common Prayer during services even when Cromwell's disapproving soldiers held a gun to his head. Wren built one of his largest parish churches on the site after the Great Fire. Unfortunately there is not much to see apart from its graceful exterior; the inside, destroyed by wartime bombs, was unimaginatively restored.

*Holborn Circus is the traffic roundabout ahead. The equestrian figure in the middle is of Queen Victoria's husband Prince Albert; it is known as the most polite statue in London because the Prince is seen doffing his hat. Take the second turning on the right, called **Hatton Garden**.*

This street is the centre of London's diamond trade, and the jewels displayed in the soft cushions of its shop windows sparkle in the sunshine. Jewellers have been here since the 1830s, but the street is also known for its curious inhabitants. The Italian revolutionary Giuseppe Mazzini lived at No.5 in the early 1840s, while at No.57 a Mr Hiram Maxim perfected the world's first automatic gun in 1884.

*Just west of Hatton Garden are the stalls and cheap cafés of Leather Lane market, an amiable if unremarkable place to pick up a sandwich or cheap clothes and electrical goods. For the purposes of this walk, however, you should look for the alley next to No.8 Hatton Garden which leads into a beautifully unspoilt street of smart Georgian townhouses, Ely Place. This private road, closed to traffic, boasts a fine gatehouse. Halfway down on the left is Holborn's most intriguing and beautiful church, **St Etheldreda's**.*

Etheldreda was a 7th-century Anglo-Saxon princess who had the distressing habit of marrying and then refusing to sleep with her husbands. When husband number two, Prince Egfrith of Northumbria, finally lost patience with her and made unseemly advances, she withdrew into holy orders and founded a double monastery at Ely in Cambridgeshire. Seven years later, in 679, she was stricken with a tumour on her neck and died. None mourned Etheldreda more than her sister, the unfortunately-named Sexburga, who campaigned ardently to have her sanctity recognized. In 695, Sexburga had Etheldreda's coffin opened and found that the tumour had quite vanished. Her skin was now quite unblemished. A miracle!

Etheldreda became Ely's special saint and was the obvious choice of patron for this double-storey church, built in the 13th century as part of the Bishop of Ely's London palace. It was by all accounts a sumptuous residence, with stunning gardens. John of Gaunt came to live here after his Savoy Palace was burned down in the Peasants' Revolt of 1381, while Henry VIII and his first wife Catherine of Aragon spent five days in 1531 feasting in the Great Hall on swans stuffed with larks stuffed with sparrows. After the dissolution of the monasteries, the palace went into decline. Elizabeth I leased part of the property to her favoured chancellor, Christopher Hatton, to whom we owe the name Hatton Garden, for an annual rent of £10, plus—a romantic touch, this—ten bales of hay and a red rose plucked at midsummer. Of all the palace buildings, only the church survived the double onslaught of the Civil War and the Great Fire. Today it is one of the oldest surviving buildings in the City and one of its few Roman Catholic churches (it was taken over by the Rosminian Order in the late 19th century).

The Gothic **upper church** is a warm, lofty room with a fine wooden-beamed ceiling and huge stained-glass windows at each end. The east window, behind the altar, is particularly striking with its depiction of the Holy Trinity surrounded by the apostles and Anglo-Saxon and Celtic saints including Etheldreda herself. The west window is much starker, portraying the martyrdom of three Carthusian priors at Tyburn in 1535 with Christ hovering over them. Both windows date from after the Second World War; their predecessors were shattered by German bombs. Downstairs, the lower church or **crypt** is much simpler, no more than a room with a plain altar and little decoration. Round the walls are stone engravings depicting the stations of the cross, while in one of the alcoves on the south side is a statue of St Blaise, the patron saint of throat diseases (he once saved a boy who had swallowed a fishbone), who is commemorated in an annual ceremony.

> The other early building in Ely Place is the **Olde Mitre Tavern**; its low, cherry-panelled rooms date back to Tudor times. At the end of the street, a gateway leads through to an alley called Bleeding Heart Yard and out on to Greville St. Unfortunately, the gate is usually shut, obliging you to return to Hatton Garden and walk round the block to the same point. Once on Greville St, cross Farringdon Rd, and continue to Cowcross St, which takes you past Farringdon station. You can carry straight on to Smithfield (see below), but you may feel like a short detour to **Clerkenwell** to the north.

Clerkenwell

By turns a centre for monks, clockmakers, gin manufacturers and Italian labourers, Clerkenwell has the feel of a cosy village with its squares, winding streets and pretty churches. Its proximity to the City made it an ideal headquarters for the knights of the Order of St John, who stayed here until the dissolution of the monasteries in the 1530s. Then in the early 17th century the digging of the New River put Clerkenwell on the main freshwater route into London and so attracted brewers and distillers. In the 19th century much of Clerkenwell was slumland, and the Victorians built forbidding prisons there to cope with the overflow from the city jails. After decades of neglect, it is now undergoing something of a revival, its grimy backstreets filling with slick new offices, converted lofts and cheap, attractive cafés.

> *From Cowcross St, turn left up Turnmill St. Follow the railway tracks, cross Clerkenwell Road and take the first right-hand turning into Clerken-well Green.*

The sites of Clerkenwell are all within easy reach from the Green, which was often used in the 19th century as a starting point for protest marches. The **Marx Memorial Library** at Nos.37–8 (*open Mon 1–6, Tues–Thurs 1–8, Sat 10–1, closed Fri; non-members are welcome to look around for free but cannot use the library or its lending facility unless they pay a modest membership fee*) has the best private collection of radical literature in the city; Lenin wrote radical pamphlets here in 1902–3. Clerkenwell Close (off to the left) leads to the attractive grey stone **St James's Church**, once part of a Benedictine nunnery but rebuilt many times over the years. The steeple, the latest addition, dates from 1849. Further up the Close (follow the signposts) is the **Middlesex House of Detention**, the site of one of the area's notorious Victorian prisons, itself a conversion of an earlier prison.

All that remains are the cellars, which offer an atmospheric insight into the damp and cold conditions, and show you where prisoners' clothes were fumigated, meals were prepared and uniforms were laundered from 1846–78.

> *Return to Clerkenwell Green, turn left and then right at the end down Jerusalem Passage. This brings you to a square and **St John's Church**.*

This was the place where the medieval knights of St John worshipped, but you would not know to look at it now. It was destroyed during the Peasants' Revolt of 1381, left to rot after the dissolution of the monasteries, converted into a private chapel and then a Presbyterian meeting house, bombed in the Blitz and finally restored and refurbished.

The 15th-century altar paintings were looted during the dissolution and only returned in 1915; the 12th-century crypt, part of the original church structure, is also well worth a visit for itself and for its alabaster effigies.

> *Cross Clerkenwell Road again and you pass underneath the crenellated stone **St John's Gate**, the only surviving relic of the priory where the Order of St John of Jerusalem lived and worked.*

The knights of St John were crusaders. Like the Templars, they set up a priory in London and built a round church inspired by the Dome of the Rock in Jerusalem. Visitors were welcome, especially the sick and the poor, who were invited to receive three days' board and lodging free of charge. Much of the original priory was burned down in the Peasants' Revolt. This gatehouse, dating from 1504, is all that remains of the rebuilding work. The rest was parcelled off and sold after the dissolution, and the fine tower was blown up to provide stone for Somerset House in the Strand. The gatehouse itself took on various guises over the ensuing centuries—home to Elizabeth I's Master of the Revels, coffee shop and newspaper office. Now it is a small museum (*open Mon–Fri, 10–5, Sat 10–4; adm*) containing relics and armour of the medieval knights and exhibits celebrating the work of the St John's Ambulance charity, a modern incarnation of the crusading order.

> *From the gatehouse, walk down St John's Lane and then St John's St and you come directly to the painted iron sheds of **Smithfield Market**.*

Smithfield has come a long way since the 14th century, when cattle was slaughtered in front of the customers and witches boiled alive for the entertainment of the populace. This is still where Londoners come to buy their meat, but nowadays it is a civil, sanitized sort of place. The carcasses arrive ready-slaughtered and are stored in giant fridges so you'll barely see a speck of dirt or blood. The covered market halls have been refurbished and are surrounded by restaurants and pubs.

Smithfield was originally a jousting field within easy reach of the city walls. The annual Bartholomew Cloth Fair started in the 12th century, and shortly afterwards drovers began bringing cattle and horses to a weekly market. After the Black Death of 1348–9, Smithfield was the city's main mortuary: the thousands of dead were shovelled into giant pits. This was also the spot where Richard II confronted the Peasants' Revolt and disbanded the mob after the murder of their leader Wat Tyler (*see* p.41). The meat market proper did not get going until the 17th century, but it rapidly became a major London institution. Pigs and cattle made the journey to London on foot from the furthest corners of the country. Cows from the Isle of Skye off the west coast of Scotland swam to the mainland before continuing the journey by road. Geese and turkeys from East Anglia would wear cloth shoes on their feet to help them survive the trek. One 18th-century drover complained: 'A pig is a sluggish, obstinate, opinionated, not very social animal and has no desire to see foreign parts.' The cattle breeders would celebrate their arrival in London by getting uproariously drunk and letting their animals run amok through the streets. As late as the 1830s, bulls were regularly seen stampeding down major roads, goring terrified residents and occasionally killing them. Around Smithfield itself, the streets were filled with the stench of blood and entrails which blocked up the gutters and infiltrated the water system. The 18th-century satirist Jonathan Swift gave a graphic description in his poem *A City Shower*:

> *Sweepings from butcher's Stalls, Dung, Guts and Blood,*
> *Drown'd Puppies, stinking Sprats, all drench'd in Mud,*
> *Dead Cats and Turnip-Tops come tumbling down the Flood.*

The market was little better in the 1840s, when Dickens described it in *Oliver Twist* as 'nearly ankle-deep in filth and mire; a thick steam perpetually rising from the reeking bodies of the cattle'. Finally, in 1855, the Victorians decided enough was enough. Cholera epidemics were becoming all too common and, under the influence of such reformers as Edwin Chadwick, the authorities started thinking seriously about hygiene.

Live animals were allowed no further into the city than Islington. The City architect Sir Horace Jones built the first covered market halls at Smithfield and linked them to London's new railway stations by underground passageway. The meat trade had entered the modern age. Only the pubs carried on as before. From 4am the market boys would sit and drink pineapple rum or 'wazzers', a Smithfield special of tea laced with whisky. Since Jones's overhaul, the market has continued in more or less the same form. Unlike other food wholesale markets such as Covent Garden or Billingsgate, there seems to be no pressure on Smithfield to move out to the suburbs. More than 1000 people still work here, shifting 150,000 tonnes of meat each year. It's an all too rare piece of real urban life in the City of London. Long may it last.

> For a pleasant detour, walk eastwards on Charterhouse St, then veer left through a grandiose set of iron gates leading into the delightfully leafy **Charterhouse Square**.

This was the site of a magnificent Carthusian monastery founded in 1370, and later of one of England's foremost private schools. Little survives of the original, and of the parts that do only the gatehouse on the northern side of the square is readily accessible. Most of the buildings are now in the hands of the St Bartholomew's Medical School. If you do manage to get in, take a look at the cloisters, the 14th-century chapel and the somewhat war-damaged 17th-century library.

Returning to Smithfield, cross through to the south side of the market and you'll see a large circular open space, half roundabout, half park, called West Smithfield. The road running south, on the far side of the circle, is Giltspur St, the original **Pie Corner** *where the Great Fire of 1666 eventually halted. At the junction with Cock Lane you'll see a 20th-century statue, the Fat Boy of Pie Corner, who marks the exact spot. His rotund figure echoes the 17th-century superstition that the Fire was divine retribution for gluttony. As you return to West Smithfield, the main building on the south side of the roundabout is* **St Bartholomew's Hospital***.*

St Bartholomew's, or Bart's as it is universally known, is the oldest hospital in London, dating back to 1123. It was founded, somewhat improbably, by Henry I's court jester Henry Rahere, who made a vow to help the sick after catching malaria on a pilgrimage to Rome. For the first 400 years it was more of a priory than a serious hospital, offering little more than prayer by way of medical help to its patients.

Medieval medicine was a haphazard affair at the best of times; pioneers such as John of Gaddesdon, who practised at Bart's in the early 14th century, administered live beetles and crickets as well as revolting mixtures of chemicals and human spittle. Few of the patients who entered Bart's ever came back out again. It was not until the 16th century, after the dissolution of the priory by Henry VIII, that Bart's devoted its full energies to medicine and employed full-time physicians. Its early practices seem horrific nowadays: the beds were infested with lice and invariably occupied by more than one patient, the windows were kept shut at all times and there was no access to hot water. It took several centuries to iron out all these problems; the hospital itself was entirely rebuilt in the 1730s by James Gibbs. In the 18th century Bart's became a pioneer in medical science and developed a prestigious teaching college with a dissecting room and displays of samples removed from patients during operations. Until the mid-19th century, when medical research finally won government sanction, students and surgeons who wanted to increase their knowledge of anatomy had to resort to body-snatching. After a night at the graveyard they would take the exhumed bodies to a first-floor room in the Fortunes of War pub on Giltspur Street and lay them out on wooden benches.

In recent years Bart's fate has hung in the balance. In 1992, an official report recommended its closure, since it served only a small local population and resources needed to be diverted to the suburbs and the rest of the country. The report caused a furore, and the hospital chapel held daily prayers for its survival. The election of a

Labour government in May 1997 raised hopes it might yet be saved; in early 1998 came the news that funds had been found to enable it to stay open.

There are guided tours of the hospital every Friday at 2pm all the year round (starting at the Henry VIII Gate on West Smithfield). The highlight is a visit to the **Great Hall** and staircase with its two **Hogarth paintings** on medical themes commissioned for the hospital: *The Pool of Bethesda* with its motley, characteristically satirical congregation of sick and eccentric figures and the rather more restrained *Good Samaritan*. The main church inside the complex is **St Bartholomew-the-Less**, a small octagonal structure by George Dance the Younger (1789). Most of its furnishings were destroyed by wartime bombing.

Finally, in the North Wing of the hospital there is a new **Museum of St Bartholomew's Hospital** (*open Tues–Fri 10–4, but call ahead to check on ✆ 0171–601 8152, as the museum is staffed by volunteers and opening hours may vary*). This contains a mixture of exhibits on the history of medicine and the history of Bart's. There are fascinating displays of amputation instruments, early syringes and stethoscopes; also a section on William Harvey, who was appointed physician to the hospital in 1609, and who went on to discover the circulation of the blood in his celebrated treatise of 1628, *Exercitatio Anatomica de Motu Cordis et Sanguinis* .

> *To see the most interesting relic of Bart's history, walk back out through the Henry VIII Gate and round to the right, to the corner of Little Britain. Just across the road is a 13th-century stone arch topped by a Tudor timber gateway, which leads to the only remaining part of Rahere's original priory, the church of St Bartholomew-the-Great.*

The original Norman church was 300ft long and included the whole area now taken up by the churchyard. By the time Henry VIII's wreckers had finished with it, only about one-third of the original building was left. It is nevertheless an impressive place. Most of the Norman arches are original, as are the vaulted wooden ceiling, font and Gothic cloister bays on the right as you come in. Much of the rest, including the porch and choir screen, was refurbished in the late 19th century.

The church is filled with peculiar relics of its past. Rahere's tomb, for example, dates not from the time of his death but from the early 16th century. The clue to the precise date is in the decoration of a crossbow in a barrel: this is a rebus indicating the name of one of the last priors of St Bartholomew, William Bolton (bolt plus tun). Bolton was given over to fits of anxiety: he was so convinced that the priory would be destroyed by floods that he moved out and set up house, Noah-like, on the highest hill he could find, out in Harrow.

Look out for a stone commemorating the 17th-century citizen Edward Cooke on the south wall. You'll notice a damp patch directly below: legend has it the stone sheds real tears, although since the installation of a radiator underneath, they have been rather more scarce. There is also a touching memorial on the northern side of the church to Margaret and John Whiting, who both died in 1681. The verse tells the story: 'Shee first deceased, Hee for a little Tryd/to live without her, likd it not and dyd.'

> *Just north of the church is a street whose name, Cloth Fair, is a reminder of the festive trade markets that took place here for 700 years. A few houses in the street survived the Great Fire, notably No.41, which has been carefully restored. The poet and London conservationist John Betjeman loved this street, and there is a pub named after him. Returning to Little Britain, turn left and then take the fourth turning on the left. This takes you past Postman's Park and the 18th-century church of St Botolph before bringing you to a busy roundabout. A pedestrian passageway leads you across and up a flight of stairs to the **Museum of London** (open Tues–Sat 10–5.50, Sun 12–5.50; adm, free after 4.30pm).*

This ambitious and fast-changing museum sets out to tell the story of London from prehistoric times to the present, drawing on a vast collection of documents and historical relics. It is an ideal place to come if you want to familiarize yourself with the basic facts about the city. It is also a tremendous resource for students and researchers, with its packed programme of workshops, lectures, temporary exhibitions and organized historical walks.

The museum is very strong on early history, particularly the Roman era, and gives a rich impression of life in the 19th century. It also has an imaginative section on contemporary London. In other areas, perhaps inevitably, the museum is a bit patchy, since the quality of the displays varies according to the illustrative material available. It is weak on the early Middle Ages, a time of tremendous turbulence in the city, and weak, too, on the excesses and grotesquerie of the 18th century. The main problem, in the end, is that the Museum's archive of documents is far richer than its collection of artefacts, and a museum can only display so much documentation before losing the interest of its visitors. Gimmicks, such as the glowing model of the city used in an audiovisual display on the Great Fire, are a rather unsatisfactory substitute for genuine items handed down by history.

That said, the museum is never boring. It is beautifully laid out over three descending levels. There are lucid explanations of the historical evidence yielded by lumps of Roman paving stone and recovered coinage. One angled window cleverly gives you a view down onto a piece of Roman wall (AD 200) on the ground outside. The most beautiful relics of the period come from the Temple of Mithras, a shrine to a Persian deity much invoked by Roman soldiers which once stood in what is now Temple Court off Queen Victoria Street. Temple treasures here include several sculptures and a small silver incense box.

Many of the best displays in the rest of the museum are reconstructions of contemporary buildings: a 16th-century grocer's shop, a cell at Newgate Prison, a Victorian pub, a Second World War bedroom kitted out with a protective cage called a Morrison shelter. London Now includes such innovative exhibits as a chunk of concrete from the notorious Ronan Point tower block in Newham (which collapsed in the 1970s), models of squatter houses in the End East, a print of Rachel Whiteread's intriguing sculpture *House* (depicting the interior of a terraced house in Hackney that was demolished shortly after Whiteread's piece won the Turner Prize in 1993) and a video of the dub poet Benjamin Zephaniah walking around London reciting his specially commissioned poem, *The London Breed*.

The museum also has a magnificent range of clothing, giving an insight into changing fashions since the 17th century. The undisputed centrepiece, though, is the **Lord Mayor's Coach**, which has pride of place at the bottom of the main staircase in full view as you descend from level to level. Built in 1757 in blazing red and burnished gold, the coach is still used every November for the investiture of the new Lord Mayor. It looks the sort of thing Prince Charming might have used to drive Cinderella home; it is covered in allegorical paintings depicting both the virtues of modesty and the glories of wealth. For all its splendour, though, you might not want to travel in it: it has no springs, only leather braces, which must make any ride distinctly bumpy. Until 1951 it also had no brakes.

> *Just behind the Museum of London, and accessible via stairways and passages, is* **Ironmonger's Hall**, *one of the most striking of the City livery company buildings. It is constructed in a mixture of styles going back to 1587, part stone and part wood, with beautiful iron fittings including the main crest-covered gateway. Return back up to the Museum of London and follow the signs to the Guildhall. Almost immediately you come to Nettleton Court, where the founder of Methodism, John Wesley, was converted in 1738. A monument in the shape of a scroll tells the story of how he felt his heart 'strangely warm'd' during a prayer meeting hosted by the bookseller James Hutton. Continue along the high walkway, and turn left at the signs for the* **Barbican Arts Centre**.

The Brave New World architecture of the Barbican comes straight out of the 1950s, all high-rise concrete and labyrinthine walkways (you will probably have got lost already, everybody does). The City's only residential area worthy of the name, rebuilt after extensive wartime bombing, would not be out of place in a 1960s television escape drama. There are some advantages to living here: the leafy balconies, the forecourts and fountains. But the development is not exactly on a human scale. Friendly-sounding buildings like the Shakespeare Tower or Defoe House are in fact monolithic skyscrapers.

The main reason for coming, apart from the dubious pleasure of gaping and shuddering, is a trip to the Arts Centre, home to the Royal Shakespeare Company, an art gallery (*open Mon–Sat 10–5.45 and Sun 12–6.45; adm*), three cinemas, a concert hall and a semi-tropical conservatory (*open on Level 3 from 12 until dusk, call ℭ 0171–638 4141 for more details*). On the way, you pass **St Giles Cripplegate** (*open Mon–Fri 9.30–5.30*), where John Milton was buried in 1674. The church itself, mostly built in the 16th century, escaped the 1666 fire but was destroyed by wartime bombs and faithfully rebuilt in the 1950s. A stretch of the Roman city wall can be seen just behind it.

> *To get out of the Barbican Centre, head for ⊖ Barbican or ⊖ Moorgate. Both are signposted ... good luck.*

Start: ⊖ *Bank.*

Walking time: *2½ hours*
not counting time inside the Tower.

VIII: The City—Bank to the Tower

The City is the heart of London, the place where the whole heaving metropolis began, and yet there is something so strange about it that it scarcely seems to be part of London at all. Tens of thousands of commuters stream in each morning, the bankers, brokers and clerks that oil the wheels of this great centre of world finance, spilling out of Liverpool Street or crossing over London Bridge towards their jumble of gleaming high-rise offices. During the lunch hour, you can see them scurrying from office building to sandwich bar to post office, a look of studied intensity stamped on their harried faces. By early evening they have all vanished again, back to their townhouses and dormitory communities, leaving the streets and once-monumental buildings to slumber eerily in the silent gloom of the London night.

This is T.S. Eliot's Unreal City, a metropolis without inhabitants, a place of frenzied, seemingly mindless mechanical activity that the poet, back in the apocalyptic early 1920s, thought worthy of the lost souls of limbo.

And yet it remains oddly fascinating, full of echoes of the time when it *was* London. Its streets still largely follow the medieval plan. Its fine churches and ceremonial buildings express all the contradictory emotions of a nation that built, and then lost, an entire empire. Its business is still trade, as it was in the 14th century, even

A Dirty Dick's
B Sri Thai
C Reynier Wine Bar
D Imperial City
E Poons in the City
F Regis Snack Bar
G Obertelli's

if it is trade of a most abstract and arcane sort. The great exchange floors for commodities, shares and bonds may have disappeared in this computer-driven global marketplace, but the City still clings on to its curious traditions and colourful ceremonies. The Guildhall, the epicentre of City power down the centuries, is a shrine to such ritual, where the fathers of commerce dress up in gaudy robes and nod reverentially to the past.

VIII: The City—Bank to the Tower

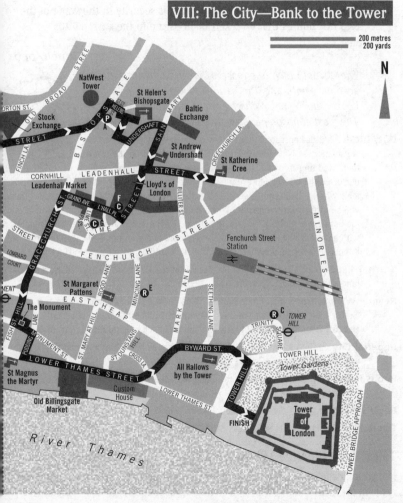

200 metres
200 yards

N

At the other end of the Square Mile, the Tower of London is a striking relic of medieval London and a reminder of the constant historical struggle between wealth creation on the one hand and the jealous encroachment of political interests on the other. The City is a weekday place only, although you won't have any difficulty getting into the Tower or Guildhall on Saturday. Many of the buildings on this walk are, regrettably, not open to the public. In some cases this is because they have lost their traditional function as trade exchanges; in others the main reason is security in the wake of the two IRA bombs that wrecked Bishopsgate in the early 1990s.

---

lunch/pubs

There's not much to choose between the fancy expense-account joints and the sandwich bars, but if you're a boozer the Reynier Wine Library is a tempting alternative. The most atmospheric place to stop is Leadenhall Market.

Dirty Dick's, 202 Bishopsgate. Dirty Dick was a well-known dandy whose real name was Nathaniel Bentley. His fiancée died on the eve of their wedding in 1787, and he never washed again. He totally neglected the house, and even left the wedding breakfast to rot on the dining room table where it had been laid out. 'It is no use,' he said, 'if I wash my hands today they will be dirty again tomorrow.' When he died in 1809, the house was in ruins even though he was worth a fortune. Rebuilt in 1870, it's now a jolly cellar bar, complete with a cabinet filled with fake mouse skeletons and a mummified cat to remind customers of the original owner. Lunch is well-cooked bar food from £5–10.

Sri Thai, Bucklesbury, Queen Victoria St. Sleek Thai restaurant with an excellent set menu lunches from £19.95 upwards.

Reynier Wine Library, 43 Trinity Square. Wine cellar deep in the city where customers choose a bottle of wine from the comprehensive 'library', and down it with cheese and pâté from the simple but tasty £10 buffet. Lunch only from £13 upwards.

Imperial City, in the basement of the Royal Exchange. A fine Chinese restaurant beneath vaulted brick ceilings. £16–35.

Poons in the City, 2 Minster Pavement. Stylish Chinese restaurant; lunch from £5 or £12 for the set meal.

Regis Snack Bar, 34 Leadenhall Market. Takeaway or sit-down sarnies.

Obertelli's, 38 and 61 Lime St Passage. Sandwiches and café-style Italian meals. £5–10.

Tales of the City: the 1980s and After

Not so long ago, the City was a club of privately-educated, discreetly-mannered gents in grey suits and bowler hats acting on behalf of respected companies and select upper-middle-class clients. 'My word is my bond,' was the ethical code that pertained right across the financial services industry: when share traders exchanged their peculiar nods and hand signals across the floor of the Stock Exchange, they were putting their honour as well as their money on the line.

How quaint and innocent that all seems now. The old certainties of the City have been shaken to the very core over the past generation or so, from the advent of floating exchange rates in the early 1970s, to the orgiastic, 'greed is good' excesses of the high-tech 1980s, to the more chastened and pragmatic atmosphere prevailing at the turn of the millennium. Where once London was the financial powerhouse of the world, the capital of an empire and issuer of the single most important global currency, it now plays a more technocratic role; it nevertheless remains, along with New York and Tokyo, one of three world centres for 24-hour trade in currencies, commodities and bonds, as well as futures and options, the new generation of financial instruments or 'derivatives'.

The pivotal moment for the City came during the Thatcher years, when it underwent not just a financial revolution but a sociological one too. As the government's priorities switched from manufacturing industry to the service sector—and financial services in particular—the old-school gents of Cornhill and Lombard Street were swept aside by a new breed of aggressive, instinctual bounty-hunters who were as likely to have pitched up from the barrows of the East End as the hallowed playing-fields of Eton or Harrow. The suits grew wider, the ties grew louder and the accents around the trading halls went sharply downmarket. While the old collieries and steelworks of Britain's industrial heartland went into terminal decline, the money here in the City got so good it was almost obscene. Seventeen-year-old whizzkids who knew how to play the foreign exchanges were taking home hundreds of thousands of pounds each month. Out went the old rituals of boardroom lunches (for wimps only) and boxes at the opera; in came champagne, cocaine and 7-series BMWs. Salaries spiralled as firms competed to hold on to their best staff; for a while new recruits were being offered 'golden hellos' as an extra inducement to join firm X rather than firm Y.

This delirium of serious money reached its height in October 1986 and the so-called 'big bang', which deregulated many financial services and, most spectacularly, moved share trading off the floor of the Stock Exchange and on to dealing-room computer screens. London, in financial terms, became no more than a geographical expression. There was nothing to stop traders in New York or Singapore buying and selling on the London markets, and they did so with relish. As a result, money moved around much faster and among far more people, leading to bigger speculations and bigger profits. Of course, it could not last and it didn't. The stock market crash of 1987, when traders wiped billions off the value of companies that they themselves had pumped up in the big bang euphoria, dealt the first swingeing blow. Then, 18 months later, British interest rates shot up in response to a general over-heating of the economy. Suddenly the banks called in their debts. Repossession and receivership became the new growth industries. Recession soon followed, and the City, burdened by a morass of fraud and corruption scandals, found itself cutting back sharply on its excesses.

Margaret Thatcher always used to say 'you cannot buck the market', and thanks to her deregulation policies this mantra turned into a self-fulfilling prophecy. On Black Wednesday in September 1992, the British government fought desperately to support the value of sterling so it could stay in the European Community's fixed-band monetary system, the ERM. The Bank of England spent billions buying up its own currency before giving in to the international forces working against it. Over in Downing Street, the cabinet listened to news of the plummeting pound on a transistor radio, and John Major, the Prime Minister, grimly drafted a letter of resignation (though he never delivered it). The billions simply moved out of the Treasury's coffers and into the speculators' pockets. It was a moment of plunderous self-destruction that came close to destroying the very foundations of the British economy.

It has taken a long time for the City to recover its equanimity. For years, some of its most august institutions, notably the Lloyd's insurance market and the ill-fated investment bank Barings, went through excruciating humiliations and many of its office buildings stood idle and empty. These days, the City is performing an uneasy balancing act over European integration: fulfilling all the conditions to join the single currency (making the Bank of England independent, for example) while attempting to keep some distance from the mainstream European economies. Life may be returning, but the brashness and supreme self-confidence are gone. The barrow-boys are still around, but they are not so noticeable in the general mingle of classes, educations and nationalities. Rather than attracting just the grasping, over-materialistic children of the Thatcher generation, the City is now something of a melting-pot for ambitious, usually well-educated young people from all over Europe, North America and Asia. Eighties boom-and-bust has given way to a gentler, more reasonable atmosphere in this sweaty boiler-room of world capitalism—multiculturalism meets the market place.

> Emerging from Bank Underground station, you find yourself at a confluence of several roads and a number of grandiose buildings: Mansion House to the south, the Royal Exchange to the east and the Bank of England on the north side stretching into Threadneedle St.

Mansion House, the official residence of the Lord Mayor, was intended to be something of a trend-setter, the first project of the Georgian era to be designed in

Palladian style. There is a story that a design by Palladio himself was proposed but rejected because the 16th-century Italian master was a foreigner and a Papist and therefore unfit to be the architect of the Lord Mayor's first permanent residence (mayors had previously lived in their own houses). Whether or not this was true, the building of Mansion House ended up being delayed not just for years but for decades. In the end George Dance's building, erected on the site of the old Stocks Market, was completed in 1752, nearly 40 years after the project was first put forward. The end result is not a tremendous success; the awkward shape of the surrounding square does not allow the eye to be drawn towards its grandiose portico, which in any case is top-heavy and unwieldy with its six Corinthian columns.

Unfortunately Mansion House is now almost always shut and more or less the only way to get in is to apply in writing for a minimum of 14 people two months in advance. Should you be lucky, the main attraction is the high colonnaded Banqueting Hall, also known as the Egyptian Hall because the column arrangement is based on drawings described as Egyptian by the ancient Roman architect Vitruvius. Stained-glass windows at either end depict scenes from London's history including the signing of Magna Carta and the stabbing of Wat Tyler, the leader of the Peasants' Revolt, by Mayor William Walworth.

> *To the right of Mansion House is a street called Walbrook, leading to the church of* **St Stephen Walbrook.**

St Stephen's is widely considered Christopher Wren's masterpiece, a sort of mini-St Paul's that is all nave and no transepts, a bit like the giant cathedral down the road. Wren in fact used this church, built in 1672–9, to test out some of his ideas for St Paul's. St Stephen's benefits from the smaller scale: the interior has a graceful intimacy as well as an architectural flamboyance often missing from Wren's coolly geometrical designs. St Stephen's was badly damaged in the war and restored a number of times since; now it has been rearranged as a single open space, circled by Corinthian columns, with Henry Moore's cream-coloured altar, irreverently nicknamed the Camembert, as its centrepiece. Note the florid pulpit with its impressive black wrought-iron canopy. Note, also, the emphasis on natural light supplied from the windows around the base of the dome—this typical Wren touch was obscured for years by some thoroughly unnecessary stained glass.

> *From Walbrook, take Bucklersbury and turn left on Queen Victoria St. On the left just before Budge Row is the site of the* **Temple of Mithras,** *the Roman shrine whose treasures are stored in the Museum of London (see Walk VII). The site is wedged in a corner of an office block. From here take the next right, Queen St, walk up across Cheapside, along King St and up to the* **Guildhall** *(open 10–5 daily except for special occasions, closed Sun Oct–April; free).*

The Guildhall is the seat of the City's government, headed by the Lord Mayor and his Sheriffs and Aldermen and composed principally of the 12 Great Livery Companies, or guilds, that nominally represent the City's trading interests. Nowadays the governing body, known as the Corporation of London, is little more than a borough council for the City, but back in the Middle Ages it wielded near-absolute power over the whole of London. Even kings could not touch it, since the guilds generated much of the nation's wealth and made sure everyone knew it. Henry III tried to impose direct rule on London in the 13th century but eventually gave up, describing the City fathers as 'nauseously rich'.

The Guildhall, first built in the 15th century, has preserved its medieval identity to a remarkable degree. Anyone wanting to join a livery company still has to be properly connected, or very rich, or preferably both. Heredity is an important consideration, just as it was in the Middle Ages. Nowadays, of course, the company names have lost some of their meaning: haberdashers and salters are not as important as they once were. But the Corporation still wields considerable power. In the mid-1980s it successfully lobbied for the abolition of the GLC, London's overarching government body, and has enjoyed greater autonomy ever since to the detriment of London's other, generally poorer boroughs. Architecturally, the Guildhall has also retained much from the medieval era, despite the calamities of the Great Fire and the Blitz. The old oak beams proved remarkably resilient on both occasions, glowing from the heat but remaining solidly in place. The building nevertheless bears the marks of countless renovations. The pinnacled façade looking onto Guildhall Yard is a bizarre 18th-century concoction of classical, Gothic and even Indian styles.

The public entrance leads to the western end of the magnificent **old hall**, giving a spectacular view of the 152ft room draped with the banners of the 12 Great Livery Companies—Mercers, Grocers, Drapers, Fishmongers, Goldsmiths, Skinners, Merchant Taylors, Haberdashers, Salters, Ironmongers, Vintners and Clothworkers. On the wall behind each banner is the coat of arms and motto of each company. They are lined up in order of importance, starting at the far end on the left and moving in criss-cross fashion up towards the western door. In medieval times, the companies were forever bickering about their relative importance. The Skinners and Merchant Taylors, in particular, had a dispute so bitter as to who was sixth and who seventh on the list that in 1484 the Lord Mayor of the time, Robert Billesden, ruled that they should take it in turns: this may be the origin of the expression *to be at sixes and sevens*. The recesses of the hall are dotted with monuments to famous British leaders, from Nelson and the Duke of Wellington to Winston Churchill. Most eccentric are the large painted limewood figures perched on the musician's gallery at the west end. These are **Gog and Magog**, giants so mythical that nobody is quite sure where they come from. One version has it that they represent the antagonistic forces of ancient Britain and Troy; another says they were the sole surviving offspring of an unholy alliance of 33 demons and the daughters of the Emperor Diocletian. What is known is that they cropped up regularly as floats in the mid-summer pageants of the 15th and 16th centuries. Since 1708 they have also stood in the Guildhall; the present models, erected after the war, are 9ft high.

> *Ask the beadle to be taken down to the **crypt**, the most extensive of its kind left in London.*

The crypt is divided into two: the eastern half, split into 12 bays propped up by blue Purbeck marble pillars, and the western half which has a magnificent vaulted ceiling. The western half is presumed to be the cellar of the original Guildhall, dating back to the 15th century or possibly earlier. It is lit by 19 stained-glass windows depicting the arms of the livery companies. Somewhere beneath the floor are the foundations of the amphitheatre that the Romans built. Excavations in 1988 revealed that the foundations of the medieval Guildhall were in fact the Roman ruins; the arena is presumed to cover the area now taken up by Guildhall Yard.

> *Giles Gilbert Scott's concrete-clad post-war re-development around the Guildhall may be no beauty, but it contains two interesting features: the Guildhall **library** (entrance on Aldermanbury), which has the most extensive collection of books and documents on London available to the general public, and the **Guildhall Clock Museum** next door (open Mon–Fri 9.30–4.45).*

Here you'll find more than 700 timepieces of all shapes and sizes belonging to the Worshipful Company of Clockmakers. Look out for the silver skull watch said to have belonged to Mary Queen of Scots, and the wrist watch worn by Edmund Hillary during the first recorded ascent of Mount Everest in 1953.

> *Walk out to the bulky Wren church, St Lawrence Jewry, and follow Gresham St. Take the second right, Old Jewry, which as the name implies was the centre of the medieval Jewish ghetto. The street also boasts some fine Georgian townhouses (in Frederick's Place) designed by the Adam brothers in 1776. Turn left on Poultry (the continuation of Cheapside) and you return to ⊖ Bank where this walk started. This time, walk straight ahead, where to your right you see the beginning of **Lombard Street**, named after the Italian bankers who taught Londoners the rudiments of financial transaction in the 13th century. On the corner of Lombard St and King William St is **St Mary Woolnoth**, an intriguing design by Nicholas Hawksmoor based on a series of squares within squares. The interior is based on the same design by Vitruvius as the Banqueting Hall at Mansion House. Just beyond the next street, Cornhill, is the classical portico of the **Royal Exchange**.*

The eight huge Corinthian pillars give this building a sense of importance to which it can no longer lay claim. The Royal Exchange was once the trading centre of the City *par excellence*, home to all of London's stock and commodity exchanges, but it lost this crucial role in 1939 when it was bought by the Guardian Royal Exchange insurance company. It now houses a number of company offices.

This is the third Royal Exchange building to occupy the site. London's first exchange was built by the merchant and Lord Mayor Sir Thomas Gresham in the 1560s; before that, incredible as it might seem, traders conducted their business in the open air in Lombard Street. In Gresham's building the commodity traders still gathered in a central open courtyard (the covered parts being occupied by shop-keepers), but at least they could repair to the arcades on rainy days. Gresham's exchange, generally reckoned to be one of the finest Tudor buildings in London, burned down in the Great Fire of 1666; fire also claimed its successor, which housed the first offices of Lloyd's of London. The present building, designed by Sir William Tite, dates from 1844, a rare example of neoclassical architecture from the Victorian era. The pediment at the front nevertheless indulges in a characteristi- cally Victorian taste for allegory: the 17 figures depicted there are all heroic portrayals of the merchant classes with an embodiment of Commerce in the very centre. Tite's Exchange comes complete with an equestrian **statue of the Duke of Wellington**, made in suitably triumphalist fashion from the melted-down metal of French guns. There is also a memorial to the war dead of London.

> *Turning north, you are confronted with the formidable stone wall of the Bank of England. The main entrance, facing you on Threadneedle St, is for official visitors only. To reach the **Bank of England Museum** (open Mon–Fri 10–5; free), follow the building round to the right into Bartholomew Lane.*

The playwright Richard Sheridan described the Bank of England as 'an elderly lady in the City of great credit and long standing'. Its record as prudent guardian of the nation's finances is well known; it rescued London from bankruptcy at the end of the 17th century, resisted the temptations of the South Sea Bubble and kept the country's economy buoyant throughout the trauma of the Revolutionary wars against France. As the bank of last resort it played a crucial role in the development of Britain's capitalist system during the 18th and 19th centuries.

But the Bank has had a tough time of it in recent years, particularly since the aban- donment of worldwide currency controls in the 1970s. The rise of virtually unfettered currency speculation has severely limited its control over the value of sterling. At the same time, the changing nature of international capital has made it increasingly hard for the Bank to monitor the activities of the commercial houses. In 1991 it closed down the Bank of Credit and Commerce International after discovering a web of bad debts and dishonest dealings that stretched well beyond English shores to Luxembourg, Abu Dhabi and beyond. Four years later Britain's oldest merchant bank, Barings, collapsed largely as a result of the uncontrolled mania of one trader based in Singapore, Nick Leeson, who badly overstretched himself in the derivatives market. In both cases, it became apparent that the Bank of England was no longer able to supervise the banking industry adequately, and it has since lost its regulatory powers to a new body called the Securities and Investments Board. In compensation, it has won independence from the Treasury and is now free to set interest rates as it sees fit. But even this role is under threat from the burgeoning single European currency and the establishment of a pan-European central bank in Frankfurt.

Architecturally, the Bank has a distinctly mixed record. At the end of the 18th century Sir John Soane, that most quirky and original of English architects, came up with a magnificently intricate neoclassical design, a veritable treasure trove of interconnecting rooms each with its own peculiarities of light and decoration. But Soane's design proved too good for the people it was built for. In 1925 the Bank governors decided they needed more space, and instead of considering an extension or a new building they simply demolished Soane's work and replaced it with an unimaginative multi-storey patchwork by Sir Herbert Baker. The great architectural critic Sir Nikolaus Pevsner called the destruction of Soane's bank 'the worst individual loss suffered by London architecture in the first half of the 20th century'. When one considers the damage wreaked by the Blitz, that is some indictment. All that remains of Soane's original work is the secure curtain wall on the outer rim of the building and, thanks to a postwar reconstruction, the first room in the museum, the **Bank Stock Office**. Beneath Soane's vaulted roof, illuminated naturally through a series of skylights, the museum's displays recount the architectural fortunes of the Bank and show off some of the original mahogany counter-tops and oak ledger-rests. You are then led through a series of rooms, culminating in Herbert Baker's Rotunda, that give an account of the Bank's history.

Up to the time of the Great Fire, most of London's banking needs were serviced by the Company of Goldsmiths. It was a primitive system which was only as good as the immediate creditworthiness of its customers. When Charles II reneged on a large debt in 1672, five banks went out of business. Sixteen years later, when James II declared war against France, the government suddenly found itself unable to raise the funds necessary to finance its armed forces. Thus it was that in 1694 a Scottish merchant, William Paterson, proposed the creation of a new joint-stock bank that would lend £1.2 million to the government in the first instance at an interest rate of eight per cent and with no fixed term for repayment. The proposal was an instant success; the money was raised in less than three weeks and soon afterwards the Bank was recognized by royal charter. As time went on, the Bank became the undisputed manager of the national debt: this rose from its initial £1.2 million to £12 million in 1700 and £850 million at the end of the Napoleonic Wars in 1815. Other innovations slowly followed. Token money evolved during the revolutionary wars against France (occasioned by an acute shortage of gold); banknotes became commonplace in the 19th century and the Bank of England became sole issuer in 1921.

The Bank's reputation for security (hence the phrase 'as safe as the Bank of England') dates from the Gordon Riots of 1780, when a detachment of horse and foot guards drove the mob away. Thereafter the government provided a permanent overnight guard called the Bank Picquet. Initially the guard's only reward was an allowance of bread, cheese and beer; they were not paid in cash until 1792. For nearly 200 years the guard was a symbol of the bank's security and wore a succession of special uniforms which you can see in the museum. The Picquet was eventually abolished, however, in 1973 and its duties handed over to a private security firm.

*Return to Threadneedle St and turn left. On the corner of Old Broad St is the building which until the Big Bang housed the **Stock Exchange**.*

Share trading has carried on in London since the 16th century, as has speculation on the value of stock. At first arbitrage and other forms of gambling were considered little better than criminal: Dr Johnson's dictionary defines a stock-jobber as 'a low wretch who makes money by buying and selling'. But legislative curbs down the centuries have done little to deter City brokers and jobbers from making a fast buck where they have seen the chance. The terms 'bull' and 'bear', denoting speculators who count, respectively, on either rising or falling prices, date from the early 18th century. Gradually speculation has won respectability as a pursuit; the Big Bang made it open to everyone. The Stock Exchange was on this site from 1801 until the advent of computer trading. Now the building, which was entirely refitted in 1972, is home to the London International Financial Futures Exchange.

*Continuing along Threadneedle St, you come to **Bishopsgate**. To the left is the soaring **National Westminster Tower**, at 600ft the second tallest building in London after Canary Wharf.*

You might not guess it at first glance, but Bishopsgate was ripped to smithereens by two IRA bombs in 1992 and 1993. On both occasions the City was emptying for the weekend and only three people were killed. But most of the buildings between Bishopsgate and St Mary Axe were gutted, and the psychological impact was devastating. The City had been so abstract a place for so long it was hard to remember that it too was made, if not out of flesh and blood, then at least out of bricks and mortar. From one day to the next the area was closed to traffic and the damaged buildings covered in scaffolding and PVC sheeting, like a hospital patient draped in bandages from head to foot. While rebuilding work was in progress you could glimpse the underbellies of these great money-generating houses writhing in almost human pain: heating ducts and girders exposed and twisted out of shape, office furniture strewn about and disfigured, strip lighting shattered and left dangling precariously from exposed wires.

The area has got back on its feet again with astonishing speed, as you can appreciate from the shiny newness of many of the office buildings. The swiftness of the rebuilding was partly a deliberate statement of defiance towards the IRA bombers, and partly testimony to the financial muscle of the Corporation of London, richest by far of the city boroughs, which footed the bill. The bombings have nevertheless left considerable scars. The Baltic Exchange, an early 20th-century shipping and cargo exchange on St Mary Axe, was disfigured beyond all recognition and is still, at the time of writing, awaiting a decision on whether it should be rebuilt. The 15th-century church of St Ethelburga within Bishopsgate was blown clean away and is probably gone forever. Curiously, the little-loved NatWest Tower, a typically in-your-face 1980s skyscraper, appeared to weather the blast rather well despite early rumours that structural damage might spell demolition.

> *Opposite the NatWest Tower is the entrance to Great St Helen's St, which in turn leads to the splendidly restored church of St Helen's (open Mon–Fri 9–5, ring the bell on the south side of the rectory, services with live music Tues 12.35 and 1.15pm).*

In the Middle Ages St Helen's was a Benedictine nunnery popular with the daughters of the rich and well-connected. As such, it was more of a career monastery than a place of great religious inspiration; indeed in 1439 the prior had to issue an order banning dance and revelry and scolding the nuns for 'kissing secular persons'. The nunnery was dissolved in 1538, and although the church survived intact it went into a long decline that lasted right up to the time of the Bishopsgate bombs. Ah, but what wonders have been achieved by restoration in the face of adversity. A rather dark, dingy church has been transformed into something approaching its original medieval splendour. St Helen's always was remarkable for its unusual twin nave; now the floor has been raised, the windows scrubbed clean, and the interior rearranged to let every corner exude its unassuming beauties—the Jacobean pulpit, the 15th-century choir stalls, the window dedicated to Shakespeare and the many brass-covered tombs, including that of Sir Thomas Gresham, founder of the Royal Exchange. The organ, which once blocked the 13th-century beams and stonework of the south transept, has been moved to a new upstairs gallery, a decision that has enhanced both areas of the church.

*Turn left outside the entrance to St Helen's and walk round to St Mary Axe at the back where you'll see the entrance to a curious underground pub called **The Underwriter**. The site of the Baltic Exchange is straight ahead of you, slightly to the left. To your right, on the corner of Leadenhall St, is the Perpendicular Gothic church of **St Andrew Undershaft**.*

St Andrew is notable for one curious feature, a memorial to London's first historian, John Stow. A 16th-century tailor with a lifelong passion for literature, Stow was already well advanced in middle age when he embarked on the original London guidebook, *A Survey of London*, an astonishingly detailed record of the buildings of the city as he found them. It was a labour of love, and one that brought him pitiful reward. On its publication in 1598, he was paid just £3, and although the book was reprinted within a year he never enjoyed a further share of the profits. 'It hath cost me many a weary mile's travel, many a hard-earned penny and pound, and many a cold winter's night study,' he wrote. By 1603 he was reduced to leaving begging bowls in the street outside his house and two years later he was dead. Stow's widow shared her late husband's tenacity and, despite her severely straitened circumstances, had a marble statue of him erected inside this church where he was buried. The City belatedly recognized Stow's contribution and initiated an annual ceremony in which the Lord Mayor removes and replaces the quill pen in Stow's right hand. The ritual continues to this day. In 1905 the original statue had become dilapidated and the Merchant Taylors' company paid for a replacement.

*Another interesting church is a few steps away to the left down Leadenhall St, **St Katherine Cree**.*

This, along with St Andrew Undershaft, was one of the few church buildings in the City to survive the Great Fire. Built in the 1620s in Renaissance style, with Tuscan columns and rounded arches, St Katherine's has no qualms about the morality of making money: it is dedicated 'to commerce, industry and finance'. Its distinctive blue-ribbed plaster ceiling is adorned with the crests of City livery companies. The Rose Window is a copy from the medieval incarnation of St Paul's and the 18th-century altar is attributed to Robert Adam.

*Looming to the left as you return to the junction with St Mary Axe is the outline of the City's most innovative and challenging building, Richard Rogers' design for **Lloyd's of London**, the world's biggest insurance market. On Leadenhall St itself, to the right, you can see a fine façade from the 1925 incarnation of Lloyd's. The entrance to the Richard Rogers building is on Lime St, the continuation of St Mary Axe, although since the IRA bombs the building has been closed to the public (group visits can be organised via the Communications Department on © 0171–327 1000).*

Insurance did not begin at Lloyd's—the Lombards introduced the idea to England in the 16th century—but Lloyd's was where it became a market. Edward Lloyd was the owner of one of London's first and most fashionable coffee-houses in the 1680s and attracted a clientèle of ships' captains, shipowners and merchants. Soon the customers were doing business, and the coffee house gradually gained recognition as the centre for marine insurance worldwide. It was a pleasant, clubbish sort of place that grew more impersonal only as the weight of business became larger. In the late 18th century the show moved away from the lingering aroma of coffee beans and into more conventional offices, first in the Royal Exchange and then, in 1925, in the first of two addresses of its own on Leadenhall Street.

In the late 1970s the British architect Richard Rogers, fresh from his success with the hi-tech Pompidou Centre in Paris, was commissioned to design a new building next door here in Lime Street. It opened in 1986. Like the Pompidou Centre, this building has all its innards—heating ducts, ventilator shafts and so on—on the outside to permit greater flexibility of space on the inside. The fuss over this idea has been very similar in both Paris and London: one joke goes that Lloyd's started out as a coffee house and ended up as a percolator. This is nevertheless a sober building, with few of the Pompidou Centre's garish colours or multi-layered interiors. It is a much narrower, taller edifice, the inside an uncluttered atrium where brokers and underwriters can get on with making money undistracted. Indeed, as another joke has it, it may be the only building in London with all the guts on the outside and the arseholes on the inside. Its most endearing features are the exterior lifts, which offer sudden dramatic views over the City, and the famous Lutine Bell, a relic from a 19th-century shipping disaster which is rung once for bad news and twice for good.

The news has been almost unremittingly bad in recent years, and the disasters have not been limited to wrecks at sea. The whole structure of the insurance market has come tumbling down as Lloyd's has posted a series of unprecedented losses running into billions of pounds. Acts of God and freak accidents in the late 1980s certainly accounted for some of the problems: hurricanes, earthquakes, the destruction of the Piper Alpha oil rig in the North Sea and the Exxon Valdez oil spill in Alaska. There were also some unfavourable U.S. court decisions on asbestosis and pollution. But the main culprit in the Lloyd's débâcle was that very Eighties phenomenon, greed. In common with other financial industries, Lloyd's dramatically broadened its base of investors, known as Names, during the Thatcher decade. The insurance market always attracted a peculiarly rarefied sort of investor because it required a declaration of wealth of at least £75,000. The advantage for Names was that they had to do little more than declare their means, and the money they put forward could be used to accumulate interest elsewhere at the same time. The disadvantages were a relatively modest rate of return from the insurance risks and a stipulation that an investor's liability in the event of loss was unlimited. For most of the 1980s nobody took this stipulation seriously; the whole point of Lloyd's was that it was safe as houses. All kinds of people decided that they wanted in on Lloyd's, for too long the preserve of the privileged upper classes, and signed themselves up like unwitting lambs to the slaughter.

In response, market-makers developed ever more sophisticated ways of siphoning off as much as possible of this new money into their own pockets. One tactic, known as the LMX spiral, was to insure and reinsure the same risk over and over again through the same syndicates, using the Names' money as collateral. It all worked like a pyramid investment scheme, drawing in ever more people until the sheer weight of exposure became untenable. A few people, mostly brokers picking up commission for every new transaction, made a killing. But when the big losses came, people left stranded at the end of chain were left facing vertiginous bills several times larger than the sum required to cover the original risk.

Names soon deserted Lloyd's in droves, severely depleting the market's capital base. In desperation, Lloyd's has now changed the rules to allow in corporate investors with limited liability. But hundreds of victims have been ruined, most of them still waiting for some kind of settlement to haul their deficit millions back to break-even point. A rescue company called Equitas has been set up, but its auditors fear that compensation claims could yet outstrip the company's capital base. The plight of the Names has not exactly won much public sympathy; after all, they are just a bunch of rich people ripped off by another bunch of rich people. But it is a sorry tale that has done untold damage to one of the pillars of London's financial establishment.

> *Turn off Lime St into Leadenhall Place and you find yourself immersed in* **Leadenhall Market**.

Leadenhall Market is a pleasant surprise: a whiff of real life among the office blocks. It has considerable charm, plenty of bustle and excellent food, particularly meat, fish and cheese. For centuries it was just another City market, but went upmarket in the 1880s when Horace Jones, who had previously cleaned up Smithfield, designed the present covered arcades. The prices match the clientèle, many of them businessmen doing some inexpert and usually extravagant housekeeping on behalf of their wives stranded in suburbia; hence the popularity of game and exotic fish. It's worth a good sniff around, though, and makes an ideal stopping point for lunch.

> *As you wander through the market, head westwards to emerge on Gracechurch St. Beneath this point once stood the Roman basilica, London's ancient law courts and town hall. Cross the junction with*

Fenchurch St and Lombard St, then carry on down Fish St Hill to the tall column known as the **Monument** *(viewing platform, accessible by spiral staircase, open April–Sept, Mon–Fri 9–5.40 and Sat–Sun 2–5.40; Oct–March, open Mon–Sat 9–3.40; adm; ✆ 0171–626 2717).*

The Monument commemorates the Great Fire of London. On its completion in 1677 it was the tallest free-standing column in the world; now it is so obscured by office buildings it is easy to miss. Parliament charged Christopher Wren and his assistant Robert Hooke with the task of erecting a memorial on or near the bakery in Pudding Lane where the fire had broken out. In the end they built a monument the same height (202ft) as the distance between its pedestal and Mr Farynor's burned out shop one street over to the east. The Monument is a simple, not to say dull, Doric column in Portland stone. Wren initially wanted something more flamboyant, but was told to keep the design sober. The only symbol of the Fire itself is the bronze urn spouting metallic flames at the very top. The Latin inscription on the north panel of the base describes the course of the Great Fire; the other panels glorify Charles II and the rapid rebuilding of the late 1660s. The view from the top is obscured by office buildings but enjoyable nonetheless. In the late 18th and early 19th century this was a favourite spot for suicides; the authorities put an end to this distressing habit in 1842 by enclosing the gallery in an iron cage.

There's nothing to see in **Pudding Lane** *any more except for some particularly ugly office architecture. You can catch a glimpse of it by taking the overhead concrete walkway which leads from Fish St Hill over the very busy Lower Thames St. Once over on the other side, pause for a quick look at the church of* **St Magnus the Martyr**, *which T.S. Eliot reckoned was one of the finest of Wren's interiors. That may be overstating it; it is another elegant Wren rectangle, topped with a tallish spire and filled with statues, gilded sword rests and other heroic paraphernalia. The church also has a fine organ built in 1712. Walking east along Lower Thames St, you come to the disused* **Billingsgate Fish Market**.

'Famous for fish and bad language,' remark Christopher Hibbert and Ben Weinreb in their *London Encyclopedia*. Since when was bad language the preserve of fishermen? It is too late to argue; there's nobody left inside Horace Jones's elegant pseudo-Renaissance building because the effing fishmongers moved out to the Isle of Dogs in the early 1970s. Citibank bought up the building in the late 1980s intending to create the biggest dealing room in the world, and got the Richard Rogers partnership to carry out an elegant conversion. But nothing ever came of it and the building has yet to reopen. There were rumours that fishermen's ice blocks left in the cellar had melted and cracked the foundations. In fact Citibank was merely sunk, like everyone else, by the post-Thatcherite recession.

Opposite Billingsgate, on the north side of Lower Thames St, is the old **Waterman's Hall**, *originally the headquarters of the Thames oarsmen. Up the hill is St Margaret's Patten's church, with its uncharacteristically plain lead steeple reflected in the mirror glass of an office building. Back on Lower Thames St, follow the traffic round into Byward St. At length, the familiar outline of the Tower of London emerges from behind the office blocks. First, though, another church,* **All Hallows-by-the-Tower**.

The 7th-century church of All Hallows was where Samuel Pepys first came to watch the Great Fire engulf the City. All Hallows survived, but it had less luck thereafter and was bombed to pieces during the Blitz. The church nevertheless possesses some remarkable remains, including a Saxon arch at the entrance to the choir and a beautifully carved font cover by Grinling Gibbons. For many years All Hallows' main fame was as the centre of the international Christian charity Toc H. The main body of the church, rebuilt in the 1950s, has a handful of memorials to the dead of the Second World War.

Byward St leads into Trinity Square, dominated by the old Port of London Authority building, a striking example of Edwardian Baroque, now occupied by an insurance broking company. According to ancient custom, the first five yards of the building belong to the crown because they can be reached by bow and arrow from the Tower of London; the insurance company pays a special tribute every year by way of rent. In the grassy square is a low stone memorial to the war dead of the Mercantile Marine. From 1388 until 1747 there was a scaffold here; but the practice of executing traitors ended after a stand holding a clutch of enemies of the last victim, the Jacobite rebel Lord Lovat, collapsed, killing 12. At the south end of the square, next to the Tube station, is a chunk of Roman wall dating from the 3rd century. From Trinity Square, turn down the arm of Tower Hill that leads to the much-signposted entrance to the **Tower of London**.

The Tower of London

The Tower *(open March–Oct, Mon–Sat 9–6 and Sun 10–6; Nov–Feb, Mon–Sat 9–5 and Sun 10–5, last adm all year round an hour before closing; adm expensive)* is one London sight that everyone knows but nobody particularly likes. 'All European cities have these lumps of dead history in them,' wrote V.S. Pritchett. 'They obstruct the mind, lie inertly across it for centuries and do no more than alert the fancy for an hour or two...' Ever since the monarchy moved out in the early 17th century, the Tower has existed principally as a stronghold of historical nostalgia, a place that owes its appeal more to romantic notions of the past than to real past events. The American novelist Nathaniel Hawthorne wrote in 1863 that for him the Tower was a 'haunted castle in a dreamland'. Modern Americans might want to compare it to the fantasy castles of Disneyland, especially if they follow the **Tower Hill Pageant** (entrance near All Hallows' Church), a 15-minute underground ghost train ride, complete with commentary, and nasty smells and sounds, past tableaux of famous episodes in London's history. This is history as theme park.

So what is the big attraction? First of all the site, which is undoubtedly one of the best preserved medieval castles in the world. By all means take your time wandering around the outside of the Tower, with its formidable ramparts, walls and turrets, and broad grassed-over moat. The **White Tower**, the keep at the centre of the complex, dates back to William the Conqueror and includes the magnificent heavy round arches and groin vaults of the 13th-century **St John's Chapel**. More importantly, the Tower corresponds to every myth ever invented about England. Its history is packed with tales of royal pageantry, dastardly baronial plots, ghoulish tortures and gruesome executions. The Tower is still guarded by quaint liveried figures, the Beefeaters, who obligingly conduct their Ceremony of the Keys at 9.45 each evening (which, as all the literature tells you, involves lots of key-clanking and praise of the monarch as the chief warder requests the opening of the gates of Byward Tower from a sentry). And, of course, the Tower contains the Crown Jewels, the ornaments worn by the monarch during the Coronation ceremony. To be honest, they are not much to write home about, but the sight of them gives thousands of royal junkies who visit every day the same kind of thrill that Elvis worshippers get catching a glimpse of the King's guitar at Graceland.

For much of the Middle Ages, a myth circulated that the Tower was built by Julius Caesar. In fact it was started by William the Conqueror, who was keen to show the people of London soon after his arrival in 1066 that he meant business. The first tower, built just to the east of the city walls, was a temporary structure made of wood; the stone keep (later known as the White Tower because it was whitewashed under Henry III) took about 50 years to complete. It was and is a phenomenally sturdy building, with walls up to 15ft thick and 90ft high. The Tower has changed hands many times but, to its credit, has never been taken by storm.

The Tower soon attracted political trouble, and plenty of it. In the 1140s the Constable, Geoffrey de Mandeville, conspired with Queen Mathilda and nearly succeeded in overthrowing her husband, King Stephen. Half a century later, Richard the Lionheart entrusted the Tower (and the kingdom) to William of Longchamp while he went away on the Crusades. Longchamp was so frightened of rebellion that he built two new towers, erected a thick fortifying wall and dug a ditch around the perimeter. It was not enough to prevent Richard's brother John seizing power; Longchamp surrendered after a three-day siege and went into exile in France. By this time, the Tower had also become the kingdom's most important jail. Its very first prisoner, Bishop Ranulf Flambard of Durham, escaped in 1101 by getting his guards drunk and lowering himself out of a window by rope. In 1244, the Welsh prince Griffith tried a similar ruse by tying his bedclothes together but his rope broke and his head was crushed between his shoulders by the fall.

Under Henry III the Tower expanded considerably and included for the first time a menagerie, complete with lions, leopards, a polar bear and an elephant. Prisoners were brought in from the river through **Traitor's Gate**, which you can still see today. During the Montfort revolt of the 1260s Henry found the Tower invaluable to protect himself from the wrath of parliament; as so often with royal prisons, the Tower was just as useful keeping the loose rebels out as it was keeping the captured rebels in. Indeed the decision to bring the Crown Jewels here in 1303 was prompted by concern for their security at Westminster. The Tower was seemingly impenetrable; the closest anyone ever got to breaching it was during the Peasants' Revolt, when the mob ransacked the kitchen, armoury and bedchambers, mockingly pulled the beards of the guards and made unseemly advances towards the Queen Mother. Four of the king's ministers were caught off guard at prayer, dragged out on to Tower Hill and beheaded. Once the revolt was over, their heads were displayed on London Bridge as an official rebuke for their carelessness.

This was the first of many bloody incidents in the Tower, culminating in the mayhem of the War of the Roses in the mid-15th century. Henry VI, who spent much of his reign either in the Tower or on the battlefield, was almost certainly murdered in the Wakefield Tower in 1471, although his rival and successor Edward IV claimed he died of 'pure displeasure and melancholy'. In 1478 Edward's brother, the Duke of Clarence, was arrested for treason and then died in the Tower under mysterious circumstances. Finally, and most notoriously, Edward's 12-year-old son and successor, also called Edward, was murdered along with his 10-year-old brother in the Garden Tower (since called the Bloody Tower) in 1483. The culprit was almost certainly the boy king's protector, Richard of Gloucester, who went on to seize the throne for himself. The events are familiar to anyone who knows Shakespeare's history plays *Henry VI* and *Richard III*. Several historians have carved out careers contesting this version of events, arguing that the modern world has been unduly influenced by Shakespeare's poetic licence. Richard, they maintain, was not a hunchbacked villain at all, but a well-meaning Lord Protector who fell victim first to machinations within the House of York and then to the propaganda machine of the Tudor dynasty which took the crown from him. There is no conclusive evidence either way. Who exactly might have murdered the Princes in the Tower, if not Richard, remains a mystery.

The dissolution of the monasteries and the rejection of the Catholic Church by Henry VIII sparked a positive orgy of blood-letting and cruelty. Victims included the liberal thinkers Thomas More and John Fisher (the latter so ill-treated in his prison cell he had to be carried to the scaffold), two of Henry's wives (Anne Boleyn and Catherine Howard, both accused of adultery), the teenage royals Jane Grey and Guildford Dudley (who posed a nominal threat to Queen Mary), the plotters who tried to put Mary Queen of Scots on the throne in the 1580s and the luckless courtier and explorer Walter Raleigh, who never quite managed to side with the right conspiracy and whose wife carried his severed head around in a red leather bag for years after his death.

Anne Boleyn opted for a sword rather than an axe, and she died so quickly that her lips continued reciting her final prayer for a split-second after her head was separated from her body (she, along with several Tudor execution victims, is buried in the 16th-century chapel of St Peter ad Vincula in the northwestern corner of the Tower). By contrast, the Countess of Salisbury was so reluctant to face her fate that she had to be tied down to keep her head on the block. Even then she could not be induced to stop hunching up her shoulders, and it took more than a dozen axe blows to sever her head. A luckier man was the Duke of Norfolk, who was saved at the last minute when Henry VIII died the night before his execution.

James I put an end to this reign of political terror when he took the throne in 1603. The Tower ceased to be a royal residence and lost some of its notoriety as a prison. But it still had great symbolic value as the repository of the Crown Jewels. During the Civil War Charles I tried desperately to retain control of the Tower, but the man he appointed Constable, Thomas Lunsford, was denounced by parliament as a cannibal and the jewels were eventually seized and most of them destroyed. The new jewels fashioned at the Restoration became the object of a bizarre plot by an Irishman called Captain Blood. Blood disguised himself as a priest and befriended the Jewel House Keeper, who was foolish enough to sell him his pistols. Blood and a group of friends then launched a raid, but were discovered in the act when the keeper's son turned up unannounced. One man shoved the orb down his breeches, while Blood flattened the crown with a mallet and tried to run off with it. The Tower guard caught up with the lot of them and hauled Blood before the king. Charles was so taken with Blood's cheek that, far from punishing him, he gave him estates in Ireland and a fat annual pension. Blood became a national celebrity. When he died years later, his body had to be exhumed to persuade the people that his death was not just another trick.

The Tower never really played much of a role again. The animals (apart from the ravens who remain to this day) were moved to London Zoo in 1835 after one of the lions attacked a guard. Prisoner numbers dwindled as the rise of democracy made treason less fashionable, although the Tower still played host to the occasional spy in wartime. Hitler's deputy Rudolf Hess spent some time here before starting his lifelong confinement in Spandau jail in Berlin. Much of this history is recounted in loving detail as you tour round the Tower, particularly by the Beefeaters who turn out to be knowledgable and willing guides. The sense of authenticity is marred, however, by a tendency to sensationalism, which manifests itself most blatantly in the over-flashy torture display in Bowyer's Tower.

Inevitably, you also will be drawn towards the **Crown Jewels**, newly housed on a lower floor of Wellington Barracks. You'll probably have to share the spectacle with the entire adult population of Cleveland, Ohio, not to mention several thousand loudmouthed Euro-teenagers, but at least there is a decent attempt at crowd control, thanks to a relatively new conveyor-belt system. As noted above, most of the collection dates from 1660 onwards, although the ampulla and anointing spoon, used to bless the new sovereign's head with oil, managed to survive the Civil War. There are two main crowns: St Edward's Crown, a heavy, somewhat unwieldy piece used only during the coronation ceremony itself; and the golden Crown of State, encrusted with 3000 gems, which was originally made for Queen Victoria and is still used for grand occasions such as the state opening of parliament. Next are the jewelled sword and spurs, also used to anoint the new monarch, followed by the orb, bracelets and two sceptres which symbolize the sovereign's secular and divine mission. The orb represents the spread of Christianity around the world, the sceptres forge the link between the monarch and his or her subjects, while the bracelets are an emblem of Britain's link to the Commonwealth. The Ring of Kingly Dignity is a sapphire mounted with rubies, while the Great Sword of State, the sovereign's symbolic personal weapon, is decorated with a lion and unicorn as well as the royal arms.

These are the main pieces of what, in the end, is a remarkably tedious collection of royal regalia. Certainly the precious stones are genuine enough, but they suggest not so much the grandeur of the monarchy as its obsession with ritual. You'll notice that many of the items were made in the 19th century or later; it was in the late Georgian and Victorian era that the monarchy lost the last vestiges of real power and sought its legitimacy instead in ceremony and the display of wealth. The Crown Jewels, and indeed the Tower of London itself, have been seconded to the task of thrilling the tourists and stirring up patriotic fervour. That is why the place seems so empty and uninteresting to writers like V.S. Pritchett. Londoners aren't conned by the trick the Tower is trying to pull, and that is surely why they largely ignore their own most famous landmark.

> *That's the end of the walk, although if you still have some energy you might want to continue to St Katharine's Dock (see p.439) just to the east of here. The nearest Undergrounds are ⊖ Tower Hill (back at Trinity Square) and ⊖ Monument, where the newspaper seller so swallows his words that* Evening Standard *reduces to just two syllables.*

Start: *Waterloo station or* ⊖ *Embankment.*

Walking time: *about 2½ hours*
not including museums, of which there are many.

IX: The South Bank and Southwark

London's South Bank conjures up images of poverty and grime, of railway junctions, wharves and raucous back-street bars. Indeed, that's how it was for centuries—the poor relation of the City, a general dumping ground for undesirable persons, trades and pastimes. Southwark, the London borough stretching from Waterloo Bridge to the other side of Tower Bridge, has seen it all: butchers, leathermakers, whores, corrupt bishops, coach drivers, actors, bear-baiters, railwaymen and dockers. Shakespeare's Globe Theatre was here, and so was the notorious Marshalsea debtors' prison. It is one of the most atmospheric parts of London, used over and over by the city's novelists, particularly Dickens.

Nowadays, the atmosphere is very much intact, but in a wholly new form. The South Bank has become one of the most vibrant, fastest-changing parts of the city. Museums and arts venues have flourished where industrial life has curled up and died. Art galleries and restaurants have moved into the derelict wharves, and trendy new housing

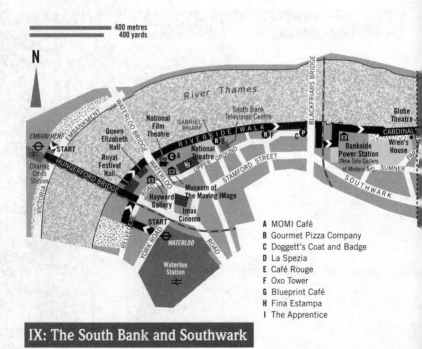

A MOMI Café
B Gourmet Pizza Company
C Doggett's Coat and Badge
D La Spezia
E Café Rouge
F Oxo Tower
G Blueprint Café
H Fina Estampa
I The Apprentice

IX: The South Bank and Southwark

developments have livened up the old railway sidings. Even the Globe Theatre is back, not quite where it was in Shakespeare's day, but almost. Best of all, these attractions are now linked by a wonderful river walkway stretching from Westminster Bridge to London Bridge and beyond—so you encounter little more than the distant rumble of traffic along the way.

Take your pick of the sights carefully, as you're unlikely to have time for everything. Of the many museums some, like MOMI or the Clink, are outstanding, while others, such as the London Dungeon, are worth giving a wide berth. You may want to consider doing the walk backwards, so you can finish up at the South Bank Centre for a concert or play in the evening.

lunch/pubs

MOMI Café, Riverside Walk, South Bank. Perfect for watching the world go by from the wooden outside tables. Good, cheap food and freshly squeezed juices. £5–10.

Gourmet Pizza Company, Gabriel's Wharf. Pizza with lovely views of the Thames from a riverside terrace. £4.75–8.50 per pie, with oodles of exotic toppings.

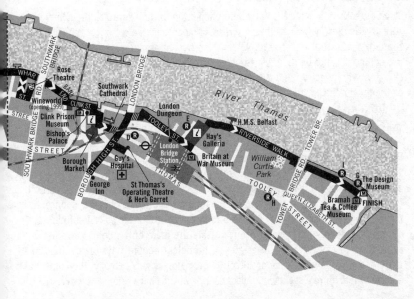

Doggett's Coat and Badge, 1 Blackfriars Bridge. Large, rambling renovated pub named after an annual boat race from London Bridge to Chelsea. Good beer and excellent river views. Food only so-so.

La Spezia, 33 Railway Approach. Classy Italian restaurant tucked away behind London Bridge station. £20–25.

Café Rouge, Hay's Galleria. Bustling café-brasserie in a converted wharf. £5–10 for a main course.

Oxo Tower: includes Bistrot 2—an informal café and bar serving cocktails and light snacks on the second floor, and the Oxo Tower Restaurant and Brasserie on the eighth floor, both managed by Harvey Nichols, with highly eclectic food. The Restaurant is more expensive and formal, with a good value but very filling set lunch for £24.50, the Brasserie and Bar cheaper and higher decibel. Both restaurants have wonderful views of the London skyline.

Blueprint Café, Design Museum, Butler's Wharf. Inventive and tasty Mediterranean cuisine attracting crowds from all over London. Worth booking (© 0171–378 7031). £20–25.

Fina Estampa, 150 Tooley Street. London's only Peruvian restaurant—tasty and delicious ceviche lunch from £15.

The Apprentice, 31 Shad Thames. A training school for chefs—hit and miss but extremely cheap, with gourmet food from £12 a head.

Twenty-first Century Thames

The South Bank is where it will all be happening in the run up to the Millennium. Already, as these words are being written, the area is in a frenzy of refurbishment, rebuilding and future planning. After much hesitation and gloomy foreboding, the project looks set to be the most exciting thing to happen to London for more than a century, wholly eclipsing the 1951 Festival of Britain, which also used the Thames as the focal point for the revival of London after the Second World War.

So be prepared to see a few new and surprising apparitions along the route of this walk. Biggest and weirdest will be the **Millennium Wheel,** a solar and wave-powered ferris wheel that will arc up 152ft into the London sky just next to Westminster Bridge (a little to the west of the start of this walk, but glaringly visible nonetheless). The area around Waterloo Station is due for a major overhaul, including a reorganization of the station itself, new pedestrian walkways lined with shops and cafés that will hug either side of Hungerford Bridge, and a huge **Imax cinema**, sponsored by the British Film Institute, that will rise up in the centre of the so-called Bullring, the distinctly unlovely mega-roundabout outside the main entrance to Waterloo notorious for its heavy traffic and armies of homeless people who take refuge in its underground subways. If the architect Richard Rogers gets his way, the South Bank Centre will acquire a spectacular glass canopy in the shape of a giant wave.

The newly refurbished Oxo Tower will be graced with a **Floating Lido** right on its doorstep, complete with Olympic-length swimming pool, aquarium-lined changing rooms and retractable roof that can be converted into a sports arena or dance floor. At Bankside, the satanic old power station is being converted into the **Tate Gallery of Modern Art**, and plans are afoot to build another pedestrian river crossing designed by Norman Foster, **Bankside Bridge**, that will connect the new gallery to St Paul's Cathedral.

*There are two ways of starting this walk. From **Waterloo station**, take the raised walkway that takes you out of the western end of the station (next to the Channel Tunnel terminus) and follow it over York Road and through the **Shell Centre**, now being converted into a residential complex called the White House. This rambling office development (it covers 7½ acres) is one of London's nastier 1960s eyesores, although to be fair to the architect, Howard Robertson, it was more than a little interfered with by the planning authorities who feared having anything too tall in central London; you'll notice it seems unduly squat. As you approach the river, turn right, take the underpass beneath Hungerford Bridge and you emerge outside the Royal Festival Hall. Alternatively, from **Embankment**, climb the stairs on to Hungerford Bridge and walk alongside the railway tracks across the river to the same point. That way you can enjoy the view towards St Paul's and the City, and also admire the nine-span wrought-iron bridge itself, a fine example of Victorian-era industrial progress (1864). By the year 2000 or so, you will be able to make the same journey along one of the two new pedestrian bridges mentioned above.*

The South Bank Centre

From the outside, the buildings lying at the heart of the South Bank Centre look rather forbidding—lumps of dirty grey concrete streaked with rain, and proof if ever it was needed that concrete does not suit the English climate.

Aesthetics apart, though, the South Bank works remarkably well as a cultural complex. Everything is easily accessible, well-signposted and free of traffic. The concerts and plays are subsidized and tickets relatively cheap. People enjoy coming not just for the scheduled events, but also to hang out in the spacious halls with their plentiful cafés, occasional musicians, elegant bookstalls, piers and river views.

The South Bank grew out of the 1951 Festival of Britain, the then Labour government's attempt to boost the nation's morale after the war with a broad range of public works projects and cultural events. The Royal Festival Hall, the South Bank's main concert venue, opened the same year. The National Film Theatre followed in 1958; the Hayward Gallery (for major international exhibitions), Queen Elizabeth

Hall and Purcell Room (also for concerts) in the late 1960s; and the three-stage National Theatre (now Royal National Theatre) in 1976.

The Festival of Britain harked back to the Great Exhibition which had taken place exactly a century earlier, but it set a very different tone. Where the Victorian extravaganza was essentially a trade fair designed to generate revenue, the Festival of Britain was a government-sponsored jamboree intended to give people a good time. One was profoundly capitalist in inspiration, the other essentially socialist. The South Bank, with its faithful and diverse audience, high artistic standards and willingness to experiment, was the product of a collectivist spirit that almost entirely disappeared from British public life after the Thatcher revolution of the 1980s. With the advent of the Heritage Lottery Fund, formed under Conservative Prime Minister John Major in 1995, money to fund new cultural projects came gushing forth after a long period of austerity. But the Lottery, as its name implies, comes with its own controversies and complications, some of which are to do with the fact that the Treasury has stipulated that all projects receiving Lottery grants must find matching funding from the private sector. In the last few years this has put heavy strains on corporate and private sponsorship, with the net result that private capital as well as public subsidies are nowadays more elusive than ever.

> The merits of the various venues are dealt with in the Entertainment and Nightlife section. The Hayward Gallery has no permanent exhibition, but puts on top-class temporary shows. The **National Theatre** foyers have excellent bookshops, particularly for drama, as well as free live concerts in the early evenings (the theatre has recently received a £32 million Lottery grant, which will enable it to build a new foyer extension and a large and elegant outdoor performance space linking the theatre to the riverside, and creating attractive vistas of the theatre itself). The **Festival Hall** has a varied programme of free lunchtime concerts (as well as the most luxurious toilets in London). All the venues have cafés: one of the nicest is the **Film Café** on the riverfront outside the National Film Theatre, which will move to the West End in 1999. Best of all is the magnificently entertaining **Museum of the Moving Image**. To enter, go through to the back of the NFT foyer (open daily 10–6, last adm 5pm; adm slightly on the pricey side but well worth the money; try to come at off-peak times otherwise you will be swamped by parties of schoolchildren).

Unless you are one of those mutants from Jupiter who never watches television, never goes to the cinema and has no interest in anything to do with communications technology or the media, you can be safe in the knowledge that you will love the Museum of the Moving Image. It's the kind of place you never want to leave:

there are just too many gadgets to twiddle with, too many games to play, too many old films to watch. Since it opened in 1988, MOMI has won stacks of awards and rightly so. Its genius is its perfect marriage of serious education and boundless fun. At every turn you get a chance to participate, whether it is by watching the curious visual effects of zoetropes and magic lanterns, or flying like Superman over futuristic cityscapes. You learn about the technology of a TV newsroom by reading the news yourself and watching the results on a video screen. Nothing in this museum is dull, not even the staff who are in fact actors dressed up in period costumes to show you round by way of dramatic vignette and comic improvisation.

If you want, you can sit all day watching pioneering films from the first decade of cinema, or admire lengthy clips from French classics from the 1930s, or watch the progression of the horror movie from *Un Chien Andalou* to *Psycho* and beyond. If it's action you seek, you can make your own cartoon, do a Hollywood screen test, or get yourself invited on to a television chat show and answer questions about your glittering career. You don't have to investigate everything: the television section, for example, is of limited interest to foreigners not weaned on BBC children's programmes like *Bill and Ben the Flowerpot Men*. But you'll find it hard to tear yourself away in less than two hours. Real fans might do better to leave MOMI for now and come back for a half-day some other time.

---

*From MOMI, turn right and continue along the River Walk past the Festival Pier. The path is decorated with a stone circle and the occasional statue, and joggers from the neighbouring offices running along in shoals of three or more. Look across the river; directly opposite, immediately to the right of Waterloo Bridge, is Somerset House (see p.261). A little further down you'll see the spire of the Temple Church above the trees. To your right, about 150 yards beyond the National Theatre, is **Gabriel's Wharf**, an attractive square set back from the river. Formed by the backs of warehouses painted in* trompe l'oeil *fashion to resemble house-fronts, it is occupied by sculpture, ceramics, fashion and jewellery workshops. There are some good cafés, bars and restaurants here if you want to stop for a drink. Otherwise continue on past a steep staircase leading down to the water called the **Old Barge House Stairs**. If it's low tide, you can walk down these and do a spot of beach-combing along the Thames. An astonishing variety of objects wash up on the shores of this conceptual artist's paradise: lots of gloves, bicycle tyres, brooms, old bottles and curiously battered pieces of wire and wood.*

Before the advent of the motor car, the river was a major transport route. These stairs would have been used as a stopping off point for watermen: boat-owners who would pick up and drop off passengers like a modern-day taxi driver. A century ago this section of the riverbank had pleasure gardens and the occasional trading wharf. Since the coming of the railways, however, it was stranded between the two main transport routes running to and from Waterloo and Blackfriars stations. Samuel Butler gave a vivid idea of the disorienting effect of the railways in the 1880s when he described the central commuter stations thus: 'See how they belch forth puffing trains as the breath of their nostrils, gorging and disgorging incessantly those human atoms whose movement is the life of the city.' The new **Thames Lido** will be moored just off here, connected to the river's edge by a 40m-long jetty. The enormous egg-shaped steel swimming pool will float on the Thames, rising and falling with the tides, and giving swimmers 360° views of the city around them.

> *The old barge house, just behind the stairs, was replaced in 1928 with the* **Oxo Tower,** *a warehouse whose top windows are shaped to spell the name of the famous savoury cubes.*

This elegant Art Deco tower was magnificently restored in 1996 and now houses over 30 designer and jewellery workshops on the first and second floors. In here you can buy work from the highest quality designers and craftsman at prices that are significantly cheaper than galleries and shops in central London. Work on show includes designer-made lights and blinds, 'painterly' carpets, hand-painted silk scarves and ties, one-off chairs and tables and, in Studio Fusion, the best enamelled jewellery and silverwork you can see anywhere in the country. Above the workshops is a laid-back café and bar (Bistrot 2) and several floors of co-op flats. At the very top of the building on the 8th Floor is a free public viewing gallery and the swish new Harvey Nichols Restaurant and Brasserie.

> *Continuing towards Blackfriars Bridge, look again at the north bank and you'll see a succession of attractive buildings.* **Sion College,** *which houses a society of Anglican clergymen, is a mock-Tudor building dating from 1886 with a large stained-glass window looking out over the river. To the east of it is the Renaissance-style former* **City of London School,** *now occupied by offices. And next to that is* **Unilever House,** *home to the chemicals and food coorporation which invented margerine. Unilever House curves elegantly round from the Embankment into New Bridge St. Just before the bridge is the* **Doggett's Coat and Badge** *pub, named after the annual boat race inaugurated in 1715 by Thomas Doggett, manager of the Drury Lane Theatre, in which teams of six dress in livery and row from London Bridge to Cadogan Pier in Chelsea. Immediately after the pub is* **Blackfriars Bridge,** *London's third river crossing, first constructed in the*

1760s and then rebuilt a century later as a magnificent structure of cast-iron lattice girders. You have to cross it by climbing up some steps and walking over the road.

The bridge had an uneventful history until 15 June 1982, when the Italian banker Roberto Calvi was found hanging from the underside with weights in his pockets and trouble aplenty on his mind. Calvi's death unleashed one of the biggest scandals in the scandal-ridden history of postwar Italy as his eminently well-connected bank, the Banco Ambrosiano, collapsed in a heap of bad debts. Nobody was spared, not even the Vatican, as it emerged that Calvi had set up murky deals and secret slush funds around the world. The Pope's banking chief Archbishop Paul Marcinckus was for a time under house arrest in Vatican City, while Calvi's crooked financial adviser Michele Sindona died mysteriously of cyanide poisoning four years later in a maximum security jail. It has never been properly established whether Calvi was murdered (as seems probable) or committed suicide (as the English courts initially chose to see it). The bridge, meanwhile, has gone back to the mundane job of ferrying cars and people across the Thames.

Next to Blackfriars Bridge Road, you'll notice the brightly painted arms of the London Chatham and Dover Railway, from which a row of fat iron piers marches across the river. Built in the 1860s to carry the railway, they were found to be impractical and abandoned in favour of the current bridge (1884–6) just downstream. The path takes you beneath the girders and tracks, then returns to the riverside and the forbidding silhouette of **Bankside Power Station** *(opening as the Tate Gallery of Modern Art in 2000, with a visitors' centre open now, Weds 12–7, entrance at 25 Sumner Street).*

This dark apparition was Sir Giles Gilbert Scott's companion piece to the power station at Battersea, built in two phases in 1937 and 1963. Currently it is being gutted and flooded with natural light via a massive glass canopy by Swiss architects Herzog & de Meuron. The canopy will span the building, add two floors to its height and give visitors spectacular views of the City across the river. The gallery inside will house three temporary loan exhibitions a year plus the Tate's modern collection—works by Picasso (*The Three Dancers*), Matisse (*The Snail*), Bonnard, Dalí, Duchamp, Moore, Bacon, Gabo, Giacometti and Warhol.

Shortly after Bankside the path widens into a cobbled road. On your right is Cardinal's Wharf; the tall white house is where Christopher Wren lived during the construction of St Paul's, which he could see rising opposite. Just beyond is a reconstruction of Shakespeare's open-air Globe Theatre.

The Globe Theatre

The original Globe was in fact a few hundred feet away from this building site, on the corner of present-day Park Street and Southwark Bridge Road. When London's first playhouse, The Theatre, was forced to move off its premises in Finsbury Fields, just north of the City, in 1598, its manager Richard Burbage had it dismantled and reassembled here on Bankside where the Rose Theatre had taken root 12 years earlier. Shakespeare helped finance Burbage's enterprise and had many of his plays, including *Romeo and Juliet*, *King Lear*, *Othello*, *Macbeth* and *The Taming of the Shrew* performed in its famous O-shaped auditorium for the first time. Bankside was the perfect location for theatrical entertainment; all manner of pursuits not deemed proper across the river in the stiff-collared City had moved here, and the area was already notorious, among other things, for its taverns and its whore-houses.

The Globe never properly recovered from a fire in 1613 and was finally demolished during the Civil War. This reconstruction was the brainchild of the late American actor Sam Wanamaker, who devoted most of his retirement to realizing the scheme, which remained unfinished when he died in December 1993 at the age of 72. The theatre finally opened for business four years later, following a remarkable fund-raising effort in which actors, politicians and members of the general public volunteered to sponsor every last paving-slab and brick.

The construction is remarkably faithful to the original, from the distinctive red of its brickwork, to its all-wooden interior and thatched roof (the first of its kind to appear in London since the Great Fire of 1666). There are a few postmodern retro flourishes, such as the theatrical masques incorporated into the design of the wrought iron gates. And a few concessions had to be made to the 20th century, particularly when it came to fire-proofing: the thatch sits on an insulating layer of fibre-glass, it is painted with special fire-proof chemicals and dotted with sprinkler nozzles that form a curious pattern along the roof edge.

If you are in London during the summer you should try to see a performance (box office ℂ 0171-401 9919) to appreciate the peculiarities of Elizabethan theatre. The huge stage, with its vast oak pillars holding up a canopy roof, juts out into the open area holding up to 500 standing members of the audience (known as groundlings). The rest of the public is seated on wooden benches in the circular galleries, giving a peculiar sense of intimacy and audience involvement. Scenery is restricted to the brightly painted curtains at the back of the stage, so actors make full use of the architecture of the theatre itself to hide, run and do battle. Again, there are a few concessions to modern sensibilities: the seating is more spacious and comfortable than in Shakespeare's day, and performances take place in the evening as well as the traditional afternoon slot with the help of discreet electric lighting.

Whether or not you come for a play, you can visit the **Shakespeare Globe Exhibition** (*open daily 10–5; adm*) which charts the building of both the original and the reconstructed theatre and offers a guided tour around the auditorium itself. Wanamaker's Globe is more than just a venue for authentic performances of Shakespeare, however: there is also a study centre and library, open to scholars and theatre performers. At the time of writing, there are also plans to build a second, indoor theatre on the site, based on an unrealized project by Inigo Jones called The Cockpit. Fund-raising is in full swing.

If Wanamaker chose this location it was mainly because the ground was free, unlike the original site of the Globe which is now the head office of the *Financial Times* newspaper. Another reason was a historical link with another aspect of Elizabethan Bankside: this was where crowds came to watch bears tear each other's limbs apart. Bear-baiting was highly popular in Shakespeare's time, and only stopped briefly during a ban imposed by the Puritans at the same time as they closed the theatres. 'The Puritans hated bear-baiting,' wrote Macaulay somewhat mischievously in the early 19th century, 'not because it gave pain to the bear, but because it gave pleasure to the spectators.' It was only towards the end of the 17th century that the barbarities of this sport impressed themselves on the authorities sufficiently to move them to ban it for good. John Evelyn describes in his diary his disgust on seeing cock-fighting, dog-fighting, bear and bull baiting in Bankside in 1670: 'One of the bulls tossed a dog full into a lady's lap as she sat in one of the boxes at a considerable height from the arena. Two poor dogs were killed, and so all ended with the ape on horseback, and I most heartily weary of the rude and dirty pastime.'

---

*Take the next alley on the right—which is actually called Bear Gardens—turn left into Park Street, and left again into Rose Alley. Through the ground-floor window of the office block at the bottom of the alley, you can see the ruined foundations of the **Rose Theatre**, the first Bankside playhouse (1587). Retrace your steps to the river and continue beneath Southwark Bridge until you reach the **Anchor Inn**.*

The inn (notice its old wooden panelling) dates back to the 17th century, when Bankside and the whole borough of Southwark were bywords for a raucous good time.The boisterous character of the area is easily explained by history. When the Romans first built London Bridge in AD 43, **Southwark** naturally developed as a small colony and market town opposite the City of London. As the City grew in wealth and importance, Southwark attracted some of the dirtier, more unpleasant trades that might have offended the rich merchants across the river. In 1392, for example, a decree was passed giving butchers the right to dump animal skins here, thus giving rise to the leather trade south of the river. In subsequent centuries, travellers often had to spend the night here because the bridge was only open at certain times. Southwark therefore developed a secondary role as a transport hub: Londoners would cross the bridge and then wait for a coach to take them southwards on their journey. With all this waiting around to do, particularly in the evening hours, inns and whorehouses (also banned in the City) were soon doing brisk business. Such brisk business, in fact, that in the 12th century the Bishops of Winchester built their palace here and took over the brothels as a lucrative sideline that they ran with extreme cruelty. For centuries much of Bankside was an unconsecrated graveyard for dead prostitutes; many of them perished in the neighbourhood's numerous private jails.

In 1556 Southwark came directly under the City's jurisdiction and cleaned up its act somewhat. The dissolution of the monasteries and the arrival of syphilis from America put paid to the Bishop of Winchester's little whoring scam. The theatres made the available entertainment a little more thought-provoking, if only for a brief period. And then local industries sprang up: in Evelyn's day Bankside was bustling with wharves, breweries, foundries and glassworks.

Southwark remained a promising, if still raucous area until the mid-18th century, when the construction of Westminster Bridge and the first Blackfriars Bridge diminished its importance as the most accessible of London's southern satellites. The arrival of the railways in the Victorian era made it even more isolated, reducing it to no more than a row of warehouses stuck between the noisy train tracks. Further decline came after the Second World War, as the London docks became obsolete and the area's wharves and warehouses closed. Today, like so many neglected areas of London, it has only its past to turn to as a source of income. Southwark is busy devoting itself to the heritage industry, opening museums and renovating its historical landmarks. This is good news for the visitor: whether it lasts remains to be seen.

> *Walk under Cannon Street Railway Bridge and you come out on Clink St, a dark, narrow alley hemmed in by the blackened brick walls of the disused wharves. From one building to the right you'll hear eerie music and mournful voices. This is the* **Clink Prison Museum***, one of London's more offbeat, not to say macabre, small museums on the site of the notorious medieval jail (open daily, approx 10–6; adm, © 0171-378 1558).*

The Clink was the Bishop of Winchester's private prison, where anyone who dared to challenge the extortion rackets he ran on Bankside would be locked up in gruesome conditions. For 400 years successive bishops acted as pimp to the local whores, known as Winchester Geese, and used the prison as dire punishment for any who tried to conceal their earnings, or work for somebody else. Incredibly, the scam was sanctioned by royal licence under Henry II; it was not until the Reformation that any-body saw fit to question the moral standards that the bishop set his flock.

The name Clink is familiar enough nowadays as a synonym for jail; it derives from a Latin expression meaning, roughly speaking, 'kick the bucket', which gives a good indication of the fate a prisoner could expect inside. Inmates were mostly prostitutes, beggars, actors and political enemies of the Bishop. Once inside, they had to pay their own way; they even had to pay the costs of being fitted with a ball and chain (it sounds a bit like modern car wheel-clamping). The only food they could buy was rotten and grossly overpriced. Well-connected prisoners could expect a certain alleviation from the suffering, but the poorest were thrown into a rat-infested dungeon called the Hole, from which few emerged alive. One medieval Chief Justice commented unsympathetically: 'Prisoner ought to live on his goods. And if he have no goods he shall live on the charity of others, and if others will give him nothing then let him die in the name of God for his own presumption and ill-behaviour brought him to that punishment.' Not surprisingly, the Clink was a much-detested institution that frequently became a target for city mobs. It was only after the Gordon Riots of 1780, in which the Clink was destroyed for the fourth time in its history, that the authorities decided it would be best not to rebuild it.

The exhibition highlights the cruelty of life in medieval Bankside, particularly the barbaric treatment of women both in prison and outside. Wives deemed too talka-tive would wear a scold's bridle, an iron gag shoved into their mouth and left there for days; sometimes the gag would be spiked. Crusaders off to the Holy Land would lock their womenfolk in chastity belts which prevented not only sexual contact but all genital hygiene. Women often died of infections or, if the belt was fitted while they were teenagers and still growing, of constriction of the pelvis. In 1537 Henry VIII ruled that women who murdered their husbands were to be boiled in a vat of oil; it was up to the executioner whether or not to boil the oil in advance.

Bankside women risked more than judicial punishment. One intriguing room in the exhibition (an X-rated section not open to children) focuses on the risks of working in the whorehouses, or 'stews' as they were known. There was little pro-tection against pregnancy, venereal disease or the flagellation devices they were forced to use. Many women believed the best way to avoid conception was to pee as hard as they could into a pot after intercourse (there is a marvellous Rowlandson print depicting this). Sexually transmitted diseases, meanwhile, prompted a whole host of crackpot remedies and cures. The 14th-century physician John of Gad-desdon proposed that women jump up after intercourse, run downstairs backwards, inhale pepper to induce sneezing, tickle their vaginal membrane with a feather dipped in vinegar and then wash their genitals with a concoction of roses and herbs boiled in more vinegar.

Just beyond the Clink Exhibition are the remains of the 13–14th-century **Bishop of Winchester's Palace** *which were discovered by accident when a warehouse on the site burned down in 1814. The best-preserved part is the 13ft-wide rose window; much of the rest perished in the Civil War when the episcopacy was suppressed by order of parliament. At the end of Clink St is a river inlet called* **St Mary Overie's Dock,** *home to the* **Golden Hinde***, a full-size reconstruction of a galley captained four centuries ago by Francis Drake and nowadays staffed by an extremely entertaining crew of actors dressed in Elizabethan costume (open daily 10–6 May–Sept and 10–5 Oct–Apr; adm; tea and coffee available. Although it looks unsailable it has crossed the Pacific and Atlantic oceans several times since it was built in 1973. Turn the corner and you'll see* **Southwark Cathedral***. You can enter through the modern annexe slightly to your left. Once inside, there is a café to the left and the cathedral entrance to the right.*

Southwark Cathedral has a past almost as chequered as the neighbourhood, suffering fire, neglect and patchwork reconstruction over a history stretching back to the 7th century. It started life as the parish church of St Mary Overie (which despite the weird name merely means 'St Mary over the river'), built according to legend by the first boatman of Southwark to ferry gentlemen to and from the City. It burned down at least twice before being incorporated into a priory belonging to the Bishop of Winchester sometime around 1220. In the Civil War it was a bastion of Puritanism where preachers denounced the Bankside playhouses as offences to the Almighty. By the 19th century it had largely fallen to pieces, and the nave was rebuilt—twice as it turned out, since the first attempt was considered an appalling travesty. By the 20th century, with a little help from the restorers, Southwark was elevated to the rank of cathedral for the whole of south London.

The architecture is still predominantly Gothic, particularly the choir, fine retrochoir and altar, making it something of a rarity in London. The oldest relic is the wooden effigy of a 13th-century knight in the north choir aisle. In a pillar in the south transept you can see a carving of the hat and coat of arms of Cardinal Beaufort, the 13th-century Bishop of Winchester responsible for the bulk of the building work. The tower is 15th-century, although the battlements and pinnacles weren't completed until 1689. The nave is the only significant portion from a later era, although you will also notice Victorian statues atop the reredos behind the altar.

Southwark has always liked to think of itself more as a humble parish church than as a grand cathedral. Shakespeare's friends and relations came to worship here and the playwright's youngest brother Edmund is buried in the churchyard. In the north aisle is the brightly painted medieval tomb of the poet John Gower (d. 1408).

John Harvard, the founder of the archetypal Boston university, was born in the parish of St Mary Overie in 1607 and has a chapel dedicated to him on the north side. To this day the cathedral has a friendly, neighbourhood feel which it cultivates through regular concerts and attention to local issues. To the left of the main entrance you may notice a memorial to the dead of the *Marchioness* disaster. The *Marchioness* was a pleasure boat hired out for a party one Saturday night in the summer of 1989. The boat was rammed and sank at a spot not far from the cathedral, and more than 50 people were drowned.

> *Leave the cathedral by the main entrance, which takes you out through the churchyard into Green Dragon Court. In front of you, between the railway bridges, are the Victorian cast-iron sheds which shelter the stalls of* **Borough Market***.*

A fruit and vegetable market started on the southern end of London Bridge as early as 1276, but was chased away to the present site in the 18th century because it caused too much traffic congestion. Curiously, the market is a non-profit organization run by the local parish; proceeds from renting out the stalls are used to give poorer residents a discount on their community taxes.

> *As you follow the churchyard railings round to the left, you get a good view of the exterior of the cathedral. Climb the steps at the end up onto Borough High Street and turn right under the railway bridge. As you continue down past the large junction with Southwark St, you'll notice that the alleys off to your left have names like King's Head Yard and White Hart Yard after the pubs that used to stand here. The third turning on the left, George Inn Yard, leads to the only coaching inn that still survives.*

The coaching inns were like the railway stations that eventually superseded them, each one providing a transport service to a specific group of destinations. Unlike railway stations, however, the inns had no fixed timetable but functioned according to demand. As a result there was often a great deal of waiting to do, and the inns made up for this by ensuring a ready supply of draught ale for waiting passengers. The **George Inn** goes back to the 16th century, although the present buildings date from shortly after the Great Fire. It is an elegant terrace of small interconnecting wooden bars looking out on a quiet courtyard, where during the summer you can see morris dancing (an old English ritual which involves wearing folklore costumes festooned with bells) and open-air productions of Shakespeare. Take a look at the 18th-century clock on the right-hand wall of the bar at the western end of the inn: this was the brainwave of one particularly parsimonious landlord fed up with coach passengers gawping through his window to find out the time. Not only did he put the clock on a side wall where it could not be seen from the courtyard, he also charged passers-by a penny for the right to look at it.

Many of the famous landmarks of Borough High St, however, are no more. Tabard Inn, which once stood on the site of modern-day Talbot Yard, is where Chaucer's fictional pilgrims gathered to tell their Canterbury Tales. The Queen Inn was owned by John Harvard until he sold up shop and went to the United States to found his famous university, while the White Hart is mentioned both in Shakespeare's *Henry VI* and in Dickens's *Pickwick Papers*. Borough High Street was also the site of many of Southwark's seven prisons, most notorious of which was the Marshalsea just off the eastern side of the High Street. The list of its inmates reads like a roll of eminent alumni at an Oxford or Cambridge college: Ben Jonson, Tobias Smollett, Leigh Hunt (who libelled George IV by calling him, with perfect accuracy, a 'portly Adonis') and Dickens's bankrupt father. Dickens himself used the prison as the fictional birthplace of his heroine Little Nell, describing it as 'an oblong pile of barrack building, partitioned into squalid houses standing back to back, so that there were no back rooms; environed by a narrow paved yard, hemmed in by high walls duly spiked at top.' Dickens wrote those words in 1856; by that time, the dreaded Marshalsea had been closed for 14 years.

> *Return back up Borough High St and turn right down St Thomas's St. No.9a is an old church tower housing the* **St Thomas Operating Theatre Museum and Herb Garret** *(open Tues–Sun and most Mons 10–4; adm).*

First of all, the tower deserves a little explanation. It used to be attached to the chapel of St Thomas's, one of the biggest hospitals in London founded on this site back in the 12th century. The hospital moved to Lambeth in the 1860s to make way for London Bridge railway station, and all the old buildings except this one were destroyed. For a century the chapel was considered a mere curiosity, an unspectacular relic from a bygone age. Then, in 1956, a historian named Raymond Russell noticed a curious hole above the tower belfry. He squeezed through and discovered a garret containing a 19th-century operating theatre, the only one of its kind to have survived in the whole country. It was restored and in 1968 turned into a museum charting the tower's history, first as a medieval garret devoted to herbal remedies, then as an operating room attached to a women's ward in the next building. It is a fascinating, if grim place; nowhere else in London will you get such a graphic insight into the horrors of medicine before the modern age.

> *You have to climb a steep winding staircase to reach the entrance and then take another flight of steps to the exhibition itself.*

One of the most gruesome reports to surface from the war in Bosnia was of surgeons in shell-battered towns reduced to performing amputations by hacksaw without proper antisepsis and without the benefit of any anaesthetic except perhaps a bottle of slivovic. The horror of it is almost inconceivable: it feels as though

Europe has been plunged back into a distant dark age. And yet we forget the astonishing pace of medical progress. Until the mid-19th century all amputations, whether in war or peacetime, were performed under such appalling conditions. Before the advent of anaesthetics and Joseph Lister's antiseptic surgery, only the most desperate of patients would dare undergo the surgeon's knife.

Back in the early 19th century, surgeons had no proper notion of hygiene and performed their operations in frock coats 'stiff and stinking with pus and blood', as the museum explains. They washed their instruments only after the operation (to wipe the blood off), but did not think to do so beforehand. The patient, who was usually tanked up on ale (for years the daily allowance was three pints per patient), would be held down by six or seven people as the knife or saw penetrated the flesh; the surgeon would then kick a box of sawdust to the appropriate spot beneath the operating table to catch the blood. The trick was to get the whole thing over with as quickly as possible: one surgeon at Guy's Hospital, Alfred Poland, once managed to amputate a leg in 37 seconds.

The centrepiece of the museum is the operating theatre itself, built in 1821 and used up until 1862 when St Thomas's moved to Lambeth. You can still see the bloodstains on the floor, and the mop and bucket used to clear up the mess. It looks like a lecture hall, with rows of seats on three sides for students and colleagues to watch the proceedings: in the days before dead bodies became widely available, watching operations was the only legal way doctors and medical students could carry out anatomical research.

The museum also gives a lightning account of the history of apothecaries and of herbal and surgical medicine in London, accompanied by a display of gynaecological instruments that would not look out of place in a torture chamber: a sharp conical metal speculum, for example, or a fearsome eight-pronged cervical dilator. For a long time St Thomas's actually had a reputation for showing great indulgence towards women. In the 15th century Mayor Dick Whittington established eight rooms where unmarried mothers could stay and deliver their offspring out of the public eye to save their reputations. Unfortunately such enlightenment did not last and in 1561 the hospital banned unmarried pregnant women, saying its job was the relief of 'honest persons, and not of harlots'.

The most famous woman in the hospital's history was Florence Nightingale, the legendary nurse of the Crimean War who set up London's first nursing school at St Thomas's in 1858. Under her influence nurses were no longer allowed to drink on duty or turn up in dirty street clothes. In her words, nurses were to be 'sober, honest, truthful, trustworthy, punctual, quiet and orderly, cleanly and neat'. So saying, albeit in strict Victorian fashion, she set the standards of nursing that are still observed today.

On the south side of St Thomas St is the second hospital built in the area, Guy's, which was founded by a former governor of St Thomas's in the 1720s. It has largely been rebuilt since the Second World War. Return to Borough High St, turn right and continue to **London Bridge**.

'London Bridge is falling down,' goes the old nursery rhyme. Too right. London Bridge has fallen down so often that there's nothing left to see. No, it's not the one on all the postcards that opens in the middle (that's Tower Bridge), although God knows there are enough tourists who haven't realized this yet (and one American who, back in the 1960s, bought the previous incarnation of London Bridge and had it reconstructed stone for stone back home in Lake Havasu, Arizona—how disappointed his friends must have been). London Bridge stopped being interesting some time around 1661, when the spikes used to display the severed heads of criminals were finally removed. It ceased to be London's one and only river crossing about a century later with the construction of Westminster and Blackfriars Bridges. Now London Bridge is nothing more than a cantilevered lump of concrete with four busy lanes of traffic on top, just one nondescript bridge among many. And it hasn't fallen down for centuries.

Time was when London Bridge burned or fell down once every 10 years or so, cutting off all contact between the City and the South Bank. For the first thousand years of its history the bridge was made of wood, and back in the Dark Ages London was full of arsonists, rabble-rousers and general butter-fingers. It fell down most spectacularly in 1014 when London was besieged by the Danes and a spineless King Ethelred had fled into the countryside. Ethelred's ally, Olaf of Norway, sailed a fleet of ships up to the bridge, attached ropes to the piles and pulled the whole structure down by rowing away as vigorously as possible. The Danes, who were holed up on the South Bank, realized they had lost their only means of entering the city and withdrew.

The first stone bridge was started in 1176 and took 33 years to complete. Its broad columns caused the river to freeze in winter and created treacherous currents in summer, making the bridge a hazardous obstacle to navigate past. All but the smallest vessels had to negotiate their way through a narrow passage in the middle where a drawbridge could be raised. On top were built houses, shops, and a chapel to St Thomas à Becket. As a saying of the time went, 'London Bridge was made for wise men to go over and fools to go under.' Accidents were commonplace: in 1428 the Duke of Norfolk and several of his cronies were drowned when their barge overturned.

Because of the bridge's strategic importance, it was frequently attacked by rebel leaders and riot mobs. The rebel baron Simon de Montfort took it briefly in 1264 (though he could not penetrate the City walls themselves), as did Wat Tyler and his peasant revolters in 1381. The bridge provided little defence for itself other than as a deterrent: in 1305 the head of the Scots patriot William Wallace (hero of Mel Gibson's *Braveheart*) appeared, parboiled and coated in tar, above the portico of the gatehouse as an example to other would-be plotters. Plenty more heads followed, sometimes scores of them at a time. After Jack Cade's rebellion in 1450 there were so many heads on display that the authorities had to call a temporary halt. The practice stopped for good when Charles II came to the throne, the restored monarch being understandably nervous about severed heads given what had happened to his father Charles I.

> *The only striking feature of London Bridge now is the building at the Southwark end,* **One London Bridge,** *a 1980s office complex in shining chrome and glass that links up with the dinky shops and restaurants of Hay's Galleria (see below). Take the steps by the bridge down into Tooley St, past the Art-Deco* **St Olaf's House.** *Tooley St is home to two of London's more garish and less successful museums. The first of them, at Nos.28–34, is the* **London Dungeon** *(open daily, 10–5.30, last adm 4.30pm; adm exp; with a Pizza Hut on the premises).*

'Enter at your peril,' says the sign above the door. It is an appropriate warning for a museum that strives to make a spectator sport out of medieval torture but can only manage the ketchup-splattered inauthenticity of a 1950s Hammer horror movie. First of all, this is not a dungeon at all, but a converted warehouse underneath the arches of London Bridge station. Secondly, there is scarcely a genuine historical artefact in the place; it is all second-rate stage design and bad waxwork for which no amount of ghoulish lighting or spooky music can compensate. For sheer kitsch, the high point is surely watching a stuffed dummy of Anne Boleyn lip-synch her 1536 execution speech. You can take a trip on the Jack the Ripper Experience (a kind of haunted house with the lights on) or a boatride through Judgment Day. You have to hand it to the Dungeon, though: the bus tours keep pouring through, come rain or shine.

> *A little further, on the same side of Tooley St, is* **Winston Churchill's Britain at War Museum** *(open daily, 10–4.30; adm exp).*

This is the kind of museum you could cook up out of a recipe book. Take a popular subject (the Second World War), add plenty of period memorabilia (books, clothes, newspaper cuttings, radio broadcasts, etc.), mix in a couple of set-piece reconstructions (an Underground station during an air raid and a bombed-out house) and top with lashings of patriotism (Vera Lynn singing *There Will Always Be An England*). There is not a drop of originality about the place. You'll see all of it, and more, at the Cabinet War Rooms in Whitehall. 'Thanks for the memory,' says the visitors' book: this is not a museum, it is a nostalgia trip. Enter, as they say, at your peril.

*Cross Tooley St. On the left are Hay's Lane and **Hay's Galleria**.*

London's oldest wharf dates back to 1651, but the present structure is dominated by the tall yellow brick façades of the Victorian dock buildings. These were covered in the 1980s with a barrel-vaulted glass roof to form a pleasant arcade of shops, cafés and restaurants. The best feature is the central fountain sculpture, *The Navigators* by David Kemp, a fantasy in which a Viking galley is overtaken by naval commanders, astronomers and modern sailors with half-umbrellas for hats.

> *Walk through the Galleria to the riverfront and turn right. Up ahead are the moorings of the battleship HMS Belfast (open daily, 10–6, closes 4.30pm Nov–Mar; adm).*

A bit of a special interest item, this. The *Belfast* was built in 1938, saw active service throughout the Second World War and took part in the D-Day landings. You are free to roam its seven floors and admire its gun turrets, decks, cabins, instrument decks and boiler room. If you've ever seen one of those old stiff-upper-lip British war films like *The Cruel Sea*, then HMS *Belfast* won't need any introduction. If you are one of those people who suddenly starts behaving like a six-year-old at the sight of military hardware, then this will be right up your alley. If not, the experience falls somewhat short of a thrill-a-minute.

> *Follow the riverfront path east of HMS Belfast. There is a fine view of the Tower across the river, and the walk takes you straight up to the beginning of **Tower Bridge**.*

Tower Bridge is one of the great feats of late Victorian engineering, half suspension-bridge and half drawbridge, linked to two neo-Gothic towers. Designed by an engineer, John Wolfe-Barry, and an architect, Horace Jones, working in tandem, it has become one of London's most recognizable landmarks. Its fame was not exactly instant; indeed, at its opening in 1894, the critics founds its evocation of medieval style crude. *The Builder* called it 'the most monstrous and preposterous architectural sham that we have ever known... an elaborate and costly make-believe.' There is still a reasonable case to be made that Tower Bridge is a kind of Victorian Disneyland, but time has mellowed its vulgarity and made it both awe-inspiring and loveable. Its two bascules, the arms that rise up to let tall ships through, weigh an astonishing 1000 tonnes each. Despite the decline of river freight traffic, the bridge still opens at least once a day on average; phone ahead (© 0171–403 3761) to find out the times. At the southern tower you can join The Tower Bridge Experience (*open daily Apr–Oct 10–6.30, 9.30–6 Nov–Mar, last entry an hour and a quarter before closing; adm*), a hi-tech retelling of the history of the bridge, plus a chance to enjoy the view from the overhead walkways and admire the giant Victorian hydraulic engines that once operated the bridge (it is now done with electric power).

*Return to the southern end of Tower Bridge and take the riverfront path eastwards. Immediately you hit upon another 1980s docklands conversion, Tower Bridge Piazza, which is built partly on the site of the old Anchor Brewhouse. On the riverfront are bronze memorials of the good old days of the docking business: rotor blades, anchors and so on. Soon you come to a large white building with a generous forecourt. This, as the signposts tell you, is the **Design Museum** (open Mon–Fri 11.30–6, Sat–Sun 12 noon–6; adm; © 0171-403 6933 for details of temporary exhibitions. The museum includes a Conran restaurant and café).*

The text to read before coming here is Walter Benjamin's *The Work of Art in the Age of Mechanical Reproduction*: the museum's abiding theme is the aesthetics of mass-produced objects. It glorifies the car, the record-player, the telephone, the vacuum-cleaner. It has lovingly collected examples from the 1920s to the present and arranged them intelligently over three smallish floors; you can even buy period phones in the museum shop.

Ah, but is this art? The museum would have us believe that it is; that art is an extension of the industrial process and, as the Bauhaus school argued, that beauty and practicality are complementary virtues. And yet the Design Museum does not feel like an art gallery. Benjamin argued in his ground-breaking essay that the more works of art are reproduced (that is to say turned into commodities in a consumer economy), the more they lose their aura as aesthetic objects. You can't help thinking that the successive models of vacuum-cleaner on display here do not glorify the aesthetics of design so much as they glorify the Hoover company that made them. They are certainly part of the *culture* of 20th-century life; that does not, however, automatically imbue them with high aesthetic value. Back in the 19th century the enthusiasms of the Design Museum would have been called commodity fetishism; now, as the world suffers its recessionary hangover from the 1980s consumer binge, it seems a rather empty sort of place. It is, incidentally, a rather pale imitation of the 20th Century Galleries in the Victoria and Albert Museum, which have a far greater array of quirkily designed everyday objects. This is, in the end, not so much a shrine to industrial art, as a shrine to industry itself.

*The complex of buildings around the Design Museum is known as Butler's Wharf. As recently as the 1950s it was a hive of trade in commodities from tea and coffee to rubber, spices, wines and spirits. The rise of container shipping sounded the wharf's death knell; now only tourism and service industries can save it. The Design Museum opened in 1989; behind it, in the Clove Building (a former spice warehouse), is the **Bramah Tea and Coffee Museum** (open daily, 10–6, closes 5.30pm Nov–Mar).*

Coffee arrived in London in the 1640s and quickly became popular among the traders and brokers of the City. 'It is a very good help to digestion, quickens the spirit and is good against sore eyes,' remarked one contemporary quaffer. The city's first coffee seller was one Pasqua Rosee, a Greek from Smyrna who came to London with the merchant Daniel Edwards and set up the Jamaica Coffee House in St Michael's Alley. Within 30 years coffee houses had become unofficial trading centres, particularly for the burgeoning insurance trade (Lloyd's of London started as a coffee house). Coffee was very much a man's drink; indeed for a long time women were not admitted to coffee houses at all.

Women were expected to drink tea, which arrived in Europe at roughly the same time, thanks to the Dutch who brought it from Java and Macao. Charles II's wife Catherine of Braganza was the first to make it fashionable in England. Thanks to her example the East India Company developed tea trade with China and made the five o'clock tea break a national ritual. The rest, as they say, is history.

This museum, the brainchild of a lifelong commodity broker called Edward Bramah, gives an engaging account of coffee and tea both as drinks and as commodities. It also shows off Bramah's astonishing lifelong collection of coffee and tea pots. They come in all shapes and sizes: monsters, hedgehogs, petrol pumps. There is even a late 19th-century teapot in the shape of Sherlock Holmes. His pipe is, of course, the spout.

> *A water inlet just to the east of Butler's Wharf brings the waterside footpath to an abrupt end.*

Just across the water is the stretch of land which Dickens called **Jacob's Island** in *Oliver Twist* and made the setting of Bill Sikes's suicide. His graphic description of this cholera-infested site led to howls of indignation from the local alderman who furiously denied that anywhere like Jacob's Island really existed. Dickens won the argument, and a few decades later one of the neighbourhood streets was renamed Jacob Street in his honour.

> *Unfortunately the only way to reach Jacob's Island, and Bermondsey and Rotherhithe beyond, is to return to Tooley St and its continuation, Jamaica Road. The pleasures of Rotherhithe are described elsewhere in this book; this walk ends here. You can either walk back to ⊖ London Bridge, or take one of two buses. The 47 returns to London Bridge and then crosses into the City; the P11 retraces the whole of this walk and takes you back to Waterloo.*

X: Exhibition London

Start: ⊖ *Hyde Park Corner.*

Walking time: *2 hours, not including the major museums, which merit up to half a day each.*

X: Exhibition London

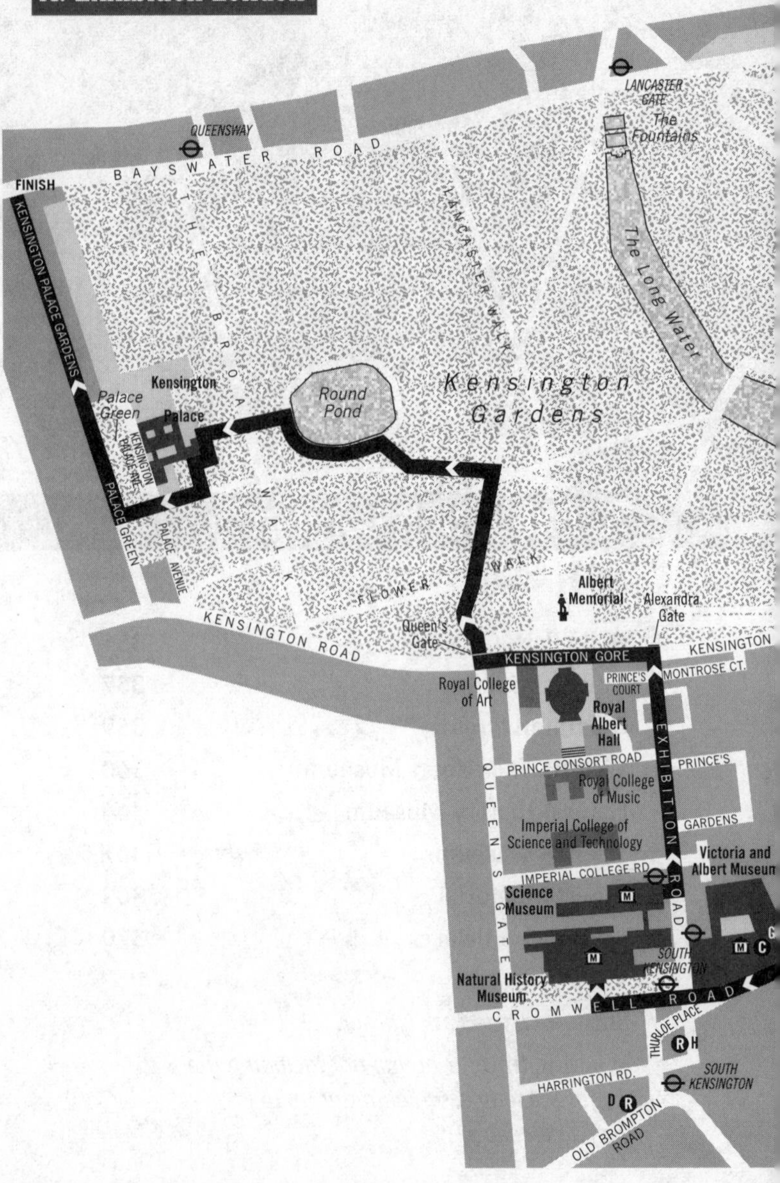

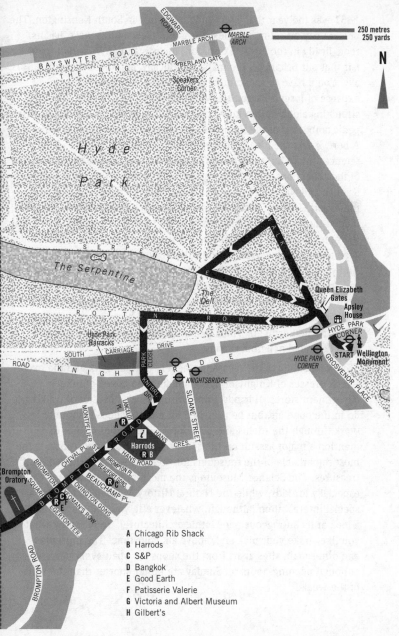

EDGWARE ROAD

MARBLE ARCH

MARBLE ARCH

BAYSWATER ROAD

THE RING

CUMBERLAND GATE

Speakers Corner

Hyde Park

PARK LANE

PARK LANE

BROAD WALK

SERPENTINE

The Serpentine

The Dell

ROAD

SERPENTINE

Queen Elizabeth Gates

Apsley House

ROTTEN ROW

HYDE PARK CORNER

HYDE PARK

Hyde Park Barracks

CARRIAGE DRIVE

SOUTH

ROAD

KNIGHTSBRIDGE

PARK CLOSE

BRIDGE

START

Hyde Park Corner

GROSVENOR PLACE

Wellington Monument

KNIGHTSBRIDGE

KNIGHTSBRIDGE

SLOANE STREET

LANCELOT PL.

MONTPELIER ST.

CHEVAL PL.

BROMPTON ROAD

A

HANS CRES.

HANS ROAD

Harrods

R B

BEAUFORT GDNS.

Brompton Oratory

BROMPTON SQUARE

BROMPTON

CHEVAL PL.

BEAUCHAMP PL.

YEOMAN'S ROW

OVINGTON GDNS.

R C

R C

EGERTON TER.

BROMPTON ROAD

A Chicago Rib Shack
B Harrods
C S&P
D Bangkok
E Good Earth
F Patisserie Valerie
G Victoria and Albert Museum
H Gilbert's

1851 was the year that everything happened in South Kensington. The present-day museum complex, the centrepiece of this walk, has its roots firmly in the Great Exhibition, the gargantuan Victorian trade fair that put Britain on the map scientifically, commercially and culturally. You'll have to spend quite a bit of time imagining the vast expanse of Joseph Paxton's Crystal Palace (now, alas, gone for ever) stretching along Rotten Row, and recreating in your mind the encyclopedic ambitions of the Exhibition's sponsors, Henry Cole and Prince Albert. It was the idea of these two men to blend the arts and the sciences into a huge international show; they were also the originators of the collections which form the basis of today's Victorian and Albert, Science and Natural History Museums. Albert's name is everywhere—the Albert Hall, the Albert Memorial, the Victoria and Albert Museum; indeed the district is sometimes referred to as Albertopolis. Cole's, on the other hand, has largely been forgotten; the only memorial to him is an annexe to the Victoria and Albert Museum which he founded. And yet each was equally important in establishing South Kensington as London's museum city, visited and loved by tourists and scholars from around the world. Before Albert and Cole, this part of London was a distant outpost of the city, the haunt of highwaymen, duellists and hardened drinkers. After them, it turned into one of London's most desirable neighbourhoods.

This walk explores the pleasant greenery of Hyde Park and the exclusive addresses of Knightsbridge, including the doyen of luxury department stores, Harrods. Otherwise, there's not a lot of walking to do in the open air, but be prepared for a tremendous amount of legwork through the rooms and corridors of the museums, not to mention a major assault on the senses. The Victoria and Albert is the most remarkable of the museums for sheer variety and value of its treasures. The Science Museum is the most immediately entertaining, especially for kids, while the Natural History Museum is more of a special interest item (although, whatever else you do, you should take a look at its outrageous neo-Gothic architecture). You'll know what you like—take your pick and, above all, your time. The museums and other main sites apart from the shops are open every day, although opening hours on Sunday are rather shorter than the rest of the week.

Chicago Rib Shack, 1 Raphael St. Friendly American restaurant. Ribs, burgers and good cocktails. £15–20.

Harrods, 87–135 Brompton Rd. There are bars and restaurants on every level, from the snackish to the extravagant. Ideal for people-watching and soaking up the atmosphere of this outrageous department store. For light refreshment, try the Health Juice Bar on the lower ground floor.

S&P, 9 Beauchamp Place. First class delicious Thai lunches from £8.95 for two courses.

Bangkok, 9 Bute Street. Another good Thai restaurant with lunch from £15.

Good Earth, 233 Brompton Road. Attractive Chinese eatery with an excellent £9.95 set lunch.

Patisserie Valerie, 215 and 256 Brompton Road. Two branches of the famous French café in Soho. Wonderful coffee and cakes.

Victoria and Albert Museum, Exhibition Rd. The café-restaurant is no great shakes but a vital stopping-off point on your way round the vast collections. In summer you can sit out in the courtyard. £5–10.

Gilbert's, 2 Exhibition Rd. Good French and English specialities. Bargain set lunches from £12.50 for two courses (closed Sat lunchtimes).

The Great Exhibition

All was bustle, life, confusion and amazement.

Henry Mayhew

The Great Exhibition of the Works of Industry of All Nations was an altogether exceptional event in the history of London—exceptional because by rights it should never have happened at all. It required imagination, audacity, bureaucratic indulgence and inventive flair, all qualities that the city's authorities have usually lacked utterly. London in 1851, though, was lucky enough to have an imaginative royal patron, Prince Albert, an outstanding organizer in Henry Cole and a designer of genius, Joseph Paxton. Albert first conceived of the show as a monument to free trade and the might of the British Empire, but also as a forum for the scientific and aesthetic achievements of the whole world. The young prince worried that Britain would recede as an industrial nation unless it became more familiar with the very latest in scientific innovation and artistic endeavour. It was a very un-British idea, coming from a prince who had been born and brought up in continental Europe, and it was not exactly greeted with universal glee. As the project got under way, doctors began writing to the newspapers warning that the influx of foreigners would spread plague and venereal disease, while protectionist members of parliament complained that the Exhibition would 'encourage the foreigner at the expense of the already grievously distressed English artisan'.

But Albert had the support of Henry Cole, one of the few enlightened bureaucrats of the Victorian age and the closest thing to a renaissance figure the era could claim. Cole had reformed the public record office, helped establish the penny post and fought for a standard railway gauge. He was a painter, an industrial designer, a journalist and magazine editor; he even published the world's first Christmas card in 1843, his most enduring legacy of all. Together, Cole and the Prince persuaded parliament to set up a special commission to organize the Exhibition. Hyde Park was agreed upon as a venue, and a competition was launched to find the best architect for a suitable building. Nearly 250 designs were submitted. At first, the 27 commissioners tried to blend the merits of all of them, resulting in a disastrous hotchpotch of a structure, taller even than St Peter's in Rome, that would have required 15 million bricks and years to construct. In the ensuing debate, the project almost foundered over the fate of the fine old elm trees along Rotten Row, which the commissioners wanted to cut down. It seemed the Exhibition would end, like so many London projects, in squabbling and penny-pinching.

Then providence intervened in the shape of Joseph Paxton, a man of whom the Duke of Wellington later said: 'I would have liked him for one of my generals.' Paxton was a brilliant gardener who had built glasshouses and arboreta for the Duke of Devonshire at Chatsworth, successfully protecting all manner of tropical plant species. In 1849 he hit upon the design formula that was to be the basis of the Crystal Palace. To protect a rare water plant from British Guiana, the Victoria Regia, he constructed a glasshouse based on the ribbed skeletal leaf structure of the lily. His hollow cast-iron columns doubled as rain-water pipes, while a system of ridge and furrow roof lights provided heat, light and ventilation. After reading about the Exhibition project in the newspapers, Paxton humbly approached Henry Cole saying he thought he could build a suitable structure that would overcome the speed and cost problems, and spare the elm trees to boot. His plan was enthusiastically endorsed, and less than nine months later his Crystal Palace—1848ft long by 408ft wide, covering 18 acres and enclosing a staggering 33 million cubic ft of space—was complete.

The Palace was essentially a glorified greenhouse, but on an astonishing scale. Paxton used 1060 iron columns supporting 2224 trellis girders, 358 trusses, 30 miles of guttering, 202 miles of sash bar and 600,000 cubic ft of timber fashioned into 16 semi-circular laminated ribs. Its centrepiece, used as a meeting point throughout the Exhibition, was a 27ft-high fountain fashioned from four tons of pure crystal glass. For the first time London was using the most up-to-date building materials, glass and iron, which had been discovered in Paris a generation earlier. The Crystal Palace was also the first major pre-fabricated building ever erected. All the parts could be made elsewhere using the latest machine tool technology. To Londoners used to the painfully slow construction of the past, the fast-rising apparition of the Crystal Palace in Hyde Park must have been extraordinary. *The Times* described the finished product as 'an Arabian Night's structure, full of light, and with a certain airy unsubstantial character about it, which belongs more to an enchanted land than to this gross material world of ours.'

The Exhibition, which opened to great fanfare on 1 May 1851, was a huge and largely unexpected popular success. In the 140 days that it stayed open, over six million entries were recorded. More than £350,000 was taken at the doors, for a clear profit of £186,000. People came by omnibus, by coach and by train from London, the countryside and the world. A young man by the name of Thomas Cook specialized in organized trips and made his name as the world's first tour operator. One 85-year-old woman walked all the way from Penzance in Cornwall with just a basket on her head for luggage. Rooms in London could not be had for love or money; Henry Mayhew describes how servants accompanying house guests from out of town were invited to sleep on kitchen tables and atop grand pianos.

In all, the Exhibition had some 100,000 objects on display. They included such innovations as the first cotton-spinning machines, cigarette rollers and wrappers, and the first soda siphon. The British section boasted the largest sheet of plate glass and the largest mirror in the world, a 2500ft-long sheet of paper, the first phosphor matches, the first cod liver oil, a pioneer model alarm clock known as a 'servant's regulator', a collapsible piano for gentlemen's yachts and a network of gutta-percha tubes intended to link a church pulpit to special pews for the hard of hearing.

The French section was more artistic than practical and featured silks, satins and tapestries from the Gobelins in Paris. The Germans sent stuffed animals, while the Canadians supplied a giant piano with room for four players at once. The Philosophical Instruments section was a treasure trove of the eccentric; there was a special walking stick with room inside for medical instruments including materials to perform an enema, and a spring-loaded 'Man of Steel' which could expand to the size of Goliath or contract to dwarfish proportions. Among the more useless exhibits were a vase made entirely of lard and mutton fat, and a specially sprung bedstead (sent in by a Mr Jones of Lombard St) that hurled its occupants on to the floor at a preset hour. The museum organizers provided a few innovations of their own, not least the world's first public conveniences, known in gloriously euphemistic parlance as Comfort Stations. These contraptions alone brought in a tidy profit of £1769.

The Great Exhibition is the key to understanding the aims and interests of the founders of the South Kensington museums; the Victoria and Albert in particular, with its mania for accumulation and eccentricity, can trace its heritage straight back to the great trade fair of 1851. The story also illustrates the great, largely untapped potential of a city like London and shows all too clearly what kind of opportunities can be taken, given enough vision and imagination. Unfortunately, succeeding generations failed to carry on where Albert and Henry Cole had left off. The biggest crime was dismantling the Crystal Palace. Paxton had actually drawn up plans to expand it and keep it as a permanent winter garden 'where multitudes might ride, walk or recline amidst groves of fragrant trees'. Others chipped in with further suggestions, the wackiest being a plan to turn it into a 1000ft museum tower to save ground space. Parliament, for reasons best known to itself, voted to pull it down, and the giant structure was eventually reassembled, in modified form, at Sydenham in southeast London. Here it fell into slow decline, was converted into a naval depot during the First World War and eventually burned down on 30 November 1936. The blaze was spectacular and could be seen as far away as Brighton on the south coast.

Despite the jettisoning of the Crystal Palace, exhibition fever continued in London for another decade after the doors closed in November 1851. Prince Albert arranged for the purchase of nearly 90 acres of land just south of Hyde Park, most of it a nursery and market garden, with a view to building a science and museum park. A second international exhibition was planned, and the architect Francis Fowke, a brilliant captain in the Royal Engineers, was commissioned to start work on the permanent buildings. The plans began to go seriously off course when Prince Albert died in 1861 at the age of just 42. The international exhibition was directly affected, and proved neither a popular nor a commercial success. Further misfortune followed with the untimely death of Francis Fowke in 1865, which put back the whole building programme. The Albert Hall opened in 1871 and the Albert Memorial shortly after, but the museums and great centres of learning had to wait years or even decades for completion. The Natural History Museum, mooted as early as 1860, was not opened until 1881; the Victoria and Albert, meanwhile, had to content itself with temporary headquarters until 1909. Buildings to house Royal Colleges of Music and Art popped up towards the end of the century in Prince Consort Road and Kensington Gore, but were unintegrated into the whole.

Albert's plans for a landscaped museum city thus gave way to the usual London mixture of bodge and compromise. The result is a higgledy-piggledy collection of buildings dotted between the park and Cromwell Road. In recent years, the architect Norman Foster has been looking at ways to relandscape Albertopolis, and hide such 1960s eyesores as Imperial College in Exhibition Road and the neighbouring extension to the Natural History Museum. As usual the problem is money; Foster is now lobbying for a smaller version of the scheme, involving a subway system and central information ticketing hall underneath Exhibition Road.

*An apology is in order for starting at **Hyde Park Corner**, one of London's more impossible traffic junctions which abruptly separates Green Park from Hyde Park. Life is made easier for pedestrians by a decent subway system linked to the Underground. The reason for starting here is to see Decimus Burton's Constitution Arch in honour of the Duke of Wellington, his Ionic Screen at the entrance to Hyde Park and Wellington's London residence, Apsley House.*

The planners got their teeth into Hyde Park Corner at around the same time that they came up with the idea for Trafalgar Square, and both projects were intended for the same purpose: to glorify Britain's victories in the Napoleonic Wars. While Trafalgar Square honoured the country's great naval commander Horatio Nelson, who died in the heat of battle, Hyde Park Corner gave pride of place to the hero of Waterloo, the Duke of Wellington, who was still very much alive and climbing the political ladder towards the prime minister's office. Wellington, unlike his great adversary Napoleon, was unfortunately one of the bigger bores in history, which might go some way to explain why he allowed such a dog's breakfast to be made of this collection of memorials to him.

Decimus Burton designed both the Greek Revival screen at the entrance to Hyde Park and the triumphal arch which now stands in the concrete island at the top of Green Park. Originally the arch was topped by a vast statue of the duke astride Copenhagen, the horse he rode at Waterloo. The bronze monster, built by Matthew Cotes Wyatt and his son James, was 30ft high, weighed 40 tons and by all accounts was revoltingly ugly. One Frenchman who saw it exclaimed: 'We have been avenged!' So reviled was the statue that it was taken down in 1882 and eventually replaced with the present quadriga depicting four horses harnessed to a chariot of peace. The architect of the quadriga, Adrian Jones, held a dinner party for eight people in the open carcass of one of the bronze horses shortly before the ensemble was completed in 1912. There had been a precedent for such an eccentric dinner half a century earlier, when the designer of a dinosaur display at the Sydenham Crystal Palace, a Mr Waterhouse Hawkins, entertained his friends in the body of an iguanadon. Nowadays Jones, like Hawkins, is remembered more for his entertainment habits than for any contribution to civic art. Wellington, meanwhile, was compensated for the loss of one statue by the arrival of another: a replacement equestrian figure was erected next to the victory arch, rather closer to terra firma this time, in 1888.

*Next to the Ionic screen is Wellington's London residence, **Apsley House** (open Tues–Sun, 11–5; adm).*

Wellington was given this house as a reward for his victories against the French, and he modestly dubbed it No.1, London (its real address being the more prosaic 149 Piccadilly). Robert Adam had built it half a century earlier for Henry Bathurst, a man generally reckoned to be the most incompetent Lord Chancellor of the 18th century. The Iron Duke succeeded in defacing Adam's original work, covering the brick walls with Bath stone, adding the awkward Corinthian portico at the front and ripping out much of the interior with the help of the architects Benjamin and Philip Wyatt. It's a slightly sterile place now, but amongst the military memorabilia and unexciting portraits you will find some excellent examples of work by Goya, Velazquez and Rubens. You feel the coldness of a man who terrified most who met him and who, according to legend, once defused a mounting riot in Hyde Park with a single crack of his whip. Sadly the museum does not own a pair of Wellington boots, the man's greatest legacy to the 20th century. The highlight is indubitably Canova's double-life-size sculpture of Napoleon, which Wellington stole from the Louvre after its megalomaniac subject rejected it. No, it wasn't that Napoleon found it too small; he was offended because the winged victory figure on the palm of one of the hands faced away from the sculpture, suggesting (so Napoleon thought, quite rightly as it turned out) that victory would finally elude him.

> *From Apsley House, cross the road and take a peek at the **Queen Elizabeth Gates** at the entrance to the park.*

This shiny web of stainless steel filigree is one of London's more recent adornments, and not exactly one of its more successful. To be frank, it is kitsch beyond belief, what with its pseudo-Victorian flower motifs and gaudily painted lion and unicorn figures beneath a rosebush; a £1.5 million exercise in what one critic called 'three-dimensional knitting'. David Wynne's gateway, opened in 1993, was built in honour of Queen Elizabeth the Queen Mother. Maybe when he designed it he was thinking of the frilly hats she likes to wear to the races at Ascot.

> *Head into the park, a remarkably large expanse of greenery for the centre of a big city. This end is rather hilly and open, giving views of the posh hotels along Park Lane up to Marble Arch. There are more trees towards Kensington Gardens, as the stretch beyond the Serpentine lake is known. For the purposes of this walk you should try to stick close to Rotten Row, the sandy horse path running along the southern edge. Its name is a corruption of the French route du roi (royal road).*

Hyde Park started out as part of the Westminster Abbey estate, a breeding ground for deer, boar and wild bulls. When Henry VIII dissolved the monasteries, he decided to keep it as a private hunting ground; it was not opened to the public until the beginning of the 17th century. William III hung lamps along Rotten Row to deter highwaymen while he made his way from Kensington Palace to St James's, instituting the idea of street-lighting in London. The park was a favourite hang-out for crooks of all kinds, and even George II was once robbed of his purse, watch and buckles while out walking. In the course of the 18th century it also became London's most popular duelling ground. The most famous encounter was between Lord Mohun and the Duke of Hamilton in 1719, on which occasion the sparring partners succeeded in fatally skewering each other at the same time. The duchess was evidently heartbroken by the death of her husband, but Lady Mohun betrayed no such emotion. She merely complained about the seconds laying her blood-spattered late husband on her best bed, so making a terrible mess of the sheets.

In 1730 Queen Caroline created the Serpentine by having the underground West-bourne river dammed. The L-shaped lake is still the park's most prominent feature, famous for its New Year's Day swims which are open to anyone foolhardy enough to jump into the freezing winter water (some years the swimmers have to break the ice before they start). The Serpentine has provided the focus for many other events, from funfairs to political demonstrations. The northeastern end of Hyde Park remains the only place in Britain where demonstrators can assemble without police permission, a concession made in 1872 in a truce between the Metropolitan Police and a succession of angry demonstrators. The spot is known as **Speaker's Corner**, and every Sunday afternoon you can hear impassioned crackpots droning on for hours about the moral turpitude of the world. Despite the fame of Speaker's Corner, it is hardly an impressive symbol of free speech. Microphones are banned, and most of the words are drowned out by the traffic on Park Lane. Nobody takes the place seriously, particularly in this media-saturated era. You can talk all you like, Speakers' Corner says; just make sure nobody can hear you.

> Be sure to return to Rotten Row and follow it to the south of the Serpen-tine. Looming up ahead on the left is one of the ugliest buildings in London, **Knightsbridge Barracks**, built by Basil Spence in the late 1960s to house the Queen's Household Cavalry and their 250-odd horses. Just before the barracks, head for the southern edge of the park and, between the children's playground and the manège, you should find the small gate that leads into Park Close, a narrow alley attractively lined with small shops and restaurants. Cross the road called Knightsbridge and continue directly along Knightsbridge Green.

There is nothing very grand about the houses of **Knightsbridge**, but the confident late-Victorian mansions fetch astronomical rents. The area has long been popular with oil sheikhs from the Gulf and the dependants of Third World dictators, who certainly contribute to the high-spending tone of the neighbourhood if not the tastefulness of its social banter. Knightsbridge was not always thus: for a long time it was a small village far from London noted mainly for its taverns, particularly the

Fox and Bull where Joshua Reynolds went boozing in the 18th century and Shelley's wife Harriet Westbrook was laid out after drowning herself in the Serpentine in 1816. It was the Great Exhibition that turned Knightsbridge into the birthplace of the late Victorian department store. **Harvey Nichols**, the most stylish (and the absolute favourite of Patsy and Edina in *Absolutely Fabulous*), is on the corner of Sloane Street and Knightsbridge. Harvey Nicks is justly famous for its weird and wonderful window displays, and fifth floor food halls, where swishly packaged exotica of every description are sold under an equally exotic steel panelled corrugated canopy with views of the Knightsbridge skyline. (If you need a break, coffee or even a drink, it's well worth making a short detour from here to the food halls' glamorous café and bar).

> The most famous department store of all, **Harrods**, is right in front of you on the Brompton Road.

Nowadays it is often mentioned in the same breath as the name of its owner, Mohammed Al Fayed—Egyptian tycoon, failed candidate for British citizenship and father of the ill-fated Dodi, last companion of Princess Diana. But its pedigree stretches back much further to the glory days of the 19th century. Henry Charles Harrod was a tea merchant from Eastcheap who set up shop in Knightsbridge in 1849. The arrival of the Great Exhibition two years later proved the foundation of his prosperity; over the next 35 years, first under his management and then under his son, Charles Digby Harrod, the business grew into a two-storey department store employing more than 100 people, selling perfume and stationery as well as groceries. The real coup, ironically, was a fire that destroyed the premises in December 1883. With impeccable sang-froid, Charles Harrod wrote to his best customers that 'in consequence of the above premises being burnt down, your order will be delayed in the execution a day or two'. He successfully made all his Christmas deliveries on time, so impressing the clientèle that in 1884 his turnover more than doubled.

The vast, terracotta-fronted palace that Harrods now occupies was built in the first five years of the 20th century, at much the same time as the first modern luxury hotels like the Savoy and the Ritz. Indeed Harrods is itself in some ways more like a five-star hotel than a mere shop; service and indulgence towards the customer are paramount, and no request is ever too much trouble. The place is kitted out to provide a fitting welcome to the noblest of princes; particularly striking are the Food Halls with their beautiful food displays and Edwardian Art Nouveau tiles in the Meat Hall depicting hunting scenes. As you wander around, you are serenaded alternately by a harpist and a piano player. You'll find just about anything on its six floors, just as long as money is no object. Should you unexpectedly run out of funds on your peregrinations, Harrods has thoughtfully provided its own bank (on the lower ground floor) as well as an automatic *bureau de change* machine enticingly placed just inside the main entrance.

The best time to come to Harrods is either just before or just after Christmas. In the run-up to the big day the windows are stuffed with magnificently over-the-top displays depicting episodes from Dickens's *A Christmas Carol* or similar classics, against a backdrop of presents bearing the unmistakable Harrods green and gold logo. After Christmas, the discreet emporium turns into a total zoo for the January sales, when many of the goodies are given discounts of 50 per cent or more. It is not the prices, though, that attract the crowds so much as the ritual. Swarms of shoppers press against the windows long before opening time, scratching and thumping for a better look. When the doormen finally let them in, they stampede through the store like a herd of buffalo. Almost immediately you hear the crash of china and glass on the second floor. The women's clothing department turns hysterical as shoppers smash and grab for bargains on designer labels. The staff are trained to keep their cool even when faced with such chaos; most of the display china is cheap and dispensable, and smashing it is all part of the fun. Film stars and international royalty usually look in on the mayhem to broaden their education; other shoppers pretend not to notice them since bumping into a celebrity is, of course, just part of their daily routine.

> Head westwards along the Brompton Road for about five minutes; the road suffers somewhat from the traffic but the shops are all impeccably elegant. Beauchamp Place, just off to the left, is filled with jewellery and china shops as well as plenty of restaurants. As Brompton Road turns into Cromwell Gardens, you will see on your right, just after Cottage Place, the vast façade of the **Brompton Oratory**.

The double-decker white stone classical façade of this heavily Catholic church contains a gaudy Baroque interior based on the Chiesa Nuova in Rome. The Oratory, like its Roman model, is dedicated to San Filippo Neri, one of the leading lights of the Counter-Reformation in the 16th century. Neri founded an informal order called the Institute of the Oratory, in which priests and lay believers were encouraged to observe basic rules of piety and worship. Cardinal Newman, who was responsible for bringing the Oratory tradition to Britain in the Victorian age, also encouraged the building of this church, designed by Herbert Gribble and completed in 1884. There is something oddly appealing about the very Italian coloured marble and relief figure work in the nave, perhaps because it seems so out of place in staid, largely Protestant London. The dome is a stunning 200ft high, and the nave, at 51ft, a good bit wider even than St Paul's Cathedral. The Oratory has always been popular with the city's Catholics, who tend to prefer it to Westminster Cathedral, built 20 years later. It is nevertheless a derivative piece of work. The statue of St Peter on the right-hand side of the nave is a copy of the seated figure in St Peter's in Rome (though the custom of kissing its extended foot while reciting a Credo was introduced by a disciple of San Filippo). The marble statues of the Apostles, by Mazzuoli, were taken from Siena Cathedral. And the portrait of San Filippo by Guido Reni, which hangs over the altar, is a copy of a picture in the saint's rooms in the Chiesa Nuova.

> Behind the Oratory, beyond a somewhat dishevelled garden and surrounded by attractive pastel-painted cottages, is the much more modest Edwardian Protestant church, **Holy Trinity Brompton** (closed except for services). Once you have returned to Cromwell Gardens, the next building after the Oratory is the Victoria and Albert Museum.

The Victoria and Albert Museum

This huge, sprawling museum (*open Mon noon–5.50, Tues–Sun, 10–5.50; adm, free after 4.30pm; note there is a second entrance on Exhibition Road*) is nominally dedicated to applied art and design, but in fact even such a broad definition does not sufficiently cover the sheer vastness of its collections. Over the years it has become the nation's treasure trove. You could liken it to a magical chest in some long-forgotten attic; but the V&A has also kept bang up to date, displaying everything from Donatello to Dalí, from medieval reliquaries to Reebok sneakers. Its former director, Sir Roy Strong, once defined it as an 'extremely capacious handbag'. Unlike most large museums, you would be ill-advised to pick and choose your way around the V&A on a first visit. To get a proper feel of it, you should aim to get hopelessly lost along its seven miles of corridors, enjoy its sheer size and wonder at its mania for accumulation.

For half a century after its foundation in the 1850s, the museum was housed in uncomfortable temporary premises nicknamed the Brompton Boilers. A mishmash of corrugated iron, cast-iron and glass, it was painted green and white on Prince Albert's orders to make it less ghastly, but remained an eyesore nonetheless. The foundation stone for a proper building was not laid until 1899 (on which occasion Queen Victoria gave the museum its present name), and construction was completed only 10 years later. Back in 1863, the museum was instructed to confine its purchases to 'objects wherein Fine Art is supplied to some purpose of utility'. The instructions were totally ignored, and today it is filled with all manner of Indian and Oriental art, silverware, armour, tapestries, plaster casts and paintings. As Roy Strong has pointed out: 'Any visitor to the Victoria and Albert Museum today is likely to be bemused as to what exactly is the central thread that animates these discrepant if marvellous collections. The answer is there is none.'

Pick up a free museum guide at the reception desk. It tells you where the most famous exhibits are, and provides detailed maps of the two main floors, plus the six storeys of the Henry Cole wing (note slightly earlier closing here at 5.30pm). There are guided tours through the day, which are recommended for an hour's concentrated stimulation. Neither the museum guides nor this book would be foolhardy enough to undertake an exhaustive description of the whole place: what follows is a broad-brush and personalized account of what to expect.

Level A: Dress

An enthralling starting point is the room dedicated to European fashion across history. Watch how the flamboyant clothes of the 17th and 18th century gradually grow more restricted by corsets and bodices, then become blander and fussier in the 19th century, turn morose in the 1930s and 1940s before exploding in new-found freedom and colour in the 1960s and beyond. On modern fashions you are sure to have your own ideas, but don't miss Vivienne Westwood's outrageous electric-blue platform shoes, which are so tall that they made supermodel Naomi Campbell trip and fall on the Paris catwalk when she revealed them to the world in 1993. The display cabinets have detailed descriptions of the rise of fashion, explaining how the Paris haute couture tradition was established by an Englishman, Charles Worth, who was personal tailor to Empress Eugénie of France. The collection pays great attention to wigs, gloves, hats, buttons, shoes and parasols as well as dresses and menswear. As the display explanation points out, 'hair sometimes reached ridiculous heights'. The magnificent headgear includes 17th-century coifs and a highly ornate Victorian cream silk bonnet. Up a spiral staircase from the dress section are **Musical Instruments**, a range of historical music boxes, virginals and a Dutch giraffe piano with six percussion pedals, as well as the usual strings, wind and brass. The most impressive piece hangs unmissably in the stairwell: an Italian double-bass dating from around 1700 which looks big enough to house an entire string orchestra.

Italy 1400-1500

The V&A calls this the greatest collection of Renaissance sculpture outside Italy. The pieces here are so disparate they could have come from some glorified car boot sale held by the great churches of Tuscany and northern Italy. There are rood sculptures and reliefs, and beautifully decorated cassones in gilt and gesso; a *Neptune and Triton* by Giovanni Bernini and *Samson Slaying a Philistine* by Giovanni Bologna. The greatest treasures are two delicate reliefs by Donatello, the *Ascension With Christ Giving The Keys To St Peter*, which may have been commissioned for the Brancacci chapel in Santa Maria della Carmine in Florence, and a *Dead Christ*

Tended by Angels, which may have been intended for Prato cathedral. Look out, too, for some of the very best glazed terracotta reliefs by Luca and Andrea della Robbia, particularly Luca's allegorical series *The Labours of the Months*, executed for the Medici Palace in Florence, and Andrea's *Adoration of the Magi*. Other artists displayed here clearly emulated the della Robbias' enamelling techniques: Donatello with his gilt terracotta *Virgin and Child* and Lorenzo Ghiberti's treatment of the same theme in pigmented stucco.

Poynter, Gamble and Morris Rooms

On your way through the Italian section you pass the world's first museum café-restaurant, where early visitors to the Brompton Boilers could drop in for refreshments. Each of the three rooms is a rich, highly decorated example of Victorian design. The Poynter Room, originally the grill room, is decked out in blue tiles depicting idyllic country harvest scenes in between allegories of the seasons and the months of the year. The Gamble Room, used for the cold buffet, is a throwback to the Renaissance with its gold and blue tiles, enamelled metal ceiling and apt quotation from Ecclesiasticus around the walls: 'There is nothing better for a man than to eat and drink.' The last room is the work of William Morris, famous for the vegetal inspiration of his wallpaper designs. The theme here is nature and greenery, with plant motifs worked into the plasterwork beneath a ceiling stencilled with gold and white patterns. All three rooms highlight the Victorian taste for bright colours, the reworking of ideas from the past and a fascination for the rediscovery of nature. All too often these preoccupations were a recipe for overblown and gaudy design; here in the refreshment rooms, however, the effect is stunning.

Plaster Casts

Two rooms, straddling the altogether disappointing collection of fakes and forgeries, are devoted to near-perfect copies of some of the most famous sculptures and monuments in the world. The effect is altogether surreal: how can you get your mind around seeing Michelangelo's *David* and *Moses*, Ghiberti's *Gates of Paradise*, Trajan's Column from Rome, the *Puerta de la Gloria* from Santiago de Compostela and chunks of Bordeaux, Aix-en-Provence, Amiens, York and Nuremberg cathedrals all in one place? The irony is that you can view many of these masterpieces better here than you would *in situ*: Ghiberti's famous doors to the Baptistery in Florence come without barriers or crowds of backpackers, while Trajan's Column is presented in two manageable if still enormous chunks, undamaged by the Roman traffic. Michelangelo's *Moses* sits higher here than in San Pietro in Vincoli in Rome, subtly altering the effects of perspective; this version also omits the chip in Moses' knee which according to legend Michelangelo inflicted upon his own supremely realistic work to see if it would cry out in human pain.

The real treat is his *David*—sneak round to the back of the pedestal and you'll see, hanging in a glass case, the plaster fig leaf the museum authorities used to hide the genitals when royal visitors came to the V&A. Such prudish protocol only stopped in the 1950s.

Oriental Art

The central section of Level A is devoted to art from the Islamic world, India, China, Japan and Korea. The most famous piece is **Tipu's Tiger** (often but wrongly spelled Tippoo's Tiger) in the Nehru Gallery of Indian Art. This is an adjustable wooden sculpture dating from 1790 in which a tiger can be seen mauling the neck of an English soldier. There are Indian sculptures of deities dating back to the 1st century BC, and paintings and artefacts giving an overview of two millennia of Indian decoration. Brightly coloured scrolls illustrate tales from Hindu mythology (for example, a rendition of the ten incarnations of Vishnu), alongside complicated geometrical patterns from the Jain tradition. There are several masterpieces from the Mughal dynasty, including a late 16th-century manuscript illustration of the life of Babur, founder of the Mughal Empire, and vivid episodes from the life of Hamza by Persian artists. From the 17th century on you see the European influence, both in the figures depicted and in the styles adopted. An interesting section on fashions in the age of empire, includes tea-caddies and European-style furniture adorned with a few oriental touches.

The Toshiba Gallery of **Japanese Art** boasts some particularly fine lacquer work: tables, trays and some amazing playing-card boxes. Look out for the ornate wicker baskets and then compare them to the late 19th-century stoneware pots fashioned in imitation of them. There are also some interesting ceramics, including a huge porcelain disc originally shown in Europe at the 1878 Paris Exhibition.

The **Chinese Art** section focuses principally on fine objects used in everyday life, particularly ceramics and a collection of ornaments and figurines used in burial ceremonies. Grander pieces include a large Ming dynasty canopied bed and a Qing dynasty embroidered hanging for a Buddhist temple. The **Korean Art** gallery also focuses on everyday objects, including some ancient metalwork, and ceramics from the Koryo and Choson dynasties that go back to the 9th century. Finally the section on **Art in the Islamic World** contains a pot pourri of carpets and prayer mats from Egypt and Turkey and finely decorated bowls and earthenware from Persia.

The Rest of Level A

Sandwiched in the middle of the oriental art sections is the **Medieval Treasury**, a beautiful collection of mainly religious artefacts from the 5th to the 15th century. The reliquaries and reliquary caskets boast highly intricate silver and gold work and delicate alabaster carving (look out in particular for the famous 13th-century

Eltenberg reliquary from Cologne). There is beautifully patterned clothwork in a number of tapestries, altar covers and two elaborate English copes, ceremonial cloaks worn by the priesthood, from the 14th century. The other remaining highlight of Level A is the **Raphael Cartoons**, sketches for the great religious and philosophical frescoes he painted for the Papal apartments in the Vatican. Dotted around the corridors of Level A are European works of all kinds dating from 1100 to 1800. For a taste of the truly mediocre, have a laugh at the British sculpture room (as Nikolaus Pevsner once remarked, the English are not a sculptural nation). Or you can take a breath of fresh air in the **Pirelli Gardens**, the central courtyard of the museum with plenty of benches and views up to the V&A's brick and terracotta turrets.

Level B: 20th Century Gallery

This series of altogether enthralling rooms is a far more engaging history of 20th-century design than the Design Museum at Butler's Wharf. The focus is on household furniture, but within that remit is everything from Marcel Breuer's pioneering Bauhaus chair to Salvador Dalí's totally frivolous lipstick-pink sofa in the shape of one of Mae West's kisses. The most recent exhibits are the most striking, even shocking: personal favourites include Shiro Kuramata's wavy chest of drawers and Ralph Bacerra's postmodern earthenware teapot, which looks like it is about to fall over but, as the display blurb explains, is in fact remarkably stable and easy to pour. A brief section on architectural design, features, amongst other things, ABK's proposal for the National Gallery extension, the one that Prince Charles called a carbuncle. Here's your chance to decide for yourself.

Tapestries

Beyond the 20th Century Gallery you have to walk through yards and yards of unexciting silver pots, metalwork and armour before reaching the tapestry collection and, in particular, the medieval series known as the **Devonshire Hunt**. Famed for their beauty, wealth of detail and high standard of preservation, these tapestries were commissioned in the 15th century for Hardwick Hall, a country mansion in southwestern England. Each of the six pieces, displayed in subdued light, illustrates a different kind of hunt: boars and bears in one, otters and swans in another and so on. Rather than dwelling on the gore, however, they are a joyous celebration of country life, blending figures of men, women and animals with a lush profusion of plants and trees.

In the *Boar and Bear Hunt*, notice the emblem in mirror writing on one woman's sleeve. It reads *Monte le désir*, underpinning the delicately erotic themes of the tapestries; the mirror effect suggests the weavers worked from the back of the cloth and failed to consider that the lettering would come out back to front when the tapestry was finished. One of the most enchanting tapestries is the last in the series, *La Main Chaude* (the warm hand), so called because it depicts a peculiar kind of guessing game: if a participant guesses wrong, the punishment is a slap on the hand.

Henry Cole Wing

This wing, named after the museum's founding director, comes closest to the chest-in-the-attic analogy: much of what is in here is junk, particularly the painting section on the fourth floor, but a bit of patient burrowing will be well rewarded. To get to it you have to go through the restaurant on Level A, which is a good opportunity for a restorative cup of tea and a slice of cake. The signs will point you to what are in fact the back stairs; hunt out the front staircase and you'll find some intriguing paintings lining the walls: Pre-Raphaelite-inspired nudes by William Etty and a series of views of Rome by Louis Haghe, an artist notable mainly because he taught himself to paint left-handed after losing his right in a childhood accident.

On the second floor is the **Frank Lloyd Wright Gallery**, a series of rooms dedicated to the great 20th-century American architect and figurehead of the modern movement. A series of displays explains Wright's predilection for prairie-style houses with low roofs and horizontal window banding. There is a mock-up of one of his interiors, the general manager's office at Kaufmann's department store in Pittsburgh, all warm woods and rational geometry. Architectural plans and photographs give a quick overview of his main works, including his masterful spiral design for the Guggenheim Museum in New York. Round the back from Frank Lloyd Wright is an intriguing section called the European Ornament Gallery, which traces design motifs through a variety of artefacts from medieval art to modern sneakers. This is the V&A having a bit of fun; in the end the links are not all that convincing but they are entertaining none the less.

Floor three is reserved for special exhibitions of prints. Floor four is crammed with mediocre painting, much of it British; try to pick out Courbet's moody seascape *L'Immensité* or Degas's depiction of a scene from Meyerbeer's *Roberto Il Diavolo*. One item you won't miss is the giant silver Jerningham Kantler wine cistern. This is, however, only a copy; the original is in the Hermitage in St Petersburg.

Skip past the fifth floor, which is a print library not open to the general public, and you come up to a light, airy exhibition of some of the best of British painting, including a clutch of Turners and a broad selection of the work of John Constable. Most people only know Constable's *Hay Wain* and his other romantic country idylls displayed in the National Gallery; here you will find watercolours of rural scenes, soft-focus portraits and even the odd (admittedly very pastoral) view of London from Hampstead where the artist lived for a time. There is also a sketch in oils for the *Hay Wain*. If you've seen the original, you may notice that the boy on a horse, included here, was later removed.

> *If you come out of the V&A by the Exhibition Road exit, you'll find yourself just across the street from the side entrance to the **Natural History Museum** (open 10–5.50 Mon–Sat and 11–5.50 Sun; adm but free after 4.30). This, however, takes you into the modern extension of the museum; if all you want is a quick glimpse of the building itself (which should not be missed), you should head for the Cromwell Road entrance around the corner.*

Natural History Museum

This place looks for all the world like a cathedral. The interior is composed of a series of vast rounded arches in brick and terracotta and its floors are linked by a labyrinthine network of staircases worthy of the grandest of Gothic structures. Alfred Waterhouse, the architect who replaced the deceased Captain Fowke, drew his inspiration from the 11th- and 12th-century church building styles of the Rhineland. It shows. His object was to induce an appropriate sense of awe in visitors coming to admire the wonders of creation. The result is way over the top, but quite glorious.

You are soon jolted out of any notion that this is a place of worship by the giant dinosaur in the central hall. This skeletal creature, a 150 million-year-old plant-eating beast called a diplodocus, that warded off predators with its giant tusks and whiplash tail, really sums up what is best and worst about the Natural History Museum. Our prehistoric friend *looks* very impressive; the trouble is, he's a fake, just a cast. Ever since *Jurassic Park*, the dinosaurs have been the museum's main attraction. The special section devoted to them is long on history but short on real skeletons of the critters themselves. One display gives an intriguing list of theories on why prehistoric monsters died out: they drowned in their own dung, they developed cataracts in their eyes, slipped too many discs, were hit by a meteor, they suffered deep depression or else, Jim Jones-like, they committed mass suicide. Maybe they were just told they would have to appear in a film one day alongside the histrionically challenged Laura Dern, and they all expired from shame.

Much of this museum resembles a science classroom at school. There are games explaining human perception and memory, interactive displays on creepy-crawlies and a very politically correct Ecology Gallery explaining the importance of the rain-forests in the world's ecosystem. All of this is fine for children, but not so great for adults who either learnt it at school, or else hated science and have no intention of learning it now. For grown-ups, the museum only really gets going with the Bird Gallery, featuring a remarkable collection of stuffed birds and wild animals from the 18th century onwards, and a geological section known as the Earth Galleries, which are filled with beautiful stones and gems, and where there's a chance to step inside the 'Earthquake Experience'. Right next to the Exhibition Road side-entrance you can really go for the broad view with an audio-visual experience called the Story of the Universe. Again, it is instructive, but not very inspiring.

The Science Museum

For sheer fun, the Science Museum (http://www.nmsi.ac.uk, entrance on Exhibition Road just above the side-entrance to the Earth Galleries; open daily 10–6; adm free from 4.30pm onwards) beats the Natural History Museum hands down.

One of the central ideas behind Prince Albert's museum city was to blend science and the arts into a single demonstration of human knowledge and endeavour. Anyone who visited the Brompton Boilers in the latter half of the 19th century would have been instructed on the interdependence of scientific invention, mechanization, design and the visual arts. But by 1898, a select committee of MPs reconsidered the matter (mainly because of space restrictions) and recommended splitting off the arts and the sciences into separate collections. The Science Museum duly sprang up in 1913, making itself quite distinct from the V &A across the road. The divide between arts and science has continued to grow ever since, but that is scarcely the fault of this museum's curators. The Science Museum has done perhaps more than any other institution in London to make itself accessible and popular, undergoing constant updating and improvement.

Children have always loved it; one of the latest gimmicks is to allow them to sleep at the museum overnight. Anyone between eight and eleven who brings a sleeping bag will be treated to an after-hours tour of the building, a choice of workshops and bed-time stories before lights out (children may also be accompanied by adults: phone the museum on ℗ 0171-938 8008 for details).

For less privileged visitors, the best place to start is with the synopsis on the mezzanine above the **Ground Floor**, giving an overview of industrial and technological progress across the centuries. Here you can disabuse yourself of a few basic misconceptions: Jethro Tull was not just a bad 1970s heavy metal band but also an 18th-century agricultural pioneer who introduced rowcrop farming. Here too, notably, is the Davy lamp which warned miners about the presence of methane gas. Nearby, the Power section gives a brief history of engines including pioneering models by Boulton and Watt from the 1780s. By the telephones is a modern reworking of Foucault's pendulum, the device which first illustrated the rotation of the earth. Then comes a Space section, complete with Second World War V2 rocket and Apollo 10 command module. Beyond, the Land Transport section traces the history of automobiles from Stephenson's Rocket to the Morris mini, the latter bisected from top to bottom. One of the most recent additions is the Challenge of

Materials, a new 'gallery of the future' whose centrepiece is a spectacular glass and steel bridge which spans the main hall of the museum, and whose exhibits celebrate British industry, manufacturing and design with such intriguing objects as a Bakelite coffin, a steel wedding dress and fashion designs by Vivienne Westwood and Hussein Chalayan.

Moving up to the **First Floor** you come to one of the highlights for children, a gallery full of interactive games called the Launch Pad. Children are taken in groups at a time to be explained the rudiments of such diverse phenomena as bicycle gears and hangovers. For grown-ups the most fascinating section on this floor is Time Measurement, tracing the technology of clocks from the first Egyptian timepieces, based on water, to modern quartz and atomic clocks. The key to the modern concept of 'clockwork' was the invention of the foliot balance, a device made of springs, cogs and a pendulum which could guarantee a regular beat; among the beautiful timepieces displayed here which employ it is a late 17th-century coster clock. Next to the tickers is Food for Thought, which explains everything you wanted to know about nutrition (and a few things you didn't—a group of see-through plastic vats, for example, demonstrating all too graphically how much urine, faeces and sweat a 10-year-old boy produces in a month).

The highlight of the **Second Floor** is the Chemistry section, exploring the history of the science through the discoveries of such pioneers as Priestley, Dalton, Davy and Faraday. Under Living Molecules you'll find Crick and Watson's metal-plate model of the structure of DNA. Further along the floor are displays on the development of computers and an overview of nuclear physics, as well as a beautiful collection of model ships. On the **Third Floor** most children head for the Flight Lab, featuring simulators, a wind tunnel and a mini hot air balloon. The main Flight section is a display of more than 20 historic aircraft, plus a collection of models and an ingenious air traffic control display. Equally intriguing is Optics, a collection of spectacles, telescopes, microscopes and the like, leading up to such modern developments as lasers and holograms. The **Fourth and Fifth Floors** are devoted to medicine. Although there are historical models aplenty (including equipment used by Louis Pasteur in the 1860s and a striking 1875 anatomical model of a horse), the main curiosity is a series of 43 full-scale mock-ups depicting key developments in medical science. Thus you see one of the first antiseptic hospital wards, surgery in a First World War trench, a 1930s dentist's office and, finally, a modern operating theatre equipped to perform open-heart surgery.

Children in need of tiring out can be taken directly to the **Science of Sport** gallery, on the ground floor, where they can see a genuine £2 million Formula 1 McLaren, or practise rock climbing an indoor mountain, try out their snowboarding skills or experience the thrills and spills of a simulated penalty shootout.

By this point you may well feel museumed out; if so, you can ditch the rest of this walk and hotfoot it to ⊖ *South Kensington, either by heading down Exhibition Road or else walking through a spooky Edwardian tiled passenger tunnel, which is well signposted. The walk continues up Exhibition Road towards the park, passing the concrete boulder that is Imperial College (part of London University) to the left and the equally horrendous concrete Church of Jesus Christ of Latter-Day Saints (headquarters of the London Mormons) opposite. As you reach the park, turn left on Kensington Road and you bump straight into the **Albert Hall** (call ✆ 0171-589 8212 for details of concert programmes and other events).*

The Albert Hall is the one building designed by the unfortunate Captain Fowke that actually made it into bricks and mortar, but it is unlikely, had he lived, that he would have been particularly pleased with it. As a concert venue it has one unforgivable flaw, an echo that has been the butt of jokes ever since the Bishop of London heard his prayers of blessing reverberate around the red-brick rotunda at the opening ceremony in 1871. There is some truth in what the wags say: this is probably the only place where modern British composers can be sure of hearing their work in performance twice. The irascible conductor Sir Thomas Beecham remarked that the hall was fit for many things, but playing music was not one of them. To be fair, it should be said that Fowke died before the foundation stone was laid and the echo may just as easily have been the fault of his successor, Colonel H.Y. Daracott Scott. Modern acoustics specialists have been trying to correct the problem with mushroom-shaped roof hangings since the late 1960s, with partial success.

For all its failings, the Albert Hall is still well-loved. Visually, it is one of the more successful Victorian buildings in London, at the same time an echo of the Coliseums of antiquity and a bold 19th-century statement on progress and learning. The high frieze around the outside depicts the Triumph of Arts and Sciences—a most Albertian theme. The Albert Hall is huge (capacity 7000 or more) and remarkably versatile; through the year it hosts symphony orchestras, rock bands, conferences, boxing matches and tennis tournaments. Every summer it becomes the headquarters of the Proms, a series of cheap concerts widely broadcast on radio and television. 'Prom' is short for promenade: originally the concerts were held in the open air and were open to all comers; now the promenaders pay a small charge to stand in a special open area in the front stalls. The Last Night of the Proms in early September is a national institution; the orchestra plays only the most patriotic of British tunes and the high-spirited audience, waving Union Jacks and banners, sings boisterously along as *Land of Hope and Glory* and *God Save the Queen* are thumped out by the orchestra and the hall's 150-ton organ.

*On the other side of Kensington Road, just inside the park, is arguably the ugliest monument in London, the **Albert Memorial**.*

The notion of honouring Albert with a memorial was mooted even before the prince's untimely death in 1861. His over-eager homage-payers had to bide their time, though, if only because Albert himself was adamantly opposed to the idea. 'It would disturb my rides in Rotten Row to see my own face staring at me,' he said, 'and if (as is very likely) it became an artistic monstrosity, like most of our monuments, it would upset my equanimity to be permanently ridiculed and laughed at in effigy.' As it turned out, the prince's fears were only too well founded. The widowed Queen Victoria launched a competition for a memorial the year after her husband's death and was personally responsible for picking George Gilbert Scott, nabob of neo-Gothic excess, as the winner. The 175ft-high monument he built is a bloated, over-decorated stone canopy housing an indifferent likeness of Albert reading a catalogue from the Great Exhibition by John Foley: a ponderous pickle of allegorical statuary and religious imagery decked out in far too much marble, mosaic panelling, enamel and polished stone. The wonder is that anyone ever liked it. In fact, it was a big hit with the Victorians and remained popular well into the 20th century. Osbert Sitwell described it in 1928 as 'that wistful, unique monument of widowhood'. It took a writer as cynical as Norman Douglas to puncture the myth. 'Is this the reward of conjugal virtue?' he wrote in 1945. 'Ye husbands, be unfaithful!'

In the 1980s, the memorial received its comeuppance. So ravaged was it by atmospheric pollution, structural movement, vandalism, water seepage and rust that it had to be put out of sight behind scaffolding and wrapped in a condom-like sheet of white metal. The government has long pondered whether to preserve it or not: at the time of writing the memorial is due to come out of hiding some time before the end of the century. If you want a close-up view anyway, check with the Visitor Centre at the base of the monument.

*The area of parkland behind the Albert Memorial is known as Kensington Gardens; the dividing line between it and Hyde Park is reckoned to be the Serpentine, which is now off to the right (head up there if you want to see George Frampton's famous statue of **Peter Pan**, which is by the lakeside towards the Bayswater Road end). Just behind the memorial is an attractive area of bushes and flowering plants known as the Flower Walk; from here you should head in a northwesterly direction towards the Round Pound, and then turn left towards the plain brick façade of **Kensington Palace**.*

Since the death of Princess Diana, Kensington Palace *(open Dec–Sept daily from 10–3.30 but closed Dec–May 1998 for a redisplay of the ceremonial dress collection; adm; includes a small café)* has become something of a shrine to her memory; this was where she, along with that other well-known royal divorcee Princess Margaret, lived after the failure of her marriage to Prince Charles. You won't be able to visit her private appartments, but the Palace offers other delights in their place. William of Orange originally moved here in 1689 because he thought Whitehall Palace, being near the river, would be bad for his asthma. He appointed Christopher Wren to spruce up what was then a relatively modest Jacobean mansion, and took on the design of the grounds, including the elegant sunken garden, himself. Two of the more embarrassing royal deaths of the 18th century took place in Kensington Palace: Queen Anne succumbed to apoplexy in 1714 after an extended bout of overeating, while George II had a violent stroke while squatting on his toilet in 1760. Queen Victoria was born here in 1819, and it was in one of the palace's bedrooms that she was woken at five in the morning 18 years later to be informed by the Archbishop of Canterbury that she was now sovereign of the empire.

The tour is divided into two sections: the historic apartments, and an exhibition of royal clothes including the coronation robes worn by monarchs from George II onwards. The most interesting aspect of the apartments is the decoration work by William Kent: a beautifully patterned ceiling in the Presence Chamber, some fine *trompe l'œil* murals of court scenes on the King's Staircase and painted episodes from the *Odyssey* on the ceiling of the King's Gallery. The Cupola Room plays clever optical tricks to make you believe the ceiling is taller and more rounded than it is; from the King's Drawing Room there is a fine view over Kensington Gardens, the Serpentine and Hyde Park.

The fashions in coronation garb charted by the special exhibition give a good reading of the changing status of the monarchy itself. The over-confident Georges wore ermine galore, particularly the profligate George IV who sported a ludicrously flamboyant white feather hat and a train as thick as a shag-pile carpet. William IV and Victoria, whose coronations went almost unnoticed by a populace more interested in democratic reform than regal pomp, were sober almost to the point of blandness. Edward VII, who helped restore the monarchy's image, showed renewed confidence with his bright military uniform and ermine mantle braided with gold. The exhibition is an unequivocal defence of the uniforms and finery associated with the royal family, but as 20th century draws to a close and the role of the monarchy in British society is increasingly questioned, one might respond with the words of one of George IV's satirists, written in 1820: 'Pageantry and show, the parade of crowns and coronets, of gold keys, sticks, white wands and black rods; of ermine and lawn, maces and wigs, are ridiculous when men become enlightened, when they have learned that the real object of government is to confer the greatest happiness on the people at the least expense.'

From Kensington Palace, you can find transport either by walking to Bayswater Road for the 12 or 88 bus, or ⊖ Queensway—a walk that, incidentally, takes you past a small dog cemetery in the northwestern corner of Kensington Gardens—or by heading south towards ⊖ High Street Kensington. In either case you may want a quick stroll down the street directly behind the palace, Kensington Palace Gardens (which the public filled with acres of flowers after Princess Diana's death in the shape of a cross).

This is one of the poshest addresses in town, home to a number of rich London families as well as embassies representing Nepal, Nigeria, Egypt, Lebanon and the Czech Republic. The Victorian red-brick architecture bears the imprint of Decimus Burton, Charles Barry and Sydney Smirke. Do be discreet though: this is a private road and you'll need to be indulgent towards the policemen who stand guard at either end.

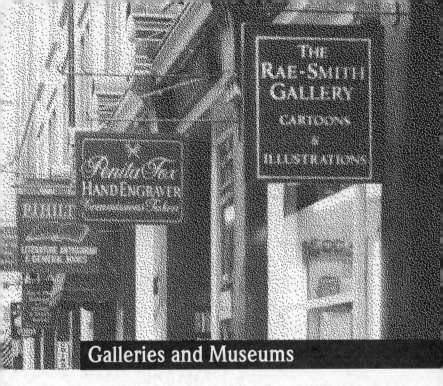

Galleries and Museums

Maybe not all the best things in life are free, but happily some of London's most celebrated museums are among the things that still are. The British Museum, which you won't find listed below because it defies categorization (but which you will find on pp.239–47), is entirely free of charge, as are the National Gallery, Tate Gallery, John Soane Museum and a host of other outstanding collections. The list below is intended to help orient you according to your interests. Page references are given where there are descriptions elsewhere in the book; otherwise a brief overview is given along with details of opening times and admission. Note also the totally subjective and no doubt rather cheeky star-rating system. Three stars are for the very best only; two stars indicate either a big museum that falls short of total wonderfulness or an outstanding museum of relatively limited focus; one star means you shouldn't go out of your way to visit; and no stars means no dang good at all.

Art Collections

★★   **Courtauld Institute**, Somerset House, The Strand, WC2, p.261.

★★   **Dulwich Picture Gallery**, College Rd, Dulwich, SE21, pp.435–6.

★   **Estorick Collection of Italian Art**, Northampton Lodge, 39a Canonbury Square, N1, © 0171-704 9522. Fascinating private collection of Italian art, mainly futurist painters including Balla, Boccioni and Carra. With a library, café and shop (*open Tues 11–6; low adm*).

★   **Kenwood House**, Hampstead Lane, NW3, pp.400–1.

★   **Marianne North Gallery**, Kew Gardens, Surrey, p.423.

★★★   **National Gallery**, Trafalgar Square, WC2, pp.138–44.

★★   **National Portrait Gallery**, St Martin's Lane, WC2, pp.200–2.

★★★   **Tate Gallery**, Millbank, SW1, pp.191–4.

★   **Thomas Coram Foundation for Children**, 40 Brunswick Sq, WC1, p.248.

★★   **Wallace Collection**, Hertford House, Manchester Square, behind Oxford St, W1 (*open Mon–Sat 10–5, Sun 2–5, free but donations welcome*).

One could not hope for a more perfect monument to 18th-century aristocratic life than the Wallace Collection, a sumptuous array of painting, porcelain and furniture housed in a period mansion called Hertford House. It is the location that makes it, the wonderfully uplifting feeling as you glide up the staircases with their gilded wrought-iron banisters and wander from one elegant, well-lit room to another.

The collection is the result of several generations of accumulation by the Hertford family, who moved to Manchester Square in 1797 because of the excellent duck shooting in the fields behind. The family's link with the art world had already begun in the mid-18th century, when the first Marquess of Hertford patronized Joshua Reynolds. The third Marquess had a penchant for Sèvres porcelain and 17th-century Dutch painting, while the fourth lived in Paris and spent his time buying up the works of Fragonard, Boucher and Watteau. Richard Wallace, who gave his name to the collection (as well as designing the Paris drinking fountains that still bear his name), was the bastard son of the fourth Marquess and acted as agent for his father in all his transactions. He later bequeathed the whole lot to the state, on condition that it remain on public view in central London.

Highlights include works by Frans Hals (*The Laughing Cavalier*), Rembrandt (*Titus*), Rubens (*Christ's Charge to Peter* and *The Holy Family*), Poussin (*Dance to the Music of Time*) and Titian (an extraordinary rendition of *Perseus and Andromeda* in which the Greek hero tumbles towards the open jaws of the sea monster with only his sword and shield to save him). Take your time around the rest of the collection to take in the finely carved wardrobes inlaid with tortoiseshell and gilt bronze, the delicate porcelain and any number of eccentric *objets d'art*.

Design and the Decorative Arts

★   **Clockmakers' Museum**, Guildhall Library, Aldermanbury, EC2, p.311.

★★   **Commonwealth Institute**, Kensington High St, W8, p.410.

★   **Crafts Council Gallery**, 44a Pentonville Rd, E3 (*open Tues–Sat 11–6, Sun 2–6; free*). Excellent exhibition of modern British crafts.

★   **Design Museum**, Butler's Wharf, SE1, p.345.

★★   **Geffrye Museum**, Kingsland Rd, E2 (*open Tues–Sat 10–5, Sun 2–5; free*). A thoroughly absorbing series of reconstructions of British living rooms from Tudor times to the present, housed in a row of former almshouses, with a new extension focusing on design.

★   **Horniman Museum**, 100 London Rd, Forest Hill, SE23 (*open Mon–Sat 10.30–5, Sun 2–5.30; free; garden open 8am–dusk*). Victorian-era curios.

★★   **Leighton House**, 12 Holland Park Rd, W14, pp.410–11.

     National Postal Museum, King Edward St, EC1. Go to the philatelic collection in the British Museum instead.

★★★   **Sir John Soane's Museum**, 12–14 Lincoln's Inn Fields, WC2, pp.276–7.

★★★   **Victoria and Albert Museum**, Cromwell Rd, SW7, pp.360–6.

★★ **William Morris Gallery**, Lloyd Park, Forest Rd, Walthamstow, E17 (*open Tues–Sat 10–1, 2–5, plus first Sun in the month 10–noon, 2–5; free*). A long way to go to see William Morris's childhood home and its fascinating exhibition on his life and work. Lots of Arts and Crafts wallpaper, stained glass, tiles and carpets. There is also an interesting collection of pre-Raphaelite paintings and drawings by Burne-Jones and Rossetti, plus a few Rodin sculptures.

Historical and Military

★★ **Bank of England Museum**, Bartholomew Lane, the City, EC2, p.312–14.

★ **Cabinet War Rooms**, Clive Steps, King Charles St, Westminster, SW1, p.176.

★★ **Clink Prison Museum**, 1 Clink St, SE1, pp.336–7.

★ **Guards Museum**, Wellington Barracks, Birdcage Walk, Westminster, SW1 (*open daily 10–4; adm*). Uniforms, weapons, and history.

★ **Imperial War Museum**, Lambeth Rd, SE1, pp.433–4.

★★ **Kensington Palace**, Kensington Gardens, W8, pp.370–1.

London Dungeon, 28–34 Tooley St, SE1, p.343. Go to the Clink instead.

★ **Museum of Artillery**, Repository Rd, Woolwich, SE18 (*open Mon–Fri, 1–4; free*). Guns and cannon from medieval times to the present.

★★ **Museum of London**, 150 London Wall, EC2, pp.300–1.

★ **National Army Museum**, Royal Hospital Rd, Chelsea, SW3, p.417.

★★ **National Maritime Museum**, Romney Rd, Greenwich, SE10, pp.449–50.

★ **Royal Naval College**, King William Walk, Greenwich, SE10, pp.448–9.

★ **Royal Mews**, Buckingham Palace Rd, SW1, pp.167–8.

★ **Theatre Museum**, Tavistock St, Covent Garden, WC2, p.207.

Winston Churchill's Britain at War Museum, Tooley St, SE1, p.343. Go to the Cabinet War Rooms instead.

Science, Medicine and Technology

★ **Brunel Engine House**, St Marychurch St, SE16, p.441.

★ **Faraday Museum**, Albemarle St, W1, p.229.

★ **Florence Nightingale Museum**, 2 Lambeth Palace Rd, SE1, p.432.

★ **Heritage Motor Museum**, Syon Park, Middlesex, p.376.

★ **Kew Bridge Steam Museum**, Green Dragon Lane, Brentford, Middlesex (*open daily 11–5; adm*). An exhibition of functioning steam pumps in an old Victorian water-pumping works, complete with tall brick chimney and a new exhibition on water and public sanitation with 'lucky holes' for viewing the London sewer system.

★ **London Planetarium**, Marylebone Rd, NW1, p.384.

★ **London Transport Museum**, 39 Wellington St, WC2, p.207.

★★★ **Museum of the Moving Image**, South Bank, SE1, pp.330–1.

★★ **Natural History Museum**, Cromwell Rd, SW7, pp.366–7.

★★ **Royal Observatory**, Greenwich Park, SE10, pp.451–2.

★★★ **Science Museum**, Exhibition Rd, SW7, pp.367–8.

★★ **St Thomas's Operating Theatre Museum**, 9a St Thomas St, SE1, pp.340–1.

★ **Thames Barrier Visitor Centre**, Unity Way, SE18 (*open Mon–Fri 10–5, Sat and Sun10.30–5.30; adm*). A brief history of flooding in London, and an explanation on how the barrier works.

★ **Vintage Wireless Museum**, 23 Rosendale Rd, SE21 (*private residence, open by appointment only on © 0181-670 3667; free*). More than a thousand old radio sets dating from 1917–46. Offers a repair service and stocks the spare parts most electrical shops ran out of decades ago.

Famous Homes

★ **Apsley House** (the Duke of Wellington), Hyde Park Corner, W1, pp.355–6.

★★ **Carlyle's House**, 24 Cheyne Row, SW3, p.416.

★ **Dickens's House**, 49 Doughty St, WC1 (*open Mon–Sat 10–5; adm*). The only one of Dickens's many London homes to survive. The furnishings have been drafted in from other Dickens homes; there is little atmosphere, merely an accumulation of hallowed objects.

★ **Dr Johnson's House**, 17 Gough Square, EC4, p.274.

★★ **Freud's House**, 20 Maresfield Gardens, Hampstead, NW3, p.403.

★ **Hogarth's House**, Hogarth Lane, Chiswick, W4, p.419.

★ **Keats's House**, Wentworth House, Keats Grove, NW3, p.403.

Children

★ **Baden-Powell House Museum**, Queen's Gate, SW7 (*open daily 8–8.30; free*). A monument to the founder of the Boy Scouts. Baden-Powell was known at school as 'Old Bathing Towel'; there's a lot of pseudo-heroic lather here that needs washing off.

★ **Bethnal Green Museum of Childhood,** Cambridge Heath Rd, E2, p.460.

★ **London Toy and Model Museum**, 21 Craven Hill, W2, p.404.

★ **Pollock's Toy Museum**, 1 Scala St, W1, p.253.

Religion

★ **Freemason's Hall**, Great Queen St, WC2, ✆ 0171-831 9811 (*open Mon–Fri 10–5 and Sat 1pm, guided tour only; free*). An intriguing PR exercise stressing Freemasonry's principles of truth and brotherly love. Lots of regalia but no elucidation of those handshakes. 'It is not a secret society,' explains a leaflet. Right, and the Pope's not Catholic.

★ **Jewish Museum**, 129–32 Albert St, NW1, p.390.

★ **Museum of Methodism**, Wesley Chapel, 49 City Rd, EC1 (*open Mon–Sat 10–4, Sun 12–2; adm*). John Wesley's house, and the noncon-formist chapel he built next door in 1778, with columns made from the masts of ships donated by George III. Lots of missionary paraphernalia, and the world's first electric chair (invented by Wesley).

Sport

★ **MCC Museum**, Lord's Cricket Ground, St John's Wood Rd, NW8, p.387.

★ **Rugby Football Museum**, Rugby Rd Stadium, Twickenham, ✆ 0181-892 2000 (*open Tues–Sat 10.30–5, Sun 2–5; adm*). Guided tour of the changing rooms and field, a history of the game and an array of trophies.

★ **Wimbledon Lawn Tennis Museum**, Church Rd, Wimbledon, SW19 (*open Tues–Sat 10.30–5 and Sun 2–5; adm*). The history of the famous tennis tournament, including the quantity of strawberries consumed by spectators, the ever-changing fashion in hemlines and a video gallery replaying great moments of the past.

One-offs

★ **BBC Experience**, Broadcasting House, Langham Place, W1, p.233.

★ **Black Cultural Archives Museum**, 378 Coldharbour Lane, SW9, p.435.

★ **Bramah Tea and Coffee Museum**, Clove Building, Butler's Wharf, SE1, pp.345–6.

★ **Fan Museum**, 12 Croom's Hill, Greenwich, SE10, p.450.

★ **London Aquarium**, County Hall, Waterloo, SE1, p.432.

★ **Madame Tussaud's**, Marylebone Rd, NW1, pp.384–5.

★ **Museum of Garden History**, St Mary's, Lambeth Palace Rd, SE1, p.433.

★ **Sherlock Holmes Museum**, 221b Baker St, NW1, p.385.

★ **Wineworld**, (*opening May 1999*) Bank End and Clink Street, SE1 (*open daily 9–7; adm*). Exhibitions on wine culture, history and vineyards.

London Area by Area

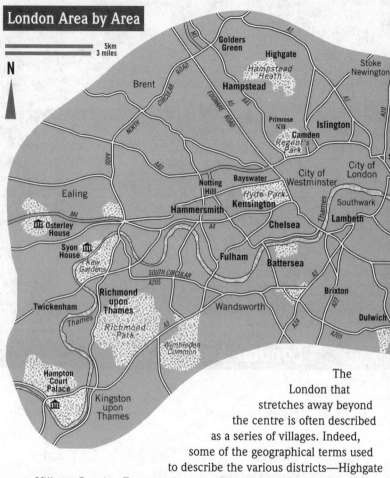

London Area by Area

5km
3 miles

N

Golders
Green

Highgate

Stoke
Newington

Hampstead
Heath

Brent

Hampstead

Primrose
Hill

Islington

Camden

Regent's
Park

City of
London

Notting
Hill

Bayswater

City of
Westminster

Sp
fie

Ealing

Hyde Park

Kensington

Southwark

Hammersmith

Chelsea

Lambeth

Osterley
House

Syon
House

Fulham

Battersea

Kew
Gardens

SOUTH CIRCULAR

Brixton

Richmond
upon
Thames

Wandsworth

Dulwich

Twickenham

Thames

Richmond
Park

Wimbledon
Common

Hampton
Court
Palace

Kingston
upon
Thames

The
London that
stretches away beyond
the centre is often described
as a series of villages. Indeed,
some of the geographical terms used
to describe the various districts—Highgate
Village, Camden Town, and so on—encourage this way of thinking,
as though the outskirts of the city were a patchwork of truly
autonomous communities separated by fields and trees. To compare
anything within the London urban area to village life is, of course,
wishful thinking; there is little of a real village's close-knit sense of
community, only hints of the unbroken greenery of the countryside,
and none of the gossiping about the neighbours. Life in Dulwich, or
Hammersmith, or Brixton is just as anonymous and alienating as in
any urban district; these places may have been villages once, but

now they define themselves almost entirely in terms of their standing and geographical position within the metropolis as a whole.

It is important when visiting outer London, therefore, not to think that you are heading off into the sticks, as you might if you strayed 10 or 15 miles out of the centre of Paris or New York. Rather you should think of yourself exploring another side of a multi-faceted city. Each outer satellite has a distinct identity of its own and a sense of integration with the whole. If there is any city in the world to which London might be compared in this respect, it is perhaps Los Angeles. LA wouldn't be LA if it were just Downtown and the surrounding area; Griffith Park, the Valley, Malibu and Anaheim are all crucial elements in its make-up, just as Islington, Hampstead and Chelsea are in London's. London may not yet have lost its sense of a centre, as Los Angeles has—several hundred years of history and culture cannot be shaken off that easily—but increasingly it is a capital of mutating shapes and uncertain form, the closest thing Europe has to a postmodern city.

Partly for this reason, the point at which central London ends and outer London begins is not easy to define. You might justifiably feel that Regent's Park, Kensington and Chelsea are really part of the centre and do not belong in this section at all. The criteria for arranging this book as it is are, in the end, ones of convenience: you cannot construct a dense inner-city walk in Islington or the East End in the same way you can in Soho or the City; the wealth of history and culture simply is not there. What you find instead is a sense of identity and atmosphere that can be described more usefully than an exhaustive list of tourist attractions.

As a visitor, you will want to head for the obvious delights of Hampstead and Greenwich. Hopefully, if you go browsing in Portobello market or out for a meal in Islington you will also take time to get a feel for the surrounding neighbourhood. In recent years, the river has come back into its own as a focus for city life, and it would be a shame to leave London without looking at the dramatic redevelopments in the Docklands, or enjoying the gentler pleasures of Richmond and Kew. Throughout, directions have been given as fully as possible—sometimes, where appropriate, in the same style as the inner London walks. Take a good map with you, though, just to make sure.

Lunch suggestions are given only where they seem useful; certain areas, like Notting Hill and Islington, are so well covered in 'Food and Drink' that it seems unnecessary to repeat the recommendations here. The occasional café or bar is nevertheless pointed out, where appropriate, in the body of the text.

North London

Regent's Park and Around

Getting There/Around

There are several Underground stations near Regent's Park, including Baker St, Regent's Park, Great Portland St, Mornington Crescent and Camden Town. Lots of bus routes also pass by, including the 13 which starts at Trafalgar Square and goes through St John's Wood towards Swiss Cottage and Golders Green. The description below suggests a route for visiting the park, starting at ⊖ Regent's Park.

Lunch

The park is ideal picnic territory. There is a decent supermarket for provisions on Melcombe St near ⊖ Baker St. For cafés and restaurants, your best bet is Regent's Park Rd or else slightly further afield in Camden. *See* 'Food and Drink' for suggestions.

Regent's Park is the most ornate of London's open spaces, a delightful mixture of icing-sugar terraces, wildlife, lakes and broad expanses of greenery. It is the most rigorously planned of London's parks, the brainchild of George IV's favourite architect, John Nash, who conceived it as a landscaped estate on which to build several dozen pleasure palaces for the aristocracy. It was meant to be the culmination of a vast city rebuilding project, of which the centrepiece was Regent Street. As detailed elsewhere (*see* Architecture and Walk IV), Nash's dreams of a new London, endowing the city with a full sense of aristocratic majesty, were tempered by a succession of objections and financial problems; Regent's Park, however, perhaps comes closest to embodying the spirit, if not quite the letter, of his plans. His stuccoed terraces around the perimeter of the park are at once imposing and playful; the handful of grand mansions inside the park exude the same air of nonchalant, summery elegance as the hunting villas and parks on the outskirts of central Rome; the park itself is beautifully manicured, giving it a curious air of exclusivity even though it is open to all; most delightfully, for the visitor, it is remarkably empty.

Originally, Regent's Park was part of the vast Forest of Middlesex that occupied much of north London. Set aside first as a royal hunting area and then as farmland, it was a major source of hay, milk and butter for the city right up to the end of the 18th century. The rapid development of the Portland estates to the south, however, made farming a poor prospect and in 1811 the Prince Regent invited Nash to build a park based on a series of concentric rings dotted with mansions and fine terraces. With the Napoleonic Wars dragging on public finances, however, Nash's original 56 mansions were reduced to a paltry eight, and some of his terraces, particularly on the north side where London Zoo now stands, had to be abandoned altogether. Nash's loss, though, is perhaps our gain; the park is more accessible and less cluttered as a result.

> One good place to enter Regent's Park (open daily 5am–sunset) is from Park Crescent, one of the most successful of Nash's terraces just to the south of the Marylebone Rd. It is at the top of Portland Place, the continuation of Regent St, and so gives you an idea of Nash's overall vision in his rethink of central London. It is also the point where Walk IV finishes, and ➔ Regent's Park emerges.

Originally Nash wanted to continue the neoclassical crescent around 360 degrees, but had to give up after his backer went bankrupt just six houses in. For a view of more terraces, all built in the same grandiose neoclassical style, cross the Marylebone Road and head up the eastern side of Regent's Park on or near the Outer Circle. First comes Cambridge Terrace, then the outrageously over-stuccoed Chester Terrace, followed by the magnificent Cumberland Terrace, with its portico of Ionic columns. On top is a bright blue and white pediment depicting Britannia and allegorical emblems of the arts, sciences and commerce.

> At this point, head into the centre of the park; try to keep Chester Rd at least vaguely in view as a guide.

Within the Inner Circle is Queen Mary's Rose Garden, a magnificent array of flowers and plants of all kinds. At the north end is the Open Air Theatre (open

May–Sept, ✆ 0171-486 2431), a magical sylvan setting for summer productions of *A Midsummer Night's Dream*. Around the outside of the Circle are some Nash-era mansions—such as Decimus Burton's The Holme—plus a few modern Georgian imitations by Quinlan Terry and others. These are among the most exclusive addresses in London, and well protected from prying visitors by imposing gates, thick bushes and state-of-the-art security systems. The US Ambassador is among the chosen few to live here. On the west side of the Inner Circle (find the path next to the open air theatre) is the Boating Lake, a wonderfully romantic stretch of water where you can rent boats of all kinds for a balmy summer afternoon's idle dreaming.

> *The bottom end of the lake curves round towards York Terrace and the park exit that leads, via the early 19th-century St Marylebone Parish Church, to the two monster tourist attractions of the Marylebone Rd,* **Madame Tussaud's Waxworks** *(open daily 9–5.30 May–Sept, with slightly later opening the rest of the year; adm exp) and the green-domed* **London Planetarium** *(open daily 10.20–5 June–Aug, and Sept–May 12.20–5; adm), both just next to ⊖ Baker St. A joint ticket is available.*

The world's most famous waxworks take some getting into. There is no escaping the horrendous queues, which are little shorter in the winter than in high season. Take plenty of consolatory sustenance (i.e. chocolate, or whatever else keeps you and your children smiling) and expect a long wait. Nearly three million people put themselves through the crush each year, although it is hard to see why—the only thing you can say in the end about a waxwork is whether it is lifelike or not—and most of the film stars, politicians and famous villains here fare pretty indifferently on that score. The royal family, displayed in a tableau on the ground floor, look particularly unconvincing. They don't so much imitate life as bad television. Back in the 19th century, of course, waxworks made more sense as they provided the only opportunity for ordinary people to catch a glimpse of the rich and famous, albeit in effigy. Marie Tussaud was a Swiss model-maker who trained with her uncle by making death masks of the victims of the revolutionary Terror in France. By the time she came to England in 1802, she had 35 wax figures to her name, which she exhibited not far from here on Baker Street (the show has occupied the present site since 1885). The Duke of Wellington was a particular fan and came often to admire the likeness of his vanquished foe, Napoleon. Madame Tussaud's hallmarks were her attention to detail, particularly in the costumes, and her efforts to keep the exhibition bang up to date with the latest celebrities and figures in the news. She even bought up George IV's coronation robes for a cool £18,000.

One of Madame Tussaud's most inspired ideas, the **Chamber of Horrors**, survives to this day. Down in the basement you'll find many of the crooks and murderers who have stalked London's streets, from the 18th-century rabble-rouser Lord Gordon, to the executed American murderer Gary Gilmore. One of the more intriguing figures down here is Hawley Harvey Crippen, a sinister-looking American doctor who poisoned his wife in 1910 and buried her under the cellar floor at their house in Hilldrop Crescent in Kentish Town.

The final section of Madame Tussaud's is called the Spirit of London, a funfair-type ride in a modified black cab featuring illustrations of London's history from the Great Fire to the swinging 1960s. Strictly for kids only (and even then...). If you have children, you might do better next door at the **Planetarium**, with its exciting and informative laser, sound and light show projected over a vast dome-shaped auditorium via a high-tech Digistar Mark 2 projector. The show explains how the solar system works, what the galaxy and the Milky Way are (apart from the chocolate bars you chomped in the queue), how earthquakes and volcanoes happen, and more.

> *Walk back past the Underground station and turn right into the top end of Baker St, the 18th-century residential avenue inextricably linked with Sherlock Holmes.*

They pick over the spoils of Conan Doyle's celebrated detective here like vultures. Among the ferociously competitive businesses is a Sherlock Holmes pub, a memorabilia shop at No.230 selling tea mugs and postcards of the original book covers, plus a **Sherlock Holmes Museum** (*open daily 9.30–6; adm*). The museum *says* its address is 221b Baker St, and certainly looks convincing enough to be the super-sleuth's consulting rooms (there is even a fake Blue Plaque commemorating him above the door). Unfortunately, though, it is really No.239; the building encompassing No.221b (which never actually existed as a self-contained address) is the glass-and-concrete headquarters of the Abbey National Building Society. This makes for much acrimony over who has the right to handle Sherlock Holmes's copious international correspondence. The Abbey National has been answering letters for years and employs a public relations officer called Gug Kyriacou to 'be' Sherlock Holmes on a part-time basis. Gug loves his job and receives 30–40 letters *a week*, mostly from children in Japan and the US. Ever since the museum started up in 1990, however, its curators Elizabeth and Grace Riley have tried to muscle in on the act, issuing Sherlock Holmes visiting cards and answering any correspondence they can persuade the Post Office to bring their way.

The museum is a lot of fun, if you enter into its spirit of artifice. You are greeted at the door by either a housekeeper (a young-looking Mrs Hudson) or a policeman. The rooms have been lovingly filled with late Victorian furniture and artefacts illustrating the Holmes stories. Most entertaining of all is the folder containing Sherlock Holmes's fan mail. Evidently schoolchildren in the United States are asked to write to Holmes as part of their homework; as a result some of the letters have a tone of almost surreal facetiousness. One begins: 'Dear Mr Dead Sherlock Holmes, I feel stupid writing to you because I know you are six feet under.'

At the top of Baker St you can either head up Park Road or else rejoin the Outer Circle. About 500 yards up, roughly parallel with the top of the Boating Lake, is the **London Central Mosque**.

This rather remarkable mosque, the glint of whose squat golden dome winks across the top end of Regent's Park, was built in 1978 as a study centre and place of worship for the city's growing Muslim population (easily the largest religious minority). The arcaded concrete outer buildings contain a rather plain grey minaret as well as the mosque itself. Take off your shoes and enjoy the sheer sense of space and light beneath the dome. There are few furnishings other than a large chandelier and thick decorated carpet, but the place exudes a sense of peace and spiritual calm.

The area to the north and west of here is called **St John's Wood**, *in many ways the archetypal London suburb.*

The avenues of St John's Wood are broad and leafy and its houses, by modern city standards, plush and roomy. The area hasn't been a wood since the Middle Ages, when the knights of St John, amongst others, acted as landlords. But since the late 18th century it has been a choice residential neighbourhood. The semi-detached house, now a standard suburban feature, was first established here by a firm of property-minded auctioneers called Spurrier and Phipps. Anyone familiar with the cover of the Beatles' Abbey Road album, the one where they walk across a zebra crossing, will know what St John's Wood looks like; Abbey Road itself, former home to the Beatles' Apple Corporation, is a 10-minute walk away down St John's Wood Road and up Grove End Road.

Ten minutes further on at the north end of Abbey Road and the junction with Boundary Road is the **Saatchi Collection** *(98a Boundary Road, open 12–6 Thurs–Sun; adm).*

Life for art students in Britain is strapped, and for many the only hope of paying off a burdensome student loan is that Charles Saatchi will descend on graduation shows like a *deus ex machina*. Saatchi—the advertising magnate whose 'Labour's Not Working' campaign helped sweep Mrs Thatcher to power in 1979—began buying up art in the 1980s, starting with early stage-managed forays into post-modern neo-expressionist artists like Schnabel and Anselm Kiefer, and moving on to conceptual art by little known British artists (many of them graduates from Gold-smiths College in Camberwell, where they were coached in the conceptual way by artist-director Michael Craig-Martin). The relationship has been a sound investment for Saatchi who has cornered the market in works by Fiona Rae, Jenny Saville, Gary Hume, the Chapman Brothers, Damien Hirst and Sarah Lucas whose value has soared as conceptual art has continued to tighten its vice-like grip on all Britain's art institutions, from the Royal Academy and the Tate Gallery to Britain's most prestigious awards to artists, the Turner and Jerwood Prizes.

The Saatchi collection here in St John's Wood is where it all started. There are three shows a year and Saatchi's pot luck approach to buying ensures that most exhibitions will be a stimulating mix of the excellent and the execrable. Whatever, you will not be disappointed by Richard Wilson's permanent installation 20:50, involving a pool of sump oil which is so still and black that it looks solid. This alone will guarantee that the long detour to the viper's nest of Saatchi is worth your while.

If you don't have time to visit the Saatchi collection, walk down St John's Wood Road (left off the roundabout at the top of Park Road) and you will see two curiosities staring across the road at each other. One is the **Liberal Synagogue**, an unprepossessing concrete block which holds popular services and Jewish cultural events; the other is **Lord's Cricket Ground**, Mecca for lovers of the world's most eccentric sport and headquarters of its soul in England, the Marylebone Cricket Club. This is not a place to come with naïve questions about overs, innings and lbw—if you don't know what these are you might find the place rather intimidating (especially if you are a woman). Cricket fans will need no introduction, however; indeed they might recognize from afar the distinctive weather vane depicting Father Time stooped over the stumps. They should try to see the small **museum** (*open during play on match days with daily tours at 10 & 11am and 12pm, by appointment at other times on* © *0171-432 1033; adm*). Highlights include the Ashes, the trophy contested in matches between England and Australia—actually the remains of a bail ritually burned after a meeting of the two sides in 1882; and a sparrow—now stuffed—which was killed by a particularly vicious delivery at Lord's in 1936.

> *Through the lower end of St John's Wood and the north side of Regent's Park runs the **Regent's Canal**, running from Paddington and Little Venice and heading off, via some underground sections, towards Camden and Islington. The whole expanse winds through some attractive residential districts, and you will see brightly decorated barges, tugs, houseboats and pleasure boats. To take a boat trip yourself, contact the Regent's Canal Information Centre at 289 Camden High Street on © 0171-482 0523, or one of the private boating companies such as the London Waterbus Company (© 0171-482 2660), which runs services on the hour from 10am to 5pm between Little Venice and Camden.*

Follow the canal on foot through the park, ducking under bridges and passing the tennis courts and jogging tracks used by the residents of the imposing 19th- and early 20th-century mansions on Prince Albert Road. Along this stretch of water a barge loaded with petrol and gunpowder exploded in October 1874, killing four crew members, destroying a bridge and damaging houses in a half-mile radius. There was no foul play involved, just good old-fashioned English incompetence.

London Zoo

*The canal brings you round to **London Zoo** (open daily March–Oct 10–5.30 and Nov–Apr 10–4; adm; the excellent value Lifewatch Season Ticket costs around £20: holders are entitled to unlimited free access to the museum for a year).*

> *The London zoo is an animal microcosm of London, and even the lions, as a rule, behave as if they have been born in South Kensington.*

Leonard Woolf

The Zoological Gardens in Regent's Park were where the term 'zoo' originated. The abbreviation, which first surfaced in the late 1860s, was immortalized in a music-hall song of the time beginning: 'Walking in the zoo is the OK thing to do'. In these post-colonial, animally-correct times, zoos are not quite as OK as they used to be. But London Zoo has responded to debate about its role with some energy. The **Bear Mountain**, once horribly overcrowded and a place of abject misery, has been redeveloped, and houses just two bears. The delightful new **Children's Zoo** is built entirely out of sustainable materials, with a Camel House whose roof is planted with wild flowers and grass seed, a wonderful touch paddock, barn, and pet care centre. A new Lottery-funded **Conservation Centre**, with exhibitions explaining eco systems and animal diversity, is due to open in mid-1998.

If Leonard Woolf was right to compare the zoo to London society, then it is also true that the fortunes of the gardens mirrored those of the British Empire. The Zoological Society of London was founded in 1826, and the zoo itself was created two years later on a plan drawn up by Decimus Burton. As the Empire stretched into the furthest corners of the earth, so the animals grew more exotic: monkeys, bears, emus, kangaroos and llamas at first, followed in due course by elephants, alligators, boas and anacondas, and joined eventually by bison, hippos, koalas and pandas. When giraffes first appeared in 1836, they created a fashion vogue for women's dresses patterned like their skin. A few years later disaster struck when the keeper of the new reptile house was bitten between the eyes by a cobra and died. A further calamity occurred in the 1870s when Alice the African elephant mysteriously lost the end of her trunk. Mostly, the zoo has nurtured and encouraged the British love of animals; its Chinese pandas, in particular, took more than their fair share of the newspaper headlines during the 1970s when the whole nation waited with bated breath to see whether they would mate or not (they did).

One of the attractions of visiting the zoo now is the fine array of well-designed animal houses—the penguin pool by Lubetkin and Tecton (1936), Lord Snowdon's spectacular polygonal aviary (1964), Hugh Casson's elephant and rhino pavilion (1965) or the recently built Macaw Aviary. On your way round you will be invited to 'adopt' any animal that takes your particular fancy. Pay £20 for an exotic breed of cockroach, £6000 for an elephant, or £30 for a part share in *any* animal, and you are assured the beast will be fed and nurtured for a year. Your name will also go on a plaque beside the animal's enclosure—you'll see plenty of these already in place.

Camden

Getting There/Around

You can walk to Camden from London Zoo (*see* above); otherwise, ⊖ Camden Town and ⊖ Chalk Farm are both on the Northern Line. Buses include the 24 from Trafalgar Square which continues to Hampstead.

Lunch

Note: does not include places listed under 'Food and Drink'.

Bar Gansa, 2 Inverness St. Unspoiled Spanish tapas bar.

Silks and Spice, 28 Chalk Farm Rd. Thai and Malaysian café-restaurant.

Crown and Goose, 100 Arlington Rd. Award-winning pub and wine bar with real ale, good food and friendly service.

Dublin Castle, 94 Parkway. Rowdy but friendly Irish pub with live music.

Camden is above all its open-air market, or rather series of markets, that have sprung up around the canal and the surrounding streets. There is something for everyone: cheap clothes, pianos, herbal cures, tarot card readings, off-beat bookshops, furniture stores, pubs and lots and lots of restaurants. At the weekends, traffic comes to a standstill as thousands of strollers, tourists and bargain hunters descend on the area. The atmosphere is very relaxed, young but not overly self-conscious or trendy. You can easily spend hours sorting through the leatherwear and second-hand records, stopping every now and again for a drink or hot snack from a street stall; later, you can head off for a meal or a spot of dancing; or you can easily escape the crowds by strolling away along Regent's Canal.

Back in the 18th century, the whole area was fields and trees and there were more cows than people. Camden acquired its name only after Charles Pratt, the first Earl Camden, bought it up for building speculation. The extension of Regent's Canal eastwards in 1816 brought coal wharves and the first merchants, a tendency towards industrialization that was confirmed with the arrival of the railways in the middle of the 19th century. Dickens, who lived in Bayham Street as a boy, described Camden in *Dombey and Son* as full of 'dunghills and dustheaps'. Soon it filled with the families of poor Irish labourers, joined over the years by Greek

Cypriots and all manner of other immigrants, lending the neighbourhood an exotic if downtrodden air which was captured in the paintings of Walter Sickert, Augustus John and other members of the so-called Camden Town Group at the time of the First World War.

Camden's modern identity as a haven for artists and small shopkeepers was established in the 1970s, when the market started and the old Victorian warehouses were slowly converted into artists' studios, music venues and restaurants. Television personalities of the 1960s, such as the playwright Alan Bennett and the doctor turned stage director Jonathan Miller, chose to set up home in Camden. The cartoonist Marc Boxer devised a long-running strip called 'Life and Times in NW1' (the Camden postcode) as a satire of the new media set descending on the district; his characters were gullible but fashion-conscious liberal lefties with names like the Stringalongs and the Touch-Paceys. A whole generation of post-1968 Londoners spent their adolescence dancing at Dingwall's nightclub (now revamped as an alternative rock venue at Camden Lock). Even the inefficiency of the local council has done nothing to dampen enthusiasm for the place—the market is London's fourth most-visited attraction.

The nerve centre of the market is at Camden Lock, just next to the canal off Chalk Farm Road (the extension of Camden High Street). Some of the stalls and shops stay open all week, but the busiest and most rewarding time to visit is undoubtedly the weekend. In the middle of the market is a covered three-storey building with narrow staircases and passages selling jewellery and crafts; in the immediate vicinity are stalls selling clothes, antiques, books and records. The stalls then continue for about 500 yards up the Chalk Farm Road, in an area known as The Stables. Some of the most interesting shops are on Camden High Street, which is really a market unto itself; the Electric Ballroom nightclub doubles on Sundays as a bazaar for cheap designer fashions and jewellery. Finally, there is a fruit and veg market on Inverness Street, between the High Street and Gloucester Crescent, which is open Mon–Sat.

One last curiosity in Camden is the newly arrived **Jewish Museum** at 129–32 Albert St, between Parkway and Delancey St (*open 10–4, closed Sat and Mon*). This celebration of Jewish life in England from the Middle Ages, formerly in Woburn House on Tavistock Square, is notable mostly for its collection of old ritual objects from London synagogues. The centrepiece is an elaborately carved 16th-century Venetian Synagogue Ark. There are also attractive illuminated marriage contracts and some Torah bells fashioned by the 18th-century silversmith Abraham Lopes de Oliveira.

The pleasure of Camden is to browse and surprise yourself. However, here are a few addresses to get started:

Just 20 years later, though, there was nothing marginal about Islington at all. Its attractive Georgian houses, offered at knockdown prices, proved irresistible to the media darlings and they set about some energetic gentrification. The Camden Passage antiques market arrived in 1964, and pub theatres led by the King's Head on Upper Street began to flourish soon after. The old Collins Music Hall burned down and was replaced with the Screen on the Green cinema. Nowadays the changes in Islington come so fast it is hard to keep track of them: a Lebanese restaurant closes there, a Cuban bar opens here. The area retains a certain self-conscious shabbiness, but that is part of its charm, a way of banishing excessive pretension or over-trendy posing. There's no danger of Islington becoming another South Kensington.

> Islington doesn't have any tourist attractions in the traditional sense of the word, just bags of atmosphere. The best way to visit is to start at ⊖ Angel and work your way slowly northwards, past the antiques shops of Camden Passage and the crowded nexus of bars and restaurants around Islington Green, up towards the quiet Georgian squares of Canonbury. If you come in the evening (and you should), consult the 'Food and Drink' and 'Entertainment' sections for further ideas.

Islington High St, which stretches north from ⊖ Angel, is a rather offputting introduction to the district since it is forever jammed with cars and heavy lorries. Soon, however, the main road broadens and the High Street veers off to the right behind a couple of converted old warehouses and into **Camden Passage**, a cobbled row of elegant antiques shops and stalls, most of which open their doors on Wednesday mornings and Saturdays only. The market is ideal for browsing, since everything looks perfect and the prices of the furniture, prints, silverware and jewellery are probably too high to consider seriously for purchase.

All the streets around here, from Upper Street across to St Peter's Street and down to City Road, are a delight for strollers—small, relatively traffic-free and packed with elegant houses, cafés and restaurants. The area to the east, along the Grand Union Canal, is particularly charming and dotted with pretty Georgian houses. In the 1950s and 1960s this was the distinctly unfashionable home of the playwright Joe Orton and his lover Kenneth Halliwell. No.25, Noel Road, where they shared a dingy second-floor bedsit, has become something of a pilgrimage site, especially since Stephen Frears's film *Prick Up Your Ears*, which told the story of their extraordinary life and violent death.

Orton, a working-class boy from Leicester, and Halliwell, a would-be artist and writer of independent means, met at drama school and decided to set up house together to write plays and novels. For more than a decade they were totally unsuccessful, although publishers picked up soon enough on Orton's quirky and scabrous humour. To amuse himself in idle moments, Orton would tamper with the covers of library books, and write faintly obscene fake blurbs on the inside of the jackets. This was childish stuff in one sense, and Orton and Halliwell were sent to prison for six months once they were caught. But the pranks showed an impishly subversive and frequently hilarious side to Orton which emerged again and again in his plays—*Entertaining Mr Sloane*, *Loot*, *What The Butler Saw*—and his other writings. Orton invented an outraged middle-class alter ego called Edna Welthorpe who wrote regularly to the national newspapers about the disgustingness of his plays. 'I myself was nauseated by this endless parade of mental and physical perversion,' she wrote after the successful opening of *Sloane*, a tale of psychological and sexual blackmail among its three characters. 'Today's young playwrights take it upon themselves to flaunt their contempt for ordinary decent people. I hope that the ordinary decent people will shortly strike *back*!'

Success for Orton, however, was the undoing of his relationship with Halliwell, who felt he had taught Orton all he knew and felt depressed and frustrated at his inability to share in the glory. Orton was good-looking, witty and popular; Halliwell was bald, running to fat and thoroughly unloved. Orton made no secret of his casual sexual encounters in lavatories and with young Moroccan boys in Tangiers; at the same time he taunted Halliwell for his own lack of sexual prowess. By the summer of 1967, with Orton in demand from everyone including the Beatles, it looked as though he might finally break with Halliwell. A desperate and deranged Halliwell responded by beating him to death with nine hammer blows to the head before killing himself with an overdose of barbiturates.

> *Return to Islington High St and cross the main road (Upper St) to Liverpool Rd and **Chapel Market**, a lively fruit, veg and clothes market which is open every day but Monday. Just to the north, back on Upper Street, is the lumbering hulk of the **Business Design Centre**.*

This rather clumsy brick building is a redevelopment of the old Royal Agricultural Hall, a fine Victorian hangar made of iron and glass used for agricultural shows and industrial exhibitions. The Design Centre now hosts conferences, the annual Islington Art Fair and other odd art shows. In 1994 a sculptress presented a life-size reclining nude of herself made entirely out of white chocolate; perhaps unsurprisingly one visitor decided to take a bite out of it, though he had the good grace to go for the elbow rather than any more delicate region.

> *On either side of the Design Centre, Upper St is packed with the restaurants and offbeat shops that characterize Islington. A little further up, where Upper St meets Essex Rd, is **Islington Green**.*

The Green is more of a meeting place than a spot of any great beauty, as the crowds in the Slug and Lettuce pub and outside the Screen cinema testify. The statue in the middle is of Sir Hugh Myddleton, architect of the New River. Heading north on Upper St, you come to the King's Head theatre pub which as a gimmick still counts money in the pre-decimal currency of pounds, shillings and pence (12 pence to a shilling, 20 shillings to a pound). The streets to the left of here, forming the beginning of the area known as Barnsbury, contain some fine Georgian town-houses. Theberton Street, not far from the pub, leads to the pale brick splendour of Gibson Square. One block further up is Almeida Street, home to the highly suc-cessful fringe theatre of the same name.

> The crowds and the trendiness factor gradually ebb away the further north you walk up Upper St. It is worth continuing for five minutes, past the town hall, to turn right on Canonbury Lane and explore one of the most unspoiled areas of Georgian housing in north London.

The name **Canonbury** recalls Islington's roots as the burgh, or district, of the canons of the priory of St Bartholomew at Smithfield. Then, as now, the most imposing building in the neighbourhood was **Canonbury Tower** on Canonbury Place, a building of mythical reputation whose history goes back to pre-Roman times; no fewer than 24 ley lines meet at the point where the central pillar of its main staircase stands. Once part of the priory, the square tower passed into the hands of a rich cloth merchant called John Spencer some years after the dissolution of the monasteries. Spencer disinherited his daughter after she escaped from the tower in a basket in 1599 to elope with her penniless lover Lord Compton; he was, however, tricked into readopting her by Queen Elizabeth, who asked him to sponsor a poor child she knew. Spencer consented, realizing too late the child was his own grandson. Lord Compton eventually took over the running of the manor, and began a tradition of leasing it out to eminent tenants. The statesman Sir Francis Bacon lived here in the 17th century, and the playwright Oliver Goldsmith in the 18th. Now it is home to the Tower Theatre, a popular repertory venue with a strong local following. Inside you can see some Elizabethan wall panelling, and plasterwork on the ceilings dating back to the end of the 16th century.

There are a few other relics from that period in Canonbury Place, for example the bolt and tun motif on the façade of No.6, which may be familiar to those who have visited St Bartholomew the Great (*see* p.299) as the rebus used by the 16th-cen-tury prior William Bolton. Most of the area, however, is now notable for its attractive Georgian buildings. Canonbury Square, one of the finest ensembles, is just a few yards to the west; another pretty row is along the New River two streets to the east of here (take Canonbury Park up to St Paul's Road, then turn back down New River Walk for the best views).

> The borough of Islington stretches quite a bit further to the north and west than the area described above. Much of it, particularly around Holloway Rd and Caledonian Rd, is very run down, riddled with

unemployment and petty crime. Two areas, however, are pleasant enough if you happen to be passing through: **Highbury,** *an area of tranquil residential streets, parks and the Arsenal football ground, and* **Stoke Newington,** *which has a handful of good cafés and restaurants as well as the Vortex jazz club. Green Lanes, which stretches up from Stoke Newington, turns into a Greek Cypriot haven beyond Finsbury Park; come on Sunday afternoons and the aroma of freshly-baked pitta bread wafts out from a cluster of delicatessens and kebab houses.* **Finsbury Park** *also has a strong ethnic character, and boasts several very cheap Caribbean and Indian restaurants along Stroud Green Rd.*

Highgate

Getting There/Around

⊖ Archway and ⊖ Highgate are both on the Northern Line and both within walking distance of Highgate village, although in both cases there is a steepish uphill walk. Local buses include the 271, which starts in Highgate village and heads down to Liverpool St Station via Highbury, and the 210 which crosses north London from Golders Green and Hampstead to Finsbury Park. It also stops in the village.

Highgate has been a genteel hilltop village, protected from the hubbub of the capital, since the 13th century. In 1593 the writer John Norden praised its 'sweet salutary air', its grassy walks and shady avenues. The village has the same attractions today, plus sturdy 19th-century houses which attract well-to-do families seeking a compromise between the big city and the anonymity of the suburbs proper. The hilly terrain and surrounding expanses of greenery give Highgate a climate all its own: often it will rain or even snow when the rest of London stays dry, and vice versa. Its main attractions to visitors are the mythical traces of Dick Whittington, the 15th-century Lord Mayor of London; and the cemetery, resting place of Karl Marx.

A good place to start is ⊖ *Archway, a busy roundabout flanked by late-opening Indian groceries and, somewhat off-puttingly, the concrete headquarters of Islington's Department of Social Security. Heading round to the north side, look up the Archway Road, which forms a deep cutting between the two halves of Highgate Hill and can on occasion turn into a ferocious wind tunnel. To the left of the Archway Road is Highgate Hill. Near the foot of the hill, on the left-hand side, is the* **Whittington Stone.**

This marks the spot where, according to fairy tale, a dejected young Dick Whittington stopped on his way out of London and was persuaded to return by the chimes of the Bow Bells prophesying his rise to Lord Mayor (*see* pp.61–3 for a dissection of that myth and a commentary on the inscription on the stone). Highgate Hill was an obvious place for storytellers to set such a scene, since it was the site of the last toll-gate in London; the precise location a little way up the hill may have coincided with that of a medieval cross outside a leper's hospice (now superseded by the Whittington Hospital). Having been fortuitously picked as the location of a fairytale, Highgate has taken great pains to honour its famous would-be wayfarer. The stone has been replaced at least twice, has been adorned with a special railing and a lamp-post, and has acquired a statue representing Whittington's faithful cat.

> *The hill leads past the Jacobean mansion Cromwell House at No.106 (now the Ghana High Commission) up to Highgate High Street, a pleasant villagey row of shops and small cafés. To the left, shortly before Bisham Gardens, is a path leading into* **Waterlow Park**.

This little-known park affords, along with Kenwood House to the west, one of the best views over London. On a clear day you can see not only the skyscrapers of the City and the Docklands, but the woods and suburban jungle of south London. From here, London looks uncharacteristically romantic, an impression helped by the grandiose Victorian architecture of Highgate cemetery in the immediate foreground. Waterlow Park itself is pleasant, but remarkable only for its tennis courts and for Lauderdale House, a 16th-century mansion used as a summer residence by Charles II's mistress Nell Gwynne and now converted into an arts centre.

> *To reach the entrance to the cemetery, return to the High Street and turn right down the steep narrow hill called Swains Lane. At the bottom there are patches of gravel on either side of the road. To the right is the grand arched entrance to the western cemetery (open for guided tours only, usually every two hours during the afternoon, © 0181-340 1834; adm), and to the left is the more mundane iron grille leading to the eastern cemetery (open daily 10–5, closes at 4pm in the winter; free).*

Highgate Cemetery has been a tourist attraction ever since it opened in 1839, both for its magnificent funereal Victorian architecture and for its views. 'In such a place the aspect of death is softened,' wrote the *Lady's Newspaper* in 1850. The western side is the older and more splendid of the two halves, a maze of winding paths leading to an avenue of mock-Egyptian columns and obelisks, and a hemicycle of tombs around a cedar of Lebanon. Winding roads and footpaths lead up to the so-called Egyptian Avenue, which you enter through an arch flanked with obelisks and mock-Egyptian columns. The avenue leads beneath a bridge to the Circle of Lebanon, a complex of tombs constructed on each side of a circular path with a magnificent cedar tree in the middle. The spire of St Michael's parish church looms above at the top of Swain's Lane. The guide will point out the eminent dead occupying these hallowed tombs; they include the chemist Michael Faraday and the poet Christina Rossetti.

The eastern cemetery, which opened in 1857 to cope with the overload of coffins from across the road, is altogether wilder and spookier (it features in Bram Stoker's *Dracula*) where the cracked tombstones are covered in creepers and ivy. Here you can roam around at will. Most people head straight for the large black bust of Karl Marx marking the place where the much-maligned philosopher was buried in 1883. The bust, with its two inscriptions, was erected in 1956, the year when the crushing of the Hungarian uprising turned many western liberals off the whole idea of communism. The visitors have kept coming regardless, admiring the two epitaphs: 'Workers of the world unite' (from the *Communist Manifesto*) and 'The philosophers have only interpreted the world in different ways; the point, however, is to change it' (from the *Theses on Feuerbach*). The eastern cemetery contains a sprinkling of other left-wing revolutionaries, mainly from the Third World, plus the remains of novelist Mary Ann Evans (a.k.a. George Eliot) and the radical conservative thinker Herbert Spencer who died in 1903. The combination of Marx and Spencer has always seemed an odd one, but thanks to the department store chain of (almost) the same name it makes a good joke because it makes everybody think of cheap underwear and naff trousers.

> *Outside the centre of Highgate—and stretching away to the north and west—are a few other curiosities, which you might want to explore if you are staying in the area.*

At the north end of Highgate, up the hill from the Tube station, are two enchanting woods, Highgate Wood and Queen's Wood, relics of the forests that once covered the whole of north London. The road between the two woods leads up to Muswell Hill, a largely residential district with an enviably high position and a number of Greek delicatessens and other small shops. No. 23 Cranley Gardens in Muswell Hill was the site of some particularly gruesome murders in the early 1980s, uncovered after human body parts were found blocking the drains. It turned out that a 37-year-old civil servant called Dennis Nielsen was in the habit of picking up young men in pubs, luring them back home, strangling them and then decorating his flat with their mutilated corpses which he used to exercise his morbid fantasies.

The park at the northeastern end of Muswell Hill contains **Alexandra Palace**, originally the reconstructed hall from the ill-fated second Great Exhibition of 1862, but much rebuilt since because of fire. It is used as a cultural and sports centre, and has fine views over the north London townscape. Due east of Highgate is **Crouch End** (walk along Hornsey Lane or Shepherd's Hill), a rather nondescript-looking corner which nevertheless enjoys an infectious community atmosphere best characterized by the King's Head pub, where comedy shows in a downstairs room draw big crowds every weekend.

The most appealing direction to take from Highgate is undoubtedly westwards, towards...

Hampstead

Getting There/Around

Hampstead village is served by a Tube station on the other branch of the Northern Line from Highgate, as well as several buses including the 46 from King's Cross and Kentish Town. Hampstead Heath is accessible from ⊖ Hampstead, ⊖ Belsize Park and, at a stretch, ⊖ Tufnell Park. If you are coming from Highgate, the 210 bus takes you as far as the junction of Spaniards Road and North End Way.

In 1814 John James Park described Hampstead as 'a select, amicable, respectable and opulent neighbourhood'. So it has remained, a pretty hilltop village of Georgian rows and Victorian mansions, inhabited by wealthy if liberally inclined families and surrounded by the vast expanse of the Heath. Throughout its history, Hampstead has provided a refuge when life in the big city has become too much. Vast crowds gathered here in 1524 when the sages were predicting a great flood that would engulf the whole of London; there were similar scenes when the end of the world was deemed to be nigh in 1736. During the Great Plague of 1665, lawyers carried out their profession and slept rough under the trees of what is now called Judges Walk. Rural-minded folk forced to spend time in the capital have always enjoyed Hampstead as a good compromise between country and city. John Constable came here and painted some distant cityscapes that were barely distinguishable in tone from his great rural idylls. No wonder: the air is so pure and the Heath so big and wild you can easily feel you are lost in the deep heart of the English countryside.

Nowadays Hampstead has an unmistakable air of *established* comfort. Like Camden and Islington, it is full of lively restaurants, bars and theatres frequented by its well-off, generally left-wing and frequently Jewish residents. But in contrast to its north London neighbours there is no sense of the new or the fleeting. Hampstead, for all its liberal credentials, is a staid and remarkably conservative place. When the androgynous pop singer Boy George bought a house overlooking the Heath in the early 1980s, his neighbours never stopped complaining about the raggedy fans beating a path to his door in the hope of a glimpse of his dreadlocks and girly outfits. A few years later, there was a similar furore over a proposed McDonalds in the High Street. The burgers finally arrived, but in a much toned-down building without the customary golden arches.

Everything in Hampstead is carefully planned and lovingly looked after, from the window boxes in the Georgian houses on Holly Hill to the inverted white-on-black street signs. The dress code, for the most part, is one of effortless chic. There are a few Islington-esque scruffs, particularly around the Everyman cinema, but they are the exception to the rule. More common are the hordes of designer teenagers driving daddy's Porsche into the village in the early evening to hook up with their equally glamorous friends for a night on the town. There is a name for this peculiar species of humanity: they are called Becs—short for Rebecca which, Hampstead being a strongly Jewish area, is one of the more common girls' names around. This is an affectionate moniker, not a racist jibe, intended to tease the gilded youth of the area for their supreme self-confidence and considerable vanity.

Hampstead's saving grace is its sense of humour. Even if you meet an 18-year-old wearing Jean-Paul Gaultier and Ray-Bans, the chances are you will be able to strike up a conversation, and crack a few jokes, before someone more glamorous than yourself comes along to distract your friend's attention. Harmless flirtation is a strong element in Hampstead's social interaction. Hang around the Dome on the High Street of an afternoon and you could find yourself being charmed by a Jewish grande dame of 50, or a computer whizz just out of high school. You won't make friends for life, but you'll have a great conversation.

For the sake of imposing some kind of order on the general sprawl, the following section describes Hampstead as though you were arriving from Highgate, that is in a semi-circle from Kenwood down to Swiss Cottage, with the village somewhere in the middle.

Hampstead Lane, the link road between Highgate and Hampstead, is lined with opulent homes with large high-walled gardens. To the north, particularly down The Bishops Avenue and to the northwest towards Hampstead Garden Suburb, are some of the most expensive properties in London. Roughly opposite The Bishops Avenue is the secluded, winding entrance to **Kenwood House** *(open daily 10–6 April–Sept, closes earlier in the winter; free).*

The unpretentious atmosphere at Kenwood is a breath of fresh air after the stuffily earnest stately homes dotted around the rest of London. The location makes it: what with the expanse of the Heath rolling away to the south and its breathtaking views over Highgate and central London. Kenwood is famous for its summer concerts held by the lake at the bottom of the garden; the orchestra sits under a white awning and the audience watches from across the water.

The house itself dates back to 1616 but was given a near-total facelift by Robert Adam in the 1760s. He stuck on the white neoclassical façade, an elegantly simple affair in stucco adorned with slim pilasters, and reworked most of the interiors including the remarkable library with its elegant curved ceiling and fluted Corinthian columns. The pictures, bequeathed by Lord Iveagh who bought the house in 1925, are dotted around the main house and library extension; they include works by Rembrandt (a remarkable self-portrait), Vermeer (*The Guitar Player*), Van Dyck, Gainsborough, Guardi, Reynolds, Landseer and Turner.

> *The hill down from Kenwood leads to Highgate Ponds, a series of open-air pools segregated by sex to encourage nude bathing. The ladies' pool, discreetly hidden behind some thick bushes, is nearest the top just off Millfield Lane; the men's pools are alongside the path nearer Highgate Road. Right down at the bottom of the Heath, should you stray that far, is* **Parliament Hill***, site of an ancient barrow where the rebel queen Boudicca is rumoured to have been buried. The view from the hill, no more than a bump compared to the heights of Kenwood, is rather disappointing, but the wind the site attracts is ideal for kite-flying. If you want to see Hampstead itself, rather than just the Heath, you might do better to stay up at the Kenwood end. Returning to Hampstead Lane, the road curves round and narrows beside a famous tavern,* **Spaniards Inn***.*

This 16th-century inn, named after two Spanish proprietors who killed each other in a duel, owes its fame to the 18th-century highwayman Dick Turpin who used to stop for drinks here in between coach hold-ups. During the Gordon Riots of 1780, a group of mobsters dropped by on their way to Kenwood, then belonging to the Lord Chancellor Lord Mansfield, which they intended to destroy. The publican offered the rioters pint after pint of free beer as an inducement to stay out of trouble. Soon the men weren't in a fit state to walk to Kenwood, let alone burn it down, and when the army arrived they were disarmed without incident. You can see their muskets hanging on the wall in the saloon bar.

> *At this point, Hampstead Lane becomes Spaniards Rd. At the junction with North End Way there is a roundabout and Whitestone Pond, and just beyond another famous pub called* **Jack Straw's Castle***, named after one of the ringleaders of the Peasants' Revolt of 1381 who is said to have taken refuge here before being caught and executed. The present building is an unimpressive fake castle erected in 1964. Just beyond the pub, North End Way becomes Heath St and you enter* **Hampstead** *proper.*

The real pleasure of Hampstead village is in getting lost in the winding dead-end backstreets lined with Georgian houses and backed by woodland. From the pond, Lower Terrace takes you past the entrance to **Judges Walk**, the legendary 'substitute' law court of the Great Plague which is now just a driveway to a couple of tumbledown houses. A little further down to the left is **Admiral's Walk**, which contains a splendid Georgian house with multi-levelled rooms and balconies, where at various times the novelist John Galsworthy and the architect George Gilbert Scott have taken up residence. Admiral's House was named after Admiral Matthew Barton, who for a long time was wrongly assumed to have fired salutes on special occasions from the improvised quarter-deck on the roof. In fact Barton never lived here. At the other end of Admiral's Walk, Hampstead Grove takes you down to **Fenton House**, a splendid brick mansion dating from 1693 (*closed for conservation work until March 1998, then open weekend afternoons all year, plus some weekdays in the summer, adm; check opening times on © 0171-435 3471*). Aside from the elegant rooms and fine garden, the house has collections of early keyboard instruments and fine porcelain.

At the bottom of Hampstead Grove, the narrow road up to the left is **Hollybush Hill**, a cul-de-sac lined with beautiful small houses including the 17th-century Hollybush pub, so called because landlords used to hang a bush outside their door to advertise their wine and beer. Just after the pub is a steep staircase plunging down towards Heath Street. Better, however, to retrace your steps and head down Holly Walk, another delightful cobbled path flanked by fine houses and a small flower-filled cemetery. At the bottom of the hill is **St John's**, an attractive 18th-century church with a tall tower and, inside, a balustraded gallery and a bust of Keats beside the lectern. Constable is buried in the churchyard. The road from the church back to Heath Street, called **Church Row**, is one of the most elegant lines of Georgian housing in London, with large, shimmering bay windows, discreetly decorated red-brick façades and ornate wrought-iron frontings.

Heath Street is one of two Hampstead thoroughfares lined with fine shops, delicatessens, cafés and restaurants. The other, the High Street, can be reached through Oriel Passage, which has an old oak tree growing in a minuscule patch of ground halfway along. Cross the High Street and you come into **Flask Walk** with its second-hand bookshops, elegant restaurants with hand-written menus, and posh tea merchant Keith Fawkes. Along with its continuation Well Walk, this is where fashionable folk came to take the Hampstead spa waters back in the 18th century. Flask Walk opens out and arrives eventually at New End Square, dominated by rather forbidding Victorian houses with their thick high walls and terracotta turrets. Turning left up the hill at New End Square, you come to **Burgh House**, a fine Queen Anne house lost in a fantastical growth of climbing plants. It houses the local history museum (*open Wed–Sun 12noon–5; free*). Mostly the exhibitions dwell on Hampstead's famous residents, including Constable, Keats and the artist Stanley Spencer. There is a friendly café in the basement.

> *Continue up the hill and you return to Heath St (the Tube station is then a few steps to the left). Before leaving Hampstead, though, you might want to visit two well-known houses a little way outside the village, one the*

former residence of John Keats, the other the last dwelling of Sigmund Freud before his death in 1939. **Keats' House** *(℗ 0171-435 2062; open April–Oct Mon–Fri 10–1 and 2–6, Sat 10–1 and 2–5 and Sun 2–5, and Nov–Mar Mon–Fri 1–5, Sat 10–1 and 2–5, and Sun 2–5; free) is in Keats' Grove, which you can reach by walking down Hampstead High St and its continuation Rosslyn Hill, then turning off of Downshire Hill and taking the first right.*

The main attraction is the plum tree in the garden, under which Keats wrote *Ode to a Nightingale* in 1819 (if you think the tree looks a bit young, you are right; it is a replacement). The house, called Wentworth Place and completed in 1816, was in Keats's time split into two halves. In all, Keats spent only two years here as a lodger of Charles Armitage Brown, a literary critic specializing in Shakespeare's sonnets. It was nevertheless an eventful time. He produced some of his best and most famous work, fell in love with Fanny Brawne who lived in the other half of the house, and contracted the consumption that was to kill him two years later at the age of 25. The house's attractions are admittedly somewhat limited. Keats used one living room downstairs and one bedroom upstairs. Memorabilia have nevertheless been strewn in every room; these include a lock of Keats' hair and some of his manuscripts and books.

The **Freud Museum** *(open Wed–Sun 12noon–5; adm) is a little further away, at 20 Maresfield Gardens. Walk down Fitzjohn's Avenue (the continuation of Heath St) and you will find it one block over to the right. If you come by Underground, then* ⊖ *Swiss Cottage is your stop.*

This is the house where Freud set up his last home after fleeing the Nazis in Vienna in 1938. Six rooms have been left untouched since the founder of psychoanalysis died of throat cancer on the eve of the Second World War. Of greatest interest is the couch where his patients lay during sessions—if, that is, it is not on loan to another museum. You can also see Freud's collections of furniture and artefacts, including some extraordinary phalluses, and watch the home movies he made of his family and dog at home in Vienna in the increasingly dark days of the 1930s.

West London

Little Venice and Bayswater

Getting There/Around

The nearest Tube station to Little Venice is ⊖ Warwick Avenue. Other useful stops in the district are ⊖ Paddington, ⊖ Lancaster Gate, ⊖ Queensway and ⊖ Bayswater. The 15 bus runs from Trafalgar Square to Paddington and on to Westbourne Grove, while the 12 and 94 run along the Bayswater Rd from Oxford St. If you want to reach Little Venice by boat from Camden or Regent's Park, call the London Waterbus Company on © 0171-482 2550.

Little Venice is an unexpectedly tranquil and atmospheric corner of London, an area of tree-lined streets, understated Victorian town houses and, above all, the canal with its colourful array of houseboats. The best way to explore it is to walk down the towpath from Regent's Park through the lower end of St John's Wood. The most colourful area is around Blomfield Road and Maida Avenue, where pretty iron bridges cross the canal. The entrepreneur and one-time hippie Richard Branson, founder of the Virgin empire, has a floating home here, along with many other Londoners who can't face the hassle of landlords, mortgage lenders and conveyancing. By all accounts, the biggest problem with the neighbours is not noise or squatting so much as making sure they don't dump the contents of their toilets into the canal.

From here it is a short walk to **Bayswater**, another Victorian-era residential area which may be of immediate interest as there is a good chance you will be staying there. There are some elegant stuccoed houses overlooking Hyde Park and on Gloucester Terrace, plus a few quiet backstreets and attractive pastel-painted mews, some of which are still used to stable horses for rides in Hyde Park. The area has a few oddities, too. The railings on the Hyde Park side of Bayswater Road are used every Sunday afternoon to display cheap paintings. What was once Christ Church in Lancaster Gate has been converted into a block of flats. The church was deconsecrated in 1978 because of the risk of structural collapse; you can still make out its spire and part of the nave on the outside of the concrete and glass redevelopment. Just around the corner in Leinster Gardens, you'll notice that the windows and front door of Nos.23–24 are painted on. To find out why, walk through the passage to Porchester Gardens and look at the building from the back: it is only a façade, put up to conceal the emerging Circle Line underground tunnel. Also nearby, at 21–23 Craven Hill Terrace, is the **London Toy and Model Museum** (*open daily 9–5.30; adm*), a diverting collection of toys from 1850 to the present, including model trains and cars, giant dolls' houses and teddy bears. There are toy train rides and a carousel in the garden. Recommended for children.

Notting Hill and Portobello Market

Getting There/Around

➊ Notting Hill is the most useful reference point for the neighbourhood, although ➊ Ladbroke Grove or ➊ Westbourne Park might be useful if you end up at the top end of Portobello market. The 12 and 94 buses come down Bayswater Rd, and the 94 continues towards Shepherd's Bush. The 15 goes down Westbourne Grove and across Portobello Rd, while the 27 and 31 both wend their way through the back streets towards Camden.

Notting Hill conjures up many images: of antiques dealers on the southern end of Portobello Road pulling a fast one on unsuspecting tourists; of young Caribbeans dancing in the streets during the annual carnival; of arty types standing in line outside the Gate cinema; of young people riffling through second-hand records and cheap jewellery underneath the A40 flyover; of Moroccans and Portuguese jabbering away in the ethnic cafés of Golbourne Road; of affluent professional families relaxing in their large gardens in Stanley Crescent or Lansdowne Rise. To say Notting Hill is a melting pot is both a cliché and an understatement. It has been an emblem of multicultural London ever since the big immigrant waves from the Caribbean in the 1950s.

Once considered irredeemably out of fashion, Notting Hill is now so hip with the liberal middle classes that it risks becoming as exclusive as the posh villas on Campden Hill on the south side of the main road. A rapid period of gentrification in the 1980s smartened things up—the once-thriving drug culture, in particular, has waned into insignificance—but it has also created barriers of class and status that the neighbourhood had always previously sought to break down. The motorway flyover has created a neat divide between the spruced-up pastel-painted Victorian houses to the south (Notting Hill proper), and the high-rise 1960s council estates to the north (dismissively described as North Kensington). Just a few years ago the contrast was nowhere near as stark. All Saints Road, for example, was once a run-down stub of a street throbbing to a reggae beat and reeking of dope. Now it is all fresh paint, trendy Middle Eastern food and bicycle shops.

The area derives its name from the Danish King Knutt, who built an encampment in the district around AD 700. For centuries Knottynghull was nothing more than fields and gravel pits, and as late as 1849 the cows outnumbered the humans three to one. In the late 1870s, the Victorians decided to make it 'the centre of a new prosperous and refined district', building a hippodrome to attract residents. But for some reason the place did not catch on and by the end of the 19th century it was considered distinctly passé. After the Second World War it was, like Soho and Brixton, a rundown inner-city area where immigrants could find plenty of cheap housing. Notting Hill became a mini-Caribbean, a fresh and exotic antidote to the sleepy calm of most of London's Victorian suburbs. The area features prominently in Colin MacInnes's London Trilogy; in *Absolute Beginners*, the Ladbroke Grove area is nicknamed Napoli because it seems so strange, chaotic and exciting.

MacInnes's book gives a potent description of the racial tensions and the eventual explosion of violence witnessed during the summers of 1957 and 1958. Thereafter, local community leaders resolved to put on an annual show to vaunt the attractions of their Caribbean culture, and by the mid-1960s the Notting Hill Carnival, held on the last weekend in August, had become a permanent fixture. For two days each year, on the Sunday and Bank Holiday Monday, the streets throb with steel bands and soca music. The crowds sway giddily to the conga while balancing glasses of Jamaican draft stout and getting pleasantly high on some choice Caribbean weed. Everywhere is the tangy smell of saltfish, goat curry, fried plantain and patties. It is not always a peaceful affair. Relations between residents and police are tense at the best of times, and every few years that tension spills out at the carnival. Either the police will do something stupid, like drag an abusive drunk by his hair down a street, or else the crowd will vastly overreact to, say, the routine arrest of a car radio thief. Many of the middle-class residents of Notting Hill pack up the family Volvo and motor the hell out on Carnival weekend—not exactly eloquent testimony to their liberal credentials, but there you are. The impeccably liberal newspaper the *Guardian* once described the carnival as an 'all-singing, all-dancing Benetton advert viewed through a haze of marijuana', and included in its list of things to expect 'the contents of someone else's pitta bread dribbled down your back in the crush; vegetarian samosas embedded in the soles of your shoes; and a bassline that will reverberate through your ribcage for days'. The carnival is something you will either love or hate.

> *Most visitors pile out of* ⊖ *Notting Hill and head straight for Portobello Market. It's worth dallying for a while, though, to look at the pretty mews-style houses on Uxbridge St and Hillgate St behind the Gate cinema, and to head up Campden Hill to peek through the box hedges at the grandiose properties overlooking Holland Park.*

This is one of the most attractive residential areas in London, especially in the springtime when the small private gardens and trees are in bloom. It is also dotted with good restaurants and pubs like the Uxbridge Arms and Malabar on Uxbridge Street. There is some fine housing on the north side of the main road, too. Walk up Pembridge Road, with its excellent second-hand record stores and cheap restaurants, and turn off to the left at the mini-roundabout up Kensington Park Road. To the left, one attractive residential park succeeds another—Ladbroke Square Gardens, Kensington Park Gardens, Stanley Gardens (with a particularly imposing tall white house at the end) and Arundel Gardens.

> *Turn right on the corner of Westbourne Grove and stroll past the rows of antique shops. One block over from Kensington Park Rd is **Portobello Road**, one of the most atmospheric market streets in London.*

Westbourne Grove forms a neat dividing line between the touristy antiques market, which takes place on Saturdays (7am–5.30pm) at the southern end of Portobello Road towards Notting Hill, and the rather shabbier furniture, food, jewellery, cheap records, books, postcards and funky bric-à-brac on sale down towards the flyover and beyond (the fruit and vegetable market is open Mon–Sat till 5pm with early closing at 1pm on Thurs). The whole street offers a view on to a tight-knit, unspoiled and resolutely individual local community where anything goes, and usually does. Anybody in London who has had any silver stolen goes to the silver market just north of Westbourne Grove on Saturday mornings to see if their wares have turned up there. Further down the street, there is a Spanish delicatessen, an Italian delicatessen and plenty of Caribbean stallholders among the very English fruit and veg sellers. You'll find headbangers, potheads and Dead Heads at record stores like Intoxica or Rough Trade on Talbot Road. Mingling among these counter-culture vultures are smarter, more self-conscious types on their way to the Travel Bookshop on Blenheim Crescent. Broadly speaking, the crowd gets more unorthodox and eclectic the further down the street you go. Under the flyover is a bric-à-brac and cheap clothes market, as well as a vegetarian café and an indoor arcade packed with home-crafted jewellery. Further north, among the ugly modern brick housing estates, you stumble across small art dealers, the excellent jazz shop Honest Jon's and the Spanish restaurant Galicia. Finally, off to the right is Golborne Road, a bustling short street divided between Portuguese and Moroccan communities. Each has its own cafés and restaurants; the Lisboa, with its home-made pastries and pavement seating, is particularly recommended and well worth seeking out.

The Iberian connection goes back to the 18th century, when a local farm named itself after a town in the Gulf of Mexico, Porto Bello, taken from the Spaniards by the British army under General Vernon in 1739. The Portobello Road was then no more than a track leading to the farm. The market arrived in the 1870s, when gypsies came to sell horses for the nearby hippodrome, but it did not boom until after the Second World War when the Caledonian antiques market in Islington closed. Nowadays Portobello is not only friendly but chatty too. Quite a change from 1928, when George Orwell lived at No.10 and was astonished to discover that his landlady had never spoken to her neighbours for fear of seeming over-familiar.

> *From the top of Portobello Rd, it is a 10-minute walk to one of the neighbourhood's great curiosities, **Kensal Green Cemetery** (open Mon–Sat 9am–dusk, Sun 10am–dusk). Walk up Ladbroke Grove (one block, or at most two, across to the left from Portobello) and turn left after the canal into Harrow Rd. The cemetery entrance, an imposing Doric arch, is opposite Kensal Green Underground and railway station.*

The Victorians dealt with death the same way that they dealt with anything that made them nervous: they turned it into a grand enterprise to the greater glory of God, art and human endeavour, and made sure they made a fast buck while they were about it. Already by the 1820s, the small established burial grounds in the centre of London had become woefully inadequate to cope with the city's mushrooming population. The bodies in the old graveyards were so closely packed and so close to the surface that they constituted a serious health hazard. So in 1830 the General Cemetery Company was founded, setting aside seven vast tracts of land on the outskirts of the city which it proceeded to turn into highly profitable commercial enterprises known, in delightfully euphemistic parlance, as 'gardens of the deceased'. Highgate Cemetery (*see* p.397) was one such concern; of the others, Kensal Green was undoubtedly the most popular, partly for its snob value as a celebrity cemetery and partly for its extraordinary Greek Revival architecture.

The large entrance arch frames an avenue leading to the Anglican Chapel, itself adorned with Doric pillars and colonnades. The chapel stands atop a layered cake of underground burial chambers, some of which used to be served by a hydraulic lift. Around the rest of the cemetery are extraordinary testimonies to 19th-century delusions of grandeur: vast ornate tombs worthy of the Pharaohs, decorated with statues, incidental pillars and arches. What made Kensal Green such a hit was a decision by the Duke of Sussex, youngest brother of George IV, to eschew royal protocol and have himself buried among the people, so to speak. Eminent fellow-occupants include Thackeray, Trollope, Wilkie Collins, Leigh Hunt and the father and son engineering duo Marc and Isambard Kingdom Brunel.

Kensington

Getting There/Around

The best Underground stations for the chunk of Kensington described below are Holland Park, High St Kensington and Earl's Court. The 31 bus goes along Kensington Church St from Notting Hill on its way down to Earl's Court; otherwise, the 9 (for Piccadilly Circus and the Strand), 10 (for Oxford St) and 52 (for Victoria) all come along Kensington High St.

Kensington has a rather posh ring to it, suggesting rich dowagers, expensive boutiques and diplomats in well-appointed Victorian mansions. But the geographical area that can lay claim to the name Kensington is far too big to be compartmentalized so easily. In theory it stretches all the way up to Kensal Green and out west as far as Shepherd's Bush, encompassing a huge variety of people and lifestyles. The poshest, most familiar part known as South Kensington, stretching from Knightsbridge to Kensington Palace, is largely explored in Walk X; what was left out there, the bit between Cromwell Road and the Old Brompton Road, is a strangely soulless if occasionally pretty suburb of stuccoed Victorian houses and small gardens populated in the main by brash Euro-yuppies working in the City. What follows is a description of Kensington's varied and distinctive centre, starting with the magic of Holland Park, past the trendy but refreshingly unpretentious shops of the High Street, and finishing up in the dog-eared whirl of Earl's Court.

*The best way to enter **Holland Park** (open daily 7.30am until half an hour before sunset) is through the wooded northern end. Take Holland Walk, a path opposite the Underground station, and look out for the first turning into the park, which is on the right after about 300 yards.*

Holland Park turns reality on its head: it seems much bigger, much wilder, much more remote than it really is. Covering only about 40 acres (a fraction of the size of Kensington Gardens, for example), it feels like something out of a magical children's story, a maze of winding paths, wooded hideaways, rolling fields and formal gardens, wild flowers, birds and even the odd peacock. The park is what remains of the estate of Holland House, a grand Jacobean mansion devastated beyond recognition during the Second World War, which survives only in truncated form, about two-thirds of the way down towards Kensington High Street.

Originally the house, built in 1606, was called Cope Castle after its first patron Sir Walter Cope, who was minister in charge of King James I's finances. Its profusion of turrets, gables and stone arcades made little impression on the king, who complained of terrible drafts keeping him awake at night when he came to stay. The house passed into the Holland family in 1624, and remained with them until financial problems and a dearth of male heirs caused them to give it up at the end of the 19th century. Its heyday was undoubtedly under the third Baron Holland (1773–1840), who along with his redoubtable wife turned it into a salon for liberal political thinkers. Regular guests included Richard Sheridan, Sydney Smith, Lord Byron, William Wordsworth, Walter Scott, Lord Palmerston, Charles Dickens and Thomas Babington Macaulay. The Hollands were generous hosts, but not averse to speaking their minds. 'Poets inclined to a plethora of vanity,' wrote the Irish scribbler Thomas Moore, 'would find a dose of Lady Holland now and then very good for their complaint.' The Hollands were also ardent supporters of Napoleon, whom they met in 1802 and stuck by even after the Duke of Wellington beat him at Waterloo; in delightfully English fashion, they sent him pots of plum jam to keep him going during his exile on Elba.

After the third Baron's death in 1840, the house went into a slow decline as the last of the Hollands allowed property developers to nibble at the edges of the estate. It was taken over after the Second World War by the municipal authorities, who preserved what they could of the house and opened the park to the public. You can see some of the ground-floor stonework of the original building, but little else. The east wing has been entirely rebuilt as a youth hostel (a wonderful place to stay if you are a student), while part of the ruined main house has been converted into an open-air theatre with an eclectic summer season of plays, concerts and opera. Around the house to the north is a series of formal gardens, including the peaceful Kyoto Garden with its still lake and lawns lined with gentle blooms. On the south side is a terrace café overlooking a cricket pitch and tennis courts—you may recognise this as the place where David Hemmings played metaphysical tennis with a group of mime artists at the end of Antonioni's *Blow Up*.

> *The tent-like building at the bottom of the park is the* **Commonwealth Institute** *(open daily 10–5; adm; © 0171-371 3530).*

The shimmering green hyperboloid roof, made of Zambian copper, is only the first of many surprises at this highly imaginative cultural centre celebrating the diversity and imagination of Britain's former colonies, now grouped together as the Commonwealth. There are three floors of galleries, each dealing with a different country, where you can pluck a sitar, sit on a snowmobile or watch a model demonstrating the digestive system of a New Zealand cow. Children love it. The Institute also has a lively programme of lectures, concerts and art exhibitions; a shop jam-packed with craft work; and a restaurant offering indigenous dishes from around the Commonwealth. A new 'interactive' attraction called The Commonwealth Experience is a vertiginous and quite scary simulated helicopter ride over rather a more visible Malaysia than in real life.

> *Outside the Institute, turn right, passing a Victorian-era hexagonal red letter box, and then right again into Melbury Rd, then left into Holland Park Rd where at No.12 you will find the wondrous* **Leighton House** *(open Mon–Sat 11–5.30; free).*

This apparently straightforward redbrick house opens into a grand extravaganza of escapist late Victorian interior design. Lord Leighton, one of the Pre-Raphaelite painters, used his imagination, his not inconsiderable funds, and the inspiration of a number of friends to create an astonishing if totally over-the-top Oriental palace here in his London home. The highlight is undoubtedly the Arab Hall, completed some 14 years after the rest of the house in 1879, which has a stained-glass cupola, a fountain spurting out of the richly decorated mosaic floor and glorious painted floral tiles which Leighton and his friends picked up in Rhodes, Cairo and Damascus. Dotted around the downstairs reception rooms, among the paintings of Leighton and his contemporaries Millais and Burne-Jones, are highly ornate details including Cairene lattice-work alcoves and marble columns decorated in burnished gold. This house is the Victorian dream of Oriental exotica made flesh, a recreation of the Arabian Nights in grey northern Europe. One wonders what it would have been like to live in: even Lord Leighton's studio has a gilded dome above its broad north-facing windows.

> *Another curious house is at 18 Stafford Terrace, two streets up on the other side of Holland Park. It is **Linley Sambourne House** (open March–Oct only, Wed 10–4 and Sun 2–5; adm).*

This was the home of Edward Linley Sambourne, a cartoonist for the magazine *Punch* in the late Victorian and Edwardian period, and a more typical if still opulent example of middle-class living of the time. The rooms are a-clutter with furniture, thick velvet drapes, portraits and prints (including much of Linley Sambourne's own work), William Morris carpets and wallpaper, lamps, vases, china, clocks and the odd stained-glass window. The sheer sense of accumulation speaks volumes about the owners' late Victorian mentality. With all these objects piled up everywhere, every step around the house has to be discreet and perfectly controlled. You can't imagine anyone relaxing for a minute.

> *Return to **Kensington High St** and turn left for the best of the shops.*

This is a really fun place to shop, and not that expensive either. At the western end of the High Street are some fairly standard clothes and shoe shops, but also a large branch of the booksellers Waterstones and the delightful children's store, the Early Learning Centre. Around the Underground station are trendier clothes shops, notably the discount designer emporium Hype DF and, almost directly opposite, the bazaar-like Kensington Market. For antiques, look around the lower end of Kensington Church Street and the cobbled passage, Church Walk, that snakes behind the Victorian-era St Mary Abbots. Some of the houses in the backstreets are quite imposing, particularly up towards Campden Hill and Notting Hill. In the other direction, just to the south of the junction of the High St and Kensington Church St, is Kensington Square, which was first laid out in 1685 and still has a few early 18th-century houses (Nos.11 and 12, for example). The square was a big artistic haunt in the 19th century, attracting the likes of Burne-Jones and the philosopher John Stuart Mill.

> *The area to the south of Kensington High St is largely residential—houses either redbrick or stucco, and not very interesting. Things liven up a bit, though, at the bottom end of the district, known as **Earl's Court** (get there by taking a bus or else walking down the Earl's Court Rd opposite the Commonwealth Institute).*

Earl's Court was named after the Earls of Warwick and Holland who had courthouses here in the 16th century. The village suburb was famous for its luxuriant fruit gardens and stayed mainly rural until the 1870s, when tall genteel houses built for wealthy London traders and importers began to spread with vegetable speed down Earl's Court Road. To most Londoners today Earl's Court means The Exhibition Centre, with its shows devoted to Ideal Homes and military parades. More curious, though, is Earl's Court's present-day population of tourists, short-term American visitors and other waifs and strays who give the area a transient and oddly exhilarating feel. Earl's Court has been variously nicknamed the Bedsit Jungle and, because of the large number of Australians around the place, Kangaroo Valley. You'll see backpackers and ageing hippies sitting in the small cafés, and street sellers brandishing copies of the Antipodean ex-pat magazine *TNT*. Earl's Court also used to be the centre of London's gay community—it boasted more late-opening bars and clubs than any other part of town, and until his death Freddie Mercury lived in the vicinity at 1 Logan Place. The relaxing of the licensing laws in the late 1980s brought about a decline in the area's fortunes, however, as the trendies moved away to Soho and elsewhere. Earl's Court—though not worth going out of your way for—nevertheless remains a quirky sort of place to stroll around or spend a quiet afternoon.

Belgravia and Victoria

Getting There/Around

Victoria Underground, bus and railway stations serve as much of the area as you are likely to want to see.

The chunk of residential London that runs from Knightsbridge down to Victoria station is known as Belgravia, a large estate of sumptuous stuccoed houses and large squares. It has featured heavily on the social agenda of London's moneyed classes ever since it was built in the first half of the 19th century, but it is all pomp and very little circumstance. Almost all the architecture between Belgrave Square and the river at Pimlico was the work of one man, Thomas Cubitt, who lost no opportunity to turn this promising area of residential London into a veritable savannah of blandness. The Victorians already hated it, calling it insipid and tawdry and giving it the disparaging nickname Cubittopolis. In the 20th century, Pimlico inspired such indifference that it turned briefly into slumland. Now the area is the domain of foreign embassies and generally worth avoiding.

You are almost bound to gravitate at some point towards Victoria Station, however, and if so you should take 10 minutes to look at London's main Roman Catholic church just off Victoria Street. **Westminster Cathedral** is a striking confection of red brick and Portland stone built according to the Byzantine style of the early Christians even though the exterior was completed in 1903. Catholicism had a long, hard road to travel to reach acceptability in Britain, and even after the appointment of the first Cardinal Archbishop of London in 1850 it was not easy to raise the funds needed to build an appropriate central place of worship. In the end, the church fathers decided to build the outside first, and leave the cost of furnishing the interior to future generations. Hence the curious effect of the interior, which is highly ornate in some places and virtually bare in others, an effect accentuated by its vast proportions—360ft long and 156ft wide (the widest nave in Britain). The sumptuous green marble pillars in the nave were cut from the same stone as the 6th-century basilica of St Sophia in Istanbul; it took two years to bring the stone to London because of a little local difficulty with the Turkish army in deepest Thessaly. Among the other features are a series of bas-reliefs in the nave by Eric Gill of the 14 Stations of the Cross, a 15th-century alabaster statue of the Virgin and Child brought over from France by an anonymous donor, a marble pulpit, and a huge *baldacchino* inlaid with mosaics, which stands on eight pillars made of yellow Veronese marble. The organ is unique because of its dual control system, which allows it to be played at either end of the cathedral. In 1903 it played a key part in the somewhat disastrous première of Edward Elgar's oratorio *The Dream of Gerontius*, based on a poem by the English Catholic reformer Cardinal Newman.

From Victoria to Sloane Square you cross more bland Cubitt buildings in Eaton Square. This is now the end of Belgravia and the beginning of ...

Chelsea

Getting There/Around

Sloane Square is your key Tube station in an area not particularly well-served by the Underground. The 137a bus heads down Chelsea Bridge Rd, while the 19 and 239 go down the King's Rd as far as Beaufort St before turning left past Cheyne Walk and across Battersea Bridge.

Chelsea was an attractive riverside community long before it was ever integrated into greater London. The humanist and martyr Thomas More made the district fashionable by moving here in the 1520s, and soon every courtier worth his salt, even Henry VIII himself, was building a house near his. The attractions of this 'village of palaces' were obvious: close to Westminster and only a short boat-ride away from the City, and yet at the same time safely concealed from the general hubbub behind a large bend in the river. By the mid-19th century, Chelsea had turned into a bustling little village of intellectuals, artists, aesthetes and writers as well as war veterans—the so-called Chelsea pensioners who lived in the Royal Hospital built by Christopher Wren for Charles II.

The almost rural calm of the district was shattered in the late 19th century, when big, brash building developments began to crowd out the intimate townhouses of Cheyne Walk and the streets just behind the river. The construction of the Chelsea Embankment in 1871–4 was particularly damaging, a disruption only exacerbated once motor cars began racing down from Earl's Court and Fulham to Westminster and the West End. As a result, Chelsea in the first half of the 20th century turned into little more than an annexe of South Kensington—a little more classy perhaps, a little more established, but just as snobbish and sterile. In the 1950s and 1960s, it became the refuge of the dying aristocracy, as films like Joseph Losey's *The Servant* (shot in Royal Avenue) showed to withering effect. In the 1980s, the sons and daughters of these last-ditch aristos mutated into a particularly underwhelming social animal known as the Sloane Ranger—a special kind of upper-class twit with deeply misguided delusions about being trendy. Male Sloanes wore corduroy trousers, striped shirts and tweed jackets, while the female of the species went in for frilly white shirts and pearls. During the week they lived off daddy's allowance and threw food around in chic neighbourhood restaurants; at weekends they all put on their wellies and Barbour jackets and decamped to the country for a spot of polo or shooting. The pre-marital Princess Diana was the prototype Sloane Ranger—giggly, not very bright and constantly on the phone to girlfriends called Amanda, Henrietta or Caroline to discuss their quest for the Ideal Husband.

Chelsea's artistic streak never entirely disappeared, however, and in the 1960s and early 1970s it flourished with a vengeance along the **King's Road**. Like Carnaby Street in Soho, the King's Road let its hair down and filled with cafés and fashion shops selling mini-skirts and cheap jewellery. Old-fashioned shops, including the delightfully named toilet-maker Thomas Crapper, were superseded by the likes of Terence Conran, who opened his first household store Habitat on the King's Road as a direct challenge to the fusty, old-fashioned goods then on sale at Peter Jones on Sloane Square. The Royal Court Theatre, opposite Peter Jones, came into its own as a venue for avant-garde writers like John Osborne (the original Angry Young Man), Edward Bond and Arnold Wesker. Mods, later replaced by punks, set the fashion tone for whole generations of young people.

Nowadays, the punks have pathos. Only a few exist—and one suspects that they are paid to patrol the Kings Road by some dubious Conan Doyle-type character in the tourist board. Meanwhile most of the boutiques have either gone upmarket or been replaced by generic highstreet chainstores. Some of the1960s spirit lives on, however, in the delightfully sprawling antiques markets on the south side of the road: Antiquarius at No.137, the Chenil Galleries at No.181–3 and the Chelsea Antiques Market at No.253. You might also want to take a look at the Chelsea Farmer's Market, with its cafés and craft shops just off the King's Road on Sydney

Street. Terence Conran has not abandoned the district either, expanding his restaurant empire with one knock-out location after another. A couple of blocks north of here, on the restaurant-lined Fulham Road, is the remarkable Art Nouveau **Michelin Building** (at No.61), which he renovated in the 1980s complete with glass cupolas and car-themed mosaics to create offices, a Conran Shop and the Bibendum restaurant.

> *The heart of old Chelsea is down by the river. Either take the bus down as far as Battersea Bridge, or else walk down Old Church St (a little beyond Sydney St and on the other side of the King's Rd) until you reach the waterfront.*

Just to the left of the bridge is **Chelsea Old Church**, which preserves the memory of Sir Thomas More, author of the humanist tract *Utopia* and the first man to lose his head for standing up to Henry VIII over his break with the Pope. The church's history goes back to Norman times, but most of it was rebuilt in classical style in the 17th century. The best-known, and oldest surviving, part is the south chapel which More built in 1528 for his own private use. In the sanctuary is a monument to More as well as a tomb containing the remains of his first wife. He originally intended to be buried here himself, as the inscription on his monument testifies, but after his execution his head was eventually buried at Canterbury Cathedral.

Outside the church is a statue of More in glorious technicolour (it was sculpted in 1969), sitting in his Lord Chancellor's robes and gazing piously across the river towards Battersea. The churchyard has been converted into a small park called Roper Gardens (after More's daughter Margaret Roper, and her husband William). The remains of one of More's properties, **Crosby Hall** (*open Mon–Sat 10–12noon and 2.15–5, Sun 2.15–5 only; free*), stands a few steps to the west, at the bottom of Danvers Street, although in More's time it was in quite a different location. It was built in the 15th century for a rich grocer in Bishopsgate in the City; the remains were moved inside this mock-Tudor building in 1927. The main hall still contains the original hammerbeam roof and oriel windows, plus a portrait by Holbein of More and his family.

Stretching to the east, just behind the Chelsea Embankment, are the delightful 18th-century brick houses of **Cheyne Walk**, one of London's most fashionable addresses for the past 200 years. Amongst the famous residents have been George Eliot, who died at No.4; Henry James, who spent the latter years of his life in Carlyle Mansions, a Victorian house standing just beyond the King's Head and Eight Bells pub; Whistler, who was living at No.101 when he produced some of his most extraordinary paintings of the Thames (*see* p.121); the writer of children's cautionary tales, Hilaire Belloc, at No.104; and Turner, himself no mean painter of the Thames, who used No.119 as a retreat where he lived under the pseudonym

Admiral or 'Puggy' Booth. The Queen's House at No.16 was shared during the 1860s by a trio of poets, Dante Gabriel Rossetti, Algernon Swinburne and George Meredith, who kept a whole bestiary of animals including some noisy peacocks that upset the neighbours no end.

The most interesting address, however, is 24 Cheyne Row just around the corner: **Carlyle's House** (*open Apr–Oct, Wed–Sun 11–4.30; adm*). Few houses in London evoke such a strong sense of period or personality as this redbrick Queen Anne building, where the historian Thomas Carlyle, author of *The French Revolution* and *Frederick the Great*, lived with his wife from 1834 until his death in 1881. It has been kept almost exactly as the Carlyles left it. Even the old man's hat still hangs on the peg in the entrance way. What strikes you about the place is how extraordinarily impractical it must have been. The staircases and corridors were horribly dark—an effect enhanced by the fact that electricity has never been installed—and Carlyle's study was a small windowless room at the top of the house which he tried unsuccessfully at one stage to soundproof. There was no running water on the upper floors, only a hand pump and a system of pulleys to bring buckets up. One imagines the couple, and Jane Carlyle in particular, being sticklers for cleanliness, hard work and thrift. Jane in fact was so strict that when Carlyle's friend Lord Tennyson came to call the two men had to smoke under the chimney so the smell would not offend her nostrils. By all accounts the couple had appalling rows; Jane was given to fits of jealousy and Carlyle, modern historians believe, may have been impotent.

> At the end of Cheyne Walk is the **Chelsea Physic Garden**, which you have to enter from the back on Swan Walk (*open April–Oct Wed 2–5 and Sun 2–6; adm*).

This wonderfully unusual garden of rare trees, plants, herbs and seeds has a history stretching back to 1676 when it was founded by the Apothecaries' Company. Some of England's first cedar trees were cultivated here in the 1680s and the hardiest of them lasted until 1903. In the 1730s the Physic Garden sent out the seeds that allowed James Oglethorpe, the colonist of Georgia, to sow the southern United States' first cotton fields. Among the wonders still visible today are the world's first rock garden, built in 1772 with old bits of stone from the Tower of London, a Chinese willow pattern tree, and a 30ft-high olive tree that once produced seven pounds of olives in a season (something of a miracle in rainy old England). The statue in the garden is of Sir Hans Sloane, the physician and philanthropist who saved the gardens from bankruptcy in 1722. Sir Hans owned large tracts of Chelsea (hence the number of streets named after him) and built up a huge collection of art and antiquities that were bequeathed to the nation after his death and provided the foundation of the British Museum (*see* pp.239–47).

*Head up Royal Hospital Rd and on your right you pass the **National Army Museum** (open daily 10–5.30; free), a disappointing exhibit illustrating the glorious exploits of the British armed forces from Henry VIII's time to the 20th century. If the gold-embroidered saddlecloth worn by the Duke of Marlborough at Blenheim turns you on, this is for you. Otherwise, head on a few more yards and turn right into the **Royal Hospital** (open Mon–Sat 10–12noon and 2–4, Sun 2–4 only, closed on Sun in winter months; free).*

Charles II took a leaf out of Louis XIV's book and created his very own Invalides for war veterans here in Chelsea. Christopher Wren (who else?) was set to work in 1682, and 10 years later he came up with this graceful building made up of three courtyards. The main block to the north contains a simple panelled chapel adorned with flags captured in battle down the centuries, and a Great Hall featuring a large painting of Charles II on horseback by Antonio Verrio. The real stars, however, are the pensioners themselves, a 400-strong group of lucky veterans whose every need is attended to from the age of 55 or so until they die. Their day-to-day uniform is navy blue, and they wear a peaked cap inscribed with the letters RH for Royal Hospital. They are generally rather eccentric and some are very old indeed. 'I keep fit by routine,' 97-year-old Sergeant Jones once told a television reporter. 'A pint of beer mid-morning and evening, same as everyone else, and always have a bath on Monday.' On special occasions they parade in scarlet frock coats and three-cornered hats; every 29 April, for example, known as Oak Apple Day, they commemorate the Battle of Worcester, from which Charles II escaped by hiding in an oak tree, by covering his statue in the south courtyard with oak sprigs.

The gardens are used every May to host the Chelsea Flower Show, a week-long display of blooms and garden design which brings out the very deep-seated English love of gardening. In recent years the event, always thought of in the same exclusive breath as the races at Ascot and rowing at Henley, has been somewhat upstaged by the less pretentious Hampton Court Flower Show in June. The eastern end of the grounds leading up to Chelsea Bridge Road was once Ranelagh Gardens, the most fashionable place for a stroll in 18th-century London. It boasted an ornamental lake, a Chinese pavilion and a large rotunda offering food, drink and myriad entertainments. 'You can't set your foot without treading on a prince, or a duke,' wrote Horace Walpole soon after the gardens opened in 1742. The historian Edward Gibbon put his finger more precisely on the Ranelagh's great attraction when he wrote that it was 'the most convenient place for courtships of every kind'. By 1803, however, the games of upper-class flirtation had gone out of fashion and the rotunda was demolished.

Chiswick and Beyond

Getting There/Around

The transport gets scarcer the further west you travel out of London. Fulham, Hammersmith and Osterley Park are all on the Underground; Chiswick House, however, is a longish walk from ⊖ Turnham Green (scene of Charles I's London defeat in the Civil War), and you might do better to go by train to Chiswick station. The 267 starts at Hammersmith and passes both Chiswick House and Syon House before heading down to Hampton Court.

The roads west of Chelsea (particularly the New King's Road and Fulham Road) lead through some pretty and affluent residential areas like Fulham and Parsons Green. The centre of Fulham, in particular, is abuzz with restaurants and upmarket bars clustered around the bottom end of North End Road market. Down next to Putney Bridge is **Fulham Palace**, until recently the official residence of the Bishop of London (*open Mar–Oct Wed–Sun, 2–5, and Nov–Feb Thurs–Sun 1–4; adm*). The 16th-century red and purple brick house includes a museum charting the history of the palace's occupants and speculation on the archaeological origins of the site, which might have been occupied by Danish or even Roman soldiers.

Up at the top of the next bend in the river is **Hammersmith**, which has a lively arts community (film and theatre at the Riverside Studios, theatre at the Lyric, live music at the Hammersmith Apollo) and an ornate bridge over the Thames, the first suspension bridge in London (1827). Hammersmith's charm is ruined somewhat, however, by the cluster of busy roads that meet at the Broadway. One of these, the Great West Road, heads off towards the M4 motorway via **Chiswick**, once a small village community but now itself rather torn to pieces by busy roads. The best, if slightly long, way to get there is along the pretty series of paths and small roads by the river.

Chiswick House (*entrance on Burlington Lane, open daily 10–6, earlier closing in winter*) was one of the first Palladian mansions in London built by the zealous Lord Burlington along with his friend William Kent in 1725–9. From 1890 to 1928 the house was used as an insane asylum, an appropriate fate, perhaps, given the opinions of the late Victorians on classicism. But the house was controversial even at the time of its construction. 'Too little to live in, and too big to hang a watch chain,' was the opinion of Burlington's enemy Lord Hervey. Modelled closely on Palladio's Villa Rotonda in Vicenza (which also inspired Thomas Jefferson's Monticello), Chiswick House is built around a central octagonal room in a series of classically-inspired geometric patterns, and topped by a shallow dome. The interior decorations, including some spectacular plaster ceilings and the sumptuous Blue Velvet Room, are by William Kent. Kent also helped design the garden, one of the first in England to break away from the formal Dutch style. It is jam-packed with classical follies including an Ionic temple, a Doric column, an avenue of urns, two obelisks and statues of Caesar, Pompey and Cicero.

Nearby, on Hogarth Lane (follow the signs), is **Hogarth's House** (*open at very weird times but essentially Thurs–Sun 1–4; © 0181-994 6757 to check*). This was where the great 18th-century painter and satirist, in the last 15 years of his life, came to get away from it all—hard to believe, given the current traffic level. It is no more than a curiosity, since the house itself is unspectacular and contains only prints of his most famous works, not the originals which are in the National Gallery, John Soane Museum and elsewhere.

A couple of miles further west in Isleworth is **Syon Park**, not so much a stately home as a kind of theme park *à l'anglaise* (*main entrance on London Road, with another off Park Road near the riverfront, open April–Sept Wed–Sun 11–4.15, Oct–Dec Sun 11–4.15, gardens open 10am–dusk daily; adm*). Here in the large if rather empty park stretching down to the river are a butterfly house, a vintage car museum and a gardening centre housed beneath an impressive Victorian domed conservatory made of gunmetal and Portland stone.

The house itself, built in crenellated stone around a quadrangle, was once part of a monastery, but was seized by Henry VIII for his own private use after his break with the Roman church. He locked up his fifth wife, Catherine Howard, in Syon House before her execution on adultery charges; a few years later the gods got their revenge when a band of dogs discovered the half-open coffin containing Henry's remains and chewed on them all night long. Since 1594 Syon Park has belonged to the Percy family, holders of the Duchy of Northumberland. At first they let it slowly decline, but then in 1762 Robert Adam was commissioned to rework the interior, and the landscape architect Capability Brown was set to work on the grounds.

The house is particularly successful, using only the bare bones of the original structure to create a sumptuous classical atmosphere. The highlights are the Great Hall, which makes up for the unevenness of the floor with a series of small steps embellished with Doric columns, and the ante-room, which has a lavishly gilded plasterwork ceiling and a multi-coloured marble floor. Osbert Sitwell once said this room was 'as superb as any Roman interior in the palaces of the Caesars'.

About a mile to the north of Syon Park is another stately home decorated by Robert Adam called **Osterley House** (*entrance from Jersey Road near ⊖ Osterley; open late Mar–early Nov, Wed–Sun 1–5; adm*). Originally the country home of Sir Thomas Gresham, the 16th-century financier and founder of the Royal Exchange, it came into its own in the 18th century when the Child banking family commissioned Adam to convert the turreted Tudor villa into a work of classical splendour. The state rooms are rich in plaster ceilings, friezes, decorated pilasters, painted ornaments and fine contemporary furniture. Horace Walpole was overwhelmed, saying the drawing-room alone was 'worthy of Eve before the Fall'. The vast gardens, sadly cut in two by the M4 motorway, are full of old oak and cedar trees, and even a lone, very ancient mulberry. The lake is pretty in summer and has been adorned recently with a floating pagoda donated by a Japanese company.

Upriver

A boat ride offers views of London you never get on dry land, but you may want to think twice about doing this whole stretch of river by boat. Charing Cross or Westminster pier to Hampton Court can take four hours; the 90-minute run to Kew may be quite long enough. There are other piers at Chelsea (Cadogan Pier), Chelsea Harbour, Putney and Richmond, which might be useful stopping-off points. As the boats are run by a plethora of competing independent companies, precise times are hard to find out unless you call the London tourist board on ℂ 0839 123432, or for upriver journeys to Hampton Court, Kew, Putney and Richmond ℂ 0171-930 4721. Otherwise you could simply go down to a pier to see, since you can be fairly sure of regular boats between 10am and 4pm. For local travel details, see individual sections below.

Westminster pier is next to one of the more melodramatic emblems of London, Thomas Thorneycroft's sculpture of Queen Boudicca and her daughters riding to defeat the Romans (see p.36 for her story). The Houses of Parliament look perhaps their most splendid from the river; the ferry allows you to see Barry and Pugin's work in great detail and also gives you a glimpse of the café terrace where MPs take their guests to tea. After Lambeth Bridge, the Tate Gallery is to the right; to the left, at Vauxhall Cross, is a shimmering post-modern mediocrity with a curtain wall of bottle-green glass studded with concrete spikes and cone-shaped trees. This is none other than the headquarters of MI5, also known as British Intelligence, and home to around 2000 of Her Majesty's spies. A mesh or Faraday Cage has been built into the framework to prevent electro-magnetic waves passing in and out of the building; but the occupants have had to resort to more old-fashioned technology (blinds) to prevent tourists using zoom lenses to video the would-be Bonds downing their gin and tonics in the bar at the front. A little further along on the south bank is Battersea, home to the Battersea Power Station built over 20 years from 1933 to 1953 by Sir Giles Gilbert Scott. Passing the new development at Chelsea Harbour, then Putney, Hammersmith, Barnes and Chiswick, you come to Kew.

Getting There/Around

✆ Kew Gardens is on the Richmond branch of the District Line; just north of the river, Kew Bridge station is on a British Rail line from Waterloo. Useful buses include the 7 from Oxford Circus and Paddington. There are several entrances to Kew Gardens, the most useful being the Victoria Gate on Kew Road, where guidebooks and free leaflets are available at the visitor centre and shop. Take sturdy shoes as there are around 300 acres of gardens to explore. The gardens are open from 9.30am until dusk and there is an admission fee. The glasshouses and other buildings open at 9.30am as well but close about 30 minutes before the open air gardens. There are guided tours in the summer at 11am.

Lunch

The gardens do it all for you. Not only is the place ideal for picnics, there is a first-rate inexpensive restaurant at the Orangery, self-service at the Pavilion (near the Pagoda), snacks at the Kew Bakery and cold drinks and ice-cream at a number of kiosks. These services are restricted in winter, but the Orangery serves food in some form all year round. At 288 Kew Road is the Maids of Honour tea room where Henry VIII is said to have bought pastries, and nearby at 1 Station Parade is the Kew Greenhouse café and opposite it the excellent Kew Hothouse restaurant (serving thick soups and delicious ciabatta).

The Royal Botanical Gardens at Kew have always been more than a collection of trees, flowers and plants; they are more like a giant vegetable laboratory, sucking up new information about the botanical world and, through the power of their research, influencing the course of human history in all sorts of unexpected ways. It was a commission from Kew to bring examples of breadfruit back from the South Seas that set the ill-fated HMS *Bounty* on its way to Tahiti in 1789. In the 19th century, Kew's laboratories first isolated quinine and, realizing it was an efficient natural antidote to malaria, recommended putting it in the tonic water with which the colonial administrators of India and Malaya diluted their gin. Kew was also involved in the development of commercial rubber and helped produce artificial fibres like rayon and acetate. It is now actively researching plant substances for the treatment of AIDS. A toxic compound called castanospermine, found in the Moreton Bay chestnut of New South Wales and in certain flowers from the central American rainforests, has been found to reduce the infectiousness of the HIV virus. In these days of receding rainforests and dwindling numbers of species of all kinds, Kew also does vital work in cataloguing and preserving plant types and developing new, genetically engineered hybrids that stand a better chance of survival in the wild.

For the visitor, Kew is a place of many wonders: 38,000 different plant species, some of them entirely extinct in the wild; vast glasshouses showing off some of the best of Victorian architecture; historic houses and buildings including Kew Palace and the Chinese Pagoda; and, above all, acres and acres of beautifully tended parkland, some of it wonderfully wild and remote, with views up and down the Thames and across to Syon House on the riverbank opposite. All year round, Kew provides a glorious array of colours: flowering cherries and crocuses in spring; roses and tulip trees in summer; belladonna lilies, heather and darkening leaves in autumn; strawberry trees and witch hazels in winter.

> *Pick up a free map at Queen Victoria Gate, which will locate all the major sites for you. It is also colour-coded for easier use.*

In the 18th century, Kew was part of the royal estates that stretched down as far as Richmond. Princess Augusta, the mother of George III, first had the idea of laying a botanical garden in the grounds of **Kew Palace** where she lived. This elegantly gabled two-storey Jacobean mansion (*open April–Sept 11–5.30 daily only; separate adm*) so endeared itself to George II and his wife Queen Caroline a generation before Augusta that they leased it for 99 years, for 'the rent of £100 and a fat doe'. The botanical garden was at first of only incidental importance to Kew; George III spent his energies commissioning a series of follies and outhouses from the architect William Chambers. These included three pseudo-classical temples, a ruined Roman arch, the handsome Wren-like Orangery, and—most striking of all—the **Pagoda**.

Chambers took his inspiration for this ten-storey octagonal tower from a visit to China in his youth. When finished in 1762, it was the most accurate rendering of Chinese architecture in Europe—although to be truly accurate it should have had an odd number of storeys. Not everybody liked it, least of all Horace Walpole, who lived across the river in Strawberry Hill. 'We begin to perceive the tower of Kew from Montpelier Road,' Walpole wrote during construction. 'In a fortnight you will be able to see it in Yorkshire.' Walpole was similarly dismayed by the fake Turkish mosque and copy of the Alhambra that originally stood next to the Pagoda; these, however, have since been demolished.

The botanical garden began to grow thanks to the enthusiasm of its keeper, Sir Joseph Banks, who organized Kew's first foreign plant-hunting expeditions and set about cultivating rare species. A cycad called *encephalartos altensteinii*, which was sent to Kew from South Africa in 1775 and now sits in the Palm House, remains the oldest glasshouse plant in the world. Near the Orangery is a beautiful maidenhair tree planted as far back as 1761. Banks's was nevertheless a small-scale enterprise, and Kew did not really take off until 1840 when it was handed over from the royal family to the state, opened to the public and expanded to more than 200 acres. The first director of the new public gardens, Sir William Hooker, put Kew on a firm scientific and research footing and founded the discipline known as 'economic botany'—botany in the service of people.

Hooker's most lasting architectural influence was to commission two great glasshouses from Decimus Burton, the Palm House and the Temperate House. The **Palm House** (1844–8) is a wondrous structure of curvilinear iron and glass, reminiscent of Joseph Paxton's ill-fated Crystal Palace, with a two-storey dome as its centrepiece. It used the latest techniques of water heating and ventilation to provide a home for palms and other exotic plant life, and had the coal for its basement furnaces supplied by underground railway from the **Campanile** built by Burton 100 yards away to the south. Now that the Palm House basement is no longer needed for coal burning, it has been converted into a display of marine life, including algae, coral and exotic fish. The **Temperate House**, built in the early 1860s and modified right up to 1898, is far bigger but more conventional in structure, using straight panes and iron rods to achieve its great height and width. Covering nearly 48,000 sq ft, the Temperate House is ideal for growing rare and exotic trees. Its oldest specimen is a Chilean wine palm brought to Kew as no more than a seed in 1846.

Kew has been expanding steadily ever since the mid-19th century. William Hooker's son Joseph, a veteran of plant-hunting expeditions to Antarctica, New Zealand and Nepal, took over as director in 1865 and established the Jodrell Laboratory to enhance Kew's research credentials. He also encouraged a young artist called Marianne North to set up a special gallery to display her collection of 832 botanical paintings based on her travels around the globe between 1871 and 1885 (see it to the left of Victoria Gate).

In this century, Kew has burst out of its original premises and taken over a stately home called Wakehurst Place in Sussex, where a broad range of plants can benefit from the more stable climate and heavier rainfall of the South Downs countryside. A number of new glasshouses have been added to the park, including the **Princess of Wales Conservatory**, containing Kew's collection of tropical herbaceous plants not least of which the incredible **Titan Arum**, which at two metres high is one of the largest flowers in the world. In 1996 the Titan blossomed for the first time, exuding a terrible stink which clung to the clothes of photographers; it flowers every two to four years in July and August, and the next blossoming is rumoured to be 1998. The newly refurbished **Museum No 1** will be opening opposite the Palm House in June 1998, and this will contain Kew's fascinating 'economic botanic collection' of wood and plant materials which have been made into useful materials for man—a 200-year-old shirt made out of pineapple fibres, from the Caribbean, and an incredible collection of Japanese lacquer boxes.

Richmond

Getting There/Around

✆ Richmond is at the end of the District Line; you can also reach it by British Rail from Waterloo, or by river. There are no really useful buses, although the 65 and 391 travel down the road from Kew.

Lunch

A pub lunch by the riverside is delightful—at the White Cross Hotel, say, or the White Swan at the bottom of Old Palace Lane. Other options include the Rose of York in Petersham Rd.

Richmond is a tranquil, affluent riverside community of attractive Georgian and neo-Georgian houses, flanked on all sides by wide expanses of greenery—Kew Gardens and the Old Deer Park golf course to the north, Marble Hill Park across the river in Twickenham, and Richmond Park to the south and east. On a sunny day it is an ideal place to walk along the river.

In medieval times, the focal point of the district was Shene Palace, a relatively modest manor house used as a lodge for the excellent hunting in the surrounding hills. The village green (today's Richmond Green) became a popular venue for pageants and jousting tournaments. Henry VII was so attached to the place that he changed its name from Shene to Richmond, after his earldom in Yorkshire, and entirely rebuilt the palace after a fire in 1497. The new Richmond Palace must have been quite something, a riot of spires and turrets which you can see reconstructed as a model in the Richmond Town Hall's small **museum** (*entrance on Red Lion Street, open Tues–Sat 11–5, and Sun 2–5, May–Oct only; adm*). Sadly, almost nothing survives of medieval Richmond in real life. A charterhouse which stood a few hundred yards to the north was destroyed during the Reformation, and the palace followed suit immediately after Charles I's execution in 1649. All that remains is a stone gateway off **Richmond Green**, bearing Henry VII's coat of arms, and the palace wardrobe, or household office, to the left just inside Old Palace Yard.

Political upheaval could not disguise the basic attraction of Richmond, and by the early 18th century building had begun again in earnest. In Old Palace Yard is **Trumpeters' House**, an elegant mansion built by a pupil of Christopher Wren and subsequently used as a refuge for Prince Metternich after the upheavals in Vienna of 1848. Further fine Georgian houses are to be found in all the neighbouring streets, such as Old Palace Terrace and Maids of Honour Row.

Today, as ever, the biggest attraction of Richmond is the riverside, which boasts, amongst other things, the elegant five-arched **Richmond Bridge** dating from the 1770s. The houses on the north side have been extensively redeveloped as a neo-Georgian terrace of shops, restaurants and offices called **The Riverside**, opened in 1988. The architect responsible was Quinlan Terry, a chum of Prince Charles much in sympathy with the Prince's traditionalist leanings. Most critics were appalled by this piece of unadventurous pastiche, while Prince Charles called it 'an expression of harmony and proportion'. The development nevertheless does its job well enough, and on summer days its layered terraces descending towards the water are crowded with strollers, sunbathers and the spillover customers of the surrounding pubs.

*From the centre of Richmond you can either walk along the river to Ham House (a good mile) or else hop on a 65 or 371 bus. To the east, up on the hill, is the beginning of the vast expanse of **Richmond Park**.*

At 2470 acres, Richmond is the largest urban park in Britain and one of the least spoiled in London. A few medieval oaks survive, as do many of the varieties of wildlife that medieval royal parties would have hunted. The deer are what make Richmond Park famous—around 350 fallow deer and 250 red deer, which do so well in the heart of London that there is an annual cull—but there are also hares, rabbits and weasels. Richmond Park also has two ponds for anglers, five cricket pitches, two golf courses, no fewer than 24 football grounds and numerous cycle paths.

At the top of Richmond Hill near the park entrance is the **Star and Garter Home**, once a humble tavern which rose to be one of the most fashionable addresses in outer London. Its Assembly Room was the setting for many a 19th-century wedding reception, and its modest bedrooms housed everyone from common wayfarers to continental royalty. In the 1860s the tavern was revamped as an imitation French Renaissance chateau, a project as unpopular as it was extravagant, and one that led to the establishment's demise at the turn of the 20th century. Used as a hostel for disabled soldiers after the First World War, it is now an old people's home. Few can enjoy its enviable views over Richmond and the river; it, however, is all too visible for a mile or more in each direction along the Thames towpath.

*Off Petersham Rd, down Sandy Lane and Ham St, is the entrance to **Ham House** (grounds open daily exc Fri 10.30–6; free; house open Mon–Wed 1–5, Sat–Sun 12–5.30; adm).*

Ham House is one of the grandest surviving Jacobean mansions in London, a magnificent three-storey redbrick house that has recently been restored to something approaching its original splendour. Built in 1610 and nicknamed the 'sleeping beauty' for its tranquil position, it became the home of William Murray, a friend of Charles I, who as a child had acted as the future King's whipping boy; that is to say, when Charles was naughty, he was the one who was beaten. In gratitude, Charles offered the adult Murray a peerage (he became the Earl of Dysart) and all the property around Ham and Petersham including this house. The highlight is the Great Hall, a wonderfully airy room decorated in blue, with a gallery overlooking the black and white checked floor. The rest of the house, some of which is still under reconstruction, boasts a profusion of tapestries, velvet drapes and plaster ornamentation on the staircases and ceilings. The gardens have retained their original 17th-century formal layout; the hedges and rows of trees intriguingly conceal the house from the river, lending an air of mystery and anticipated pleasure as you approach from the ferry stop.

Twickenham

Getting There/Around

Twickenham is just the other side of the river from Richmond, and within easy walking distance. St Margaret's Twickenham is the next railway station down the line from Richmond, and the handiest for Marble Hill Park. Useful buses include the 33 and 290 from Hammersmith and the 90 from Richmond. You could also take a train here from Victoria. If you come by car, park at the bottom of Orleans Rd, which is much more convenient than Beaufort Rd on the north side of Marble Hill Park. In the summer, a boat company called Hammerton's operates a very cheap ferry, for foot passengers only, from Ham House to Marble Hill.

Lunch

Picnic by the river at the bottom of Marble Hill Park. Otherwise the best bets are in Richmond back over the river.

Twickenham is a pleasant enough suburb, famous for its rugby stadium but hardly known at all for its wonderfully lush river front bordered by the grounds of Marble Hill House and those of its truncated neighbour, Orleans House. From the Twickenham side of Richmond Bridge you can enjoy a delightful mile-long walk along a stretch of the Thames that seems almost entirely rural. **Marble Hill House** (*open daily 10–6, earlier closing in winter; adm; © 0181-892 5115*) is a simple white Palladian villa built in 1729 for Henrietta Howard, the 'exceedingly respectable and respected' mistress of George II. Henrietta could not stand the pressure of life at court, where she had to negotiate a tricky path between her lover and her influential husband, and so with a little help from the royal purse she set up home here, some 10 miles out of central London. The house is rather empty, having been neglected for 200 years and depleted of most of its furniture. But the park is open and very green, affording the broadest possible view of the river. A series of annual open-air concerts is staged here every summer; it is a delightful venue when the weather holds.

Twickenham was briefly fashionable at the turn of the 19th century as a refuge for royalists fleeing the French Revolution. One such fugitive, the Duke of Orléans, later restored as King Louis Philippe, set up home next to Marble Hill Park in **Orleans House** and lived there from 1800 to 1817. The house, attractively set in a woodland garden, had been built a century earlier for one of William III's ministers. Its best feature, and the only one to survive, is James Gibbs's neoclassical Octagon Room, which has some fine plasterwork and a black and white checked floor now used as an outsize chess board. The room, plus a modern extension, has been turned into an art gallery (*open 1–5.30 Tues–Sat, 2–5.30 Sun, closing at 4.30 every day from Oct–Mar; free*).

> *About a mile to the southwest, and well worth a visit if you have the chance, is Horace Walpole's Gothic fantasy of a house, **Strawberry Hill** (on Waldegrave Rd—take the 33 bus from Richmond; open April–Oct for guided tours Sun 2–3.30pm, also by appointment the rest of the week on © 0181-240 4114; adm).*

This is generally believed to be the first building of the Gothic Revival in England, although the laconic Horace Walpole was less earnest about his project than later fanatics like Augustus Pugin. For 50 years after he bought the property in 1749, Walpole set about building what he himself termed 'a little plaything of a house, the prettiest bauble you ever did see'. He stole ideas and ornaments from any Gothic source he could lay his hands on—exterior battlements, Tudor chimneys, quatrefoil windows and fireplaces based on archbishops' tombs. For the Long Gallery he copied nothing less than the fan-vaulted ceiling of the Henry VII chapel at Westminster Abbey. Who knows how much Walpole's imagination was responsible for the late 18th-century vogue for Gothic horror novels; he certainly scared *himself* to death. One night he dreamed of a mighty armoured fist appearing at the top of the stairs—an image he used as the starting point of his novel *The Castle of Otranto*. Strawberry Hill was extended in the 19th century by one of Walpole's successors, Lady Frances Waldegrave; it is now a Roman Catholic college called St Mary's.

Hampton Court

Getting There/Around

If you don't travel by river (by far the most pleasant but slowest means), go by train from Waterloo to Hampton Court station, or else catch a bus: the 267 comes from Hammersmith and the R68 from Richmond.

Not much around, except snacks. The park is ideal for picnics, however.

Hampton Court Palace (*open Mon 10.15–6, Tues–Sun 9.30–6, earlier closing mid-Oct–Mar; adm*) is one of the finest Tudor buildings in England, a place that magnificently evokes the haphazard pleasures and cruel intrigues of Henry VIII's court. We are lucky to have it. Oliver Cromwell meant to sell off its treasures and let it go to pieces, but then fell in love with it and decided to live there himself. A generation later, Christopher Wren had every intention of razing it to the ground to build a new palace; only money problems and the death of Queen Mary prevented him from wreaking more damage than he did.

It is not usually considered polite to say so, but Wren did nobody any favours with his work at Hampton Court. Not only did he maul many of the original Tudor features, he replaced them with an endlessly boring series of royal apartments built in the same workaday, if well-proportioned style that he adopted for his legal buildings at Middle Temple and Lincoln's Inn. Now Hampton Court is, stylistically speaking, a palace at war with itself. Wren's classicism sits awkwardly in its Tudor surrounding, the result of a hostile but unsuccessful takeover bid; it cramps but fails to supersede the sophisticated grace of the original.

Hampton Court started as the power base of Henry VIII's most influential minister. Cardinal Thomas Wolsey bought the property from the Knights of St John in 1514, one year before he became Lord Chancellor of England. As his influence grew, so did the palace: at its zenith it contained 280 rooms and kept a staff of 500 busy, constantly entertaining dignitaries from around Europe. Seeing the grandeur to which his chief minister was rapidly allowing himself to become accustomed, Henry VIII grew nervous and threatened to knock Wolsey off his high perch. Wolsey responded in panic by offering Hampton Court to the monarch; Henry was unimpressed and at first snubbed him by refusing to take up residence there. Wolsey was then given the impossible task of asking the Pope to grant Henry a divorce from his wife, Catherine of Aragon. When he failed, his possessions were seized by the crown, he was arrested for high treason and eventually died as he was being escorted from his archbishopric in York to London. It seems Hampton Court haunted him to the end. All his life, Wolsey had refused to set foot in Kingston, the town across the river from the palace, in the belief that it would bring him bad luck. As he lay on his deathbed in Leicester, he found out to his consternation that the constable of the Tower of London where he was headed was a certain Mr Kingston.

Henry first got interested in Hampton Court as a love nest for himself and his new flame, Anne Boleyn. The two of them moved here even before Henry had annulled his first marriage and set about effacing every possible trace of Wolsey. They removed his coat of arms, since restored, from the main entrance arch and renamed it **Anne Boleyn's Gateway**—a magnificent red brick structure with octagonal towers at either end. In 1540, Henry added a remarkable astronomical clock, and renamed the main courtyard within Clock Court.

Hampton Court was where Henry retreated to block out the dark consequences of his bruising politics. While Thomas More, the main opponent to Henry's break with the Catholic Church, languished in the Tower on the night before his execution in 1535, Henry was living it up at his new palace watching Anne Boleyn dance her heart out. More predicted, with devastating accuracy: 'These dances of hers will prove such dances that she will spin our heads off like footballs, but it will not be long ere her head will dance the like dance.' Anne lasted just one year before succumbing to the intrigues at Hampton Court and ending on an executioner's block on trumped up charges of adultery. Henry did not seem unduly perturbed, and the night after her death he supped at Hampton Court with his prospective third wife, Jane Seymour, wearing a feather in his cap.

The mid-1530s were Hampton Court's heyday. Henry built the **Great Hall**, with its 60ft-high hammerbeam roof and its stained-glass windows, amended right up to the end of his life to include the crests of each of his wives, even the ones he repudiated or executed. The king also established the gardens, planting trees and shrubs, notably in the Pond Garden, and built a **real tennis court** which still survives in the outhouses at the northeastern end of the palace. Hampton Court began to turn sour for him after Jane Seymour died in 1538 while giving birth to his much anticipated son and heir, Edward. Thereafter Henry grew cantankerous and paranoid, a mood not exactly lifted when he began suffering from ulcerations in his legs and found it difficult to walk. Edward led the greater part of his unhappy short life at Hampton Court; it is said that his mother's ghost appears occasionally on the east side of Clock Court, dressed in white and holding a lighted taper.

For a century after Henry's death, Hampton Court continued to thrive. The Great Hall became a popular theatrical venue, and the state rooms filled with fine paintings, gold-encrusted tapestries, musical instruments and ornaments. Charles I built the gardens' fountains and lakes as well as the long waterway, originally cut to provide the palace with water at the expense of neighbouring communities. Charles also accumulated a vast collection of art including the wonderfully restored *Triumph of Caesar* series by Mantegna which hangs in its own gallery at the south end of the palace.

By the time William and Mary came to the throne, appreciation of Tudor architecture had waned considerably. The apartments at Hampton Court were considered old-fashioned and uncomfortable, and Christopher Wren was drafted in to build an entirely new palace to rival Louis XIV's extravaganza at Versailles—a project that, perhaps fortunately, never saw the light of day. The bulk of Wren's work is at the eastern end of the palace and centres around the cloisters of **Fountain Court**. The new apartments were decorated by the likes of Antonio Verrio, James Thornhill, Grinling Gibbons and Jean Tijou in sumptuous but stilted fashion; the **Chapel Royal** was also rebuilt, with only the Tudor vaulted ceiling surviving from the original. The best work carried out under William III was in the gardens, notably the lines of yew trees along the narrow strips of water, the herb garden (now beatifully restored) and the famous **maze**. Originally the maze was considered a religious penance to impress upon ordinary mortals the labyrinthine complications of a life in the service of Christ. Now it is a popular diversion, particularly for children too small to peer over the hedges to see what is coming next.

South London

The novelist Angela Carter once described London as 'two cities divided by a river'. So gaping is the north-south divide that grown men have been known to weep at the prospect of crossing the Thames into unknown territory. Even taxi drivers get nervous, especially late at night; like the reluctant Charon demanding an obol to ferry the dead across the river Styx to hell, they generally need some heavy encouragement to take you to the wrong side of town. It's not as though one half of London is impossibly dangerous or immoral, it's an instinctive thing. You just *know* if you are a north-of-the-river or south-of-the-river sort of person. By and large north Londoners are a bit more bohemian and adventurous, a touch more extrovert if you like, and this leads them to assume that south Londoners are only interested in their homes and gardens and in leading a steady, unruffled existence. South Londoners know that they are innately superior to everyone, and don't even bother explaining why.

From the visitor's point of view, the north bank of the Thames is where nearly all the city's history and most of its fun and activity is to be found. The historian Walter Besant once described south London as 'a city without a municipality, without a centre, without a civic history'. Almost nothing south of the river, apart from the immediate vicinity of the Thames embankment, is worth any more than a cursory detour. Districts like Clapham and Forest Hill, with their spacious Victorian houses, elegant parks, good restaurants and easy access to the City, may seem attractive to house-buyers but a tourist would get bored in five minutes. Like all urban sprawls, much of the south London cityscape is monotonous, run-down, poorly served by public transport and depressing. Too many district high streets have the same cluster of generic shops, the same rickety pub, the same takeaway, the same queue at the bus stop, the same lorries rumbling down the main road. Look around and you could be in Peckham, or Tolworth, or Thornton Heath (or 'Fort Neath' as residents call it). Who knows which? Who cares?

Below is a description of the areas you might want to care about. The south Thames embankment area are dealt with largely in Walk IX and in the Downriver and Upriver sections. Otherwise, Lambeth has some interesting museums, Brixton has a lively Caribbean market and thriving nightlife and Dulwich an interesting picture gallery.

Lambeth

Getting There/Around

You can walk to most of the sights from Waterloo station or Westminster Bridge. Also useful are ⊖ Lambeth North and ⊖ Elephant and Castle (which despite the interesting sounding name—derived from Eleanor of Castile—is a shopping centre cum stinking swimming pool—a ghastly pink coloured architectural monstrosity and probably the most hated building in London). The handiest bus is the 109, which starts at Trafalgar Square and continues on past Brixton.

Lunch

Your best bets are Pizzeria Castello (20 Walworth Road in the Elephant & Castle shopping centre and considered by many to be the best pizzeria in London); the South Bank Centre (the café at MOMI or The Archduke wine bar in Concert Hall Approach, for example); The Fire Station, an all-day café-restaurant on 150 Waterloo Rd; or Livebait, a sophisticated fish restaurant based in an old pie and mash shop at 41 The Cut (© 0171–928 7211 for reservations).

Lambeth was slumland for most of the 19th century, and although it has smartened up somewhat since, it is certainly no beauty. 'The people are poor and there are a lot of rag shops,' George Orwell wrote in 1933 in *Down and Out in Paris and London*. In popular folklore, the area is known for spawning the word 'hooligan' (the Fagin-like pickpocket Patrick Houlihan, also called Hooligan, thrived here in the 1890s along with his band of young apprentices) and for inspiring the famous music-hall number, *Doing the Lambeth Walk*, which comes from Lupino Lane's folklore musical about Cockney life, *Me and My Girl*. You can still visit Lambeth Walk, a quiet street market off Lambeth Road near the junction with Kennington Road, although the Victorian music halls that used to thrive here are long gone. Otherwise, the borough is a sprawl of council houses and railway lines, enlivened only by a couple of interesting museums, the so-called 'Waterloo churches' built to commemorate the British-led victory over Napoleon in 1815 and Lambeth Palace, official London residence of the head of the Anglican Church, the Archbishop of Canterbury.

To the left of Westminster Bridge is **County Hall**, a grand grey stone public building in the pompous Edwardian 'Wrenaissance' style. Until 1986 it was the headquarters of the Greater London Council, the elected city government that proved such a threat to Margaret Thatcher that she abolished it. The GLC's last leader was a radical but popular left-winger, Ken Livingstone, who infuriated the Conservative government by pursuing the kind of tax-and-spend policies it abhorred; he ploughed funds into the arts and the capital's public transport system, making both more efficient and cheaper than at any time since. This was anathema to Thatcher's free-market approach, and given County Hall's position directly across the river from the Houses of Parliament, a highly visible political embarrassment to boot. 'Red Ken' revelled in his role as *enfant terrible* and posted the number of London unemployed on a huge banner around his building's concave riverfront terrace, in full view of government ministers opposite.

Although London may now be getting a new city government, its seat will no longer be at County Hall, which is being converted into a multi-purpose centre for residential housing, hotel accommodation and conferences. The basement already houses one of London's newer attractions, the **Aquarium** (*open Mon–Fri 10–6, last adm 5pm, Sat–Sun 9.30–7.30, last adm 6.30pm; adm*). Here, in spectacular three-storey fish tanks set among kitsch Roman ruins, you can say hello to sharks, stingray, octopus, sea bass, cuttlefish, umbrella-like jellyfish and wondrous shoals of sea bass. The Aquarium is primarily entertainment and unfortunately fails to tell the visitor much about either the fish or the environment.

Just south of here, near the top of Lambeth Palace Road, is the entrance to the new St Thomas's Hospital and, on the right as you go in, the **Florence Nightingale Museum** (*open Tues–Sun 10–5, last adm 4pm; adm*). You won't learn much more about the founder of modern nursing here than at the Old St Thomas's Operating Theatre (*see* pp.340–1), but the museum nevertheless builds up a vivid image of her life and times. Here are the letters, childhood books and personal trophies that the 'Lady with the Lamp' brought back from the Crimean War. You can also see a reconstructed ward from the Crimea, contemporary nurses' uniforms and some of the equipment they used. 'Nursing is a progressive art, in which to stand still is to go back,' Florence Nightingale said towards the end of her long life (she died, aged 90, in 1910). Her influence is still being felt today.

At the bottom of Lambeth Palace Road is **Lambeth Palace** itself, which dates back to 1190 but was largely rebuilt in neo-Gothic style by Edward Blore in the 19th century. It is not open to the public. Before Westminster Bridge was built in 1750, Archbishops of Canterbury would travel to parliament and back by horse ferry, a somewhat hazardous mode of transport since the many church riches they carried in their horse-drawn carriages had a tendency to sink the boat. The most interesting visible feature of the palace is the red-brick Tudor gatehouse, completed in 1501. Right up to 1842, alms were distributed directly to the poor of Lambeth here; now the archbishopric writes an annual cheque to the local council instead.

On the corner of the Lambeth Bridge roundabout is the parish church of **St Mary-at-Lambeth** with its unusual Museum of Garden History (*open Mar–Dec, Mon–Fri 10.30–4 and Sun 10.30–5; free*). The plants on display were first gathered by Charles I's gardener John Tradescant, who is buried in the churchwith his son. You can also see gardening tools dating back to the ancient world. The church, largely rebuilt in 1852 but still based on its 14th-century precedent, is curious for other reasons too. It contains the only full-immersion font in London. It is the last resting place of Captain Bligh, of *Mutiny on the Bounty* fame. And in the south chapel is a stained-glass window commemorating a medieval pedlar who grew rich when his dog unearthed great treasure while scratching around one day on a piece of waste land in the area. The pedlar left an acre of land to the parish when he died, but asked for the window for him and his dog in return.

Turning left onto Lambeth Road, you come to the park containing the **Imperial War Museum** (*open daily 10–6; adm but free after 4.30pm*). Until the First World War this was the site of the notorious Bethlehem Royal Hospital for the insane, better known as Bedlam, where inmates were kept like zoo animals in cages and cells. In the 17th and 18th centuries the public was admitted free of charge to laugh at the lunatics as they were whipped into submission by their keepers, a barbaric practice that was curbed when it emerged that the king himself, George III, was going mad. The building is now used to illustrate Britain's wartime experiences from 1914 to the present day.

Despite the intimidating pair of artillery cannon at the entrance, this museum does everything it can to illustrate the human side of war, not just the military hardware. Certainly, there are plenty of Zeppelins, Lancaster bombers, Cruise missile launchers—there is even a distasteful flight simulator for which visitors cough up extra money to 'experience' a World War Two bombing mission. Fortunately there are also exhibits on rationing and air raids, sound and light shows illustrating the terrors and privations of life in a First World War trench, and artworks including Henry Moore's drawings of London during the Blitz. Try as it might, however, the museum ultimately fails to convey the sheer barbaric awfulness of war and can't help wrapping the experiences it depicts in a coat of patriotic nostalgia. The weapons are there to be admired, and the fortitude of the combatants to be accepted regardless of the rightness or otherwise of their struggle. There is a dearth of material on other countries' experiences of war, although to the museum's credit it recently staged a fascinating and truly powerful exhibition of paintings by Bosnian children, while down in the basement a clock counts down the lives which have been lost in wars all over the world, a number which the museum estimates will reach 100,000 million by 1999.

Brixton

Getting There/Around

⊖ Brixton is at the end of the Victoria Line, and served by buses including the 3, 109 and 159 from Trafalgar Square and Lambeth.

Lunch

Around the market is a cluster of small cafés and stalls selling snacks. One of the more popular is the Satay Bar, serving cocktails and delicious Indonesian cooking near the Ritzy Cinema at 447 Coldharbour Lane. Inside the market itself you'll find the Pizzeria Franco at 4 Market Row (good calzone as well as pizza) and the vegetarian Café Pushkar at 16a Market Row.

Come to Brixton in the afternoon to soak up the atmosphere of the market and the surrounding streets before heading off for a concert at the Academy or clubbing at the Fridge. There's not much to see but lots of distinctive local character. Brixton is often called the Afro-Caribbean capital of London—exciting and exotic if down-at-heel and even a little dangerous. That impression is not quite right, since around two-thirds of Brixton has in fact always been white; two of its more famous sons are David Bowie (who certainly passes muster on the exotic front) and former Prime Minister John Major (who doesn't, even though his father, as a circus trapeze artist living on Coldharbour Lane, probably did).

It is nevertheless the Caribbean community that gives Brixton its particular flavour. Immigrants from Jamaica and neighbouring islands took advantage of the cheap if dilapidated housing around Railton Road as early as 1948, and they kept coming during the 1950s and 1960s. In the 19th century, the area had been known for its music halls, and these were now converted into warehouses or music venues like the Academy. Unlike Notting Hill, however, the area did not benefit from gentrification or the arrival of media trendies. The Brixton riots of 1981, sparked by economic recession and a profound disgust among the local black population for a

a Window and a portrait of the artist's son Titus), Rubens (a suggestive pictur
Venus squirting milk into Cupid's mouth), Van Dyck, Poussin, Watteau, Canal
and Raphael. Curiously, the gallery's founders, Sir Francis Bourgeois and N
Desenfans, chose to have their mausoleum placed among the pictures in full v
of visitors. It is based on an engraving of an Alexandrian catacomb, publishe
England in 1809.

Downriver

Getting There/Arou

Boats leave either Charing Cross or Westminster Pier every half an hou
so (less often in winter) between about 11am and about 5pm, and sto
any number of piers including Swan Lane in the City, London Bridge
Katharine's Dock, Canary Wharf, Greenland Dock (in the Surrey Qua
Greenwich and the Thames Barrier. Your best bet is to go down to on
the main piers to check times, since every ferry company runs a differ
and often changing schedule. Otherwise call the London Tourist Bo
recorded river service information line on © 0839 123432, or for Do
river services to Greenwich, the Tower and the Thames Barrier
© 0171–930 4097.

You can see a great deal of the Docklands by taking the overland Do
lands Light Railway (DLR) from Bank or Tower Gateway to its terminu
Beckton (call © 0171–918 4000 for 24-hour travel information). This
vated railway is exactly like the futuristic monorail in Truffaut's *Faren*
451, and a ride on it—sitting next to the driver where you get panora
views as you go, and getting on and off to explore as you fancy—makes
an extremely entertaining day out in itself. (You can also buy a *Sail and*
Ticket for around £7.20—this entitles you to a day's unlimited travel
the DLR plus a riverboat trip from Westminster or Greenwich Piers, a
discounted entry to the National Maritime Museum at Greenwich, 1
Royal Observatory and The Queen's House (*see* Greenwich, below).
other details of Underground stations and bus lines, see separate entr
under each district. The Docklands includes an extensive network of cy
routes (maps available at tourist centres), and you can pick up a useful f
street map of the area and other tourist information from the Tourist Bo
Centre at DLR Canary Wharf.

To head downriver from the Tower is to enter a different world— more in tu
with the Emerald City in *The Wizard of Oz* than the London described in the r

of this book. The converted Docklands show the face of a city of the future: a vision of shimmering high-rise glass and steel reflected in the lapping tides of the River Thames, a Phoenix risen from the ashes of the derelict wharves and warehouses of a bygone age. It's disorientating, endlessly surprising, pock-marked by building sites, mud and cranes, and—in terms of sheer visual impact—extraordinarily impressive.

What is this? A successful large-scale property development? In *London*? There's a catch, of course. The Docklands were built without a shred of planning or civic sense and as a result were a spectacular financial flop. So keen was Margaret Thatcher's Conservative government to see private enterprise flourish back in 1981 that it lifted all planning restrictions and waived local taxes on investors for the first 10 years. In consequence, the development failed to respect its environment and the wishes of local people, many of whom were pushed out of their modest homes to make way for a higher-class breed of resident. Furthermore, nobody—least of all the government—thought to provide proper services or adequate transport links, so the gleaming palaces were almost impossible to get to or live in. When recession struck at the end of the 1980s, hundreds of speculators went bust because they simply could not attract tenants, even at cut-price rates.

The place, now a subject in itself on the National Curriculum, has become a bit of a ghost town:office blocks with bland reflective façades, impersonal shopping centres the same as you find in any New Town suburbia, luxury housing estates where the main luxury is a near-total absence of an identity. But let's not be too negative. The free-market ideological baggage that came with Docklands, the lack of planning that stemmed from it and—last but not least—the social prejudice that automatically turns the London middle classes off anything east of Aldgate Pump, have all acted as blinkers preventing the critics from recognizing the area's potential. And potential it certainly has.

Normal people are still able, just, to live amidst this Yuppyville-sur-Tamise, and there is a real chance to build a broad-based waterside community along the lines of Seattle or Vancouver. That is what the once aggressively Thatcherite but now chastened London Docklands Development Corporation has worked towards, though God knows it has been a slow process, especially given that everyone has lost so much money. The eastern extension of the Jubilee Underground line is at last opening in 1998, though at vastly inflated cost and with only a reduced service at first. The Docklands Light Railway will one day extend south to Lewisham. Shops and restaurants are appearing, as are the first stirring of community life, including an annual fish fair in September. These are small victories, but if they keep coming the Docklands could still become the most exciting city development in Europe.

in 1724. It has also been the subject of diabolical rumours. Why was it not consecrated for six years after its completion? Why is there a pagan symbol, a pyramid, in the churchyard? Hawksmoor's surviving papers provide no clues, and speculation still rages. The interior of the church, a rectangle containing an elongated Greek cross, is intact although many of the fittings were added after a fire in 1850.

Limehouse (named after the lime kilns which used to operate here) bears the vestiges of the mini-Chinatown it was before the 1980s property bonanza and it has a little-publicized reputation for good cheap Chinese restaurants. In the 19th century the area was considered an iniquitous den of vice; this was where Oscar Wilde set the opium-smoking scene in his novel *The Picture of Dorian Gray*. More recently, Limehouse has acquired political overtones. It was here that four senior members of the Labour Party, including the youthful Limehouse resident David Owen, decided to set up a more centrist breakaway group called the Social Democratic Party or SDP, in 1981. It was not a portentous move. The SDP fizzled out by 1988, David Owen became one of the most hated figures in British politics, and in the meantime the split in the centre-left vote allowed the common enemy of both the SDP and Labour, Margaret Thatcher's Conservatives, to win two more general elections.

Rotherhithe

Getting There/Around

Rotherhithe is on the short East London Underground line (which you can join from the DLR at Shadwell) and will eventually be on the Jubilee Line extension too. The P11 bus from Waterloo Station to London Bridge is the handiest other means of transport.

Lunch

Two obvious possibilities: the Mayflower pub (117 Rotherhithe St) or the Angel pub (101 Bermondsey Wall East), both with fine views over the river, the Angel being the better bet for food.

Rotherhithe was where the Pilgrim Fathers set out for America in their ship the *Mayflower* in 1620. You might think hordes of American tourists come to pay homage to their forefathers, but in fact Rotherhithe is a delightfully unspoiled, relatively unknown part of riverside London and one of the most successful of the Docklands redevelopments. The old warehouses have been repaired but not tarted up, the streets have been kept narrow, and the green in front of St Mary's Church lends an air of village-like cosiness. There are no hi-tech modern buildings in Rotherhithe, just good views of the ones in Wapping and on the Isle of Dogs.

ginally Rotherhithe was part of the estate of the great abbey of Bermondsey, ich was destroyed at the Reformation. The monks used to drink in a tavern ed The Salutation, since renamed **The Angel**. The present pub was built, prob-y in the 17th century, as a drinking haunt for sailors. A trapdoor was built into floor over the river, which must have been useful for smugglers; however, the orious Judge Jeffreys brought a halt to the hanky-panky by coming to the Angel vatch the hangings at Execution Dock directly across the river.

e departure of the Pilgrim Fathers is commemorated in the **Mayflower** pub, ich is partly built out of the broken up segments of the original ship and has a del of the vessel hanging outside its front door. Because of its tourist clientele, pub is allowed to sell postage stamps, including American ones. This was prob-y the tavern where Captain Christopher Jones and his crew spent the night ore their departure for the Americas. Within two years, the ship came back from expedition, and Jones was eventually buried, along with the three co-owners of *Mayflower*, in the churchyard of **St Mary's** opposite. The church itself, which s attractively rebuilt in the 18th century, contains a plaque to Jones as well as ains of the *Fighting Temeraire*, the battleship whose demise was so poignantly tured by Turner in his famous painting in the National Gallery.

herhithe acquired a new cause for celebrity in the early 19th century, when rc Isambard Brunel made it the starting point for the first tunnel to run beneath Thames. Brunel was born in France and fled the Revolution with a forged pass-t. Although a talented engineer—he invented a system of pulley blocks still embered today—he had no financial sense and spent far too much of his own ney on his work. The Duke of Wellington had to haul him out of debtors' prison tart the tunnel from Rotherhithe to Wapping. The job took 18 years, from 1825 1843, and nearly ended in disaster on five separate occasions when the roof ed in. You can see the bright red pump that Brunel used to suck out the water, well as a number of other memorabilia at the **Brunel Engine House** a little to east of St Mary's (*open by appointment on* © *0171-252 0059 or* © *0181-748 34; adm*). The Thames Tunnel is now used by the East London Underground e; it is not to be confused with the adjacent Rotherhithe Tunnel, built for road fic in 1908.

:ause of its isolation on a bend in the Thames, Rotherhithe became rather dilapi-ed after the Second World War. Its recent redevelopment, however, has racted a modest number of artists and artisans, and by the river is an intriguing lpture park called The Knot Garden.

*Southeast of Rotherhithe, if you can bear the noisy walk down Lower Road and off to the left down Redriff Road, are the old **Surrey Docks**, part of which have been converted into a yachting and pleasure-boat*

enthusiasm. Olympia and York could justifiably feel let down by the Conservative government that invited them in on such generous terms but then lifted barely a finger to help when they ran into trouble. The Department of the Environment made vague noises about moving into Canary Wharf, as the French transport ministry had done at the similarly troubled Grande Arche at La Défense outside Paris. But it never happened. To compound the misery, in the early evening of 9 February 1996 a huge IRA bomb explosion at Canary Wharf, killed two people and damaged 1 million square foot of office space—at the time of writing repair works are still going on.

> *The Pelli tower is closed to visitors, which is a shame because the view from the 50th floor is quite stunning. See if you don't know anyone who works there; otherwise try posing as the representative of a big company interested in renting office space. Chances are, though, you'll have to content yourself with walking round the surrounding plazas and craning your neck up to the heavens.*

> *The rest of the Isle of Dogs is best visited by DLR train. As you travel out of Canary Wharf and south you will see on your left an elegant cantilevered pedestrian bridge linking Heron and South Quays, and in the distance building works on the **Millennium Dome** in North Greenwich—at the time of writing, these look like circus poles rising into the sky. No one is quite sure what will go inside the ill-fated dome, and as delays increase on the complicated Jubilee Line extension, no one is sure how anyone will get there (although emergency shuttle trains will probably run from Stratford and Westminster).*

The **Isle of Dogs** is a peninsula defined by a tight loop in the river and criss-crossed by artificial waterways. There is no hard evidence that it ever had any association with dogs, although there are folktales that the royal kennels were once kept here. Most likely, 'dogs' is a corruption of 'docks'; after all, that was what provided the area's livelihood from 1802 until the second half of the 20th century. The southern end of the Isle of Dogs is littered with failed upmarket residential estates as well as a sprinkling of older lower-class council houses. You get a keen sense here of the social dislocations brought about by the redevelopments. Most troubling is the rise of the extreme right-wing British National Party which has exploited tension between whites and the local Bengali community. A BNP candidate, Derek Beackon, briefly held a local council seat for the Isle of Dogs in 1993–4, sounding alarm bells throughout the country. In the run-up to his election, a 17-year-old Asian boy was beaten up to within an inch of his life by a neo-Nazi white gang. Racist attacks remain all too common, particularly on grim estates like Cascades, a bold but failed experiment in layered high-rise housing by Piers Gough.

e **Storm Water Pumping Station** on Stewart Street off Marsh Wall is well
rth a visit—but to get there you will have to get out at South Quay and walk
ng Marsh Wall (about 10–20 minutes). Built by John Outram in 1988, the enor-
us pump station looks like an outsized Chinsese temple, and is one of the most
cessful buildings in the Docklands. Inside the terrorist-proof station, storm
ter from the Isle of Dogs flows into an underground chamber, and from here is
nped into a massive concrete surge tank from where it drains by gravity into the
ames. At the same time a propeller fan in the apex of the pediment rotates at 16
n to expel any sewer gases that build up inside the station. (If pumping stations
ite you, you may also like to make the longish trip to Royal Victoria DLR station
Royal Docks to see Richard Rogers' Pump House on Tidal Basin Road—a brightly
oured concentric drum structure which discharges waste water from 25m-deep
nels into the Thames.)

rther south, **Mudchute** is one of a number of city farms dotted around east
ndon, a 32-acre patchwork of vegetable allotments and open fields. Among the
m's much-loved inhabitants are a one-legged chicken called Nelson and a llama
led Gazza after the English footballing hero Paul Gascoigne. Here you will also
d a riding school for all ages, and a café. A little further down Eastferry Road is
and Gardens, a small riverside park with an outstanding view across the river
Greenwich (although the classical symmetries of the view through the Royal
spital to the Queen's House and the park have been marred by the tall roof
tension to the park's tea house). You can walk over to Greenwich through the
t tunnel built in 1902 beneath the river, its two onion-domed brick towers
rking the entrances at either end.

> *The Docklands redevelopments continue out east all the way to London*
> *City Airport and beyond, featuring hi-tech office architecture by the likes*
> *of Richard Rogers and I. M. Pei, which for the moment remain rather*
> *stranded as building works continue to develop an 'urban village' and a*
> *university campus on land where the **Royal Docks** (the Royal Victoria*
> *and the Royal Albert Docks) used to be.*

Greenwich

Getting There/Around

The most pleasant way to reach Greenwich is by ferry; failing that, take the
DLR to Island Gardens and walk through the foot tunnel. There are British
Rail trains from Charing Cross, Cannon St and London Bridge to Greenwich (a bit off to the west) or Maze Hill (a bit off to the east). The 188 bus
also goes to Greenwich from Waterloo. The weekend tends to be crowded,
especially on Sundays when the market is in full swing, but it is also the

King William Walk takes you to the iron gate (on the left) leading to **Royal Naval College**, *which stands on the site of the old Palace of* centia (open daily 2.30–5.30; free). The Pepys Building inside the coll is now home to the The Millennium Visitors' Centre, which has an exh tion on the bizarre Millennium Dome being built in North Greenw (open Mon–Fri 11–7, and Sat–Sun 10–6).

Charles II's first thought when he restored the monarchy was to rebuild Placen but he didn't have the money and gave up soon after the foundation stone was la Queen Mary had another idea after she witnessed the terrible wounds inflicted British sailors at the battle of La Hogue in 1692: she commissioned Christopl Wren to clear the ruins of the old palace and build a naval hospital. This promptly did, leaving only a Jacobean undercroft, used for wine and coal stora from the original structure. Mary and Wren did not enjoy an altogether happy c laboration, since Mary insisted that the Queen's House should be visible from t river (something that was never the case when Placentia was still standing), a that the path of the Deptford to Woolwich road, which at the time ran through middle of the building site, should be undisturbed. As a result, Wren and his s cessors, Hawksmoor and Vanbrugh, were obliged rather against their will to co up with a design based on four entirely separate buildings. The final result, with majestic neoclassical façades overlooking the river and pepper-pot towers at t back, was described by Dr Johnson as admirable but 'too much detached to ma one great whole'. The naval pensioners grew to dislike it, too, though not for architecture so much as the corruption of its administrators. 'Columns, colonna and friezes ill accord with bully beef and sour beef mixed with water,' complair one Captain Baillie in 1771. The hospital was eventually closed, and the Ro Naval College, which had been based in Portsmouth, moved here in 1873.

Only the chapel and Painted Hall are open to the public. The former is based o design by Wren, but was entirely refurbished by James Stuart after a fire in 1779 has an intricate plaster-moulded ceiling, and a fine painting of *St Paul at Melita* Benjamin West above the altar. The **Painted Hall** is a magnificent ensemble three rooms painted in opulent style by James Thornhill, the man who also de rated the cupola of St Paul's. Greenwich is the overall theme, whether expressed allegorical depictions of battleships, or in portraits of the great astronomers—Tyc Brahe, Newton and the first astronomer royal, John Flamsteed. The culmination Thornhill's work is the rather absurdly patriotic ceiling in the first of the rooms, t Great Hall, which shows William and Mary, all temperance and dignity, handin cap of liberty to the prostrate figure of a conquered Europe. Thornhill spent the b part of a quarter-century completing these decorations and, given that he was pa £1 per foot for the walls and £3 per foot for the ceilings, can't have done badly c of it. Nevertheless, he painted a rather tongue-in-cheek self-portrait at the foot of one of the walls with one hand held out—presumably for more money.

> *Return to King William Walk and take the next left past the top of the Naval College, Romney Rd. To your right is the entrance to the Queen's House and the National Maritime Museum (oprn daily 10–5; adm).*

The **Queen's House** was Inigo Jones's first experiment in Palladian architecture after his return from Italy in 1615. James I's wife Anne of Denmark was the queen in question, who wanted her own private villa as an extension to the Palace of Placentia. For years after Anne's death in 1619 the house languished unfinished, but the project was taken up again by Queen Henrietta Maria in 1629. So happy was she with the final result, completed in 1640, that she nicknamed it her 'house of delights' and returned to live in it as the Queen Mother after the Restoration. The building is a textbook exercise in Palladian classicism—simple and sober on the outside, and full of 'licentious imaginacy', as Jones put it, on the inside. We can't entirely appreciate Jones's intentions, since his original H-shape was filled in with the addition of a couple of first-floor rooms in 1662. Not all the interior decoration was completed by the time of the Civil War, and many of the fittings that were already in place—including paintings by Rubens, Raphael and Van Dyck— were filched and sold off by the Roundheads. Much of the further decay which the Queen's House suffered in the 18th and 19th centuries has been reversed, however, thanks to a recent restoration bringing the building back to something close to its 1660s state.

The centrepiece is the **Great Hall**, a perfect 40ft cube immediately inside the main entrance with an elegant gallery at first floor level. At first sight it looks as though the original ceiling fresco, *The Arts of Peace* by Gentileschi, has been reinstated after a long exile at Marlborough House. In fact it is a computer-enhanced photographic copy, the original having proved too difficult to move back because bits of it are missing. What is genuine, however, is the **Tulip Staircase** at the eastern end of the hall, a wrought-iron helix staircase which twists its way up to the Queen's Bedroom. This was the first open-well staircase to be built in England, or as Jones put it, the first with 'a vacuum in ye middle'. The floral decorations on its banister are not in fact tulips at all, but fleurs-de-lys in honour of Henrietta Maria, daughter of King Henry IV of France.

The Queen's House is now at the centre of the **National Maritime Museum**, whose side wings are connected to the main house by colonnades constructed in 1807 to commemorate Nelson's victory over the French at Trafalgar two years earlier. Nelson is not so much celebrated as hero-worshipped in this museum, in apparent fulfilment of Richard Sheridan's dictum that 'the period of Nelson's fame can only be the end of time'. Relics of the famous admiral include the uniform in

was relatively easy, as it could be ascertained from the angle of the Pole Star to
horizon. But longitude was something else. Scientists knew what they needed
dependable and portable watch or clock with which to work it out. But for a
thing other than the shortest journeys no such timepiece existed. So acute did
problem become that 'to find longitude' became a synonym for an impossible tas

In 1754, parliament issued a Longitude Act, offering a reward of £20,000 to t
person who could crack the problem. The first proposals ranged from the sublim
to the ridiculous. One was to line barges around the world and have them set
flares simultaneously every night at midnight. Another was to sprinkle a spec
magic 'powder of sympathy'on a pack of dogs who were to be sent to the four c
ners of the world; one of them would be stabbed in London every day at noon, a
all the others would then howl in vicarious pain.

It was a Yorkshire clockmaker called John Harrison who eventually broke t
impasse. He constructed his first marine clock, based on a double pendulum,
1730 and continued perfecting it all his life. Each of his four prototypes took ye
to produce, and by the time he came up with the prize-winning model in 1772
complete with bimetallic strip to compensate for temperature changes, caged ro
bearing and grid-iron pendulum—he was already 79 years old. Captain Cook to
Harrison's clock to Australia and called it his 'trusty friend'.

The museum gives an engaging account of all this, and takes the history of bo
navigation and time up to the present, including the landmark 1884 Washingt
conference that selected Greenwich as the Prime Meridian, and the invention
atomic clocks based on the nine billion vibrations per second of a caesium ato
The observatory itself is also worthy of note, particularly Flamsteed's original obs
vatory, the **Octagon Room**, which was designed by the professional astronom
and architect Christopher Wren. The room, where Flamsteed kept his telescop
and tested the rotation of the earth with a 13ft pendulum, is one of Wren's fin
achievements, a model of geometric simplicity and airy beauty which by his ow
admission was built 'for the observer's habitation and a little for pomp'. Flamstee
beautiful collection of 17th-century Persian astrolabes is also on display, as is a c
temporary painting of the soon to be destroyed Palace of Placentia.

> *Head down to the river on the eastern side of the park. At the wate*
> *edge at the end of Park Row is the **Trafalgar Tavern**, one of the venu*
> *for the so-called whitebait dinners.*

Every year on the Sunday after Whitsun, 18th- and 19th-century cabinet minist
gathered at an inn in east London for a banquet of whitebait and other fish caug
in the Thames. Tories opted for the now defunct Ship at Blackwall, while t
Liberals took to the Trafalgar Tavern as soon as it was built in 1837. Water poll
tion soon tempered the ministers' appetite for whitebait, however, and the dinn

ceased to be a regular event after 1868. The pub, which was refurbished as a tourist attraction in 1965, still serves whitebait when it is in season from Feb to July, though not from the Thames.

Next door, under the shadow of a power station is an attractive row of 17th-century almshouses known as **Trinity Hospital** (*open by appointment only*). The chapel has a fine Flemish stained-glass depiction of the crucifixion and ascension; among the hospital's other possessions are some preserved rats from the Great Plague of 1665.

The East End

Getting There/Around

✆ Liverpool St is a handy starting point for visiting Spitalfields. Other Underground stations in the area are Aldgate, Aldgate East and Whitechapel. Buses aren't very practical unless you plan to stray a long way east; the 15 comes from Paddington, Oxford Circus and Trafalgar Square and continues along the Commercial Rd to Limehouse and Poplar.

Lunch

If you come on Sunday morning (a good time to visit in general) you'll find plenty of snacks in Petticoat Lane market, including jellied eels (an acquired taste) at Tubby Isaac's famous stall at the bottom of Goulston St. Near Liverpool Street at 15 St Botolph Street is the Barcelona Tapas Bar. Spitalfields market has takeaway couscous. Otherwise, try one of the many licensed and unlicensed cheap Indian restaurants on Brick Lane or else bagel and lox or salt beef at the famous Brick Lane Beigel Bake open 24 hours at 159 Brick Lane.

> *Who knows the East End? It is a shocking place... an evil plexus of slums that hide human creeping things; where filthy men and women live on penn'orths of gin, where collars and clean shirts are decencies unknown, where every citizen wears a black eye, and none ever combs his hair.*

Arthur Morrison, *Tales of Mean Streets*

Back in the 1880s and 1890s when Arthur Morrison was writing his rather sludgy novellas of working-class life in London, the East End was almost entirely cut off from the rest of the city. Victorian maps of London tended to leave the area out, like so much uncharted territory in a godforsaken corner of the British Empire. In 1902, the visiting American novelist Jack London could not find a cab to take him

Stand in the middle of this shiny shop, restaurant and office development, and you appreciate the bizarre mixture of your surroundings. The centre itself, completed in 1991, is all red and green marble and cantilevered iron girders. To one side you see the glass roof of Liverpool Street station and the steady stream of commuters in suits heading to and from work; on the other side is a grimy old railway tunnel and beyond a horizon of derelict warehouses. The Broadgate Centre expresses much of the consumer optimism of the 1980s, with its open-air ice rink, rock waterfall and incidental modern sculpture (including a particularly off-putting reclining figure of a woman with bloated short legs, called the *Broadgate Venus*). In 1990 it became the headquarters of the European Bank for Reconstruction and Development, the French-inspired institution that was supposed to breathe new economic life into the post-communist economies of eastern Europe. Within a couple of years, however, its first chairman Jacques Attali was forced to resign for spending almost as much time and money on kitting out the atrium in Carrara marble as on organizing worthwhile loans. The whole centre has suffered from the recession that brought about Attali's demise and, apart from the few businessmen who come for expense-account lunches at its upmarket restaurants, it has rather a forlorn air.

*On the other side of Bishopsgate begins the grid of streets lined with Georgian houses called **Spitalfields**.*

Spitalfields was, as the name implies, originally the grounds of a medieval hospital, and remained more or less rural until the mid-17th century. It first drew attention to itself as a centre for religious nonconformity; the first Baptist chapel popped up in the district in 1612, a trend encouraged when French Protestants started settling in the area after 1685—some 60,000 of them in all. Under the French influence, Spitalfields became established as a centre of fine silks, and its prosperity was enhanced by heavy Huguenot investment in the Bank of England, which was set up in 1694 largely to cover the costs of war against the Protestants' sworn foe, Louis XIV. Today the prosperity is gone, and the only relics of the French presence in Spitalfields are the street names—Fournier Street, Fleur-de-Lys Street or Nantes Passage—and the fine Georgian brick houses in which the silk merchants once lived. Silk-weaving declined dramatically as a trade in the 19th century, partly because of the unsuitability of the English climate for mulberry trees which attract the silkworms in the first place, mostly because of the advent of machine-woven cotton. The 50,000 weavers engaged in the trade in 1824 had dwindled to just 3300 by 1880. Cloth is still an important trade in Spitalfields, but nowadays it is mostly worked on by Bangladeshis labouring for slave wages in backstreet sweat-shops. There is something sad, almost ghostly, about roaming the old streets now.

One of the most extraordinary addresses in Spitalfields, and indeed in all of London, is **Dennis Severs' House** at 18 Folgate Street (*open first Sun in the*

onth 2–5pm; adm; and also for evening performances three times a week with a
ecial Silent Night on the first Monday of each month when the house is lit by
ndles and no one speaks, so that a 'silent poetry' is created; adm exp;
0171–247 4013 for times and booking). This is not so much a house as a the-
e, a place which offers a glimpse back into the past not by showing off
ell-preserved artefacts and objects in the way that National Trust homes do, but
forcing you to feel your way into the atmosphere of bygone eras, from neo-clas-
al to romantic. The artifice is evident even from the outside, where you can see a
ged canary next to a gas lantern in the ground-floor window and, three flights up,
painted ghost peering down into the street. Inside, each room is a living tableau,
ovingly constructed still-life time machine, where sheets are rumpled, candle
ax is congealed on the floor and last week's vegetables sit half-eaten on the tables.
ou are encouraged to touch things, feel things, smell things and become part of
e novel surroundings even at the risk of spooking yourself.

e master of ceremonies is Dennis Severs himself, a mildly eccentric ex-pat Amer-
n lawyer who dropped out of the southern Californian rat race in the late 1970s
d bought this house as a way of getting back in touch with himself and with the
st. According to him, most historians and academics are 'dead from the neck up'
cause they are obsessed with objects and facts, not feelings. He is like a film
ector or obsessive painter, forever rearranging his rooms to seize a particular
oment—the middle of a meal, say, or preparations for bedtime. In his startlingly
ginal evening performances (for which you should book several weeks in
vance since only eight people can attend at a time), Mr Severs evokes the lives of
e generations of occupants of the house, the fictional Jervis family, through a
xture of sound effects, light, still-life décor and sheer acting bravado. Emma
ompson came here to prepare for *Sense and Sensibility*; others, including Severs
nself, have described the performances as being 30 years ahead of the British art
ovement. The effect is almost that of a seance; spectators can be so shaken up by
e conjuring tricks with the past that they occasionally collapse with shock. Mr
vers calls this 'perceiving the space between the eye and what you see'. Or, to
ote his motto, *aut visum aut non*—you either see it or you don't.

> At the end of Folgate St, turn right on Commercial St, and almost imme-
> diately on the left-hand side is the **Ten Bells** pub.

is pub used to be called the Jack the Ripper but was forced to change its name in
88 under pressure from feminist groups who objected to what they saw as its
orification of violence against women. It is still the starting point for any number
Ripper walks and tours, and *the* place to buy your serial killer tee-shirts and com-
emorative mugs. The link with the Ripper is rather tenuous, apart from the
nveniences of geography—his second victim, Annie Chapman, was murdered

That brings this mini-tour of the East End to a close. There are, however, a number of curious sights a little further afield. These include:

Columbia Road Flower Market (*off the Hackney Road about three-quarters of a mile north of Liverpool St Station, open 8am–1pm Sun morning*): Columbia market was set up in 1869 as a covered food market set in a vast neo-Gothic palace. The traders preferred to do their business on the street, however, and the venture failed. The shortlived market building was knocked down in 1958 to make room for the lively, modern, highly successful flower market. As well as a wide range of cut flowers and pot plants, you can buy home-made bread and farmhouse cheeses and enjoy the small cafés that line the street.

Bethnal Green Museum of Childhood, Cambridge Heath Road (*near ❺ Bethnal Green, open Mon–Thurs, Sat 10–5.50 and Sun 2.30–5.50; free*): This extension of the Victoria and Albert Museum is housed in the building once known as the Brompton Boilers where the decorative arts collections were kept during the 1850s (you'll notice the very Victorian mosaic frieze on the outside depicting Agriculture, Art and Science). Inside are some extraordinarily intricate children's toys, notably dolls' houses, train sets, puppet theatres and board games; a shame, however, that they are displayed in such gloomy cabinets. (Cambridge Heath Road, incidentally, leads up to the East End extension of the Grand Union Canal and the western end of Victoria Park, the biggest piece of greenery in east London).

Whitechapel Art Gallery, Whitechapel High St (*open Tues–Sun 11–5, late opening until 8pm on Wed; free*): A lively gallery focusing on contemporary and avant-garde work, housed in an interesting Art Nouveau building designed by Charles Harrison Townsend at the turn of the 20th century. It was the brainchild of Samuel Barnett, a local vicar who believed education could help eradicate the appalling poverty in the East End and founded the adult education institute Toynbee Hall on Commercial Street as well as this gallery. Jackson Pollock and David Hockney both held exhibitions here early in their careers.

Food and Drink

they chewed with their mouth closed, and kept their elbows off the tableclo
Cleanliness remained a problem, however. The Duc de la Rochefoucauld remar
at the end of the 18th century that 'even in a nobleman's house, where serva
were plentiful, napkins and dishcloths decidedly were not.'

The class divisions over food turned into a full-scale political and economic crisi
the early 19th century. The Corn Laws of 1815 protected middle-class farmer
the detriment of smaller land-owners, and a run of poor harvests in 1817, 18
and 1819 compounded the problem. Food prices soared, and violent anti-gove
ment demonstrations multiplied. The advent of canned food in the 1820s depri
working people of fresh vegetables and fruit; at the same time, basic foodstuffs su
as bread continued to be adulterated. A groundbreaking book of 1820, called *T*
tise on the Adulterations of Food and Culinary Poisons, carried a quotation fr
the second Book of Kings on the front cover: 'There is DEATH in the Pot'. So gr
was the furore caused by the book's publication that its author, a German im
grant writing under the name F. Accum, was forced to flee to his homeland
avoid criminal prosecution.

The quality of food slowly improved after the repeal of the Corn Laws in 1846.
by this time many ordinary city-dwellers had simply forgotten how to cook, a
standards of preparation plummeted—hence all those overboiled joints of meat a
vegetables deplored in the anonymous *Memoirs of a Stomach*. Tinned food v
supplemented by a lot of jam and treacle, particularly after the mass production
Golden Syrup started in 1880. Working-class Londoners munched their v
through a lot of ready-made pies, industrial sliced bread and fish and chips. 1
middle and upper classes also lost their interest in food, as the new gentleme
clubs (*see* pp.152–3) privileged male chumminess over gastronomic excellence.

The two world wars of this century instilled a Spartan attitude to food across m
of the social spectrum. The dizzy spirit of national pride following the Battle
Britain and the Blitz led people to believe that the strictures of rationing were g
for the character and that decent food was a sign of decadence. A certain kind
Englishman actually relished the disgustingness of spaghetti rings and wob
industrial jelly, and terrorized children who showed the slightest reluctance to
up. Bad food was considered a national asset, not a cause for embarrassme
Eating out, even in the prosperous decades after 1945, was considered a lux
only the very rich could afford. At best people would grab a pie or a sandwich
lunchtime, or pop out for a quick İndian or Chinese takeaway. Restaurant st
dards were abysmally low: all rubbery meat and soggy vegetables, served up
waiters who could not care less. The shops were not much better, taking foreve
stock basic items: dried pasta was first seen circa 1960, and fresh fruit juice o
became widely available around 1982.

The last 25 years, however, have seen a revolution in eating habits in London. Britain's entry into the European Economic Community (as it then was) in 1973 and the subsequent boom in foreign travel finally woke people up to the possibilities of good healthy eating. Travellers came back from holiday revolted by the bland regime of sliced white bread and tinned baked beans and began asking in the shops for wholemeal bread, fresh basil, pine nuts, lemongrass and mangoes. In London, at least, they found what they were looking for, largely thanks to the Indian, Chinese and Mediterranean communities who had always made these things available to the few who were interested.

By now, the revolution has penetrated the British hinterland and broken down many of the class barriers that once associated good food with the gluttonous rich. Not that all the problems have disappeared. Britain is the birthplace of Mad Cow disease, almost certainly the result of brutally commercial farming practices; every now and again scares arise over unsafe eggs or listeria epidemics. Greasy chips and tinned carrots still form a large part of the national diet. But such habits are rapidly being exposed as a needless form of self-flagellation. This is now a country where cookery programmes on television are beginning to outnumber detective serials and soap operas. London's trendier neighbourhoods are filling to bursting point with new cafés, lunch-spots and designer eateries. The opening of a high-profile new restaurant is a full-blown media event, the fads and fancies of modern cuisine a constant subject of society gossip. The fusty old establishments have been forced to change or die. Spaghetti houses, bistros, vegetarian cafés and tapas bars (as well, unfortunately, as fastfood burger joints) have made eating out accessible to a far broader range of people than ever before; at the same time, at the upper end of the market, top-class chefs have developed a new brand of British cuisine that improvizes, occasionally brilliantly, on ideas taken from around the world. The standard of restaurant food in London is now higher overall than in Paris, and far more varied than anywhere else except perhaps New York.

In the midst of all the changes, traditional English food has become something of a sideshow in the great London beanfeast, and perhaps deservedly so given its shoddy history. You are most likely to encounter it over breakfast, particularly if you stay in a hotel or guest house. A full English breakfast, if you can face it first thing in the morning, will keep you going all day: a deceptively harmless-looking glass of fruit juice to start, followed by cereal or porridge, followed by a huge fry-up of bacon, egg, sausage, tomato and fried bread, followed by oodles of toast and marmalade washed down with a limitless supply of tea. In some of the classier establishments you might also get offered black pudding, kippers (smoked herring) or kedgeree (a mixture of smoked fish, rice and hard-boiled eggs). This is an intimidating prospect minutes after you have rolled out of bed, and not one, you might be

Covent Garden are undoubtedly the most fertile areas, although there are excellent selections in Notting Hill, Fulham, Camden Town, Islington and Hampstead.

The one drawback is money—eating out in London is an expensive pleasure. There are some incredible bargains to be had, but overall you are lucky to get away with much less than £25–35 per head for a decent evening meal, roughly half as much again as you would in Paris, Rome or a number of North American cities. One reason for this is the wine, which can be cripplingly expensive without being especially reliable: watch out. Meal prices should be inclusive of tax (VAT), but an extra cover charge (no more than £2) may be added in swankier places. Look carefully to see if service is included. If not, leave an extra 10–15 per cent of the total, preferably in cash. As for prices, the listings below divide restaurants into the following categories, according to the price of a full meal with wine and service:

> **luxury: more than £50**
>
> **expensive: £35–50**
>
> **moderate: £25–35**
>
> **inexpensive: £15–25**
>
> **cheap: under £15.**

All but the cheapest establishments will take cheques or credit cards. If you are paying with plastic, the total box will inevitably be left for you to fill, in anticipation of a fat tip. Don't feel under any pressure, especially if service is already included.

Soho — *map A*

expensive

❶ Alastair Little, 49 Frith St, W1, ℗ 0171-734 5183 (*closed Sun and Sat lunchtime*). One of the first and also the best of nouvelle British cuisine restaurants. The freshness and simplicity of the ingredients is echoed by the minimalist, positively bare-essentialist decor. The menu changes according to what's fresh in the market. There are generally six main courses, though fish and shellfish feature prominently.

❷ The Gay Hussar, 2 Greek St, W1, ℗ 0171-437 0973 (*closed Sun*). Velvet-upholstered, Hungarian restaurant, famous for its wild cherry soup, goulash and dumplings, served on thick red-and-white china. The stylish, intimate setting is much beloved by the old left of British politics, as the Labour posters, trophies and signed biographies of boasted regulars attest. The unchanging menu is calorific and filling and diametrically different from the culture of nouvelle cooking.

moderate

❸ L'Escargot, 48 Greek St, W1, ℗ 0171-437 2679 (*closed Sat lunch, all day Sun*). This one-time bulwark of the Soho scene has reopened under new management, serving high quality, classic French food under the gaze of high modern art (Picassos, Mirós, Chagalls). The first floor dining room is more

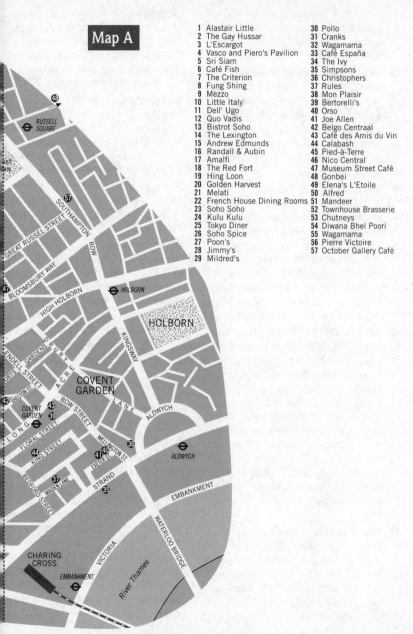

Map A

formal than the magnolia room below, but both serve exquisite dishes in daring sauces. A speciality is *feuilleté* of snails served with bacon.

❹ Vasco and Piero's Pavilion, 15 Poland St, W1, ✆ 0171-437 8774. Sophisticated, friendly Italian restaurant serving immaculately presented dishes, e.g. grilled breast of guinea-fowl with juniper berries. Cheaper two- or three-course set menus. Truffles from Umbria available in season.

❺ Sri Siam, 16 Old Compton St, W1, ✆ 0171-434 3544. Modern, minimalist and hip, a combination unusual in a Thai restaurant. The sleek, cream walls, adorned here and there by banana and palm leaf themes, host throngs of diners in the evening, although it can be empty at lunch. There are elaborate four course menus but also more modest displays. Service can be almost over-attentive.

❻ Café Fish, 39 Panton St, SW1, ✆ 0171-930 3999 (*closed Sat lunch, all day Sun*). Although there is an underlying old French character to this bustling bistro, the accent is fish, obviously. And you can order fish and shellfish in most cooked forms, be it chargrilled, steamed, meunière or fried, or sometimes even marinated. You can also have them in breadcrumbs with chips if you, like many English people, prefer the aqueous creatures a little more unrecognizable before you eat them.

❼ The Criterion, 224 Piccadilly, W1, ✆ 0171-930 0488. A magnificent, art-deco, gold mosaic interior, originally opened in 1870 and recently re-launched with Marco Pierre White as chef. The place has seen much drama—suffragettes met here in the 1910s when women were not allowed into pubs. While the service is sometimes impatient and the room crowded, the food is exquisite without being exotic—oysters with celeriac *remoulade,* Savoy cabbage *ancienne,* or blackberry soufflé.

❽ Fung Shing, 15 Lisle St, WC2, ✆ 0171-437 1539. Beautiful, delicate, mainly Cantonese Chinese food, served with style in a bright lemon, blond-wood-panelled dining room; there is also an airy veranda at the back. The menu has recently been overhauled to include some more traditional Chinese dishes. Although there is a boosted vegetable section, one of the classic dishes is braised suckling pig.

❾ Mezzo, 100 Wardour St, W1, ✆ 0171-314 4000. Reputedly one of the biggest, trendiest restaurants in Europe, which opened in 1995 to loud acclaim by the media, partly because of the prestige of the designer and owner, Sir Terence Conran. The basement restaurant is overpriced, and the service (not surprisingly given the sheer size) is erratic, but the place definitely has style and class. Prepare for noise. A high standard of cooking: fillet of beef, pesto and *pommes frites*; salmon, pickled eggplant and ewe's milk yoghurt.

❿ Little Italy, 21 Frith St, W1, ✆ 0171-734 4737. An offshoot of the famous Bar Italia, which was for many years the only place selling real espresso in London. The restaurant has a comparable authenticity that some of the more fashionable places may lack. Photographs of boxers adorn the walls. A long menu, with unusual dishes of the day, like meatloaf steamed in tomato sauce, as well as simpler, sometimes more successful dishes.

⓫ Dell'Ugo, 56 Frith St, W1, ✆ 0171-734 8300. A big statue sticks out of one of the windows to beckon you in. A three-storey building, each level being a separate, different restaurant. The ground floor hosts a fashion-conscious under-30s crowd. The upper floors are calmer and serve more serious dishes. A vast diversity of eclectic combinations and styles on the menu.

⓬ Quo Vadis, 26–29 Dean St, W1, ✆ 0171-437 9585 (*closed Sat lunch, Sun lunch*). Lime green airy interiors with meticulous table decoration. Positively serene compared with the new, trendy bustling bistros. Recently more upmarket with the advent of the ubiquitous Marco Pierre White as chef. French food with Mediterranean influences: fresh snails *bourguignon*, rock oysters, frogs legs with a *coulis* of parsley and garlic. Downstairs from Karl Marx's old digs.

inexpensive

⓭ Bistrot Soho, 64 Frith St, W1, ✆ 0171-734 4545. Newly renovated bistro, joining two adjacent venues into one, with a warm, earthy but modern interior. Specialities include ballontine of oxtail and aubergine with onion purée or pig's head with spinach gnocchi, but there are also less outré numbers in vegetable and meat. Mainly French inspired.

⓮ The Lexington, 45 Lexington St, W1, ✆ 0171-434 3401 (*closed Sat lunch, Sun*). Modern European food: 2 course set menu for £10 which includes broad-shouldered dishes like roast pheasant and chorizo or suckling pig with butter bean and morel stew. There are also less expensive combinations. Warm, purple and faintly psychedelic with modern art. Jazz pianist at night.

⓯ Andrew Edmunds, 46 Lexington St, W1, ✆ 0171-437 5708. Simple, beautifully prepared dishes at low prices. Queues at the door, which makes the service understandably frenzied. Old-fashioned frontage, hard benches and restless sawdust effect belie the modern ethos and originality of the cooking. Menus change weekly, but dishes might include smoked haddock with saffron mash, or slow cooked lamb shank with couscous.

⓰ Randall & Aubin, 16 Brewer St, W1, ✆ 0171-287 4447. An old Victorian butcher's shop (of the same name) converted into an oyster and champagne bar, with a rôtisserie; the original tiled interior has been preserved. Specializes in seafood and spit-roasts, also langoustines, crabs, whelks—the ingredients can be made into sandwiches to order.

⓱ Amalfi, 29–31 Old Compton St, W1, ✆ 0171-437 7284. Known as one of the longest standing cheap and cheerful eating dives in Soho, even if the prices are edging upwards. A cheap option is to choose from the 11 types of pasta and 10 sauces. The design refers at all times to the Amalfi coastline and the blue skies of the Mediterranean. Downstairs are four arched grottoes.

⓲ The Red Fort, 77 Dean St, W1, ✆ 0171-437 2115. Northern Indian restaurant. Excellent Tandoori and Mogul specialities such as quail and a Rajasthani smoked kebab of fresh salmon. Recently refurbished decor has upped the prices. Indian food festivals occasion special menus.

⓳ Hing Loon, 25 Lisle St, W1, ✆ 0171-437 3602. Despite miniature quarters, the food is very good, the menu endless.

One can even have spiced duck's kidneys. Economic meals—that is the 'specials' of the day—are usually challenging, and delightfully done.

⓴ Golden Harvest, 17 Lisle St, WC2, ✆ 0171-287 3822. A new Chinese restaurant, offering excellent food at low prices, served in a delicate (verging on the dainty), low-lit environment. The owners are also Chinatown's fishmongers, so fresh fish is easily guaranteed: including pomfret and carp.

㉑ Melati, 21 Great Windmill St, W1, ✆ 0171-437 2745 (*open all day*). Lively and authentic Indonesian restaurant—soups, satays and coconut desserts attracting young crowds but also families and self-absorbed couples. A diversity of tastes and a long, reliable, tested menu with exotica such as *cumi cumi istimewa* (a stuffed squid in dark red, sweet soy sauce).

㉒ French House Dining Rooms, 49 Dean St, W1, ✆ 0171-437 2477 (*closed Sun*). Dark, worn wooden rooms above a pub of the same name. Atmospheric, 1920s ambience, much frequented by literati and associates. Excellent French food, sometimes with British influences, e.g. duck confit with cucumber, mint and spinach.

㉓ Soho Soho, 11–13 Frith St, W1, ✆ 0171-494 3491. Mediterranean (especially Provençale) cooking both upstairs and downstairs. Downstairs is a cheaper brasserie/rôtisserie and a bar. Wild boar and more challenging platters are served upstairs, in a more sober environment. Modern look, lots of white, and tiled floors.

cheap

㉔ Kulu Kulu, 76 Brewer St, W1, ✆ 0171-734 7316. Sushi is hand-made at this busy Japanese eating spot, where it is hard to get a stool in view of the queues—but it's a tiny space anyway. A long, narrow conveyor belt runs along the counter and the food is served on colour coded plates. Also non-sushi dishes.

㉕ Tokyo Diner, 2 Newport Place, W1, ✆ 0171-287 8777 (*open from 12 every day—all 365*). Japanese fast food—sushi and Japanese curries. Although prices have risen, it's still one of the cheapest Japanese eateries in London. Noodles (about £5), *donburi*—rice and various toppings (£4–£6). Ingredients are fresh and crisply cooked. Good service, authentic décor, no tips.

㉖ Soho Spice, 124–126 Wardour St, W1, ✆ 0171-434 0808. One of the few Indian restaurants in Soho. Radiant blue and magenta colour scheme and wooden effect make for a modern Indian look. Good standard food, although choice can be limited. A hint of Thai influence. Genial service; also a bar.

㉗ Poon's, 27 Lisle St, W1, ✆ 0171-437 4549. Recently expanded, this has lost some of its chaotic caffness. Famous for high-quality 'wind-dried' meats—especially the duck. Also good, hearty soups.

㉘ Jimmy's, 23 Frith St, W1, ✆ 0171-437 9521 (*'sometimes' closed Sun*). Moussaka and chips, as eaten by the Rolling Stones, among others, in the 1960s, is a mainstay of this basement Soho institution. Unchanging décor, green lino and cheap prices for standard Greek Cypriot dishes, like *taramá*, *afelia* and the like. Cosy in winter, hot in summer.

㉙ Mildred's, 58 Greek St, W1, ✆ 0171-494 1634 (*open all day*). Eclectic wholesome vegetarian fare from Brazilian casserole to Chinese black bean vegetables and vegetarian sausages. Vegan daily specials. Also seasonal organic produce and even organic wines. Good Sunday brunch. Swift, welcoming service.

㉚ Pollo, 20 Old Compton St, W1, ✆ 0171-734 5917 (*open all day*). Cheap student dive near Leicester Square. Good Italian menu. Despite the name, there is little emphasis on chicken. Extremely popular, crowded and frenetic. People flock in groups and bunch up on scuffed red benches in wooden booths.

㉛ Cranks, 8 Marshall St, W1, ✆ 0171-437 9431. Popular, pioneering vegetarian restaurant with several branches around London. Warm, apricotty interiors. Good vegetarian food—roasted vegetables and couscous—and definitely tasty salads, quiches, pies. Self-service.

㉜ Wagamama, 10A Lexington St, W1, ✆ 0171-292 0990. Wagamama, now an institution in Bloomsbury, has opened a new branch in Soho. The philosophy of this Japanese noodle bar is 'positive eating, positive living'. Hi-tech, efficient, fast service on long communal tables. Long queues do not diminish the experience.

㉝ Café España, 63 Old Compton St, W1, ✆ 0171-494 1271. Plain, authentic little Spanish restaurant—a far cry from

self-conscious, un-Spanish tapas bars that have cropped up all over London. Good generous portions of Galician and Castilian dishes, emphasizing fish. Popular even among Spaniards. Specially delicious paella.

Covent Garden   *map A*

expensive

㉞ The Ivy, 1 West St, WC2, ✆ 0171-836 4751. The moody oak panels and stained glass dating from the 1920s are offset by vibrant modern paintings. The menu caters for elaborate as well as tamer tastes. Salmon fishcakes on a bed of leaf spinach is a signature dish. Takes orders from 12–3 and 5–12—which ensures a diverse clientèle, but particularly popular amongst the theatre comers and goers as well as the players. Sister establishment to Mayfair's Le Caprice.

㉟ Simpsons, 110 Strand, WC2, ✆ 0171-836 9112. The ultimate, old-fashioned English restaurant, ideal if you like your roast beef and Yorkshire pudding served by deferential, tail-coated waiters in a posh, aristocratic environment. Once a gentlemen's club and also a chess club, the ethos of which is preserved and refined. Also serves 'The Great British Breakfast' which includes the 'ten deadly sins' of liver, black pudding, sausages and the like.

㊱ Christophers, 18 Wellington St, WC2, ✆ 0171-240 4222. The opulent curved stone staircase in the foyer recalls a 19th-century pleasure dome—reinforced when one realizes that this was once London's first licensed casino (and later a high-class brothel). Up the stairs, in the dining hall, a more restrained elegance pervades. As an American restaurant, the menu emphasizes steaks and grills, but there are also seafood inspirations (crab chowder or fried oysters) and beautiful roasts.

moderate

㊲ Rules, 35 Maiden Lane, WC2, ✆ 0171-836 5314 (*open all day*). The oldest restaurant in London (established 1798), with a long history of serving aristocrats as well as actors. Formal and determinedly old-fashioned, panelled in dark wood and decorated with hunting regalia. Specializes in game of the season: even rarities such as snipe, ptarmigan and woodcock. Dress smart.

㊳ Mon Plaisir, 21 Monmouth St, WC2, ✆ 0171-836 7243. Jumbled, old bohemian charm, reminiscent of a convivial Rive Gauche brasserie, and a cluttered yet capacious dining area, thronged with rushing, Gallic waiters. Appetizing, well-presented French provincial dishes, especially seafood. Classic signature dishes include *coquilles St. Jacques meunière, gratinée à l'oignon*, steak tartare, crème brûlée, and also home-made foie gras.

㊴ Bertorelli's, 44a Floral St, WC2, ✆ 0171-836 3969 (*closed Sun*). Conveniently located for opera-goers, 'Bert's' serves a broad range of proven Italian favourites, but also a more radical catalogue of Italian dishes, from *maltagliati* served with pumpkin, cream, chorizo, French beans and grated chili cheese, to antipasti of deep-fried mozzarella, roasted peppers and smoked eel, or lean pork stuffed with sultanas and pinenuts.

㊵ Orso, 27 Wellington St, WC2, ✆ 0171-240 5269 (*open all day*). High quality Italian fare, served in a graceful, terracotta, Venetian dining room. Mainly Tuscan food, interestingly and daringly interpreted, like pizza with goat's cheese and roasted garlic and oregano, or *puntarelle* with anchovy dressing. Osso buco is another speciality. The walls are covered with photographs of the great and the good who frequent the place—actors, royalty, jetsetters, etc.

㊶ Joe Allen, 13 Exeter St, WC2, ✆ 0171-836 0651. Started out as an American restaurant, serving hamburgers and steaks, but now embraces modern British and European too. The result is a long menu, lacking character—but there are some delights, particularly if you're into monster puddings. Joe Allen's is traditionally a venue to be seen in and also for star-gazers. Rollicking atmosphere with last orders at 12.45am.

inexpensive

㊷ Belgo Centraal, 50 Earlham St, WC2, ✆ 0171-813 2233. A huge railway depot of a restaurant in gleaming metallic '90s style, along the lines of the Pompidou Centre, whose motto is 'delight in all your inside functional apparatus'. Mussels are the heart of the idea, but also other Belgian essentials like lobster and steak tartare. 100 different beers. Throbbing trendcity.

㊸ Café des Amis du Vin, 11–14 Hanover Place, WC2, ✆ 0171-379 3444 (*closed Sun*). A cheap, quiet French brasserie, favoured by theatre goers. Caters for all tastes, from omelettes to stuffed trout. More formal upstairs dining room. A little pedestrian, but solid. Service can be slow.

㊹ Calabash, Africa Centre, 38 King St, WC2, ℓ 0171-836 1976 (*closed Sat lunch, all day Sun*). Dishes from all over Africa are served at this basement restaurant under the Africa Centre. A surprisingly institutional feel pervades the dining room, partly because of the collegey canteen. *Egusi* (stew of beef, melon, shrimps cooked in palm oil) from Nigeria, couscous from the Maghreb, *dioumbre* (okra stew) from Ivory Coast, or *yassa* chicken (grilled chicken with lemon, onion and pepper) from Senegal, with lots of fried plantain.

Bloomsbury/Fitzrovia   *map A*

expensive

㊺ Pied-à-terre, 34 Charlotte St, W1, ℓ 0171-636 1178 (*closed Sun*). Excellent French restaurant with Italian touches. Neutral setting. The seafood first courses and the game are highly recommended. Prices have been kept in check after some allegations of overpricing, but luxury cooking survives nonetheless, such as quails' egg salad. Cheaper set menus at lunchtime.

㊻ Nico Central, 35 Gt Portland St, W1, ℓ 0171-436 8846 (*closed Sat, Sun*). Although this restaurant is no longer run by Nico Ladenis, the standards, as well as the good deals in the set menus, remain. Mostly Provençal-inspired creations. Sometimes smallish portions, but beautifully cooked, with interesting ideas such as boudin blanc with caramelised apple galette, and red snapper with couscous. Dream puddings.

moderate

㊼ Museum Street Café, 47 Museum St, WC1, ℓ 0171-405 3211 (*closed Sat, Sun*). Sleek and spartan, emphasizing the '90s predilection for scarce décor. Excellent, unusual items, although standards are reputedly variable. Sample dishes include salad with *confit* of guinea fowl with roasted beets and walnut vinaigrette, and penne with roasted red peppers and saffron and basil cream.

㊽ Gonbei, 151 King's Cross Rd, WC1, ℓ 0171-278 0619 (*closed Sun*). One of London's cheaper, but still excellent, Japanese restaurants. Only open in the evening (6–10.30). Delicious set dinners; also à la carte choices. Sushi is particularly recommended, as is noodle soup with tempura.

㊾ Elena's L'Etoile, 30 Charlotte St, W1, ℓ 0171-636 1496 (*closed Sat lunch, all day Sun*). This historic Fitzrovian locale has appropriated Elena Salvoni's name to its title in tribute to her personal contribution to the Etoile. Faded grandeur and old photographs of fêted regulars serve as the backdrop. But the menu is no longer only traditional French fare: some modern touches especially in the Eastern influence of some recipes.

inexpensive

㊿ Alfred, 245 Shaftsbury Ave, WC2, ℓ 0171-240 2566 (*closed Sat lunch, all day Sun*). A modern angle on old British favourites. Stark, no-nonsense décor with duck egg blue and nut brown walls and formica tabletops. This serves to underline the delicacy of the cooking. Straightforward dishes like roast pork combine with imaginative accompaniments like marinated artichoke.

51 **Mandeer**, 21 Hanway Place, W1, ℗ 0171-323 0660 (*closed Sun*). Appetizing vegetarian food from Gujarat and Punjab, including puffed lotus seeds and tofu curry. The place has been serving vegetarian dishes of this ilk since 1961. There are about five *thalis*—complete meals—several being suitable for slimmers.

52 **Townhouse Brasserie**, 24 Coptic St, WC1, ℗ 0171-636 2731. A fusion of modern French and international cooking, e.g. seafood tempura in French batter. Somewhat cramped quarters even though there is plenty of space. Fizzing and boozy atmosphere, and huge portions.

cheap

53 **Chutneys**, 124 Drummond St, NW1, ℗ 0171-388 0604 (*unlicensed*). One of several extraordinarily cheap, vegetarian Indian restaurants along this narrow street just behind Euston Station. Watch out for unexpectedly high service charges.

54 **Diwana Bhel Poori**, 121 Drummond St, NW1, ℗ 0171-387 5556 (*unlicensed*). Another Drummond Street Indian institution, which is widely thought to have the edge over its main competitors along the road. Reliable southern Indian fare, especially the snacks like *papri chat* and *sev poori*. Less reliable curries.

55 **Wagamama**, 4 Streatham St, ℗ 0171-323 9223 (*closed Sun, no credit cards*). The first branch. See entry under Soho.

56 **Pierre Victoire**, 11 Charlotte St, W1, ℗ 0171-436 0248. A remarkably successful chain of bargain bistros serving set menus for knock-down prices. Some

short cuts are inevitably taken with the cooking—but you can get an excellent, wholesome three-courser for remarkably little.

57 **October Gallery Café**, 24 Old Gloucester St, WC1, ℗ 0171-242 7367. Eclectic inspiration from around the world; busy, cosy and friendly. Two or three course meals for highly reasonable prices. A limited choice—but usually a vegetarian option. A courtyard to skulk in in summertime.

Marylebone   *map B*

moderate

1 **Stephen Bull**, 5–7 Blandford St, W1, ℗ 0171-486 9696 (*closed Sat lunch, all day Sun*). An excellent, original voice amongst the multi-faceted strains of modern European cooking. Like Alistair Little, Bull believes strongly in simplicity in cooking, and emphasizes fresh ingredients and unfussy, non-gimmicky presentation. The result is highly sophisticated. A strong commitment to seafood, e.g. fillet of sea bass with baby fennel, hollandaise and oyster sauce.

inexpensive

2 **Singapore Garden**, 154–6 Gloucester Place, NW1, ℗ 0171-723 8233. A spacious, light basement venue under Regent's Park Hotel, serving Singaporean Chinese food. Sometimes very hot, but very successful seafood dishes. The service is very friendly, the environment a touch staid. Try the fried seaweed and squid and the mild fish curry.

3 **Sea Shell**, 49–51 Lisson Grove, NW1, ℗ 0171-723 8703. Arguably the best fish and chips in town. Fresh and crisp, and popular too. Fine home-made fish cakes and, more's the rarity, home-made tartare sauce. Clean and attractive. Café-style eating as well as takeaway.

❹ Union Café & Restaurant, 96 Marylebone Lane, W1, ✆ 0171-486 4860 (*closed Sun, brunch served on Sat*). Another restaurant preaching simplicity, with great verve. Delicious salads; organic, free-range produce is guaranteed, where appropriate. Non-puritanical puddings.

Mayfair/St James's   *map B*

luxury

❺ Connaught Hotel Grill Room, Carlos Place, W1, ✆ 0171-499 7070 (*closed Sat, Sun*). Steaks, grills, as well as unusual French delicacies are a treat in this most exclusive of surroundings. High quality but not wildly adventurous. A fine, apple-green room, chandeliers, banquettes. Serious but friendly waiters with impeccable sensitivity.

❻ Le Gavroche, 43 Upper Brook St, W1, ✆ 0171-408 0881 (*closed Sat, Sun*). Albert Roux is one of the most revered cooks in Britain, the first this side of the Channel to win three Michelin stars. He has now delegated much of the cuisine to his son, Michel, but standards are still de luxe. Extraordinary creativity, from the sautéed scallops to the coffee cup desert. It doesn't however come cheap—recently one customer reputedly spent £13,500 on dinner for three.

❼ Suntory, 72–3 St. James's St, SW1, ✆ 0171-409 0201 (*closed Sun*). One of the best, most expensive Japanese restaurants in town, with a Michelin star

and also prices to remind you of the fact. You can eat in the old-fashioned, black beamed, paper screened dining room—or in a private room. Very delicate sushi—which usually comes as a six-course meal.

expensive

❽ Al Hamra, 31–33 Shepherd Market, W1, ✆ 0171-493 1954. Sophisticated if rather overpriced Middle Eastern restaurant in the heart of the cosmopolitan chic of Shepherds' Market, where you can sit 'out' in the summer months. The idea is to select a meze of different dishes from the 48 different delicacies—*batrakh* (fish roe with garlic and olive oil) and *makdoue* (aubergines stuffed with walnuts and spices) are particularly recommended.

❾ The Greenhouse, 27a Hay's Mews, W1, ✆ 0171-499 3331 (*closed Sun*). The principal idea behind this restaurant was to resurrect stale old English recipes into new categories. Liver and bacon or sponge pudding may sound dull, but they come to life here. Signature dishes include fillet of smoked haddock with Welsh rarebit on a tomato and chive salad.

❿ The Square, 6–10 Bruton St, W1, ✆ 0171-839 8787 (*closed Sat, Sun lunch*). The Square has moved to a new Mayfair address, equally sleek and modern. Constantly changing menu, with strong emphasis on fish. Try the delicious seared tuna with niçoise dressing.

⓫ Le Caprice, Arlington House, Arlington St, SW1, ✆ 0171-629 2239. Fashion victims crowd this modish but imaginative restaurant. Essentially 'modern

Regent's Park

MARYLEBONE

BAKER STREET

MARYLEBONE ROAD

REGENT'S PARK

SHROTON ST.

HAREWOOD AV.

MARYLEBONE

LISSON GROVE

COSWAY ST.

PADDINGTON STREET

MARYLEBONE HIGH STREET

NEW CAVENDISH STREET

PORTLAND PLACE

GREAT PORTLAND STREET

YORK STREET

CRAWFORD ST.

BAKER STREET

CHILTERN STREET

MANCHESTER STREET

BLANDFORD STREET

MARYLEBONE LA.

SEYMOUR PLACE

GEORGE STREET

GLOUCESTER PLACE

WIGMORE STREET

CAVENDISH SQUARE

EDGWARE ROAD

UPPER BERKELEY ST.

SEYMOUR STREET

OXFORD STREET

BOND STREET

NEW BOND STREET

MADDOX ST.

BAYSWATER

MARBLE ARCH

PARK

UPPER BROOK STREET

SOUTH AUDLEY STREET

DUKE STREET

DAVIES STREET

Grosvenor Square

Grosvenor Street

CONDUIT

BRUTON ST.

Berkeley Square

ADAM'S ROW

MOUNT STREET

SOUTH FARM ST.

HAY'S M.

DERMERY ST.

GREEN ST.

CHARLES ST.

QUEEN ST.

CURZON ST.

WHITEHORSE

GREEN PARK

SHEPHERD ST.

Hyde Park

PARK LANE

PARK LANE

OLD PK LN.

PICCADILLY

Green Park

N

500 metres

500 yards

478

Map B

1 Stephen Bull
2 Singapore Garden
3 Sea Shell
4 Union Café & Restaurant
5 Connaught Hotel Grill Room
6 Le Gavroche
7 Suntory
8 Al Hamra
9 The Greenhouse
10 The Square
11 Le Caprice
12 Wiltons
13 Quaglino's
14 Sofra
15 Bentley's
16 Mulligans'
17 Zen Central
18 Down Mexico Way
19 Condotti's

British' food, but eclectic choice, with lovely starters such as squash risotto and a variation on Middle Eastern meze.

⑫ **Wiltons**, 55 Jermyn St, W1, ✆ 0171-629 9955 (*closed Sat lunch*). A traditional old English address, with fish and game specialities. A positively Edwardian air, with sporting prints in the hall and few evident modern accessories—that applies to the menu too. Unreconstructed British cooking. Jacket and tie essential.

moderate

⑬ **Quaglino's**, 16 Bury St, SW1, ✆ 0171-930 6767. Modern, designer restaurant in a converted, sunken ballroom, with mainly Italian menu. Polished and gleaming, it is another facet of the growing Conran empire. The menu is equally design conscious, although there is a large choice. Good shellfish.

⑭ **Sofra**, 18 Shepherd Market, W1, ✆ 0171-493 3320. Excellent Turkish restaurant with all the usual meze dishes, a crushed wheat salad and delicious sticky filled pastries. An emphasis on fresh ingredients ensures high quality at reasonable prices. A slightly 'packaged' design effect—but this does not deter hordes of tourists.

⑮ **Bentley's**, 11–15 Swallow St, W1, ✆ 0171-734 4756 (*closed Sun*). Good-value English seafood restaurant, with excellent oysters. A steady emphasis on traditional cooking is moderated by some exotic flashes from the Far East. Non-seafood dishes include maize-fed chicken with black pudding.

⑯ **Mulligans'**, 13–14 Cork St, W1, ✆ 0171-409 1370 (*closed Sat lunch, all day Sun*). Hearty Irish cooking, but a new management has incorporated lighter dishes (such as smoked fish, or blue cashel cheese and artichoke and spinach salad), especially at lunch time. But you can still find beef cooked in Guiness, and other Irish favourites. Wicked puddings, particularly the black and white one with apple and ginger chutney.

⑰ **Zen Central**, 20–22 Queen St, W1, ✆ 0171-629 8103. More inventive than your average Chinese restaurant and gaining popularity all the time. Pekinese, Cantonese and Szechuan specialities. Branches in Hampstead and Chelsea.

inexpensive

⑱ **Down Mexico Way**, 25 Swallow St, W1, ✆ 0171-437 9895 (*closed Sun lunch*). London does not excel in Mexican food but this is one of the better addresses in town. Fish with chilli and almond, and lime-cooked chicken provide welcome variations on the usual enchiladas. Also a more up-market ambience than usual.

⑲ **Condotti's**, 4 Mill St, W1, ✆ 0171-499 1308. A smart pizza parlour with white linen table-cloths and chic waitresses. Otherwise the pizzas are regular and juicy as opposed to thin and crusty. At lunch time it is full of business clients, but in the evening it jollies up.

luxury

❶ **Clarke's**, 124 Kensington Church St, W8, ✆ 0171-221 9225 (*closed Sat, Sun*). A Californian restaurant to the extent that there is an emphasis on fresh produce. The set menu changes nightly, including salad of roasted pigeon with water cress, blood orange and black truffle dressing, and chargrilled turbot

with chilli and roasted garlic mayon-
naise, sea cale and leaf spinach. Small,
intimate, nearly prissy room, but
cooking is precise and professional.

moderate

❷ **Phoenicia**, 11–13 Abingdon Rd, W8,
℗ 0171-937 0120. Swish, carpeted
Lebanese restaurant attracting smartly
dressed customers. Delicious meze
selections—excellent *basturma* (smoked,
cured Lebanese beef) and falafel—but
portions can be modest. Makes much of
pudding too: a variety of fresh cream and
pastry dishes are given a dousing in aromatic syrups.

❸ **Boyd's**, 135 Kensington Church St,
W8, ℗ 0171-727 5452. British dishes
with flashes of Mediterranean and
French inspiration. Great sauces with a
variety of meat, fish and seasonal game,
e.g. seared venison with orange and red-
currant sauce.

❹ **Wódka**, 12 St. Alban's Grove, W8,
℗ 0171-937 6513 (*closed Sat, Sun
lunch*). This site has been a Polish restaurant since the 1950s—but the current
proprietor of this newish venture is
intent on modernizing the image of
Eastern European food in London. Plain
interior with jazz backdrop. A list of 30
different vodkas and *eaux de vie*; also a
daily changing set lunch at low prices.
The result is both classy and professional.

❺ **Cambio de Tercio**, 163 Old
Brompton Rd, SW5, ℗ 0171-244 8970.
Exuberant contemporary Spanish
cooking: delicate paella, skate wings, salt
cod, octopus. Intensely popular; best to
book ahead. Strong references to the
bullring in the decorative theme. Some
excellent real tapas too to start with—
jamón serrano with *fino* or *manzanilla*.

inexpensive

❻ **The Gate**, 51 Queen Caroline St, Hammersmith, W6, ℗ 0181-748 6932
(*closed Sat lunch, all day Sun and
Mon*). First-rate vegetarian restaurant
with mouth-watering fennel mousse,
wild mushroom cannelloni and teryaki
aubergine. Sunflower walls and a leafy
courtyard make an attractive ambience.

❼ **Lou Pescadou**, 241 Old Brompton Rd,
SW5, ℗ 0171-370 1057. Jolly atmosphere, friendly waiters. Provençal-
cooked fish on the pricey side but reli-
ably good: fish soup, mussels, monkfish,
turbot, sea bream, langoustines with
cream and garlic.

cheap

❽ **Polish Air Force Association Club
and Restaurant**, 14 Collingham Gardens, SW5, ℗ 0171-370 1229. Set
three-course meal from £5.20. Atmospheric basement club founded after the
War, filled with flying memorabilia,
catering to local Poles but welcoming
visitors. Hearty Polish cooking: *pierogis*,
sauerkraut, meatballs: also *golonka*
(pig's knuckle) and jam pancakes or cake
for pudding.

❾ **La Pappardella**, 253 Old Brompton
Rd, SW5, ℗ 0171-373 7777. Crowded,
high-decibel, good-value, ultra-friendly
Italian: 18 varieties of pizza, also pasta,
veal, fish.

Chelsea and Fulham   *map C*

luxury

❿ **La Tante Claire**, 68 Royal Hospital
Road, SW3, ℗ 0171-352 6045 (*closed
Sat, Sun*). Classic French cuisine, with
three Michelin stars to its name. Lots of
goose, foie gras and duck, as well as

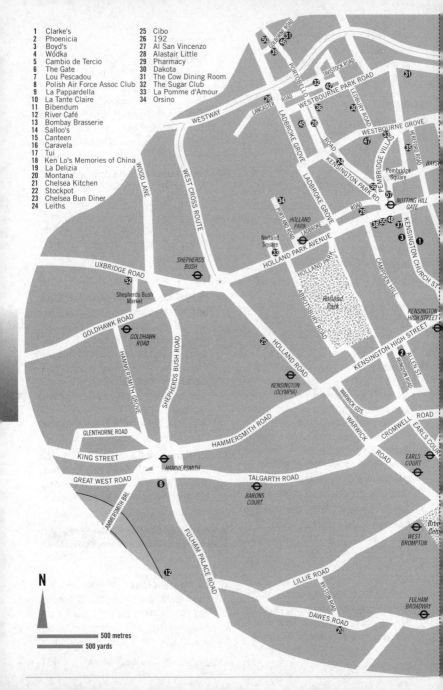

1	Clarke's	25	Cibo
2	Phoenicia	26	192
3	Boyd's	27	Al San Vincenzo
4	Wódka	28	Alastair Little
5	Cambio de Tercio	29	Pharmacy
6	The Gate	30	Dakota
7	Lou Pescadou	31	The Cow Dining Room
8	Polish Air Force Assoc Club	32	The Sugar Club
9	La Pappardella	33	La Pomme d'Amour
10	La Tante Claire	34	Orsino
11	Bibendum		
12	River Café		
13	Bombay Brasserie		
14	Salloo's		
15	Canteen		
16	Caravela		
17	Tui		
18	Ken Lo's Memories of China		
19	La Delizia		
20	Montana		
21	Chelsea Kitchen		
22	Stockpot		
23	Chelsea Bun Diner		
24	Leiths		

N

500 metres
500 yards

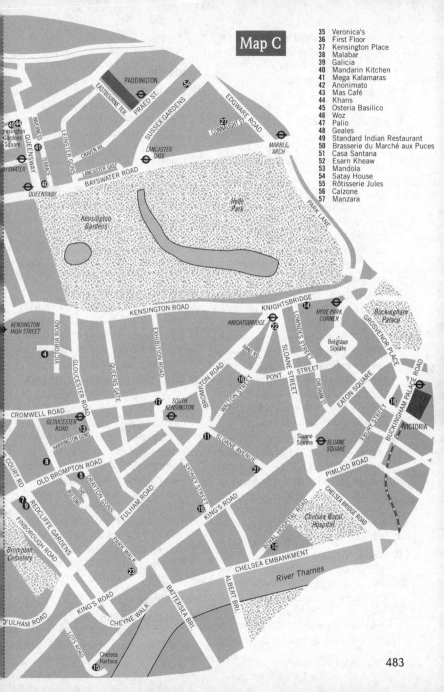

Map C

35 Veronica's
36 First Floor
37 Kensington Place
38 Malabar
39 Galicia
40 Mandarin Kitchen
41 Mega Kalamaras
42 Anonimato
43 Mas Café
44 Khans
45 Osteria Basilico
46 Woz
47 Palio
48 Geales
49 Standard Indian Restaurant
50 Brasserie du Marché aux Puces
51 Casa Santana
52 Esarn Kheaw
53 Mandola
54 Satay House
55 Rôtisserie Jules
56 Calzone
57 Manzara

483

other Gascon-inspired compositions, prepared with delicacy and style. *Galette de foie gras au Sauternes et échalottes rôties* is one of chef Pierre Koffman's signature dishes.

expensive

⓫ **Bibendum**, Michelin House, 81 Fulham Rd, SW3, ℗ 0171-581 5817. Excelling in ultra-rich French regional food, set in the sumptuously restored art deco Michelin building (ex-headquarters of the tyre manufacturers, designed by an untrained architect in 1905, and restored by Conran in 1987). The oyster bar downstairs, with a shorter fish-oriented menu, is cheaper though less grand.

⓬ **River Café**, Thames Wharf Studios, Rainville Rd, W6, ℗ 0171-381 8824 (*closed Sun dinner*). Simple, very tasty Italian food in a splendid riverside setting designed by Richard Rogers—and then re-designed by him. Rogers' wife, Ruthie, and her friend Rose Gray, are the chief chefs—and they have written a series of highly influential cookbooks to illustrate their vision and style.

⓭ **Bombay Brasserie**, Courtfield Close, Courtfield Rd, SW7, ℗ 0171-370 4040. Near Gloucester Rd. Unlike most Indian restaurants in London, this is posh, in sumptuous colonial décor, and gastronomically flawless. Largely north Indian menu, including some unusual tandoori dishes. Beautiful veranda.

⓮ **Salloo's**, 62–4 Kinnerton St, SW1, ℗ 0171-235 4444 (*closed Sun*). Succulent grilled meats are the speciality at this superior Pakistani restaurant. Beautifully prepared marinades, and terrific tandooris. Reputedly one of the best Pakistani restaurants in the capital, although

the classy location definitely helps. Good wine list too.

moderate

⓯ **Canteen**, Unit 4G, Harbour Yard, Chelsea Harbour, SW10, ℗ 0171-351 7330. Part owned by the actor, Michael Caine, a resident of the harbour. Postmodern setting with playing-card upholstery. Dishes include *velouté* of artichokes, spinach and chestnut ravioli, and peppered duck breast, roast baby vegetables and pineapple *jus.*

⓰ **Caravela**, 39 Beauchamp Place, SW3, ℗ 0171-581 2366. Lively Portuguese restaurant with a guitarist and singers to serenade you as you eat your salt cod or charcoal-grilled meats. Dark blue and intimate setting. Rich puddings.

⓱ **Tui**, 19 Exhibition Rd, SW7, ℗ 0171-584 8359. A cool atmosphere but warm service and a fine array of Thai specialities including rich soups brought simmering to your table.

⓲ **Ken Lo's Memories of China**, 67–69 Ebury St, SW1, ℗ 0171-730 7734 (*closed Sun*). Minimalist décor, but maximalist cooking. Ken Lo, one of Britain's best-known Chinese restauranteurs, who died a few years ago, founded this esteemed establishment which offers a stunning gastronomic tour of China to delight your eyes and satisfy every stomach. His daughter, Jenny Lo, has opened a similiarly impressive Chinese eatery, building on her father's inspiration, at Jenny Lo's Tea House, 14 Eccleston St, SW1, ℗ 0171-259 0399.

inexpensive

● **Del Buongustaio**, 283 Putney Bridge Rd, SW15, ℗ 0181-780 9361 (*closed Sat lunch in winter*). Tasty Italian regional specialities at very reasonable prices. Emphasis on seasonality: monthly changing menus, knowledgeably researched, e.g. baked goat with prosciutto, roasted vegetables, rosemary and marjoram.

⑲ La Delizia, Chelsea Farmers' Market, Sydney St, SW3, ✆ 0171-351 6701. Good pizzeria with attractive outdoor seating and elegant indoor rooms. Often very crowded. Thin crust pizzas come ready-sliced so they can be conveniently shared about.

⑳ Montana, 125 Dawes Rd, SW6, ✆ 0171-385 9500. Cooking from the American southwest (despite the name): subtle chilli flavours, and lots of cumin, squash, tortilla and pumpkin. Some highly original combinations such as Navajo rabbit and fig *quesadilla.* Sophisticated blue and purple colour scheme.

cheap

㉑ Chelsea Kitchen, 98 King's Rd, SW3, ✆ 0171-589 1330. Continental food and wine for less than £10. This venue has been known since the 1960s as a jostling, studenty joint for knock-down prices—a haven of cheapness in the posh streets around Sloane Square.

㉒ Stockpot, 6 Basil St, SW3, ✆ 0171-589 8627. Three-course meals for not much more than a fiver. Strains of school dinner. Hardly makes pretensions at culinary art, but the quality isn't actually bad.

㉓ Chelsea Bun Diner, 9a Limerston St, SW10, ✆ 0171-352 3635. Set meals from £5.50. Bring your own alcohol. American-style all-day breakfasts, also burgers and pastas from 200 item -long menu. Excellent value, no credit cards.

Notting Hill — map C

luxury

㉔ Leiths, 92 Kensington Park Road, W11, ✆ 0171-229 4481 (*closed all day Sun, lunch Sat–Mon*). An ultra-neutral environment, verging on the bland. This is doubtless to emphasize that the culinary delights on offer are not to be competed with. Presentation is as expert as the combination of ingredients: modern, inventive and elegant. Roasted scallops and spiced lemon couscous amount to high art.

expensive

㉕ Cibo, 3 Russell Gardens, W14, ✆ 0171-371 6271. Highly imaginative pasta sauces (wild mushrooms and broad beans for instance), and duck ravioli, as well as many other unusual interpretations of Italian food. Thick, multi-coloured, individualized porcelain, and naked Renaissance ladies on the walls. Intimate and classy.

㉖ 192, 192 Kensington Park Rd, W11, ✆ 0171-229 0482. Once the early stamping ground of embryonic chefs such as Alastair Little. Now a very trendy French brasserie where food plays second fiddle to the posing: models and actors and the like come in their droves. Dishes include sea bass on samphire with *beurre blanc* and chives; duck confit with mash and apple sauce.

㉗ Al San Vincenzo, 30 Connaught St, W2, ✆ 0171-262 9623 (*closed Sat lunch, all day Sun*). Spicy southern Italian food prevails at this efficient and friendly establishment. Simple cooking, but some eccentric components are added to unlikely subjects, such as parmesan with lamb. Intimate, tiny room. Good wine list.

28 Alastair Little, 136A Lancaster Rd, W11, ✆ 0171-243 2220 (*closed Sun*). New branch of famous Soho establishment (*see* above). Even more minimalist, but food just as marvellous.

29 Pharmacy, 150 Notting Hill Gate, W11, ✆ 0171-221 2442. The ultimate in tasteful conceptual art: a restaurant and café/cocktail lounge designed by formaldehyde artist Damien Hirst, with the help of a few consignments of pill-boxes and specimen jars from St Mary's Hospital, Paddington. Waiters are dressed in hospital gowns designed by Prada. A small menu, including spit-roast gambas and roast suckling pig, and a trendy, arty crowd.

30 Dakota, 127 Ledbury Rd, ✆ 0171-792 9191 (*closed Sun*). Increasingly popular amongst the great and the good of Notting Hill, this is one of the best in the area. Modern, elegant US cuisine boasting an impressive (delicious corn bread) menu. Impeccable service.

moderate

31 The Cow Dining Room, 89 Westbourne Park Road, W2, ✆ 0171-221 0021. The relaxed, almost countrified, atmosphere at the upstairs rooms above the trendy pub (of the same name) belies the precision cooking. Global inspiration but strong French strain, particularly in the sauces.

32 The Sugar Club, 33A All Saints Rd, W11, ✆ 0171-221 3844. One of the hippest places in swinging London. Globally inspired dishes with particularly good contrasting textures and tastes, e.g. grilled scallops with sweet chilli sauce and crème fraîche; spicy kangaroo salad

with coriander, mint, peanuts and lime chilli dressing. Leafy garden.

33 La Pomme d'Amour, 128 Holland Park Avenue, W11, ✆ 0171-221 4498 (*closed Sat lunch, all day Sun*). Precise modern French restaurant with constantly changing menu. Succulent sauces; pristine atmosphere.

34 Orsino, 119 Portland Rd, W11, ✆ 0171-221 3299. Sibling restaurant to Orso's and thus shares many of the latter's characteristics. Terracotta walls, Venetian blinds and simple but interesting and innovative cooking with Tuscan roots, like veal escalopes with sun dried tomatoes, sage and white wine; roast turbot with lime leaves and new potatoes.

35 Veronica's, 3 Hereford Rd, W2, ✆ 0171-229 5079 (*closed Sat lunch, all day Sun*). A restaurant that has unearthed historical and regional British dishes—spring lamb with crabmeat or calf's liver and beetroot—and even relaunched recipes that date from the 14th century, sometimes adapting them to more modern tastes. Elizabethan puddings, Reform lamb...

36 First Floor, 186 Portobello Rd, W11, ✆ 0171-243 0072 (*closed Sun eve*). Fantastical—some might say pretentious—upmarket brasserie above a loud drinking place with a broad range of interesting concoctions, including chorizo, Thai fishcakes and guacamole, and verging on the weird with coffee-smoked ostrich fillet with mango sushi. The room itself is a haven of calm in this boozy, happening end of Portobello.

37 Kensington Place, 201 Kensington Church St, W8, ✆ 0171-727 3814. Sleek, airy, noisy, modern dining room with bold garden frescoes and 'eclectic

European' cuisine. The highest quality ingredients; venison, sirloin steak, wild sea trout, sorrel omelette. Full of publishers lunching out with their favoured writers and journalists.

⊕ Malabar, 27 Uxbridge St, W8, ✆ 0171-727 8800. Quiet northern Indian restaurant with sumptuous, but unchanging choices. Very popular with Notting Hill regulars. Modern and wooden inside with white-washed alcoves. Dishes are served on large, shiny stainless-steel plates. Sleek, deferential waiters all dressed in black.

⊕ Galicia, 323 Portobello Rd, W10, ✆ 0181-969 3539. Galicia jostles with a rum mixture of authentic 'Gallego' locals and a trendy crowd of 'Gatey Mates' (Notting Hill Gate fashion fiends). But the produce, the waiters and the 'feel' are uncannily real. Excellent paella and seafood options.

⊕ Mandarin Kitchen, 14–16 Queensway, W2, ✆ 0171-727 9468. An increasingly popular Chinese restaurant, with fish you can pick out of the fish-tank. Mainly Cantonese food, in spite of its name. One of the best Chinese joints outside Chinatown.

⊕ Mega Kalamaras, 76–78 Inverness Mews, W2, ✆ 0171-727 9122 (closed Sun). A high-quality, very friendly Greek restaurant. Good seafood and a wide variety of vegetarian dishes as well as the hearty meat standards. Its smaller, cheaper twin Micro Kalamaras is in a basement next door.

⊕ Anonimato, 12 All Saints Road, W11, ✆ 0171-243 2808. Imaginative, inventive menu drawing on the unusual and the familiar (ostrich, seafood, ravioli). Blends trendy Italian and Pacific elements in airy, unfrenetic surroundings.

inexpensive

⊕ Mas Café, 6–8 All Saints Rd, W11, ✆ 0171-243 0969 (closed lunch Mon–Fri). Swinging, bustling, loud, ultra-trendy restaurant. Starts buzzing late. Mediterranean food like baby squid; definite high-quality spicy cooking to boot. Brunch offered on weekends, where you can see people working off their hangovers.

⊕ Khans, 13–15 Westbourne Grove, W2, ✆ 0171-727 5420. Hectic, helter skelter Indian restaurant; frantic waiters collide with waiting queues. Noise drowns intimacy, and yet the main dining room preserves its charm—painted clouds waft all about you and palm trees act as columns. Delicious food.

⊕ Osteria Basilico, 29 Kensington Park Rd, W11, ✆ 0171-727 9372. Intensely popular, hence intensely noisy restaurant with warm ochre walls. New wave Italian dishes that are now becoming the norm, like spaghetti with fresh lobster and tomato, and linguine with spiced salami, parmesan, tomato and basil. Wooden kitchen tables and chairs, and echoey floors. Brazen staff.

⊕ Woz, 46 Golborne Rd, W10, ✆ 0181-968 2200 (closed Mon lunch). In spite of the jokey name, this is a serious venture with serious Mediterranean food and a fixed menu. Sample dishes include pan fried chicken livers with rocket and balsamic vinegar, and Tunisian spinach salad served with poached skate. Airy ground floor room with interesting abstracts, cosier basement.

⊕ Palio, 175 Westbourne Park Grove, W11, ✆ 0171-221 6624. Cool yellow and black décor with big round staircase winding through to the first floor; jazz wafts through the rooms; dark and intimate and yet noisy. Italian food in bold combinations.

㊽ **Geales**, 2 Farmer St, W8, ✆ 0171-727 7969 (*closed Mon*). Superior fish and chips (deep-fried in beef dripping for a touch of class). Very busy. Photographs of famous customers from the world of rock 'n' roll.

㊾ **Standard Indian Restaurant**, 17 Westbourne Grove, W11, ✆ 0171-229 0600. First-rate tandoori restaurant with excellent pickles and friendly service. Unassuming name and room belie the high quality of the food.

㊿ **Brasserie du Marché aux Puces**, 349 Portobello Rd, W10, ✆ 0181-968 5828 (*open all day*). Inventive, café-style restaurant (the name means flea-market brasserie, as it's near Portobello market). Serves eclectic menu including an extraordinary haggis in filo pastry with quince purée. Old-fashioned but popular.

(51) **Casa Santana**, 44 Golborne Rd, W10, ✆ 0181-968 8764 (*no credit cards*). Neighbourhood Portuguese restaurant (Madeiran to be precise)—meat stews and smoked cod—with bags of character and good if somewhat inconsistent food. Triumphant desserts and Madeiran beers.

(52) **Esarn Kheaw**, 314 Uxbridge Rd, W12, ✆ 0181-743 8930 (*closed Sat and Sun lunch*). High quality, authentic, northern Thai food at very reasonable prices just west of Shepherd's Bush. Thought by some to be one of the best Thai restaurants in London; thick sticky rice and unusual sauces like *koong pad* oyster sauce. The only grimness is the long, unpleasant Uxbridge Rd.

cheap

(53) **Mandola**, 139–141 Westbourne Grove, W11, ✆ 0171-229 4734 (*unlicensed*). Delightful Sudanese restaurant which has had to expand to cope with demand. Simple wooden décor with a few African exotica. Strong Arabic overtones to the dishes: *filfilia* (mixed vegetable stew), *addas* (lentil stew dressed with caramelised garlic; *fule* (boiled dried broad beans).

(54) **Satay House**, 13 Sale Place, W2, ✆ 0171-723 6763 (*closed Mon*). Small, intimate shop front serving delicious Malaysian food—most of the customers appear to be Malaysian which suggests authenticity. Strong flavours and a broad range of delicious recipes, chargrilled, baked and marinated. Karaoke on a Saturday night in the basement is popular amongst Malaysians too. Photographs of Malay pop stars adorn the walls downstairs as inspiration.

(55) **Rôtisserie Jules**, 133A Notting Hill Gate, W11, ✆ 0171-221 3736 (*closed Sat lunch, all day Sun*). A very welcome new venture in cheap but good restaurants. Good free-range chicken and other meats, with huge portions. Three courses for a very modest bill. Two other branches in Bute St, SW7, and 338 King's Rd, SW3.

(56) **Calzone**, 2A Kensington Park Rd, W11, ✆ 0171-243 2003 (*open all day from 10am*). Wide thin-crusted pizzas. The antidote to Pizza Express (whose pizzas are juicier)—particularly if you dislike chain restaurants. Calzone is situated in an interesting, curved glass-fronted room overlooking the juncture of four roads. The goldfish bowl of Notting Hill?

57 **Manzara**, 24 Pembridge Rd, W11, ✆ 0171-727 3062 (*open all day*). Good, cheap Turkish restaurant with a wide selection of meze dishes. Sometimes sloppily cooked—as in oily or over-done—but good value and some definitely tasty, fresh choices.

Camden *map D*

moderate

1 **Café Delancey**, 3 Delancey St, NW1, ✆ 0171-387 1985 (*open all day*). Charming, discreet French restaurant with robust, attractively presented dishes. Caters for all types. Brasserie food: venison but also snacks and soups.

2 **Lemonia**, 89 Regent's Park Rd, Primrose Hill, NW1, ✆ 0171-586 7454 (*closed Sat lunch and Sun eve*). Popular Greek Cypriot restaurant with a delightful conservatory for simulated *al fresco* dining in the summer. Very high standard Greek food, especially fish, although a particularly good *spanako pita* with fresh mint. Much charm all round.

3 **Belgo**, 72 Chalk Farm Rd, NW1, ✆ 0171-267 0718. Slightly pricey Belgian *moules et frites* in a fashionable setting: original version of Belgo Centraal (*see* under Covent Garden).

inexpensive

4 **Vegetarian Cottage**, 91 Haverstock Hill, NW3, ✆ 0171-586 1257 (*evenings only except Sun when open all day*). Excellent vegetarian Chinese restaurant, with inventive dishes including 'duckling' made entirely of soya, and water chestnut pudding. Essentially seeks to provide Buddhist vegetarian dishes—

sometimes variable, but wonderful when good.

5 **Paphos Restaurant**, 43 Pratt St, Camden, NW1, ✆ 0171-485 7266. Good *loukamika* sausage and grilled kebabs at a veritable 'little Greece'—during the day you can find a deli, a bakery and even a Greek tailor nearby.

6 **Cheng Du**, 9 Parkway, Camden, NW1, ✆ 0171-485 8058. Spicy Chinese Szechuan cooking in the heart of Camden. Often mixes Szechuan with more modern Chinese cooking. Attentive service, quiet ambience.

Hampstead *map D*

moderate

7 **Café des Arts**, 82 Hampstead High St, NW3, ✆ 0171-435 3608. Classy French cooking and a beautiful 17th-century building make this one of the most appealing restaurants in north London. An open fire and wooden panelling impart warmth.

inexpensive

8 **Byron**, 3A Downshire Hill, NW1, ✆ 0171-435 3544. Elegant but simple English restaurant with good fishcakes and trimmings and excellent traditional Sunday lunches. Romantic Georgian townhouse setting, and long swirling taffeta curtains give a stagey feel. Cheap lunches in the week.

Islington *map D*

moderate

9 **Granita**, 127 Upper St, N1, ✆ 0171-226 3222 (*closed Mon and Tues lunchtime*). Eclectic Islington restaurant,

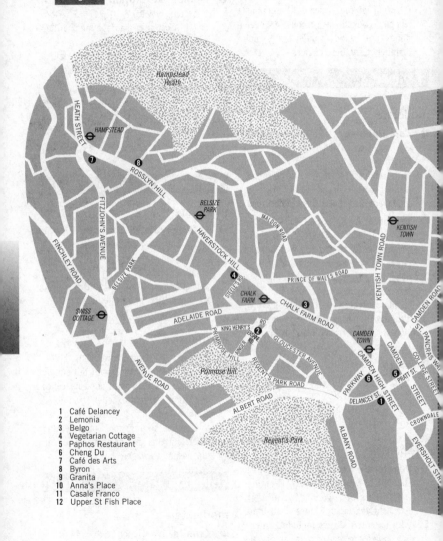

Map D

1 Café Delancey
2 Lemonia
3 Belgo
4 Vegetarian Cottage
5 Paphos Restaurant
6 Cheng Du
7 Café des Arts
8 Byron
9 Granita
10 Anna's Place
11 Casale Franco
12 Upper St Fish Place

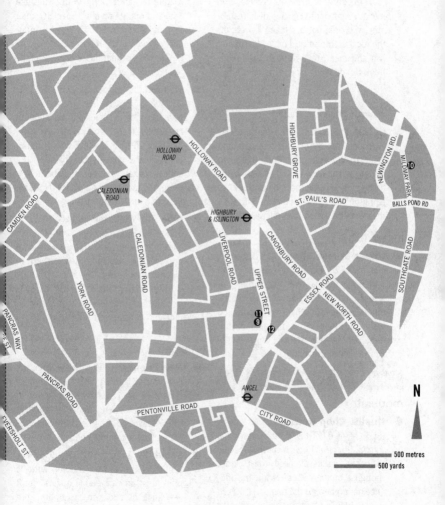

HOLLOWAY ROAD

HOLLOWAY ROAD

CALEDONIAN ROAD

HIGHBURY GROVE

NEWINGTON RD.

MILDMAY PARK

⑩

ST. PAUL'S ROAD

BALLS POND RD

CAMDEN ROAD

HIGHBURY & ISLINGTON

SOUTHGATE ROAD

CALEDONIAN ROAD

LIVERPOOL ROAD

CANONBURY ROAD

ESSEX ROAD

NEW NORTH ROAD

YORK ROAD

UPPER STREET

⑪
⑨

⑫

PANCRAS WAY

F ST.

PANCRAS ROAD

ANGEL

EVERSHOLT ST

PENTONVILLE ROAD

CITY ROAD

N

500 metres
500 yards

with imaginative polenta, fish and meat dishes. Tony Blair is reputed to have dined here with Gordon Brown when they decided who should go for the leadership of the Labour Party in 1994.

⑩ Anna's Place, 90 Mildmay Park, N1, ✆ 0171-249 9379 (*closed Sat eve, Sun eve*). A real oddity: a Swedish restaurant, and one that has made a mark on the local community. Lots of marinated fish and meat, plus home-made bread. Book in advance, especially for the terrace tables which are especially delectable in summer and heated in winter. Cottagey interior.

⑪ Casale Franco, 134–7 Upper St, N1, ✆ 0171-266 8994. Great pizza and spicy Italian cooking—from pizzas to grilled vegetables—in this bare-brick hangar of a restaurant in an alley off Islington's main street. Popular post-theatre place. Often long queues.

inexpensive

⑫ Upper St Fish Shop, 324 Upper St, N1, ✆ 0171-359 1401 (*closed Sun*). Superior chippie with the option of grilled or poached fish as well as the traditional deep-fried. Plain wood panelled walls decorated with pictures of the mop-like former house dog, Hugo. House special is halibut.

Smithfield/East End

moderate

● **Quality Chop House**, 94 Farringdon Rd, EC1, ✆ 0171-837 5093 (*closed Sat lunch*). Superior English specialities like fishcakes, game pie and roast lamb, though a modern Mediterranean influence has crept onto the menu. All served in the highly atmospheric rooms of a former 19th-century working-class men's club—hence the hard wooden benches—whose features are preserved delightfully. Extremely popular, especially at Sunday brunch.

● **Stephen Bull**, Smithfields, 71 St. John St, EC1, ✆ 0171-490 1750. Innovative Mediterranean cooking, with dishes like crab and orange ravioli. Especially good fish and seafood. Strong Spanish influence, as well as Latin American *ceviches* (uncooked but marinated fish, generally in lime juices or chilli).

● **St. John**, 26 St. John St, EC1, ✆ 0171-251 0848 (*closed Sat lunch, all day Sun*). A converted smokehouse, still with an industrial feel to it. Hearty, meaty, ingenious British cooking with a difference: every conceivable part of the animal (trotters, oxheart, bone barrow) is presented in interesting dishes. No fussiness, thin on sauces, crisp vegetables.

● **Alba**, 107 Whitecross St, EC1, ✆ 0171-588 1798 (*closed Sat, Sun*). Quietly excellent Italian restaurant, specializing in polenta, risotto and other northern or Piedmontese dishes. The only drawback is the location, next to the hideous labyrinthine quarters of the Barbican. Pink and minimalist inside.

inexpensive

● **New Friends**, 53 West India Dock Rd, E14, ✆ 0171-987 1139. Tasty Chinese restaurant well worth the trek out to Limehouse, where many Londoners simply never go. The barbecued pork is particularly recommended.

● **Seoul**, 89 Aldgate High St, EC3. The subtle delights of Korean food, with its mild meat and vegetable dishes, don't get much of a look-in in London, but here it is cheap and courteously served.

- **Frock's**, 95 Lauriston Rd, Clapton, E9, ✆ 0181-986 3161. Opens 11am, with an evening menu every day except Sun. Wine bar-cum-restaurant with excellent Sunday brunch-style food. The only drawback is its distance from the centre of town. You have to take a 277 bus from ⊖ Mile End.

- **The Peasant**, 240 St John St, EC1, ✆ 0171-336 7726. A gaudy pub converted into an interesting restaurant —the aim being to make country food sophisticated, with delicious results. Upstairs you move from purple and blue Victoriana (the pub décor) to a white, pristine, wooden room. The food has Italian leanings. A delightful experience.

cheap

- **F. Cooke**, 9 Broadway Market, E8, ✆ 0171-254 6458 (*open all day, closed Sun*). An authentic East End pie and mash shop that goes back nearly 100 years. The present owner, Bob Cooke, is the grandson of the first owner. Original façade was destroyed in the Blitz in the Second World War.

- **Nazrul**, 130 Brick Lane, E1, ✆ 0171-247 2505 (*open late*). One of a number of incredibly cheap, unlicensed Bengali Indian restaurants on and around Brick Lane. Getting a little too well-known for its own good, but still outstanding value.

South of the River

luxury

- **Le Pont de la Tour**, Butlers Wharf, 36d Shad Thames, SE1, ✆ 0171-403 8403 (*closed Sat lunch, Sun eve*). The flagship of Terence Conran's little restaurant empire at Butlers Wharf, with high-class French food and views of the river, Tower Bridge and the City. Everything, even the bread, is home-made. Chic but relaxed.

moderate

- **RSJ**, 13a Coin St, SE1, ✆ 0171-928 4554 (*closed Sat lunch, all day Sun*). Flamboyant, innovative French cooking, with a certain amount of global influence from Thailand and elsewhere. Extremely popular. Predominantly Loire wines. Delightful upper rooms.

- **Blueprint Café**, Design Museum, Butlers Wharf, Shad Thames, SE1, ✆ 0171-378 7031 (*closed Sun eve*). French and Italian food at the Pont de la Tour's less expensive sister establishment. Recently refurbished to include a new conservatory to emphasize the terrific views over the river and Tower Bridge, as well as Canary Wharf.

- **Buchan's**, 62–4 Battersea Bridge Rd, SW11, ✆ 0171-228 0888. Just over Battersea Bridge, a popular wine bar and restaurant with a Scottish slant. The seasonal menu ranges from steaks, pheasant and wild boar to seafood, soufflés and salads.

- **Ransome's Dock**, 35 Parkgate Rd, Battersea, SW11, ✆ 0171-223 1611. With its canal-side view, this periwinkle-blue converted warehouse provides an inventive modern-English menu with seasonal dishes. Good-value lunch and monthly changing menu. Reliable good cooking. Relaxed.

- **Riva**, 169 Church Rd, Barnes, SW13, ✆ 0181-748 0434. It is worth making the journey to this foodie shrine, where the variations on Italian recipes are of a high standard: San Daniele ham and pears, bresaola with goat's cheese.

inexpensive

- **Pizzeria Castello**, 20 Walworth Rd, Elephant and Castle, SE1, ✆ 0171-703 2556. Extremely popular pizzeria near Elephant and Castle, with filling deep-pan pies and lots of cheap beer to wash them down. Framed prints by local photographers.

- **The Fire Station**, 150 Waterloo Rd, SE1, ✆ 0171-620 2226 (*closed Sun eve*). This former fire station has had its basic features preserved and been converted into an extremely fashionable restaurant, just opposite the Old Vic theatre. Serves excellent warm salads and Mediterranean dishes. Service a bit slow, especially in the afternoon.

Further Afield

inexpensive

- **Istanbul Iskembecisi**, 9 Stoke Newington Rd, N16, ✆ 0171-254 7291 (*open most of the night till 5am*). Lively Turkish restaurant in an interesting and little-known neighbourhood north of Islington. Iskembecisi is a server of tripe soup usually served in the early morning to work off the hangover, but there is also more habitual Turkish cooking on offer.

- **Afric Carib**, 1 Stroud Green Rd, Finsbury Park, N16, ✆ 0171-263 7440. The name says it nearly all: cheap African and Caribbean dishes, including an interesting snail stew. A dominance of Nigerian cooking with dishes like *egusi* and fish pepper stew.

- **Bar Bella**, 1 Park Rd, Crouch End, N8, ✆ 0181-348 5609. A lively Mexican bar-cum-restaurant-cum hang-out. Lots of burrito snacks and paellas, and also non-Mexican dishes like chicken satay. Tiled floors and wooden effect. Good vegetarian options.

- **Madhu's Brilliant**, 39 South Rd, Southall, ✆ 0181-574 1897. The drab suburb of Southall has a huge Indian community, and here they show-case the very best their cuisine can offer at extraordinarily low prices. This is just one example. Northern Indian dishes, as well as Indo-African concoctions like *muchhuzi kuku*, a chicken curry in a big pot.

- **The Patio**, 5 Goldhawk Rd, W12, ✆ 0181-743 5194. Eccentric Polish restaurant, run by an ebullient blonde as if you're dropping in to her home for dinner. A lot busier since some rave write-ups in the London listings guides, but they still do a 3-course evening menu for an amazing £9.90, including a free flavoured vodka if Ewa likes the look of you.

- **Viet Hoa Café**, 70–2 Kingsland Rd, E2, ✆ 0171–729 8293 (*open Tues–Sun 12–3.30 and 5.30–11*). First-rate Vietnamese food, from steaming bowls of soup to spicy prawn dishes, in a bustling studeny atmosphere. You have to sit at long tables with other diners and there isn't much in the way of décor, but service is deferential and efficient and the fare is unfailingly delicious. Plenty of Asian faces around, as well as stragglers from the jazz and trendy pubs of Hoxton Square down the road.

Restaurants by Type

Classic French
L'Escargot, 48 Greek St, W1, p.467
The Criterion, 224 Piccadilly, W1, p.470.
French House Dining Rooms, 49 Dean St, W1, p.472.
Pied-à-terre, 34 Charlotte St, W1, p.475.
Nico Central, 35 Gt Portland St, W1, p.475.
Elena's L'Etoile, 30 Charlotte St, W1, p.475.
Connaught Hotel Grill Room, Carlos Place, W1, p.477.
Le Gavroche, 43 Upper Brook St, W1, p.477.
La Tante Claire, 68 Royal Hospital Rd, SW3, p.481.
Bibendum, Michelin House, 81 Fulham Rd, SW3, p.484.
Leiths, 92 Kensington Park Road, W11, p.485.
La Pomme d'Amour, 128 Holland Park Avenue, W11, p.486.
Café des Arts, 82 Hampstead High St, NW3, p.489.
Le Pont de la Tour, Butlers Wharf, 36D Shad Thames, SE1, p.493.
RSJ, 13a Coin St, SE1, p.493.

Stylish modern European
Alastair Little, 49 Frith St, W1, p.467.
Mezzo, 100 Wardour St, W1, p.470.
The Lexington, 45 Lexington St, W1, p.471.
Andrew Edmunds, 46 Lexington St, W1, p.471.

Randall & Aubin, 16 Brewer St, W1, p.471.
Soho Soho, 11–13 Frith St, W1, p.472.
Belgo Centraal, 50 Earlham St, W1, p.474.
Museum Street Café, 47 Museum St, WC1, p.475.
Stephen Bull, 5–7 Blandford St, W1, p.476.
Townhouse Brasserie, 24 Coptic St, WC1, p.476.
Union Café & Restaurant, 96 Marylebone Lane, W1, p.477.
Le Caprice, Arlington House, Arlington St, SW1, p.477.
Quaglino's, 16 Bury St, SW1, p.480.
Clarke's, 124 Kensington Church St, W8, p.480.
River Café, Thames Wharf Studios, Rainville Rd, W6, p.484.
Canteen, Unit 4G, Harbour Yard, Chelsea Harbour, SW10, p.484.
192, 192 Kensington Park Rd, W11, p.485.
Alastair Little, 136 a Lancaster Rd, W11, p.486.
The Cow Dining Room, 89 Westbourne Park Road, W2, p.486.
The Sugar Club, 33A All Saint's Rd, W11, p.486.
Kensington Place, 201 Kensington Church St, W8, p.486.
Pharmacy, 150 Notting Hill Gate, W11, p.486.
Anonimato, 12 All Saints Rd, W11, p.487.
Mas Café, 6–8 All Saints Rd, W11, p.487.
Woz, 46 Golborne Rd, W10, p.487.
Belgo, 72 Chalk Farm Rd, NW1, p.489.

Granita, 127 Upper St, Islington, N1, p.489.

Quality Chop House, 94 Farringdon Rd, EC1, p.492.

Stephen Bull, Smithfields, 71 St. John St, EC1, p.492.

The Peasant, 240 St John St, EC1, p.493.

Blueprint Café, Design Museum, Butlers Wharf, Shad Thames, SE1, p.493.

The Fire Station, 150 Waterloo Rd, SE1, p.494.

Global

Dell'Ugo, 56 Frith St, W1, p.471.

The Ivy, 1 West St, WC2, p.473.

October Gallery Café, 24 Old Gloucester St, WC1, p.476.

First Floor, 186 Portobello Rd, W11, p.486.

Brasseries

Bistrot Soho, 64 Frith St, W1, p.471.

Mon Plaisir, 21 Monmouth St, WC2, p.474.

Café des Amis du Vin, 11–14 Hanover Place, WC2, p.474.

Pierre Victoire, 11 Charlotte St, W1, p.476.

Brasserie du Marché aux Puces, 349 Portobello Rd, W10, p.488.

Rôtisserie Jules, 133A Notting Hill Gate, W11, p.488.

Café Delancey, 3 Delancey St, Camden, NW1, p.489.

Frock's, 95 Lauriston Rd, Clapton, E9, p.493.

Swish Fish

Café Fish, 39 Panton St, SW1, p.470.

Randall & Aubin, 16 Brewer St, W1, p.471.

Sea Shell, 49–51 Lisson Grove, NW1, p.476.

Bentley's, 11–15 Swallow St, W1, p.480.

Lou Pescadou, 241 Old Brompton Rd, p.481.

Geales, 2 Farmer St, W8, p.488.

Upper St Fish Shop, 324 Upper St, Islington, N1, p.492.

British

Quo Vadis, 26–29 Dean St, W1, p.471.

Simpsons, 110 Strand, WC2, p.473.

Rules, 35 Maiden Lane, WC2, p.474.

Alfred, 245 Shaftsbury Avenue, WC2, p.475.

The Greenhouse, 27a Hay's Mews, W1, p.477.

The Square, 6-10 Bruton St, W1, p.477.

Wiltons, 55 Jermyn St, W1, p.480.

Bentley's, 11–15 Swallow St, W1, p.480.

Boyd's, 135 Kensington Church St, W8, p.481.

Veronica's, 3 Hereford Rd, W2, p.486.

Byron, 3a Downshire Hill, Hampstead, NW1, p.489.

St. John, 26 St. John St, EC1, p.492.

Buchan's, 62–4 Battersea Bridge Rd, SW11, p.493.

Ransome's Dock, 35 Parkgate Rd, Battersea, SW11, p.493.

Italian

Vasco and Piero's Pavilion, 15 Poland St, W1, p.470.

Little Italy, 21 Frith St, W1, p.470.
Amalfi, 29–31 Old Compton St, W1, p.471.
Pollo, 20 Old Compton St, W1, p.473.
Bertorelli's, 44a Floral St, WC2, p.474.
Orso, 27 Wellington St, WC2, p.474.
La Pappardella, 253 Old Brompton Rd, SW5, p.481.
Del Buongustaio, 283 Putney Bridge Rd, SW15, p.484.
Cibo, 3 Russell Gardens, W14, p.485.
Al San Vincenzo, 30 Connaught St, W2, p.485.
Orsino, 119 Portland Rd, W11, p.486.
Osteria Basilico, 29 Kensington Park Rd, W11, p.487.
Palio, 175 Westbourne Park Grove, W11, p.487.
Alba, 107 Whitecross St, EC1, p.492.
Riva, 169 Church Rd, Barnes, SW13, p.493.

Chinese
Fung Shing, 15 Lisle St, WC2, p.470.
Hing Loon, 25 Lisle St, W1, p.471.
Golden Harvest, 17 Lisle St, WC2, p.472.
Poon's, 27 Lisle St, W1, p.472.
Singapore Garden, 154–6 Gloucester Place, NW1, p.476.
Zen Central, 20–22 Queen St, W1, p.480.
Ken Lo's Memories of China, 67–69 Ebury St, SW1, p.484.
Jenny Lo's Tea House, 14 Eccleston St, SW1, p.484.
Mandarin Kitchen, 14–16 Queensway, W2, p.487.
Vegetarian Cottage, 91 Haverstock Hill, NW3, p.489.

Cheng Du, 9 Parkway, Camden, NW1, p.489.
New Friends, 53 West India Dock Rd, E14, p.492.

Indonesian/Malaysian
Melati, 21 Great Windmill St, W1, p.472.
Satay House, 13 Sale Place, W2, p.488.

Japanese
Wagamama, 10A Lexington St, W1, p.473.
Gonbei, 151 King's Cross Rd, WC1, p.475.
Wagamama, 4 Streatham St, p.476.
Suntory, 72–3 St. James's St, SW1, p.477.

Eastern European
The Gay Hussar, 2 Greek St, W1, p.467.
Wódka, 12 St. Alban's Grove, W8, p.481.
Polish Air Force Association Club, 14 Collingham Gardens, SW5, p.481.
The Patio, 5 Goldhawk Rd, W12, p.494.

Scandinavian
Anna's Place, 90 Mildmay Park, Highbury, N1, p.492.

Middle Eastern
Al Hamra, 31–33 Shepherd Market, W1, p.477.
Sofra, 18 Shepherd Market, W1, p.480.
Phoenicia, 11–13 Abingdon Rd, W8, p.481.
Manzara, 24 Pembridge Rd, W11, p.489.
Istanbul Iskembecisi, 9 Stoke Newington Rd, N16, p.494.

American
Christophers, 18 Wellington St, WC2, p.473.

Joe Allen, 13 Exeter St, WC2, p.474.

Clarke's, 124 Kensington Church St, W8, p.480.

Montana, 125 Dawes Rd, SW6, p.485.

Chelsea Bun Diner, 9a Limerston St, SW10, p.485.

Dakota, 127 Ledbury Rd, W11, p.486.

Mexican
Down Mexico Way, 25 Swallow St, W1, p.480.

Bar Bella, 1 Park Rd, Crouch End, N8, p.494.

African
Calabash, Africa Centre, 38 King St, WC2, p.475.

Mandola, 139–141 Westbourne Grove, W11, p.488.

Afric Carib, 1 Stroud Green Rd, Finsbury Park, N16, p.494.

Conveyor Belt Sushi
Kulu Kulu, 76 Brewer St, W1, p.472.

Tokyo Diner, 2 Newport Place, W1, p.472.

Spanish/Portuguese
Café España, 63 Old Compton St, W1, p.473.

Cambio de Tercio, 163 Old Brompton Rd, SW5, p.481.

Caravela, 39 Beauchamp Place, SW3, p.484.

Galicia, 323 Portobello Rd, W10, p.487.

Casa Santana, 44 Golborne Rd, W10, p.488.

Greek
Jimmy's, 23 Frith St, W1, p.472.

Mega Kalamaras, 76–78 Inverness Mews, W2, p.487.

Lemonia, 89 Regent's Park Rd, Primrose Hill, NW1, p.489.

Paphos Restaurant, 43 Pratt St, Camden, NW1, p.489.

Irish
Mulligan's, 13–14 Cork St, W1, p.480.

Korean
Seoul, 89 Aldgate High St, EC3, p.492.

Thai
Sri Siam, 16 Old Compton St, W1, p.470.

Tui, 19 Exhibition Rd, SW7, p.484.

Esarn Kheaw, 314 Uxbridge Rd, W12, p.488.

Vegetarian Only
Mildred's, 58 Greek St, W1, p.473.

Cranks, 8 Marshall St, W1, p.473.

Mandeer, 21 Hanway Place, W1, p.476.

Chutneys, 124 Drummond St, NW1, p.476.

The Gate, 51 Queen Caroline St, Hammersmith, W6, p.481.

Vegetarian Cottage, 91 Haverstock Hill, NW3, p.489.

Indian/Pakistani
The Red Fort, 77 Dean St, W1, p.471.

Soho Spice, 124–6 Wardour St, W1, p.472.

Mandeer, 21 Hanway Place, W1, p.476.

Chutneys, 124 Drummond St, NW1, p.476.

Diwana Bhel Poori, 121 Drummond St, NW1, p.476.

Bombay Brasserie, Courtfield Close, Courtfield Rd, SW7, p.484.

Salloo's, 62–4 Kinnerton St, SW1, p.484.

Malabar, 27 Uxbridge St, W8, p.487.

Khans, 13–15 Westbourne Grove, W2, p.487.

Standard Indian Restaurant, 17 Westbourne Grove, W11, p.488.

Nazrul, 130 Brick Lane, E1, p.493.

Madhu's Brilliant, 39 South Rd, Southall UB1 1SW, p.494.

Vietnamese

Viet Hoa Café, 70–2 Kingsland Rd, E2, p.494.

Pizza Parlours

Condotti's, 4 Mill St, W1, p.480.

La Delizia, Chelsea Farmers' Market, Sydney St, SW3, p.485.

Calzone, 2A Kensington Park Rd, W11, p.488.

Casale Franco, 134–7 Upper St, Islington, N1, p.492.

Pizzeria Castello, 20 Walworth Rd, Elephant & Castle, SE1, p.494.

Dead Cheap

Pollo, 20 Old Compton St, W1, p.473.

October Gallery Café, 24 Old Gloucester St, WC1, p.476.

Polish Air Force Association Club, 14 Collingham Gardens, SW5, p.481.

Chelsea Kitchen, 98 King's Rd, SW3, p.485.

Stockpot, 6 Basil St, SW3, p.485.

Chelsea Bun Diner, 9a Limerston St, SW10, p.485.

F. Cooke, 9 Broadway Market, E8, p.493.

Nazrul, 130 Brick Lane, E1, p.493.

Cafés, Teahouses and Snack Foods

Ever since the rise of the City coffee house in the 17th century, London has been addicted to the relaxed charm of café culture. These days it seems to be labouring under one of its periodic illusions that Britain enjoys a Mediterranean climate: pavement cafes, along with al fresco dining, are all the rage. You will soon discover the new vogue for coffee, whether at one of the city's many Italian-style espresso bars or at the even newer chains offering much the same thing Pacific Northwest style: skinny wet caps and the rest, sharpened up with a flavoured syrup if you so desire. Back indoors, you will still find a cosy kind of establishment geared towards the English ritual of afternoon tea and cakes. Tea, being the quintessential English drink, tends to be delicious; you'll be given a bewildering choice of varieties.

Soho and Covent Garden

❶ **Bar Italia**, 22 Frith St, W1 (*open Mon–Thurs 7am–5pm; 24 hrs Fri–Sun*). The café with the best coffee in town and it knows it. The mirrored bar, complete with TV showing Italian soccer games, could have come straight from Milan or Bologna. The seating is a bit cramped, but at least there are tables on the pavement. Better to stand.

❷ **Patisserie Valerie**, 44 Old Compton St, W1 (*open Mon–Sat 8–8; Sat 8–7, Sun 10–6*). Excellent French cakes and coffee. You may have to wait for a seat.

❸ **Bunjie's Coffee House**, 27 Litchfield St, WC2 (*open 12pm–11pm, exc Sun*). Eccentric beatnik café, named after the founder's cousin's hamster. Vegetarian food and good coffee.

❹ **Maison Bertaux**, 28 Greek St, W1 (*open Mon–Sat 9am–8pm; Sun 9–1, 3–8*). Mouthwatering pastries in a slightly cramped upstairs tea-room which is always crowded.

❺ **Java Java**, 26 Rupert St, W1 (*open Mon–Thurs 9.30am–10pm; Fri–Sat 10.30am–11pm; Sun 1pm–9pm*). Old French haunt frequented by international youth reading free magazines. Good coffee, unusual cakes.

❻ **Est**, 54 Frith St, W1 (*closed Sun*). Loud, young bar with trendy crowd and somewhat steep prices.

❼ **Freuds**, 198 Shaftesbury Ave, W1. Trendy basement bar with young, studenty atmosphere and intriguing menu design.

❽ **Beatroot**, 92 Berwick St, W1 (*open 9–7*). Cheerful, down-to-earth vegetarian eat-in/takeaway café where you choose your size of food box and have it filled with any selection of hot dishes and salads from the food bar. Great puddings too—try the pineapple and coconut crumble or the sugar-free fruit cake.

Mayfair, Kensington, Chelsea

❶ **The Ritz**, Piccadilly, W1, ✆ 0171-493 8181. Tea sittings at 3pm and 4.30pm daily. The fanciest, most indulgent tea in town, served in the sumptuous Edwardian Palm Court. Worth splashing out, but you'll definitely need to book.

❷ **Browns Hotel**, Dover St or Albermarle St, W1. Tea served 3–6pm daily. Very snobbish traditional English hotel serving tea to all-comers, as long as you dress to fit the part. A snip cheaper than the Ritz.

❸ **Harry's**, 19 Kingly St, W1 (*open all night*). London's only all-night diner, with hearty fry-ups and reasonable coffee, featuring an eccentric cast of weirdos and insomniacs. During the day and early evening it serves Thai food. There's often a queue.

❹ **Patisserie Valerie**, 215 Brompton Rd, SW3. Branch of the Soho French patisserie.

❺ **Muffin Man**, 12 Wright's Lane, W8. Quaint all-day café just off Kensington High St. A variety of set teas include, as you would expect, homemade muffins galore.

❻ **Stravinsky's Russian Tea House**, 6 Fulham High St, SW6. Enormous selection of teas, plus eastern European pastries, at very reasonable prices.

❼ Amandine, 122 Wandsworth Road, SW6. Excellent bread, cakes and Belgian chocolates served in a spacious tea-room.

Notting Hill and Around

❶ Julie's, 137 Portland Road, W11. Multi-levelled and multi-purpose establishment with eccentric décor that is part café, part wine bar and part restaurant. The place is at its best for afternoon tea when it is neither too expensive nor too pretentious.

❷ Cullen Patisserie, Kensington Church St, W8, and 108 Holland Park Avenue, W11. Pastries made by the Roux brothers, served in a shocking pink environment. The Kensington Church St branch has more sitting space.

❸ Maison Bouquillon, 41 Moscow Road, W2. Slightly drab café which nevertheless boasts wondrous cakes made in the bakery next door.

❹ Grove Café, corner of Portobello Rd and Westbourne Park Rd, W11. First floor café with a terrace overlooking the market. Good coffee and newspapers to browse in the morning or afternoon.

The City, East End and around

❶ Mermaid, Puddle Dock, EC4. Basic café and self-service restaurant in one of London's more modern theatres.

❷ Brick Lane Beigel Bake, 159 Brick Lane, E1. Round-the-clock bagels. Always crowded, even at three in the morning.

❸ Whitechapel Café, 80 Whitechapel High St, E1. Wholefood café inside the Whitechapel Art Gallery.

❹ Café Rongwrong, 8 Hoxton Square, N1. Beatnik café in one of London's trendiest east London squares. An old warehouse, full of graphic designers and video artists. Atmospheric, in spite of moody owner.

North London

❶ Louis Patisserie, 32 Heath St, Hampstead, NW3. Famous Hungarian tea-room which has been a haunt of middle-European emigrés for decades. Wonderful cheesecake and cream cakes brought on a tray for you to choose from.

❷ Everyman Café, Holly Bush Vale, Hampstead, NW3. Atmospheric basement café beneath north London's best established rep cinema.

❸ The Coffee Cup, 74 Hampstead High St, NW3. Dazzling menu including delicious raisin toast. Good for watching the beautiful people walk by outside.

❹ Wisteria, 14 Middle Lane, Crouch End, N8. Pretty garden for afternoon tea.

❺ Carmelli's, 128 Golders Green Rd, NW11. The best bagels in London, in the heart of Jewish Golders Green, though you can't eat them on the premises.

South of the River

❶ MOMI Café, South Bank Centre, SE1. A nice place to spend half an hour on a summer evening, with a view over the river and various street performers to distract you. The food and drink are fine, but not great.

❷ Annabel's Patisserie, 33 High St, Wimbledon, SW19. Old-fashioned tea-room-cum-brasserie in the genteel atmosphere of Wimbledon.

❸ **The Gallery Tearooms**, 103 Lavender Hill, SW11. Scones and cucumber sandwiches at tea-time in Clapham, with brunch on Sundays and restaurant food the rest of the time.

❹ **Tea-time**, 21 The Pavement, SW4 (*closed Sun*). Cakes, sandwiches and set teas at the top end of Clapham Common.

❺ **Kew Greenhouse**, 1 Station Parade, Kew. Cakes and pastries near Kew Gardens.

Drunk for a Penny, Dead Drunk for Two

Drink suits the English: it relaxes them, unbuttons their inhibitions and tends to make them rather witty. Unfortunately, though, it also makes them drunk. For as long as the ale has flowed, the country has been trying to decide whether it likes or abhors its high alcohol consumption. Puritans and reactionaries have periodically tried to blame all the ills of society on the drunken lower classes, saying they are immoral dogs who should have their drinking habit flogged out of them. At the same time, sozzled eccentrics have spent years of their lives contemplating the meaning of life through an alcoholic haze; most of London's great writers and poets have spent a large proportion of their free time down at the boozer.

Certainly, the traditional image is of working men chucking down pint after pint in the pub, while their wives swig away at the gin bottle at home; the middle-classes, meanwhile, sipping wine at smart dinner parties and downing the odd discreet glass of port or brandy. The image, though, is inaccurate, distorted by class prejudice and wishful historical thinking. No social class has been immune from the evils of drunkenness, certainly not in London. The rich are every bit as rambunctious as the working classes after they have had a few (think of all those all-male dining societies which trash restaurants and beat up beggars). If the poor have traditionally put away a lot of alcohol, it has been as much a response to the appalling social conditions in which they have found themselves as any natural inclination to rot their livers and sink into an early grave. Alcohol has oiled the wheels of the English class war for centuries; its role, though, has never been straightforward.

Ale was the universal drink of the Middle Ages, more common and more widely available than water. This lukewarm form of beer was cheap and relatively weak— even hospital patients would down two or three pints a day without serious side-effects. In the 14th century taverns would be inspected by so-called ale-conners, who would deliberately splash beer on their bench or chair before sitting down. If their cloak stuck to the bench, they knew the ale had been adulterated with sugar and fined the landlord. Wine, which had to be imported from France or further afield, was restricted to the upper classes. Vintners, too, were often suspected of tampering with their produce; in 1350 a wine merchant called John Penroe was sentenced to drink as much of his adulterated wine as he could, then had the rest poured over his head.

London's real drinking problems began in the 17th century, with the introduction of Dutch genever, later known simply as gin. The spirit had a diabolical attraction to working people: it was very cheap, tasted better than beer (which was often watered down or adulterated) and was less likely to make them ill in the short term than water, which came straight from the Thames and was polluted with excrement, animal carcasses and the effluent of the city's fledgling industries. Gin consumption soared, and quickly became an excuse for class prejudice. Daniel Defoe satirized the working man thus: 'Ask him in his cups what he intends. He'll tell you honestly, he'll drink so long as it lasts and then go to work for more.' The politician William Temple went as far as to suggest that the best remedy for drunkenness would be to cut wages and increase working hours, thereby robbing workers of the time and the wherewithal to down their gin. But while the more affluent classes condemned gin drinking, many also made sure they derived a tidy profit from it. The constables who were supposed to keep an eye on the ginshops and alehouses often supplied gin themselves on the side, and so had no incentive to stop people drinking it. At the end of the 17th century, Londoners were getting through 600,000 gallons of gin per year. In 1727 the figure had jumped to 3.5 million gallons, and by 1735 6.5 million gallons. In 1736 parliament tried to impose a duty of one pound per gallon but the law was ignored. Bootleggers without licences undercut the official sellers, and anybody who informed on them was hunted down and killed by angry mobs. In 1751 the novelist Henry Fielding, then chief magistrate at Bow Street, remarked: 'Should the drinking of this poison be continued in the present height during the next 20 years, there will by that time be few of the common people left to drink it.' The same year, the government finally succeeded in introducing duties on gin, and consumption began to level out.

It seems astonishing that Britain managed to create an empire at all in the 18th century, let alone start the industrial revolution. Aristocrats may have shunned gin but they went gaga over punch (favoured by the Whig party), claret (the Tories' tipple of choice) and cognac. The throne was occupied by one lush-head after another. The inaugural banquet for William of Orange and Queen Mary at Whitehall in 1689 turned into such an orgy of inebriation that, according to one French observer, 'there was not a single one that did not lose consciousness'. Queen Anne was particularly partial to brandy, and eventually died of apoplexy brought on by excessive eating and drinking. George IV was also fond of a drop or two and spent his wedding night in a drunken stupor in a fireplace.   •

In their few sober moments, the authorities continued to worry about the gin problem and mounted a campaign, echoed in the newspapers, to bring back beer drinking for the sake of the nation's health. 'Beer and porter [an old word for dark ale] are the natural beverage of the Englishman,' opined *The Times* in 1829, 'the increase of gin-drinking and that of suicides, murders and all kinds of violence are contemporaneous.' The Duke of Wellington solved the problem in one fell swoop in 1830 with his Beer Act, which abolished all duty on beer and slashed the price of licences for beer retailers and inn-keepers. Within a year, 31,000 beer licences had been issued, and the nation's drinking habits changed for ever.

The pub as we know it today was a Victorian invention, a place riddled with class prejudice and moral overtones. Respectable gentlemen who a century earlier had happily eaten and drunk in chop-houses and taverns did not set foot in pubs at all; indeed the secretary of White's Club, Algy Burke, boasted in 1896: 'The class I deal with and the class I associate with and the class I know do not go into public houses.' But even within the pub, there was a class divide between the lounge or saloon bar (for well-dressed patrons) and the public bar (for riff-raff). It was not long before the Victorian moralists barged in. In 1872, under the influence of the Temperance Society, strict licensing hours were introduced. The Society ensured that children would be kept out of pubs, whether for drinking or not, thereby encouraging the menfolk to get even drunker in the secure knowledge that their families could not see what they were up to.

The temperance crusaders managed to hold sway for much of the 20th century, and generations of drinkers had to suffer strictures imposed during the First World War to discourage munitions workers from getting drunk while handling high explosives. The licensing laws were not relaxed until the late 1980s, when at last it was possible to buy a drink in the afternoons. By that time there had been many other changes, too. Cafés and wine bars had begun to challenge the traditional tippler's bastion, the pub, and the pubs themselves had become less class-conscious and more welcoming to women and children. By now, the partitions dividing the saloon from the public bar have nearly all been removed, although you might still see the words in the stained glass of the door. By and large, the level of drunkenness has gone down and the atmosphere improved immeasurably. Gone are the days when fat, prematurely aged men would nibble crisps, play darts and crack dirty jokes; now they are more likely to bring their wives and take part in pub quizzes and karaoke nights.

At the same time, however, down-sizing, the health kick and the advent of Perrier water have stripped alcohol of some of its appeal. You'll still find people downing five or six pints and calling it a quiet night, but they are becoming the exception rather than the rule. The recession of the early 1990s caused London boardrooms to ordain employee sobriety at lunchtime in the interests of a productive afternoon, and the habit has stuck. The tradition of bar-room wits holding forth (and keeping the inevitable bar-room bores at bay) has waned, and long liquid lunches are largely a thing of the past. No doubt drinking fizzy water and alcohol-free beer is good for the health, but in London of all places it feels a little joyless.

Pubs

The London pub—gaudily decorated with gleaming brass, ornate mirrors and stained glass—is still an essentially Victorian establishment, at least to look at. Even recently-built pubs eschew modern decor in favour of mock-Tudor beams, leaded windows and reproduction hunting prints. Some of the Victorian atmosphere of discipline and moral vigilance persists, too. Licensing hours, although now much extended, are still rigorously enforced; the landlord usually rings a bell when it is time to drink up, like a fussy schoolmaster calling his pupils to order. Gone, however, are the days when the pubs closed just when you were feeling thirsty; you can now drink without interruption between 11am and 11pm every day except Sunday, when there is still a break from 3–7pm. Many pubs in outer London still close every afternoon, however.

Beer is still the drink of choice. British beer is admittedly an acquired taste—stronger, darker and flatter than lager and served luke-warm rather than stone cold—but easy to get hooked on in time. Unfortunately, London pubs are being swamped, like everywhere else, with generic multinational lagers—Carlsberg, Heineken, Budweiser and the rest—which for the most part are fizzy, cold and desperately bland. This is far from good news for traditional local breweries, who are fighting an energetic rearguard campaign with the help of CAMRA, the Campaign for Real Ale. CAMRA's influence has been greater in country pubs and the cities of northern England than it has in London, where wine and American-style cocktails are more popular than in the rest of the country; in the capital you will nevertheless find decent bitters like Fullers London Pride and Youngs, and creamy, full-bodied ales like Theakston's, Abbot and Ruddles.

The following list is necessarily short, since few London pubs really shine above the rest. Most of them make the list because of their location—overlooking the river, maybe, or in a quiet row of Georgian houses—or because of a particular historical association. You'll notice their eccentric names, which date from a time when most drinkers were illiterate and recognized pubs only by their signs. Hence the preponderance of coats of arms (King's Arms, Queen's Arms, Freemasons' Arms etc) and highly pictorial appellations (Wheatsheaf, Dog and Duck, Nag's Head, Slug and Lettuce etc). One thing to look out for is the name of the brewer that owns the pub. If the sign says 'Free House', that means the pub is independent and generally has a better range of beers. Quite a few London pubs are venues for theatre or concerts; where the entertainment is the main attraction, you will find them in the Entertainment section rather than here.

Soho, Covent Garden, Fitzrovia

❶ **Lamb and Flag**, 33 Rose St, WC2. One of few wooden-framed buildings left in central London, dating back to the 17th century, with low ceilings and a lively atmosphere. The pub was for a long time nicknamed the Bucket of Blood because it staged bare-knuckled fights. Now you just have to knuckle your way past the crowds at the bar.

❷ **Dog and Duck**, 8 Bateman St, W1. Soho's smallest pub. Customers spill out on to the pavement in the summer, and huddle round the log fire in the winter.

❸ **The French House**, 49 Dean St, W1. Meeting-place for De Gaulle's Free French during the Second World War; now adorned with pictures of famous Frenchmen. The wine, of course, is excellent.

❹ **The Sun**, 63 Lamb's Conduit St, W1. A beer-lover's paradise: 15 real ales and the chance to tour the cellar with the landlord.

❺ **Fitzroy Tavern**, 16 Charlotte St, W1. Dylan Thomas's main drinking haunt; see the literary mementoes on the walls downstairs.

Holborn and Fleet Street

❶ **Cittie of York**, 22 High Holborn, WC1. The longest bar in London. Cosy, separate booths, ideal for winter lunchtimes.

❷ **Ye Olde Cheshire Cheese**, Wine Office Court, 15 Fleet St, EC4. Dr Johnson's old haunt, with atmospheric beams but disappointing food.

❸ **The Eagle**, 159 Farringdon Rd, EC1.

New wave pub with less emphasis on drinking and more on food, good atmosphere and general hanging out.

East End

❶ **Ten Bells**, 84 Commercial St, E1. The original Jack the Ripper pub, with oodles of memorabilia. Marred by the tourist coaches who drop in during the evening but friendly enough at lunchtime.

❷ **The Ship and Blue Ball**, 13 Boundary St, E2. First-rate organic beer from the independent Pitfield brewery. Try the brand called Dark Star.

❸ **Town of Ramsgate**, 62 Wapping High St, E1. The pub where the merciless 17th-century Judge Jeffreys finally got his come-uppance. Friendly East End atmosphere, with a riverside garden and view of the post where smugglers and pirates used to be condemned to hang in chains for the duration of three high tides.

Southwark, Rotherhithe, Greenwich

❶ **Anchor Inn**, 1 Bankside, SE1. Superior food and excellent river views in this ancient Bankside institution where fugitives from the Clink prison next door used to hide in cubby holes.

❷ **Old Thameside Inn**, Clink St, SE1. Shantymen perform sea shanties at lunchtime on the last Sunday of the month at this pub with attractive riverside views from a concrete terrace.

❸ **The Angel**, 101 Bermondsey Wall East, Rotherhithe, SE16. The pub where Captain Cook had his last drink before sailing to Australia. Notable for its ship's wheel, smugglers' trapdoor and balcony overlooking Tower Bridge and Execution Dock.

❹ The Mayflower, 117 Rotherhithe St, SE16. Inn from which the Pilgrim Fathers set out for America, and the only place in Britain where you can buy US postage stamps. There's a long jetty from which to admire the river. Avoid the indifferent food.

❺ Trafalgar Tavern, Park Row, Greenwich, SE10. Famous for its Whitebait Dinners, at which cabinet ministers and senior public figures would hold informal chats over seafood from the Thames. River pollution ended the tradition in 1914, though you can still eat rather indifferent whitebait from the pub menu. Nice views.

Islington, Highgate, Hampstead

(For Camden pubs, *see* p.389).

❶ Slug and Lettuce, 1 Islington Green, N1. Popular meeting point in central Islington with decent pub grub and a beer garden.

❷ King's Head, 115 Upper St, Islington, N1. Popular Islington pub, where the money is still counted according to the old pre-decimal system of pounds, shillings and pence. The pub theatre is excellent and the atmosphere is very genial.

❸ Canonbury Tavern, 21 Canonbury Place, Islington, N1. Delightful garden pub with an unusual court for playing *pétanque*.

❹ The Flask, 77 Highgate West Hill, N6. Friendly pub dating back to the 17th century at the top of Highgate Hill, with a garden and good food.

❺ The Bull, 13 North Hill, Highgate, N6. A large tree-lined garden and patio are the most attractive features of this former drinking haunt for painters such as Hogarth and Millais.

❻ Spaniards Inn, Spaniards Road, Hampstead Heath, NW3. Reputed as a highwayman's pub patronized by Dick Turpin and a host of scurrilous scribblers including Byron and Shelley. Wonderful garden and, of course, the expanse of Hampstead Heath just across the road.

❼ The Holly Bush, 22 Holly Mount, Hampstead, NW3. Idyllic pub with five low rooms grouped around an old wooden bar.

❽ Freemasons Arms, 32 Downshire Hill, Hampstead, NW3. Huge garden and terrace, fountain and pitch to play the ancient game of pell-mell. Gets crowded.

West London

❶ Ladbroke Arms, 54 Ladbroke Rd, Notting Hill, W11. Very popular pub with flower-lined patio. Don't bring the car as there's a police station next door and they'll nick you for drink-driving in no time.

❷ Queen's Head, Brook Green (West Kensington), W6. Old coaching inn overlooking a green, with a beer garden at the back.

❸ Anglesea Arms, 15 Selwood Terrace, SW7. Good beer in this local Chelsea haunt.

❹ Havelock Tavern, 57 Masbro Road, W14. Happening pub serving high-quality pub food.

❺ King's Head and Eight Bells, 50 Cheyne Walk, Chelsea. Enjoy the antiques displays in this 16th-century building. There are views of the Battersea peace pagoda across the river.

❻ Dukes Head, 8 Lower Richmond Rd, Putney. Fine views along the river, though you have to put up with plastic cups if you sit outside.

❼ The Ship, Ship Lane, Mortlake. The place to watch the end of the Oxford and Cambridge boat race in April. Fine river views and a tranquil setting the rest of the year.

❽ The White Cross, Cholmondeley Walk, Richmond. A pub that turns into an island at high tide. Enjoy the real fires and good food.

Southwest London

❶ The Ship, Jews Row, Wandsworth. Wonderful river views and great food including summer barbecues (except Sun evening).

❷ Hope and Anchor, 123 Acre Lane, Brixton. Good home-made food and a garden to enjoy a summer drink.

Where To Stay

There is only one word to describe London's hotels and that word is *nightmare*. Accommodation, although improving slowly, is on the whole shamelessly expensive and shamelessly shoddy. You can pay up to £80 for an ordinary double room with no guarantee of quality or even basic hygiene; and you can pay up to twice that without even approaching the luxury category. There is no universal rating system, and the variously sponsored star or crown systems are so unreliable as to be virtually useless. So your best bet is to dust down your address book and see if there isn't anybody in London who might be able to put you up. If that fails, don't lose heart: there are some cheap deals available, and some surprisingly enjoyable establishments. You must, however, be very wary of the pitfalls.

If at all possible, try to arrange accommodation from your home country. Flight and accommodation packages cover a wide price range and can work out to your advantage. Otherwise, try the numbers below. You can usually confirm your booking by giving a credit card number or sending a fax. The London Tourist Board also operates a telephone credit card booking service on ℂ 0171–824 8844 which is open Mon–Fri 9.30–5.30. If you turn up in London without a room in your name and you get nowhere ringing the numbers listed below, you can line up outside a tourist office and try your luck there. Try Victoria station forecourt, Liverpool St station, the underground concourse at Heathrow Terminals 1–3, or one of the following local tourist offices: Greenwich (ℂ 0181–858 6376), Islington (ℂ 0171–278 8787) or Richmond (ℂ 0181–940 9125). Commission for all booking services is around £5. If you are travelling out of high season (i.e. not the summer), try haggling a bit and you might negotiate your own discount. Weekend rates are common, and if you stay for a week you might get one night free. You can further save your pennies by declining breakfast (a possible £10 saver, *see* Food and Drink for other places to go) or by asking for a room without a bath. In the cheaper establishments, the corridor bathrooms are usually better than the *en suite* kind, so this is not much of a sacrifice. The following internet address may also be useful: hotels www.demon.co. uk/hotel-uk/excindex.html.

Most hotels are in the West End and around, Kensington, Chelsea, Earl's Court and west London. Try to avoid streets like Sussex Gardens in Bayswater, which is something of a hotel ghetto and rather miserable for it. Finding somewhere quiet can be a problem, especially in the busy summer months, but as a broad rule of thumb you will be disturbed less the further you are out of the centre. The best places to stay are in districts like Notting Hill and Holland Park, or else by the river—don't forget the newer hotels in the Docklands. Bloomsbury offers some excellent bargains as well as the proximity of the British Museum.

Prices given below are for a normal double room for one night, but—again—find out about discounts before dismissing a place as too dear. Remember that space is tight, so book as far in advance as possible, whatever the category of accommodation. Hotels are graded by price, as follows:

∞∞∞∞∞	**luxury (£200 and over)**
∞∞∞∞	**very expensive (£150–200)**
∞∞∞	**expensive (£100–150)**
∞∞	**moderate ((£60–100)**
∞	**cheap for London (under £60)**

Luxury (mostly Mayfair)   map A

∞∞∞∞ **Brown's**, 19–24 Dover St W1,
❶ ✆ 0171-493 6020. Old fashioned English establishment, with the air of a country house and impeccable, stiff-collar service. Attractive if smallish rooms. £235–695 + VAT.

∞∞∞∞ **Claridges**, Brook St W1, ✆ 0171-629
❷ 8860. Art deco bedrooms, black and white marbled foyer and a touch of royal class at London's most celebrated smaller luxury hotel. £255–£2,450 + VAT (the latter for a 2-floor penthouse).

∞∞∞∞ **Connaught**, 16 Carlos Place W1,
❸ ✆ 0171-499 7070. Attentive service commands a troupe of loyal devotees. An air of calm exclusivity presides. Outstanding restaurants; personalised formality. Book in writing well in advance. £225–310 + VAT.

∞∞∞∞ **Dorchester**, 53 Park Lane W1,
❹ ✆ 0171-629 8888. Triple-glazed

rooms (to foil the Park Lane traffic) and views over Hyde Park, plus a dazzling choice of fine restaurants and acres of gold and marble. £270–300 + VAT.

∞∞∞∞ **Hyatt Carlton Tower**, 2 Cadogan
❺ Place SW1, ✆ 0171-235 1234. De luxe mod cons, marble bathrooms, a stone's throw from Harrods, with a well-equipped health club, swimming pool and spacious rooms. £190 + VAT.

∞∞∞∞ **Ritz**, Piccadilly W1, ✆ 0171-493
❻ 8181. Marble galore, gorgeous rococo carpets, plus glorious views over Green Park if you pick your room right. *Ancien régime* luxury. £275–300 + VAT.

∞∞∞∞ **Savoy**, Strand WC2, ✆ 0171-836
❼ 4343. A sleeker, more business-like luxury here. *Fin de siècle* dining room: a favourite venue for afternoon tea. Many restaurants and bars and discreet good service. £280 + VAT.

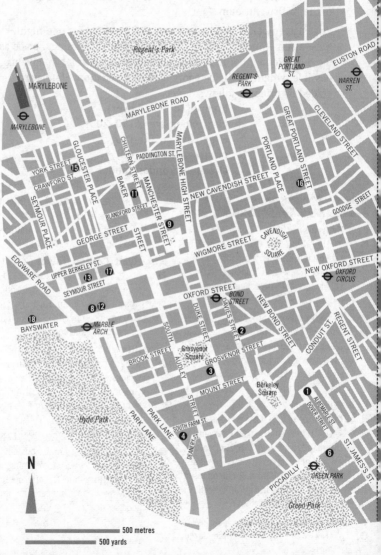

Map A

Regent's Park

MARYLEBONE

MARYLEBONE

GREAT PORTLAND ST.

EUSTON ROAD

REGENT'S PARK

WARREN ST.

MARYLEBONE ROAD

YORK STREET

CRAWFORD ST.

GLOUCESTER PLACE

15

CHILTERN STREET

PADDINGTON ST.

BAKER STREET

MARYLEBONE HIGH STREET

PORTLAND PLACE

GREAT PORTLAND STREET

CLEVELAND STREET

16

GOODGE STREET

NEW CAVENDISH STREET

11

BLANDFORD STREET

MANCHESTER STREET

9

SEYMOUR PLACE

GEORGE STREET

WIGMORE STREET

CAVENDISH SQUARE

EDGWARE ROAD

UPPER BERKELEY ST.

13   17

SEYMOUR STREET

NEW OXFORD STREET

OXFORD CIRCUS

OXFORD STREET   *BOND STREET*

DAVIES STREET

DUKE STREET

NEW BOND STREET

CONDUIT ST.

REGENT STREET

8   12

18
BAYSWATER

MARBLE ARCH

SOUTH AUDLEY STREET

BROOK STREET

Grosvenor Square

GROSVENOR STREET

2

3

MOUNT STREET

Berkeley Square

1

ALBEMARLE ST.

DOVER STREET

ST. JAMES'S ST.

Hyde Park

PARK LANE

DEANERY ST.

SOUTH FARM ST.

4

6

PICCADILLY

GREEN PARK

Green Park

N

500 metres

500 yards

512

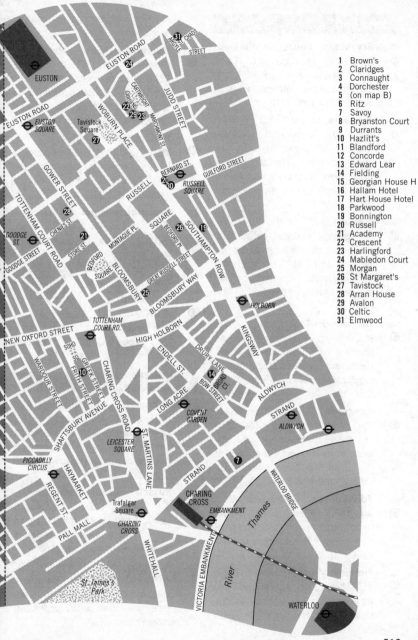

1 Brown's
2 Claridges
3 Connaught
4 Dorchester
5 (on map B)
6 Ritz
7 Savoy
8 Bryanston Court
9 Durrants
10 Hazlitt's
11 Blandford
12 Concorde
13 Edward Lear
14 Fielding
15 Georgian House H
16 Hallam Hotel
17 Hart House Hotel
18 Parkwood
19 Bonnington
20 Russell
21 Academy
22 Crescent
23 Harlingford
24 Mabledon Court
25 Morgan
26 St Margaret's
27 Tavistock
28 Arran House
29 Avalon
30 Celtic
31 Elmwood

∞∞ **8** **Bryanston Court**, 56–60 Great Cumberland Place W1, ✆ 0171-262 3141. Business-like hotel with few frills but a pleasant atmosphere and an open fire in winter. £110.

∞∞ **9** **Durrants**, George St W1, ✆ 0171-935 8131. A former 18th-century coaching inn preserving many old-fashioned touches including silver plate covers in the restaurant. Rooms are simple, a few on the small side. £125.

∞∞ **10** **Hazlitt's**, 6 Frith St W1, ✆ 0171-434 1771. Small Georgian rooms with some four posters and claw-footed iron baths in the former home of essayist William Hazlitt. Palm trees and classical busts adorn the premises. £148 + VAT.

∞∞ **11** **Blandford**, 80 Chiltern St W1, ✆ 0171-486 3103. Simple bed and breakfast style hotel, offering decent rooms and a copious morning meal, in a quiet side street near Baker St station. £80.

∞∞ **12** **Concorde**, 50 Great Cumberland Place W1, ✆ 0171-402 6169. Plain and inexpensive but light and efficient, under the same management as the Bryanston Court. With self-catering options. £78.

∞∞ **13** **Edward Lear**, 28–30 Seymour St W1, ✆ 0171-402 5401. Named after the nonsense-verse writer. Small hotel with a homey feel. Informal but efficient. £60–85.

∞∞ **14** **Fielding**, 4 Broad Ct, Bow St WC2, ✆ 0171-836 8305. A pretty good deal for central London, right opposite the Opera House. Smallish rooms and a tiny reception area: a parrot greets you on your way in. £85.

∞∞ **15** **Georgian House Hotel**, 87 Gloucester Place W1, ✆ 0171-935 2211. Spacious rooms with personality; quietly high standards and good prices. Great discounts on 'student' rooms up 3 or 4 flights of stairs. £80.

∞ **16** **Hallam Hotel**, 12 Hallam St W1, ✆ 0171-580 1166. Quiet, businesslike hotel just around the corner from the BBC. Some rooms have views of the Telecom Tower. £93.

∞ **17** **Hart House Hotel**, 51 Gloucester Place W1, ✆ 0171-935 2288. Superbly run hotel in a Georgian mansion overlooking Portman Square, with remarkably large rooms for the area. £69–85.

∞ **18** **Parkwood**, 4 Stanhope Place W2, ✆ 0171-402 2241. Family-run hotel with slightly worn furniture but attractive prices. Charming Georgian mansion near Hyde Park. £85.

∞∞ **19** **Bonnington**, 92 Southampton Row WC1, ✆ 0171-242 2828. Renovated Edwardian establishment with bland furniture but warm management. Plenty of beds, relatively easy to book. £75–133.

∞∞ **20** **Russell**, Russell Square WC1, ✆ 0171-837 6470. Extravagant Gothic Revival architecture and an atmosphere to match. A renovated ballroom. Friendly service. £160.

∞ **21** **Academy**, 17–21 Gower St WC1, ✆ 0171-631 4115. Enjoy the atmosphere of a Georgian townhouse. Cosy library and small paved garden. An antique charm. £120.

Crescent, 49–50 Cartwright Gardens WC1, ✆ 0171-387 1515. Use of the garden and tennis courts a big plus here, as is family atmosphere. Old-fashioned and good value. £73.

Harlingford, 61–3 Cartwright Gardens WC1, ✆ 0171-387 1551. Floral-print wallpaper adorns the simple rooms. Access to tennis courts possible. £60–75.

Mabledon Court, 10–11 Mabledon Place WC1, ✆ 0171-388 3866. Clean but unexciting hotel near King's Cross with reasonable rates. £60–70.

Morgan, 24 Bloomsbury St WC1, ✆ 0171-636 3735. Beautifully furnished bed and breakfast style hotel, with warm atmosphere and excellent breakfast. Next to British Museum. £70.

St Margaret's, 26 Bedford Place WC1, ✆ 0171-636 4277. Clean, fresh hotel with a plant-filled dining room and a wide variety of large, well-proportioned rooms. £54–60.

Tavistock, Tavistock Square WC1, ✆ 0171-278 7871. Large rooms, a good location, art deco finishes but impersonal atmosphere and tour-group clientele. Views over Tavistock Square garden a plus. £70.

Arran House, 77–9 Gower St WC1, ✆ 0171-636 2186. Wonky floors and a lovely rose garden add charm to this otherwise no-frills guest house. In-house laundry and use of kitchen including microwave. £47.

Avalon, 46–7 Cartwright Gardens WC1, ✆ 0171-387 2366. Bright, old-fashioned Georgian house in a beautiful crescent packed with similar establishments. Drying and ironing facilities. £52–65.

Celtic, 61–3 Guildford St WC1, ✆ 0171-837 9258. Simple, unexciting family-run bed and breakfast. No private bathrooms but cheap at around £48. Street rooms can be noisy.

Elmwood, 19 Argyle Square WC1, ✆ 0171-837 9361. Basic but very cheap, in a lovely square near the new British Library. Not far from King's Cross. £32.

Bayswater, Notting Hill map B

Hempel, 31–5 Craven Hill Gardens W2, ✆ 0171-298 9000. New luxury hotel designed by Anushka Hempel. Takes minimalism to its logical, most exotic extreme. Pure white blank foyer interrupted only by otherworldly flames and Thai ox-carts. £220–770 + VAT.

Halcyon, 81 Holland Park, W11, ✆ 0171-727 7288. Modern but traditional, in a large, renovated Holland Park mansion house. Popular with showbiz and media people. Rated restaurant and bars. £165–250 + VAT.

Pembridge Court, 34 Pembridge Gardens W2, ✆ 0171-229 9977. Elegant Victorian townhouse, fastidiously deconstructed; but flourishing vegetation and an interesting collection of Victoriana in frames. Next to Portobello market. £160.

Whites, 90 Lancaster Gate W2, ✆ 0171-262 2711. Stucco palace overlooking Kensington Gardens. Rebuilt behind the façade for modern tastes in traditional guise. Deferential service. £220.

Map B

Portobello, 22 Stanley Gardens W11, ℰ 0171-727 2777. Victorian Gothic furniture conceals all-mod cons comfort including a health club. Idiosyncratic rooms. A touch pokey. £140–220.

Ashley, 15–17 Norfolk Square W2, ℰ 0171-723 9966. Maniacally clean and quiet hotel, ideal for families or business people looking for peace. Party animals stay away. Bulletin board has hints on sightseeing. £63.

Byron, 36–8 Queensborough Terrace W2, ℰ 0171-243 0987 (toll-free number in US ℰ 1-800-448 8355). Young, friendly atmosphere in this smart hotel full of sunshine and flowers, just a stone's throw from Kensington Gardens. £96.

Delmere, 130 Sussex Gardens W2, ℰ 0171-706 3344. Smart building on an otherwise miserable street of hotels. Some tiny rooms, but others are spacious and comfortable. £98.

Gate, 6 Portobello Rd W11, ℰ 0171-221 2403. Well-appointed, no nonsense hotel in plum location among the antique shops of Portobello Rd. £65–72.

Kensington Gardens, 9 Kensington Gardens Square W2, ℰ 0171-221 7790. Attractive rooms, good bath facilities and a light, pleasant breakfast room make this a good mid-range choice. £65.

Abbey House, 11 Vicarage Gate W8, ℰ 0171-727 2594. Simple, spacious rooms in this delightful Victorian town house in a quiet square. Preserves many original features. Cheap at around £60.

Border, 14 Norfolk Square W2, ℰ 0171-723 2968. No-nonsense hotel with simple, cheap facilities, in a square full of other similar hotels. £56.

Garden Court, 30–31 Kensington Gardens Square W2, ℰ 0171-229 2553. Simple bed and breakfast with nice views over the square at the front and gardens at the back. Well located next to Queensway and not far from Portobello. £48–72.

Lancaster Hall (German YMCA), 35 Craven Terrace W2, ℰ 0171-723 9276. Sounds grim and looks awfully generic, but the rooms are clean, the location excellent. £68.

Mornington, 12 Lancaster Gate W2, ℰ 0171-262 7361 (toll-free number in US 1-800-528 1234). Scandinavian-run hotel with serious but professional staff. Nice library. Next to the Football Association, so lots of soccer types around. £115.

Ravna Gora, 29 Holland Park Avenue W11, ℰ 0171-727 7725. Palatial Holland Park mansion turned slightly dilapidated bed and breakfast, with a talkative Serbian owner. £50–60.

South Kensington   map B

Blakes, 33 Roland Gardens SW7, ℰ 0171-370 6701. Richly decorated hotel with four-poster beds and antique lacquered chests. Birdcages and carved giraffes to boot. £155–220 + VAT.

The Gore, 189 Queen's Gate SW7, ℰ 0171-584 6601 (toll free in US ℰ 1-800-528 1234). Gothic and Edwardian décor, plus hundreds of old prints, make this an atmospheric stopover. £165.

Number Sixteen, 16 Sumner Place SW7, ✆ 0171-589 5232. Charming Victorian house with a garden and fountains, plus large reception areas and rooms with balconies. Posh B&B. £150–190.

Aster House, 3 Sumner Place SW7, ✆ 0171-581 5888. Silk-wall décor and lots of flowers all over this award-winning hotel. Light breakfast alternatives to the usual bangers, bacon and egg. £115–145.

Claverly, 13–14 Beaufort Gardens SW3, ✆ 0171-589 8541. Lovingly detailed and award-winning hotel, with attractive rooms and an imaginative breakfast featuring waffles and fresh juices as well as bacon and eggs. £110.

Cranley, 10–12 Bina Gardens SW5, ✆ 0171-373 0123 (toll free in US ✆ 1-800-553 2582). American-run hotel converted from three elegant town houses. Style, great attention to detail thanks to antiques and designer fabrics, and a view from the top of the pinnacle of St Paul's. £140.

Five Sumner Place, 5 Sumner Place SW7, ✆ 0171-584 7586. The feel of a country home in the heart of London, with a stunning conservatory-style breakfast room. Smart but unpretentious. Quiet. £110 + VAT.

Hotel 167, 167 Old Brompton Rd SW5, ✆ 0171-373 0672. Attractively decorated Victorian corner house with young clientele. £90.

Knightsbridge

Diplomat, 2 Chesham St SW1, ✆ 0171-235 1544. Elegant rooms and suites up and down a glass-domed stairwell. Copious buffet breakfast and just a short walk to Beauchamp Place and Harrods. £115–125.

Wilbraham, 1 Wilbraham Place, Sloane St SW1, ✆ 0171-730 8296. Very English establishment just off Sloane Square, with Victorian décor and attractive wood panelling. £70–129.

Victoria/Pimlico

Ebury Court, 28 Ebury St SW1, ✆ 0171-730 8147. Labyrinthine corridors connect the beautifully laid out rooms in this long-established neighbourhood favourite. £115–135.

Collin House, 104 Ebury St SW1, ✆ 0171-730 8031. Clean, hospitable bed and breakfast behind Victoria station. Homey but fresh. £55–65.

Enrico, 77–9 Warwick Way SW1, ✆ 0171-834 9538. Basic but comfortable hotel in Pimlico. £30–45.

Oak House, 29 Hugh St SW1, ✆ 0171-834 7151. Small rooms with basic catering facilities for only £35. Breakfast is in your room. No advance booking, so roll up early in the day.

Earl's Court/Fulham

Hogarth, 35–37 Hogarth Rd SW5, ✆ 0171-370 6831 (toll free in US ✆ 1-800-528 1234). Part of Best Western chain, a hotel with full amenities near Earl's Court Exhibition Centre. Busy but friendly. £105–124.

Beaver, 57–9 Philbeach Gardens SW5, ℡ 0171-373 4553. Simple, attractive establishment, pool table and cheap car parking. Plush lounge with polished wooden floors. Lovely street. £30–70.

Pippa Pop-Ins, 430 Fulham Rd SW10, ℡ 0171-385 2458. A real oddity: a hotel for children aged 2–12. Leave them here and they will play to their heart's content. Available also for daytime child-minding. £40–50 per child. (Max stay: 3 days.)

Elsewhere

Tower Thistle, St Katharine's Way E1, ℡ 0171-481 2575. Not a great beauty, but ideally placed next to the Tower overlooking the river. Ultra-modern fittings and every conceivable comfort (including meeting rooms). £155–175.

Clarendon, 8–16 Montpelier Row, Blackheath SE3, ℡ 0181-318 4321. A bit of a way out, but a comfortable Georgian hotel with all mod cons including free parking and a beautiful view over Blackheath and Greenwich Park. £55–150.

Dorset Square, 39–40 Dorset Square NW1, ℡ 0171-723 7874 (toll free in US ℡ 1-800-543 4138). Restored Regency building between Madame Tussaud's and Regent's Park with beautiful furniture and a strong cricket theme because of the nearby Lord's ground. £98–180 + VAT.

La Gaffe, 107 Heath St, Hampstead NW3, ℡ 0171-435 4941. Charming bed and breakfast above an Italian restaurant in a former shepherd's cottage. Bedrooms reached via a precipitous stairway. £50–75.

Swiss Cottage, 4 Adamson Rd NW3, ℡ 0171-722 2281. Olde worlde atmosphere with lots of antiques, reproduction furniture and even a grand piano. Good location near Hampstead and Camden. £75–85.

Hampstead Village Guesthouse, 2 Kemplay Rd NW3, ℡ 0171-435 8679. Family household just a step away from Hampstead Heath. Lots of books and pot plants, plus fridges in your rooms. £35–65.

Bed and Breakfast

The bed and breakfast is a British (and Irish) tourist institution: you get to stay in someone's house, enjoy their company and eat a slap-up breakfast for a fraction of the cost of a hotel. In London the system works less freely than in the rest of the country, and you will have noticed that some of the hotels listed above have a distinctly B'n'B flavour to them. The least certain way of finding a B'n'B is by going to one of the tourist offices listed at the top of this chapter. A safer bet is to go through one of the following agencies:

Bulldog Club, 15 Roland Gdns SW7, ℡ 0171-341 9495. Will fix you up in palatial surroundings in the city or the country—at a price of course.

Uptown Reservations, 50 Christchurch St SW3, ℡ 0171-351 3445. Offers homes in Knightsbridge, Chelsea and similar neighbourhoods.

Host and Guest Service, 103 Dawes Rd SW6, ℡ 0171-385 9922. Agency with 3000 homes on its books all over London. £14.50–35 per person per night.

- **London Homes**, 6 Hyde Park Mansions, Flat G, Cabbell St NW1, ✆ 0171-262 0900. A wide range to choose from, for as little as £18 per person.

- **London Homestead Services**, Coombe Wood Rd, Kingston, Surrey, ✆ 0181-949 4455. Minimum stay three nights for as little as £15 per person. Book early.

- **Stayaway Abroad**, 71 Fellows Rd, Hampstead NW3, ✆ 0171-586 2768. Slightly more expensive, but a classier service as a result.

Student Halls of Residence

A number of university halls of residence throw open their doors to foreign visitors during the long summer holiday from July to September and can be excellent value (£25 for a double room per night). Conditions are obviously a bit spartan, and you won't be able to cancel bookings very easily, but try the following addresses:

International Students House 229 Great Portland St W1, ✆ 0171-631 3223. Strictly for students only, but excellent value for money, with access to a whole range of student amenities.

King's College Campus Vacation Bureau, 552 King's Rd SW6, ✆ 0171-928 3777. Agency for seven halls of residence all over London.

John Adams Hall, 15–23 Endsleigh St WC1, ✆ 0171-387 4086.

Northampton Hall, Bunhill Row EC1, ✆ 0171-628 2953.

Ramsey Hall, 20 Maple St W1, ✆ 0171-387 4537.

Walter Sickert Hall, 29 Graham St N1, ✆ 0171-477 8822.

Youth Hostels

Not necessarily much cheaper than the cheapest B'n'Bs. You can get a full list of addresses from the YHA Shop in Covent Garden (14 Southampton St, ✆ 0171-836 1036).

The most scenic locations are without doubt **Holland House**, ✆ 0171-937 0748, slap bang in the middle of Holland Park in a converted Jacobean mansion, and **Highgate Village** (84 Highgate West Hill, ✆ 0181-340 1831).

Self-Catering

Only really worth it if you are numerous, or if you are staying for several weeks. Try the following agencies:

Aston's, 39 Rosary Gardens, South Kensington, SW7 ✆ 0171-370 0737.

Butlers Wharf Residence, Gainsford St, ✆ 0171-407 7164. A chance to stay in one of the luxury flats built in the failed Docklands property boom of the 1980s. Very close to Tower Bridge and bang next to the Design Museum.

Kensbridge Hotel Group Flat Rentals, ✆ 0171-589 2923. Flats all over South Kensington.

Camping

Naturally, this condemns you to staying far from the centre, but it is certainly the cheapest way to stay in (in? more like near) London. Here are some sites:

Abbey Woods Caravan Club Site, Federation Rd, Abbey Wood, SE2 ✆ 0181-311 7708.

Caravan Clubsite, Crystal Palace Parade, ✆ 0181-778 7155.

Hackney Camping, Millfields Rd, Hackney Marshes, ✆ 0181-985 7656.

Lee Valley Park, Picketts Lock Centre, Picketts Lock Lane, ✆ 0181-803 6900.

Tent City, Old Oak Common, East Acton, ✆ 0181-743 5708.

Entertainment and Nightlife

No matter how much their city seems to fall apart around them, Londoners never forget how to enjoy themselves. The city has world-beating reputations in at least two departments—theatre and music—and also boasts excellent comedy venues, dance venues and nightclubs. The arts scene has undergone considerable upheavals in recent years, largely because of deep cuts under Margaret Thatcher and the consequent need to rely ever more heavily on corporate sponsorship. But it is currently enjoying something of a boom thanks to the National Lottery. Lottery money is providing much of the wherewithal for the Millennium celebrations and is galvanising many young groups of artists, actors or film-makers eligible to apply for a piece of the considerable cake. Nothing this exciting is going on anywhere else in Europe. It is not all good news, however. The Lottery may encourage new projects, but a loophole in the rules means its funds cannot be used to subsidise existing concerns. As a result a handful of thriving, but indebted theatre companies face closure, and the Royal Opera and Ballet—bled dry during the 1980s—face a deep financial crisis.

The indispensable guide to the week's events is the listings magazine *Time Out*, which appears on Tuesday afternoon or Wednesday morning; it provides addresses, descriptions and reviews of everything that moves or is scheduled to move over the following seven days. The magazine isn't perfect, tending to overhype celebrities and the latest fashion fads, but it has no serious competition—don't buy the rather limp *What's On* and certainly don't be tempted by the freebies left lying around hotel lobbies, which won't tell you anything. The national newspapers have more complete reviews than *Time Out*, of course, and give digests of what's on in their weekend editions, but their listings are usually pretty patchy. The *Guardian*'s Saturday Guide (a separate booklet) is probably the best of the bunch.

Most of the West End theatres, as well as a good smattering of cinemas and nightclubs, are clustered around Soho and Shaftesbury Avenue. Some of the most interesting nightlife, however, takes place well away from the centre of town: jazz and fringe theatre in Islington, nightclubs in North Kensington or Brixton, comedy way up north in Crouch End or down south in Clapham. If you venture far afield, or if you have a long way to get home, you'll need to think carefully about transport. The Underground system dries up soon after midnight, and taxis can be hard to find in more remote parts of London. Night buses head to and from Trafalgar Square, each service usually leaving once an hour. If these aren't convenient (and they certainly aren't all that pleasant), you may have to resort to a minicab. Don't let yourself be cajoled into taking a minicab off the street; not only is it illegal for drivers to solicit business this way, it may not be safe for you either. Instead, phone one of the numbers listed on p.8.

Theatre

Foreign visitors will find the cast lists of plays showing in London disconcertingly familiar: it looks as though the villains and eccentrics of Hollywood have mounted a takeover. In fact, the London stage is where actors like Anthony Hopkins, Ralph Fiennes and Alan Rickman come home to roost when they are not making megabucks in the movies. Those Californian casting directors know very well that London boasts the best serious stage acting anywhere, a reputation it has built up meticulously over several centuries. Why should this be, especially in so unsentimental and mercantile a city as London? Wade through the voluminous literature on the English stage and you'll find all sorts of theories. It is the richness and versatility of the English language, claim some. It is the character of the people, say others; precisely because the English are so reserved in real life, they manage to put on a convincing masquerade of emotion on stage. Maybe there is some truth in these assertions, but a more concrete reason for London's theatrical success lies in its history and the early chance it had to perform plays in a public arena. A little digression is in order...

A One-Act History of the London Stage

The first public playhouse was called simply The Theatre, and it was established in Finsbury Fields just outside the City in 1576 by a travelling player called James Burbage. The City fathers deemed theatre and all other entertainments distasteful and refused to allow them within their walls. Generations of travelling players and minstrels had, however, built up a demand for public performance. Burbage had little difficulty in raising audiences for his enterprise, and the whiff of naughtiness made his theatre all the more attractive. Within a generation theatres were thriving all over town, particularly in Bankside where the likes of Shakespeare, Marlowe and Ben Jonson first had their plays produced. Elizabethan theatres were round, open to the skies and made of wood, with audiences either crammed into the standing space beneath the tall jutting stage or packed tight into the galleries piled four or five storeys high. You can get a good idea of what they were like from a visit to the reconstructed Globe Theatre on Bankside (*see* p.334).

Performances were rowdy affairs, and it was not long before the Puritan movement was denouncing theatre as degenerate. 'Satan hath not a more speedy way and fitter school to work and teach his desire, to bring men and women into his share of concupiscence and filthy lusts of wicked whoredom, than those plays and theatres,' wrote William Prynne. When the Civil War began in 1642, Cromwell's Roundheads closed down every company, vandalized theatre buildings, ripped up costumes, imprisoned actors and fined theatre-goers. But the very excess of puritanical zeal proved a blessing in disguise; the first thing Charles II did after the collapse of the Commonwealth and the restoration of the monarchy in 1660 was to revive and fund the public playhouses as a symbolic political gesture.

Charles' King's Company, based in Covent Garden, introduced ideas the monarch had picked up from the court theatre of Louis XIV during his exile in France. Thus London acquired its first scenery and its first women on stage. Shakespeare's generation had used boys with unbroken voices to play all the female roles, but now actresses proved a big hit; indeed the leading lady of the day, Nell Gwynne, became the king's mistress. Acting techniques remained somewhat eccentric: players would happily talk between lines and greet their friends in the audience in mid-speech. In serious plays, the emphasis was very much on grand rhetoric rather than realism. The audiences didn't mind. If they liked a speech, they would weep and gnash their teeth in appreciation. If they didn't, they would start a riot.

Only in the 18th century did naturalism catch on, thanks largely to the actor-manager David Garrick whose awesome control of voice and gesture inspired the French philosopher Denis Diderot to compile an entire theory of stagecraft. The march towards modernity gathered further pace in the early 19th century, when auditorium lights went down for the first time during performances to heighten the theatrical illusion. Character actors like Edmund Kean came triumphantly into their own, broadening the appeal of the theatre and turning it into a major emotional experience. '[Kean's] great merit consists in having a soul which cannot only be touched, but fired with passion, and a countenance which can indicate the most rapid changes of the soul,' one contemporary critic wrote.

After Kean died in 1833—on stage, during a performance of *Othello* at the Covent Garden Theatre—there was a brief period of decline in which even Shakespeare went out of fashion. The Victorians disapproved of acting, thinking it immoral, and put on a flurry of mediocre shows whose only lasting curiosity was their absurd titles—*My Wife's Dentist*, *The Negro of Wapping*, *I Have Eaten My Friend* or *The Phantom Breakfast*. Then, in the 1880s, the great classical actors Henry Irving and Ellen Terry pulled London out of its thespian doldrums. A clutch of ornate new theatres was built (particularly around Shaftesbury Avenue) which vied with each other for technical and well as dramatic brilliance. Straight plays were soon competing with musicals, grand spectaculars and operas featuring casts of thousands and stage props including live elephants.

London really has not looked back since, its stages rightly appreciated for craftsmanship, fine attention to detail and, by and large, intellectual integrity. Its playwrights have pioneered no theatrical movements—England boasts no equivalent of Pirandello or Brecht—but have nevertheless turned out compelling and challenging dramas of a quality not seen in any other European city. Likewise, West End actors have rarely become major international stars, but still command enormous respect on Broadway and in Hollywood where their performances win awards by the bucketful.

Aside from the many successes, the history of the London stage is also peppered with much-relished stories of the bizarre and the disastrous. Down the years there have been *Hamlet*s performed without a Hamlet, props and stage effects that go catastrophically wrong and scathing battles between critics and actors. The writer Charles Lamb was so embarrassed by the première of his own play *Mr H* in 1806 that he ended up booing and hissing at it himself. In 1870, the dilettante playwright Lord Newry made the fatal mistake of providing real picnic hampers for a scene in his play *Ecarte*. The first-night cast became riotously drunk on champagne, started mumbling or shouting their lines and were eventually booed off stage. There was no second night. The reviews were not as scathing, however, as one notice for a show at the Duchess Theatre at the turn of the century called *A Good Time*. The critic wrote simply: 'No.'

What to See and Where to Go

The major commercial theatre companies are concentrated in the West End, just as the main New York stages are grouped together on Broadway. Two distinct traditions are forever jostling for attention, the straight play and the musical. Shakespeare is of course a perennial favourite, along with Chekhov, Shaw and Noel Coward, but in pure terms of seat numbers the darling of the British musical, Andrew Lloyd Webber, is way ahead in the popularity ratings. Lloyd Webber's shows, from *Joseph and the Amazing Technicolour Dreamcoat* through to *Sunset Boulevard*, have been running without interruption in London for the past quarter century. At the time of writing his *oeuvre* is occupying no fewer than four major theatres—cause for celebration, perhaps, if you enjoy his brand of harmless flummery, but a pity for all the talented new writers and actors being pushed out of the West End as a result. Lloyd Webber's flagship theatre, the Palace on Cambridge Circus, has for the past few years been showing a musical he did not write himself, the smash hit *Les Misérables*. Just across the road at the St Martin's is the longest-running show in London, Agatha Christie's *The Mousetrap*, which has been on in one theatre or another since 1952. Longevity is no guarantee of quality, and you'd do well to give this wooden and outdated tourist attraction a wide berth.

Established playwrights, such as Tom Stoppard, David Hare, Harold Pinter, Tony Kushner and David Mamet, are increasingly turning to the off-West End theatre companies to stage their work. The most consistent and reliable of these is the three-stage **Royal National Theatre** on the South Bank, which puts on superb versions of the classics as well as showcasing high-quality new writing. The RNT is followed closely by the **Royal Shakespeare Company**, based at the Barbican, which concentrates mainly on the Bard and his contemporaries. The **Royal Court** in Sloane Square and **Lyric** in Hammersmith are excellent venues for new work, while experimental shows and reworkings of established plays are the hallmark of the **Almeida** in Islington, the **Hampstead Theatre** or the **Donmar Warehouse** in Covent Garden.

The **fringe** is always active, and occasionally you can find first-rate shows in draughty halls or upstairs rooms in pubs. If you are in London during the summer, don't forget about open-air venues like the **Globe Theatre, Regent's Park, Holland Park** and the garden of the **Royal Observatory** in Greenwich, where you can enjoy Shakespeare (particularly *A Midsummer Night's Dream*) and lively modern comedies.

Practical Details

Most performances start at 7.30pm or 8.00pm, with matinées usually scheduled on Wednesdays and Saturdays. By far the best way to book is through the theatre itself. At most places you can pay by credit card over the phone, then pick up the tickets just before the curtain goes up. **Ticket agents** charge stinging commissions, usually 22 per cent, although they can be a necessary evil to get into the big musicals (try Ticketmaster on ✆ 0171–344 4444 or First Call on ✆ 0171–420 0000). The Royal National Theatre offers a limited number of cheap tickets from 10am on the day of the performance (get there early as there are often long queues), and the Society of London Theatre has a ticket booth in Leicester Square *(open 2.30–6.30pm, or noon–6pm on matinée days)* with half-price tickets for West End shows that night. If all else fails, you can try for returns in the hour before the performance starts; students can get a hefty discount this way.

A Few Addresses

There's not a lot of point recommending individual theatres, as the quality of each production cannot be guaranteed, but the following addresses—most outside the West End—should give you some pointers. The telephone numbers are for the box office:

Royal National Theatre, South Bank, ✆ 0171-928 2252. The National has three stages—the large apron of the Olivier, the conventional proscenium at the Lyttleton and the smaller, cosier Cottesloe. An evening here not only guarantees top-notch theatre; you can enjoy foyer concerts, browse through the bookshops and linger in the cafés with views out over the Thames. Highly recommended.

Barbican Arts Centre, Silk St, Barbican, ✆ 0171-638 8891. The Royal Shakespeare Company, based both in London and in Shakespeare's birthplace, Stratford-upon-Avon, has two stages here, the conventional Barbican Theatre and the more experimental Pit. Standards are excellent and well worth the byzantine complications of finding the venue in the first place (*see* p.301).

Royal Court, Sloane Square, ✆ 0171-565 5000. The major venue for experimental or counter-cultural writing, made famous by Shaw and Granville-Barker in the 1920s and kept prominent by the likes of Edward Bond, Caryl Churchill, Howard Brenton and Hanif Kureishi. The Theatre Upstairs on the first floor is one of the better fringe venues in town (both theatres being refurbished at the time of writing, and temporarily relocated to the West End).

Wyndham's, Charing Cross Rd, ✆ 0171-369 1736. One of the more reliable West End addresses, with plenty of serious productions that attract big-name foreign actors like John Malkovich and Dustin Hoffman.

Theatre Royal Haymarket, Haymarket, ✆ 0171-930 8800. Unadventurous choice of plays, but impeccable production and acting standards in this early 19th-century theatre built by John Nash. Maggie Smith, Vanessa Redgrave and Ian McKellen are regular stars here.

Old Vic, Waterloo Rd, ✆ 0171-928 7616. The former home of the National Theatre has come down in the world a bit, but still puts on good productions. Recently refurbished. Peter O'Toole caused a sensation here in the early 1980s by playing Macbeth for laughs in a near-incoherent drunken slur. The theatre was packed out every night, but the management was scandalized and O'Toole has never been asked back.

Donmar Warehouse, Earlham St, Covent Garden, ✆ 0171-369 1732. Excellent venue where many distinguished young directors have cut their teeth.

Lyric Hammersmith, King St, ✆ 0181-741 2311. Hosts many regional and foreign theatre companies. Home also to the smaller, experimental Studio.

Hampstead Theatre, Avenue Road, ✆ 0171-722 9301. Actors and audiences often mingle in the bar after the show at this friendly neighbourhood theatre, which is often a springboard for prestigious West End productions.

Theatre Royal Stratford East, Gerry Raffles Square, Stratford, ✆ 0181-534 0310. High-quality drama in a crumbling Victorian palace in the midst of grey tower blocks. Well worth the long trip out east.

Almeida, Almeida St, Islington, ✆ 0171-359 4404. A fringe theatre that has acquired a formidable reputation. Stages different productions every 6 or 7 weeks. Often produces its own plays but also reworks classical pieces.

King's Head, 115 Upper St, Islington, ℗ 0171-226 1916. Eccentric pub (*see* 'Food and Drink', p.507) with popular theatrical tradition in a charming, thespian back room. Serves a 3-course dinner in the theatre just before the curtain rises (metaphorically speaking, because there is no curtain).

The Gate, 11 Pembridge Road, Notting Hill, ℗ 0171-229 0706. Excellent pub theatre that features new plays as well as ambitious reworkings of the classics, including Greek tragedy. Currently in danger of closure.

BAC (Battersea Arts Centre), 176 Lavender Hill, ℗ 0171-223 2223. Lively theatre venue south of the river.

The Globe, New Globe Walk, ℗ 0171-401 9919. Opened for business in 1997, this lovingly reconstructed version of Shakespeare's original London theatre puts on three or four Elizabethan productions each year, most of them by the Bard, in a season that lasts from May until September. It's proving popular, so book early (box-office opens around January once the programme has been fixed). Lots of audience participation and period high jinks (like jesters with firecrackers attached to their feet). Watch out for rain and cold, though, as the theatre is open to the skies (*see* p.334 for more on the theatre itself).

Regent's Park Open Air Theatre, Inner Circle, Regent's Park, ℗ 0171-486 2431. Open-air theatre from May to September. Bring a blanket and umbrella to keep the worst of the English summer at bay.

Holland Park Theatre, Holland Park, ℗ 0171-602 7856. Has a shorter open-air season, from June to August, but with all manner of productions including opera.

Opera and Classical Music

London has classical music coming out of its ears: two major opera companies, five world-class orchestras, lunchtime concerts, summer festival concerts, open-air concerts. For generations, classical music in Britain was tinged with class prejudice, being a pursuit of the educated upper-middle classes who turned up their noses at the philistine hordes who couldn't tell their Handel from their Haydn. The barriers have broken down somewhat, partly because stars like Luciano Pavarotti and the punk violinist Nigel Kennedy have brought classical music to the masses, and partly because the steady decline of state funding has forced orchestras and opera companies to pull in whatever audiences they can find. One London orchestra or another is forever in danger of closure, and severe financial constraints mean that the English National Opera (currently at the Coliseum) might have to move in with the Royal Opera and Royal Ballet at the newly refurbished Covent Garden opera house when it reopens. You'll still find the snobs lurking in the foyers of the Festival Hall and on the rarefied airwaves of the BBC's classical station Radio 3. But you'll also find a wealth of unpretentious, dedicated young performers and audiences, especially in smaller concert venues like the Wigmore Hall. London's weakness is undoubtedly in contemporary and avant-garde music; programmers tend to play very safe, with a preponderance of Mozart, Beethoven and Brahms. A steady stream of new works is nevertheless performed at the summer Promenade concerts at the Albert Hall. Anyone with a strong interest in contemporary music should also head for the Aldeburgh Festival in Suffolk, which was established by Benjamin Britten and takes place every July.

The following addresses are for the main concert and opera venues; again, you should check *Time Out* to see what is playing.

Royal Opera House, Covent Garden, ✆ 0171-304 4000. Britain's leading opera venue is right up there with the Met, the Staatsoper and La Scala, but constant financial and political problems have not only pushed up prices almost as high as the top C in the Queen of the Night's bravura aria from Mozart's *Magic Flute*, they have put the very future of the theatre in doubt just when it is due to emerge from an exciting and long overdue renovation. At the time of writing, the plan is to rename it the Covent Garden Theatre and bring the English National Opera under its roof from down the road at the Coliseum. Check the papers for the latest news.

London Coliseum, St Martin's Lane, ✆ 0171-632 8300. Home to the English National Opera, which performs in English to high musical standards and with infectious enthusiasm. Much cheaper (from £8, top price around £40) and far less pretentious than Covent Garden. Regrettably, the ENO may be forced to move out because of deep financial problems (*see* above).

South Bank Centre, South Bank, Belvedere Rd, ✆ 0171-921 0600. Three first-rate concert halls under the same roof: the Royal Festival Hall, boasting its own organ and room for as many musicians and singers as any musical work might demand; the Queen Elizabeth Hall, which is smaller and a little more adventurous in its programming; and the Purcell Room, for chamber music only. The larger halls also host occasional jazz, rock, dance and even small-scale opera performances.

Barbican Centre, Silk St, ✆ 0171-638 8891 or 638 4141. Home to the London Symphony Orchestra and English Chamber Orchestra. Excellent acoustics make up for the out-of-the-way venue.

Royal Albert Hall, Kensington Gore, ✆ 0171-589 8212. Hosts the Promenade concerts, or Proms, which run every year from July until early September. The Proms are an eclectic platform for music old and new, and for unknown as well as established performers. The seats are removed from the area in front of the stage, leaving an open space in which people either stand or sit on the floor for as little as £3 per person. Queues form in the hours before the performance begins; bring a cushion to soften the bum-numbing effects of the Kensington pavements. You can also book conventional seating in advance, at regular concert prices (up to around £30). The Last Night of the Proms is a raucous affair at which the all-English orchestra plays all-English music, and the all-English audience sings along to the national anthem and *Rule Britannia*. (*see* p.369).

Wigmore Hall, 36 Wigmore St, ✆ 0171-935 2141. An intimate venue with excellent acoustics that attracts solo performers like guitarist Julian Bream or prima donna Jessye Norman. The tickets are very cheap—between £6 and £20—and sell out very fast.

Sadler's Wells, Roseberry Ave, ✆ 0171-278 0563. A somewhat unfashionable venue for all kinds of music, including the infectious if supremely silly late Victorian operettas of Gilbert and Sullivan performed by the D'Oyly Carte company in April and May.

St John's Smith Square, Smith Square, Westminster, ✆ 0171-222 1061. Thomas Archer's fine baroque church is the best lunchtime concert spot in town. Other good lunchtime venues include St James's Piccadilly (usually on Mondays at 1pm), St Martin-in-the-Fields in Trafalgar Square (which boasts its own excellent chamber orchestra), St Bride in Fleet St, St Michael's Cornhill (organ recitals), St Sepulchre-without-Newgate (mainly piano recitals on Fridays) and the magnificently restored St Helen's, Bishopsgate.

Kenwood House, Hampstead Lane, ✆ 0171 973 3426. From June to September, enjoy idyllic outdoor concerts beside a lake at the top of Hampstead Heath. Highly recommended. Other open-air summer venues include Holland Park (for opera), Hampton Court and Marble Hill House in Twickenham (Sunday evenings only).

Dance

London puts on everything from classical ballet to performance art. Covent Garden (*see* above) is home to the highly accomplished Royal Ballet, which is cheaper and much less snooty than the Royal Opera in the same building; while the London Coliseum (*see* above) hosts the English National Ballet, at least for now. Sadler's Wells (*see* above) used to have its own ballet company too, but it decamped to Birmingham in 1990; the theatre nevertheless puts on an eclectic dance programme that has recently included both the mime artist Lindsay Kemp and the National Ballet of Cambodia. Two other addresses worth knowing about are the **ICA** on the Mall (✆ 0171–930 3647), arguably the most avant-garde address in town; and **The Place** (17 Duke's Rd, Bloomsbury, ✆ 0171–380 1268), which is also home to the London Contemporary Dance School. Every autumn, from mid-October to early December, London stages a festival called Dance Umbrella, which provides a showcase for performers from around the world.

Jazz

Jazz came to London in the 1950s, largely thanks to the effort of the late Ronnie Scott and his excellent club in Soho, and it has gone from strength to strength ever since. Venues used to be pokey, smokey and cheap; now they are smartening up, perhaps a shade too much since they are starting to offer fancy food and drink at extraordinarily high prices. The music has not suffered yet, however, and continues to flow until the not-so-early hours of the morning. Check *Time Out* for jazz concerts in pubs and foyers of the larger theatres. Note that many clubs charge a (usually nominal) membership fee. You may find it hard to book for the more popular shows at Ronnie Scott's, for example, if you are not already a member.

Ronnie Scott's, 47 Frith St, W1, ✆ 0171-439 0747 (*closed Sun*). The prime jazz venue in town, with a steady flow of big names and a suitably low-key, laid-back atmosphere. Book if you have time, and get there early (around 9pm) to ensure a decent seat. Admission is £15, but worth it.

Blue Note, 1 Hoxton Square, N1, ✆ 0171-729 8440. A serious-minded, highly popular jazz venue with special African and Latin American dance nights at weekends.

100 Club, 100 Oxford St, W1, ✆ 0171-636 0933. Lively basement venue with an eclectic mix of trad and modern jazz, as well as blues, swing and rockabilly. The Sex Pistols gave one of their first performances here in the mid-1970s.

606 Club, 90 Lots Rd, Fulham, ✆ 0171-352 5953. Seven-nights-a-week basement club where young musicians are invited to jam with the players on the night's billing. Late-night restaurant licence. 8.30–2am.

Jazz Café, 5 Parkway, Camden, ✆ 0171-916 6060. Typical of the new-style jazz club, a slick venue with plush dinner-table seating (food optional). The music is first-rate.

Duke of Wellington, 119 Balls Pond Rd, Dalston. Free admission, free jazz. The venue is small, so arrive early.

Bull's Head, 373 Lonsdale Rd, Barnes, SW13, ✆ 0181-876 5241. Top-notch bands in a riverside setting.

Vortex, Stoke Newington Church St, ✆ 0171-254 6516. Friendly first-floor jazz bar featuring many local north London bands.

Pizza Express, 10 Dean St, Soho, ✆ 0171-437 9595. Be-bop to accompany your pizza; an unlikely setting, but a congenial one which boasts its own resident band as well as many prestigious visitors. Branch at **Pizza on the Park**, 11 Knightsbridge, off Hyde Park Corner.

Rock, Pop and World Music

Back in the 1960s and 1970s, London was a major centre for rock music, with the emergence of The Who, The Yardbirds, The Rolling Stones, David Bowie, T Rex and finally the Sex Pistols. It has come into its own again recently, thanks to Britpop groups like Blur, Pulp and Oasis, and still has an enviable array of clubs and concert venues that attract every major artist (and plenty of more offbeat acts) from around the world. By and large, the big Madonna/Michael Jackson venues like Wembley Stadium are impersonal and have terrible acoustics, while smaller, more specialized clubs like the Africa Centre or the Mean Fiddler are infinitely more rewarding and cheaper too. Posters and press adverts will tell you how to buy tickets. You'll probably have to go through a ticket agency (*see* Theatre section above) for the bigger acts, otherwise go directly to the venue. Once again, *Time Out* will have all the details, including reliable recommendations on the week's best shows.

Wembley Stadium, Empire Way, Wembley, ✆ 0181-900 1234. Appalling views, appalling acoustics, appalling transport links. If the big acts insist on coming here, it is mainly because of the seating capacity (up to 100,000); but as Madonna would be the first to tell you, size isn't everything. Only the Live Aid concert of 1985 and the Free Nelson Mandela bash of 1988 generated something approaching atmosphere. Otherwise, only the sledge-hammer lyricism of U2 or Bruce Springsteen can ever get through to audiences. Bring a telescope.

Wembley Arena, same address as above. The indoor neighbour of the stadium, with all of its problems but with a seating capacity of only 13,000.

Royal Albert Hall, Kensington Gore, ✆ 0171-589 8212. The iffy acoustics and somewhat grandiose Victorian architecture are more than compensated for by intelligent programming—folk-rock and R'n'B by the likes of Bonnie Raitt, Eric Clapton etc.

Brixton Academy, 211 Stockwell Rd, Brixton, ✆ 0171-924 9999. Much more like it. Raw, raucous music in a crumbling art deco setting. Sweaty but exhilarating.

Forum, 9–17 Highgate Rd, Kentish Town, ✆ 0171-344 0044. Formerly known as the Town and Country Club and arguably the best rock venue in town; an excellent blend of high-quality facilities and first-rate bands.

Shepherds Bush Empire, Shepherds Bush Green, ✆ 0181-740 7474. Similar-sized venue to the Forum, with seats upstairs. Attracts big names; great atmosphere.

The Grand, Clapham Junction, St John's Hill, ✆ 0171-738 9000. Newish rock venue with great view of the stage from the bar. Sister establishment to...

The Mean Fiddler, 24–28a High St, Harlesden, ✆ 0181-961 5490. Ace setting for Irish folk and new country artists. Well worth the schlepp out to unfashionable Harlesden.

Weavers Arms, 98 Newington Green Rd, ✆ 0171-226 6911. Roots music, from Cajun to Celtic, with plenty of folk and country too.

Africa Centre, 38 King St, Covent Garden, ✆ 0171-836 1973. Groovy atmosphere and infectious African music. Cheap and great fun.

Camden Palace, 1a Camden Rd, ✆ 0171-387 0428. Tuesday night features new indie bands. Dancing the other nights of the week.

Hammersmith Apollo, Queen Caroline St, ✆ 0171–416 6080. A big-name venue, which puts on stage shows as well. Excellent sound and good views of the stage.

Subterrania, 12 Acklam Rd, Ladbroke Grove, ✆ 0181-960 4590. Funk, jazz, soul and rap, interspersed with new songwriter nights, make this one of the more unpredictable and enjoyable spots in west London. Hot rubber rooms.

The Venue, 2a Clifton Rise, New Cross, ℂ 0181-692 4077 (*open Fri, Sat*). Specializes in indie music, with dancing late into the night after the main band has gone home.

Bunjies, 27 Litchfield St, Covent Garden, ℂ 0171-240 1796 (*music Wed, Fri, Sat*). Laid-back café setting for old-hippy acoustic performers.

Comedy Clubs

Comedy has been all the rage in London since the early 1980s, and clubs have been sprouting with amazing speed all over town. Traditionally, stand-up comedy was restricted to music halls or to working-men's clubs in the industrial towns of northern England. Performers were generally fat and male, and cracked jokes in dubious taste about blacks, big tits and mothers-in-law. The only 'sophisticated' comedy was the zany brand pioneered by the Footlights revue at Cambridge University and developed by the likes of Peter Cook, Dudley Moore and Monty Python. These were middle-class, well-educated performers who despite a strong anti-establishment streak appealed mostly to their own kind. Comedy, like everything else in Britain, was divided along class lines.

All that changed with the advent of the Thatcher government in 1979. A new counter-culture of politically aware comedy sprang up, making what jokes it could out of industrial decline, growing gulfs between rich and poor and the 1980s culture of greed and self-advancement. Performers from a broader social and racial spectrum, including Lenny Henry, Rowan Atkinson, Harry Enfield, Ben Elton, Rik Mayall, Jo Brand and Josie Lawrence, soon became established stars, both on television and in some cases in feature films too. All of them started out in London's comedy clubs, particularly the Comedy Store in Leicester Square (since transferred to new premises) which opened in 1979, the year of Thatcher's election. The comedy club circuit has expanded considerably since then, and established performers mingle easily with new talent in more than 20 major venues. Sit in the front rows at your peril, as you are likely to be roped into the act and insulted or humiliated (in the best possible taste, of course). Some of the humour is a bit parochial, revolving around British adverts and television programmes, but many acts are truly inspired. Usually several artists will contribute to a single evening, so if you don't like one there's not long to wait for something better. Anyone who has never experienced John Hegley's surreal poetry or Arthur Smith's deadpan delivery has a treat in store; look out for the up-and-coming Paul Foot.

Comedy Store, Haymarket House, Oxendon St, ℂ 01426 914433. Stand-up on Fri and Sat, improv on Wed and Sun. The most famous comedy club of them all has got a bit slick for its own good and the hefty admission fee (around £8) reflects that. The standard remains very high, however.

Jongleurs, The Cornet, 49 Lavender Gardens, Clapham, ✆ 0171-564 2550. Top acts on Fri and Sat nights. Worth booking well in advance.

Hackney Empire, 291 Mare St, Hackney, open Fri, Sat, ✆ 0181-985 2424. Comedy with a political edge in a fine Victorian theatre.

East Dulwich Cabaret, East Dulwich Tavern, 1 Lordship Lane, open Thurs–Sat, ✆ 0181-299 4138. Pub venue with excellent acts.

Downstairs at the King's Head, 2 Crouch End Hill, ✆ 0181-340 1028. One of the least pretentious comedy clubs in town, with a warm atmosphere encouraged by the very funny compères. Open Sat, Sun.

Red Rose Cabaret, 129 Seven Sisters Rd, Finsbury Park, ✆ 0171-263 7265. Top acts at knock-down prices in a slightly iffy area. Open Fri, Sat.

Cinema

London cinemas are a bit like the British film industry—bursting with potential, forever on the verge of a real breakthrough, but poorly looked after and often disappointing. The mainstream cinemas are on the whole unfriendly and very expensive (£7 or more for a ticket, regardless of whether the venue is a plush auditorium with THX Dolby sound or a cramped backroom with polystyrene walls). The multiplex has hit London in a big way, for example at the Warner and Empire in Leicester Square or at Whiteleys in Queensway. For no discernible good reason seats tend to be numbered, which means confusion breaks out just as the main feature is starting, and the audience rarely settles down until 10 minutes into the first reel. There has been a flurry of interest in new British and independent cinema in recent years, thanks to *Four Weddings and a Funeral, The Full Monty* and the darkly humorous work of the Scottish director Danny Boyle (*Shallow Grave, Trainspotting,* etc). But Hollywood blockbusters still grab more than their fair share of the market. The gruesomely untalented Kevin Costner stares down from every billboard, and yet the work of some of the most challenging British directors—Mike Leigh, Nicolas Roeg or Ken Loach—might not make a first-run cinema at all.

On the plus side, the arthouse and repertory sector is reasonably healthy, showing subtitled foreign-language films as well as the classics of American and British cinema. Prices are lower than first-run cinemas—£4–5 is normal—and can be lower still if you pay a membership fee and return regularly. The National Film Theatre offers the broadest range, while clubs like the Everyman attract a fiercely loyal clientele.

Film censorship in general is very strict, and in some cases the British Board of Film Classification cuts out footage it finds offensive without alerting the audience. Films are graded U (family films), PG (parental guidance recommended), 12 (nobody under that age), 15 (ditto) or 18 (ditto). The system is governed by crazy pseudo-puritanical rules that border on paranoia—the very first film to be censored in Britain, back in 1898, was a close-up of a piece of Stilton cheese. Don't ask why. Steven Spielberg's dinosaur thriller *Jurassic Park* was given a PG rating despite its self-evidently disturbing effect on children, while an intelligent classic like Robert Altman's *McCabe and Mrs Miller* is lumped along with pornography and Kung Fu in the 18 bracket.

Odeon Leicester Square, Leicester Square, ✆ 0181-315 4215. London's plushest venue, which premières major Hollywood productions, often with royals and film stars in tow. Even more expensive than the average mainstream cinema, with interminable adverts before the main feature. Rather go to...

Odeon Marble Arch, 10 Edgware Rd, ✆ 0181-315 4216. The biggest screen in London, with a top-notch sound system to boot. Shows Hollywood spectaculars but also old classics like *Spartacus* and *Lawrence of Arabia*.

Prince Charles, Leicester Place, ✆ 0171-437 8181. This former soft-porn cinema has smartened up its act and shows a constantly changing schedule of cult classics at £2 a seat. Surely this can't go on... take advantage while you can.

Curzon Mayfair, 38 Curzon St, ✆ 0171-465 8865. Cinema showing art or foreign films. A more relaxed venue is its sister-cinema, the **Curzon West End** at 93 Shaftesbury Ave, ✆ 0171-369 1722.

Metro, 11 Rupert St, ✆ 0171-437 0757. Two-screen cinema that shuns Hollywood fare in favour of independent productions.

Renoir, Brunswick Centre, Brunswick Square, ✆ 0171-837 8402. The most adventurous of central London's cinemas, showing lots of foreign films and the best of British and American independents.

Screen on the Hill, 203 Haverstock Hill, Belsize Park, ✆ 0171-435 3366. Very popular first-run and art cinema with excellent coffee at the bar. Affiliated cinemas include the rather cramped **Screen on Baker Street** (96 Baker St, ✆ 0171-935 2772) and the more commercial **Screen on the Green** (83 Upper St, Islington, ✆ 0171-226 3520).

Gate, 87 Notting Hill Gate. ✆ 0171-727 4043. Classy west London cinema with lively Sunday matinée line-ups. First-run films and classic revivals.

National Film Theatre, South Bank, ✆ 0171-928 3232. The mecca of London's film junkies and main venue for the annual London Film Festival each November. Lots of old and new films always showing in rep, with special seasons, for instance of Iranian cinema, to liven up the proceedings.

Everyman, Hollybush Vale, Hampstead, ✆ 0171-435 1525. London's oldest rep cinema with an excellent bar downstairs. Lots of old favourites and a dedicated, studenty audience.

ICA Cinémathèque, Carlton House Terrace, The Mall, ✆ 0171-930 3647. The wackiest film selection in town, with the emphasis on the avant-garde, especially feminist and gay cinema.

Clapham Picture House, Venn St, ✆ 0171-498 3323. Cheap and appealing cinema showing intelligent recent releases. A rare cinematic high spot south of the river.

Phoenix, 52 High Rd, East Finchley, ✆ 0181-444 6789. Rather out of the way but very lovable old rep cinema, showing interesting double-bills.

French Institute, 17 Queensberry Place, South Kensington, ✆ 0171-828 2144. A good place to catch up on Gabin, Godard *et compagnie*.

Goethe Institute, 50 Princes Gate, Exhibition Rd, ✆ 0171-411 3400. Shows a broad range of German-language cinema, sometimes without subtitles.

Nightclubs and Discos

From the hot and sweaty to the cool and sophisticated: London has about 150 clubs and discos providing anything from big-band swing to rap and techno. The London club scene always used to be hampered by the country's strict licensing laws. Now, however, you should be able to drink alcohol until 3am at most establishments and carry on dancing, with the help of vitamin-enriched fruit juices, until dawn or beyond. The main handicap is price: it usually costs around £10 to get into a club, and £2 or £3 more to buy a drink.

Annabel's, 44 Berkeley Sq, ✆ 0171-629 1096. One of the most exclusive clubs in town, with a strict members-only policy so you'll need to be well connected (and well-dressed) to go.

Bar Rumba, 36 Shaftesbury Ave, ✆ 0171-287 6933 (*open 10pm–3am*). Lively bar and club. Latin nights Tues and Sun, Acid and House music the rest of the week.

Bohemia, Apple Tree Yard, Duke of York St, St James's (*open 10.30pm–3.30am except Mon 6pm–midnight*). Studeny House-inclined club with theme nights called Prozak (Fri) or Someone's Yearning (Sat).

Café de Paris, 3 Coventry St, ✆ 0171-734 7700 (*open Fri, Sat only 10pm–6am*). Waltz and foxtrot all night in this 1920s ballroom bombed during the Blitz and now restored. Lots of red velvet.

Equinox, Leicester Square, ✆ 0171-437 1446 (*closed Sun*). Vast venue (room for 1500) which plays chart and dance standards, with lasers to liven up the atmosphere.

The Fridge, Town Hall Parade, Brixton Hill, ✆ 0171-326 5100 (*open Tues–Sat*). Funky music and a packed dancefloor. Mainy gay nights, but open to all.

The Gardening Club, 4 The Piazza, Covent Garden, ✆ 0171-497 3153 (*closed Sun*). Varied music during the week; House dominates at the weekends.

Gossips, 69 Dean St, ✆ 0171-434 4480 (*closed Sun*). Atmospheric dark cellar with wide range of music. Thursdays feature Gaz's Rockin Blues, a mix of blues and funk. Cheap entry (£5–7).

Heaven, Villiers St, ✆ 0171-930 2020. Excellent club with multiple bars, dance-floors, laser shows and crazy lighting. In theory a gay venue, but most nights very cool about anyone who wants to come.

Hippodrome, Cranbourn St, ✆ 0171-437 4311 (*closed Sun*). Vastly popular club just off Leicester Square, attracting a large crowd of non-Londoners. Entertainment includes trapeze artists and fire-eaters.

Legends, 29 Old Burlington St, ✆ 0171-494 2271 (*open Wed–Sat*). Cool-paced, elegantly designed club which livens up at weekends with House music.

Limelight, 136 Shaftesbury Ave, ✆ 0171-434 0572 (*closed Sun*). A converted church that blasts out Garage and House music six nights a week.

Madame Jo Jo's, 8–10 Brewer St, ✆ 0171-734 2473 (*closed Sun*). Outrageous transvestite cabaret. Camp and colourful but a bit touristy.

Ministry of Sound, 103 Gaunt St, Elephant and Castle, ✆ 0171-378 6528 (*open all night Fri and Sat only*). Expensive, but very trendy and always packed. A New York-style club with lots of Garage and House music. Expect long queues. Unlicensed, but then again you'll be too busy dancing to drink.

Paradise Club, 1–5 Parkfield St, Islington (*open all night Fri and Sat only*). A must for the inexhaustible: the Paradise Club has a 24-hour party licence. Hosts occasional all-male rubber and leather nights and transvestite floorshows.

Powerhaus, 1 Liverpool Rd, Islington, ✆ 0171-561 9656. Cheap (£5–7) place to hear live indie music, followed by dancing until late.

Stringfellow's, 16 Upper St Martin's Lane, ✆ 0171-240 5534 (*open Mon–Sat 9.30pm–3am*). Politicians, film stars and models theoretically come here, but so do lots of tourists dressed up in their smartest togs for one of London's posher night spots. Decent food.

Turnmills, 63 Clerkenwell Rd, ✆ 0171-250 3409 (*open all night Sat, Sun only*). Everything from funky jazz to explicit gay love-ins.

Wag Club, 35 Wardour St, ✆ 0171-437 5534 (*closed Sun*). Everything from live rock to funk and hip hop. A young trendy club spread over two floors.

Gay Bars

London's main drag centres on Old Compton St and adjoining streets in Soho, where passing media suits mingle freely with shaven headed, body-pierced fashion queens. Past squabbles between restaurateurs and Westminster Council over tables thrust onto wobbly narrow footpaths may have been resolved; the result is an untidy but lively compromise. The tidal pink pound has seen the rise and demise of many places to be seen in; what follows is a snapshot of the current scene. For gay clubs, *see* above. *See also* p.19 for other addresses.

The Box, 32–34 Monmouth St, Covent Garden (*open Mon–Sat 11–11, Sun noon–10.30*). Café by day and lively bar by night, attracting a young mixed crowd. Women only on Sun.

First Out Café Bar, 52 St Giles High Street, Covent Garden (*open 10am–11pm*). Great veggie food served at this café bar, the first of its type in the West End. Women only on Fri eve.

Freedom, 60–66 Wardour St, Soho (*open 9am–11pm*). Large café bar serving good food and cocktails to a trendy crowd posing in designer gear. Downstairs club open until 2am.

Ku Bar, 75 Charing Cross Road, Soho (*open Mon–Sat noon–11pm, Sun 1–10.30 pm*). Popular with young, scene-loving crowd.

Kudos, 10 Adelaide St, Covent Garden (*open 11–11*). Brasserie and bar, popular with smart or after-work crowd. Free bus to The Fridge (*see* under 'Nightclubs', above) leaves at 11.15pm.

The Retro Bar, 2 George Court, Adelphi (off Strand), Covent Garden (*open noon–11pm*). Karaoke, '70s and '80s music and regular DJs in this friendly, traditional gay bar.

Rupert Street, Rupert St, Soho. Large, stylish, trendy new bar, with similarly stylish and upmarket clientele.

The Yard, 57 Rupert Street, Soho. Good food and cabaret attracting mixed stylish crowd. Outdoor courtyard a bonus in summer.

The Village, 81 Wardour St, Soho (*open Mon–Sat 11.30am–11pm, Sun noon–10.30pm*). Stylish bar on two floors.

Wow Bar, Glasshouse St, near Piccadilly (*open Sat eve only*). Popular lesbian bar.

Shopping

London...a kind of emporium for the whole earth

Joseph Addison

London has been a cosmopolitan place to shop since the Romans traded their pottery and olive oil for cloth, furs and gold back in the 1st century AD. Until comparatively recently the best shopping was for the rich, channelled through prestigious department stores such as Harrods, or smaller establishments in St James's and South Kensington offering exceptional service and attention to detail. The Carnaby Street spirit of the 1960s changed that, and now you can find cheap clothes and jewellery, unusual music and exotic food all over town in flea markets and gaily coloured shops. Carnaby Street itself, regrettably, has long since sold its soul to the cause of tourist kitsch, but you will find its successors in Covent Garden, down the King's Road, around Notting Hill and at Camden Lock market. Thanks to the 1990s design boom, some of the dingier old addresses have been spruced up and transformed, San Francisco-style, into dinky pastel-coloured boutiques selling the work of idiosyncratic small artisans. In London at least, the encroachment of chainstore blandness appears to have hit its limit.

The major department stores and prestige stores are famous enough to need no introduction. Have a good look by all means at Harrods or Liberty's or Fortnum & Mason, but think hard about price and quality before whipping out the old credit card. Often you will find the same thing for much less elsewhere. Neither of the two classic shopping districts is ideal—Knightsbridge is snooty and expensive, while the area around Oxford Street and Regent Street is *very* crowded and noisy. Both areas reach a fever pitch of activity before Christmas and during the winter and summer sales, that is, January and July. So don't be afraid to look further afield.

A note on VAT: if you leave Britain for a non-EU country within six months of arriving, you are entitled to a refund on the Value Added Tax, or VAT, that you have paid on any goods you have bought. You must pick up a form in the shop where you make your purchase, and then hand it in at the airport when you leave the country. Since the rate of VAT is 17.5 per cent, this is well worth the hassle, especially with larger items.

Opening hours: *see* 'Practical A–Z', p.27.

Department Stores

Harrods, Brompton Rd. A shopping institution of such proportions that it demands to be seen (*see* p.358). Whether you want to buy anything is another matter. Exotic foods, kitchenware, silverware and toys are all excellent, clothes rather less so. Look out for bargains on mundane things like CDs during the sales.

Selfridge's, 400 Oxford St. London's number two store promises money back if you find an article cheaper elsewhere. There are also perfume and make-up demonstrations and a travel agent's in the basement.

Liberty, Regent St. A labyrinth of a store with warm wooden interiors. Famous for its print scarves, also good for women's fashion, china, rugs and glass.

Harvey Nichols, 109–125 Knightsbridge. High-class fashionwear, plus an excellent food hall on the fifth floor floor made famous by TV's *Absolutely Fabulous*.

Fortnum & Mason, 181 Piccadilly. Prestige British produce, mostly food, displayed with the tourist market very much in mind. More pleasing to the eye than the purse.

Marks & Spencer, 458 Oxford St and branches all over London. Suppliers of cheap, comfortable clothes and underwear to the nation—and the world now that the store is setting up abroad. Don't overlook the food section, either, with excellent pre-prepared dishes and stunningly good ice-cream that beats Haagen Dazs for both quality and price.

Antiques

There are no hard and fast rules about buying antiques in London, except that you should keep a sharp eye out and haggle like crazy. Go where there are clusters of shops, so you can compare quality and price. Head for **Camden Passage** in Islington; the west end of Westbourne Grove and the south end of **Portobello Road** in Notting Hill; **Gray's Antique Markets** at 58 Davies Street in the West End; **Kensington Market** just off Kensington High Street; the **Bermondsey Antiques Market** on the corner of Long Lane and Bermondsey Street; **Antiquarius** at 131–141 King's Road; or the **Chelsea Antique Market** a bit further along at 245–253 King's Road. Gray's is probably the smartest, Portobello the most touristy (though not if you head into the sidestreets), Chelsea the least classy and Bermondsey the one for professional antiques hawks. For market opening times, *see* under 'Markets' below.

Art

Serious art buyers should head for Bond St and Cork St in Mayfair, where there are any number of dealers such as **Waddington** (10 Cork St), **Richard Green** (4 New

Bond Street) or **Christopher Wood** (141 New Bond St). This corner of town is also home to the prestigious auctioneers Sotheby's (34–35 New Bond St) and rivals Phillips (101 New Bond St). You'll find cheaper art dotted all over London, for example at the Bayswater Rd open-air art market which takes place on Sundays. The Contemporary Art Society organizes a market every autumn at **Smith's Galleries** at 56 Earlham St, Covent Garden, where you can pick up excellent contemporary works for as little as £100. For photography, head for the **Photographers' Gallery** at 5–8 Great Newport St just next to Leicester Square, which has the largest collection for sale in the country.

Books

Charing Cross Road is the traditional centre of the London book trade, although the pressure of high rents is pushing many original establishments out into other areas like Notting Hill. The once-gentlemanly publishing and book trade has become something of a cut-throat environment. Stores no longer stock the eclectic range of titles that they once did, preferring to focus on titles they know will sell in large numbers. The abolition of the Net Book Agreement that fixed retail prices has made mainstream titles considerably cheaper, but it has also intensified competition between sellers, favouring the big chains at the expense of the smaller specialists.

On the plus side, many assistants still give expert advice on titles and subjects. Browsing is not only tolerated, it is welcomed; letting yourself drift for hours from shelf to shelf is one of the great pleasures of the London bookshop.

Dillons, 82 Gower St and many branches. London's best-stocked bookshop in the heart of the university district, with titles spread out over four floors.

Waterstones, 121–5 Charing Cross Rd and many branches. Probably the best chain overall, with an outstanding selection at every branch.

Books Etc, 120 Charing Cross Rd and many branches. The most commercial of the quality chains, but strong on crime fiction and film screenplays. Charing Cross Rd has a permanent bargain basement.

Crime in Store, 4 Bedford St. Specialist crime and mystery bookshop, including many US titles unavailable elsewhere in Britain.

Grant & Cutler, 55–7 Great Marlborough St. Uneven, but nevertheless the best bookshop in London for obscure and not so obscure foreign-language books.

The European Bookshop, 5 Warwick St, off Regent St. Makes up for Grant and Cutler's deficiencies, especially in French literature in which it excels.

The Travel Bookshop, 13 Blenheim Crescent, off Portobello Rd. A delightful store for browsing or gift-hunting.

Travellers' Bookshop, 25 Cecil Court, off Charing Cross Rd. An atmospheric shop in a Georgian building, with a broad range of travel titles.

Books for Cooks, 4 Blenheim Crescent. Another delightful specialist store, with a small restaurant for morning coffee or a light lunch to go with your gastronomic browsing.

Offstage, 37 Chalk Farm Rd. Excellent theatre bookshop, with extensive film and general media sections too.

Stanfords, 12–14 Long Acre. Map specialist, indispensable if you are travelling to the Third World where maps are virtually non-existent. Also travel guides, travel literature and walking guides.

Silver Moon, 64–8 Charing Cross Rd. cialist women's bookshop.

Zwemmer, 80 Charing Cross Rd. London's leading art bookshop.

Henry Pordes, 58–60 Charing Cross Rd. One of many secondhand and antiquarian booksellers on the Charing Cross Rd and its offshoot, Cecil Court. More secondhand books can be found at Camden Lock and Greenwich Markets (*see* below), and in the streets to the south of the British Museum.

Clothes

It was an Englishman, Charles Worth, who founded the fashion industry during the 19th century. Unfortunately, he did most of his work in Paris, leaving London with a reputation for well-cut gentlemen's suits and little else. The fashion breeze is beginning to blow back to this side of the Channel, though, and designers led by the likes of Vivienne Westwood and Alexander McQueen are putting England and London back on the map. You'll find the latest fashions around Covent Garden, South Molton Street (near ↔ Bond Street), St Christopher's Place (on the other side of Oxford St) and Knightsbridge. Classic menswear can still be found around Savile Row in Mayfair and in St James's, although the styles on offer are beginning to look impossibly old-fashioned; suffice to say that one of the biggest contemporary fans is the puddingy French politician Edouard Balladur.

A note on sizes: Britain is, as on so many details of daily life, completely out of kilter with the rest of the world on clothes sizes. It would take a chart of military proportions to explain it all exhaustively; suffice to say here that the numbers tend to be bigger than in the US for women's clothes (for example, a British 10 is an 8 in the US), and slightly smaller for men's clothes, particularly shoes. The British and continental European scales bear almost no relation to each other at all. Seek advice from the store in question, and make sure you try everything on anyway.

Classic Menswear

Aquascutum, 100 Regent St. Raincoats, cashmere scarves and endless sober suits. Clothes to last, not look hip in.

Burberry, 18–22 Haymarket. Home of the classic overcoat.

Church's, 163 New Bond St. Solid, sober shoes to last half a lifetime.

Gieves and Hawkes, 1 Savile Row. One of the last gentlemen's outfitters in Savile Row. Unwavering attention to detail.

ouse, 2 Brompton Rd. Classic
...ns, from socks to knitted ties, plus
...h kilts and all the paraphernalia.

...l and Asser, 69–72 Jermyn St.
One of many old-fashioned clothing
boutiques on Jermyn Street, with lots of
shirts and silk ties.

Fashion names

Browns, 23–7 South Molton St. Centre of a
burgeoning empire of fashion shops
along this bijou pedestrian street off
Oxford St. Lots of famous labels, not all
of them unaffordable.

Duffer of St George, 29 Shorts Gardens,
Covent Garden. Very trendy menswear
store, selling streetwear and clubwear.

Jones, 13 Floral St, Covent Garden. At the
cutting edge of fashion; here Gaultier
and Galliano are old hat.

Katherine Hamnett, 20 Sloane St. The
queen of the outsize tee-shirt has a wide
range of formal and casual wear.

Michiko Koshino, 70 Neal St, Covent
Garden. Glad rags suitable for the high-
class club circuit. Cool and dazzling.

Paul Smith, 40–4 Floral St, Covent
Garden. High-class gloss on the bovver-
boy look. Mostly for men, but there is
now a women's collection too.

Vivienne Westwood, 6 Davies St. The
punk queen of British fashion offers real
clothes as well as eccentric pieces of tai-
loring art.

Discount Designer Wear

70, 70 Lamb's Conduit St. Mostly
menswear, with a range that can be surprising both in quality and in price.

Designer Sale Studio, 241 King's Rd. Last
season's collections at up to 70% off.

Discount Designer Clothes Store, 14
Proctor St, Bloomsbury. Knock-down
prices on the conservative end of the
fashion industry's output.

Hyper Hyper, 26–40 Kensington High St.
Indoor market-style showcase for young
designer talent, a place to snatch the
trendy stuff before it becomes really
trendy (and expensive).

Vivienne Westwood, 40–41 Conduit St.
Cast-offs from the shop around the
corner in Davies St. Up to 75% off.

Mid-range

Jigsaw, 65 Kensington High St and
branches. Youth fashion of slightly variable quality. At its best both stylish and
practical.

Oasis, 13 James St (Covent Garden) and
branches. Stylish, fashionable wom-
enswear at reasonable prices.

Next, 54–60 Kensington High St and
branches. Next is short for 'Next to
absolutely everything', or at least it
should be, given the number of branches
all over London. Safe but perfectly
acceptable clothes covering a wide
range. Worth sniffing around.

French Connection, 56 Long Acre, 11
James St and branches. Chain store with
an imaginative flair.

Mash, 73 Oxford St. Copies top fashions
effectively and cheaply.

Monsoon, 33d King's Rd and branches.
Strong-coloured fabrics with an oriental
influence. Mostly for women.

Natural Leather, 33 Monmouth St,
Covent Garden. Leather jackets, jeans
and bags.

Paco Life in Colour, Trocadero Centre, 122 King's Rd and at Whiteley's on Queensway. Bright, well-designed sweaters.

Sonico, 47 Oxford St. Jeans galore at competitive prices.

Second-hand

The Cavern, 154 Commercial St, Spitalfields. Lots of unworn originals.

Glorious Clothing Company, 60 Upper St, Islington. Discarded fashions from the 1960s onwards.

Clothing Accessories, Jewellery

Bead Shop, 43 Neal St. Everything to make your own jewellery.

The Button Queen, 19 Marylebone Lane. The name says it all.

Electrum Gallery, 21 South Classic jewellery from world—at a price.

Fred Bare, 118 Columbia Rd. hatter open on Sunday, so worth popping in after a visit to the Columbia Road flower market.

Hat Shop, 58 Neal St. Vastly popular shop with a huge range of headwear but not much room to try things on.

Gohil's, 246 Camden High St. Belts galore.

James Smith and Sons, 53 New Oxford St. Classic umbrellas to last a lifetime, or as long as it takes for you to leave it on the bus.

Thimble Society of London, Grays Antique Market, 58 Davies St. Antique and modern thimbles. Bizarre bizarre.

Details, 4a Symons St, SW3. Original jewellery shop.

Food

Most Londoners shop for food exclusively at supermarkets. Among the big chains, Sainsbury's wins the prize for the biggest, most stylish branches. Its Cromwell Rd outlet, next to Gloucester Rd, is so posh you virtually have to dress up to go; in Camden (at 17 Camden Rd) it is housed in an impressive, spanking new building designed by Nicholas Grimshaw. The best quality fruit and veg is still to be found in the street markets, particularly Berwick St in Soho and Portobello Rd (between Colville Terrace and Westbourne Park Road). For delis and specialist shops, try the following:

Epifani, Alba Place (off Portobello Rd). Smaller scale Italian deli with delicious home-made ciabatta and the best *pizza a taglio* in town.

Garcia and Sons, 248 Portobello Rd. Spanish deli: unusual cheeses, great olives.

Loon Fung Supermarket, 42–4 Gerard St. Chinese food galore in the heart of Chinatown.

Paphos, 43 Pratt St, Camden. Little Greece including a deli and a restaurant.

l's Yard Wholefood Warehouse, off Shorts Gardens. Organic everything in Covent Garden.

Neal's Yard Dairy, 17 Shorts Gardens. More than 70 varieties of cheese, matured and served with love.

Paxton and Whitfield, 93 Jermyn St. Impeccable, old-fashioned cheese shop with specials of the day and nibbles at the counter.

Rococo, 321 King's Rd, SW3. Zany chocolate shop; an Aladdin's cave of edible delights.

Hi-fi, Computers and Photographic

Tottenham Court Rd is the address to head for. Visit plenty of shops, ask to see write-ups in the trade magazines to back up the recommendations and haggle the price down as far as you can. North Americans will find prices rather high, but Europeans will be astounded at how cheap everything is. Only a couple of specific addresses to recommend:

Cornflake Shop, 37 Windmill St. Particularly friendly shop just off Tottenham Court Rd, mainly for hi-fi.

Hi-fi Care, 245 Tottenham Court Rd. Accessories shop. Very useful for extension cords, speaker cable and all those other things you can't usually find.

Keith Johnson and Pelling, 93 Drummond St (behind Euston station). Particularly well-stocked camera and equipment store, mainly for professionals.

London Camera Exchange, 112 Strand. Excellent for photographic equipment, repairs and specialist developing.

Household Design

You'll find lots of furniture, kitchen and bathroom fittings in the big department stores. Here are a few more addresses to consider:

Conran Shop, Michelin House, 81 Fulham Road. Baskets, chairs, lighting, even notebooks are all beautifully designed and presented in this tremendous art deco building.

Falkiner, 76 Southampton Row. Fine paper including plentiful stock for artists and printmakers.

Habitat, 196 Tottenham Court Rd. Everything for the house, from glasses and corkscrews to fitted cabinets. Cheap and practical.

Heal's, 196 Tottenham Court Rd and 234 King's Rd. Upmarket sister to Habitat, with innovative designs for furniture, beds, lighting, etc.

Italian Paper Shop, 11 Brompton Arcade. Beautiful Florentine paper and stationery.

Kitchen Ideas, 70 Westbourne Grove. Excellent range of pots, pans, glasses and knicknacks.

Muji, Shelton St, Covent Garden, and branches. Minimalist Japanese store selling kitchen equipment and stationery.

Richard Kihl, 164 Regent's Park Road, Primrose Hill. Designer and antique decanters, corkscrews and other drinking equipment.

Space, 214 Westbourne Grove, Notting Hill. Top-notch British-designed furniture; lots of stainless steel and perspex.

Waterford Wedgewood, 173 Piccadilly. Classic English/Irish crystal and bone china. Not to everyone's taste by any means.

Music

Anyone from North America might baulk at the CD prices, but there can be no complaints about the sheer range of record stores in London, beating anywhere else in Europe hands down. People inevitably gravitate towards the two big mommas in the centre of town: **Tower Records** at Piccadilly Circus and the **Virgin Megastore** on the corner of Oxford St and Tottenham Court Road. More interesting are the specialist stores around Berwick St, Soho, selling dance and indie music. Or try the following:

Black Market, 25 D'Arblay St, Soho. Wide range of club dance music.

Honest Jon's, 278 Portobello Rd. Atmospheric cavern of a store jampacked with jazz records and memorabilia.

Mole Jazz, 291 Pentonville Rd. Another mecca for jazz fans, near King's Cross.

Music Discount Centre, 58 Rathbone Place and branches. Classical music—big range at low prices.

Music and Video Exchange, several addresses on Pembridge Rd and Notting Hill Gate and branches elsewhere. Wide-ranging stock of second-hand CDs, records and tapes, giving you good-as-new quality for knock-down prices.

Ray's Jazz Shop, 180 Shaftesbury Ave. New and second-hand jazz.

Rough Trade, 130 Talbot Rd, off Portobello Rd. Punk and alternative music.

Stern's, 293 Euston Rd. The place for African music and unusual jazz.

The Virgin Megastore has a good stock of sheet music for rock and pop; for classical try **Boosey and Hawkes** at 295 Regent St or **Chappell's** at 50 New Bond St. One of the better places for musical instruments, surprisingly enough, is Harrods. A big specialist store is **Blanks** at 271–73 Kilburn High Road which has everything from bagpipes to African drums. Rock musicians should head for **Denmark St** off Charing Cross Rd. Andy's Guitar Workshop at No. 27 will mend instruments too.

Perfume and Body Care

Body Shop, 32–4 Great Marlborough St and several branches. Extremely successful, ecologically conscious high street shop devoted to natural beauty.

Crabtree and Evelyn, 6 Kensington Church St and branches. Herbs and fruit scents, all beautifully packaged. Ideal for gift-hunting.

Culpepper Herbalists, 8 The Market, Covent Garden. Herbs, spices, bath salts and pot-pourri, mostly taken from home-grown sources.

Floris, 89 Jermyn St. Old-fashioned, long established perfume shop.

Neal's Yard Remedies, 15 Neal's Yard. Lots of oils and homoeopathic remedies, all very natural.

Penhaligon's, 41 Wellington St, Covent Garden. Own-brand eau de toilette and other fragrances. Also delicious air freshener sprays.

South Molton Drug Store, 64 South Molton St. Cheap end-of-line cosmetics.

Tea and Coffee

The tourists generally flock to **Fortnum & Mason** (*see* above). For something different, try:

Algerian Coffee Stores, 52 Old Compton St, Soho. Aromatic and friendly.

H.R. Higgins, 79 Duke St, Mayfair. Purveyor of fine coffee to Her Majesty the Queen. Evokes the atmosphere of the old Jacobean coffee houses.

Tea House, 15 Neal St. Every conceivable type of tea.

Unusual

Arthur Middleton, 12 New Row, Covent Garden. Antique globes, microscopes.

Blade Rubber, Neal's Yard. Every kind of rubber stamp.

Broadhurst Clarkson, 63 Farringdon Rd. Telescopes.

Candle Makers' Supplies, 28 Blythe Rd, West Kensington. Made-to-order candles.

The Kite Store, 48 Neal St. Kites.

Knutz, 1 Russell St. Adult joke shop: ozone-friendly fart spray and edible condoms.

Left-Handed Shop, 57 Brewer St. Famous shop with customized can openers and mugs for the differently dextrous.

London Weather Centre Shop, 284 High Holborn. Everything you wanted to know about the weather, plastered on tee-shirts and mugs.

Singing Tree, 69 New King's Rd. Dolls' houses.

Chess Shop, 69 Masbro Road. Sells everything conceivable associated with chess.

Teddy Bear Shop, 153 Regents' St, W1. Sells handmade (English) teddy bears. Traditional ones as well as more modern varieties.

Street markets are one of the best things about London. They are where the city comes alive, showing off the vitality and variety of the neighbourhoods lucky enough to have them. Many are described in the main sections of this book; what follows is a list of what to expect and details of opening hours.

Bermondsey, Bermondsey Square and Long Lane (*open Fri 5am–2pm*). Where professional antiques dealers come to pick up their wares. Arrive early (and that means very early) and you can find a bargain.

Berwick Street, Soho. Outstanding fruit and veg (*open every day except Sun, with lunchtime closing on Wed*).

Brick Lane, Whitechapel (*open Sun morning*). Very popular market where East End barrows try to offload their junk, especially furniture and old books. Keep a hard nose and you can haggle a real bargain.

Brixton, Electric Avenue (*open daily except Sun, with lunchtime closing on Wed*). London's biggest Caribbean market, with music, exotic vegetables, goats' meat and wafting spices.

Camden Lock, between Camden High St and Chalk Farm Rd (*open Sat and Sun*). A weekend institution, with an array of books, clothes, records and assorted antiques by the canal. Huge crowds guarantee a festive atmosphere, and there are lots of excellent refreshments on hand.

Camden Passage, Islington (*open Wed and Sat only*). High-class antiques market in a quiet street next to the bustle of Upper St.

Chapel Market, Islington (*closed Mon and at lunchtime on Thurs and Sun*). An exuberant north London food market,

with excellent fish and, as a sideline, lots of household goods and cheap clothes.

Collectors' Market, in the basement car park at Embankment Place, Charing Cross station (*open Sat morning*). Intriguing setting for trade in stamps, coins, military memorabilia, Mercury phonecards and just about anything else you might want to collect.

Columbia Road, Shoreditch (*open Sun morning*). The city's best flower market.

Greenwich, College Approach, Greenwich (*Sat and Sun only*). Lots of crafts, books, furniture and coins and medals. Worth a detour.

Leadenhall Market, The City (*open Mon–Fri*). A high-class market with lots of fish and game, under Horace Jones's late Victorian glass roof.

London Silver Vaults, 53–64 Chancery Lane (*open 9.30–5.30 Mon–Fri; 9.30–12.30 Sat*). A cluster of underground shops, protected at night by a formidable steel security door, with antique and modern silver galore.

Petticoat Lane, Middlesex St, Whitechapel (*open Sun morning*). Leather, cheap fashion and household goods at London's most famous Sunday market. Look out for the jellied eel and whelk sellers on the fringes.

Portobello Road, Notting Hill (*open Mon–Sat, with lunchtime closing Thurs; antiques Sat only*). Perhaps the most atmospheric market in London. The southern end is stuffed with antique dealers, while the northern end is a mixed bag of design shops, cafés, food stalls, jewellery stands, record stores and more. Has a real neighbourhood feel, culminating in the wonderful half-Portuguese, half-Moroccan Golborne Road.

Walthamstow, Walthamstow High St (*every day except Sun*). Way out in the back of beyond of northeast London is the city's fastest-growing street market, with food, clothes and assorted junk at rock-bottom prices.

Sports

The English have a peculiar knack for inventing games and then failing dismally at them in international competition. Football (that's soccer, not the US variety), tennis and cricket all originated on the fields and meadows of merry England; nowadays, though, all the country seems to produce is an endless string of plucky, or not so plucky, losers. Ask English people about their national sporting pride and they will hark back nostalgically to the country's sweetest moment of victory in the 1966 World Cup final. Nowadays the national football side has to struggle to qualify for the World Cup, much less actually win it. The only sports in which the British really dominate internationally are darts and snooker—both about as far away from real exercise as you can get.

London is nevertheless rich in sports facilities and venues thanks to its extensive parkland and plentiful supply of ponds, reservoirs and lakes. It boasts several first-rate venues, including Wembley for soccer, Twickenham for rugby, Crystal Palace for athletics, Lord's and the Oval for cricket, and the mythical lawns of Wimbledon for tennis. London has no fewer than 11 professional soccer teams, roughly six of them in the top division. It has two major cricket teams, Middlesex and Surrey, and any number of rugby sides.

The number of last resort you should call with any sporting query, whether for participation or spectating, is **Sportsline** on ✆ 0171–222 8000.

Spectator Sports

Soccer

Soccer is the English national obsession, with a season lasting from mid-August through to May. The best place for a foreigner to start watching is probably on television, where you get a feel not only for the games but also the peculiar mixture of national pride, mixed metaphor and self-derision displayed by the commentators. Traditionally the two strongest London sides are Arsenal (stadium at Avenell Rd in Highbury, ✆ 0171-704 4000) and Tottenham Hotspur (stadium at White Hart Lane, Tottenham, ✆ 0181-365 5050). Major international fixtures are played at Wembley Stadium in northwest London (✆ 0181-900 1234).

Cricket

A game surely invented to be incomprehensible to the uninitiated, cricket incites great passions in its most ardent fans and sheer tedium in nearly everyone else. Games last at least a day, and can at international level go on for five days, with no guarantee of an outcome at the end. A certain type of Englishman revels in the game and lives for the sound of the red leather ball cracking against the willow of the bat.

It would be foolhardy to attempt an explanation of the rules, which defy description, at least on paper. Atmosphere's the thing, and a visit to Lord's or the Oval usually provides plenty of good drink and conversation as well as an introduction to the world of silly mid-offs, follow-ons, googlies, chinamen, long legs and short legs.

During international matches (called Test matches) you will hear people in parks and bars listening avidly to the ball-by-ball commentary on BBC radio. Cricket unseen is even more abstracted than the real thing, but at least the commentators show a certain potty enthusiasm and good humour. Most of the time they pore over old statistics and thank kindly listeners who have sent them fruitcakes.

Lord's, St John's Wood Road, ✆ 0171-289 1611. The most famous cricket venue in the world, and home to the original governing body of the sport, the Marylebone Cricket Club, as well as the local side, Middlesex.

The Oval, Kennington, ✆ 0171-582 6660. Home to Surrey, this vast pitch usually hosts the last Test match of the summer.

Rugby

Rougher and more complex than soccer, rugby football involves hand as well as foot contact and is played with an ovoid ball. International fixtures are held at Twickenham in southwest London, ✆ 0181-892 8161. Not far away are the home grounds of two of the best London sides, Harlequins (Stoop Memorial Ground, Craneford Way,

Twickenham, ✆ 0181-410 6000) and Rosslyn Park (Upper Richmond Road, Priory Lane, ✆ 0181-876 6044).

Athletics

Major meetings take place at Crystal Palace Stadium near Sydenham in southeast London, ✆ 0181-778 0131.

Tennis

The Wimbledon lawn tennis championships take place in the last week of June and the first week of July. You'll need to apply nine months in advance for a seat on the Centre Court or Number One Court—they are allocated by ballot. However, if you turn up early in the competition you'll see plenty of action on the outside courts, and can enjoy strawberries and cream under the pale English sun. **All England Lawn Tennis Club**, Church Road, Wimbledon, ✆ 0181-944 1066.

Horse Racing

The closest race courses are at Sandown Park in Esher, Surrey (✆ 01372-463072), Kempton Park nr Hampton Court (✆ 01372-470047), Epsom race course, also in Surrey and venue for the Derby in early June (✆ 01372-726311), and Ascot in Berkshire, where the Queen turns up along with cohorts of aristocratic horse-lovers for the Royal meeting in June (✆ 01344-622211).

Greyhound Racing

The ultimate working-class pastime is to go to the dog races at the weekend. The dogs chase a dummy rabbit round the track while the betting punters look on nervously between rounds of beer. One of the most famous venues is at Walthamstow in north-east London (© 0181-531 4255). You won't catch any of the Ascot crowd there.

Croquet

The Hurlingham Club in Ranelagh Gardens, Fulham (© 0171-736 3148) hosts the annual British Open Championships every July. Very English in a sedate sort of way, croquet is the modern version of pell mell, the ball-through-the-hoop game that transfixed the aristocracy in the 16th century.

Boxing

There's plenty of boxing through the year at the Albert Hall (© 0171-589 8212). Otherwise you could try the East End club at York Hall (Old Ford Road, Bethnal Green, © 0181-980 2243).

Sports Activities

General Workouts

Most London clubs charge an annual membership, so are impractical for temporary visitors. All London boroughs have public sports centres which are much cheaper—ask Sportsline for your nearest one.

The following may also be of interest (all public sports centres except The Harbour Club):

Queen Mother Sports Centre, 223 Vauxhall Bridge Road, Victoria, © 0171-630 5522. Swimming, squash, gym and aerobics, etc.

The Oasis, 32 Endell St, Covent Garden, © 0171-831 1804. Ditto—with open air swimming pool which is even popular in winter among stalwarts.

Chelsea Sports Centre, Chelsea Manor St, © 0171-352 6985. Everything from badminton to yoga, via canoeing, netball and sub-aqua.

The Harbour Club, Water Meadow Lane, Fulham, © 0171-371 7700. Upmarket private club where Princess Diana used to exercise.

Boating

Regent's Park Boating Lake, © 0171-486 7905. Rent a boat during the summer and idle away a few hours on either the large adult or the tiny children's lake between the Inner and the Outer Circle of Regent's Park. Cheap and wonderful.

Dance

Danceworks, 16 Balderton St, Mayfair, © 0171-629 6183. High teaching standards, with entrance fees for any time from an hour to a year.

Pineapple, 7 Langley St, Covent Garden, © 0171-836 4004. Another first-class dance studio for all categories.

Go-Karting

Daytona and Indianapolis Raceways, 54 Wood Lane, Shepherd's Bush, © 0181-749 2277. Crazy name, crazy sport. Expensive but trendy.

Golf

There are courses at Richmond and all round the outskirts of town. Call the Golf Foundation on ✆ 0181-367 4404 or Golf Events on ✆ 0171-237 3636.

Horse Riding

Ross Nye, 8 Bathurst Mews, Bayswater, W2, ✆ 0171-262 3791. For riding in Hyde Park.

Wimbledon Village Stables, 24a High St, Wimbledon, SW19, ✆ 0181-946 8579. Good for beginners, with the whole of Wimbledon Common and Richmond Park in which to roam free.

Ice Skating

Queens Ice Skating Club, 17 Queensway, W2, ✆ 0171-229 0172. Lessons, ice discos and more at London's most famous club.

Ski-ing

Don't laugh: the former chemical waste dump in Beckton in Docklands has been sealed and converted into a 200m dry ski slope called the Beckton Alps; ✆ 0171-511 0351 for details.

Snooker

Centre Point Snooker Club, Centre Point, New Oxford St, ✆ 0171-240 6886. Open all day and most of the night.

Squash

Almost impossible to play without joining a private club. If you know a member or are staying in London long enough to make it worth joining, try Cannon Sports Club next to Cannon St station in the City, ✆ 0171-283 0101, or Lambs Squash Club by the Barbican, ✆ 0171-638 3811. There are also courts below the Dolphin Square apartment/hotel complex in Pimlico, where membership is relatively cheap (✆ 0171-798 8686).

Swimming and Watersports

The foolhardy can break the ice on the Serpentine on New Year's Day; the really foolhardy can try the foul waters of the Thames. The rest of us still have plenty to choose from—public pools run by each borough (ask Sportsline for your nearest one) or clubs like The Oasis.

There are some superb outdoor venues for summer, notably the Highgate and Hampstead Ponds on Hampstead Heath. The Hampstead Pond, which is mixed-sex, is best reached from East Heath Road. The single-sex Highgate Ponds are accessible from Millfield Lane. Check also for the opening of the Thames Lido at Bankside (see p.332). Other council-run lidos worth trying are Tooting, Brixton and Parliament Hill (lidos are large unheated open-air pools, usually built in the '30s).

For more energetic water sports, try the following:

Docklands Watersports Club, Gate 14, King George V Dock, Woolwich Manor Way, E16, ✆ 0171-511 7000. Wet-biking and jet-skiing.

Princes, Clockhouse Lane, Bedfont (near Heathrow Airport), ✆ 01784-256153. Waterski-ing, jet-ski-ing and table-ski-ing.

Surrey Docks Watersports Centre, ✆ 0171-237 4009. Sailing, windsurfing, canoeing and sub aqua among the empty office blocks of Docklands. A surprisingly attractive venue.

Tennis

There are courts in virtually every London park—check with Sportsline for details and booking procedure. Battersea Park has some of the cheapest courts, while Holland Park has the trendiest. Most charge a membership fee, but this may entitle you to play at other London venues. Often you have to book in person. Give up all thoughts of playing at Wimbledon, unless you have lots of money, impeccable connections and plenty of time for your membership to be considered.

Tenpin Bowling

Rowans, 10 Stroud Green Rd, Finsbury Park, ✆ 0181-800 1950. For a little late-night exercise.

Children's London

Children have traditionally come somewhere beneath dogs and horses on the scale of human affection in England. The Edwardian short story writer Saki frequently depicted them as malicious pests, while George Bernard Shaw—who admittedly had none of his own—compared them unfavourably to farmyard animals; chickens, he said, were at least cheaper to keep. A rather more progressive way of thinking has held sway in recent times, but still the prevailing view is that children should be neither seen nor heard in public. If some pubs, bars and restaurants now admit children, and even provide high chairs and nappy-changing facilities, it is more out of a sense of obligation than any real enthusiasm. Nevertheless, there is plenty to keep children occupied and amused in London, whether they remain under their parents' supervision or are farmed out to specialist care. Aside from the ideas listed below, you can find out more through Kidsline on ✆ 0171–222 8070, or the London Tourist Board's special children's information line on ✆ 0839–123404.

Look out for child reductions; anyone under 14 should qualify most of the time, and under-16s a fair bit. The transport network insists that 14- and 15-year-olds have a photo pass to qualify for child fares, so have passport photos at the ready. Note that under-16s are not allowed to buy cigarettes, and that under-18s can't buy or consume alcohol in public.

Sights

Children are a diverse bunch, and in principle there is no reason why they shouldn't enjoy nearly all the adult sights recommended in the rest of this book. Attractions specially designed for children stand or fall on their overall quality, not just on their appeal to a specific age-group. So there is no excuse to fob your children off with, for example, the noisy trash of the Trocadero Centre and the other attractions around Piccadilly Circus; they are no less tacky an experience for them than they are for you. Among the most popular and absorbing sights for children are: the Science Museum (where they can even spend the night), the Natural History Museum, the Museum of the Moving Image, the Commonwealth Institute and the three museums devoted to the younger generation: Pollock's Toy Museum in Fitzrovia, the Bethnal Green Museum of Childhood and the London Toy and Model Museum in Bayswater. Avoid such crowd-pullers as the London Dungeon and Madame Tussaud's. The former is horribly inauthentic and overblown, while queuing at the latter will try the patience of all the family to breaking point. For gore and ghoulishness, try instead the Clink Exhibition in Southwark or the Tower of London. Note that children under 14 are not allowed into the Old Bailey, and that infants are barred from the Houses of Parliament.

The parks are of course great for children. They can swim and row on the Serpentine in Hyde Park, play in playgrounds in Regent's Park and Kensington Gardens. They can fly kites and go on nature trails on Hampstead Heath, and they can play mini-golf at Alexandra Park up in north London. A number of parks including Battersea Park, Holland Park and Alexandra Park have special play areas for the under-fives called One O'Clock clubs where your littl'uns will find sandpits, paddling pools, climbing frames and toys galore. Battersea Park also has a children's zoo with ponies to ride, monkeys, pygmy goats and a pot-bellied pig. London Zoo, at the top end of Regent's Park, is still going strong thanks to a fat cheque from the Emir of Kuwait. The Chessington World of Adventures in Surrey (✆ 0372–729560) is a theme park as well as a zoo, with runaway trains, rollercoasters and a circus. The Windsor Safari Park, once very popular with children, has closed down, but it is now Europe's first Lego park outside Denmark, called Legoland.

Entertainment

Options are many: funfairs in the parks during the summer (see *Time Out* or ask in a tourist office for details); Punch and Judy shows at Covent Garden; children's films at the National Film Theatre, the Barbican and the ICA; and a daily schedule of sometimes first-rate children's television programmes in the late afternoons on both BBC and ITV. At Christmas time there are pantomimes galore all over London. Among the big West End shows, Andrew Lloyd Webber's musical extravaganza on roller-skates, *Starlight Express* (check for venue and book early), is usually a hit with children. During the rest of the year there are children's shows at the following theatres:

Little Angel Theatre, 14 Dagmar Passage, Islington, ✆ 0171-226 1787. A delightful puppet theatre.

Polka Theatre for Children, 240 The Broadway, Wimbledon, ✆ 0181-543 0363. A complex for the under-13s including the main theatre, a playground, two shops with cheap toys and an adventure room for under-5s.

Unicorn Theatre for Children, 6 Great Newport St, Covent Garden, ✆ 0171-836 3334. London's oldest children's theatre.

Rainforest Café, 20 Shaftesbury Avenue, ✆ 0171-434 3111. Exciting rainforest eating place which will delight children, and an inspired alternative to the ubiquitous McDonalds. (Not only for children.) Top floor is a retail area.

Shopping

No lack of outlets to shop *for* kids: for most emergency toy or clothing needs you should be satisfied by the many branches of the Early Learning Centre, Mothercare, Toys R Us, Next, Baby Gap or Gap for Kids. As for shopping *with* kids, here are a few hardy perennials:

Hamleys, 188 Regent St. One of the world's great toyshops with loads of puzzles, computer games, teddy bears and gadgets. The escalators alone can keep kids happy for hours. Expensive, though.

Harrods, Old Brompton Rd, Knightsbridge. The Christmas window displays and the toy department on the fourth floor are both big draws.

Davenport's Magic Shop, Charing Cross Underground Shopping Arcade. Masks, practical jokes and hardware for professional magicians.

Doll's House Shop, 29 The Market, Covent Garden. Everything for your child's doll at this delightful basement boutique.

Dillons, Trafalgar Square branch. Lots of children's books and a chequered floor where you can play noughts and crosses.

Virgin Games Centre, 100 Oxford St. Jigsaws, computer games and more.

Childminding

Childminders, ✆ 0171-935 3000. An agency with a network of babysitters, nurses and infant teachers.

Universal Aunts, ✆ 0171-738 8937. Provides babysitters, entertainers, people to meet children off trains, and guides to take children round London.

Pippa Pop-Ins, 430 Fulham Rd, ✆ 0171-385 2458. This award-winning hotel for 2–12 year olds provides a crèche, nursery school and babysitting services.

Living and Working in London

London undergoes a radical transformation as you graduate from visitor to resident. All of a sudden the talk is not of attractions or atmosphere but of *areas*—are you an Islington person, or a Clapham person, north-of-the-river or south-of-the-river, West End or East. Where you live and where you work shape the persona you project to others. Given London's historical (and continuing) obsession with property and class, perhaps this is not surprising. But a whole dinner party's worth of conversation about house prices in W11, the desirability of Stoke Newington, flat conversions and conveyancing—a more common occurrence than you might suspect—can get rather trying.

After a while, though, your emotions become impossibly entangled in the place and your likes and dislikes are raised to the level of deep passion. The Underground becomes not just bad but unbearably, indescribably appalling; the traffic monstrous, the prices outrageous. A favourite theatre or shop, on the other hand, becomes an object of deep affection, and your whole personality seems to suffer when it closes down or changes management. Everyone gets caught up in the latest fads, the newest restaurants, the high-society gossip, the best plays, exhibitions and films. London is many things, but it rarely leaves its citizens cold.

Living close to your workplace can make all the difference in a city where public transport is one of the biggest gripes. If you have a job in the City, areas you should consider include Islington, Bloomsbury, Clapham and parts of the East End and Docklands. There is little in the way of housing in the City itself, Soho or Mayfair, so the knack is to find somewhere far enough out of the centre to be pleasant but not so far as to be a chore. Many foreigners make the mistake of settling in South Kensington, which is overpriced and short on character. They would do much better to hunt further north around Notting Hill, Camden or Hampstead, or, if they are looking for something cheaper, Kilburn or Stoke Newington. South of the river, there are lively communities in Clapham, Battersea and parts of Brixton, and some quieter, pleasant suburban communities beyond. Greenery is a big consideration, especially for families, and you can't go very wrong in places like Greenwich, Richmond and Highgate, as long as you can afford them.

Citizens of European Union countries can stay in Britain as long as they like and do not need a work permit. There is no such thing as an identity card, and most of your documents, from academic certificates to your driving licence, should be recognized without too much hassle, though you might do well to check with your embassy or consulate.

Everyone else has to do a bit of legwork, although the bureaucracy is by and large far more straightforward than in the rest of Europe. If you are staying for more than six months, you will have to regularize your residence status with the Home Office (equivalent of the Interior Ministry) at its distinctly charmless Immigration and Nationality Department in Croydon in the depths of south London (full address: Lunar House, Wellesley Rd, Croydon, © 0181–686 0688, open Mon–Fri 9am–5pm). Staff will want to know all about your financial means, work intentions and the rest. If you don't have a job or a course of study lined up in Britain before you arrive, you may be in for a hard time.

In any case, if you intend to work you need a permit. Pick up a form called OW1 from any Jobcentre and send it in to the Department of Employment (address on the form). Be warned that without a British employer to sponsor you, you may not get very far at all. There are, however, special arrangements for young people from the United States and Commonwealth countries. Commonwealth citizens aged 17–27 can get a stamp in their home countries declaring them to be a 'Working Holiday Maker', which entitles them to do part-time work for up to two years. US students can get a blue card enabling them to work for six months. Apply for one before you leave for Britain through the Work in Britain department of the Council on International Educational Exchange in New York, © 212–661 1414.

Once you have a job, you need to worry about social security and tax. For the former, you need a National Insurance number which you can obtain through your local Department of Social Security office. For the latter, you need a document called a P45, which you can get through your employer if you have one, or through the DSS if you are self-employed. The self-employed will have to make careful enquiries into which category they fall; if you are lucky you can just pay a flat rate of social security (around £5.50 a week) and hand your financial details to an accountant who will calculate your tax liability for a modest commission-based fee. Company employees will have to worry about none of this: tax and social security contributions are deducted from their pay packet.

Finally, you'll need to register with a doctor in your area. This is well worth the effort as it will entitle you to a home visit should you need one. Your nearest

Family Practitioner Centre will have lists of general practitioners. Here are some numbers of the health authorities for likely areas of London:

Camden and Islington, ✆ 0171–383 4155

City and East London, ✆ 0171–739 6566

Kensington, Chelsea and Westminster, ✆ 0171–725 3333

Lambeth, Southwark and Lewisham, ✆ 0171–716 7000

Finding Somewhere To Live

If you have the money and the time to make it worthwhile, buying a flat or house is by far the best option. It works out far cheaper in the long run, and gives you the chance to organize your own furniture. Rented accommodation is of generally poor quality, almost always comes with furniture included and can be cripplingly expensive. Either way, you will find it very difficult to avoid dealing with an estate agent unless you can get your hands on a property through word of mouth. Few landlords take much more than a financial interest in their properties and find it much easier to leave the whole process to the professionals.

Renting: Check the ads in the *Evening Standard* or the weekly exchange magazine *Loot*, especially for stuff at the lower end of the market. The small ads in *Time Out* also advertise accommodation, particularly flatshares, and you might strike it lucky with an advert in the window of a general store in the area where you want to live. If you manage to avoid an agent, so much the better. In any case, you should be ready to show some proof of means and maybe a letter from an employer. Rents are quoted at weekly rates, but are generally paid monthly. You'll need to pay a month's rent up front, plus another month as a deposit. You will also have to pay local taxes, currently known as council tax (a watered down version of the dreaded poll tax that helped to make Margaret Thatcher so unpopular). If you go through an agency, you may not have to pay any fee directly, but you'll notice that the rental cost will be quite a bit higher, so you end up suffering anyway.

Buying: Go to estate agents in the area you are interested in. Also, check out *Loot*, *The Evening Standard* and the Sunday newspapers. Quality varies enormously, so take your time. Make thorough enquiries about service charges, ground rents and so on, and remember that off-street parking is a highly prized asset in London. Eventually you will have to have a solicitor and a surveyor to take you through the process of acquiring a property. You can arrange a mortgage through a building society (the British equivalent of a Savings and Loan bank), though you should take expert advice on the best financial package to suit your needs.

Finding A Job

The sky-high unemployment of the 1970s and 1980s has eased considerably, so finding a job is not as hard as it once was. The best ads are in the second section of the *Guardian* (a different work sector for each day of the week); a lot of part-time and temporary work is advertised in the *Evening Standard*. Teachers should buy the *Times Education Supplement* or, if applicable, the *Times Higher Education Supplement*; they should also do the rounds of London's language schools, starting with International House at 106 Piccadilly, ✆ 0171–491 2598, which has lists of reputable establishments other than itself. If you type halfway decently, you can easily get work temping as a secretary—just look at the many ads for agencies in the *Evening Standard* and in Underground train carriages. The pay gets better the more machines you know how to operate and the more languages you know; what's more, assignments rarely last more than a week or two, so time off is very easy to arrange. More arduous is hotel, restaurant or bar work. There is a Jobcentre at 3 Denmark St, ✆ 0171–497 2047 or ✆ 0171–323 9190, specializing in hotels and catering. Otherwise, do the rounds of obvious areas like Soho and you should strike lucky, particularly in the summer months. Finally, there is plenty of *au pair* work, which comes with all the usual caveats. Pick up the magazine *The Lady*, which is jampacked with ads.

Useful Addresses

Adult Education: check with the University of London about courses on ✆ 0171-580 1122. See also the 'Floodlight' guide, available in newsagents. One of the best private institutions is Morley College, 61 Westminster Bridge Rd, ✆ 0171-928 8501.

Alcoholics Anonymous: 7-day answerphone on ✆ 0171-352 3001.

Book Search: Dillons Out of Print Book Search Department (Durham branch), ✆ 0191-384 2095, will help track down anything that is out of print.

Camera and Video Hire: Leeds Film and Hire, 20–22 Brunswick Centre, Bloomsbury, ✆ 0171-833 1661.

Dress Hire: Moss Bros at 27 King St, Covent Garden, ✆ 0171-240 4567, or 88 Regent St ✆ 0171-494 0666, for dinner jackets and formal wear; Costume Studio at 6 Penton Grove, Islington, for fancy dress; Contemporary Wardrobe at The Horse Hospital, Colonnade, Bloomsbury, for period and modern fashions.

Domestic Help: The Cinderella Agency will provide house cleaners, dinner servers, cooks, cat sitters or dog walkers at standard rates; ✆ 0181-676 0917.

Dry Cleaning: the biggest, and most reliable, chain is Sketchley's. Check the phone book for your nearest branch.

English-language courses: to brush up on your English, consult International House (*see* above, ✆ 0171-491 2598) for lists of reliable schools.

Fancy Deliveries: champagne or chocolates for a loved one provided by Basket Express (℗ 0171-289 2636); a basket of fruit by Telefruit (℗ 0171-403 0555).

Hair Care: chains like Vidal Sassoon or Toni and Guy have branches all over London. One dirt cheap establishment is Cuts at 39 Frith St. For something more fashionable, try Trevor Sorbie, 10 Russell St, Covent Garden.

Laundry: there are launderettes all over London, about half of them by now called My Beautiful Laundrette after Stephen Frears's film. Usually you can either wash and dry yourself (bring plenty of change and preferably your own powder), or else, for a modest extra charge, leave your clothes and pick them up at the end of the day (a 'service wash'). For high-class washing with guaranteed same-day service and home collection and delivery, try the Danish Express Laundry at 16 Hinde St off Oxford St, ℗ 0171-935 6306.

Libraries: Public libraries are one of the great joys of London, wonderful places to visit whether you just want to read the morning papers, borrow a potboiler for the holidays or sit down to some serious research. Every borough has at least one library (check the phonebook for your nearest), but you can link up to the lot of them via computer and ask for titles to be delivered to your local branch. The range of books available is remarkable, better by far than anything continental European cities can offer. The best reference library is the Westminster Public Library at 35 St Martin's Street, WC2, ℗ 0171-798 2036, with its free internet and e-mail facilities. Other good ones include Battersea Refer-

ence Library, Lavender Hill, SW11, and Chelsea Reference Library, Old Town Hall, King's Road, SW3. If you are looking to join a private library, you can do worse than the London Library in St James's Square (℗ 0171-930 7705, or ask for details at the door), with its ample collections and wonderfully hushed atmosphere.

Locksmith: Chiswick Security, ℗ 0171-630 6500, or North London Locksmiths, ℗ 0181-800 6041.

Manicure: Super Nail of Los Angeles, 101 Crawford St, ℗ 0171-723 1163.

Packing Companies: The Packing Shop, Broughton St, Battersea, (℗ 0171-498 3255) will deliver gifts and fragile objects anywhere around the world. For furniture and general removals, try Radford International (freight company), ℗ 0181-208 1677, for a start. Do shop around though, since certain agencies offer different rates and services for different countries.

Photo Development: Boots Chemists have a reliable one-hour or overnight service (branches all over London). You could also try Sky Photographic at Ramillies St (in Soho) and 17 Southampton Row, WC1.

Pizza Deliveries: loads of places all over town, as there are for Indian food. If you are in west London, Pizza Place on ℗ 0171-289 4353 is excellent.

Shoe Repairs: The Complete Cobbler, 28 Tottenham St (℗ 0171-387 2234) and 253 Eversholt St, Camden.

Turkish Baths: Porchester Baths, Queensway, ℗ 0171-792 2919; Ironmonger Row Baths, Ironmonger Row, Finsbury, ℗ 0171-253 4011.

Day Trips

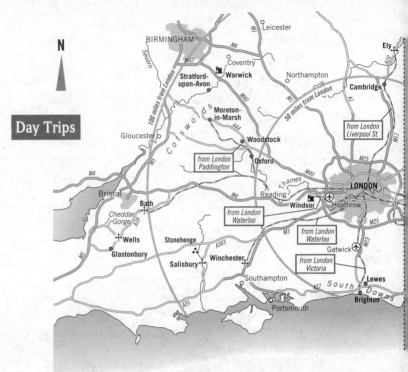

N

BIRMINGHAM

Leicester

Coventry

Stratford-upon-Avon Warwick

Northampton

Ely

Cambridge

from London Liverpool St.

Gloucester

Moreton-in-Marsh

Woodstock

from London Paddington

Oxford

Reading

Windsor

Heathrow

LONDON

Bristol

Bath

from London Waterloo

Thames

Cheddar Gorge

Wells

Stonehenge

from London Waterloo

Glastonbury

Salisbury

Winchester

Gatwick

from London Victoria

Lewes

Southampton

South Downs

Brighton

Portsmouth

Day Trips

England is so small that you arrive just about anywhere in three or four hours. In the time it takes to cross London, you could be most of the way through a train journey to Manchester or York at the other end of the country. So the notion of a day trip is a flexible one. Here are a few brief suggestions for places no more than an hour and a half away; a complete rundown would fill another book.

Windsor

Trains leave from Waterloo (direct) or Paddington (change at Slough) and take 35–50 mins. There are also Green Line buses from Eccleston Bridge behind Victoria station. Tourist office on © 01753–743900.

A fire at **Windsor Castle** in November 1992 was the culmination of what Queen Elizabeth II called an *annus horribilis* of scandal and misfortune. Now the castle (© *01753–831118, open daily 10–5, 10–4 in winter; adm exp*) has been meticulously restored for millions of pounds and is back on its feet—a medieval fortress inhabited and embroidered by the monarchy for the last 900-odd years. The highlight is the castle itself, a vast complex of crenellated towers, turrets and loopholes. Inside you can tour some of the royal apartments, decorated with Holbeins, Rembrandts and Van Dycks from the Royal Collection; St George's Chapel, with its magnificent Perpendicular vaulted ceiling, where 10 sovereigns including Henry VIII are buried; and the extraordinary **Queen Mary's Dolls' House**. Arguably the most intricate in the world, it took 1500 craftsmen three years to build it for the future Queen Mary at the end of the 19th century.

Down the road from the castle, near the river Thames, is **Eton College**, the most exclusive private boys' school in the country. The 15th-century buildings are fine, but the real attraction is the sight of adolescent boys who talk like Prince Charles and run around in tailcoats and bow ties.

Oxford

Trains leave from Paddington and take an hour. The best bus is the Oxford Tube which leaves from Grosvenor Gardens near Victoria. Tourist office on ℡ 01865–726871.

The home of England's oldest university is a wondrous cluster of soft yellow sandstone buildings and 'dreaming spires' that rise romantically out of the mist on damp autumn mornings. Oxford is a bustling town, a place of many facets and diverse culture. The university, which dates back to the 12th century, is a surprisingly unacademic place. For centuries, its main function was as a meeting place for the sons of the influential and the wealthy; exams were not introduced until the early 19th century, and even today many students spend a disproportionate amount of time on the river, acting in student plays or debating in the Oxford Union, a misleadingly named private club that fancies itself as a mini-parliament. Terms are short (just eight weeks), lectures are optional, and the only structured teaching in many subjects is a weekly one-on-one session between student and tutor.

The university is split into colleges, fortified mini-monasteries that are medieval in inspiration if not always in architecture. All have a chapel, student lodgings, courtyards and well-manicured lawns. The most beautiful include **Magdalen** (very romantic), **Merton** (idyllic by the riverside), **Christ Church** (imposing if a little flashy), **New College** (with a winding alley leading to the main gate, great gargoyles and a great Epstein sculpture in the chapel) and **All Souls** (especially Hawksmoor's superb north quadrangle and old library, which you can see through the railings in

Radcliffe Square even if the college is shut). You should also visit the Bodleian Library, particularly the **Divinity School**, one of the most beautiful examples of Perpendicular style; admire the views up and down the High Street; and take a punt—a flat boat propelled by a long pole—along the Thames, known locally as the Isis.

Six miles north of Oxford in Woodstock is John Vanbrugh's **Blenheim Palace**, built for the ancestors of Winston Churchill (*© 01993–811325, open daily 9–4.45; palace closed in winter 31 Oct–16 March but the park is open all year round; adm*). The slightly forced Versailles-like splendour of its buildings is more than compensated for by the lush and vast landscaped park.

Stratford-upon-Avon and the Cotswolds

There are trains from Paddington to Stratford and Moreton-in-Marsh (although these involve a number of changes, usually at Oxford, Didcot, Banbury or Leamington Spa) and National Express coaches, which take nearly four hours from Victoria coach station. To see this area properly, you really need a car. Stratford tourist office on © 01789–293127.

Stratford is one of the bigger tourist cons in the world; all it boasts, apart from its excellent theatre run by the Royal Shakespeare Company, is a handful of pretty cottages that have been shamelessly exploited as a Shakespeare heritage trail. The Bard was certainly born in Stratford, but whether he was really raised in the so-called Birthplace Museum is open to question. Come for the theatre, and perhaps for Anne Hathaway's attractive thatched cottage at Shottery one mile out of town; but otherwise you would do better to explore the surrounding countryside. These gently rolling hills, known as **the Cotswolds**, are dotted with pretty sandstone villages with names like Broadway, Stow-on-the-Wold, Upper and Lower Slaughter and Chipping Campden, which date back to Tudor and Jacobean times. Tourism has made them a bit too twee for their own good in recent years, but they nevertheless make a delightful day out. North of Stratford is **Warwick Castle** (*© 01926–495421, open daily 8.45–6, earlier in winter; adm*). Dating back to the Norman conquest, it has an atmospheric dungeon and torture chamber, complete with horrifying instruments, and an extensive park landscaped by the ubiquitous Capability Brown.

Cambridge

Trains leave from Liverpool St and take just over an hour. Buses leave from Victoria coach station but can get stuck in the north London traffic. Local bus information on © 01223–423554; tourist office on © 01223–322640.

Founded by renegade students from Oxford and still known by its rival as 'the other place', central Cambridge consists almost entirely of its university and is rather quiet and cerebral as a result (although it is becoming increasingly known as a centre for computer technology). Its most beautiful colleges—made of whiter stone than Oxford's—are lined in a row, with gardens rolling down towards the bank of the river Cam. The riverside, with its views of St John's, Trinity, Caius (pronounced 'Keys') and King's, is known as **The Backs**; it has a special magic that makes the trip to Cambridge worthwhile all on its own. **King's College** has a 15th-century Perpendicular chapel of extraordinary beauty, a riot of fan vaulting illuminated by elegant tall windows. The chapel choir, which performs regularly, is one of the most famous in the world. Other worthwhile sights include the brick and stone buildings of **Jesus College**, on the other side of town, and the **Fitzwilliam Museum** which has some valuable Roman and Greek artworks.

Northeast of Cambridge is **Ely**, with its fine cathedral. Behind the Norman front is a unique and extraordinary octagonal tower in the Decorated style. There are also traces of the vast Saxon abbey where St Etheldreda (*see* p.293) made her name.

Bath

> *Trains leave from Paddington and take 80 minutes. National Express buses leave from Victoria coach station and take up to three hours. Tourist office on ✆ 01225–477101.*

Bath has the finest array of Regency architecture in the country, the result of the town's popularity as a spa and gambling retreat in the latter half of the 18th century. It is a place of elegance and refinement, set in beautiful rolling country-side. The balming effects of the local spring water were first appreciated by the Romans, who built the baths (*Aquae Sulae*) that give the town its name. You can visit the bubbling underground source as well as the **Roman baths** and Georgian **Pump Room** built on top (entrance on Stall St). Next door is the magnificent 16th-century **cathedral**, with two Jacob's ladders on either side of the main façade (note that some of the angels of the ladder are upside down, this being the only way the sculptor could think of showing them in descent). The rest of the town is a remark-ably unified ensemble of 18th-century architecture, much of it the work of John Wood. **Royal Crescent** at the top of the town is a majestic sweep of 30 curved houses incorporating 114 Ionic columns. The Avon riverside is also delightful, notable for Robert Adam's splendid **Pulteney Bridge**.

Near Bath is the picture-postcard village of **Castle Combe**, with its old stone houses and rickety tea-rooms alongside a babbling brook. The countryside of Wilt-shire, Avon and Somerset is enchanting in general. If you have a car you might want to combine Bath with **Wells** (great cathedral), **Glastonbury** (famous for its ancient ruins and hippyish music festival), and the **Cheddar Gorge** (where the cheese originally came from). East of Bath is **Salisbury**, with another fine cathedral much painted by Constable, and **Stonehenge**, the celebrated prehistoric stone ring, atmospherically situated in the middle of Salisbury Plain.

Winchester

Trains leave from Waterloo and take just over an hour. Tourist information on ✆ 01962–840500.

Winchester was the capital of Wessex in Saxon times, growing rich on the wool trade, and at one stage even took over from London as the most important city in England. The city is now dominated by its magnificent **cathedral**, at 556ft the longest medieval church in Europe. Begun in 1079, it was worked on over several centuries; the original Norman arches of the nave are concealed behind an elaborate web of 14th-century Perpendicular tracery. The high point of the interior is the choir, with its magnificent wooden stalls. The stained-glass window in the north aisle pays homage to Jane Austen, who had a house in College Street and died there in 1817.

From the cathedral it is a short walk to the other main attraction of Winchester, its prestigious private **school** which dates back to 1382, when the then bishop, William of Wykeham, first accepted boys for religious and secular instruction. Now it is one of the most exclusive fee-paying 'public' schools in the country. The gateway in College Street (guided tours available) leads to a series of medieval and Gothic Revival courtyards where pupils work and live. The school's brightest pupils, known as scholars, dress up in shirt, tie and academic gown, while non-scholars wear straw hats and conventional jackets. The chapel, in Chamber Court, has a remarkable fan tracery roof built by Hugh Herland, the late 14th-century craftsman who also worked on Westminster Hall. The grounds, where pupils play cricket, soccer and a weird mud-spattered game called Winchester football, extend to the south towards some Saxon barrows around St Catherine's Hill.

Brighton

Trains leave from Victoria and take just under an hour. Tourist information on ✆ 01273–292599.

Brighton is a town of many facets. On the one hand, it is an old-fashioned English seaside resort of grand hotels on the front, ice-cream vans, hurdy-gurdy players, old men with rolled-up trousers on the pebble beach and lovers strolling along the pier; on the other, its cafés and nightclubs have an unmistakably young and trendy feel. For years Brighton was where married men used to come for dirty weekends with their lovers; they still come, although the town is now better known for its large gay community. Brighton is a town of more innocent pleasures too. One speciality, evoked in the famous novel by Graham Greene, is rock, a hard, coloured stick of peppermint-flavoured sugar. The streets behind the waterfront have been attractively pedestrianized and make for pleasant strolling. Further inland, John Nash's Taj Mahal-esque **Royal Pavilion**, was built for George IV as a kind of Regency Disneyland. Spurned by the Victorians, it is now fully restored and open to the public.

Try, too, to explore the beautiful countryside of the Sussex Downs in Brighton's hinterland. **Lewes**, the county capital, is particularly picturesque, as are smaller villages like Steyning; near Lewes is **Glyndebourne**, an attractive country house famous for its outstanding (but very expensive) summer opera season.

Canterbury

Commuter trains leave from Victoria and take around one hour 20 minutes. National Express coaches take even longer (around two hours). Tourist information on ✆ 01227–766567.

Canterbury is the cradle of the Anglican Church, the place where St Augustine came to convert King Ethelbert of Kent in 597. The **cathedral** bears traces of every medieval style from Norman to Perpendicular. Two tremendous towers at the western end lead you into the nave, which was entirely rebuilt by Henry Yevele in the 14th century. In the northwest transept is a slab in the pavement marking the spot where Archbishop Thomas à Becket, Henry II's 'turbulent priest', was murdered in 1170. Other attractions include a fine Roman mosaic floor in Butchery Lane, the Saxon remains of St Augustine's abbey, the Norman King's School and some well-preserved sections of medieval wall, especially the Westgate.

Leeds Castle

Take a train from Victoria to Bearsted (the castle is in the southern country of Kent, not in the northern city of Leeds), where a coach will take you to the castle; National Express also runs a bus service from Victoria coach station. Castle open daily 10–5, 10–3 in winter; adm; ✆ 01622–765400. Joint train and admission tickets are available from Victoria and all other stations on the way.

If you visit only one of the many stately homes dotted around London, this is where you should head. Its Norman ramparts are built, Chenonceau-like, over two islands in a lake formed by the River Len surrounded by verdant meadows and trees. For hundreds of years Leeds was a favourite royal residence; it now boasts an elegant series of state rooms; an eccentric collection of medieval dog collars; a park landscaped by Capability Brown with lakes, waterfalls, nature reserves and herb gardens; and, best of all, an enchanting maze (bigger and better than Hampton Court's) with an intricately carved underground grotto at its centre.

Language

Language in London is all about class. Despite the levelling effects of television and social mobility, the elite remains suspicious of the way that ordinary Londoners talk, and the feeling is mutual. Pernickety middle-class folk despise the double negatives, dropped l's and h's and swallowed consonants of the Cockney dialect, which they think of as unforgivably bad English; in return, ordinary people poke fun at the preciousness of society ladies in their Kensington drawing rooms who talk about *snare*, when what they mean is the white stuff that falls out of the sky on an exceptionally cold day. London is a city divided by a common language.

At best, upper-class English people regard Cockney as quaint, the kind of thing that is amusing to hear as long as it is on stage or in the street, not in one's own home. More usually they find it despicable. The very term Cockney, traditionally used to denote anybody from the East End, the heart of working-class London, is in its origin disparaging. Derived from the Old English for 'cock's egg', it was used by Chaucer to mean a spoiled child and by Shakespeare to denote a fool. Pierce Egan, in his classic 1821 study *Life in London*, defined the Cockney as 'an uneducated native... pert and conceited, yet truly ignorant'—an attitude that neatly sums up Professor Higgins's opinion of his young charge Eliza Doolittle in George Bernard Shaw's *Pygmalion* (later turned into the hit musical *My Fair Lady*). 'A woman who utters such depressing and disgusting sounds has no right to be anywhere—no right to live,' he says as he embarks on his wager to teach her the sounds and sophistications of 'proper' English.

In fact, from a historical point of view, it is Eliza who speaks the more proper English. The London dialect known as Cockney has been around since before the Norman invasion of 1066. As the philologist M. MacBride wrote in 1910, three years after *Pygmalion* was first performed: 'The London dialect is really, especially on the south side of the Thames, a perfectly legitimate and responsible child of the old Kentish tongue... The dialect of London north of the Thames has been shown to be one of the many varieties of the Midland or Mercian dialect, flavoured by the East Anglian variety of the same speech, owing to the great influx of Essex people into London.' The ruling classes have always sought to distinguish themselves from the rabble with a more rarefied form of speech, but Received Standard English as we now understand it—that is to say, talking posh—dates back only to the late 18th century. It was the 'public' schools, the private establishments where the élite pay to send their children, which set the agenda in speech and writing. In standardizing the English language's notoriously irrational spelling habits, the schools set the rules to suit themselves, paying scant attention to considerations of either etymology or current usage. Thus it was that *often* gained its t, *assault* and *vault* gained their l's and *advantage* and *advance* their d's. Etymologically there is no justification for these additions, and yet when Cockney-speakers drop any of them they suffer the indignity of being told they do not speak properly. The Cockney use of *remember* to mean remind, or *learn* to mean teach, is generally frowned upon by the chattering classes; and yet it was perfectly acceptable in Elizabethan times and crops up in Shakespeare.

The class war over language reached its height with the arrival of broadcasting in the 1920s. The BBC became the unofficial arbiter of correct speech, and since most of its producers and announcers had been to public school, the soft, drooling vowels of the English upper classes became the linguistic benchmark for the nation. If you've ever seen Pathé wartime newsreels or films like *Brief Encounter*, you'll know how hilariously fake this 'correct' speech sounded, as though everyone had half a dozen marbles stuffed into their cheeks. Cockney, on the other hand, was deemed common and generally kept off the airwaves except as an illustration of the quaintness of working-class life. When television first came into its own in the 1950s, Cockney speech was often subtitled as though it were a foreign language. It was not until the 1980s that regional or working-class accents became acceptable in broadcasting.

At the same time as Cockney was being derided in the corridors of power, a whole folklore about it was building up among those who supposedly despised it the most. Even today, you'll often hear public school-educated voices mimicking the *innits* and *yerwots* of Cockney dialect, or holding lengthy disquisitions about the peculiarities of rhyming slang (on which more below). There is even a theory that the affectations of upper-class English speech derive from the imperfect imitation of working-class accents. What really set off the fad for Cockney folklore was the rise of the music hall at the end of the 19th century. Working-class performers like Albert Chevalier, who wrote the classic Cockney song *My Old Dutch*, created a folksy version of the East End with which to entertain middle-class audiences. This was a world of pearly kings and queens wearing jackets sewn with a thousand buttons (originally the traditional costume of the costermonger, or barrow seller) and toothy old men plucking at ukeleles. Needless to say, this world did not have much to do with reality, but soon enough well-to-do Londoners were coming out with phrases like *put a sock in it* or *keep yer 'air on* and finding it endlessly amusing. The folklore Cockney—crafty, cheeky and all right for a laugh—started popping up all over the place, in plays like *Pygmalion*, in films like *Alfie* (starring that ultimate Cockney performer Michael Caine), and in musicals like *My Fair Lady*, *Underneath the Arches* and Lupino Lane's *Me and My Girl*, which is still doing the rounds in the West End and on Broadway today. In fact, *Me and My Girl* might be said to be the definitive Cockney musical. The plot revolves around a group of Cockneys who baffle a group of aristocrats with their peculiar expressions. The aristocrats quickly catch on, however, and soon they are joining in the fun and coming out with best rhyming slang. All mutual suspicion melts away and in the end everybody joins in for a rousing grand finale of reconciliation.

In fact rhyming slang, more than any other aspect of Cockney, highlights the disparity between the language of the stage and the speech of ordinary people. It seems to have originated in the first half of the 19th century. Henry Mayhew, in his *London Life and the London Poor* of 1851, remarked on 'the new style of cadgers' cant... all done on the rhyming principle'. The idea was that criminals could talk without fear of being betrayed by police narks, and that stallholders in Smithfield and Billingsgate markets could converse about prices without their customers understanding them. In other words, the whole point of rhyming slang was that it should be exclusive and comprehensible only to a chosen few. As soon as *Me and My Girl* popularized expressions like *apples and pears* (stairs) or *Dicky Dirt* (shirt), there was no point in using them any more on the street. Other exclusive languages emerged, including Billingsgate backslang in which the letters of a word were simply reversed (for example, *reeb* to mean beer or *delo woc* for old cow). But these, too, were soon worn down by overuse. The English language is now littered with relics from Cockney sub-dialects. You'll commonly hear Londoners of all classes talking about *taking a butcher's* (butcher's hook, look) or accusing each other of telling *porkies* (pork pies, lies). The word *yob*, meaning hooligan, was originally Billingsgate backslang for boy.

No kind of language or dialect remains fixed, but changes and grows with usage. Cockney has been modified with every new influx of immigrants, be they Huguenots, Jews, Pakistanis, Bengalis or West Indians. Expressions like *wicked*, meaning either super-cool or excitingly dangerous (*man, that shirt is wicked*; *whatever you put in those drinks is wicked*); or *serious* as a synonym for 'lots of' (*serious money, serious trouble*) are Caribbean in origin. More recently London speech has been vastly influenced by American English as used in films and on television (*no way, beat it, movie*, etc). Geographically, Cockney has spread from the East End all over London and beyond into the Kent and Essex suburbs. Most significantly, the erosion of the working class since the 1970s has created profound shifts in the usage of Cockney dialect. The emergence of a new category of upwardly mobile entrepreneurs in the Thatcher era changed the whole definition of Standard English. Public-school accents have catapulted out of fashion in favour of a more populist middle register, largely dictated by television. At the same time, many people from working-class backgrounds have worked hard to smooth off the rough edges of their accent to make themselves more socially acceptable. The two old registers are beginning to meet somewhere in the middle. The result has been studied by linguists and christened New London Dialect or, more vulgarly, Estuary

English after the Thames Estuary that divides Essex and suburban Kent. Tory cabinet ministers and even Princess Diana have been caught referring to *foo'bauw* and *St Pauw's Caffedraw*. Suddenly it is trendy for middle-class Londoners to say *cheers* instead of the usual thank you, and *motor* or even *mo'er* instead of car.

It is hard to say what the significance of this linguistic shift is. Certainly, it suggests that the relaxing of class strictures has led to a corresponding shift in speaking habits. But it does not signal the end of the class war over language, or at least not yet. For all the new Estuary speakers on television and in the House of Commons, deep prejudices about language still remain. It is easy enough to tell, just from turn of phrase or use of grammar, whether an Estuary speaker is a middle-class person going downmarket or a working-class person striving to go up. The social codes have become more complicated to read, but they are still very much there. They depend primarily, now as in the past, on education. Public schools are still very much in the business of grooming rich children to take their place in the élite, while the state system continues to be eroded by inadequate resources and an ingrained inferiority complex. The difference in accent between the two systems may be diminishing, but the gap in linguistic culture remains as broad as ever. As long as Britain's education system is divided along class lines into a private and a public sector, the linguistic battle is unlikely to go away.

A Cockney Glossary

The main characteristics of Cockney speech have not changed all that much, although a good deal of the vocabulary has modified or disappeared in recent years. Broadly speaking, its salient features are:

dropped h's:	as in *'orrible, 'Ackney, 'oppit!* for horrible, Hackney, hop it (clear off)
swallowed consonants:	as in *bu'er, bo'le, dau'er* for butter, bottle, daughter
dropped l's:	as in *baw, St Pauw* for ball, St Paul
f for soft th:	as in *fink*, nuffink for think, nothing
v for hard th:	as in *bruvver, muvver* for brother, mother
multiple negatives:	as in *you ain't never done nuffink for nobody*

Here is a short and very incomplete glossary of Cockney words and phrases:

bat n. price in a market, as in *to pay the full bat*

beef n. disagreement or argument, as in *to 'ave a beef.*

bird n. woman, as in *yer bird's a bit of all right*

bloke n. man, as in *me bruvver's a smashin' bloke*

blotto adj. drunk (now in general use)

blow yer top phr. to get very angry

bonce n. head, synonym for *nut* or *noddle*

boozer n. pub. *Down the boozer* means at the pub

boss-eyed adj. cross-eyed

bread-basket n. stomach

brickie n. bricklayer

clippie n. ticket collector, bus conductor

clod'opper n. twit, fool

cock n. term of endearment, as in *wotcher cock!*. A bit old-fashioned. Alternatives include *mate*, *mush* and *tosh*.

coffin nails n. pl. cigarettes. Also *Irish jigs* (rhyming slang for cigs)

conk n. nose. Also *schnozzle*, *hooter*

cor blimey! interj. Expression of surprise. Synonyms include *strewth* (from God's truth), *strike a light, love a duck, stone the crows* etc etc

coppah n. policeman, from the verb *to cop* meaning to snatch. Less polite variants include *fuzz*, *pig*, *filth*.

cuppa n. cup of tea

ear'ole n. ear, or side of face generally, as in *to slug someone round the ear'ole* Also *lug'ole*

flag n. shirt, as in *I've ironed me flag*

flap n. pocket

flappers n. ears

gob n. mouth. **I'm gonna smash yer gob** means I'm going to beat you up

goner n. dead person. To *be a goner* means to be a marked man, or to die. Other phrases for dying include *conk out, peg out, push up the daisies, turn yer toes up, kick the bucket*

gumption n. intelligence, as in *use yer gumption*. See also *loaf*

guv or **guv'nor** n. polite way of addressing important people or customers

innit adv. multi-purpose word stuck on the end of sentences for effect, a bit like *n'est-ce pas* in French, but not so classy. As in *it's bleedin' freezin', innit?* Similar words include *innee* and *dinn'I*

keep yer 'air on phr. don't get over-excited

kisser n. mouth

learn vb. teach, as in *I'm gonna learn yer good'n'proper*

lolly n. money. Also *dosh*

London dressing phr. old-fashioned way of describing soot

London flit phr. to *do the London flit* means to move house surreptitiously (usually overnight) without paying the outstanding rent

loaf n. head, as in *use yer loaf*

mate n. most common term of endearment (see *cock* above)

moggy n. cat

mo'er n. car

the moon's wet phr. it's going to rain

nosh n. food

nut n. head. *It did me nut* means it annoyed or frustrated me

oi! interj. used to get attention, as in *oi, you!*

'oky-poky man n. old word for an ice-cream seller who came round on a bicycle

'oppit! vbl phrase. clear off, scram

'oppin' the wag vbl phr. playing truant

peepers n.pl. eyes

put a sock in it! phr. keep the noise down, shut up

put wood in the 'ole, to, vbl. phr. to shut the door

preggers adj. pregnant. Also *up the pole, in the puddin' club*

punter n. customer, client of any kind

scarper vb. run, scram, clear out. Rhyming slang (from Scapa Flow, go)

scrump vb. old-fashioned word for steal

spark n. electrician. Also, clever person as in *a bright spark*

spiv n. dishonest person, usually a well turned out hustler rather than a petty thief Also *wide boy*

spud n. potato. Also *tayter*

swede-basher n. person from the country

to talk peas over sticks or

to talk right cut glass phr. to talk posh

tallyman n. debt-collector

tizz n. fuss, bother, as in *to get into a tizz*

turf accountant n. bookmaker

up the dancers adv. upstairs

wallop n. to hit, esp. parents hitting children

wotcher n. hello

yer wot? phr. I beg your pardon?

Rhyming Slang

As explained above, rhyming slang is more folklore than reality. Nevertheless, some phrases have entered the language and others, although never said with a straight face, are still well-known enough to merit entries in dictionaries. There are two types of rhyming slang: straight rhymes with the original word, such as *mince pies* for eyes or *pig's ear* for beer; and abbreviations or contractions of the original phrase, which take longer to work out. For example, *on 'is Jack* meaning on his own (Jack, Jack Jones, own) or *nanny* for coat (nanny, nanny goat, coat). Here are some of the better known and more colourful phrases:

Adam and Eve believe

apples and pears stairs

Artful Dodger lodger

Barnaby Rudge judge

battle cruiser boozer (pub)

bell ringers fingers

board'n'plank Yank

borassic out of cash (borassic lint, skint)

Brahms and Liszt a little the worse for drink (incidentally, also the name of a wine bar in Covent Garden)

bricks'n'mortar daughter

Cape of Good 'Ope soap

Charlie twit, fool, as in *'e made me feel like a right Charlie* (derivation probably Charlie, Charlie Ronce, ponce)

Crimea beer (also *pig's ear* or *far'n'near*)

daisy roots boots

dicky bird or **Richard III** word, as in *don't believe a dicky that man tells yer*

Dicky Dirt shirt (Dicky Dirt's was the name given to a chain of cheap clothing stores in the 1970s, though the phrase came first)

Dunlop tyre liar

elephant's trunk drunk

fairy snuff fair enough

fisherman's daughter water

flounder'n'dab cab

four by two Jew

Fourth of July tie

frog'n'toad road

Gawd forbids kids (also, *saucepan lids*)

glass case face, as in *shut yer glass case*

Khyber Pass arse (or *North Pole* for arsehole)

Mae West chest

mince pies eyes

Mrs Thatcher equalizer in soccer (Thatcher, matcher)

nanny coat (nanny goat, coat)

needle'n'thread bread

pot'n'pan old man (husband)

Rosy or **Rosy Lea** tea (Rosy Lea was a gypsy who told fortunes by reading tea-leaves)

swear'n'cuss bus

titfer hat (tit for tat, hat)

trouble'n'strife wife (also, *fork'n'knife*)

turtles gloves (turtle doves, gloves)

Vera Lynn gin (also *needle'n'pin*)

West Ham reserves nerves, as in *you get on my*

whistle and flute suit

Further Reading

So many books have been written about London there is even one called *Blimey! Another Book on London* (by an ex-cab driver; not really recommended). They vary from the scholarly to the trivial, from the brilliant to the banal. Most are no good at all. Few really explain London to the uninitiated, and fewer still do so in a readable or entertaining fashion. So be warned, but not deterred. If you have room in your suitcase for only two books (apart, of course, from this one), take V.S. Pritchett's *London Perceived*, a sharp outsider's view of the capital, and Jonathan Raban's brilliant evocation of life in the metropolis, *Soft City*. If it is a reference work you are after, you cannot do better than Weinreb and Hibbert's doorstopper of a volume, *The London Encyclopedia*, which combines accurate history with lively anecdotes. It was much consulted in the preparation of this book. As for novels, if you can stomach Dickens— and not everyone can—you should go for him; he is, after all, the king of London novelists. In contemporary literature, try Hanif Kureishi's *Buddha of Suburbia* or Martin Amis's *Money*. Neither will leave you indifferent; if you are not outraged, you will be in for a treat.

General

Davies, Andrew, *The East End Nobody Knows*, Macmillan 1990. A series of compelling thumbnail sketches of this neglected corner of London.

Gray, Robert, *A History of London*, Hutchinson 1978. Excellent overall introduction.

Hobsbawm, Eric and Ranger, Terence (eds), *The Invention of Tradition*, Cambridge University Press 1983. Essays examining the myths of English history, with a first-rate piece on the royal family.

Morton, H.V., *In Search of London*, Methuen 1951. A genial guide written by an old pro in the art of travel writing.

O'Connor, Anthony, *Clubland: The Wrong Side of the Right People*, Martin Brian and O'Keeffe 1976. A hilarious portrait of the decline of the London club.

Porter, Roy, *London: A Social History*, Hamish Hamilton 1994. An extensive, well-written if slightly bloodless overview from medieval times to the present.

Pritchett, V.S., *London Perceived*, Chatto 1959. Brilliant if severe portrait of the city.

Raban, Jonathan, *Soft City*, Harvill/Harper Collins 1988 (first published 1974). Beautifully written meditation on life in big cities in general, and London in particular.

Rumbelow, Donald, *The Complete Jack the Ripper*, W.H. Allen 1972/87. The best introduction to the enormous literature on the subject.

Weinreb, Ben and Hibbert, Christopher (ed), *The London Encyclopedia*, Macmillan 1993. Exhaustive, informative and entertaining, if weak on modern London.

Wilson, A.N. (ed), *The Faber Book of London*, Faber 1993. Engaging literary anthology of the Big Smoke, far better than the many name-dropping 'literary companions' to London.

Architecture

Barker, Felix and Hyde, Ralph, *London As It Might Have Been*, John Murray 1982. An entertaining romp through London's half-realized projects and hare-brained schemes, including a plan to straighten the Thames, a helicopter landing pad on top of Liverpool Street station and an overhead monorail along Regent Street.

Jencks, Charles, *The Prince, The Architects and New Wave Monarchy*, Academy 1988. Excellent survey of the row caused by Prince Charles's 'carbuncle' speech.

Olsen, Donald J., *Town Planning in London* (1964) and *The City as a Work of Art* , (1986) Yale University Press. Intelligent, academic tomes on 18th- and 19th-century London.

Pevsner, Nikolaus, and Cherry, Bridget, *The Buildings of England* (three volumes on London), Penguin. Exhaustive survey of every street and building of interest. Still the benchmark by which to measure more recent publications.

Rogers, Richard and Fisher, Mark, *A New London*, Penguin 1992. A manifesto for the future of the city by one of its leading architects and the Labour Party's spokesman for the arts.

Summerson, John, *Georgian London*, Barrie and Jenkins 1988 (first published 1948). The best book about London's golden age, now with sumptuous photographs.

London in Literature

Amis, Martin, *Money,* Penguin 1984, and *London Fields*, Penguin 1989. Sharp if overly self-conscious satires of the greed and corruption in 1980s London.

Boswell, James, *A London Journal* (1763), Heinemann. How Johnson's biographer first came to London and who he slept with. Racy stuff.

Conan Doyle, Arthur, *Sherlock Holmes Stories* (an;). The atmosphere of late Victorian London pervades these ingenious tales of exotic knavery and brilliant detection.

Conrad, Joseph, *The Secret Agent* (1905), Penguin. Moody spy thriller based on the bomb blast that killed a French student in Greenwich Park in 1894.

Dickens, Charles, *Sketches by Boz* (1837), *Oliver Twist* (1838), *Bleak House* (1857), *Our Mutual Friend* (1865) (loads of editions). The most London-oriented of Dickens's books, from his early collection of journalism (*Boz*) to his murky tale of money and riverside skullduggery (*Friend*).

Forster, E.M., *Howards End* (1910), Penguin. The London middle classes and their obsession with property. Beautifully written.

Grossmith, George and Weedon, *The Diary of a Nobody* (1884). A satirical view of a pompous lowly clerk and his household in Holloway.

Kureishi, Hanif, *The Buddha of Suburbia* (1991), Faber. The growing pains of a south London boy with a Pakistani dad who fancies himself as a visionary.

MacInnes, Colin, *City of Spades* (1957), *Absolute Beginners* (1958) and *Mr Love and Justice* (1960), Allison and Busby. Vibrant trilogy charting the multicultural London of the postwar years.

Orwell, George, *Down and Out in Paris and London* (1933) and *Nineteen Eighty-Four* (1948), Penguin. Two very different views of London, one a piece of unflinching reportage on the homeless, the other a totalitarian nightmare.

Rushdie, Salman, *The Satanic Verses* (1988), Viking/The Consortium. Among other things, a rich, fantastical picture of 1980s London from an immigrant standpoint.

Smollett, Tobias, *Humphrey Clinker* (1771), Penguin Classics. Smollett's somewhat rambling traveller's tale with some brilliant scenes set in London.

Stevenson, Robert Louis, *The Strange Case of Dr Jekyll and Mr Hyde* (1886), lots of editions. This diabolical short story neatly echoes the dual face of London itself.

Wilde, Oscar, *The Picture of Dorian Gray* (1891), Penguin. Decadence, art for art's sake and murder most foul in 1890s London.

Woolf, Virginia, *Mrs. Dalloway* (1925), Penguin. A day in the life of a politician's wife struggling to assert her identity as she roams London in preparation for a party.

Index

ABK (Ahrends Burton and Koralek) 139, 364
Adam brothers 91, 259–60, 311
Adam, Robert 91, 159, 311, 316, 356, 400–1, 574
Adelphi 91, 259–60
Syon and Osterley 419, 420
Adelphi 91, 259–60
Admiral's Walk 401–2
Admiralty Arch 149
Ahrends Burton and Koralek (ABK) 139, 364
airports 2–3
Al Fayed, Mohammed 358
Albany 226
Albert, Prince 96, 350, 351–2, 354, 360, 367
Albert Memorial 95, 370
statues 293, 370
Albert Hall 369, 531, 534
Aldgate Pump 459
Alexandra, Queen 161
Alexandra Palace 398
All Hallows-by-the-Tower 320
All Saints Margaret St 95, 232
All Souls Langham Place 233
Almeida Theatre 528, 529
Amis, Martin 117
Anchor Inn (Bankside) 335, 506
André, Carl 194
Angel pub (Rotherhithe) 440, 441, 506–7
Anne, Queen 151, 160, 161, 191, 371, 503
statue 285–6
Anne Boleyn, Queen 42, 178, 323, 343, 428–9
Annigoni, Pietro 202
Anrep, Boris 140
Antonello da Messina 141
Apsley House 355–6
Aquarium 432
Archer, Jeffrey, Lord 183, 264
Archer, Thomas 191
architecture 81–102
Arup Associates 289
Asprey's 229–30
Athenaeum 93, 154
Attlee, Clement 188
Auerbach, Frank 192
Austen, Jane 574

Bacerra, Ralph 364
Bacon, Francis 194, 216, 333
Baden-Powell House Museum 377
Bagehot, Walter 77–8
Baily, E.H. 137
Baker, Sir Herbert 313
Balla, Giacomo 374
Bank of England 99, 276, 312–14
Bank of England Museum 312–14
bank holidays 27
banks 26–7
Bankside Power Station, Tate Gallery of Modern Art 329, 333
Banqueting House, Whitehall 86, 87, 173–4
Barbican Arts Centre 301–2, 528, 529, 531
Barry, Sir Charles 137, 155, 275, 372
Palace of Westminster 94, 178, 179, 180
Barry, Charles Jnr 435
Barry, Edward 208
Bath 573–4
Battersea 420
Battersea Power Station 99, 420
Bayswater 403–4, 515–17
Bazalgette, Sir Joseph 52, 54, 258
BBC 25–6, 233
BBC Experience 233
Beatles 125, 131, 224, 226, 386
bed and breakfast accommodation 520–1
Bedford, Francis Russell, 4th Earl of 86, 203, 204
Bedford Square 247
Bedlam 433
Beeby, Thomas 289
Beefeaters 321, 324
beer 505
Belfast, H.M.S. 344
Belgravia 412–13
Bellini, Giovanni 141
Belloc, Hilaire 415
Bentham, Jeremy 252
Berkeley Square 91, 230–1
Bernini, Giovanni Lorenzo 361
Berwick St 216–17, 551
Bethnal Green Museum of Childhood 460
Betjeman, Sir John 300

bicycle, travel by 9, 23
Big Ben 180–1
Billingsgate Fish Market 319
Bird, Francis 286
Birkbeck College 252
Bishop of Winchester's Palace 336, 338
Bishopsgate 314–15
Black Cultural Museum 435
Blackfriars Bridge 332–3
Blackheath 520
Blair, Tony 58, 174, 183, 272, 392
Blake, William 189, 192–3
Blanche, Jacques-Emile 201
Blenheim Palace 572
Blitz 55–6, 78, 218, 286
Bloomsbury 235–54
Bloomsbury Square 89, 238
eating and drinking 236–8, 475–6
hotels 514–15
Bloomsbury Group 238–9, 251, 254
Blore, Edward 163–4, 188, 433
boat trips 9–10, 387, 420, 436
Boccioni, Umberto 374
Boleyn, Anne *see* Anne Boleyn
Bologna, Giovanni 361
Bond St 228–9, 231
Bonfire Night 63–4, 65
Bonnard, Pierre 333
Borough Market 339
Boswell, James 109, 110, 151, 205
Boucher, François 375
Boudicca, Queen 36, 401, 420
Bow Bells 288
Bow St Magistrates' Court 209–10
Bow St Runners 68, 209–10
Bramah Tea and Coffee Museum 345–6
Branson, Richard 404
Breuer, Marcel 364
Brewer St 217
Brick Lane 453, 455, 458–9, 551
Brighton 574–5
British Broadcasting Corporation (BBC) 25–6, 233
British Library 241, 242, 249–50
British Museum 93, 102, 239–47

British National Party 444
Britpack 123–4, 149, 216
Britten, Benjamin 130
Brixton 57, 69, 434–5, 551
  lunch/pubs 434, 508
Broadcasting House 233
Broadgate Centre 455–6
Brompton Oratory 359–60
Brooks Club 159, 160
brothels 71, 336, 337
Brown, Denise Scott 139
Brown, Lancelot 'Capability' 419,
  573, 576
Browning, Robert 189
Brown's Hotel 229, 500, 511
Brunel, Isambard Kingdom 408
Brunel, Sir Marc Isambard 408,
  441
Brunel Engine House 441
Buckingham Palace 92, 93, 162–
  7
Burgh House 402
Burlington, Richard Boyle, 3rd
  Earl of 90–1, 190, 227–8, 418
Burlington Arcade 227
Burlington House 91, 227–8
Burne-Jones, Sir Edward 193,
  376, 410, 411
Burton, Decimus 270, 355, 372,
  384, 388, 423
  Athenaeum 93, 154
  Hyde Park Screen 93, 355
buses 4, 6–7
Business Design Centre 394
Butler's Wharf 345, 493
Butterfield, William 95, 203,
  232
Byrd, William 126

Cabaret Mechanical Theatre 206
Cabinet War Rooms 176
Café Royal 226
cafés, teahouses and snack food
  351, 499–502
Calvi, Roberto 333
Cambridge 572–3
Camden 389–91, 489
Camden Lock 390, 551
Camden Passage 393, 551
Camden Town Group 121–2,
  390
Campbell, Colen 228
camping 521–2
Canaletto, Antonio 120, 142, 436
Canary Wharf 101, 442–4
Canonbury 395

Canonbury Tower 395
Canova, Antonio 166, 356
Canterbury 575
car, travel by 4–5, 8–9, 23
Caravaggio, Michelangelo Merisi
  da 143
Carlton House 139, 149, 154,
  225
Carlton House Terrace 149, 151
Carlyle's House 416
Carnaby St 231–2
Caro, Anthony 192
Caroline, Queen 51, 161, 186
Carrà, Carlo 374
Carracci, Annibale 161
Carroll, Lewis 250
Carter, Sydney 242
Cartwright Gardens 250
Casson, Sir Hugh 389
Castle Combe 574
Catholics
  anti-Catholic feeling 46–7, 50,
    63–5
  churches 29, 294, 359–60,
    412–13
Cato Street Conspiracy 68
Cavell, Edith 200
Cecil Court 202
cemeteries 397–8, 407–8
Cenotaph 175
Centre Point 100
Cézanne, Paul 143, 261
Chadwick, Edwin 52, 53–4, 250,
  297
Chamberlain, Joseph and Neville
  188
Chambers, Sir William 167, 261,
  422
Chandos House 91
Changing of the Guard 150
Channel Tunnel 3, 4, 5
Chapel Market 394, 551
Chaplin, Charlie 218
Chapman brothers 123, 386
Charing Cross 101, 136
Charing Cross Road 212
Charles I, King 43–4, 86, 161,
  179, 323, 425–6, 429
  and Banqueting House 119,
    173
  portraits 119, 142–3, 166
  statue 136, 172
  trial and execution 44, 173,
    178
Charles II, King 44–7, 126, 151,
  159, 173, 343, 451, 526

building works promoted by 47,
  155, 417
  portrait 417
  statue 215
Charles, Prince of Wales 77, 78,
  79, 162, 282
  on architecture 101, 139, 249,
    289, 425, 443
Charterhouse Square 297
Chartist movement 53
Chaucer, Geoffrey 106, 189, 250,
  340
Cheddar Gorge 574
Chelsea 413–17, 420
  Chelsea Old Church 415
  Chelsea Physic Garden 416
  eating and drinking 481–5,
    500–1, 507–8
  Royal Hospital 417
Chelsea Harbour 101, 420
chemists 20
Chesterfield St 230
Chesterton, G.K. 114–15
Cheyne Walk 415–16
Chichester, Sir Francis 447
childminding 562
children's London 559–62
  museums for children 377
Chinatown 217–18
Chirico, Giorgio de 194
Chiswick 418–19
  Chiswick House 91, 418–19
Christ Church Greyfriars 288–9
Christ Church Spitalfields 90, 458
Christ the King, Church of 251
Church Row (Hampstead) 402
Churchill, Sir Winston 55, 176,
  181, 182, 184, 226, 343
  portrait 201
  statue 176
Cibber, Caius Gabriel 215
cinema 122–3, 536–8
City 265–74, 279–324
  eating and drinking 280–2,
    306, 501
City of London School 332
City Temple 293
Claude Lorrain 142, 166
Cleopatra's Needle 258–9
Clerkenwell 295–6
climate 15–16
Clink Prison Museum 336–7
Clockmakers' Museum 311
Cockney dialect 577–84
Colcutt and Hemp 260
Cole, Henry 350, 351, 352, 365

National Film Theatre 330, 501, 536, 537
National Gallery 93, 101, 138–44, 364
national holidays 27
National Lottery 330, 524
National Maritime Museum 449–50
National Portrait Gallery 200–2
National Postal Museum 289, 375
National Sound Archive 250
National Theatre 330, 528, 529
National Westminster (NatWest) Tower 100, 314, 315
Natural History Museum 354, 366–7
Neal St 210
Neal's Yard 210
Nelson, Horatio, Lord 136–7, 287, 449–50
Nelson's Column 135, 137
Nereid Monument 243–4
New Bond St 231
New River 43, 295, 392, 395
Newgate Prison 290–2
newspapers 23–4, 72–3, 271–3, 439
Newton, Sir Isaac 188, 192, 250
Nicholson, Ben 192
nightclubs and discos 538–9
Nightingale, Florence 341, 432
Nineveh, royal lion hunt reliefs from 243
Nolde, Emil 194
Northcliffe, Alfred Harmsworth, Lord 274
Notting Hill 404–6
  eating and drinking 485–9, 501, 507
  hotels 515–17

Oates, Titus 47, 64
Old Bailey 289–91
Old Barge House Stairs 331
Old Bond St 228–9
Old Compton St 216
Old Royal Observatory 451–2, 528
Olympia and York 443, 444
One London Bridge 343
opera 126–9, 208–9, 530–2
Orleans House 427
Orton, Joe 393–4
Orwell, George 99, 116, 248, 253, 392, 407, 431

Osterley House 419–20
Outram, John 445
Owen, David, Lord 440
Oxford 571–2
Oxford St 232
Oxo Tower 332

painting 117–22
Palace Theatre 212
Palace of Westminster 94–5, 177–84, 420
Pall Mall 152, 154–5
Palladianism 86, 90–1, 227–8, 309, 418–19, 426, 449
Palmerston, Henry Temple, Lord 175–6, 188, 201, 226
Paolozzi, Eduardo 192, 250
parking 8
Parliament, Houses of 94–5, 177–84, 420
Parliament Hill 401
Parliament Square 176–7, 184
Parthenon frieze 244
Pasmore, Victor 122, 193
Paternoster Square 289
Paxton, Sir Joseph 96, 351, 352, 354
Peabody Estates 98
Peasants' Revolt 41, 260, 296, 322, 342–3, 401
Peel, Sir Robert 53, 68–9, 188
Pei, I.M. 445
Pelli, Cesar 101, 442, 443
Pennethorne, James 98
pensioners, discounts for 30
Pepys, Samuel 46, 106, 107, 184, 189, 271, 462–3
Percival David Foundation of Chinese Art 251
Peter Pan statue 370
Petticoat Lane 453, 455, 459, 551
Picasso, Pablo 144, 333
Piccadilly Circus 222–3, 225
Pie Corner 298
Piero della Francesca 141
Pilgrim Fathers 440, 441
Pimlico 412, 519
Pitt, William, the Younger 188
Plague, Great 44–6, 399, 401
Planetarium 384, 385
policemen 17–18, 53, 67–70
Pollock, Jackson 194
Pollock's Toy Museum 253
Pope, Alexander 108, 228
Port of London Authority building 98, 320

Portland Vase 246
Portobello Road 406–7, 551
post offices 27–8
Poussin, Nicolas 142, 166, 375, 436
Pre-Raphaelites 193
Prince Henry's Room 85, 270–1
Prince Regent see George IV
Princes in the Tower 189, 322
Promenade concerts (Proms) 369, 531
Public Record Office 98, 275
pubs (see also under areas) 505–8
Pudding Lane 46, 319
Pugin, Augustus Welby 94–5, 178, 179, 180, 183
punk movement 131, 414
Purcell, Henry 126–7
Purcell Room 330, 531

Queen Elizabeth Gates 356
Queen Elizabeth Hall 330, 531
Queen's Chapel 161–2
Queen's Gallery 167
Queen's House 86, 449

Raban, Jonathan 106, 109
radio 24, 25–6, 377
Railton, William 137
Raleigh, Sir Walter 323, 447
Ranger's House 451
Raphael 138, 365, 436
Regent St 92, 220–2, 224–6, 232–4
Regent's Canal 387, 389, 392
Regent's Park 92, 93, 225, 382–4, 388
  open air theatre 383–4, 528, 530
religion (see also Catholics; Jews; Muslims) 29–30
Rembrandt van Ryn 142, 166, 247, 375, 401, 435, 571
Reni, Guido 360
restaurants 466–99
Reynolds, Sir Joshua 202, 358, 375
  grave 200
  paintings by 143, 192, 201, 228, 248, 401
  statue 228
rhyming slang 579, 583–4
Richard II, King 41, 173, 186, 296
  portraits 140–1, 188
  tomb 188

Shaftesbury Avenue 98
Shakespeare, William 334–5,
  338, 526, 527, 528
  at Stratford-upon-Avon 572
  memorials to 189
Shakespeare Globe Exhibition
  335
Shaw, George Bernard 206, 250,
  254, 577
Shaw, Richard Norman 160
Shell Centre 100, 329
Shelley, Percy Bysshe 104–5,
  231, 358
Shepherd Market 230
Sheppard, Jack 290
Sheridan, Richard Brinsley 189,
  208
Sherlock Holmes Museum 385
shopping 27, 391, 541–52
Sickert, Walter 74, 121–2, 193,
  201, 390
Sidney St, siege 69
Simpson, John 289
Sion College 332
Sir John Soane's Museum 92,
  276–7
Sloane, Sir Hans 240, 416
Sloane Rangers 414
Smirke, Sir Robert 93, 138, 162,
  208, 226, 240, 241, 261
Smirke, Sydney 228, 240, 242,
  270, 372
Smithfield, eating and drinking
  280–2, 492–3
Smithfield Market 296–7
Smithson, Peter and Alison 160
Smollett, Tobias 104, 205, 340,
  463
Snowdon, Anthony Armstrong-
  Jones, Lord 388–9
Soane, Sir John 89, 92, 96, 174,
  179, 276–7
  Bank of England 99, 276, 313
  Dulwich Picture Gallery 435–6
  Sir John Soane's Museum 92,
  276–7
Soho 213–18
  eating and drinking 198–9,
  467–73, 500, 506
Soho Square 215
Somerset House 261
South Bank 325–46
  eating and drinking 327–8,
  493–4, 501–2
  South Bank Centre 100, 102,
  328–31, 501, 531

South Kensington 351, 352–3,
  359–68, 408–9
  hotels 518–19
Southampton, Thomas
  Wriothesley, 4th Earl of 88–9
Southwark 325–46, 506–7
  Southwark Cathedral 85,
  338–9
Speaker's Corner 357
Spence, Sir Basil 357
Spencer, Herbert 398
Spencer, Stanley 192, 193, 402
Spencer House 91, 159
Spenser, Edmund 189
Spitalfields 454, 456–7
  Spitalfields Market 458
sports 553–8
squares 88–90
Staple Inn 85, 278
Star and Garter Home 425
Steer, Philip Wilson 193
Stirling, James 191
Stock Exchange 307, 314
Stoke Newington 396, 494
Stonehenge 574
Storm Water Pumping Station
  445
Stow, John 316
Strand 260, 262
Stratford-upon-Avon 572
Strawberry Hill 427
Street, George Edmund 95,
  263–4
street markets 551–2
Stuart, James 159, 448
Stubbs, George 192
student discounts 30
student halls of residence,
  accommodation in 521
suburbs 97–9, 380–2
Sullivan, Sir Arthur 68, 129
Surrey Docks 441–2
Swift, Jonathan 108, 297
Swinburne, Algernon 416
synagogues 29, 387
Syon Park 419

Tallis, Thomas 126, 450
Tate Gallery 191–4
Tate Gallery of Modern Art
  (Bankside) 329, 333
taxis 7–8
Taylor, Sir Robert 275
Tecton 388
Telecom Tower 254
telephones 31

television 24, 26
Temple Bar 265
Temple Church 85, 270
tennis 378, 555
Tennyson, Alfred, Lord 189
Terry, Ellen 203, 250, 526
Terry, Quinlan 101–2, 384, 425
Thackeray, William Makepeace
  408
Thames 328, 332
  boat trips 9–10, 420, 436
  tunnels below 441, 445
Thames Lido 329, 332
Thatcher, Margaret, Lady 57–8,
  72, 154, 272, 283, 308, 432,
  435
  portrait 201
theatre 525–30
  for children 561
  Theatre Museum 207
Thomas, Dylan 253
Thomas Coram Foundation for
  Children 248
Thomas Neal's Arcade 210–11
Thorneycroft, Thomas 420
Thornhill, Sir James 286, 430,
  448–9
Tiepolo, Giovanni Battista 261
Tijou, Jean 430, 450
Tintoretto, Jacopo 141
Tippett, Sir Michael 130
tipping 32
Tipu's Tiger 363
Tite, Sir William 312
Titian 138, 375
toilets 32
Torrigiano, Pietro 287
Tottenham 57, 69
Tottenham Court Road 98, 253
tourist information 32
Tower Bridge 344
Tower Hill Pageant 321
Tower of London 38, 85, 118,
  320–4
Townsend, Charles Harrison
  460
Trafalgar Square 92, 93, 94,
  135–8
trains 3–4, 7
Trench, Frederick William 94
Trinity Hospital 453
Trocadero Centre 224
Trollope, Anthony 189, 250, 408
Trooping the Colour 150
Trumpeters' House 424
tube see underground system